TEMPORAL PILLARS

TEMPORAL PILLARS

Queen Anne's Bounty,
the Ecclesiastical Commissioners, and the
Church of England

BY

G. F. A. BEST

CAMBRIDGE
AT THE UNIVERSITY PRESS
1964

PUBLISHED BY

THE SYNDICS OF THE CAMBRIDGE UNIVERSITY PRESS

Bentley House, 200 Euston Road, London, N.W.1
American Branch: 32 East 57th Street, New York 22, N.Y.
West African Office: P.O. Box 33, Ibadan, Nigeria

Printed in Great Britain by
WILLMER BROTHERS AND HARAM LTD.
BIRKENHEAD.

To my Mother
and to the memory of
my Father

PREFACE

This is the history of two institutions about which little has yet been written. It is also, by a consequence that seemed inescapable, a history on a smaller scale of some of the less written-about relations between the Church of England—the larger institution which Queen Anne's Bounty and the Ecclesiastical Commissioners were, in 1704 and 1836 respectively, created to serve—and the ancient joint kingdom of England and Wales within whose legal and social framework the established church held its property and did its work. Nevertheless, Queen Anne's Bounty and the Ecclesiastical Commissioners stand in the foreground. The former enjoyed an independent existence from 1704 to 1948. Proposals for its union with the Commissioners were frequently made from the eighteen-thirties onwards, and so similar were the functions which each was performing that it is as impossible as it would be improper to write about one without writing about both. And yet, right up to their union at last in 1948 to make up the present body of Church Commissioners, they retained their own individualities and cherished their different official traditions. I hope that I have not wholly failed to divide my pages in fair proportion between them and that church establishment of which they were such important parts.

So many people have in one way or another helped me to write this book since I started, five years ago, to work on it in the intervals between teaching and preparing to teach, that it has not been easy to decide how to thank them. The best way has in the end seemed to pay here my grateful respects to those to whom my debt is greatest; to excuse the brevity of these prefatory acknowledgments by remarking that in many cases I shall be more specific later on; and to insist that nobody holds any responsibility at all for the use or misuse to which I may be thought to have put their help.

In the first place I must thank the Church Commissioners for having invited me to write the book, and thank Sir James Brown and Sir Mortimer Warren in particular for having made my visits to No. 1

Millbank so pleasant and profitable. At the same time I must point out that this is in no way an official history; I have been left free to write it exactly as I chose, and given every facility to do so. To Mr Alan Savidge, an Assistant Secretary there, I owe a very special debt, as will in due course be made clear; and I have been much assisted in different ways by Mr E. J. Robinson, Miss C. Lancashire, Mr James Shelley, Mrs H. D. Ashley, and other members of the Commissioners' staff.

I must acknowledge my indebtedness to three scholars in particular. The first is Dr George Kitson Clark of Trinity College, Cambridge, whose teaching and example drew me towards the study of history in the first place, and to whom I—along with so many others who try to write history—owe more than can easily be said. The second is the late Dean of Winchester. Anyone who sets out to write about the Church of England in the eighteenth century must become familiar with the sight of Dr Sykes's pioneer footprints leading through those plains of rational piety to one or other of his published monuments, from which, as from their author, while he was Dixie Professor at Cambridge, I have learnt so much. The third is Dr R. W. Greaves, of Bedford College, London University, to whose friendship and good counsel I have long been indebted, and whose kind criticisms of my manuscript gave me an opportunity to get many things right, or put them differently.

I am grateful to the Archbishop of Canterbury and the Trustees of Lambeth Palace Library for letting me use the Tenison papers and the 'Notitia Parochialis'; to the Ipswich and East Suffolk Record Office for access to the Pretyman-Tomline Collection deposited by the owner, Mr G. Pretyman; to the Lincolnshire Archives Committee for access to their collection of Bishop Kaye's papers; and to the Earl of Harrowby, Colonel E. H. Goulburn, the Marquess of Cholmondeley, and Sir Fergus Graham, Bart., for access to their family papers, and permission to use them. Several archivists and librarians have notably eased my researches; I recall with especial gratitude the help afforded me by Miss Gollancz at Kingston and Mrs Varley at Lincoln, by the Librarian of Oriel College, and by the staff of the University Library at Cambridge.

Among the many who have (sometimes no doubt without realizing it) helped me, I should particularly wish to name and thank Dr J. D. Walsh, the Rev. Dr John Kent, the Rev. Dr Owen Chadwick, Pro-

Preface

fessor W. L. Burn, Dr J. H. Plumb, Mr Mark Whittaker, Dr Diana McClatchey, Dr Esther de Waal, Dr Anne Whiteman, Professor David Spring, Mr David Joslin, Mr Charles Wilson, Canon Charles Smyth, the Rev. Dr W. Pickering, the Rev. R. A. K. Runcie, Dr R. Robson, Professor Bruce Dickins, my pupils at Trinity Hall, and my mother.

There seem to be no other specific debts to acknowledge, but very many that can be treated generally. I have been much helped from time to time, as I suppose we all have, by casual contributors of odd hints, references, suggestions, criticisms. Often small in themselves, they add up through the years to a mountain of indebtedness. I can best notice it by admitting my general gratitude to friends and colleagues at Cambridge, London, Oxford and Harvard; but especially to those at Trinity Hall during the six years of my fellowship there. Many of them have been helpful in other ways than as providers of so many of the ideas for the putting of which into one's own words the over-generous might give one credit for being 'original'. With my wife at their head, they have provided that happy and stimulating background to work which makes labour less laborious, and life itself worth living.

G.F.A.B.

EDINBURGH
September 1961

ix

CONTENTS

xi

Contents

ABBREVIATIONS

Parliamentary Papers

These are generally referred to as 'P. Ps.', thus: P. Ps. 1869, XLI, 630, meaning page 630 of the 41st volume of Parliamentary Papers for the year 1869. The only exceptions to this rule are reports of Commissions or Committees having special relevance to the subject of this book and therefore much used. These are they:

Report of the Commissioners of Inquiry into the Ecclesiastical Revenues of England and Wales, 1835 (P. Ps. 1835, XXII, 15–1060): here referred to as 'Ecclesiastical Revenues Commission'.

Reports from the Commissioners appointed to consider the State of the Established Church, with reference to Ecclesiastical Duties and Revenues: here referred to as 'Ecclesiastical Duties and Revenues Commission'.

First Report, 1835	P. Ps. 1835, XXII, 1–13
Second Report, 1836	P. Ps. 1836, XXXVI, 1–44
Third Report, 1836	*Ibid.*, 47–60
	(with 28 unpaginated maps of dioceses following)
Fourth Report, 1836	*Ibid.*, 61–78
Fifth Report, 1837	P. Ps. 1837–8, XXVIII, 9–22

Report from the Select Committee on First Fruits and Tenths, and Administration of Queen Anne's Bounty, 1837 (P. Ps. 1837, VI, 1–75): here referred to as the '1837 Committee'.

Reports from the Select Committee on the Ecclesiastical Commission, 1847 and 1848 (P. Ps. 1847, IX, 1–282; P. Ps. 1847–8, VII, 523–end): here referred to as the '1847–8 Committee'.

Reports (first, second and third) from the Royal Commission appointed to inquire into the State and Condition of the Cathedral and Collegiate Churches in England and Wales: here referred to as the 'Cathedrals Commission'

First Report, 1854	P. Ps. 1854, XXV
Second Report, 1855	P. Ps. 1854–5, XV, 35–8

Third Report, 1855   *Ibid.*, 39–107

Reports (first, second, and third) *from the Select Committee on the Ecclesiastical Commission, etc.*, 1856: here referred to as the '1856 Committee'

    First Report   P. Ps. 1856, XI, 1–504
    Second Report   *Ibid.*, 505–508
    Third Report   *Ibid.*, 509–end.

Reports from the Select Committee on the Ecclesiastical Commission, 1862–3 (P. Ps. 1862, VIII; 1863, VI, 43–301): here referred to as the '1862–3 Committee'.

Report from the Select Committee on Queen Anne's Bounty, 1868 (P. Ps. 1867–8, VII, 467–615): here referred to as the '1868 Committee'.

Report from the Joint Select Committee on Queen Anne's Bounty, 1900–1901 (P. Ps. 1900, VIII, 79–254; 1901, VII, 313–479): here referred to as the '1900–1 Committee'.

Other abbreviations regularly used

Hansard n.s.	Hansard, new series
Hansard/3	Hansard, 3rd series (similarly for 4th and 5th)
Brit. Mus. Add. MSS.	British Museum, Additional Manuscripts
C.C.F.	Church Commissioners File
D.N.B.	*Dictionary of National Biography*
H.M.C.	Historical Manuscripts Commission
P.R.O.	Public Records Office
S.P.D.	State Papers (Domestic)
V.C.H.	*Victoria County History*

Early eighteenth-century dates are given in the New Style.

INTRODUCTION

Within the past two hundred and fifty years (not to mention any longer period) both the ends pursued by the Church of England and the means by which it has sought to attain them have been greatly changed. It would be surprising if this were not so, since everything else that matters most in the life of the nation, its economy, its social structure, its political habits, has been revolutionized in the same period of time; but the fact is worth emphasizing all the same, because so many of the cherished beliefs and traditions of the loyal Church of England man tend to obscure it. The reforms in ecclesiastical administration (dominant among them the institution of the Ecclesiastical Commissioners), the rise of new church parties, changed fashions of church building, decoration and services, are not the only and perhaps not the most fundamental changes that have taken place. They are only, so to speak, internal changes. More radical in the long run, though far less swift and conspicuous in any one generation, are the changes in the Church of England's external relations, in its social and constitutional status.

About 1700, the Church of England was much more than a church in the strict, religious sense of the word. It was a political institution and a social institution as well; its possessions, its ubiquity, its history, combined to make it dominant, head, shoulders and body, among the other institutions of the state. Its standing in society at large was further secured by the nature of its ideological environment, for at that time the idea of God was (in sharp contrast to the present time) a real one to the great majority of men, commonly entertained by the adult mind, inevitably instilled into the child, so naturally and easily that it seemed intuitive. Certain of the protestant dissenters objected that this God was not best served by an established church, but they were few in number. There seems to be no doubt that to most men the idea of a religious establishment came with no more difficulty than the idea of God Himself. Not until after the middle of the century did any substantial bodies of opinion gather to support the dissenters' arguments, or to assert, what was hardly yet mentionable in public at the beginning of the century, that establishments of religion were wrong because religion itself was a fraud. In 1700, religion was still an element in which the greater part of the nation breathed naturally. It moreover still provided (as it had done since the conversion of the Anglo-Saxons) the common framework of ideas about law and society. Political and other 'secular' disputes almost inevitably took on some religious savour, partly, doubtless, because causes looked (as they still do look) better if they could sail under Christian colours, but partly also because few causes then could ever be wholly either 'secular' or 'spiritual'; the distinction was not clear, outside libraries of divinity; every topic of social and political interest brought religious connexions and implications in its wake. It is not surprising therefore that the Church of England, towering over the few other visible churches and dominant among the various 'establishments' of the state, the repository of the national faith, should have been accepted also as a natural apanage of politics, as the cement of society and the censor of morals. It is not surprising either, that its material circum-stances and working efficiency should have been matters of keenest interest to other influential persons besides the upper clergy.

'Church reform' is a subject which in the middle of the twentieth century need worry none but churchmen; it has become their private affair. 'Church reform' in the eighteenth or early nineteenth centuries, however, concerned everybody, and its fate was settled in the national legislature. It is as instruments of church reform that both Queen Anne's Bounty and the Ecclesiastical Commissioners come into English history. Incomparable though they were in scale (for the Bounty began as, and long remained, a very small concern), their lives ran through similar courses. Each was founded to promote a particular measure of church reform, each stayed on to carry many burdens other than those for which it was originally designed, and each became a permanent administrative department. Each was conceived in a time of religious revival and political excitement and bore marks of parenthood which ensured it the hostility of certain elements in society. Mainly as a result of the opposition, each was substantially modified within a few decades of its beginning, and put upon a less controversial, and possibly a less effective, footing.

Between them, they saw the Church of England through several revolutions. With the theological revolutions, and with the rise and fall of church parties during the period in question, they were only indirectly concerned. With the thorough-going reforms in the church's administration, however, they became much involved, at both the giving and the receiving end. For the revolutions in the church's territorial and financial organization, which transformed the virtually medieval system of 1700 into something recognizably up-to-date and fairly serviceable by the end of the nineteenth century, they had much direct responsibility.

These revolutions in the life and structure of the church itself ran alongside a complete change in its relations with the state and with society. The character of its establishment changed; men came to look on it with different eyes, and to dare to attack it, in the course of the nineteenth century, as on the whole they did not dare in the eighteenth; the kind of justifications offered for its establishment were not the same in 1850 as in 1750, and were different again by 1950. The Church of England in 1700 had a pronouncedly political character. This was taken to be quite natural and proper by all except the Independents, Baptists, Quakers and remoter sectarians, whose views, however interesting and perhaps alarming they might appear on paper, could generally be ignored in practice. The Whigs, who ought not, if they had followed the views of their preceptor Locke, to have set much store on an establishment, showed no signs of wishing to undo it. Their prize preacher, Hoadly, taught the complete irrelevance of all visible churches whatever; but this did not prevent him from picking the ripest plums his own church had to offer. The truth is, that the established church was far too important a part of the political and social structure of the country for any man of property, not committed by religious scruples to dissent, lightly to abandon. Politicians wrangled over its appointments: if they were on the side of the administration, they deplored the disloyalty of those clergymen who sympathized with the opposition; if they were on the opposition side, they would say that the church was being prostituted by the men in power. This was all very unpleasant, perhaps unspiritual. Some really pious clergy, whether they inclined to any or none of the existing parties, were apt to regret these concomitants of establishment. But there was no point in disputing the propriety of establishment itself. Politicians would not, and most men who cared for the political stability of the nation could not, do without it.

In the course of the nineteenth century the Church of England, like the civil service, was to a considerable degree taken out of politics. Most of the many preferments in the Crown's gift came to be given for reasons additional to political ones. Party still came into it, but it was often ecclesiastical party, as prime ministers tried to strengthen the one they thought more helpful, or to placate each in turn. On the one hand it became increasingly *infra dig.* for ministers of the Crown to appoint the ecclesiastically unworthy; on the other, the structure of politics was so changing that little advantage could be gained from appointing for political reasons; and the purity of the church gained both ways.

The other great reform in which Queen Anne's Bounty and the Ecclesiastical Commissioners participated was a social one. The reforms in the church's territorial organization and financial administration were not important for its own internal prosperity alone. The changes wrought between 1700 and 1880, in the way parishes were actually run, churches built or repaired, and clergy paid, were of much larger importance, because to begin with all these mundane matters, small individually but together of the very essence of the church's life and character, were spread about the social scene in a higgledy-piggledy confusion, inextricable from the ordinary concerns of the laity. Gradually the church's rights and properties were sorted out and put in a separate compartment. This was a gigantic work, and it was effected to some degree by Queen Anne's Bounty, but mainly by the Ecclesiastical Commissioners, who thus assisted in a national social change of, over the decades, revolutionary proportions. A vast acreage of church property, mixed up all over the country with lay property, and more than twenty thousand buildings, were transferred from the management of nearly as many individuals, and the ivy-like clutches of the ancient local authorities, to the ultimate control of a single body of statutory commissioners. This great change has been accompanied by the conversion of an indescribably complicated system of laws and customs into a simple set of office regulations. It has put order into chaos, and made orderly and useful that which was irresponsible, inefficient and unpredictable.

The reform of the national church: the modification of its relations with the state: the transition from a medieval to the modern pattern of law and local government: it is with these organic changes in the structure of English life and institutions in mind that the history of Queen Anne's Bounty and the Ecclesiastical Commissioners must be read.

4

Introduction

It is a remarkable fact that palpable inefficiency and failure to do its work properly, by the standards of the more conscientious of each successive generation, have been almost continuously characteristic of the Church of England ever since the Reformation.[1] It is even more remarkable, that although the causes of the inefficiency remained perfectly clear and constant, nothing effective was done to right them between the reigns of Elizabeth and Victoria. Historians have not failed to pay proper attention to these material defects, charting their causes and consequences in the successive accepted phases of our national history, but no one seems yet to have considered the persistence of these defects through so long a period of years as a phenomenon in itself. Surely it is at least superficially astonishing, that while the governing classes of the nation never ceased to proclaim their loyalty to the Church of England and their reliance upon its establishment, reforming prelates found exactly the same things wrong, recommended much the same reforms, and died without achieving them, generation after generation. 'Scarce any of our most Gracious Kings and Queens from the Reformation,' wrote Erasmus Saunders in 1721, 'scarce any of our wisest and best Patriots in every Reign, who have not express'd a tender Concern for them.'[2] But nothing was done. Whitgift's list of admitted defects was no different from Laud's. Burnet and Gibson found things no better, and their *agenda* could have been adopted *in toto* a century later by Bishops Blomfield and Kaye, in whose generation at last real reforms were made. Little of lasting value or vital effect was done between Whitgift's days and Blomfield's. The first church reform movement was doomed from the start by its involvement in politics. The second faded out with the coming of the Hanoverians, leaving a few institutions of which the least inadequate was Queen Anne's Bounty. Only the third movement for church reform really got anywhere, through the founding of an institution to conduct church reform as its regular, full-time, business. The institution in question was that of the Ecclesiastical Commissioners.

Sometimes one suspects that historians, writing about institutions old

[1] With the medieval period I am not concerned, but I believe that the church was open to much the same kind of material criticisms before the sixteenth century as after.

[2] *View of the State of Religion in the Diocese of St David's* (new edition, 1949), p. 99.

5

and vanished, must see them less as they really were than did contemporaries who knew them when the blood still ran warm in their veins. Of Queen Anne's Bounty and the Ecclesiastical Commissioners, I do not think this is necessarily the case. The modern ecclesiastical and social historians who have remarked upon their activities (and many have done so) seem to have understood their general characters perfectly well, better, often, than they were understood in the eighteenth and nineteenth centuries. Sheer physical difficulties such as the slow transmission of news, the expense and hazard of travelling, the decrepitude of ecclesiastical administration, kept the workings of Queen Anne's Bounty mysterious to many of the eighteenth- and early nineteenth-century clergy; in Victoria's reign the facts and figures relative to the two bodies in question were not difficult to come by but misunderstandings still clouded their public standing—misunderstandings with roots deep in political or religious party prejudice, much more damaging and difficult to shift than misunderstandings based on ignorance alone, and much more proof against the arguments of statesmen and Blue Books. My researches have produced nothing very unexpected, little that will alter in any important respect what is regularly said of them in books about the English church and clergy; in this respect, I have simply been able to construct out of the great mass of material available a larger, deeper and I hope more colourful picture of what they did and how they did it.

It is perhaps strange, that two such bodies, whose general position in history is so well known and the materials for whose histories have not been difficult of access, should have escaped detailed investigation until within the last ten years. It seems to have needed their demise as separate entities in 1948 before either was accorded the dignity of anything in hard covers, although gritty little official histories of each had been published just after the First World War[1] and Sir James Brown published at the end of the Second an admirably readable and comprehensive sketch of the Commissioners' history.[2] Then came two works, to each of which I owe much. In 1955 Mr Alan Savidge published his monograph *The*

---

[1] L. T. Dibdin and S. E. Downing, *The Ecclesiastical Commission, a sketch of its History and Work* (1919), and W. R. Le Fanu, *Queen Anne's Bounty: a sketch of its History and Work* (1921). F. G. Hughes's revised edition of the latter was published in 1933.

[2] *Number One, Millbank: the Story of the Ecclesiastical Commissioners* (1944).

Introduction

Foundation and Early Years of Queen Anne's Bounty. Little can be added to what he has written on the subject, and my own briefer account of the period 1700–36 is based very largely on his. It is a great pleasure to acknowledge the excellence of his book and the unfailing kindness with which he has received my applications for help over the past five years and allowed me to use his book; from which I have taken most of the factual detail in chapters I and III about the Bounty's foundation and early history. The other work to which I refer remains unpublished: the Oxford doctorate thesis of Dr F. M. G. Willson (formerly of Nuffield College, at present at the University College of Rhodesia and Nyasa-land), *A Consideration of the Experience, in Britain, of Administrative Commissions represented in Parliament by non-Ministerial Commissioners, with special reference to the Ecclesiastical Commission, the Charity Commission and the Forestry Commission.* It is deposited in the Bodleian Library, and I have availed myself so freely of his permission to use it that a good deal of what I say about the Ecclesiastical Commissioners' constitutional problems during their first half-century is drawn from his analysis and conclusions; in which however I have not always concurred. I must let this statement of my general debt stand in place of more detailed acknowledgments in the notes to chapters VIII and IX. One other book there is that treats the Commissioners (in their early years) with care and respect—Olive J. Brose's *Church and Parliament: the Reshaping of the Church of England, 1828–1860,* published in 1959; but of that I need say little here, since the bulk of my own work on the period and topics of our overlap was done before hers came out. We have inevitably used much of the same material. Not so inevitably, some of our conclusions and 'interpretations' are very similar: compare, for instance, our accounts of the constitutional revolution of 1828–32, and of the importance of Peel and Blomfield.[1] In our views of the origins of the Commissioners, however, and our analyses of the general character and problems of the third church reform movement, we differ greatly.

Outside the parts of the subject where Mr Savidge and Dr Willson have anticipated me, I have drawn mainly from 'primary' sources in as much detail as the nature of the task has demanded, and time and material made possible. Obviously I have not examined every source of

[1] Chapter v to VIII below, passim, and my article on the former and its consequences for the established church in *Theology,* LXII (1959), 226 ff.

any degree of relevance. The institutions in question cover nearly two hundred and fifty years of history; they have always been more or less prominent in the life of the English Church through these years, have often excited the minds and even passions of the nation's legislators and judges, and have now and then been dragged from their cool and sequestered official vales of life into the noisy world of newspaper head-lines and questions in the House. Scarcely a year of the nineteenth century passed without a parliamentary paper about them; they were the subject of debates in the Convocations and the Church Assembly as well as Parliament, they entered the discussions of diocesan synods, con-ferences and societies in that busy world of local politics and endeavour of whose share in the Victorian achievement we are still far too ignorant. Not only newspapers and well-known periodicals like the *Quarterly* and *Church Quarterly Reviews* reviewed their activities, but also the myriad and (often) short-lived organs of ecclesiastical zeal and prejudice which line the 'dead periodicals' shelves of large old libraries in a dusty silence peculiarly alien to their producers. Ever since the eighteen-forties their work has been familiar to every clergyman and many pious laymen, a surprisingly large proportion of whom, as one recognizes with a kind of weary admiration, became articulate in book, pamphlet, or letter. Their collected records in the offices of the Church Commissioners at Millbank, though incomplete (especially as regards the Bounty) are, as may easily be imagined, voluminous.

It is doubtful whether a Mabillon or a Mommsen, or even one as industrious as 'Castell, Professor at Cambridge, who, during seventeen years, accounted that day a holiday in which he did not employ from sixteen to eighteen hours upon his gigantic works',[1] would have felt it necessary to go through all that *might* throw up something of relevance from this fathomless mine. Certainly I have not been through a ten-thousandth part of what lies there; but most of it is either matter of legal record or routine business, and I believe, after having searched and sifted it with the help of men whose working lives are passed in its company, that nothing of importance to the main theme of this book remains to be discovered there.

If those parts of the book dealing with the internal history of Queen Anne's Bounty and the Ecclesiastical Commissioners are mainly based on

[1] Pusey, *Remarks upon the prospective and past benefits of Cathedral Institutions*, p. 53.

'primary' sources (in which I include parliamentary papers and debates), the same claim cannot be made in respect of all the parts which are meant to put them into their natural context and to assess their ultimate significance. These two institutions were central to the administrative machinery of the established church. They mattered a great deal in the life of the church. They mattered in a yet larger field, in the life of the nation as a whole, in proportion as the church itself mattered; and for many of the decades under discussion, the Church mattered a very great deal. Of the Church of England in the eighteenth and early nineteenth centuries, its establishment was the grandest single feature. The Church of England's character was mainly determined for the greater part of those centuries by the fact of its establishment; which meant, not whatever theory of establishment might be put forward to explain or justify it, but the whole framework of laws, traditions, usages and (so far as one can detect them) assumptions that in fact made up its establishment at any given moment. This was the setting in which most Englishmen before, say, 1870, were familiar with the Church of England. It mattered in the ordinary course of life to a degree now to many people incredible; it lay inescapably across the workaday paths of the lawyer, the politician, the magistrate, the farmer and his labourer; it could scarcely be avoided by the man of property, the ratepayer, the lover, the father, and the corpse.

I have only managed to place my history of Queen Anne's Bounty and the Ecclesiastical Commissioners into this huge setting by enlisting the aid, and standing often on the shoulders, of others. Whether this has led to shallowness or misrepresentation is for my critics to say; I have preferred to risk going wrong on the right lines to staying safe on what would have been, I think, the wrong ones.

One other feature of the book needs to be explained. Its texture is not consistent all the way through. The period from the seventeen-seventies to the eighteen-seventies is treated in greater depth and detail than the periods before or after. This is simply because that period was so crucial in both the history of the Church of England and the development of English society. If one is trying to study the two together and to mark their interrelations, those years assume an air of paramount importance. Inevitably also, they were years of particular interest for the history of Queen Anne's Bounty and the Ecclesiastical Commissioners. The

Bounty Board came then to have a greater proportionate share in the life of the church than it had done previously or was ever to do again, and the Commissioners did their greatest work, and laid the foundations of all their subsequent labours, in their first, vigorous, and controversial half-century. The period enclosed by the birth of Blomfield and the death of Tait forms the heart of my book. As to the last period, from the eighteen-eighties to 1948, I admit at once the relatively sketchy and limited nature of my treatment, especially on the economic and financial developments. Yet the work of both institutions became ever more heavy and complex and the problems with which they had to grapple were often awkward and interesting. Historians of the twentieth-century church will find in my last chapter many gaps, and as many invitations to fill them.

CHAPTER I

THE ORIGINS AND ESTABLISHMENT OF QUEEN ANNE'S BOUNTY

The modern debate on church reform was, by the end of the seventeenth century, already more than a hundred years old. Ever since Elizabeth's successful settlement of the church establishment had given churchmen a chance clearly to see and take stock of its material defects, much had been recognized as needing reform, and little had been done about it; with the result that, to many serious-minded subjects of the later Stuarts, it was obvious that religion was not being efficiently and ubiquitously taught, that the clerical order was too often held in contempt and poverty, and that social order was imperilled. Only at one period since the Reformation had church reform been undertaken on anything better than a piecemeal plan, and that was during Cromwell's ascendancy. A programme of church reform undertaken under such auspices was un-likely to recommend itself to the royalist Anglicans who came back into their own with Charles II. The Presbyterians cannot have improved their chances at the Savoy Conference when, to the Episcopalians' argument that the insufficiency of so many livings stood in the way of enforcing residence, they replied, 'When the Usurper would quickly have brought Livings to that competency, as would have maintained able Preachers; we may not question, whether just Authority will do it?'[1] But all that 'just Authority' did was to restore to royalists those parts of their estates—advowsons, impropriations, tithes and glebes—that had been made over by 'the Usurper' to the augmentation of poor parishes, thus casting many hundreds of them back into the destitution from which they had been temporarily rescued.[2] The hopes so reasonably entertained by earnest reformers, that opportunity might be taken by the legislature to make the restoration of the old establishment something of a renova-tion as well, were thoroughly disappointed. King and parliament both

---

[1] White Kennet, *Case of Impropriations*, p. 259.
[2] 13 and 14 Charles II c. 25.

spoke enthusiastically of voluntary contributions towards the relief of poor clergy and in their separate ways encouraged it—the king and the Primate by exhortations and even mild menaces, parliament by altering the law so as to facilitate and protect gifts of lands or tithes;[1] but otherwise it was a restoration of the defective old system under the old laws and institutions, less only the one institution that could, perhaps, if wisely managed and harmoniously accommodated to the common law, have become a standing instrument of reform—the Court of High Commission. It was, moreover, marked by 'the tacit abandonment of every attempt to resume church property secularized at the Reformation, or to increase tithe payments'.[2] Nothing indeed was more perfectly restored after the Interregnum than the inconveniences and anomalies of the old administration.[3] So far as putting its house in order went, the church was worse off after the Interregnum than before it.

Yet the spirit of improvement was neither dead nor sleeping in the later seventeenth century. It seems, on the contrary, to have been active and effective. Several factors combined about this time to quicken it. The growth of towns was already in some places patently outstripping the provision of church accommodation. Nonconformity, in its new position as an external force standing over against the church, was another cause for worry. A deficiency of resident clergy or regular services mattered a lot more, now that there were rival religious institutions for people to go to if they disliked, or were repelled from, the establishment.

A further stimulus to serious thought about church reform must have been that 'religious revival' which marked the later Stuart and very early Georgian period, manifesting itself chiefly in voluntary and semi-official societies for the improvement of popular morals, the pursuit of personal sanctity, or the achievement of specified philanthropic objects, and leaving among its more obvious gifts to subsequent generations the

---

[1] See the king's letters to the bishops and dignitaries, mid-1660 and June 1667; Archbishop Sheldon's letter of 17 September 1670, and the statutes 17 Charles II c. 3 ss. 7 and 8, and 29 Charles II c. 8; all conveniently given and explained in Kennet, *op. cit.* pp. 253–5, 266–8 and 271–5.

[2] Christopher Hill, *Economic Problems of the Church*, p. 240.

[3] The whole of the material side of the Restoration has been well described by Anne Whiteman, in 'The Re-establishment of the Church of England, 1660–1663', in *Trans. Royal Hist. Soc.*, 5th series, v (1955), 111 ff.

S.P.C.K., the S.P.G., and (which was at least as important from the church's point of view in the eighteenth century) the Corporation of the Sons of the Clergy. This 'revival' seems to merit closer investigation than it has yet received.[1] The motives behind it were of the mixed kind that is inevitable whenever more than one section of society is involved. The search for personal salvation ran without difficulty into anxiety for the salvation of others; which itself easily shaded off into a concern for social order and political stability that came easily into the 'revival' from merely prudential motives. No less mixed were the objects of this movement; and prominent among them was the material reform of the established church.

I. THE CONDITION OF THE CLERGY IN THE LATE SEVENTEENTH CENTURY

Without doubt, the church's main material defect in this period was the poverty that brought contempt upon so many of its clergy and inefficiency into so much of its work. There were not yet those extreme disparities of income that marked the later eighteenth and early nineteenth centuries. Nevertheless the contrast was sufficiently stark and lamentable between those with at least a settled sufficiency, and those without it; a contrast from every point of view deplorable. One at least of the relevant points of view represents a state of mind which was natural enough—was indeed instinctive up to about 1800, but which the democratic and egalitarian tendencies of modern times have made rather unfashionable. The social structure of the seventeenth and eighteenth centuries was such that a poor clergyman—a clergyman whose clothes, family, place and manner of living, pronounced him poor—might labour under grievous disadvantages. His poverty would cripple his pastorate in many obvious ways. He would lack books and the society of educated persons; he would have nothing but words to give to the afflicted; he would be driven to supplement his inadequate income by taking on other jobs—one or two additional curacies, perhaps, or school teaching, hack-writing, or farming. Lacking the means to fee a lawyer,

---

[1] See Dudley Bahlman's recent study *The Moral Revolution of 1688* and Garnet V. Portus's pioneer work *Caritas Anglicana* (subtitled, *An Historical Inquiry into those Religious and Philanthropical societies that flourished in England between the years 1678 and 1740*).

he would be powerless to resist exploitations of his unhappy position and encroachment upon the rights of his church; 'Ministers are terrify'd, and forced to submit . . . rather than be at the expense of a Suit at Law', wrote the experienced author of *The Clergyman's Vade-Mecum*, 'where the Controversy is at last to be decided by twelve Laymen, whereof sometimes half are *Dissenters*, and professed Adversaries to Men in Holy Orders'.[1]

But beyond these disabilities, it is clear from the comments of contemporaries that he would also, unless he were quite exceptional, lack the respect and confidence of his flock. Clerical poverty ultimately meant 'that their Labours have no Influence upon the Minds of Men, except it be those very few that are able to distinguish their Characters from their Circumstances'.[2] 'It is not uncommon', complained one clergyman at the Festival of the Sons of the Clergy, 'for a person of considerable Birth, and of extraordinary Merit in all respects, to be trampled on, and abused, together with his Wife and Children, by illiterate, unmannered, purse-proud Peasants, purely because he is poor, and a Clergyman'.[3] 'A poor clergy', wrote Burnet, 'may be scandalous, but must be both ignorant and contemptible'.[4] Adam Smith later gave his testimony to the same fact. 'Nothing but the most exemplary morals', he said when discussing the clergy, 'can give dignity to a man of small fortune.'[5]

The lack of a 'settled [i.e. fixed, permanent, and impersonal] pro-

[1] 5th edition, 1723, p. 145. The widow of the vicar of 'Hartyn', Sussex, explained in 1719 to the Clergy Widows and Orphans Corporation that her poverty was largely due to her husband's 'being Oblig'd to contend with a Rich and Powerfull Adversary for the Rights and Dues of his Vicaridge; and tho' after a long and expensive suit He recover'd a very considerable Addition to his Vicaridge, yet He was thereby so impoverish'd that He could not appear abroad by reason of the Debts he had thereby contracted.' (E. H. Pearce, *Sons of the Clergy*, 2nd edn., 1928, p. 143).
[2] Robert Nelson, 'Address to Persons of Quality and Estate', in *Works*, p. 264.
[3] Joseph Trapp, *The Dignity and Benefit of the Priesthood*, pp. 50–1.
[4] Memorial to the King, c.1696: cited by Savidge, *The Foundation and Early Years of Queen Anne's Bounty*, p.13.
[5] *Wealth of Nations*, Everyman edition, II, 292. It seems possible that the period between, say, the Reformation and about 1800 forms an interlude between an age in which the clergyman could at any rate hope to enjoy the respect due to his priestly prerogatives, and an age in which the 'dignity of labour', if not actually better appreciated, is at any rate much more talked about; it is certain that, whatever the

vision' for many clergy was a cognate matter which added to the worries felt by serious churchmen about the state of the established church. Lacking such security, clergymen too easily became 'mean and stipendiary ministers . . . who, wholly depending for their necessary maintenance upon the good will and liking of their auditors, have been and are thereby under temptation of too much complying and suiting their doctrine and teaching to the humour rather than the good of their auditors; which hath been a great occasion of faction and schism, and of the contempt of the ministry. . . .'[1] This was always one of the main charges alleged by establishment men against dissenters—that the dissenting minister, financially dependent upon his congregation's support, could not tell them the truth when it hurt as could the ideal establishment minister whose income came from endowments. So deeply was this argument embedded in the establishment state of mind, that it was still being used in the nineteenth century, when it was safe for all, except some still subject congregations of the countryside, to keep out of earshot of the official distributor of wholesome home-truths. Whitgift and Laud had been much troubled by the growth of subscription-lectureships, by which the Puritan laity got the kind of sermon they wanted and a good many clergy made a reasonable living. From the Restoration onwards pew-rents, especially in private chapels, greatly worried good establishment men as tending to introduce one of the key features of dissent. It added a further and powerful incentive to such a reformation as would give to every clergyman a decent basic stipend, the source and payment of which was (in theory) completely irrelevant to his popularity or otherwise.

So unpredictable and unsystematic was the organization of the church that it is difficult to say positively which classes of clergymen were the worst off in the late seventeenth century. There were plenty of exceptions to every rule. It was rare for anyone with the title of Rector to be

reason, a poor clergyman's poverty in this period was felt likely to interpose a social, 'conventional' barrier between him and his flock, quite apart from its manifold other consequences. We should err if we supposed that many men of the Stuart and Georgian period thought, with George Herbert, that conscientious drudgery was patently divine.

[1] Thus the preamble to the Act for uniting Churches in Cities and Towns Corporate, 1665, 17 Charles II c. 3, repeated with only verbal differences in the Act which established Queen Anne's Bounty, 1704, 2 and 3 Anne c. 11.

destitute; but the title of Vicar was a very uncertain guide to real income. A vicar would often enjoy by prescription, over and above most of the small tithes (which might themselves in the right district be quite lucrative), some of the great tithes, of hay or wood perhaps, or even a portion of the corn-tithe.[1] But he might fare very ill, especially if his parish was in a town where the ancient tithe-right had dwindled into a contentious claim to garden produce, or been commuted into a money-payment that had stood still while the value of money fell.

The class of curates was most generally poverty-stricken[2]. These poor men would usually come into one of four categories. First, there were stipendiary curates, men employed by non-resident incumbents, and rewarded by the incumbent with a stipend which a weak-kneed statute of 1713 attempted to keep above £20 a year.[3] They might or might not be resident in the parish they were paid to serve. Second, there were those who might, for want of a better word, be called 'temporary curates'—clergy engaged to tend sequestered livings, or to take the legal minimum of services in a parish whose incumbent was sick, moribund, demented or imprisoned. Many incumbents might be *in effect* non-resident without being quite so by formal legal standards; or they might be non-resident by the legal standard and yet succeed in avoiding legal notice; and in either case their curate would be of the 'temporary', not the stipendiary, kind. Third were the assistant curates, whose identity did not become merged in that of the stipendiary until the nineteenth century. These men were curates in the present-day understanding of the word, assisting incumbents who resided and looked after their own churches. (This could of course mean, in the period we are dealing with at present, being assistant to a stipendiary curate). There were, finally, the perpetual curates. If this term merely meant a curate who was never anything other than a curate, it would mean little enough, for of most curates this was unhappily true; but in fact a perpetual curate was unlike

[1] *Clergyman's Vade-Mecum*, 5th edn., 1723, p. 266.

[2] Of course there were exceptions to this rule. No doubt you could find around 1680 some parallel to William Sellon who was, at the time of his death a century later, deriving over a thousand a year from his several posts as curate of the united parishes of St James and St John, Clerkenwell; joint evening preacher at the Magdalen chapel; and alternate afternoon lecturer at St Andrew's Holborn and St Giles in the Fields. (See John Nichols, *Literary Anecdotes of the 18th Century*, VIII (1814), 492.)

[3] 12 Anne St. 2 c. 12.

the other types of curate in being himself an incumbent, with an incumbent's usual advantage of a freehold in his living for life. Probably this was the only advantage a perpetual curate had; for the chief characteristic of a perpetual curacy was, that its small (vicarial) as well as its great (rectorial) tithes were completely appropriated (or impropriated—the words were practically interchangeable) and the incumbent was supported by a fixed money payment or 'pension' paid to him by the impropriator. The amount paid was usually very small; and the perpetual curate's lot was the more unhappy in that, certainly lacking tithe-rights and probably lacking glebe, he could never hope to increase his income by the common means of 'improvement'.

The small amount, and sometimes also the uncertainty, of salaries was not the only cause of so much clerical poverty, though usually the main one. For one thing, it must be remembered that the clergy lacked official pensions until towards the end of Victoria's reign, when pensions were placed within the range of the more affluent. If they had private means, or had gained enough and to spare from lucrative livings during their years of health and activity, they could easily enough resign and retire; it was however much more usual to hang on to the end, and employ a curate or curates. But only the most prosperous clergy, those who could get hold of stalls and sinecures and make pluralism really pay (as it certainly did not in every case), could manage so comfortably. 'The utmost that Clergymen in the best circumstances can generally expect to do', said an anonymous early eighteenth-century pamphleteer, 'is to live decently in a private way, and to educate their children in such a manner, as by their Industry, and a small Portion, they may be able to live above contempt when their parents are Dead'.[1] This writer's business was to stick up for the clergy; but he hardly overstated his case. For most clergymen, far from being able to put anything by or to provide modestly for their dependents, were hardly able to make ends meet, and besides having sons to educate and daughters to endow, they would very likely (it is all too easy to forget this) have unmarried daughters to support as well as wives. For such, there was no alternative but to stay on to the bitter end; which is what they mostly did. The plight of the clergy in this domestic quarter of their lives was so extreme as to attract the

[1] *The value of Church and College Leases considered; and the Advantage of the Lessees made very apparent*, 3rd edn., 1729, p. 20.

attention of a Whig politician soon after the accession of George I, when good liberty-loving protestants were looking for means of attaching the clergy more firmly to the House of Brunswick. Rewards for loyalty—tangible, enviable, remunerative rewards—were the most obvious means; and one of Walpole's correspondents, as free from illusions about human nature as about the state of the clergy, proposed to reduce the clergy to 'continual dependence' by instituting in each diocese a fund to provide for pensions of twenty or thirty pounds a year for the widows of those who qualified during their life-time by showing 'a due regard to the Publick Interest'. No other scheme could work so well. The husband would 'bestir himself, to secure so great a Comfort to his wife, when he is gone; and his Wife would not fail to remind him of it, in Season and out of Season: so that Loyalty would be propagated by Curtain Lectures, and every new Addition to the Family would add new force to the Argument'.[1] Nothing came of this subtle project, so that the relief of clergy widows and children, as of sick and disabled clergy, was left in the hands of the Corporation of the Sons of the Clergy and its local, diocesan imitators, who did their best to provide small pensions for a few lucky widows, and cheap or free education and apprenticeship premiums for their children; but their operations can never have touched more than the skirts of the problem. Worry on account of these perils and endeavours to avert them worked together to increase the wretchedness of the poor clergy and to lessen the church's material efficiency.

'Dilapidations' were another cause of misery and hardship, which remained to vex all classes of clergy and to oppress all but the richest until Queen Anne's Bounty and the Ecclesiastical Commissioners together intervened just after the First World War. Each successive incumbent, being responsible at law for the upkeep of the residence house, had a right to claim from his predecessor (or predecessor's executors) the sum of money estimated as necessary for bringing the house into a state of good repair; it was the same for bishops in respect of their palaces, deans of their deaneries, and so on.[2] It was hardly to be expected that the two parties should often agree. When, for example, Parson Woodforde went

[1] A Proposal for the Regulation of the Clergy of England, in the Cholmondeley (Houghton) Papers, 78/1.

[2] For an illustration at episcopal level, see *The Diary of Francis Evans*, ed. David Robertson, pp. 48–51.

to Weston Longeville his valuer's initial estimate of the dilapidations was £175 2s. 6d. and his predecessor's widow's valuer's estimate was £26 9s. od.[1] The intrinsic justice of a claim for dilapidations was only one, and the least important, of the factors that affected its settlement. About 1800 an anxious clerical author affirmed that 'the mode of estimating dilapidations is as vague and as various as caprice and power can make it; and their amount is in general in proportion to the power of oppression on one side, or of resistance on the other'.[2] He said that things were worse than they used to be, and it is possible that this was so. Demands for dilapidations would naturally go up in the combined circumstances of a rising standard of respectability for the clergy, and a campaign to repair or provide residence houses so that they would cease to be so common and unanswerable an excuse for non-residence. In some cases, indeed, the parties came easily to an agreement.[3] But the system of dilapidations was never anything but an aggravation and a blight, that lowered the church's vitality and, at the very best, imposed charges of unpredictable amount upon its ministers, or on their widows or executors.

Then there were fees. No clergyman could hope to escape the payment of fees. In general, the more exalted the station, the more expensive the ticket to it, in the shape of fees to be paid at each stage of the process, and for each necessary document. The curate reached his haven at less expense than the bishop, and probably escaped the archdeacon's and bishop's modest visitation fees ('procurations' and 'synodals') that now and then fell upon the incumbent. Crown livings were particularly costly to take up, because so many extra formalities had to be undergone. It cost one of Walpole's beneficiaries £44 17s. 6d. to run his presentation to the sinecure rectory of Gedney, Lincolnshire, safely through the course of public offices; and he had the ordinary diocesan and parochial expenses still to come.[4]

A bishop's expenses on taking possession of a see were truly formid-

---

[1] Woodforde only got what he wanted after initiating an action in the ecclesiastical courts: the whole transaction may be followed in his *Diary*, ed. Beresford, I, 155, 171, 173, 182, 187, 191 ,and 194.

[2] *Six Letters to the Archbishop of Canterbury on Dilapidations*, pp. 2–3.

[3] See e.g. a 1730 example in Benjamin Rogers's *Diary*, ed. Linnell, pp. 17–18.

[4] Cholmondeley (Houghton) papers, 78/5. This sum was made up thus: Secretary's Office for warrant, bill and stamps, £13 2s. 6d.; 'To the Clerk as usual', £1 1s. od.; Office keepers, 5s.; Signet Office, £4 10s. 6d.; 'usual gratuity to the Clerk there',

able, so elaborate were the formalities and so magnificent his station. William Fleetwood, who became bishop of Ely in 1714, kept an exact account of his expenses.[1] They included £58 12s. 0d. for 'the Congé d'élire passing through all the offices'; £10 15s. 0d. for the dean and chapter's registrary 'for bringing the Instrument up' ('I gave it him, because he was said to be a poor and honest man, but I knew it was an imposition...'); £52 13s. 4d. for the royal assent; £55 1s. 10d. to Doctors' Commons for managing his 'confirmation' in Bow Church, and £32 5s. 0d. for their library 'by way of composition for a dinner usually made on that occasion'; £106 10s. 4d. when he did homage, 'and would have been £5 more, had there been any Groom of the Stole'; £10 10s. 0d. for three seals; £78 1s. 6d. for the restitution of the temporalities; £10 15s. 0d. 'for passing all these Instruments'; and £12 11s. 6d. for his inthronization at Ely. This total was £427 6s. 2d., and it seems not to have been the whole. In 1837 it was stated that 'the secretary's bill to the bishop, including the fees paid in the first instance, averages about £700.'[2] Their first-fruits were also very heavy. Fleetwood's were £2,134. Bishop Hooper, on his translation to Bath and Wells in 1704, asked for a special allowance of extra time to pay them, since the charges he had been put to on taking possession had absorbed almost the whole of his income.[3] When Van Mildert went to Durham in 1826, he was 'obliged to borrow to a considerable extent, and he insured his life at a considerable premium, because he was a bad life and he paid an additional sum; but altogether it was a source of great concern and anxiety to him'.[4] No wonder bishops sometimes viewed translations with mixed feelings, and hung on to as many other sources of income as they could. Even the curate was caught for fees, when he took out his license. Any eighteenth-century edition of Chancellor Burn's *Ecclesiasti-*

£1 1s. 0d.; Privy Seal Office, £3 3s. 0d.; 'usual gratuity to the Clerk there', £1 1s. 0d.; Office keeper, 5s.; Lord Chancellor's Office, £2 12s. 6d.; stamps, £3 1s. 0d.; fees of great seal, £6 14s. 6d.; Clerk of Presentations, £1 1s. 0d.; porters, 10s.; poundage, etc., 4s. 6d.; 'for soliciting the Presentation through the several offices as usual', £5 5s. 0d.

[1] See his 'Memoranda', 1714–23, in the Ely Diocesan Registry, A 6; described in A. Gibbons, *Ely Episcopal Records*, pp. 10–14.

[2] 1837 Committee, Q. 694.

[3] Savidge, p. 46.

[4] 1837 Committee, Q. 699.

cal Law, under the headings 'Fees' and 'Stamps', will show how fee-ridden, from the highest to the lowest, were the English clergy.[1]

Onerous also were the taxes which the clergy had to pay. Tithes were chargeable to the poor-rates, and a clergyman who took his tithe in kind could not escape them. If they were let out, of course, the lessee paid the rate. What the law was in the case of a *modus*, the author of the *Clergyman's Vade-Mecum* could not make out: 'I don't find any Book-Cases relating to this matter, but I fear that in some Places, poor Vicars, for want of good Advice or for Peace-sake, or thro' the Terror of Great Neighbours, are obliged to pay . . .'[2] It seems all too likely that this was so. From church-rates the clergy were, not unnaturally, exempt. But they were assessed to the land-tax from its very beginning, and their heaviest burden of all, in the late seventeenth century—a burden from which the laity was wholly free—was that they had to pay first-fruits and tenths.

2. FIRST FRUITS AND TENTHS

First-fruits and tenths were royal taxes on ecclesiastical dignities and benefices, the first-fruits being the sum of money paid on entry into possession of any one of them, and tenths being a recurring annual charge of much smaller amount. A few of the clergy had enjoyed exemption from first-fruits and tenths since the sixteenth century,[3] but to most, including the great majority of the least prosperous, they were burdensome. They were peculiarly distasteful too, as being a mulct upon ecclesiastical revenues for completely non-ecclesiastical purposes. In the beginning it had not been wholly so. What the popes of the later middle ages did with such proportion of their revenues from the English clergy as they succeeded in getting out of the country was indeed open to the criticism that the money could have been better employed; but at any rate its spending was in ecclesiastical hands. This was no longer true when

---

[1] See further, Erasmus Saunders, *View of the State of Religion in the Diocese of St. David's*, new edition, 1949, p. 69.

[2] *Op. cit.* pp. 310–11.

[3] I Eliz. I c. 4 released all vicarages under £10 a year and all parsonages under ten marks a year from first-fruits, and the dean and canons of Windsor from both first-fruits and tenths; and the archbishop of Canterbury and the bishop of London were released from payment of the latter, by royal grant under 1 Eliz. I c. 19 s. 2.

the *whole* of this revenue was taken over by Henry VIII in 1534, as a necessary part of his assertion of total national independence of the Pope of Rome. Henry's royal supremacy over his national church stretched deep and wide, but, once it was apparent that he was holding on to the first-fruits and tenths as a permanent additional source of revenue, and not merely taking care of them while some appropriate religious or charitable use was found for them, no one could seriously maintain that they were serving a better purpose after Henry's Reformation than before it.

To this insult was added the injury of a new, and higher, valuation for these unpopular taxes. In the great *Valor Ecclesiasticus* of 1535 (alias *Valor Beneficiorum*, alias *Liber Regis*) King Henry's Commissioners assessed the actual value of each dignity and benefice, in order that there should be no mistake as to the sums due to his new agency for their collection, the Court of First-Fruits. This assessment, which naturally grew increasingly unrealistic as time went by, remained the basis for their collection until what was left of them ceased to be collected at all, in 1926.[1] The machinery of their collection was, however, soon altered. Queen Mary abolished the Court of First-Fruits, and ceased to collect them altogether; tenths (for which the Court of First-Fruits had also been responsible, receiving them from the bishops whose job it was to arrange for their collection in their dioceses) continued to be collected by the bishops, but now that the Court had disappeared they paid them into the Exchequer. Elizabeth at once revived the collection of first-fruits but not the Court. Two Exchequer departments, the Board of First-Fruits and its subordinate the Board of Tenths, became the collecting agencies, and remained so until 1837.[2]

As for the revenue from first-fruits and tenths, which came to something like £17,000 a year, none of Henry's successors did anything better with it than he had done. Only the Long Parliament dealt with it justly; in 1649 it was transferred to trustees for the benefit of preachers,

---

[1] White Kennet says, in the glossary to his *Parochial Antiquities*, under the head 'Vicaria', that they were originally unrealistic—to the church's damage—in at least one respect, viz. that the value of vicarages was computed as if the vicar received the whole of the great as well as the small tithes.

[2] Savidge cites the following statutes: 26 Henry VIII c. 3, 32 Henry VIII c. 45, 2 & 3 Edward VI c. 2, 7 Edward VI c. 4, 1 Mary St 2 c. 10, 2 & 3 Philip and Mary c. 4, and 1 Eliz. I c. 4.

ministers, and schoolmasters: as if, wrote Kennet, 'the usurping Powers
. . . had been contriving by one good Act to atone for many evil'.[1] In
1660, along with every other sensible reform of the Interregnum, it went
back into its former channels; with the agreeable result that by the end of
the century most of it was appropriated to the payment of royal pensions
to persons great and small, deserving and not so deserving, and a good
deal of it was going to the support of families founded, on the wrong side
of the blanket, by Charles II. In 1705, when it was vital to know exactly
what the incomings and outgoings on this account were, the Exchequer
certified that it had to support pensions to the value of £10,950 a year.
Some of these pensions look more like official salaries, and some of the
remainder of the revenue went to meet running expenses of government,
as, for example, the secret service. A small amount of this casual expenditure might have gone to ecclesiastical persons or purposes, but of the
pensions at least Savidge says that 'with none can any connexion with
the Church be established'.[2] None of this was, as one might innocently
have supposed, hush-hush. All was open and above board. Bishop
Burnet could therefore openly and safely voice his opinion, that the uses
made of the first-fruits and tenths amounted to sacrilege.

It was probably not so much the thought that by these taxes they were
compulsorily aiding and abetting sacrilege that distressed the clergy, as
the manner in which they were collected. Their administration was
corrupt and inefficient, and in consequence produced an infinitely greater
degree of annoyance to the clergy and harm to the church than if it had
worked efficiently and fairly. So bad was it, that a historian of the
Treasury and Exchequer in this period has been moved to describe it as
'perfectly scandalous'.[3]

The First-Fruits Office (a department of the Exchequer) was in the
Middle Temple, nominally manned by a comptroller (a patent office
created early in James II's reign, in an attempt to check fraud and waste),[4]
a remembrancer (whose conversion into a patent sinecure office was
achieved in 1680 for the benefit of Charles II's bastard the Duke of
Grafton), a deputy remembrancer, a receiver, two clerks, two deputy

---

[1] *Case of Impropriations*, p. 382.   [2] Savidge, p. 34.

[3] S. B. Baxter, *The Development of the Treasury 1660–1702*, p. 119.

[4] See Baxter, *op. cit.* p. 120. This office quickly became a sinecure but must originally
have been quite important.

chamberlains, and two auditors. It was into this amply staffed office that both first-fruits and tenths were paid; the manner of their collection, however, differed. That of the first-fruits was the less scandalous, though hardly the more efficient.

First-fruits were paid straight into the Office by the clergy concerned. The Office was supposed to know from whom to expect first-fruits by receiving lists of institutions to dignities and benefices from the bishop's registrars each half-year. In practice, according to the deputy remembrancer about 1708, such lists came only irregularly and were often incomplete when they came.[1] New incumbents could spread their payment over two years, by giving bonds to the First-Fruits Office, guaranteeing four half-yearly payments. One would have thought that this was a welcome relief to them, as not only making payment more manageable for the hard-pressed but also saving those who were 'lawfully evicted, removed or put out' within two years, and the families of those who died within the same period, from a very unfair burden; but that they could be viewed in a different light is made clear by Kennet, who speaks sourly of 'the multiplied charge and trouble of *Four* several Bonds for the distinct Times of Payment', and of the clergy's being 'denied the Ease of paying down their Composition in one entire Sum, except they answer'd the Fees for the said several Bonds'.[2] Bishops were not statutorily entitled to this relief, but seem to have been able, since the sixteen-nineties anyway, to get time to pay if they were in real difficulties.[3]

The one feature of the first-fruits system that impressed itself upon the clergy at the end of the seventeenth century as really disagreeable ('a continual Burden and Terror') remains to be mentioned. This was 'the invention of a *fifth Bond* . . . for a future Account to be called for, upon any Review and fuller Valuation'; which amounted to a blank cheque for the payment of any further sum that would make the nominal first-fruits more realistic. Kennet's account of its origin[4] runs thus: 'Within a few years after the Restauration of King Charles II, when Taxes became great, and yet publick Necessities were still greater; *then* a certain statesman reassum'd the thoughts of raising the payment of the First-Fruits

[1] Savidge, pp. 40–1.   [2] *Case of Impropriations,* p. 303.
[3] Savidge, pp. 45–6; and A. Tindal Hart, *William Lloyd,* p. 151.
[4] The only account I have succeeded in finding.

and Tenths by a new extended Valuation: But he had not Courage to begin the Practice; he took the safer way of contriving to lay a Foundation for it. And so he clandestinely brought in the demand of a *Fifth Bond*, to be sued and recovered at some other time, when a Parliament should be willing, or the Prerogative able, to do it.' The clergy remained in fear of it (especially 'when by the hasty Instruments of Popery, some broad Intimations and even express Menaces were liberally given to us on this Account') 'till they were honourably delivered from it' by Queen Anne, as part of her Bounty, in 1704.[1]

The collection of tenths was altogether a more complicated business, and was managed on different lines. It was done under the bishops' superintendence in their separate dioceses. They appointed sub-collectors, whose business it was to pay the diocesan tenths into the Exchequer each year and hand in also a list of defaulters (the 'non-solvents') for the Exchequer's slow remorseless debt-collecting machinery to start work on. Corruption, fraud and extortion riddled the system, partly because some at least of the Exchequer officials and sub-collectors (the latter being often menial men) were ready to be corrupt, partly because the continual arrears of so many of the clergy invited the practice of frauds and extortions.

It is easy to see why so many fell into arrears. A few of the most ignorant might not even know of the existence of this tax on their livings. Some newcomers to livings would not know exactly how much they had to pay. The sub-collector would only succeed in bringing in a fraction of what was due on his annual circuit. Bishop Blackall of Exeter estimated it at no more than a third or a quarter when he denounced the whole rotten system in 1710;[2] and then some clergymen would not succeed in finding the sub-collector when they brought their tenths into the diocesan capital. Arrears of tenths piled up during vacancies and sequestrations, and became a very real bar to the acceptance of a presentation. The longer a vacancy went on, the longer was it likely to continue. It was because of this, and because poor clergymen were unable to pay

---

[1] Kennet, *op. cit.* pp. 303, 400–1. The form of the four usual bonds may be seen in Gill and Guilford, *Rector's Book of Clayworth*, pp. 11–12. Of the fifth bond, the rector said in 1672 that it 'was not well understood for what it should be, but was thought to be to fetch in more monies, in case there should happen to be a new valuation of livings before the first-fruits were paid'. [2] Savidge, pp. 39–40.

off long accumulations of arrears, that the tenths system worked so much harm.

Nor were the arrears merely the sum of the tenths for the number of years in question. Once a clergyman had been certified 'non-solvent' he had to pay not merely the tenth, but also a fee on it; and so for each ensuing year, until he (or his successor) at last caught up by paying what had become a very substantial sum. Whatever the arrears fees *ought* to have been, they seem in fact usually to have been 19s. or 19s. 4d. on each year's arrears, of which, when it was levied, 5s. 8d. went to the first-fruits officials and the rest was kept by the sub-collector. It was obviously in their own interests for both the diocesan collectors and the Exchequer officials to let as many clergymen get into arrears as possible; which is as likely as sheer inefficiency to explain why so many were so deep in trouble.

If Humphrey Prideaux can be relied on, it was only about 1670 that the 19s. screw began to be applied. In 1679 he found himself in six years' arrears on his Welsh sinecure, and vented his indignation in a letter to a friend. 'About seven years since, the knavery of some officers in the Exchequer had brought it to this, that if any incumbent should neglect his payments of tenths he was forthwith charged with 19s. for the neglect each year; but on complaint made this abuse was rectifyed and an order made' that the fee on each arrear should be 5s. 8d. merely. 'But the diocese of St David's being a great way off, those rogues of the Exchequer think they may play their old tricks among the poor Welch-men without control.'[1] It was, alas for the poor clergy, not only upon the poor Welchman that these exactions were laid, nor was the abuse rectified in the seventies. The sub-collector of Salisbury diocese was being instructed by the First-Fruits Office to collect the larger arrears' fees about 1710.[2]

Since we know on the evidence of the sub-collectors concerned that in the diocese of Lincoln there was no process for arrears between 1692 and 1706, nor in the diocese of Worcester between 1700 and 1709, it would seem that this particular line of extortion was workable only when the sub-collector wanted it to work.[3] But there was evil also in the

---

[1] Letter of 18 June 1679 in *Letters of Humphrey Prideaux to John Ellis*, pp. 67–8.
[2] Savidge, p. 38.
[3] *Ibid.* One of these sub-collectors, moreover, Francis Evans of Worcester, was patently an honest man: one can hardly read his *Diary* and think otherwise.

hearts of Exchequer officials. They too got something out of arrears' fees. They could, moreover, take bribes from clergymen in difficulties to hold off the dread Exchequer proceedings 'till they happen to drop off, leaving the whole burden of all the arrears in tenths, together with a dilapidated house, on their successors'.[1]

Such was the system of first-fruits and tenths in the late seventeenth century. It was one of the most obvious abuses and embarrassments of the established church; and it was the only one to be adequately reformed. The Exchequer's gains from the poorer clergy were negligible and by no rational plan of government could they be judged worth the great trouble, inconvenience, and injustice that their efficient collection involved. Accordingly we find, early in the reign of James II, a group of poor ministers in the diocese of Lincoln petitioning the king for relief from their burden of arrears of tenths ('accrued chiefly through the fault of their predecessors') and having their petition granted, once it had been ascertained by reference to the Exchequer and to their bishop that their livings really were small ones. Nor was that the end of the affair. The Lords of the Treasury were further authorized, 'in all cases where they shall be satisfied by the certificate of a Bishop or other attestation that a rectory or vicarage is of small value not exceeding £30 a year (reckoning by the utmost and most improved valuation) and that divers years' arrears of tenths are incurred thereupon', to discharge the arrears as long as the cure was duly served. Other cases from Lincoln, and similar cases from other dioceses, are recorded in the *Calendars of Treasury Books*.[2] The Treasury Lords got a reliable list of livings under £30 a year in arrears, from bishop, registrary, or sub-collector, and directed the Remembrancer of First-Fruits and his auditors to discharge them. Under William and Mary this sensible work continued, and so also under Anne, in a grander style. Encouraged apparently by Archbishop Sharp of York,[3] she instructed the Lord Treasurer in the summer of 1703 to carry on with the discharge of arrears on these poor livings; a clause was attached to the Queen Anne's Bounty Act of 1704, abolishing the fifth bond for payment of first-fruits and cutting the conventional four down

---

[1] Bishop Blackall's letter, cited above, p. 22. Baxter, *op. cit.*, p. 120, further alleges that the Exchequer officials used to take bribes for compounding long-standing arrears for a smaller, manageable, sum.

[2] Most of them are noted by Savidge, p. 20.   [3] Savidge, p. 20.

to one; all small livings of £50 a year or less were permanently discharged from both first-fruits and tenths (whether they had been in arrear or not) by statute in 1707 and 1708;[1] and by the latter statute also the bishops received the same facilities as the lower clergy, for spreading the payment of their first-fruits over a period (four years), and for an abatement if they vacated the see meanwhile. The machinery of collection also cried out for reform, and received it in 1717. This reform is better considered as part of the story of Queen Anne's Bounty proper, to which we may now turn.

3. 'THE GOVERNORS OF THE BOUNTY OF QUEEN ANNE FOR THE AUGMENTATION OF THE MAINTENANCE OF THE POOR CLERGY' INCORPORATED

Anne's succession to the throne had been eagerly looked forward to by zealous churchmen, who expected her to show a greater ecclesiastical concern than William had done. In her first speeches she repeatedly undertook to protect the church, and to attend to the clergy's welfare; moreover her fairly prompt action to hasten the discharge of arrears of tenths from poor livings seemed to testify to her sincerity. Kennet, writing only a few months later, noted all these things and continued: 'After all these publick Testimonies of Her Majesty's Pious Zeal and Affection for the Church, there was but *one* greater in Reserve, of which Her Majesty was pleased to give the glorious Example, in an Act of Bounty and perpetual Beneficence to the poorer Clergy; by devoting a constant Fund of Charity, out of her own Revenues, for the *Augmentation of small Vicarages and other insufficient Cures*. This was to redeem our happy Reformation from the only Reproach that had been cast upon it, the *Alienation of Church-Livings*.'[2]

Kennet's was only one of the many pens employed in the seventeenth century to deplore the way clerical property had been secularized at the Reformation. It was not the dissolution of the monasteries (to use the popular but not quite accurate description), nor the Crown's sale and gift of monastic land to private lay individuals, that was objected to. Abusing the monastic principle and tracing its nefarious workings in medieval England was only a standard convention of historical and antiquarian writing; the monasteries and chantries were well abolished,

[1] 5 and 6 Anne c. 24 and 6 Anne c. 27. [2] *Case of Impropriations*, p. 356.

and the religious orders with them. But a clear distinction was drawn between that property the monasteries more or less legitimately owned and that which they had illegitimately taken over; namely, above all, the tithes and glebes of the secular, the parochial, clergy, so commonly impropriated by monasteries, colleges, and chapters. This property, it was widely felt except by those who owned it, ought to have been restored to its original owners, or steps should have been taken to ensure that at any rate its special character and purpose should be respected. There was one school of thought (never lacking representatives from Archbishop Grindal to Bishop Phillpotts, from Sir Henry Spelman's *Tithes too hot to be touched* to Charlotte Yonge's *Pillars of the House* and J. M. Neale's *Ayton Priory, or, the Restored Monastery*) which held that the common law's celebrated respect for property rights ought neither to stand in the way of legislation to restore impropriated rectories and vicarages to the use of incumbents, nor to prevent bishops from compelling impropriators to deal fairly with the clergy at whose expense they were profiting, as apparently they had done in the fifteenth century, and as they might apparently still be expected to do under the provisions of 31 Henry VIII c. 13. Many proposals were made, under Elizabeth and the Stuarts, for one or other of these objects, most of which can be easily traced by reading together White Kennet's *Case of Impropriations* (the most serious work of the Stuart period on the subject) and Christopher Hill's *Economic Problems of the Church* (the only serious modern work). Kennet was able to produce, for the encouragement of the good-natured, plenty of examples of impropriators who had *voluntarily* done the decent thing—assisted thereto since 1665 by Section 7 of 17 Chas II c. 3.[1]

Despite the force of these arguments and examples impropriations remained secure with their owners, to be dealt with as they pleased. Tithes indeed proved, in the historical long run, too hot to handle; but in the opposite sense from Spelman's. It was not the class of impropriators but Queen Anne who stepped forward to save the English Reformation from reproach by returning to the use of the church the revenues from first-fruits and tenths, so long kept from it.

The idea of returning the first-fruits and tenths was not a new one.

---

[1] A clause enabling impropriators to augment parsonages or vicarages without license of mortmain, tacked irrelevantly onto an Act for Uniting Churches in Cities and Towns Corporate.

For obvious reasons it required more tactful handling than the idea of restoring impropriations. The monarch was not to be accused of sacrilege as lightly as a squire, a don, or a bishop. Nor was the value of the property at stake anything like as much. Yet the same principle could be discerned behind each, and the two campaigns should be considered as close blood-relations.

Savidge investigates as fully as one could wish the origin of the idea of Queen Anne's Bounty, and sees no reason for doubting Bishop Burnet's claim that the notion was his. Burnet was among the most active and original church reformers of the time and knew almost everybody who was anybody. He tells us that he first suggested it to Queen Mary, who was favourable. After her death he secured William's support and that of several of his ministers, neared success in 1698, and was again very near it when William died.[1] With the idea thus widely broadcast, it cannot have been difficult for others of similar mind with Burnet, and better standing with the new queen, to revive the project early in Anne's reign. It seems almost certain that the persons responsible were Archbishop Sharp, as pious and straightforward and almost as busy a prelate as Burnet; Sidney Godolphin the Lord Treasurer, intimately concerned as head of the financial department of government; and possibly, if Swift's word is to be accepted, Robert Harley, who was Speaker of the House of Commons at the time. Early in January 1704 a plan of action was being drawn up by Godolphin and Sharp, with Anne's encouragement. On Monday, 7 February, one of the Secretaries of State, Sir Charles Hedges, communicated the Queen's design to her loyal Commons.

Her Majesty having taken into her serious consideration the mean and insufficient Maintenance belonging to the Clergy in divers Parts of this Kingdom, to give them some Ease, hath been pleased to remit the Arrears of Tenths to the poor Clergy. And for Augmentation of their Maintenance, Her Majesty is pleased to declare, that She will make a Grant of her whole Revenue arising out of First-Fruits and Tenths, as far as it now is, or shall become free from Incumbrances, to be applied to this purpose; and if the House of Commons can find any proper Method, by which Her Majesty's good Intentions to the poor Clergy may be made most effectual, it will be a great Advantage to the Publick, and very acceptable to Her Majesty.[2]

[1] Savidge, pp. 13–15, relies on Burnet's *History*, Clarke and Foxcroft's *Life o̷ Burnet*, and certain manuscript sources, whose correct references are Bodleian MSS. D. 23 fos. 112–15, and Bodleian Add. MSS. A. 191 fo. 121, dated 22 November 1701.

[2] Cited in Kennet's *Case of Impropriations*, pp. 358–9.

The Commons received this proposal with suitable gratitude. A bill was brought in and, after a good deal of debate, given the royal assent on 3 April. Its most important section was the first, which enabled the Queen to set up a corporation to take over her revenues from first-fruits and tenths and apply them to the augmentation of the poor clergy's incomes; which corporation was duly founded, by charter under the great seal, on 3 November 1704.[1]

It remains only to consider the motives that lay behind Anne's and her government's action—why the deed was done, and at that time. To admit, even to expect, the operation of other motives than pure disinterested generosity, is not necessarily to derogate from the virtue of the Act. The Crown need not have given away this regular revenue. Admitting that a revaluation of first-fruits and tenths would have been far too unpopular a measure to carry through, the machinery for collecting them on their existing basis could easily have been improved and the revenue increased that way, if the government had really wished it; and it would be a mistake to suppose that early eighteenth-century governments were anything like as rich in proportion to their subjects as those of the present day, or as prodigal in their expenditure of public money. £17,000 a year, improvable to perhaps £20,000 without much trouble, was quite good money in 1704. Just how much Anne had to do with it is doubtful. If the idea had not been put into her not too intelligent head by Burnet[2] or Sharp or whoever in fact it was, she would presumably not have moved in the matter. It seems impossible to decide how much was due to her, how much to her ministers.

The establishment of Queen Anne's Bounty, as a gesture of good will and generosity towards the church, was at any rate politically well-timed. A large proportion of the clergy, especially the dignified and better-off parochial clergy, were disgruntled. In the great Convocation controversy the bishops (at least the Whig majority of them) and the lower clergy were set in violent opposition to each other. Twice had the Tories' pet Occasional Conformity bills, intended equally to harass the dissenters and protect the church establishment, been rejected by the House of Lords. Burnet himself admits that the Bounty was politic as well as generous. 'This time was perhaps chosen', he says, 'to pacify the angry clergy. . . .'[3] It seems likely enough. A later witness adds colour to

---

[1] Appendix 1; Savidge pp. 16–26.   [2] See Savidge, p. 14.   [3] Savidge, p. 19.

Burnet's evidence. Whether accurate or not, he is at any rate worth citing. The Earl of Egmont, a sensible and serious churchman so far as one can judge, records in his diary that early in 1734 he and Dr Ven got talking at dinner of Burnet's *History*. The Doctor remarked that Burnet doubtless had something to do with the Bounty: 'but the secret of that affair was as follows. At the time her Majesty made that grant the Pretender had wrote over that if he came ever to wear the Crown he would restore the first-fruits and tenths to the clergy. This happening when a new Parliament was to be called, the Ministry apprehending that the clergy would bestir themselves in elections in favour of the dis-affected persons to her Government, advised her Majesty to do the thing herself.'[1]

Baxter further suggests that the scandalous inefficiencies and corrup-tions of the First-Fruits Office 'may have made it somewhat easier for Queen Anne to be bountiful'. On the whole, the government must have breathed more freely when this revenue was finally abandoned in 1704[2]. A government unpopular with the clergy might, indeed, have felt safer once this revenue had been ostentatiously made over to clerical purposes; but it is difficult to see that government interest was otherwise involved. The Exchequer continued to be fully responsible for the collection of the revenue for over another century, and there was apparently no intention in 1704 of reforming the system of collection at all—that only came after 1710, as a result of the Governors' discovery, through their own bitter experience, of its scandalous character. On the administrative side, surely, government—considered in a vulgar, secular sense—only lost by it. They continued to get the kicks, while losing all the ha'pence.

But what government lost in cash and convenience it gained in popu-larity and support. This must have been the consideration that made the royal bounty palatable to hard-headed politicians, and additionally agreeable to the benevolent. Nor can it have been the indigent clergy's gratitude that the government most valued. Grateful these poor men doubtless were—the more so, in their ignorance of the difficulties the Governors would encounter and the number of years that would pass

---

[1] Egmont's Diary, 8 March 1734. H.M.C., *Egmont MSS*, v, 49–50. 'Dr Ven' was probably Richard Venn, Rector of St Antholin's in the City, a prominent high church divine and intimate of Bishops Hare and Gibson, who would have been unlikely to retail fables.   [2] *Development of the Treasury*, pp. 119, 121.

before any drops of the Bounty trickled through to them. But politically and socially these poor men were negligible. The men who mattered were the cathedral dignitaries, the fellows of colleges, the London clergy and the very country parsons whose social and economic positions were such as to put them personally beyond both need and qualification for the Bounty. What was there in it that appealed to them?

To this class of clergy her Bounty might well have been apparent principally in the clause of the statute that abolished the fifth bond and reassured them (the better off they were, the more they needed reassurance) that first-fruits and tenths 'shall hereafter be answered and paid by them according to such rates and proportions only as the same have heretofore been usually rated and paid'. A writer in the *Edinburgh Review*, 1823, alleged that by thus releasing themselves from fear of this revaluation, the richer clergy 'completely overreached' the simple queen. 'If the real purpose of this Act of Anne had been to augment the small livings, nothing could have been more reasonable than to do it, by enforcing the legal claim for the first-fruits and tenths on the holders of the large benefices.'[1] Nothing more reasonable, indeed, to a smart, shrewd, anticlerical Whig of the early nineteenth century; but the idea does not seem to have been as popular in Anne's time as it became after 1770. Kennet says that the idea of a revaluation was mooted in the reigns of Elizabeth and James I, before it turned up again with Charles II; but in these cases it seems to have been proposed simply for the Crown's benefit.[2] The only instance he quotes of a proposal to use such a revaluation in conjunction with a redistribution of ecclesiastical revenues, he denounces as the work of 'a Pestilent Writer' whose honesty he doubts.[3] The reviewer's thinking was too unhistorical and the support for his case too slight to make it convincing and Savidge is right to dismiss it as 'rather exaggerated';[4] but it might be a mistake altogether to dismiss the possibility of the richer clergy's having indeed had some interest of this

---

[1] *Ed. Rev.* xxxviii (1823), 152.

[2] As it certainly was by 'Mr. Thompson, Merchant in Bow Lane', who at some date in the seventeen-thirties sent Walpole 'A Scheme to Raise a perpetuall Annual Fund of £110,000 at least, for the Publick Service, by a new Survey of all Ecclesiasticall Livings and Benefices in England. . . .' Cholmondeley (Houghton) Papers, 78/19.1 and 2.

[3] *Case of Impropriations*, pp. 398–401.   [4] Savidge, p. 114.

kind in the Bounty, along with the Edinburgh reviewer's arguments for it. They need not have feared a revaluation and redistribution for their poor brethren's benefit in order to have been relieved at the fifth bond's removal and the statutory declaration that first-fruits and tenths would continue to be taken at their *Liber Regis* values. It seems, moreover, that one may be in danger from using the term 'Queen Anne's Bounty' in an unhistorical sense. By the seventeen-twenties, indeed, 'Queen Anne's Bounty' meant what it has meant ever since—the Crown's generosity towards the poor clergy, by making over its first-fruits and tenths to improve their incomes, and by discharging the smaller livings from payment of first-fruits and tenths altogether. At the start that was not its whole and only meaning. It did not include the absolute discharge of small livings until 1707–8; and it did mean the abolition of the fifth-bond. This latter provision was as bountiful in its way as the returning of the first-fruits and tenths to church purposes, and it could well have gone far to engage the clergy's enthusiasm and loyalty. One would dearly like to know who, and what, lay behind the addition of this clause to the bill on Wednesday, 1 March; the *Commons' Journal* merely says, 'A Clause was offered to be added to the Bill, that there shall be but one Bond given for Payment of the First-Fruits, instead of the Five Bonds formerly required, and given by the Clergy.'[1] It is true that the several 'official' expressions of clerical gratitude for the promise of the Bounty harp only on the Crown's relinquishing the first-fruits and tenths;[2] but the final form of the statute was not known when these expressions were made; and in any case they are patently so very 'official' and flowery, that they are no more to be trusted as accurate accounts of what they purport to represent, than commemorative painting of the same period—for example, Thornhill's 'Arrival of George I'. They are full of the buoyant and beautiful extravagance of the baroque.

[1] *Journals of the House of Commons*, XIV, 364.

[2] E.g. the Addresses presented by the Upper and Lower Houses of the Canterbury Convocation and by the Convocation of York; and Atterbury's sermon to the House of Commons on the day of thanksgiving for the queen's accession, cited by Kennet, *op.cit.* pp. 360-370; and also addresses from the clergy diocese by diocese.

CHAPTER II

THE CHURCH, THE LAW, AND THE LAITY IN THE EIGHTEENTH CENTURY

Before proceeding with the study of Queen Anne's Bounty and its history in the eighteenth century, it is necessary to examine, first, the actual legal and constitutional position of the church as it stood within the whole property-owning, law-abiding commonwealth; and then the church's property and the way it was managed.

Such expositions of the relations of the established church with the state as were put forward in the early eighteenth century were of a rather different character from those made later. The difference is important because it was a measure of a gradual shift in the actual position of the established church within the country at large, and it was due mainly to a necessity, which had not existed earlier, of defending the very principle of 'an establishment of religion', as such, instead of simply the establishment as it existed.

This necessity to think and argue philosophically about the connexion of church and state seems to have arisen and to have been pressed upon churchmen mainly by the fact that it was not until the later eighteenth century that the separation of church and state was proposed by men of any substantial political importance. It required, after all, a large measure of detachment from the ideals dominant among the ruling classes to dispute the propriety of an institution so important among them as the Church of England. Such detachment came naturally to the early Independents and the seventeenth-century sectaries, but such persons, once shorn of the dreadful strength given by membership of the New Model Army, when they had reverted to their former insignificant status, were socially and politically unimportant. The 'interests' restored to power after 1660 needed not to worry much about the dissenters' peculiar views on church and state.

Even so, the first step was taken in 1662 towards creating an 'interest' whose views could not for long be ignored. The Act of Uniformity of that year excluded from the established church the bulk of the Presbyterian nonconformists who believed in the necessity and naturalness of a connexion of church and state no less strongly than the Episcopalians. They held to this belief after their exclusion, hoping at first that the turns of the political wheel would bring in such a reform of the Church of England as to enable them to be comprehended within it. But circumstances conspired to kill this hope, and to remodel completely the theory of church and state that sustained it. The Corporation and Test Acts largely prevented them from acquiring those stakes in the public life of their country which would at any rate have helped keep them true to their old ideals; various episodes of the Glorious Revolution made it clear that comprehension was finished as a practical possibility, and that toleration was all they could look forward to; and once the practical possibility of being again part of the established church had vanished, it was only a matter of time before the principle upon which established churches rested should begin to appear questionable.

By the reign of George III, and partly because of radical changes of direction in nonconformist theology, this change of principles had happened in the most advanced dissenters, and was steadily leavening the general lump. The consequence was, that the very existence of the established church *qua* established church was challenged by men whose arguments were worth considering, either because of their ostensible reasonableness and philosophical basis, or because of their potential political influence. This challenge was at first addressed by intellectuals to intellectuals, but the progress of the French Revolution soon showed to what practical results such intellectualizing might lead. The defenders of the church had to add to their traditional repertoire, expositions of the principle of establishment in general, and of the English church establishment in particular. As to the former, more general, question, they argued often from first principles, discoursing largely of the infancy of society, human nature, and the constitution of the moral and political order. Whether they used the word 'alliance' or not, they often owed a good deal to Warburton, whose most enduring (though involuntary) gift to English thought seems to have been the idea, very popular in the nineteenth century, that 'establishment' meant a state's looking over the assortment of churches available, choosing one, and 'establishing' it. As to the latter, the justification, more particularly, of the principles of the English church establishment, they argued largely from the social and constitutional advantages resulting from it, and rested as often on Burke and Paley, as in the more general argument they had rested, sometimes without knowing it, on Warburton.

Being thus free of the several burdens and temptations which oppressed those who wrote to justify and explain the establishment later on, how did men in the early eighteenth century see their church establishment and its relation to the state? The answer is, that they saw it mainly in terms of law; terms, that is to say, which *ipso facto* ruled out the possibility of tidy systematization and clear exposition. The law was every Englishman's principal household god. The majesty and sanctity and almost inexpressible complication of English law not merely controlled but actually constituted the constitution. Law was then paramount in many ways which subsequent developments have obscured. Most of the functions of government we have learnt to call administrative were then entrusted to judicial bodies and carried out by strictly legal processes. The contribution of unwritten rules to the practical running of a constitution was scarcely recognized, and so far as such rules were recognized, they were condemned as illegal practices, tending to corruption or despotism. The laws of England, virtually, *were* the constitution, and the Church of England was but one—the largest single one by far, but still only one among many—of the legal establishments which formed it. The church's part in the constitution, consequently, and its relations with the other parts, could only be defined and described in terms of its laws, and these were so mixed up and confused with those concerning the 'state'—the non-ecclesiastical side of the constitution— that it needed a strong sense of the church's essential separateness (which in practice of course existed in respect of its temporal interests as well as its divine origin and responsibilities) to carry clerical expositors through such a jungle of legal complications to an ultimate exposition of how exactly the established church sat in relation to the state.

The best known, most complete, and only thoroughly systematic such exposition was Edmund Gibson's great *Codex Iuris Ecclesiastici Anglicani: or, the Statutes, Constitutions, Canons, Rubricks and Articles of the Church of England, methodically Digested under their proper Heads*. To it, the learned author prefixed 'An Introductory Discourse, concerning the Present State of the Power, Discipline, and Laws, of the Church of England', which gave an account of the existing relations of church and state, and so clearly indicated the respects in which Gibson thought them unsatisfactory that much vulgar and some respectable criticism was thenceforth levelled at him for having pitched the claims of the clergy too high.[1]

Gibson's intention had been neither polemical nor, strictly, practical. He told his friend the Master of University College, '... it would be a great imprudence in me and an injustice to the design, should I go out of my way to make that a party book ..., the subject of which in its own nature is equally the concern of the clergy in general'.[2] Nor was the *Codex* as it first appeared in 1713, a folio volume of over 1400 pages, likely to be either purchaseable or serviceable to the majority of the clergy. Gibson was aware of this circumstance, and only the very great pressure of business that rested on him after his translation to London prevented him from further digesting his mountain of material into 'a plain analytical system of English Ecclesiastical Law in the nature of an Institute' for the use of the ordinary clergy and ordinances—something that would at once explain the church's position as an establishment, and help the clergy find their way about it.[3] In intending such a book Gibson was actuated by the knowledge, gained doubtless in his remarkably painstaking performance of his duties first as archdeacon and then as bishop, that without such legal aid the greater number of the clergy were helpless to understand, what were in fact only opposite sides of the same thing, their own personal rights and those of their church.

Many manuals were compiled with a view to rescuing the ordinary clergyman from the legal complications and perils which encompassed him. They correspond exactly to the even more numerous books written to guide the Justices of the Peace through their legal problems and obligations, and as if to emphasize their similarity, the best known of each class was written by the same hand. Richard Burn, chancellor of the diocese of Carlisle, published his *Justice of the Peace and Parish Officer* in

---

[1] See chapter III, below, p. 96 .

[2] A letter of 15 June 1710, cited from the Ballard MSS. by N. Sykes, *Edmund Gibson*, p. 66.

[3] Sykes, *Gibson*, p. 70n. A shorter *Codex* was published by Richard Grey in 1730.

1755, and his *Ecclesiastical Law* in 1760.[1] Each was produced with a severely practical purpose, and the contents were arranged under subject-headings; so that it was only a few seconds' work for the anxious ecclesiastic to locate the law on everything that could possibly come up in the course of his professional life, from Abbot, Abeyance and Acolyth, to Usurpation, Usury and Wills.

The complexity of this body of ecclesiastical law (which ran to four volumes of over 400 pages each by the sixth edition in 1797) might well alarm us, as it certainly alarmed Burn's clerical contemporaries. It was in no way surprising to the men of the eighteenth century that their ecclesiastical and temporal laws should have been so thoroughly intertwined and mutually dependent. It was as true in the later eighteenth century as it had been for the preceding millenium, that 'the Temporal Law and the Ecclesiastical Law are so coupled together, that the one cannot subsist without the other';[2] and only in the early nineteenth century did the parliament, which alone had the power to tackle such a task, set about the untying of this old and crusted knot. Political thought and, in some respects, social practice were more and more marking the distinction between secular and spiritual throughout the late seventeenth and eighteenth centuries; but, as Gibson remarked in his Introductory Discourse, the functions of government included equally 'the Administration of Ecclesiastical Matters (under the Prince, as Supreme Head of the Church)' and 'the Administration of Temporal Matters (under the same Prince, as Supreme and Sovereign in the State)'; a plan of government so admirable and ancient that, it could not be 'described better, than in the words of a known Statute, made in the Twenty-fourth year of King *Henry* the Eighth, and commonly called, the Statute of Appeals'.[3]

Such was the theory of the constitution. In practice the administrations of ecclesiastical and temporal matters were far indeed from the ideal distinctness and equality which Gibson, like Whitgift and Laud before him, would have wished them to possess. The course of the ecclesiastical law was far from smooth, and far from clear. It was expensive and

---

[1] After the manner of all good law books, they survived their author by many years. The former went into its 29th edition in 1845, and the 9th edition of the latter was brought out by Robert Phillimore in 1842.

[2] A dictum of Sir Edward Coke's, appropriately set on the title pages of Fraser's 6th edition of Burn in 1797.　　　　　　　　　　　　　　　[3] *Codex*, p. xviii.

dilatory and its operations were in many ways irrational and unfair. It attracted the attention of many generations of reformers both clerical and lay, one of the toughest of whom, on failing to improve the ecclesiastical court in which he himself presided, was moved to the despairing reflection that 'that which is crooked cannot be made straight'.[1] The ecclesiastical legal system criss-crossed with the secular legal system, becoming for many practical purposes a single system with it. This development, the progress of which through the years is clear enough, moved at least one good eighteenth-century Englishman to lyric heights in applause of so clear an exemplification of the wisdom of the Almighty, so admirably concordant with the general fitness of things. 'It is the glory of the present age [wrote Burn, with a deprecatory glance at the Elizabethan and Jacobean squabbles between the champions of the two systems] that these ferments have at length subsided ... Persecution hath departed to its native hell, and fair benevolence hath come down from heaven. The distinctions which were introduced during the plenitude of papal power have fallen away by degrees; and we shall naturally recur to the state wherein popery took us up, in which there was no thwarting between the two jurisdictions, but they were amicably conjoined, affording mutual help and ornament to each other.'[2] Thus the general incapacity to entertain the ideas of 'church' and 'state' in isolation was concretely reflected in the state of the laws of England, and actually experienced by the many Englishmen who, in that very law-conscious and lawyer-ridden age, willy-nilly went to law.

So largely did these two jurisdictions walk on common ground that it was difficult to say what were essentially ecclesiastical, and what temporal, matters: 'one of the greatest Temporal Difficulties, that belong to the Profession, is', remarked the author of the *Clergyman's Vade-Mecum*, 'that you are under such a Multitude and Variety of Laws and Rules, and those of a different sort, *Ecclesiastical* and *Civil*, which do often interfere, and clash with one another; insomuch, that the most learned Lawyers in many Cases, are not yet agreed as to the Rights and Duties of Church-Men....'[3] The ecclesiastical and temporal laws not merely clashed and interfered but poached on each other's proper (as one would have

---

[1] Foxcroft, *Supplement to Burnet's History*, p. 503.
[2] The conclusion of his section on Courts: 6th edition (1797) II, 52–3.
[3] 1723 edition, Preface.

thought) territory. Thomas Brett, a humble non-juring clergyman, had the impression in 1701 that 'the Ecclesiastical Courts as they are now managed ... have much more Temporal than Spiritual belonging to 'em'.[1] His impression was confirmed by the most acclaimed constitutional lawyer of the century. According to Blackstone, 'the spiritual courts ... continue to this day to decide many questions which are properly of temporal cognizance';[2] while Burn, who much admired him, described the same phenomenon from the other end by saying that 'indeed most ecclesiastical matters of considerable consequence are now usually determined [in] the courts of *equity*, in the exchequer, and in the chancery'.[3] The principal subjects of this shared or disputed jurisdiction were tithes, wills, and matrimonial causes, and the many forms and occasions of action which appertained to all three of them; and only the third was to any real extent the business of the ecclesiastical courts alone. As to both tithes and wills—matters with which every landowner and man of property was bound to be familiar—it depended very much upon the circumstances of the case and the discretion or prejudice of the litigant whether it was taken to the ecclesiastical or the temporal court in the first instance. The rector of Clayworth, for example, being refused tithes on their wages by several servants in his parish in 1683, at first intended to go to law in the church court, as he had done successfully in the same cause a few years earlier. But their masters stood by them and 'told them that all I could do to them, was to excommunicate them, which was only their not going to Church etc. So, beginning to think that to proceed with them in the spiritual court would be of small effect, I was persuaded to put in a bill against them in the Exchequer.'[4] Most tithe causes in the eighteenth century were in fact decided in the exchequer, while most actions of probate and administration stayed on the ecclesiastical side; but there were numerous exceptions, of which the relevant pages of the legal manuals will sufficiently apprise the patient inquirer. (Burn's section on Wills is by far his largest, and amounts to nearly a quarter of the whole work. Tithes come next, and a good way behind them come close together, in this order, Marriages, Colleges, Popery, and Church). Even if an action was commenced on the ecclesiastical side, it was by no means

[1] Thomas Brett, *An Account of Church-Government and Governors*, p. 20.
[2] *Commentaries on the Laws of England*, Book III, ch. 7.
[3] Preface, p. xxvi.   [4] Gill and Guilford, *op. cit.* pp. 60–1.

41

certain to stay there. By the issue of prohibitions the temporal courts could interrupt the progress of any case, examine it, and take it over if it offerred any of the exceedingly numerous grounds for so doing.

The ecclesiastical and temporal courts were thus, to a great extent, concurrent jurisdictions, offering complementary or even rival roads to judgment; and the scales were weighted in favour of the latter, by their possession of the weapon of the prohibition. This weapon further strengthened their natural superiority (which was fortified by their refusal to recognize the ecclesiastical courts as 'courts of record')[1] by enabling them to interfere also with those classes of case which were normally the ecclesiastical courts' independent business—divorces, for example, church rates, or even so thoroughly ecclesiastical a matter as the deprivation of delinquent clergy or the refusal to institute the unfit.[2] There was, in fact, no proceeding in the ecclesiastical courts which the temporal could not scrutinize by a prohibition, and there were a great many grounds entitling them to take over part or the whole of any case to which their attention was thus drawn. One cannot but conclude that the temporal courts enjoyed a substantial superiority over the ecclesiastical; and that if few voices joined themselves to Gibson's in protest, it was not because this ultimate superiority was not clear to the men of the eighteenth-century establishment, but because as the century wore on more and more of them accepted it as proper, and believed no harm could come of it. The terms in which Blackstone concludes his refutation of 'that groundless notion, which some are too apt to entertain, that the courts at Westminster Hall are at open variance with those at doctors' commons', are most revealing. They show at once how well-grounded that notion was, and why so clear-sighted a man could say they were groundless. 'It is true', he admitted, 'that they are sometimes obliged to use a parental authority, in correcting the excesses of these inferior courts, and keeping them within their legal bounds; but on the other hand, they afford them a parental assistance in repressing the insolence of contumacious delinquents, and rescuing their jurisdiction from that contempt, which for want of sufficient compulsive powers would other-

[1] Secker's 1750 Charge, in his *Eight Charges*, p. 140.
[2] For example, the patron and his presentee to a living could compel a bishop to justify his refusal before the temporal courts on every ground save the unimportant one of illiteracy.

wise be sure to attend it.'[1] In other words, the temporal courts lent the aid of secular penalties, and officers to enforce them, to their ecclesiastical counterparts, whose only penalty of excommunication would otherwise stand unsupported, and be only as effective as a rough, tough, rationalistic, priest-despising people were likely to let it be. It is curious that Blackstone should have supported his contention, that the temporal courts did not in fact dominate the ecclesiastical, with the example of an activity which he described as the compassionate loan of 'a supporting hand to an otherwise tottering authority'.

Thus, in the actual working of the constitutional partnership of ecclesiastical and temporal jurisdictions, the temporal held a firm superiority. All the way up the ladder of courts spiritual—from the archdeacons' courts, two, three or four of them in each diocese, through the bishops' consistory courts to the provincial courts at York and London—every action went forward under the shadow of the prohibition; and even those that reached the provincial courts and might thus be presumed to possess a peculiarly ecclesiastical character ('being purged from all Temporal Matter before they arrive there, by Prohibitions pray'd on one side or the other, upon the least pretence or colour of such mixtures')[2] were liable to be brought at the last to the mixed jurisdiction of the Court of Delegates, appointed by the king under the great seal to hear the final appeals in ecclesiastical cases, and sure to include laymen (lay peers, high court judges, or civilians of Doctors' Commons) as well as bishops.[3] A judgment by the Court of Delegates on an ecclesiastical case was nearly analogous to a statute of ecclesiastical application made by

[1] *Commentaries*, Book III, ch. 7.

[2] Gibson, *Codex*, p.xxi.

[3] It had practically always been thus. Gibson's search of the records seemed to show that no laymen had sat among the Delegates till 1604, and very few before 1639; but later research has shown that Gibson was mistaken, that in the great majority of cases before 1640 the civilians acted alone, and that in only two of the cases whose records survive from the period 1558–1640 did bishops sit alone. The figures for cases involving discipline or doctrine—that is, the most specially ecclesiastical cases—are: 1689–1714, 26 heard by bishops, judges and civilians, 13 by judges and civilians alone: 1714–50, 8 cases by the former mixture, 19 by the latter, and 20 by the former plus peers: between 1751–1838, all but one were heard by judges and civilians alone, and that one was heard by judges, civilians and a peer; bishops appeared in none at all. See Stubbs's Historical Appendix to the Report of the Ecclesiastical Courts Commission, 1883, in P.Ps. 1883, XXIV, 121.

parliament. Representatives of the spiritualty were present in both bodies; but the laity generally preponderated, and the monarch was supreme over all.

The supremacy of the monarch; the unquestioned superiority of statute over the other kinds of law; and the temporal courts' undisputed right to interpret statutes: these powers between them certainly made the church courts (and hence the whole ecclesiastical administration) theoretically subject to the temporal courts, and to the laity at large. In practice, the ultimate fact of the subjection was considerably obscured and limited by a number of factors, the most significant of which were the chronic incapacity of most men at that epoch to appreciate the facts of sovereignty, and that reverence for inherited customs and laws which seems to have prevented most men from even beginning to think of altering them by act of the sovereign power and so turning history into a new, chosen course. (In the early nineteenth century these things became differently understood, with startling results in both church and state—among them the Ecclesiastical Commissioners). Only the frequent issue, and infallible efficacy, of prohibitions kept men constantly in mind of that ultimate superiority of the temporal courts which lay potential in the constitution.

There were many other ways in which the laity participated in what one might have thought exclusively ecclesiastical affairs. The most obvious were not the least important. The laity bore directly on the clergy through the king's government, through parliament, and through the law courts. The first of these is so obvious as scarcely to need further mention. The last prelate to hold a high post in the administration was John Robinson, Lord Privy Seal and joint-plenipotentiary at the peace-making at Utrecht in the last years of Anne; and no more signal an illustration of the possible effect of secular politics on church affairs could be given than the disreputable fact that the putting to sleep of Convocation in 1717 for nearly a century and a half 'was, in the proper and literal sense of the phrase, a *coup d'état*', for which the king's ministers were directly responsible.[1] More constantly the clergy felt the hand of the laity heavy on them through parliament and the law-courts. Sometimes the church was openly insulted and put down by its own nominal members, who often discovered a convenient distinction between the

[1] Norman Sykes, *William Wake*, I, 144.

interests of the church and those of Christianity. Parliament always contained an element of this kind, and in the second and third decades of the eighteenth century, when the clerical order generally seems to have been held lower in public esteem than ever before or since, this element sometimes actually succeeded in carrying both houses with it. No statute has ever been passed more ostentatiously in defiance of the church's interests and wishes than the Mortmain Act of 1736.[1] More often the laity, when busying itself with church affairs, was apt to appear in the character of the candid friend, anxious only to help the church in its difficulties, and claiming a clearer understanding of their causes and remedies than the church itself. Whenever the church became involved in political controversy, a strong party of 'friends of the church' sprang up in parliament to defend it; and, naturally enough, both their motives for defending the church, and their proposals towards that end, were largely determined by the fact that almost always the church was endangered not alone, but in common with the interests which they were in parliament to represent. The cry of 'the church in danger!' was a dangerously easy one for the cynical or self-interested to employ to whip up support for their cause and dress it respectably, and there can be no doubt that it was often so used.[2] On the other hand, it is certain that very often when men cried 'the church in danger!', they really believed it was. The charges to which they probably lie open are not moral but intellectual—not hypocrisy and lack of scruple, but excess of excitement and conservatism, and a failure (from which, if they lived between 1714 and 1830, they could hardly escape) to understand the church's essential spiritual independence and purpose.

From a parliamentarian's standpoint, indeed, it seemed not merely prudent but morally obligatory to give the church that strong support which acts of parliament alone could give it. The established church was the national church, and it was parliament's business to know what went on in every part of the nation, and to legislate according to need. The

---

[1] 9 George II c. 36. See chapter III, below, pp. 103–4.

[2] e.g. by the Tory 'high-fliers' in Anne's reign, on whom see especially G. V. Bennett, *White Kennet*, chapters 4 and 5; and by those who, for whatever reason, opposed the Whigs during the years of the 'Catholic question', and were described by Southey, who ought to have known, as 'a base crew, the hired retainers of party, and other noisy hunters after preferment . . .' *Essays Moral and Political*, II, 280.

church ought surely to be thankful for statutes designed especially to help it do its business (e.g. statutes facilitating the recovery of tithes and church-rates) or, what was surely better still, to do its business for it, like the acts of 1606 'for repressing the odious and loathsome sin of Drunkenness'[1] and 1697 'for the more effectual suppressing of Blasphemy and Profaneness'.[2] Here were serious moral failures threatening the social order, the proper business of the church courts but too widespread and weighty for them to cope with. Some of the clergy, especially during the campaign for the 'reformation of manners' between 1689 and 1714, urgently invited from the laity in the legislature an assistance that the laity was not at all loth to give—on its own terms.[3] How could a true friend of the church better show his loyalty than by supporting legislation that came to the church's rescue? And yet such gestures from the laity were not without sinister implications, which Edmund Gibson, a far more clear-sighted defender of ecclesiastical independence than most of his brethren, did not fail to discern. A statute on an ecclesiastical concern could mean, first, that the laity was usurping the clergy's right to determine church policy; and it might, in the second place, be taken by the ordinary man to supply the whole argument for obedience to it— whereas it was probably only repeating and reinforcing under new stronger penalties, an ecclesiastical law already existing. On a short-term view, it might help the church; but in the long run, it worked to edge the church off its proper ground.[4]

The laity's monopoly of the offices of the administration and the high courts of justice, and its massive preponderance in the legislature, thus placed it conveniently for imposing on the clergy its own view of any matter on which the views of laity and clergy might conceivably differ; and its connexions with the clergy, and opportunities for influencing them, went further and deeper still, in directions less obvious.

First, the patrons of over half the benefices in England were laymen. It would be possible, by dint of much drudgery, to find out the exact number of lay patrons about 1831, when Rivingtons published a list of

[1] 4 James I c. 5.   [2] 9 & 10 William III c. 32.
[3] See Bahlman, *The Moral Revolution of 1688, passim.*
[4] See the whole of the last section of Gibson's Introductory Discourse, in the *Codex*, pp. xxx–xxxi.

all the patrons under the title *Patroni Ecclesiarum;* but even that figure would be of no particular significance, because livings were constantly changing hands. The figures given in, or to be deduced from, published works before that date make possible only approximate estimates, which are quite sufficient to show that the laity held a very large number of advowsons indeed.[1] According to the census of 1821, the clergy (i.e. the bishops, the colleges of Oxford and Cambridge, the deans and chapters of the cathedrals, and the various collegiate churches like Windsor and Wolverhampton) presented to 3,026 rectories and vicarages. The Crown (i.e. the prime minister, the Lord Chancellor and the Chancellor of the Duchy of Lancaster) presented to 1,048: and 'private individuals' to no less than 6,619. This figure includes private individuals in orders as well as laymen, and it presumably includes clergymen who presented to benefices by virtue of their offices (e.g. prebends or incumbencies of populous, sub-divided parishes), but it is unlikely that the allowances made in respect of these bring the whole below 5,000; which makes up half the number of parish livings without bringing in the Crown livings as well to swell the lay total. These figures are approximate for the early nineteenth century. The parochial system certainly by then comprised many more parishes than in the early eighteenth century; and since the greater part of these were created by the division of existing parishes, which almost always gave the new presentation to the incumbent of the 'mother-parish', the proportion of lay to clerical patrons must have been heavier about 1700 than a hundred years later. Whoever bears in mind the figure of 5,000 livings, as a rough estimate of the number in the patronage of private lay individuals in the eighteenth century, cannot be far wrong.

Yet this preponderance of the laity in church patronage mattered less than it might have done, because of a general similarity between the social conduct of clergy and laity, which governed their behaviour as patrons of livings as in so much besides. The eighteenth-century clergy-man was not expected to be unlike the responsible laymen of his own class. He might possibly be better educated, but the education would have been of a similar kind, for there was little special professional

[1] See the *Quarterly Review*, XXIX (1823), 554. Shine and Shine, *The Quarterly Review under Gifford*, p. 85, say that the article was probably by the Reverend Edward Edwards.

education for the clergy at this epoch. He was absorbed so fully by the common social ideas and conventions of his age and his class that in the later eighteenth and early nineteenth centuries, when it became necessary to work out coherent political philosophies of church and state, this natural identification of the interests of the educated clergy and laity was seized on and glorified as an example of how an established church really should work. The clergyman, unless he were seriously affected by Evangelicalism, could farm, shoot and fish like his lay neighbours and relations. If he could afford it he took his family to London in the season, or to one of the spas. He married and begat children and shared with his lay contemporaries that sacred regard for the promotion of family interests which marked the generations of Walpole and the Pitts. He found his sons jobs in the church or out of it, as seemed most promising; if his patronage was extensive enough he helped his sons-in-law to good jobs in the church as well; and there was no reason whatever why he should not put a son, son-in-law, or any other ordainable male in whom he might happen to be interested, into a safe living, by the simple expedient of buying an advowson or a next presentation in the open market.

There were nevertheless certain reasons why the impression made by a lay patron on his presentee should be different from that of a clerical. In the first place, the lay patron was likelier to live near at hand, and was often the local squire. In that case he, his family and servants would occupy the most prominent, and most comfortably furnished, places in church, and in the nineteenth century at least (it does not seem to have been so in the eighteenth) he would be one of the churchwardens. Many, perhaps all, of the congregation would be his tenants. He would be the natural head of all parochial charities. Projects for the decoration or improvement of the church over and above what the churchwardens could finance from the church-rate would depend on his leadership, and the repairs of the chancel would very likely be his sole responsibility, as lay rector. If he were a Justice of the Peace as well, the whole of the institutions of the parish, secular as well as ecclesiastical, would naturally centre on him and become only as efficient or inefficient as he chose to make them.

A resident lay potentate in whose person were combined such legal, economic, and informal but effective powers of serving friends and influencing people, could not but mean much, for good or evil, in the life of the incumbent, whether patron or not. Of all that a squire-cum-patron could do in a parish in about 1700, and the gratitude which an independent and strong-minded incumbent could feel towards him without loss of self-respect, White Kennet's elaborate 'Epistle Dedicatory' to his *Parochial Antiquities*, 'To the honoured Sir William Glynne, Baronet, Patron of the Churches of Ambrosden and Burcester', may serve as an example. Kennet's account of the first and second baronets deserves quotation in full. It is gracefully introduced in the form of an apology for the recording of antiquities, which, in due course, for future generations, the events of the present would become: . . .

For will not your Posterity rejoice, to find upon Record the good and laudable Deeds of their Predecessors? Will it not divert them to read, How the first Baronet of their Name rais'd a beautiful and regular Seat at *Amersden*? How he kept there a Hospitable and well governed House, and by his Prudence and Charity, reform'd a rude and licentious People? How he rescued the Patronage of this Church from the hands of One, whose principles betrayed Him into no Affection for it? How he twice conferr'd the same Church with no regard to interest or importunity? How, out of his own proper soil He enlarged the bounds of the Church-yard: and made a like addition to the adjoining garden of the Vicar? How by his Countenance and kind Endeavours, He recovered an Estate (before embezzled) to the proper pious use of supporting and adorning the Parish Church? How He was pleas'd to accept a share in that new Trust, and what a conscience he made in the discharge of it? How just he was to the interest and the honour of his other Church at *Burcester*? How he fill'd it with an Incumbent of exemplary Goodness, and serviceable Learning? And how he made it a greater Beauty of Holyness, by giving a very noble Service of Communion-Plate, and, all other decent Ornaments for the Lord's Table, and the Pulpit?

The second baronet (to whom the book was dedicated) was not less worthy than the first: 'he was often projecting and promoting the strength and beauty of his Parish Church, and set an Example of constant Access to and good Behaviour in it! . . . He was encouraging and assisting the improvement of the Vicar's Manse, and making some augmentation to his slender portion of Glebe . . . [and] in a neighbouring Church of his Patronage, for the two first Turns of Presentation, he referr'd the choice of fit Persons to the sole judgement of the Bishop, and by such Deference did his Lordship and Himself most particular Honour.' The letters of Patrick St Clair to his friend, patron and neighbour Ashe Windham usefully illustrate another kind of entirely happy patron-presentee relationship.[1]

St Clair was thirteen years older than his patron, was rector of the living to which he had been presented, and held another with it; whereas Kennet was only a vicar.

This relationship could, however, as easily be unhappy, discreditable, and harmful. 'For livings being trusted in the most part in the disposal of the gentry', wrote Humphrey Prideaux to his brother-in-law about 1690, 'and they having gotten a trick of selling, it hence comes to passe, when a patron hath a living void, he goes about seeking one that will be perjured for it; whence it comes to pass that the worst men that are bred in the Universities get all the livings . . .'[2] If a person had livings to dispose of, there were bound to be clergy who would, of free choice or harsh necessity, accommodate themselves to that person's likings with a view to attracting his patronage. They would be drunken with the sots, bawdy with the lecherous, flattering to the vain, fawning to the proud, and careful above all to make it clear they would never cross their prospective patron's views or interests. Men in orders far outnumbered the benefices and curacies available, and it was small wonder that hungry young graduates were prepared to 'embrace dishonourable proposals'[3] and that even decent men went 'creeping and cringing to wealthy Tables, where either we must become perpetual Parasites and Flatterers, or expect to be receiv'd with Coldness or Superiority';[4] nor was it surprising that they should tend somewhat to conceal their higher principles (supposing them to have had any) in company in which . . . 'A due Regard to a Man's Character, and the natural Obligations that arise from it, is called *Pride*. A decent Reproof of the Wealthy and Proud, is called *Ill-Manners*. A just Censure of the Dissolute and Licentious is called *Ill-Nature:* and talking the Language of Scripture, natural Religion, Reason and Philosophy, is called *Impertinence* and *Pedantry*.'[5]

Other illustrations may be given of how sedulously a presentee might regard his patron's every whim, and appear therein to fall rather short of

---

[1] The letters run from 1729 to 1741 and are published with a delightful commentary by R. W. Ketton-Cremer, *Country Neighbourhood*.

[2] *J. R. Pine-Coffin MSS*, H.M.C. III (1876), 378.   [3] S.P.D. 1661-2; 27 June 1661.

[4] Thomas Stackhouse, *The Miseries and Great Hardships of the Inferior Clergy, in and about London*, p. 97.   [5] John Hildrop, *The Contempt of the Clergy considered*, p. 23.

what his more independent-minded contemporaries might regard as proper. The non-resident vicar of Waterperry, Oxfordshire, assured his patron—the squire—that in selecting a curate he would choose 'one who will pay attention to his duty, and endeavour to make himself agreeable to you . . . I hold myself bound in *Honour* to consult *your Comfort*'.[1] Another example, drawn from the same period, is perhaps better known; as indeed it should be, for so perfectly exemplifying a state of mind and a relationship that are timeless. The rector of Hunsford, near Westerham, Kent, on first introducing himself to his cousins in Hertfordshire, wrote, 'I have been so fortunate as to be distinguished by the patronage of the Right Honourable Lady Catherine de Bourgh, widow of Sir Lewis de Bourgh, whose bounty and beneficence has preferred me to the valuable rectory of this parish, where it shall be my earnest endeavour to demean myself with grateful respect towards her Ladyship, and be ever ready to perform those rites and ceremonies which are instituted by the Church of England.' Nor did his cousins on closer acquaintance with him find his practice to fall short of his professions, for the good rector told them that his patroness 'had been graciously pleased to approve of both the discourses which he had already had the honour of preaching before her', and that one of his principal duties had been to 'make such an agreement for tythes as may be beneficial to himself and not offensive to his patron'.[2] Almost contemporaneously the incumbent of Frocester and Nympsfield, in Gloucestershire, was soliciting the succession to both livings for his son. He assured the patron, 'should you grant it, and should you proceed in your enclosing plan, you may depend upon his acting as I should do', i.e. complaisantly.[3] Thirty years later Bishop Gray of Bristol admitted in the House of Lords that many a clergyman omitted to prosecute just claims for tithes out of 'a feeling of gratitude for patrons from whom he has derived preferment'.[4]

Mr Collins's care not to offend his patron in respect of his 'tythes' serves to introduce the first of the two rather hidden ways in which the

---

[1] A letter of February 1815, cited by Diana McClatchey, *Oxfordshire Clergy 1777–1869*, p. 6.

[2] Jane Austen, *Pride and Prejudice*, vol. i, chapters 13, 14 and 18.

[3] Cited by Esther A. L. Moir in her Cambridge doctorate thesis, *Local Government in Gloucestershire 1775–1800* (1955–6), p. 98.

[4] *Mirror of Parliament*, 1831, p. 880a, debate of 15 March.

laity, as landowners and patrons, participated in the affairs of the clergy. Either as landowners, and hence tithe-payers, or as tithe-owners—tithes being a species of property, which could be inherited, bartered, bought or leased—the laity were intimately interested in the principal means of clerical support. Many laymen were rectors of parishes, usually though not inevitably of the parishes to which they presented; and as rectors they owned the great tithes there as perfectly as they owned any other freehold property.[1] Whether as 'impropriators' of tithes (as rectors who were not also incumbents were known) or as holding them by lease (which was exceedingly often done) the laity were as bound to care about the state of the law on tithes as were the clergy, and long and loud were the latter's complaints from the sixteenth century onwards that parliament legislated on tithes with the lay owner's rather than the ecclesiastical owner's situation and interest in mind.

It was not only by their parliamentary supremacy that the lay land-owning interest asserted its rights over tithes to the clergy's disadvantage. It might seriously inconvenience the clergyman within the parish itself. A rector might, like Mr Collins, feel bound to come to easy terms with the squire to whose great tithes he was entitled; a vicar might feel the same compulsion in respect of the small tithes due to him from the squire or the lessee of the rectory, which often meant land as well as tithes. 'It is no unusual thing for patrons (very little to their credit) to present a clergyman to a living upon condition of his accepting a rent-charge or fixed annuity in lieu of tithes; or upon condition of his never raising his tithes upon the patron's tenants above a given rate in the pound; or obliging him to consent that such and such farms and lands (often those occupied by the patron himself) shall be tithe-free.'[2] Many were the in-terferences to which an incumbent might be subjected by an uncongenial impropriator or his lessee, by virtue of the other rectorial rights accom-panying the title to the great tithes. For example, the lessee of the great

---

[1] Laymen had been rectors of parishes since the dissolution of the monasteries, when the monastic properties, rectories and all, had been given or sold by the Crown to lay as well as ecclesiastical supporters; since when they had been circulating in the property market, becoming sometimes separated from the advowsons which had originally gone with them, and sometimes split into two or more parts.

[2] *The State of the Established Church, in a series of Letters to Mr. Spencer Perceval* 2nd edn., London, 1810), p. 96.

tithes of Wellington, Somerset, a violent and primitive character, repeatedly broke into the church and wrought his will in the chancel, wherein, as he imagined, he was undisputed master. He 'clandestinely caused a key of the church door to be made', and when the vicar put on a new lock, broke the door down. When the vicar fortified the door against such assaults, the lessee broke in through the belfry door and the gallery; and finally, when the resourceful vicar had fortified these as well, 'the workmen, under his [the lessee's] orders, stript off part of the roof from the top of the chancel, and broke through the ceiling. . . .'[1]

Besides all this, lay patrons turned their powers as owners of advowsons and next presentations even further to their advantage by exacting 'resignation bonds' from their presentees. These bound the bond-giver in a stated sum of money to resign from the benefice within a certain limited period after being given notice by the patron.[2] They were convenient means of keeping livings warm for sons or relatives not yet of age, or of 'enslaving [incumbents] during Life to the Will and Pleasure of Patrons, and particularly of tempting them to submit to all the most unreasonable Agreements and Compositions for Tithes, which can be propos'd'.[3]

The scale upon which resignation bonds were demanded and given hardly allows of statistical or other incontestable demonstration. That they were common cannot be doubted. All the law books deal with them, and refer to the many cases in the temporal courts by which the legal borderline between permissible and impermissible bonds was established. By canon law and by a statute of 1588[4] simoniacal contracts for benefices were illegal. The statute declared void presentations 'for any sum of money, reward gift profit or benefit directly or indirectly, or for or by reason of any promise agreement grant bond covenant or other assurance of or for any sum of money' etc.; and yet the temporal courts (in whom alone rested the power of interpreting statutes) decided that general bonds of resignation, of the kind already described, fell outside the terms

---

[1] *Jarratt* v. *Steele*, in the Court of Arches, 27 January 1820: 3 Phillimore Ecc. 167–70; 161 English Reports 1290–1.

[2] An example of a resignation bond may be found in any of the first six editions of Burn, at the end of the section on Simony.

[3] Gibson, *Directions given . . . to the Clergy of his Diocese*, 1724, p. 39.

[4] 31 Eliz. I c. 6.

of the statute and were legal. They accordingly protected the givers and takers of resignation bonds, and our certainty that there continued to be many such through the seventeenth and eighteenth centuries is based, partly on the number of cases in the temporal courts, and partly on the unflagging denunciations of the practice by the more zealous church leaders, who maintained that whatever the temporal courts might allow, their clergy ought to feel in conscience bound not to take advantage of it—or to be taken advantage of by it—because it constituted simony and went against the oath taken by all incumbents at their institution to a benefice.[1] In the sixteen-seventies Zachary Cawdrey denounced them as a new and modish form of simony; 'that which the present age may glory in, as the product of its own more fruitful invention, are the *Bonds* for *Resignation*, the evil effects whereof are like to multiply from year to year . . .';[2] and about the same time Sir Simon Degge went so far as to say that 'hardly a living was possessed without them'.[3] In 1695 Bishop Stillingfleet published a small but meaty book with the intention 'to give a stop, if possible, to a Dangerous and Prevailing Practice; and so much the more Dangerous, because it is managed with so much Secrecy . . .'[4] That the bonds were kept as dark as possible was only to be expected. Bishops rarely received certain information about them, and even when they were certain that bonds had been given, they experienced 'extreme difficulty [in] discovering the real purpose for which they are used'.[5] They were furthermore deterred from refusing institution to the peccant presentee by the knowledge that their attempts to enforce ecclesiastical discipline in this respect (as in others) would be rendered nugatory by the temporal courts. They could only exhort both parties in the case to better behaviour, warning the clergy against confusing the standards of the temporal with those of the spiritual administration, and pointing out to them that what was *legal* could still be a sin; and urging patrons, on the

[1] Pursuant to the 40th Canon of 1603; 'I, N.N., do swear, that I have made no Simoniacal Payment, Contract or Promise directly or indirectly, by myself or by any other' etc. etc.

[2] *Discourse of Patronage*, p. 25.

[3] Mr Justice Nares's speech in the House of Lords, on Ffytche's case, 1783, cited in the 6th edn. of Burn (1797) III, 359.

[4] *A Discourse concerning Bonds of Resignation of Benefices*, pp. i and 105. In the following year Dean Willes published, anonymously, his *Unlawfulness of Bonds of Resignation*.

[5] Case of the Plaintiff in *Bishop of London* v. *Ffytche*, §6, in Harrowby MSS ci, fo. 146.

other side, to forego worldly considerations in filling their livings, and to select men only for their religious seriousness and pastoral diligence.

It is much to be doubted whether these repeated exhortations made much impression upon those who read and heard them. The hardened and worldly would continue to go as far as the temporal courts allowed, and the spectre of unemployment must have forced many clergymen of good character to submit to the terms imposed by patrons whose good-will could, temporarily at any rate, save them from the workhouse and the debtors' gaol. But beyond this there were circumstances to make even the virtuous and disinterested view resignation bonds favourably. Men are, generally speaking, virtuous and disinterested only in the terms set by their age and upbringing, and men of property in the eighteenth century were swept along by strong twin currents which separately and together worked to encourage them to find justifications for the giving and taking of these bonds. Family interest was the first. A layman could not do better for a second or third son, and a dignified clergyman would probably not think of doing better for a first, than to give him a living. There might be one in the family, 'the family living'; and if there were not a living in the family already, a few thousand pounds would quickly bring one. This living was a piece of the family property, to be handed down to posterity unwasted. The son for whom it was destined would perhaps be brought up to a sense of its responsibilities (which were not, after all, dissimilar from those admitted by his father even if his father were only a lay landed proprietor), and might promise to become an admirable clergyman after the fashion of his time. What could be wrong with putting a 'warming-pan' into the living until the son was old enough to take it? And how else could the living be kept available, if the right of presentation lapsed to the bishop after six months? Such arguments were fair ones and could well be entertained by perfectly scrupulous laymen. Thomas Secker, in character one of the best bishops of a not very saintly age, came down against resignation bonds of any kind whatsoever; but he understood the force of the arguments for them in cases of family livings, and included them in his general denunciation only with some reluctance.[1]

[1] See his 1747 Charge, in *Eight Charges*, pp. 93–116. Almost the whole of this Charge is on the subject of resignation bonds. He followed Stillingfleet's clear exposition of it closely, and concluded that 'Benefices ought neither to be given, nor

The other main line of argument for resignation bonds, morally less attractive but in practice equally compelling, was drawn from the politics of the age. Patronage was the indispensable currency of eighteenth century politics. He who had much of it could be great: he who had little could still be important: and he who needed it would surely make himself useful. To the politician and the landowner, confirming their influence in government and neighbourhood, church livings were all one with the other species of patronage, which gratified friends, rewarded servants, and placated enemies, and if a suspicion ever crossed their minds, that a clergyman ought to be picked for other and more personal qualities than his degree of relationship to a political associate, it could speedily be banished by the moral reflection, that a decent performance of the prayer-book services was within anyone's capacity; that the position, like almost all official positions at that time, could be performed by a possibly more conscientious deputy (in this case, of course, a curate); and that whatever Noodle's personal demerits might be, the country's good in the current emergency depended upon his getting the living which could only be cleared for him by Foodle's resignation. It was perhaps a pity, and rather worldly, but how otherwise could men of the world be governed?

One other line of argument was occasionally followed in the advocacy of general resignation bonds. It could be said that in themselves they were, morally, neutral; their purpose might be sinister, but it could equally well be honest, a *pactio honesta;* the conditions imposed by the patron might in fact be residence and the diligent discharge of duty, matter even for complaint by clergy conscious of their freehold and impatient of their superiors. The bishops in Convocation, 1531, had been petitioned by the lower house not to exact such bonds.[1] Bishop Burnet used resignation bonds to secure higher clerical standards in his diocese, but his action was already anachronistic. What discretionary powers a bishop might have used and expected his clergy to respect in the early sixteenth century had lost their force by the late seventeenth. Many incumbents who took Burnet's bonds did not take them seriously; his

accepted, with any other Condition or Promise, than that of doing our Duty in Relation to them. This Engagement is always understood, whether it is expressed or not: and no other should either be required or complied with.'

[1] See Charles Gore (ed.), *Church Reform*, p. 206.

enemies raised the cry of simony; and his colleague Stillingfleet turned against him, pronouncing his tactics at once obsolete and dubious.[1] After this episode, the upper clergy seem entirely to have abandoned the defence of resignation bonds, and this particular argument for them was used only by the lay patrons, who set some gloss of respectability on their self-interest by instancing worthy examples, like Burnet's, and implying that lay patrons too might wish to protect themselves and their parishioners from a backsliding pastor.

The state of the law on resignation bonds was much changed in 1783, when the precedents of over two centuries were reversed. The case, *Bishop of London* v. *Ffytche*, celebrated in legal and constitutional history as the last time that bishops spoke and voted as judges in the House of Lords, began in 1780 when the bishop, Robert Lowth, having heard of a certain presentee's giving a bond to a patron, and having wrung from the presenter himself an admission that he had indeed done so, to the tune of £3,000, refused to institute. The patron promptly brought a writ of *quare impedit* against Lowth in the court of Common Pleas, little doubting that, following all the precedents, the bishop would be made to knuckle under. So at first it seemed. The case went against Lowth in the Common Pleas, and against him again when he appealed to King's Bench. But he was determined not to succumb. He appealed to the House of Lords, an eminence to which such cases had not previously been taken,[2] and was successful. General resignation bonds were pronounced illegal.[3]

It was taken for granted that bonds to resign in favour of specified

[1] Clarke and Foxcroft, *Life of Burnet*, p. 294.

[2] See Lowth's scarce *Letter to the Clergy of his Diocese*, 1784, p. 4.

[3] The majority, 19 to 18, was made up of 18 bishops and Lord Chancellor Thurlow. The minority was wholly lay. The whole case is interesting and a little mysterious. Why should Lowth have persisted in what must have appeared to the general public a foredoomed failure unless he was confident of success at the last? He admitted to his clergy that he proceeded 'with the utmost caution. I consulted certain persons of the highest authority, both in the Civil and Ecclesiastical Law. . . . I would take no step in so important a business without the approbation of the most Reverend the Archbishops . . . [who] were pleased to express their approbation of it.' (*Op. cit.* pp. 4–5). It looks as if Lowth was acting in collusion with Lord Chancellor Thurlow. Thurlow's support must have been the *sine qua non* of victory because Mansfield and Kenyon, lawyers of equal distinction, were on Ffytche's side: see *Parliamentary History*, XXIII, 893–4, and Eldon's decision in 3 Bingham 501 at 598; 130 English Reports 606 at 644.

persons remained legal. They were perfectly so about 1811, when that quintessential layman John Dashwood assumed that Edward Ferrars was to hold the living of Delaford only 'till the person to whom the Colonel has really sold the presentation, is old enough to take it'.[1] The run of John Dashwood's thoughts when he learnt of Colonel Brandon's presentation of Edward Ferrars nicely illustrates the way a well-off worldly layman might regard church patronage. 'Really!—Well, this is very astonishing!—no relationship!—no connexion between them! —and now that livings fetch such a price!—what was the value of this?' 'About two hundred a year.' 'Very well—and for the next presentation to a living of that value—supposing the late incumbent to have been old and sickly, and likely to vacate it soon—he might have got I dare say— fourteen hundred pounds. And how came he not to have settled that matter before this person's death? *Now* indeed it would be too late to sell it, but a man of Colonel Brandon's sense!—I wonder he should be so improvident in a point of such common, such natural, concern!...I suppose, however—on recollection—that the case may probably be *this*. Edward is only to hold the living till the person to whom the Colonel has really sold the presentation, is old enough to take it. Aye, aye, that is the fact, depend upon it.'

The taking of such bonds continued without a check until 1827 when another decision in the House of Lords, in the case of *Fletcher* v. *Lord Sondes*, threw all into confusion. A bond to resign in favour of the patron's brother was adjudged illegal on several grounds, the most cogent of which was the impossibility, as things then stood, of ensuring that the person named in the bond in fact succeeded. A statute was hurriedly passed at the instance of the Archbishop of Canterbury to protect the 'large number' of patrons and incumbents who were left exposed to the penalties for simony[2] and in the following year the law was placed on the footing which lasted until this century by a statute legalizing bonds in favour of near relations by blood or marriage, and bringing them into such an official light of day as to make sure that they were used for that purpose only.[3] The legalization of these bonds, which

---

[1] Jane Austen, *Sense and Sensibility*, vol. 3, ch. 5.   [2] 7 & 8 George IV c. 25.
[3] 9 George IV c. 94, An Act for rendering valid Bonds, Covenants, and other Assurances for the Resignation of the ecclesiastical Preferments, in certain specified Cases.

secured lay patrons in what was after all the principal advantage of owning a living, marked a sad falling-off from the standards proposed for the church by Gibson and Secker; but it is clear from the report of the debate that the laity would accept nothing less. The Solicitor-General, Tindal, who was in charge of the bill, more or less admitted that it was simply an acquiescence to *force majeure*. 'The intention of this bill', he said, 'is to enable the holders [sic] of benefices, whether lay or clerical, to provide for their families as they are enabled to do with other species of property. . . . [It] will only render legal that which is now practised in defiance of the law, and . . . in a most objectionable manner.' It was better, he said, to make that legal and above-board which would otherwise be managed clandestinely or by the detestable expedient of appointing the aged or the dying to livings whose speedy vacation was desired. Several members thought the bill did patrons an injustice. Only one recorded speaker, the eminent civilian Dr Lushington, ventured to object to it on spiritual grounds.[1]

There are plenty of signs that many of the clergy in the late seventeenth and early eighteenth centuries resented their enforced subordination to the laity, on both personal and theological grounds. In the late eighteenth and early nineteenth centuries such resentment is much less commonly encountered. When this change of attitude occurred, and why, are questions of the greatest interest and importance, which involve the theory of establishment that came to be generally accepted in the years of the great church reform movement.

Probably one reason why the clergy gave up complaining about the hold the laity had over them and the way they exercised it, was that once Convocation had been anaesthetized, and Bishop Gibson, that bold and strenuous asserter of their rights, had fallen out of official favour, they were more completely defenceless. Convocation, in its last days, had little real political power, but it was active and not without influence, bearing witness to a certain independence and to the special authority of the clerical order. It provided, moreover, a focus for the clergy's awareness of their own interests and a potential means of promoting them. Unfortunately, church reforms promoted by the clergy opened to lay eyes a flame-tinted prospect of clerical ascendancy. The more active and

[1] *Mirror of Parliament*, 1828, pp. 2394–5, 2525, 2583–4.

efficient it was proposed to make the church, the surer was it to be at the expense either of the layman's pocket or independence. In the early eighteenth century the clerical order was still intact and apart. Bancroft and Laud had lost their long battle against the Puritans and common lawyers, but there was still plenty of fight in a spiritual estate which could inspire a Kennet to research into *Parochial Antiquities* and a Gibson to the compilation of his enormous *Codex*. Of the clergy's vigorous will to survive in their historic independence, the optimistic and far-reaching activities of the last sitting Convocations give evident witness. In these circumstances therefore church reform almost inevitably promised to strengthen the clergy as against the laity.[1] The greater part of the English laity as represented in parliament and at the bar was not, apparently, prepared to tolerate this, and so very little was done.

The ending of sitting Convocations removed the thin screen that had, sometimes, stood between the clergy and the mixed supremacy of monarch and parliament. Few voices were heard between 1730 and 1830 to lament its dormancy. Parliament was accepted as the proper legislature for the spiritual as well as the temporal estate. Indeed, by the beginning of the nineteenth century 'the three estates' was usually understood to mean 'king, Lords and Commons'. The spiritual estate had evaporated.[2] Moreover, no clergyman of anything like Gibson's force and influence spoke out in public for the clergy's claims until the eighteen-thirties, when such bishops as Phillpotts and Blomfield on the one hand, and the

[1] I am speaking still of the reforms suggested by leading 'official' clergy. The reforms sought by the Puritan interest before the civil war, although often nominally the same, were put in quite a different class by the motives underlying them. If the Puritans had succeeded in turning the course of history into their desired channel, the relations of clergy and laity would have been very different. As things turned out, however, their characteristic type of clerical-lay co-operation remained exceptional before the civil war, and disappeared soon after it.

[2] High church writers regularly took it upon themselves to remind the public what 'the Three Estates' originally were, but they underestimated the antiquity of its misinterpretation. A. F. Pollard discussed the concept in his *Evolution of Parliament*, chapter 4, and showed that it was as old as 1401. In the 1788 Regency debates, it seemed to be accepted by both sides of the house (see Lecky's *History of England in the 18th Century*, ch. 16). By 1822 it was perfectly natural for a valiant supporter of the Protestant constitution, when Canning's Roman Catholic Peers Bill got through the lower House, to 'thank God, that there were three estates of this realm—the King, Lords and Commons'. (Sir Thomas Lethbridge, 17 May 1822, *Hansard* n.s. VII, 673.)

Oxford preachers of the apostolic succession on the other, revived ideas of clerical prerogative in ways that essentially differed but in practice often overlapped.[1] The clergy had to 'acquiese' in the layman's supremacy, partly because they had no choice.

Much more important was the evolution of a new establishment apologetic. The necessity for this derived mainly from the existence of the nonconformists. In the first place, tolerant Protestants could not comfortably enforce religious test laws upon peaceful and patient fellow-Protestants without justifying them. Further, towards the end of the century the establishment had to be defended against a fast-growing host of critics and enemies who tended to be neither peaceful nor patient. But the expositions of the establishment that were produced in response to these late eighteenth-century pressures were quite different from those produced earlier. The great social, economic and intellectual changes of the eighteenth century worked together to alter the relations of clergy and laity, to approximate them increasingly to one another, and thus to produce a new version of establishment theory, emphasizing the social affinities of clergy and laity, tending to glorify their inter-connexions and mutual dependence, and making it easier to forget, if they wanted to, that the laity still were ultimately in control. But of course they might not wish to forget it. Shute Barrington said in the House of Lords, when he was still near the beginning of his very long episcopal career, 'that the clergy . . . felt and acknowledged the blessings of an establishment fixed and ascertained by law. Incorporated with the laity, connected in one common interest, citizens of the state holding their property by the same laws, they must be mad indeed could they for an instant forget the obligations they owed to a lay legislature, or enter-

---

[1] I deliberately except the old High Church Party, *alias* the Hackney Phalanx. They certainly sometimes spoke in quite uncompromising terms about the clergy's indefeasible powers and rights—see, for instance, Daubeny's *Guide to the Church*, or W. F. Hook's early sermons—but they were really fundamentally committed to the alliance of church and state *in the form that it took after the last echoes of Gibson's voice had died away*. The constitutional revolution of 1828–1833 sufficiently shook them to enable them to follow Blomfield's line over national education in the late thirties; but they never could adopt the Tractarians' ways of thinking, for all their fame as the handers-down of the doctrine that formed the basis of the Tractarian position. The voice of Hackney might now and then have been the voice of Gibson, but its hand was the hand of Cornwallis.

tain a thought of engaging in a combat which must terminate in their inevitable ruin.'[1]

There was in this change an economic factor, namely that the clergy benefited as property owners from that prodigious increase in the national income which had been promoted by agricultural and industrial improvement, and by the great increase in the returns of foreign trade. The clergy's state was not unimproved by the Industrial Revolution; but it was the steady and increasing improvement in agricultural methods, organization, and productivity, that brought most help to such of the clergy as benefited at all.

Almost the whole of the revenues of the eighteenth-century establishment came more or less directly from land. There was no fixed rule or system in the church's financial structure. Each individual clergyman was likely to be supported in a unique fashion; pluralities, politics, patronage, the varying customs and conditions of parishes and benefices, the success or failure of the corn harvest and the other crops, the harshness or leniency (or, to look at it another way, the efficiency or weakness) shown in the collection of dues, the energy used in augmenting or multiplying the sources of income—all these factors and more besides determined what each individual clergyman got. In general the parochial clergy drew their incomes from tithes, the profits of glebes, and possibly the rents of the nominal parsonage. Bishops and the cathedral and collegiate clergy were likely to draw their official incomes as bishops, canons and fellows from one or a combination of a variety of sources— tithes (usually impropriate), rents, leases and so on.

All these various sources of income were 'improvable'. Again and again throughout the eighteenth century the word 'improvable' and the concept of 'improvement' occur, in private correspondence, in official documents, in contemporary commentaries. 'Improvement' was obviously a subject of engrossing interest, and not from base motives alone. For although much of the increased value of benefices was naturally absorbed in the provision of comforts for incumbents and fortunes for their families, much also went to the education and relief of the poor, the restoration of churches, and, perhaps most valuable of all, the making of residence-houses fit for gentlemen to live in. In consequence of the 'improvement' of the sources of so many clergymen's incomes between

[1] 30 March 1781, in *Parliamentary History*, XXII, 66.

1700 and 1830, their opportunities for usefulness, though not so often their popularity, were certainly enlarged.

A few examples may helpfully illustrate what was going on. The value of the Durham prebends swelled by between three and four hundred per cent between 1687 and 1766, mainly by means of modernizing the leases on their estates and raising the fines for their commencement or renewal.[1] The value of the see of Durham seems likewise to have been steadily increased, for good public or dubious private reasons, by all the bishops from Cosin to Barrington, who raised the fines and, less commonly, the rents on their estates, took advantage of ancient legal rights (this was Bishop Talbot's speciality) and made the most of the new opportunities coming from the coal that so plentifully underlay them.[2] The fellows of St John's College, Cambridge (a corporation like any cathedral chapter, getting its income from the same kind of sources), were drawing an annual dividend about 1690 of £10 a year or less; by 1750 it was over £20, by 1780 over £50, by 1810 over £110.[3] Of the living of Staplebridge, Dorset, it was written in 1831 that 'Dr. Colman [who went there in 1773] raised it from £300 to £700; and Mr. Bradford at his first going [1795] advanced it to £1000 a year.'[4] Catterick's new vicar in 1748, trying to heal the breaches introduced into parochial society by his non-resident and quarrelsome predecessor, 'contented himself with a very moderate commutation in lieu of tithes

[1] Since 'fines' will repeatedly be mentioned in the course of this narrative, the uninstructed reader should note exactly what they were. There was nothing of the punitive about them. They were simply single sums of money paid by tenants for leases, as distinct from the more familiar annual payments of rent. The amount of the fine was calculated in proportion (a) to the acreage and merit of the land, (b) to the period of years for which the lease ran. This latter might be either a specified term of years, or 'three lives'—i.e. until the death of the longest lived of three persons named in the lease. As a 'system' it was extraordinarily complicated and hazardous; but most church estates, and some laymen's, were in these years leased under it.

[2] Edward Hughes, *North-Country Life in the 18th Century*, especially pp. 130–2 and ch. 7, and the Spearmans' *Enquiry into the Ancient and Present State of the County Palatinate of Durham* (1729)—a lavish and documented indictment of the 'improvement' process, most of it by one who had suffered grievously at the hands of Talbot and his son-in-law secretary Dr Sayer.

[3] H. F. Howard, *Account of the Finances of St John's College*, Appendices VII and VIII. I have struck averages from a period of 20 years pivoted on the year stated.

[4] John Lamb, *Masters's History of the College of Corpus Christi*, pp. 452–3.

and never . . . cleared more than one hundred and eighty or two hundred pounds per annum by the living; although it has since been raised by some of his successors, who have not resided, and consequently have cared little about the feelings or improvement of their parishioners, to upwards of fourteen hundred pounds per annum'.[1]

Such enrichments of country livings were usually due to the imposition of tithe on land newly brought into cultivation or up till then exempt from tithe; to the breaking of old compositions or 'moduses' for tithes and their replacement by dues more nearly approaching a tenth of the land's value; or to the ordinary business of enclosure, which seems generally to have worked out to the tithe-holders' advantage, whether tithe was retained in kind, commuted for money-payments, or extinguished in exchange for extra allotments of land. Few enclosure acts can have been passed unless the holder of at any rate the great tithes approved. Sometimes the rector and the lord of the manor were the only petitioners for enclosure; the rector's name is rarely missing from the petition; and the House of Lords often amended enclosure bills to the church's greater advantage.[2] Contemporary and modern writers seem alike agreed that between 1780 and 1830, with very few exceptions, the clergy on the whole did well out of enclosure.[3]

In what proportions each of these three main causes was responsible for the 'improvement' of so many livings, it is impossible in the present state of the subject to say. The most startling results, on present evidence, appear to have come from the extension of tithe-rights; but they were possibly less common than the quieter business of enclosure so familiar to the men of George III's reign. The enrichment that could follow an extension of tithe-rights was certainly remarkable. At Dodington, near March, there occurred what must have been a most striking improvement. This was a very large parish which in Henry VIII's reign, at the time of the valuations that went into the *Liber Regis*, was worth only a modest £22 5s. 0d. Drainage, enclosure, and a series of successful lawsuits, raised it to about £5,000 by the end of the French wars, and over

[1] Mrs Catharine Cappe, *Memoirs*, p. 20. She was the vicar's daughter.

[2] W. E. Tate, *Notts. Parliamentary Enclosures*, pp. 10–14.

[3] See e.g. E. C. K. Gonner, *Common Land and Inclosure*, pp. 79,316; V. Lavrovsky, in the *Economic History Review*, IV (1932–4), 288; W. G. Hoskins, *The Midland Peasant*, pp. 250–4; and Diana McClatchey, *op. cit.* ch. 8.

£7,000 by the eighteen-forties.[1] Dodington was exceptional; but many other fenland livings naturally profited from the draining and reclamation of land for farmings. When Wisbech high fen, 'from being common and waste land, became drained and enclosed . . . the tithe thereof was claimed by the Dean and Chapter [of Ely], who have since enjoyed it'.[2] The vicar of Wisbech in 1803 decided to challenge the long-standing composition for his tithes, and after a five-year suit in the exchequer, established his claim to tithe in kind and consequently became worth '£2,000 per annum and upwards'. At Elm, two miles to the south-east, the same thing happened in 1824, and after a negligible two-years exchequer suit, the unhappy parishioners found their moduses converted into a proper tenth.[3]

An election advertisement in the *Cambridge Chronicle*, 23 July 1830, addressed to 'Brother Freeholders!', said 'there is not a Clergyman but when he comes to a living in the neighbourhood of Wisbech, instead of thinking of the 'one thing needful', he advances the tithes; and we submit for the sake of peace'. How much peace could really come to a parish on these occasions is matter for speculation. Advancement of tithes must often have aided the spread of nonconformity. One school of establishment apologists liked to believe that the payment of tithes in kind—even full tithes—made a kind of physical link between the parson and his flock such as promoted amicable relations and a precious sense of mutual dependency. But the laity has never much liked paying tithes. Where and when tithe in a certain unchanging form had been paid time out of mind, acquiring such inevitability and naturalness as to become an accepted part of the life of the community, it obviously could subsist with friendly relations between a decent resident parson and his flock, and the pleasant customs of the tithe-feast ('My Frolic for my People to pay Tithe', as Parson Woodforde called it)[4] and the harvest-home would seal their

---

[1] D. & S. Lysons, *Magna Britannia* II (1810), 177; W. Gooch, *General View of the Agriculture of the County of Cambridge*, p. 67 and note; *V.C.H.*, *Cambridgeshire*, IV, 113.

[2] William Watson, *Historical Account of Wisbech*, p. 247.

[3] *Ibid.* pp. 247 and 496–7. Further intimations of the consequences of tithe-raising in the Wisbech district may be found in Charles Vancouver, *General View of the Agriculture in the County of Cambridge*, especially pp. 165–71, 186.

[4] *Diary*, I, 193. Rowlandson did a gay picture of such an occasion, reproduced in Dorothy Marshall, *English People in the 18th Century*, opp. p. 64. Another contemporary pipe-dream of this genre, in the style of Morland, is reproduced in A.

compact of amity. But the conditions that could make tithe seem tolerable were so often lacking between 1700 and 1830, when the productivity of land was rising all the time, and new land and new crops were coming into cultivation; the producers were as anxious to retain the full amount of their increasing profits as ecclesiastics were anxious to share in them. Whenever the views of the two parties could not be reconciled by agreement or arbitration, there was but one resource—the law; which meant in most important cases the Court of Exchequer.[1] Law suits bred expense and bitterness, even when they were of the 'friendly' variety. Usually they were most unpleasant. Mrs Cappe, returning to her native parish of Long Preston in 1810, found that 'the Vicar . . . had never been there but to take possession; and was engaged in a law-suit, with many of the principal parishioners, in the hope of raising the value of the living'.[2] Things were as bad at Waterbeach when the vicar, 'being well-advised by able and friendly lawyers, set himself about . . . filing a Bill in the Exchequer, against a very rich and potent adversary, in which, by indefatigable application and at no small hazard he happily succeeded, and thereby more than doubled the value of the Living';[3] and Herbert Marsh, who made so many enemies in the course of his professorial and episcopal careers, must have made them also as a Norfolk rector, when he invited the occupiers of his united parish of Terrington St Clement's and Terrington St John's to purchase their tithes—or else! It is alleged that from his Cambridge fastness went out a circular letter couched in singularly forbidding language and concluding thus: 'Let the Occupiers, therefore, who are disposed to refuse, well consider these things, before they suffer the 25th of March to pass without signing the agreement. I have made fair proposals, and warned them of the inconvenience they

---

Tindal Hart, *The Country Priest in English History*, opp. p. 89. It shows a very pretty cottager presenting her pretty son and a tithe-pig to a portly parson who looks as if he would like to eat both.

[1] The great quantity of tithe-suits in the Exchequer seems never to have been studied except by J. A. Venn, *The Foundation of Agricultural Economics*, especially pp. 154–60. The very interesting things he there says about them, even without any other indications, make it clear that the study of eighteenth-century tithe-law, with its changing rules and policies, its origins and consequences, will be a most rewarding subject for research.

[2] *Memoirs*, p. 371.

[3] [Robert Masters] *Short Account of the Parish of Waterbeach*, p. 37.

themselves will sustain if they reject them. I have therefore done my duty to my parishioners, and shall have the satisfaction of remaining free from reproach if, after all, I should be compelled to transfer my right to a lessee. I am, gentlemen, your most obedient servant, Herbert Marsh.'[1]

Lessees were particularly feared. They leased the tithes as a commercial proposition, and would let no circumstances of hardship or misfortune stand between them and their full legal due. 'Let them know', wrote one improving clergyman to his steward when his parishioners were not being co-operative, 'if they won't do what is reasonable, I shall farm the tythes out to the best bidder'.[2] Even a fairly tough clergyman, so long as he was resident and could ascertain the facts, would not squeeze blood from a tithe-payer with the remorselessness of a lessee.

'Improvement' as a consequence of enclosure was altogether a quieter business, though as a rule less immediately and strikingly profitable. There seems to have been a noticeable growth in the scale of clerical farming in the later eighteenth century, most of which must have come in consequence of enclosures. In the debates on the Non-Residence Bills of 1801-3 clerical farming was often discussed. It is clear that many of the clergy were farming not only their glebes (which enclosure might have made very large) but other lands as well. It was a question how much farming they should be allowed or encouraged to do. The poorer clergy 'endeavouring to make up the deficiency of their frequently very scanty incomes, by taking small farms'[3] were in altogether different case from the richer, large-scale farmers, for whom other excuses had to be found. Sheridan spoke in glowing terms of an Essex clergyman whose zeal for agricultural improvement, going along with his pastoral diligence and exemplary life, had actually civilized and made prosperous a previously impoverished and lawless countryside.[4] Sir William Scott, who was promoting the bills in order to bring the law on clerical farming and non-residence up to date, read at length from a letter he had received from 'two most respectable clergymen of the West of England' who justified full freedom to farm as no more than a sensible accommodation to the growing prosperity and enlightenment of society; agriculture, they concluded, was 'so far from an illiberal pursuit, that it is hard to say how any

[1] W. Dealtry, *Examination of Dr Marsh's 'Inquiry'*, pp. 71-2 n.
[2] *Letters of Dean Spencer Cowper*, ed. Edward Hughes, p. 21. Letter of 20 June 1742.
[3] 9 June 1801: *Parl. Hist.* xxxv, 1549.   [4] *Ibid.* pp. 1552-3.

clergyman can employ his hours of relaxation (and such hours must occur in every profession) with more innocence to himself, and benefit to the public, than in the moderated study and practice of its various branches'. With these sentiments, Scott said, he felt inclined to agree.[1] He gave a pleasing picture of his ideal establishment at work: . . .'the moderated and subordinate practice of farming supplies many means of cheap subsistence for the clergyman and his family; many means of easy kindness and hospitality to his poorer parishioners; many opportunities of distinguishing the industrious and well-disposed by the favour of employment; and many motives of pleasing attachment to the place, which furnishes the healthy and amusing occupation of his vacant hours.' Personal debasement had to be guarded against;[2] but '. . . in the example of the illustrious Hooker tending his sheep on Barham Downs, I think I see that even some of its humble occupations may be performed without degradation.'

This allowance or even encouragement of clerical farming about the end of the eighteenth century was significant in two respects. It was only one of the several means by which the more fortunate or pushing clergymen seem to have been able to improve their economic position and, on the basis of that, their social status; and it indicated the social ideal at which the clergy, both by intention and through circumstances, tended to aim—the life of the country gentleman. The national pattern of gentility was more exclusively based on the idea of the country gentleman, the landed proprietor, in the eighteenth century than ever before or since, and it would have been natural enough for the clergy, as their order *as a whole* rose in social status and repute through that century, to have approximated more and more to that very attractive ideal which a century and more of unremitting urbanization has only made to seem, in retrospect, the more delightful. Most of the clergy whose rising or risen incomes enabled them to live as gentlemen were, anyway, country clergymen, who did not see and pursue the ideal from afar, but knew it closely and could conceive of no other. The poverty of so many town livings, whose large populations and influential positions (often as forts beleaguered by nonconformity) gave them a greater natural importance than equally poor country livings, was a constant theme of church re-

[1] 7 April 1802: *Parl. Hist.* XXXVI, 474–7.
[2] i.e. the Trulliber type of parson, whose awful example was often cited.

formers from the Restoration onwards, and was indeed one of the principal causes of Queen Anne's Bounty, whose augmentations gradually and moderately 'improved' a great many of them—a particular blessing, inasmuch as they were exceedingly unlikely to be 'improved' in any of the staple ways already mentioned. Besides, no clergyman who could avoid it (unless—and this came to be a most important exception—he were an Evangelical) wanted to spend the whole of his time in a town living. Bishops and prebendaries of town-sited cathedrals, and the better-off ministers of town parishes, seem all generally to have felt it necessary to retire to the country for at least part of the year, and to have held in commendam or plurality the country benefice that made such rural respite possible. The industrial, commercial town was viewed as a deplorable social monster until well into the nineteenth century, and the kind of parochial ministry it required was always contrasted unfavourably with that appropriate to the countryside. The country parish, and the life of the country gentleman—these were the ideals that the bulk of the clergy, and virtually all the dignified clergy up to about 1815, wanted to realize.[1]

There were other factors besides the 'improvement' of so many livings that helped to raise the social status of the clergy and tie them closely to the landed gentry. A contributory factor was undoubtedly that the ancient claims to some kind of disciplinary and moral authority over the laity, by virtue of orders and ecclesiastical jurisdiction, were no longer enforced. Gibson's *Codex* was their eighteenth-century swan-song. 'The Laity have little now to apprehend from Church-Authority', remarked an intelligent clergyman in 1779, 'unless the presentment of a country Church-warden for any irregularities of life be esteemed formidable. Canons framed by a Convocation have been declared by the greatest lawyer of his age[2] not binding on the Laity; and justly declared so, because not issuing from the Legislature, to which they are subject; and the Ecclesiastical Courts, if they seem ever so little to exceed their due bounds, are immediately corrected by the Courts of Common Law.'[3] In an age when respectable clergy danced attendance at court, farmed their glebes with science and zeal, and took their place on the bench of

---

[1] For further consideration of this theme, see chapter IV below, esp. pp. 165–8.

[2] i.e. Lord Hardwicke.

[3] John Sturges, *Considerations on the Present State of the Church Establishment*, pp. 73–4.

magistrates; and when noble names were as common on the bench and in the close as county names were in the close and in all the richer livings of the land—then there could no longer be any danger of clerical ascendancy, merely because the concept of a separate, independent clerical estate had evaporated from popular thinking. The objections which peers and courtiers, broad-acred gentlemen and social-climbing city-men had felt to the low-born, professional prelates of Jacobethan England, vanished before the titled and well-connected bishops of George II's and George III's reigns. Church and state, which had nearly split apart in the revolutions of the seventeenth century, were brought back into close connexion with each other; clergy and laity adopted the same ideals and almost the same conduct; the spiritual and temporal estates became again what they had always been in medieval theory, twin dimensions of an indivisible unity.

One consequence of this was that nominally 'C. of E.' laity ceased to use about the clergy the opprobrious and insulting language that was so often heard between 1700 and 1736. The contempt and disregard which seems to have been a common upper-class attitude towards the mass of the clergy in the early eighteenth century changed slowly through condescension to the respect and even admiration which was increasingly voiced in the early nineteenth. Such of the laity as were not frenzied by anti-clerical prejudice became, as it were, *sure* of the clergy; and, confident that the clergy could never again lord it over them, found the way clear to recognizing an identity of interests and affinity of opinions with the clergy that had never appeared so clearly before.

Consequently also, in these circumstances, church reform took on a tamer colouring. There was no longer talk, no longer even any implicit possibility, of the clerical estate gaining at the expense of the laity. The church dropped its pretensions to be regarded as an extraordinary body, capable, in the last resort, of breaking its bonds to the state and standing splendidly alone. Canon law turned from scratching to licking the hand that held it; and sank, from its pretensions to independent origins and supernatural authority, to the status in practice of a department of the common law of the land, and a generally subordinate one at that. Clergymen forced to defend their rights were very likely better looked after by the secular than the canon lawyers; the rights they defended at law were usually rights of property, for the rigorous upholding of which in respect of all men the English constitution was at that time eminently concerned. The protection given by the rule of law to church property was acclaimed by church publicists as one of the happiest circumstances of establishment.

The upper classes furthermore came to discover special reasons for cementing their alliance with the clergy in the last third of the eighteenth century. Political radicalism and social unrest, threatening the régime of conservatism and class subordination, made it increasingly necessary that the certainty of the 'divine rewards and penalties' awaiting respectively the virtuous and vicious in the next world should be well and ubiquitously preached. The revolution in France, and the enthusiastic interest in it so widely shown at first in England, conclusively sealed that holy alliance between the upper orders in church and state already well in being before the Revolution began. Clergy and gentry often sat side by side on the magistrates' bench: the number of clerical J.Ps. grew steadily through the eighteenth and early nineteenth centuries until it comprised about a quarter of the whole.[1] It was about 1780, rather than 1793, that they began to show and to proclaim the identity of views and policies that marked their relations in the period of the French wars, and to congratulate themselves on their social and moral assimilation; which was often, indeed, very striking. It had come about 'accidentally', but under the pressure of certain social and political threats and uncertainties, those concerned looked into it with new interest and saw that it was good and capable of logical defence and exposition. Nothing less than the hand of God can have worked so happy a consummation; and so Burke and his numberless followers evolved from their empirical knowledge of the system something resembling a full-dress theory of church and state, related as much to the social as to the political structure of the state, and triumphantly tied them together.

It was the main point of the Burkean theory to glorify the actual (and often 'accidentally' arrived at) connexions and inter-dependencies of clergy and responsible laity as if they constituted a work of supreme, supra-human wisdom, that fixed the best imaginable political system (itself a mixture of secular and ecclesiastical) in an immovable position by identifying it with a stable and sensible hierarchical social structure.

[1] S. & B. Webb, *English Local Government* I (*The Parish and the County*), 350–9; *British Magazine*, March 1832, p. 66.

'Church and state', said Burke, 'are ideas inseparable in [Englishmen's] minds';[1] one of his followers said they were 'one and the same thing in different aspects'.[2] Their formal, political and legal adjustment to one another was so neat and so profound that, said Bishop Van Mildert in 1825, 'It may be easy to say, this is a spiritual right, and that a temporal right; this is an exercise of civil power, and that of ecclesiastical; but when you come to apply these to individual cases, they will be found so blended together, as to render their separation always difficult, sometimes unpracticable. And this', he triumphantly concluded, 'is in reality the main foundation of that alliance between church and state, which exists in almost every well-constituted government, and which sustains the fabric of the British Constitution.'[3] 'The complicated interweaving of Ecclesiastical and Civil Offices which is effected by the English Law', wrote another high churchman, 'renders it difficult to distinguish clearly between them.'[4] One of the several maxims that Lord Eldon never tired or repeating was Hardwicke's dictum that 'Christianity is part of the law of England.' Another way of proving the excellence of the English version of a church-state relationship was illustrated by Lord Liverpool when he remarked that the church's hierarchial system 'was unequal and of a mixed complexion, and therefore more consistent with the other parts of our constitution'.[5]

The social adjustment of church to state was seen to be equally close and happy. The clergy were drawn from every class (even the poorest boy of promise, so long as he was fortunate enough to go to a good parish school and come under the notice of a churchman affluent and charitable enough to help him on, could get to Oxford or Cambridge as a sizar) and so the church's ministry operated at each level of the social structure in nice adaptation to the minds and circumstances of each class of the laity—bishops and canons, often themselves of aristocratic birth, catering for the nobility, and so on down the scale to the penurious and perpetual curates who could speak to the condition of the lower orders.

[1] *Reflections* (World's Classics edition, 1907), p. 109.

[2] William Palmer, *Narrative of Events connected with the Tracts for the Times* (1883), p. 37. Palmer was too clear-sighted to believe they were still so: he was instancing what he called an 'antiquated theory'.

[3] *Hansard* n.s. XIII, 696, 17 May 1825.

[4] Richard Hurrell Froude, 'Fragment on the Erastians'; in his *Remains* III, 389.

[5] *Hansard*, XXVI, 299, 21 May 1813.

'So long as the Body Politic consists of various ranks and degrees of men, and exhibits various inequalities of wealth and influence, and is even found most to prosper where these take root and flourish—so long will it be found requisite that the diffusion of *Religion* throughout the entire mass of the community should be provided for by a system of Polity somewhat analogous to the existing distinctions in civil life.'[1] Moreover, the clergy and the responsible laity were finely attuned to one another; their interests, intellectual and economic as well as political, were so similar; they were both intimately interested in the ownership and use of land, and the life of the countryside; and their educations had been conducted on exactly the same lines, and in the same institutions. Much was made of the clerical predominance over education 'from infancy to manhood', and of the way that clergy and laity read the same books and lived the same life at the universities. It was considered a positive strength of the English system that the clergy were not educated in seminaries as an order apart.

A particularly telling example of this line of apologetics is Burke's explanation of the common custom of having clerical tutors, which lent itself so readily to the criticism of both the anti-clerical and the ultra-pious. Burke saw nothing ridiculous, degrading or hypocritical in the way clergymen attached themselves to aristocratic families as tutors to the scions of the house and made their way in the world (and in the church, sometimes as far as a remunerative bishopric) through the patronage that thus came their way as long as they continued to prove congenial. There can be no doubt that this kind of attachment was often degrading and worldly. But hear Burke's account of it: 'Even when our youth, leaving schools and universities, enter that most important period of life which begins to link experience and study together, and when with that view they visit other countries, instead of old domestics whom we have seen as governors to principal men from other parts, three-fourths of those who go abroad with our young nobility and gentlemen are ecclesiastics; not as austere masters, nor as mere followers; but as friends and companions of a graver character, and not seldom persons as well born as themselves. With them, as relations, they most commonly keep up a close connexion through life. By this connexion we conceive that we attach our gentlemen to the church; and we liberalize the church

[1] William Van Mildert, *Charge to the Clergy of the Diocese of Durham*, 1831.

by an intercourse with the leading characters of the country.'[1] This way of putting it was thoroughly characteristic of the establishment apologetics of this period (and not a little characteristic also of conservative apologetics for the unreformed parliament). The existing state of things might, indeed, look silly or base to an outsider, but how well it worked in practice! And what a marvellous—surely a providential—arrangement it was, to bring so happy an issue out of so much confusion! Rash and impious must be the man who would venture to intervene in a concern that providence had clearly made its own.

So deeply rooted was this inclination to see the hidden hand of the divine wisdom in every circumstance of the establishment that even the age-old and hitherto undisputed material abuses in the church's system, its inequalities of income (which had become all the more pronounced through the eighteenth century) and consequent non-residence and pluralities, found their apologists and justifiers. By the early nineteenth century (when at last the size of the problem was better known, and the will and the wealth to tackle it were ready and waiting for direction) the progress of church reform was in no small degree obstructed by the tendency of so many of the real reformers themselves to indulge in this same apologetic language, especially when they were replying to attacks from outside. It was *good*, they said, that clerical incomes were so unequal. The plums of the profession (or, as the clearer-sighted put it, the prizes in the lottery) acted as incentives to the ambitious and rewards for the meritorious. Without some lucrative posts to offer, how could you expect men of birth and talent to enter the profession at all? What would have seemed obstacles to Bancroft or Burnet, and what certainly seem so to us, appeared to them almost as a fact of nature. Churchmen became complacent about the church's social and political position in the middle and later eighteenth century. Material abuses and defects of two centuries' standing ceased to alarm and sadden as they had done earlier on. It is significant that men seriously concerned with church and state discovered excellencies in the messy, disjointed, layman-dominated state of the church instead of inquiring how it might be made rational, efficient, and within its proper limits independent. What had been in the early seventeenth century only second-best, temporary apologies for pluralities and income inequalities, became in the later eighteenth century

[1] *Reflections, ed. cit.* p. 109.

74

positive arguments in their favour. The evils attendant upon the patron-age system, which had earlier seemed so enormous and were to seem so again in the nineteenth century, were played down, and all kinds of arguments used to show that both official and private patronage had much to be said for them. For pluralities, non-residence, and the lavish use of curates, equally plausible reasons could be advanced, which were no different from those put forward by Whitgift in 1584 or by Sherlock in 1737,[1] but which now fitted in beautifully with the conservative orthodoxy of their time. A non-resident might put an excellent curate in charge of his living. A good curate was much better than a bad resident incumbent. A curacy formed an admirable first step in a clerical career; it gave the beginner a chance to learn his job and to show his mettle. When defended on grounds like these a large measure of non-residence almost seemed an indispensable element of a good parochial system.

It was only the Evangelicals who brought into this world of mutual admiration and self-congratulation an alien note of 'melancholy not unnoticed, and of ample power to chasten and subdue'. There was of course a growing band of reformers from the end of the eighteenth century, who brought the church's material deficiencies before the public and by emphasizing the damage they did to the establishment gradually made it clear to all but the most reactionary churchmen (who, as it unhappily turned out, were thickest upon the ground in colleges and chapters) that the kind of arguments advanced in palliation of abuses simply would not do. By no means all, not even most, of these reformers were Evangelicals. Nor were Evangelicals as such necessarily bound to take the more advanced reformers' view of the church's failings; their political opinions, social position, and actual experience of the workings of the system, often inclined them to moderation. But their characteristic attitudes nevertheless had that in them that jarred with the outlook of such as Paley, Burke and Van Mildert. They were against anything that kept a parish clergyman from complete devotion to his ministry, whether it was pinching poverty, a zeal for farming, or a taste for metro-politan or academic society. The standards they set for clergymen were high and peculiar. Others complained with some justice that Evangelical

[1] See Christopher Hill, *Economic Problems of the Church*, pp. 228, 232–3; and Sherlock's anonymous *Considerations upon Pluralities, Non-Residence, and Salaries of Curates, passim.*

parsons, after sorting out the sheep from the goats by a rigorous presentation of 'the gospel system', too often left the goats out in the cold; but there can be no doubt that they usually tended the sheep with affectionate diligence. Their sermons had to be fresh and potent, their weekdays were filled with visits and prayer-meetings, their attentions were constantly requisitioned by the many national societies which their party wholly or partly ran, and they were pretty well the only clergymen who deliberately organized local clerical meetings between 1760 and 1830.

Evangelical clergymen were acutely conscious of their separateness as an order. They had recaptured, though in a different style and from quite a different source, that sense of the clergyman's essential difference from the layman which had on the whole gone out with Gibson and with the non-jurors. Of course this difference did not consist in the sacerdotal prerogatives of priesthood. No set of Anglicans have ever more clearly and forcibly stated the authentic protestant case against sacerdotalism. But Evangelical clergymen seem generally to have felt a peculiar kind of responsibility for the salvation of the souls of their flock and to have gone about achieving it by more exclusively spiritual means. There was no trace, no hint, of Pelagianism about them. The records of their ministries never give the impression that obedience to all constituted authorities and a regular routine of prayers and worship were about all that the parish minister could expect of his flock. It would be unjust to say that Evangelical clergy were absolutely, in their own language, more 'serious' than the rest. It is no more than truth to admit that Evangeliclas in general evinced their seriousness more seriously, and shied away from behaviour, dress, and talk that tended to depreciate or conceal their high calling. They thus at once emphasized their distinction from their brethren and their disagreement with too complete and easy an identi-fication of interests between clergy and laity—a distinction and a dis-agreement which were also to some extent marked by the lesser degree of attachment that many of them showed towards the life of the country-side and the ideal of the country parish. This readiness to serve town parishes was regarded as a little unnatural in them; it was also regarded with disapproval, sometimes quite reasonably, as an indication of a preference for preaching and praying with sheep (sheep whose fleeces, moreover, might be very golden) from neighbouring parishes instead of the less exciting devotion to the mixed sheep and goats of their own parishes which the non-evangelicals liked to claim as *their* ideal. In this way also the Evangelicals broke step with the majority of their contemporaries.

Yet in their co-operation with their own laity, and sense of fellowship, even equality, with them, the Evangelicals were wholly of their own time. This often so amicable partnership of clergy and laity in the joint management of their christian society and maintenance of their prized constitution in church and state, more than anything else, characterized the establishment in the last half-century of the unreformed parliament.[1] Influences and ideas flowed naturally to and fro between them; and it is on this account that we must go some way beyond Christopher Hill's perfectly correct statement, that the period between the Restoration and the early nineteenth century was 'the age of the dependence of the parson on the squire, a dependence which was fundamentally an economic dependence, although it was also in part an economic alliance'.[2] The alliance, where it existed at all, was always likely to be much more than economic.

[1] Dr Sykes has some excellent remarks upon this 'Laicisation of religion' in *Church and State in England in the 18th Century*, pp. 379–80.
[2] *Economic Problems of the Church*, p. 351.

CHAPTER III

QUEEN ANNE'S BOUNTY IN THE EIGHTEENTH CENTURY

I. STARTING TROUBLES, 1704-17[1]

The first few years of Queen Anne's Bounty were entirely occupied in preparations for later usefulness. Great indeed was the disappointment of those needy clergymen who had imagined in 1704 that substantial and swift aid would soon be brought to them. The obstacles that stood between them and the Bounty Board (a convenient alternative term for Queen Anne's Bounty, used since quite early days) were many and vexing. It took the Bounty more than ten years to get going properly. This was not because of any failure of energy or intelligence on the Governors' part but partly because their constitution had fundamental flaws in it, partly because they encountered difficulties which few could have foreseen, and partly because other difficulties, which must certainly have been foreseen, proved, in the event, less tractable than had been hoped. The first augmentations were not made until 1714; and when in 1719 John Ecton, one of the Board's principal officers, published his *State of the Proceedings of Queen Anne's Bounty*, one of his avowed objects was to show 'the true Reason why this Noble Charity took effect no sooner, which may serve to remove the Prejudices some People may lie under, touching the Management and Disposal of that Charity, which now begins to brighten and shew itself in the remotest Corners of this Kingdom'.[2]

Queen Anne's Bounty was a legal corporation, resting on combined acts of crown and parliament, and allowed a strictly circumscribed measure of independence in the management of the business for which it was created. The business parts of the first, 1704 charter,[3] after listing the governors, giving them the usual legal powers of a corporation and

---

[1] This section is largely based on Savidge's *Foundation and Early Years of Queen Anne's Bounty*, to which the interested reader is referred for further detail.

[2] 2nd edition, 1721, pp. xi–xii.   [3] Appendix I.

transferring the whole responsibility for the first-fruits and tenths to them, defined what was to constitute a quorum at their quarterly general courts; empowered them to appoint committees, and call in advice from outside; and provided that the 'rules, methods, orders, directions and constitutions' they drew up for the execution of their trust should, after being 'approved, altered or amended' by the Crown, acquire the force of law. The main business of the second charter, sealed on 5 March 1714,[1] was to alter the definition of a quorum and tabulate twenty rules and orders; which, together with those new or amending rules and orders that were added as the years went by (signed always, 'by his majesty's command', by one of the secretaries of state), laid down very exactly the lines on which the Bounty was to be run.

There seems to have been some alteration or amendment made by government to this first, basic set of rules and orders proposed by the Board; why, and how, it is impossible now to ascertain.[2] But there was no trouble about granting the Board's request for an amendment of the quorum requirements, which proved one of the chief obstacles to progress. The first charter flew altogether too high, in insisting on the attendance of some of the busiest public men in London. They often could not make it, and the early minute books show how greatly the governors' will to get on with the job was frustrated by the absence of essential members.[3] In January 1710 therefore, when in obedience to the queen's commands the Board drew up and presented to her an account of their work to date[4] they took the opportunity to solicit a modification of the charter in this particular, 'the Obligation we lie under by our Constitution, of holding no Court without the Assistance of a Bishop, a Privy-Councillor and a Judge or Queen's Council, [having] so often put a stop to our doing any Business, either in *Winter*, when Your Majesty's Service in Parliament, Councils, or Courts of Justice, requires their Attendance: or in *Summer*, when the Lords the Bishops are visiting their respective Dioceses, and the Judges in their Circuits, and Your Majesty's Court and Council remov'd from Town. . . .' The quorum requirements were accordingly modified in the second charter; all that was now needed was a bishop, or a privy councillor, or a judge or Q.C., plus any

---

[1] Appendix 2.   [2] Savidge, pp. 54–8, 65–6.   [3] Savidge, pp. 64–5.
[4] The 'Humble Representation', printed in Ecton's *State* (1721), pp. 106–11, and Savidge, pp. 135–7.

six others; and to make up a quorum on this basis presented little difficulty.[1]

Difficulties in getting a quorum delayed the transaction of business; but the very possibility of transacting business at all depended on other factors, and it was among some of these that the main sources of delay were found. Only one of the Board's preliminary tasks seems to have been accomplished with reasonable speed.

They had to find out which benefices needed augmentation. The first charter required them to compile a list of livings under £80 a year, with their distances from London, 'and which of them are in towns corporate or market towns, and which not, and how [they] are supplied by preaching Ministers, and where the Incumbents have more than one living;' and placed at their disposal the ordinary means of ascertaining such facts, by royal writs instituting local commissions of inquiry. The governors preferred to work through the bishops (and the ordinaries of exempt jurisdictions—*alias* 'peculiars': i.e. independent enclaves within the dioceses, where the administration and jurisdiction came under some other person than the diocesan bishop), probably because they already possessed a good deal of information of this kind and were thought able to get what was wanted more accurately and quickly. The inquiries were commenced early in 1705, and the results were 'received, made into a book, and presented to the Queen in December 1707'.[2] Another and partly overlapping body of information on livings was compiled under the Act of 1707, which authorized the discharge from first-fruits and tenths of livings under £50 a year. Again the bishops and ordinaries were employed to amass and certify the information; but it was actually to be collected by commissions of inquiry, three or more to each diocese, for whose assistance a set of 'Directions for the better Execution of the Commission . . .' were drawn up by a committee of governors with the help of Ecton (then assistant to the remembrancer of first-fruits), Willis the dean of Lincoln, the attorney-general and the Lord Chief Baron of the Exchequer. This information was given to the Exchequer, became the basis of the Board's work of augmentations, and was made available to the world at large in 1711 when the capable and helpful Ecton (by then deputy remembrancer) published it in his *Liber Valorum et Decimarum*. The appearance of this useful work marked something of an epoch in the

[1] Savidge, p. 66. [2] Savidge, p. 53.

history of the English church because it was the only official information on the actual value of livings to be collected between Henry VIII's *Liber Regis* and the parliamentary returns of the early nineteenth century;[1] and its publication was intended not merely to enlighten and inform, but also to direct the abounding benevolence of the age to a set of particularly deserving objects, and to stimulate private individuals to emulation of their monarch. Its worth as an account of actual values was unfortunately limited, and became increasingly so as it went through successive editions. It gave the actual present values only of those livings under £50 a year which had been certified to the Exchequer; for the rest, it reproduced the *Liber Regis* valuations and taxes. As the editions went by, some additions were made to the former class, as bishops discovered and certified other poor livings, and it is evident that the celebrated antiquary Browne Willis, who produced the edition of 1754, had had access to the 1707 book of livings under £80 a year, for he included the values of such in the latter class. John Bacon's edition of 1786 gave a good deal of further information, but was still imperfect. It needed the determination and authority of a worried sovereign legislature to do again in the eighteen-thirties as thorough a job as had been done by a determined sovereign monarch three hundred years before.[2]

Such information was an indispensable preliminary to any augmentation work on more than a local scale. It was moreover the only way conclusively to prove, in the teeth of the niggardly and the anticlerical, how much clerical poverty there was. Kennet acutely felt the need of something better than his own and other people's guesses;[3] and it is interesting that just after he had mentioned this in the suggestive concluding section of his book, and just as the new-born Bounty Board was beginning to collect particulars of livings under £80 a year, a freelance clergyman should have circulated, or at any rate begun to circulate, 'To the Reverend the Ministers of every Parochial Church or Chappel in England' a request for all the vital facts and figures about their cures. 'The Account you'll be pleased to give of these or the like Particulars',

---

[1] For the inquiries of that period, see below, p. 199-203.

[2] Ecton saw his book through the editions of 1711, 1723, and 1728. It then came out as *Ecton's Thesaurus Rerum Ecclesiasticarum* in 1742, 1754, 1763 and 1788. In 1786 it appeared in the guise of John Bacon's *Liber Regis;* for which, see p. 120.

[3] *Case of Impropriations,* pp. 403–5.

he promised, 'shall be faithfully applied to the service of the Publick.' His design was to publish an account of 'the Present State of Parish Churches'. Nothing came of it. Perhaps too few ministers replied, perhaps he heard of the Bounty Board's similar activities and feared (needlessly, as it would now appear) to put his own work in competition with theirs. There remains of his enterprise the 'Notitia Parochialis' in the Lambeth Archives, indexed by Ducarel the archivist in 1762 and described by him as 'very curious and extremely valuable . . . an exact account of the state of 1,606 parish churches in 1705'. This excellent private venture is a telling piece of evidence of the enthusiasm that existed for church reform at this time.[1]

Nothing could be done in the way of augmentation until the number and quality of the deserving cases were known. Since they were not known until 1708 or 1709, four or five years of delay might have been thus accounted for. But to have money going out, it was necessary first to have money coming in. The Board's main trouble through the first ten years or so of its life was that its revenue was uncertain and encumbered and, moreover, irksome and costly to collect; and its debtors were as happily placed, from their own point of view, as its creditors, in that they could often (and with good statutory precedent behind them) get out of paying, whereas its creditors were expressly entitled by statute to get paid to the uttermost farthing.

The encumbrances on the revenue were the pensions and salaries with which it had traditionally been saddled. There were thirteen of them still going in 1704. The Bounty Board was made responsible for paying them throughout their natural terms of life or buying their beneficiaries out. Some of them had fallen years in arrear; the arrears in fact amounted to more than a whole year's revenue; and every penny had to be paid.[2] This part of Queen Anne's Bounty's early business took time and money, and was not well understood by the public—nor, one may guess, by the families of the expiring pensioners, who might otherwise have hoped that public money would continue to flow discreetly in their direction.

More distressing by far to the Bounty Board than their thirteen creditors were their innumerable debtors. 'We found', they said in their Humble Representation to the queen early in 1710, '. . . that there was a very great Sum of Money due from the Clergy and their Predecessors.

[1] Appendix 3.   [2] Savidge, pp. 33–6.

... We have therefore spent much Time in our enquiry after the same, and in distinguishing between the sperate [sic] and desperate Debts of the Clergy...' The difficulties here were vast, and Savidge shows very clearly with what energy and boldness they pursued their often distasteful and embarrassing task and how at last they got out of the wood.[1] It cannot have been pleasant for the bishops to have to press legal proceedings against brothers and fathers in God, their widows and executors; and it was awkward in the extreme that the co-operation of the government department to which they were inexorably harnessed was imperfect and laggardly. Some of the Exchequer officers were prompt and sympathetic; Ecton at least deserves to be ranked among the best civil servants of his day. Others were inefficient and inattentive, and had moreover a sinister interest in keeping even the most desperate debts going as long as they could. The Board cut their way out of some of their difficulties by discharging the livings under £50 a year; which got rid of nearly four thousand actual or potential debtors, but diminished their revenue by over £3,000 a year. It may be doubted whether they would have had recourse to quite such drastic surgery had not the weight of arrears been so heavy, their consequences for the church's efficiency so deplorable ('many Persons have refused to take Institution of their Livings, lest they should be obnoxious to the Great Debts contracted by several of their Predecessors, and thereby ruin themselves and their Families'),[2] and the prospects so dim of ever, under existing conditions of management, avoiding the recurrence of such arrears in future. For here lay the Board's most vexing problem, in the First-Fruits office of the Exchequer. Their whole revenue came through that office, and they had to work with it. Their minutes show that they themselves were enterprising and businesslike; but their tie to the First-Fruits Office meant they had always one foot stuck in the mud.

By 1711 or so, they were chafing against this yoke and seeking means of escape from it. Savidge describes the various schemes they considered for the better collection and quicker delivery of their revenue—one of them a proposal to cut the First-Fruits Office out altogether.[3] This was evidently too startling a measure to be acceptable, and insufficiently careful of existing Exchequer interests. But their yearnings were not wholly unrewarded. In 1717 the attorney-general introduced into the

[1] Savidge, pp. 36–7, 42–51.   [2] 'Humble Representation', § 5.   [3] Savidge, p. 48.

House of Commons 'an Act for the better Collecting and Levying the Revenue of the Tenths of the Clergy'.[1] It had been drafted by the admirable Ecton and its merit must have been that it effected a decent compromise between what the interested parties separately sought.[2] While leaving the collection and delivery of their revenue wholly in the hands of the Exchequer, it simplified the tenths part of it—which gave by far the more trouble—by substituting for the old apparatus of bishops and sub-collectors a single receiver of tenths, who was to receive the tenths and pay them into the First-Fruits Office, where they would join the first-fruits and become available to the Bounty's treasurer. This new office was of a curious borderline kind. In fact subordinate to the First-Fruits Office of the Exchequer (to whom its receipts were paid, and in whose hands continued to rest the pursuit, or non-pursuit, of arrears), appointment to it was by the Crown; yet the man appointed had to take oath before the governors, who also fixed his salary and helped pay for the establishment of his office in the Middle Temple; and the first man to hold this bridge was none other than Ecton, appointed at the governors' recommendation. Between the three offices thus concerned with the administration of Queen Anne's Bounty—the old First-Fruits Office, a part of the Exchequer; the new Tenths Office; and the Bounty Board itself—there was thus constructed some degree of physical dependence, to which the practice of officials holding posts in plurality in two or even in all three of the offices, begun just after Ecton's appointment as the first receiver of tenths, gave blood and sinew and, as it turned out, practical efficiency.[3]

By this act of 1717, therefore, Queen Anne's Bounty was at last put upon a satisfactory footing. Its task had been prescribed, and its basic constitution laid down, in the first charter of 1704; its constitution made workable, and a code of rules and regulations added, by the second charter, for the accomplishment of its task. Statutes in 1715[4] improved this code, and in 1717 remedied a fundamental defect in the financial organization. No changes comparable to these were made for a hundred and twenty years.

[1] 3 George I c. 10.
[2] Savidge, p. 49.
[3] See below, p. 118.
[4] 1 George I c. 10; see below, p. 90.

84

Queen Anne's Bounty in the Eighteenth Century

2. TWO STEPS FORWARD, ONE STEP BACK

The purpose for which Queen Anne's Bounty existed was simply to 'augment the maintenance' of the poor clergy. This and no other end was prescribed for it in its foundation charter. The means however were not laid down. All that was said was that the governors should 'consider, consult, advise, agree upon, draw up, prepare, and propose in writing' to the Crown 'such proper and necessary rules, methods, directions, orders and constitutions' as should seem suitable for the running of the Board, the security of their revenues, and 'the distributing, paying, and disposing of the same and all other gifts and benevolences that shall or may be given to the said Corporation for the charitable ends aforesaid. . . .' The years from the accession of the first George to the death of the fourth passed peacefully enough in the Bounty's offices, as their tolerably efficient routine of business ensured that they did all that their charters and contemporaries asked of them. Even after 1780, when the tide of reform first touched, then rocked, and finally swept away their barque, their business was nothing like as heavy and various as it became in the later nineteenth century. After the first world war its activities expanded once again, with almost explosive force. 'Since 1920', wrote its secretary in his preface to the 1933 edition of the Board's official pamphlet history, 'duties have been entrusted to the Corporation by Parliament far exceeding in importance and magnitude the whole of the duties which were being performed by it when the first edition was published . . .'[1] But it is difficult to resist the conclusion that for all the extensions of its staff and business, Queen Anne's Bounty never quite recaptured the quiet glory of its first, Hanoverian period. It was not, indeed, faultless, and its mills ground rather slowly; but its work was good and solid, and for each man who had complaints to make about it there were a dozen to bless it. It was the church's only central executive office and, after 1717, the church's only functioning representative organ, until 1836. It was remarkable, perhaps unique, in the early eighteenth century, as existing for no other purpose than that of steady change and improvement in a key part of the constitution, and as a standing testimony to these possibilities.

The Board's main duty, then, was the distribution of the first-fruits

---

[1] W. R. LeFanu, *Queen Anne's Bounty*, ed. Hughes, p. 7.

and tenths revenue (which settled down at something over £13,000 a
year, after paying the Exchequer's fees) among the poor clergy. The
governors promptly set up a committee 'to prepare and draw up rules
and orders'. This committee was of indeterminate composition, but
frequently included among the six or seven who normally came,
Archbishops Tenison and Sharp, Bishops Burnet and Dawes (while he
was bishop of Chester, 1708-14), Deans Willis and Fogg of Lincoln and
Carlisle respectively, and a law officer or two.[1] Early in 1707 they produced a draft code of rules, which Savidge thinks must have been that
submitted to the queen along with the 'Humble Representation' in
January 1710.[2] These proposals having proved unacceptable, for no
known reasons, discussions on the subject continued and another code
was produced by the committee three years later, adopted by the
General Court of 15 January 1713 and after a long delay in the government offices embodied in the second charter, of 5 March 1714.[3]

This basic code underwent a good many alterations in detail as the
years went by, but its leading principles remained unchanged for a
couple of centuries. The governors, who could have decided to bring the
poorest or most deserving benefices up to a reasonable annual value by
paying them so much a year, adopted instead a slower but in the end
further-reaching method of augmentation. Rule 1 laid it down that
augmentations were to be 'by the way of purchase, not by the way of
pension'; rule 2, that they were to consist of sums of £200, 'to be invested
in a purchase at the expense of the Corporation'. Needy benefices were
thus to receive in due course (rule 3 stated that those under £10 a year
would be dealt with first) capital grants of £200 apiece, with which
land should be purchased so that the income of the living would be permanently augmented by the amount of the rent which the incumbent
could get for that land. In the long run, many more benefices would
profit from the Bounty under this plan of distribution than if the whole
of the Board's annual revenue had been appropriated to one happy batch
of deserving cases; but it meant, in the short run, that only a few at a
time could taste the royal bounty. The amount of money available for
distribution was much sooner exhausted in any given year by its expenditure in lots of £200 (to give a poor living about £10 extra a year) than
by lots of say £20 or £30. It ought to be put to the Board's credit, that,

[1] Savidge, p. 69.   [2] Savidge, p. 54.   [3] Savidge, p. 55.

already under fire for having done nothing for ten years, they chose the longer-term plan of operation, when the alternative would have brought a quicker return of popularity and would, moreover, have opened a convenient door to jobbery and log-rolling, had the governors felt inclined in that direction.

The other rules equally marked the direction and style in which the governors thought fit to proceed. The livings under £10 a year were to be selected by lot—Crown livings first, then the rest; and when there were no livings left under £10 a year, another group should be dealt with in the same style and brought up to whatever pitch had been decided; and so on again until, some hundreds of years ahead, no clergyman should lack a decent subsistence. This was their main principle, and the very poorest were given priority accordingly; but to this principle they admitted an important exception. To make their money go further, they set out to attract private benevolence to their aid by offering sums of £200 for livings under £35 a year, 'where any persons will give the same or greater sum or value in lands or tithes' (rule 4). The rest of the rules were concerned not with principle but procedure. For the information of the public and the encouragement of benefactors, they were at once published in the *Gazette* and circulated among the clergy; the first of the Bounty's augmentations were made several months later—nine to meet benefactions, on 8 October, and nineteen by lot, on 22 October 1714;[1] and some defects in the rules, which it took experience of their operation to discover, were corrected by act of parliament in the year following.[2] This done, the Bounty was well away.

The principles underlying the Bounty's work of augmentations up to the early nineteenth century may be listed thus:

(1) augmentation by capital grants (instead of 'pensions');

(2) the investment of these grants in land;

(3) the division of poor benefices into two classes: (a) a superior class, those under £35 a year, to aid which private benefactors were invited; (b) the rock-bottom class, to be augmented whether private benevolence was interested or not;

(4) the choosing by lot the benefices in the latter class.

[1] Savidge, pp. 59–60.
[2] 1 Geo. I. c. 10, An Act for making more effectual Her late Majesties Gracious Intentions for Augmenting the Maintenance of the Poor Clergy.

With the first principle it is difficult to quarrel. Given the fact of a fixed annual revenue with which to be benevolent, the governors chose the way to spread their benevolence over the furthest field and the longest period.[1] Nor can any criticism be made of their determination to spread their resources further still by linking their grants to those of private individuals. The duty of charitable giving was widely regarded by the affluent and there was an ever-increasing quantity of money in the country looking for charitable employment. It was only sensible of the governors of the Royal Bounty to use so conspicuous and royal an example for the encouragement of others.

What is more open to criticism is the way in which the governors selected the objects of their benevolence. It is certain that some extremely deserving cases were left out, and some not so deserving brought in. A living whose actual annual value was less than £10 a year was obviously in need of help; but among livings in that category, some would be more needy than others, and it might well be that, if all the circumstances (population, area, patronage, possibilities of uniting with adjacent parish, and so on) were only taken into account, some benefices in this category would seem to need help less than others whose emoluments were larger. Yet the rules confined the Bounty at first to the under-£10-a-year class only (except for those in the special class that was eligible for grants to meet private benefactions), provided for no examination of their particular circumstances, and had no better means of selecting them than by lot. This was not the best way to go about it; and there is plenty of evidence that some at least of the governors would have preferred a different procedure. The draft rules of 1706/7, for example, were better in two respects. They proposed a distribution of the Bounty among dioceses, in proportions 'agreeable to their respective wants', and a difference in the qualifications for livings within and beyond sixty miles from London—those within this radius being eligible if they were under £15 a year, instead of £10 (presumably because the spiritual and social needs of this part of England were thought greater).[2] This was sensible.

---

[1] Humphrey Prideaux, who was obsessed by impropriations, thought that they should buy up a batch of impropriations yearly and restore them to their proper owners. (*An Award of King Charles I . . . and Vindication of Personal Tithes*, pp. 64–5.) This would have worked in the same way.

[2] Savidge, p. 54.

It made distinctions. So did Tenison, whose views on the rules were made known to the committee in the spring of 1711. He wanted the Board to distinguish between active and worthless incumbents, at least of Crown livings; to refuse augmentations when livings were held in a prosperous plurality; and to prefer onerous parishes to under-populated.[1] Kennet, too, had favoured this last distinction. 'Is it fit to be consider'd', he asked, 'whether the first objects of this Publick Bounty, should be Market-Towns, and specially those that are most Populous, and nearest to the City of London?'[2] Burnet also was certainly in its favour; he never ceased to bewail the particularly poor showing the church made in the market towns. Bishop Wake of Lincoln in 1713 pointed out to the Board that some of the poorest benefices in his diocese 'might wholly be united with others, and spared any augmentation at all'; he proposed that all the other bishops should join him in drawing up lists of parishes thus suitable for union, and they could then, economically, get one comprehensive act of parliament to sanction the lot. Here was more sensible, dynamic, reform-mindedness; but the gleam of light disappears almost at once. 'Nothing came of Wake's suggestion.'[3]

It is clear, then, that ideas of the right sort were not lacking. It is not clear why nothing came of them. Possibly, the Crown lawyers, whose part in the drafting and passing of the rules (as, indeed, in the whole of the Bounty's early life) was great, were chary of allowing the Board anything that resembled a discretionary power, and perhaps suspicious also of clerical pretensions.[4] Some dioceses, moreover, were much better run than others; and any one could have realized that schemes requiring to be worked through the diocesan machinery were in for trouble. The governors may have decided to postpone the handling of these matters for a few years. They could, after all, scarcely go wrong in first of all making sure that every living in the national church, whether onerous or held in plurality or not, was worth at least *ten* pounds a year.

It must also be remembered, that between 1704 or so and 1716 the outlook for the church-reformers was set fair. Hoadly and the *Independent Whig* were still below the horizon; Tenison or Sharp would not have been foolish to have thought, 'One step at a time—*solvitur ambulando*—

---

[1] Savidge, p. 55.   [2] *Case of Impropriations*, p. 406.   [3] Savidge, pp. 111–12.
[4] But Gibson, who became the temporal lawyers' bugbear, only became a bishop in 1716.

some at least of these improvements can be made later on, once the Bounty is properly established.' So promising were the reforming activities of Convocation in these years while the rules were being drawn up that, indeed, even such a survey of the diocesan and parochial situation as began to be made early in the next century, and which would have been a prerequisite to an ideal management of the Bounty, can hardly have been an impossibility. It would have been a big thing to attempt, and no doubt it would have been but indifferently executed; but that such a study was absolutely impossible at that time, we are forbidden to believe by the examples, first, of the Board of Trade's inquiry into poor law expenditure in 1696, which was made through the bishops and drew answers from over 4,000 parishes,[1] and, second, of the ambitious scheme for fifty new churches in greater London, launched by parliament in 1711 on the basis of statistics provided by Convocation. The same machinery could presumably have been used for the collection of statistics from all over the country.

No evidence, however, seems to be available to explain why none of these things was done and why the Bounty Board thus set off at a disadvantage; nor can we do more than guess why the Bounty's basic rules, as codified in the charter of 1714, were in some ways so palpably defective. The act of 1715 did not much improve them. It recognized that many poor livings yet remained to be discovered and added to the augmentations list, and provided means for this to be done; but what it gave with one hand it took away with the other, for it expressly stipulated that no revaluations were ever to be made of the livings certified to the Exchequer as being under £50 a year in 1707-8. It strengthened the parochial system and upheld its own principles by insisting that all churches, curacies and chapels augmented should become (if they were not so already) 'perpetual benefices', thus giving their ministers the normal parson's freehold and protecting them (after making them a little more worth protecting) from corrupt exploitation by their patrons; and that patrons, rectors, and ministers of 'mother-churches' should not take the opportunity of a grant from the Bounty to reduce the stipend or 'pension' they had been in the way of paying to their vicars or curates. Another clause was certainly suited to strengthen church administration in general. Donatives (i.e. livings so completely in a patron's gift that his

[1] S. and B. Webb, *English Local Government* VII (1927), 109, 153.

presentee took possession of the living without any reference to the bishop or ordinary ceremony of institution or induction) were normally exempt from episcopal jurisdiction; they were in themselves 'peculiars'; they were often handled and served disgracefully, and nothing short of an act of parliament could touch them. Section 14 of the act provided that a donative, once augmented, should cease to be exempt and should come within the bishop's jurisdiction; but, again, the virtue of this provision was at once sapped by the one following, which made the patron's consent a necessary condition of augmentation, and so ensured that although the donatives of good patrons might slowly be brought into the common diocesan system, donatives belonging to bad patrons would almost certainly stay outside.

This extreme respect for the rights and advantages of patrons and impropriators (often but not necessarily the same persons) introduces the last significant point in which the Bounty's guiding principles were debateable. It could be said—and radicals later on were often to say it—that Queen Anne's Bounty existed mainly to put public money into private purses. Their augmentations by lot increased the value of livings, the advowsons of the majority of which were in private hands. As the value of a living went up, so did the value of the advowson or the next presentation; which was sheer gain to the lucky patron. He was not made to bear a share in the cost of the improvement, unless he were patron of a donative, and then he only *might* be, under section 16 of the 1715 act. Nor was he, except in the special case of donatives, compelled to do his duty by the parish from which he derived such benefits. He was left, if he was the impropriator, in undisturbed enjoyment of his revenues, and bound only not to diminish the sum he customarily paid the incumbent, if he paid such a sum at all. With augmentations to meet benefactions, it was much the same. The values of advowsons were bound to go up, and no conditions whatever were attached to patrons' ownership of them. Unless they were themselves the benefactors (in which case their net gain was still large) they were in effect receiving unmerited gifts from the public funds and from the charity and generosity of private benefactors, who were often the incumbents themselves.[1]

The principle of private patronage was actually further strengthened in 1715 by the act's making it possible for Queen Anne's Bounty to

[1] And who might, of course, own the advowson, and be their own patrons.

negotiate a benefactor's acquisition of the patronage of the living he was helping. They must have had in mind mainly small vicarages and curacies and daughter-churches in ecclesiastical patronage. It is almost inconceivable that a lay patron would part with his patronage in order to benefit the parson; particularly in view of the fact that if he really wished to see the parson in better circumstances, the remedy lay in his own hands.[1] It is impossible in the present state of knowledge to say whether more harm than good resulted to the parishes involved in these transfers; but it seems very likely that they lent themselves to simony and corruption. One instance of this is averred by the historian of the huge parish of Whalley, in Lancashire. Whalley was one of the parishes that showed up in its worst light the establishment's failure to refashion its parochial system. Very extensive, and the scene of some of the most rapid expansions of population and industry of modern English history, it only expanded its religious provisions by the common device of chapels-at-ease, their patronage being in the hands of the vicar of the old parish church, the 'mother-church'. The vicar of Whalley (himself presented by the Archbishop of Canterbury) enjoyed the patronage of more than a dozen chapelries within his parish, which were so poor that they cannot have been of much use to him, socially or politically. It is therefore easy enough to understand that he was ready to part with some of them to benefactors. The vicar from 1703 to 1738 parted with them only on terms advantageous to himself. Whalley's laborious historian says of him that he was 'a needy man, of whom I have but too convincing proofs that he took money for the presentations to curacies, etc. . . . By his means too, and not without a valuable consideration, the patronage of six, if not seven, of the curacies was alienated from the vicarage under the 1st George I.' These chapelries would appear to be those of Altham St James, Church Kirk, Clitheroe, Downham, and Newchurch-in-Pendle, augmented by Queen Anne's Bounty and Nathaniel Curzon Esq. in 1722, and described by Bacon as in the patronage of Asheton Curzon Esq. in 1786; Brimley St Peter, augmented similarly by Edmond Townley in 1724, and owned by a patron of the same name in 1786; and Padiham St Leonard, augmented by Pierce Starkie Esq. in 1730, and in

---

[1] The appropriate 'Form of Grant of the Nomination to a small Augmented Benefice', given in Ecton's *State* (2nd edn. 1721), pp. 250–3, envisages a lay knight's acquisition of the patronage of a bishop's impropriate rectory.

1786 in the patronage of Le Gendre Starkie Esq. Such extensive private trading in the church's goods might seem to a modern eye to prove the case against private patronage, but the lesson drawn from it by the vicar's accuser (who was writing about 1790) is so different that it constitutes a salutary warning against rushing to unhistorical conclusions. This lamentable affair, he says, 'appears to have operated as a warning to the dignified patrons of the living of Whalley, never more to intrust so poor a benefice with so rich a patronage annexed to it, in the hands of any but a man of property'.[1]

Parliament's only interference with the Bounty between 1717 and 1803, came in 1736. Once the encumbrances had been cleared, the rules established, and the revenue secured, the way was clear to the Bounty's career of quiet usefulness. Offers of benefactions abounded, to such an extent 'at first that they exceeded the Governors' power to cope with them'.[2] The better to handle them, the rules were altered in 1718 so as to include livings of up to £50 a year (as against the original £35), and to enlarge the proportion of their revenues available for meeting benefactions from the original one-third to two-thirds. Thus better adjusted to the age of benevolence and private property, Queen Anne's Bounty prospered. Savidge's summary of its achievements up to the disagreeable and depressing crisis of 1736 may be cited as it stands. 'In the whole period, 921 benefactions were completed. To meet benefactions, 905 grants were voted, and a further 231 by lot brought the total up to 1,136. As very few benefices had more than one grant in this period, it may be taken that about 1,100 benefices, with incomes below £50, were augmented. Benefactions in money came to about £159,107, and the nominal value at twenty years' purchase of benefactions in lands, tithes, rent-charges, or stipends was £35,328, making up £194,435. The grants voted amounted to £227,200, including £46,200 by lot, so that the gain [the *capital* gain, that is] to benefices was about £421,635.'[3] This remarkable achievement did not, alas!, increase the Bounty's popularity where it most mattered, in the Houses of Parliament.

The reputations of the clerical profession and the established church seem to have reached their lowest ebb in the seventeen-thirties and

[1] T. D. Whitaker, *History of the Original Parish of Whalley and Honour of Clitheroe* (4th edition, 1872–6), I, 214, and Bacon's *Liber Regis*.   [2] Savidge, p. 86.   [3] *Ibid.*

-forties. The church—that is to say, that section of the clergy that was aware of, and concerned for, the church's spiritual functions—was on the defensive, and at the nadir of its standing, at least among those who mattered. 'Since the days of the Lollards', wrote Mark Pattison, 'there had never been a time when the established ministers of religion were held in so much contempt as in the Hanoverian period, or when satire upon churchmen was so congenial to general feeling.'[1]

These years mark also a low ebb of public decency, order, and principle. It cannot indeed be more than suspected that England's condition in these respects was absolutely worse than anything earlier or, for some decades anyway, later. An age with a Gay and a Hogarth to illustrate its seamier sides may just be unfortunately placed for enjoying posterity's admiration. But then an age may have to have some remarkably seamy sides in order to call forth the powers of a Hogarth and a Gay. The question is at any rate arguable.

Upon the lower orders of society several forces were at work, to improve their condition and raise their level of thought and conduct. The spirit of philanthropy never slept, and one of its proudest metropolitan monuments, the Foundling Hospital, was chartered in 1739; but philanthropy of this socially-static, utilitarian variety was by this time an old-established habit, a style of respectability, and there were elements of truth in the extreme charges brought against it by the promoters of the Mortmain Bill in 1736, that it was something of a craze and a fashion, often missing the real needs of society and 'made use of only as a Cloak for the Vanity, the Pride, and the Ambition of private Men, who have got into, or expect to get into the Management of what they call charitable Foundations'.[2] The early Methodists and Evangelicals, the Moravians and their like, were beginning to work, quietly, and (so far as mobs and magistrates would let them) unostentatiously among those who did *not* count in high society and politics, providing for them (often it was providing for *themselves*) the spiritual sustenance and moral guidance that the national church and all the social and educational institutions it kept under its wing were incapable of providing. Of course there were many decent parsons and curates up and down the country, working within

---

[1] Mark Pattison, 'Tendencies of Religious Thought in England 1688–1750', in *Essays and Reviews* (1860), p. 315; Norman Sykes has endorsed this, in *Gibson*, p. 183.

[2] *Gentleman's Magazine*, VI (1736), 753: see also pp. 722 and 751.

the parochial system and combating wickedness and vice in their ordinary way of business. We have incontrovertible evidence concerning some such; it would be fair to assume there were many more. But little of this patient, unenterprising dutifulness showed itself in the higher orders of the clergy, by whom alone, if by anybody, the great would consent to be counselled, and by whose showing naturally enough the church as a whole, in that hierarchical, snobbish, and materialistic society, was judged. At *this* level—exceptions like Gibson, Secker, and Butler duly admitted—the church showed little qualification for leading its nominal flocks into better ways. Indolence, worldliness, and embarrassed self-consciousness marked too many of the upper clergy. While the good among them were on the defensive, the indifferent and the bad were often too comfortable to care.

It was, not unnaturally, part of the cant of the church's enemies to pick out the evils that the better clergy themselves admitted, and to make much of them. This was obvious and superficial; it sounded good and kept up a fine head of moral steam; but few of the church's critics in parliament and the press were really concerned to do it good. That came later in the century. In the reigns of the first two Georges, and more especially in that of George II, their concern was rather to do the church harm. For a mixture of political and ideological reasons they conceived it as a danger and a menace, a potential tyranny, and they blamed the clergy for 'not caring to be subordinate to the laity'.[1] Their endeavours were entirely to clip its wings and limit its ambitions.

Much of this hostility was anti-clericalism pure and simple. But it was anti-clericalism of a peculiarly English kind, able to seem more *really* Christian than the clergy, and to show its superior charity by defending dissenters and particularly Quakers (of whom Secker in his 1750 Charge complained as 'unwearied in labouring to render us odious, and surprisingly artful in recommending themselves to the Great') against the 'harsh exactions and proud assumptions' of the established clergy. The clergy of the established church ran grave risks if they attempted to tell the upper orders what to do; their job between 1660 (to look no further back) and the middle of the nineteenth century anyway was to help the upper orders to tell the lower orders what to do. 'Civil and religious liberty', the great Whig war-cry, had a very special meaning. Thus a

[1] H.M.C., *Egmont MSS*, IV, 108: Egmont's Diary, 15 October 1730.

Whig grandee like the second duke of Argyll ('Argyll, the state's whole thunder born to yield, And shake alike the senate and the field') could make the best of all worlds when he concluded some fine anti-clerical remarks in 1736 by saying that he thought a rich clergy was 'inconsistent to the precepts of Christianity and to Liberty'.[1] He could claim credit for his piety, by making a stand for true religion; he proved his unimpeachable whiggery; and he showed how sound a man of his age he was, by declining to let the church have anything, except on his own conditions.

But the latent anti-clericalism of the English upper classes, strong and seductive though it was in essence, could not have made such a showing against the church in the early Hanoverian period unless it had been given something to bite on. Far-fetched and hysterical though anti-clericals' allegations against church and clergy often are, they usually have some pretexts and causes beneath all the hot vapours of suspicion, envy, distrust and pride; you can hardly indict a whole class of men without at least an imagined justification.

First, there were the lawyers. The temporal lawyers had no cause for fearing the ecclesiastical law if it would but stay in its proper place, really (though not too ostentatiously) subordinate, where Coke had pretty well succeeded in putting it. Certain grounds offered themselves at this period for fearing a *revanche* by the canon lawyers—not substantial grounds by any means, for the legal and even more the political circumstances were such as to render any threat of this kind rather abstract—but enough to encourage and enliven a tendency already existing. Their fears were roused by one individual in particular. That individual was the formidable Edmund Gibson. A large party in the state were given sufficient reason to hate him for most of this period simply on account of his political influence. From the early twenties to about 1737 Gibson was the administration's ecclesiastical confidant, by far the most influential and active of the bishops, likened to Laud and known as 'Walpole's pope'; and by the common rules of eighteenth-century politics, his connexion with Walpole by itself attracted to Gibson the detestation of all who, from conviction, policy, or malice, detested Walpole.

But Gibson was not only 'Walpole's pope'. He was also 'Dr Codex', a popular butt of the satirists and a stock character in lampoons. His *Codex*

[1] H.M.C., *Carlisle MSS*, p. 169.

achieved a celebrity outside church circles which can have been achieved by few other books of such concentratedly ecclesiastical content. It was like Tract 90 and *The Ideal of a Christian Church* of the eighteen-forties— it became a talking point for the laity at large, and inflamed all sorts of people who had not read it. The *Codex* was felt to be a magazine of menaces to much that liberty-loving Englishmen held dear. It is not easy to separate what Gibson said in the *Codex* from what he said and did first as a business-like archdeacon and then as an influential bishop; but the substance of the popular indictment of 'Dr Codex' was that he sought to restore to Convocation powers of independent action that would flout the royal supremacy—and it was at any rate true, that no prelate was more anxious than he to give that failing institution a stimulant, and keep it alive and useful; that he sought to reform the ecclesiastical courts and so make them more effective for the harassment of the laity—which might indeed have been the result, though not the main intended result, of that reform of their courts which Gibson and many sensible con- temporaries certainly wanted; and lastly, that he maintained that the church's canons were binding on the laity as well as the clergy—which was perfectly true, and was made tolerably clear towards the end of his 'Introductory Discourse concerning the present state of the Powers, Discipline and Laws of the Church of England'.[1] This last was the worst possible heresy to the common lawyers and it gave much offence; the great Lord Hardwicke himself led the attack on it;[2] while Michael Foster (another sound common lawyer, anti-clerical and erastian to his finger-tips) mounted a frontal assault on the whole of Gibson's position in his *Examination of the Scheme of Church-Power laid down in the Codex . . .*, 1735.[3] Gibson was politic enough not to publish the long memorandum he wrote in reply to Hardwicke's judgment.[4] There can be no doubt that, however much his *Codex* has helped clergymen and historians busy

[1] See the *Codex*, pp. xxviii–xxx.
[2] See his judgment in *Middleton v. Crofts*, 2 Atkyns 650.
[3] His book was well-known and effective enough for a 3rd edition of it to be reprinted as the seventh item in *Tracts for the People; designed to vindicate Religious and Christian Liberty*, 1840. What seems to have been another attack by Foster on Gibson was answered by a writer using the pseudonym 'Richard Hooker' in letters to the *Weekly Miscellany* and the *Gentleman's Magazine*, 1733–5, printed in the latter, III, 182–3, 284–6, IV, 152–3, and V, 364–5.
[4] Sykes, *From Sheldon to Secker*, pp. 203–4.

on their own private occasions, it did the church nothing but public harm in the critical decades just after its publication.

The real substance of the anti-clerical campaign, however, lay not in these matters, which were often so extravagant, but nearer to men's purses and honest English hearts. What they really feared for was their property. The more far-sighted or imaginative of the campaigners did not pretend that the church's natural bent for intellectual and spiritual autocracy (natural, because to the anti-clerical mind natural in *any* church) could be indulged until it was much more independent and powerful than the facts about 1730 showed it to be. The real dangers were thus prospective; but events about this time gave them some grounds (slight enough; but a little went a long way) for sharpening their vigilance. One of these was Gibson's brave success in 1734 in marshalling the bench so stoutly as to bar the Socinian Rundle's way to an English see. The anti-clerical in every Whig was horrified. Whether Rundle was a heretic or not was immaterial; what mattered was the principle of the thing—was the Crown to appoint the heads of the church or not? 'Surely this must be a melancholy reflexion to those who are naturally jealous of the power of the church; for this step shows they [the bishops] expect at least a *nolumus* to any man the K[ing] shall think fit to promote to the purple . . . if this doctrine of the Bench be allowed as an established maxim, 'twill be adding an Ecclesiastical independent power in the State, which might prove more dangerous to Liberty than even a Military one; as of all tyranny, that practised by those in black have [sic] in all ages and nations been most destructive of Liberty, Commerce, and everything to make society agreeable to life.'[1] This anguished reference to commerce introduces another argument by which the case against church 'encroachments' was dressed up in the garb of national interests. Men used the classical mortmain argument against ecclesiastical property, that not much good came out of it for anybody else; it was withdrawn from the land market (not a very scrupulous argument in the mouths of men who believed in entails!), and clergy never used their land as intelligently as laymen. Acre for acre, and pound for pound, they said, lay property was more use to the commonwealth than ecclesiastical.

[1] From a letter of Sir Thomas Robinson to the Earl of Carlisle, in H.M.C., *Carlisle MSS*, p. 131. It was apropos of this affair that Gibson was likened to Laud, by a correspondent of the *Gentleman's Magazine*, IV, 152–3.

But for most men it was not necessary to gild their case against the church with arguments like this. Their generation took it for granted, that what was good for the landed interest was good for the nation.

Such anti-clericalism as abounded in the extremely protestant, property-worshipping period with which we are concerned could have fed on very scant actual evidence of the church's rapacity; and there was in fact more than enough tinder to kindle fears so inflammable. Many of the steps that clergymen took, or (as was more often the case) recommended to be taken, for the bettering of the church's material condition, involved treading on laymen's corns, as they had done when Whitgift and, much more, Laud, had tried to take them before the civil war. In the first place, tithes. The church's tithe-rights were forever being eroded by the setting up of moduses and compositions, as well as by sheer neglect; and this process had only to go a little way for it to need a thick-skinned parson, and probably also a good lawyer, to check it and recover the disappearing rights. The business of doing so was sure to be unpleasant but a parson was bound to attempt it if he were to do his duty. Gibson (and not he alone, of course) reminded his clergy about moduses 'which have already swallowed up so large a share of the Patrimony of the Church beyond the Possibility of a Retrieve, and which therefore ought to be immediately broken . . .'.[1] Secker encouraged his clergy courageously to shoulder the burden and the risk of these actions by pointing out that out of 700 suits for tithes brought by the clergy into the Exchequer Court between 1660 and 1713, 600 had been decided in their favour.[2] But at what cost of serenity and reputation were not such battles won! In other respects, too, the church-reformers alarmed the property-owning laity by the way they talked of tithes. There were, for instance, suggestions still being made that tithes ought to be paid on income and personal property, in town as well as country.[3] Kennet's and

[1] *Directions given . . . to the Clergy of his Diocese*, p. 39.

[2] 1750 Charge, in *Eight Charges*, p. 129. On p. 125 he put his finger on a like abuse. 'Glebe lands have been blended with temporal Estates: and Pretences set up, that only such a yearly Rent, far inferior to the real Value, is payable from them.'

[3] See for example what Egmont's friend Judge Probyn said at the coffee-house on 16 October 1730, in the former's *Diary*, I, 110–11; Prideaux's *Vindication of Personal Tithes*, a work often referred to in early eighteenth-century church polemics; and William Webster, *The Clergy's Right of Maintenance vindicated from Scripture and Reason*, pp. 40–1.

Prideaux's writings about the moral obligation of impropriators to restore to the church what was only its due made uncomfortable reading; and it was possibly under their encouragement that Philoclerus wrote to the *Grub Street Journal* early in 1733, that 'In an estate acquir'd by the private Fraud of the Father, the Children know not, perhaps, to whom to make Restitution, but in this case, Tythes in their own Nature carry upon them the indelible Badges of Levi.'[1]

Another part of the church-reform movement in this period was the compilation of correct terriers (i.e. statements of individual churches' legal rights and dues, more especially, as the name signifies, its lands and tithes); and this also went to alarm the laity. It was the kind of precaution that no layman in his right mind neglected to take, but what was prudence in a layman became, of course, avarice in a parson, and could not be judged on its merits. Just as there had been much endeavour made to draw up and safely preserve accurate terriers in the days of Whitgift and Laud, so was there a second phase of endeavour in the early eighteenth century.[2] Convocation several times concerned itself about terriers in these hopeful reforming years, complaining of omissions and proposing stricter regulations. No doubt many parsons and church wardens duly set about making new terriers; and no doubt the result was often to frighten and offend their parishioners. One early terrier-maker not only met an hot opposition but had a scurrilous anonymous letter put in at his door 'concernd . . . as much at our desire of a Terrier, as the Papacy at Luther's reformation'.[3]

The 'improvement' of their properties, of course, by whatever means it was conducted, was likely to make the clergy odious; and there is some evidence that, although 'improvement' was a process never wholly at rest, it attained an unprecedented notoriety just about this time. It was not the recovery or extension of tithe-rights that created the rumpus so much as the means by which bishops, chapters, prebendaries and colleges were improving the landed estates by which they were so largely financed. All manner of sharp practices were alleged against them;

---

[1] *Gentleman's Magazine*, III, 132.

[2] See D. M. Barratt, *Ecclesiastical Terriers of Warwickshire Parishes*, I, p. xv. She further remarks that this Tenison-Gibson phase 'appears to be the last nation-wide effort to collect them before the present century'.

[3] Gill and Guilford, *op. cit.* p. 72.

52687

'indefatigable Pains are taken, and Devices and Pretexts hitherto unheard of are used to levy money on Tenants of Church and College Lands: we are visited not for our Manners, but our Manors', wrote one angry sufferer.[1] What stuck more in the laity's throat than anything else was the impudence of these clergymen in trying to manage their estates as efficiently as hard-headed laymen managed theirs. The clergy traditionally had the reputation of easy landlords, easy to swindle and easy-going in their ways. As the value of land rose through the sixteenth and seventeenth centuries the rents on church lands had hardly altered; and the main expedient by which the clergy increased their receipts from their lands, the raising of the 'fines' for renewals of leases, was unsatisfactory in every way, besides lending itself to scandalous abuse.[2] Church leases had usually been long ones for three lives or 21 years, renewed as became necessary on fairly easy terms. Tenants thus became accustomed to a soft régime, and were apt to be indignant when a much larger fine was demanded than had been paid for the last renewal, even if their clerical landlord was only doing in his more cumbersome way what lay landlords would have been thought fools not to do. They were also aggrieved by the accompanying movement to shorten the terms of leases, from 3 lives to 21 years, and from 21 years to 7.

A less contentious device by which their lessors could more efficiently exploit church lands was by the employment of professional, or at least full-time, stewards and estate-managers; but this was probably not happening much before the middle of the eighteenth century.[3] The

---

[1] 'Everard Fleetwood' (i.e. Samuel Burroughs), *Enquiry into the Customary Estates and Tenant Rights of those who hold Lands of the Church*, p. 4.

[2] For three representative scandals of this kind, spread over the years, see (1) *Humphrey Prideaux's Letters to John Ellis*, pp. 140–41, of the year 1684; (2) Edmund Pyle, *Memoirs of a Royal Chaplain*, p. 127, for a scandal that did not quite come off in 1747; and (3) most startling of all, the case of prebendary Christopher Wilson, 1768, circumstantially set down in John Nichols, *Literary Anecdotes of the Eighteenth Century*, IX (1815), 519–24.

[3] Edward Hughes, *North Country Life in the 18th Century*, pp. 328–9. The dean and chapter of Ely seem to have enjoyed the services of such an officer after 1733; he was not a lay professional but the diocesan-registrar-cum-cathedral-precentor, and he became virtually the chapter's full-time agent. See Reginald Gibbon, 'The Order Book of the Dean and Chapter of Ely, 1729–1769', in *Church Quarterly Review*, CXXIV (1937), 256–7.

stepping-up of fines was the staple and offensive method, and it had been going on (at what pace our present ignorance of ecclesiastical economic history prevents us from saying) at least since the Restoration. In the early seventeen-thirties, it was a matter of intense public interest.[1]

One other pretext was available for this extraordinary outcry against 'church encroachments' that broke out in the early thirties. The colleges of the ancient universities were busy acquiring advowsons.[2] The reason usually given was the plausible one that only by parking fellows out on college livings (which would be sure to take them) could the blood circulate as freely as the port at their high-tables, and fellowships be cleared for newcomers. But this argument was of course only good for the first generation that had the opportunity of using it. It was valid while the college was actually acquiring livings, and was very likely a credit to the generation that thought of it, but would cease to hold as soon as the fellowship had at its disposal as many livings as it could possibly need. Lord Egmont's group of friends, who met so regularly to discuss the affairs of the day, touched on this subject, and on one intimately connected with it, in the autumn of 1730. 'We talked of Queen Anne's act for augmentation of livings, which most of the company said

---

[1] The important writings seem to have been *The Value of Church and College Leases considered*, 1718, 1722, 1729; John Smart, *Tables of Interest Discount and Annuities*, the 1726 edition of which made a set at Queen Anne's Bounty and was answered by Ecton in the 3rd edition of his *Liber Valorum*, 1728, Preface pp. ix–x; [J. and G. Spearman], *Enquiry into the Ancient and Present State of the County Palatine of Durham*, 1729; then in 1731 Samuel Burroughs's heavyweight attack under the pseudonym Everard Fleetwood, and the works of the three who held the bridge against him: W. Derham, *Defence of the Church's Right in Leasehold Estates*, 1731; [H. Gally], *The Reasonableness of Church and College Fines Asserted*, 1731; and [Roger Long], *The Rights of Churches and Colleges Defended*, 1731.

[2] This was often alleged and never denied. I have investigated a few cases, and it seems to have been true enough. Clare College, which had only 12 livings in 1736 (*Warren's Book*, ed. A. W. W. Dale, p. 115), had apparently bought ten of them only recently (B.M. Add. MSS. 35640, fos. 84–5). Of the 52 livings acquired by St John's College, Cambridge, between 1267 and 1867–9, 38 came between 1690 and 1736 (H. F. Howard, *Finances of St. John's*, Appendix V). Corpus Christi College, Cambridge, held 10 in 1831; 3 of these dated from the Middle Ages, 2 from the reign of Elizabeth, and 5 from the period 1712–21 (John Lamb, *Masters's History of Corpus*, p. 427 ff.). A spate of bequests for the purchase of advowsons in the period 1715–36 is indicated by W. C. Costin, *History of St John's College Oxford, 1598–1860*, pp. 175–6, 185–6.

would prove of dangerous consequence in the end, as also of the Universities buying up advowsons and presentations.' They thought the assurance of comfortable livings enjoyed in rotation was bad for learning; and 'Besides, as many livings are thus sold by lay proprietors, so far is diminished the laity's power over the clergy.'[1] Eighteen months later, similar anxieties were expressed by a correspondent of the *London Journal*. He was good enough to say that the clerical order was good on the whole, and ought not 'to be *restrained* from anything, but *putting Restraints* upon others, and *increasing in Lands*. This ought to be guarded against, because they are buying in the *great Livings* and *perpetual Advowsons* all over the Kingdom, and so in Time, may get such an *Overbalance of Lands*, as to become *independent* of the Crown.'[2]

Egmont's friends thought that the Bounty 'would prove of dangerous consequence in the end', because they saw it as a self-acting machine for turning lay property into church property. Some of the facts on which the case against the Bounty rested were correct, some much exaggerated. It was true that the act of 1704 enabled persons to make over or bequeath to the Bounty, and the Bounty freely to receive and apply to its proper ends, any amount of property, 'the statute of mortmain, or any other statute or law to the contrary, notwithstanding'.[3] This was a considerable privilege. Corporate bodies normally had to apply to the Crown for license to hold land up to a certain amount; and when property up to that amount had duly been acquired, another license could be applied for. Even if licenses in mortmain were automatically granted, the Bounty's exemption from the necessity of getting them meant that the Crown's law officers had no regular means of checking the quantity of its possessions. The anticlerical imagination thus evoked a spectre of the church steadily taking over property so as to raise all livings first to £50 a year, then to £100, and then to higher values still, based on a prodigious acreage of land. No one at this stage of the Bounty's history seems to have thought it possible or desirable to invest the augmentation grants not just in land but in stocks. Had they done so, the Bounty might perhaps have been less unpopular.

The main campaign against the church may probably be said to have opened in 1730 with a demonstration against the church's reclamations

[1] Conversation of 15 October 1730, in H.M.C., *Egmont MSS*, IV, 108–10.
[2] Reprinted in the *Gentleman's Magazine*, II, 621.   [3] 2 and 3 Anne c. 11 s. 4.

of dormant tithe-rights.[1] Then came Samuel Burroughs's pseudonymous *Inquiry* in 1731, and the several replies to it. Some time early in the thirties came the merchant Thompson's proposal to Walpole, already mentioned, for a realistic revaluation of first-fruits and tenths and their application to 'the Publick Service'.[2] In 1733 Sir Nathaniel Curzon introduced into the lower house a bill designed to cleanse and cripple the ecclesiastical courts; and the same session saw an attempt to control the levying of church rates. In 1734 the Rundle affair kept the anti-clericals at fever heat, and in 1736 they purged their long-pent feelings by boiling over into the unsuccessful Quakers' Tithes Bill (which, like the attempted Close Vestries bill of 1716 and the Church Rates bill of 1733, would have transferred jurisdiction over cases in which the church was intensely interested from the ecclesiastical to the magistrates' courts) and the successful Mortmain Act. The former attracted the more attention. It elicited dozens of petitions from the clergy besides a couple of 'very short smart pamphlets' in the best style of Augustan polemics, 'the one written against the Quakers by Sherlock, Bishop of Salisbury, and entitled *The Country Parson's Plea;* the other for the Quakers, entitled *The Quaker's Reply to The Country Parson's Plea,* and written by Lord Hervey.'[3] But it was the bill 'to restrain the disposition of lands, whereby the same become inalienable', and to stop the draining away (real or imaginary) of lay lands into the possession of religious and charitable corporations, that really mattered.

In the debates upon this bill,[4] one particular note, perennially characteristic of both the anti-clerical and the protestant states of mind, was sounded again and again; and it was a note that boded particularly ill for the Bounty. The laity feared that the clergy, unless legally prevented, would intimidate them as they lay dying into bequeathing more property to the church than they would have thought proper at any less

[1] There were, of course, anticlerical gestures in parliament before that. The Close Vestries bill of 1716, and Arthur Onslow's motion 'to restrain the two Universities ... from purchasing new Advowsons and Presentations of Benefices' in March 1725, were of the same character. See Sykes, *William Wake,* II, 112–13, and *History and Proceedings of the House of Commons from the Restoration to the present time* (1742–3), VI, 337.

[2] Above, p. 33.   [3] Lord Hervey's *Memoirs of the Reign of George II,* II, 531.

[4] Except where a different reference is given, quotations from these debates of 1736 are drawn from the accounts given of them in the *Gentleman's Magazine,* VI, 718–31, 745–54.

awful hour. Deathbed repentance, if it took this material form, was equated with weak-mindedness, and provisions against it were made out to be as much in the interests of the dying man as they were certainly in the interests of his family; the danger of 'practices upon dying men' had been anticipated by some of the opponents of the act of 1704; and now, 'one of the greatest intentions of the Bill . . . was to prevent the erroneous judgments of dying cowardice, to prevent persons on their death-beds from making their families miserable, from the mistaken notion of saving their souls, by donations to the Church'.[1]

The case against 'death-bed devises' rested on the assumptions that men did not usually make their will until they were at death's door ('a time when very few men can really be said to be in their right senses'), nor did they give much away at any other time. The Bounty took legal advice as to the effects of the bill and were told that it would be 'an absolute bar to the granting of any land estate to the Bounty, and probably to the granting of any legacy in money or personal estate';[2] and yet the bill only said that gifts of lands etc. 'to uses called *Charitable Uses*, to take place after their death', would not be legal unless properly completed at least twelve months before the giver's death. This would not prevent men from assisting the Bounty's work by gifts during their lifetime; nor, except for the unfortunate class of 'languishing and dying persons', did the bill make the passage of land into mortmain any more difficult than it had been before. Since the majorities in both houses were so much concerned with the dangers following the accumulation of land in mortmain, and had every chance to make the bill suit their ends, it therefore looks as if they were satisfied they had achieved them by requiring men to perform their acts of generosity with their property openly, in the days of their health and vigour. Obviously they assumed that such acts would not be common.

It must be remembered that the disposition of the greater part of a

[1] From Sir Thomas Robinson's description of the debate, in H.M.C., *Carlisle MSS*, p. 169. The belief, that putting money into clerical hands and beyond your own control was an error of judgment, died hard. Over a century later, 'when Pusey was called upon to give evidence in Court in a case of alleged lunacy, he was asked in cross-examination whether a person who gave away large sums of money to religious objects could be considered capable of managing his property. He gravely answered that he could be so considered.' (H. P. Liddon, *Life of Pusey* I, 331).

[2] Savidge, p. 103.

man's property was often controlled by entails, settlements, trusts and jointures; the amount of property free to be devised by will would thus commonly represent much less of a man's whole possessions than it does today, and might often consist only of personal chattels and cash. Leaving the making of the will until the end is to that extent the more intelligible.

The debates on this delicate subject, as summarized by *The Gentleman's Magazine*, make interesting reading.

It is certain that a Power to dispose of a Man's Estate at his death in such Manner as he may then think best, is a great Incitement to Industry and Frugality, and consequently a great Encouragement to Trade in every Country where it is established; and we may observe that the Trade and Riches of this Kingdom have increased more in the two Centuries since this natural Right was restored, than it did in many Ages before. It is a Power coveted by every Man, because when he has any Estate, and a Power to dispose of that Estate by Will, while he lives, he may expect to meet with a proper Regard and Attendance both from his next Relations, and all those who happen to be near him, whereas, take this Power from him, and he may very probably in his last Sickness or Extremity be neglected by his next Heirs, and despised by all his Servants.' . . . 'Whether a Man's next Heirs have any natural Right to succeed to his Estate after his Death, is not the Question now before us; I hope it will be granted they have at least a more natural Right than any other Person natural or political; and I am sure the giving or leaving it to them, or to any other Persons natural, is more charitable than the giving it to any charitable Use or Corporation whatsoever; because when the Estate comes to private Persons, they will be enabled to contribute the more to the parish Charities in the respective Parishes they belong to, which are the only Charities that are, or ever can be properly applied [because they were the only ones whose administrators could fully know the histories and merits of the applicants]' . . . 'There-fore, as a sincere Christian, as a true Lover of the Church of England, without being an Admirer of ecclesiastical Power, and as a good Subject, I must be for laying at least that Restraint upon such Donations which is proposed by the Bill now before us. And one of my chief Reasons for being so, is, lest the Clergy of our Established Church should be tempted and instructed to watch the last Moments of dying Persons, as insidiously as ever the *Monks* and *Friars* did in the darkest Times of *Popery* and *Superstition*. . . . The Clergy of our Church . . . are but Men, and Men are in all Ages and in all Countries, generally speaking, indued with the same Passions, and the same Affections; It is Education and Opportunity only that makes the Difference. The Opportunity is already given, and their Education will soon begin to be turned towards making the best of that Opportunity, if not speedily prevented. Arguments of such Donations will never be wanting when Men are pinched by the Messengers of Death: Nay, many weak Men may at such a Time be made to believe, that such a Donation will be an Atonement for a whole Life spent in Wickedness and Oppression.

These persuasions, so pleasant to the ears of that anti-clerical, ultra-protestant assembly, told as much against the other ecclesiastical charities concerned (e.g. the metropolitan charity schools, the Corporation of the Sons of the Clergy, and the S.P.C.K.) as against Queen Anne's Bounty; but the Bounty came in for some special attentions from Lord Hervey, whose motives were mixed and may have been entirely malignant. He had many old scores to pay off against Gibson (as had also the Duke of Argyll), and not only was Gibson one of the two bishops who had dared to defend the church against its detractors (the other was Sherlock of Salisbury) but he was also well known to be dominant at the Bounty Board and director-in-chief of its affairs.[1] Hervey managed to bring in every argument, good and bad, that would particularly discredit the Bounty. He denounced the bishops and the richer clergy for fattening on pluralities, sinecures, and overmighty revenues, while poor parsons and curates were scurrying and scraping to save themselves and their wretched families from starving. He exploited the popular antipathy to the ideas of 'episcopal ambition' and 'ecclesiastical pretensions', which went down well in a house in which every lay speaker except Lords Abingdon and Strafford 'spoke tartly, and I may say rudely, against the Bishops and clergy in general'.[2] (It had been the same in the Commons, where 'everybody that spoke for them [i.e. the anti-clerical bills] gave the Bishops and the parsons very hard as well as very popular slaps'.)[3] He made much play with statistics, fantastically purporting to show that unless its progress was halted and its management put on a different footing, the Bounty would help the church eventually to become 'mistress of all the land estates in England'. Sir Thomas Robinson thought that these were 'very judicious calculations' of Hervey's.[4]

Thus, largely through the mischief of one lay lord, the Bounty met with a set-back in the thirty-second year of its activity. Its petition to be excepted from the provisions of the act was rejected, although the petitions of the two universities and Eton, Winchester, and Westminster colleges were allowed. 'Lord Hervey laid open all the mismanagements in the fund called Queen Anne's Bounty, which was given for the augmentation of small livings and, by the disposition made of it, had

[1] See Hervey's *Memoirs*, II, 540–1, and Savidge, p. 68.
[2] Egmont's Diary, 5 May 1736: H. M. C., *Egmont MSS*, v, 269.
[3] Hervey's *Memoirs*, II, 535.
[4] H.M.C., *Carlisle MSS*. p. 169.

never been properly applied according to the intention of Parliament, or with common justice to the poor clergy. He made this out so clearly to the House, by the calculations he had made of what this Corporation had received and, showing how those receipts had been disposed of, that in consequence of these representations the House of Lords addressed the Crown to inquire into this affair and to give the Corporation new rules and restrictions for their future proceedings; which, in consequence of this address, next summer was done in Council.'[1] Hervey also succeeded in giving Gibson a fall from which he never quite recovered. Up to 1736 he had been the undisputed strong man on the Bounty Board, and Archbishop Wake had, for whatever reason, stayed away. The minutes give mute witness to a notable consequence of Hervey's victory. The General Court on 17 May 1736 was the last but three that Gibson ever attended; and the archbishop began to attend, and take the chair, regularly from March 1737 onwards.[2]

The Mortmain Act[3] limited the Bounty's powers to receive benefactions, and the Board made appropriate alterations in its printed benefaction forms.[4] The Privy Council, duly executing on the king's behalf the Lords' request that he would take the Bounty's rules into consideration and alter them if necessary,[5] met in committee, called for accounts and papers from the Bounty, and ordered that the alterations, made to rules 4 and 9 in 1718 and 1725[6] should be cancelled, since they did not serve the original purpose of the Bounty, the relief of clerical poverty. The Bounty was back where it had started. 'Henceforth, they were not to be allowed to receive bequests from the dying and not to look at offers of help for benefices over £35; and as the cutting off of these sources of supply would leave the Governors, themselves, with more money for grants than there would be benefactions to secure, it was natural as well

[1] Hervey's own account of his exploit, in his *Memoirs*, II, 536.

[2] Gibson thereafter attended only the meetings on 7 March 1737, 3 September 1744, and 7 July 1746, and there can be little doubt that he was only present at the last two, which were both in the dead season, because he had been specially called in to make up a quorum.

[3] 9 George II c. 36, An Act to restrain the Dispositions of Lands, whereby the same became unalienable.

[4] Savidge, p. 104.

[5] House of Lords Journals, XXIV, 665, 667: 6 and 10 May 1736.

[6] See above, p. 93 and Savidge, p. 87.

as right to restore the original preponderance of grants to the benefices not over £10, mainly by lot.'[1] Early in 1747, the category of known livings under £10 a year being nearly exhausted, the limit for augmentation by lot was raised (as it had from the first been envisaged that it should in due course be raised) to £20 a year;[2] and ten years later, 'in order to preserve, in some degree, and continue a difference in point of value between cures which may be augmented by benefaction, and those to be augmented by lot with the Royal Bounty alone', the Bounty was enabled to make grants to meet benefactions for cures up to the value of £45 a year;[3] in 1788 the figures for the two categories were stepped up to £30 and £50 a year respectively.[4] Apart from these small unadventurous modifications, proper and natural enough as the Bounty ground away at the extremer forms of clerical poverty and as the anti-clerical vapours of the thirties gradually dispersed, the rules remained unchanged until after 1800.

Mr Savidge's summary of the consequences of the events of 1736 and 1737 is clear and just. 'Whether the moral and practical gain from concentrating on benefices up to £35, and among these, on those of £10 or less, offset the material loss of benefaction money which the Governors were not allowed to receive, is impossible to say. If action had been taken to press home the attack in the Lord's debate on pluralities, on disproportionately rich livings, on the traffic in advowsons, and the suggestion that the way to relieve poverty in the Church was by some curtailing of these and the re-distribution of endowments, the new orders to the Governors would have been carried out as part of a general reform in the Church economy. But nothing of the sort was done. . . . If the Governors had merely been enjoined, or had thought fit themselves to take account of pluralities and the population of the parishes concerned, some definite pattern of improvement would at least have been followed. But as it was, the change in the incidence of augmentation[5] seems simply a change from one uncertain method to another.'[6] The amount of money flowing into the augmentation of benefices certainly fell off, and the governors left the parts of their system that were obviously

---

[1] Savidge, pp. 104–5.   [2] Letters Patent signed 21 February 1747.
[3] Letters Patent signed 26 April 1757.   [4] Letters Patent signed 9 July 1788.
[5] i.e. from a preponderance of grants to meet benefactions, to a preponderance of augmentations by lot.   [6] Savidge, pp. 105–6.

susceptible of improvement unimproved for over thirty years. Embarrassed and distressed by their treatment in connexion with the Mortmain Act, they were thankful to find the accomplishment of much good still within their powers. As the last surviving veterans of the second period of church reform departed their world, they took to heart the favourite maxim of that world's master-politician, and hoped that, if they behaved like sleeping dogs, they would be allowed to lie.

3. THE MEN AND THE MEANS

The evidence for the Bounty's domestic history, of how it was run and who ran it, is unfortunately scanty. Its records have suffered grievous loss in the course of their transmission from office to office and year to year and only one species of them, the minutes, has come down to us complete and unbroken. The minutes, like most minutes, are disappointing. They record only the decisions taken, never the discussions that must have gone first; still less do they give any inkling of what went on at Bounty meetings besides the transaction of the official business. For light on these matters one has to look to the lives and letters of the Hanoverian bishops, and doing so, one wishes they were even half as plentiful and copious of those of the nineteenth century. These outside sources are not very helpful. The other inside sources, besides the minutes, are ineloquent and bitty. The early letter books ('In' 1705–22, and 'Out' 1705–18) of which Mr Savidge was able to make such good use, seem to be the only survivors of that class except for one isolated 'Out' letter book for 1807–11. It is indeed unlikely that the Bounty's correspondence continued to be as interesting as it was early on, when there were discoveries to be made and principles discussed. The 1807–11 book is a chronicle of very small beer. The rest of the surviving material is almost useless—little of it, no set or run of anything, and what there is, entirely secondary to the minutes and the published accounts (i.e. Ecton's various books, and those in the Parliamentary Papers). A few office papers and accounts from this later period survive in the Public Record Office but they are of the same character.

The minutes are dull also, because the Bounty's regular work was for the most part of a commonplace routine character. They indicate that the general courts and their committees now and then (but principally after 1770) discussed more unusual matters; and it is certain that the bishops, when met together at the Bounty office, sometimes took the opportunity to discuss matters that had no connection with the Bounty at all. But the *regular* business of the office, the work conducted by the clerks and deputies under the secretary's eye, was sealed off from the chops and changes of contemporary affairs. The rules for benefactions and augmentations hardly changed. The other changes in the offices were so slight that a clerk of the original establishment, miraculously restored to life at the close of the century, would have been able to pick up very much where he left off fifty or sixty years before.

(i) The Men

The Bounty's first home was in 'the New Buildings joining to the Banqueting House' in Whitehall, which Mr Savidge describes as 'a small, mean, featureless two-storied structure' adjacent to Inigo Jones's magnificent banqueting house on its south side, and on the site of the present Royal United Service Institution.[1] The governors petitioned the queen for the use of them as almost their first piece of business (they met in 'the Prince's Chamber joining to the House of Lords') and the queen graciously went so far beyond the mere granting of their petition as to order 'that the Lord Chamberlain would furnish those Rooms out of the Royal Wardrobe'.[2] Whether these rooms, where the general courts met for nearly thirty years, were also the scene of the Bounty's routine business, is not clear. In the list of names and addresses of the Board's officers which Ecton appended to his *State of the Bounty*—a production that was at least as much of an advertisement as an *apologia*—the new buildings do not appear. He appears to be referring inquiries to their home addresses or offices elsewhere; his own office, as receiver of the first-fruits, was in the Middle Temple. Whatever office accommodation there may have been in Whitehall proved inadequate. In 1725 the secretary was instructed to lease chambers in the Middle Temple and buy office equipment for them. Seven years later the governors themselves were told by the Treasury to look for some other meeting-place; and after a year in the St Martin's Library, Castle Street, Westminster, they decided to find some more permanent premises in the same district for their meetings, where the secretary could also reside and have his office.

[1] Savidge, p. 71. These 'new Buildings' were demolished in 1792.
[2] Ecton, *State of the Bounty* (1721 edn.), p. 2.

The secretary accordingly found them a house on the west side of Dean's Yard, Westminster, where they met for the first time in March 1735. There they remained until the end of their independent existence, rather more than two centuries later.[1] At the time of its greatest activity, after several rebuildings, it was to house a staff of well over 200.

To start with, the Bounty's establishment consisted merely of its secretary and treasurer and their clerks, whom they had to pay out of their salaries which, if they received them at all, were not large. The first treasurer, indeed, Archbishop Tenison's cousin Edward, held the office (which was to begin with almost a sinecure) as a public service, and took nothing for his pains. There was more however for his successor after 1708; and both he and the secretary received from the governors about £100 a year, on an average, until they were fixed at £120 by the second charter in 1714.[2] The burden of work naturally increased but it cannot have been onerous at any stage of the eighteenth century, except perhaps at rare crises like 1736, when accounts and lists were suddenly and peremptorily demanded. In 1837 the whole business of the Bounty, by that time two or three times as heavy as it was in 1800, was conducted, under the secretary-treasurer (the offices were consolidated in 1831), by only three clerks and a messenger. It is true that they were rather over-worked, having only two days holiday a year and often working over-time; and that the secretary-treasurer 'scarcely ever had a holiday'.[3] But even so the secretary-treasurer managed to hold down several other jobs outside his hours of 10 till 4,[4] thus doing as his predecessors had done from the very beginning.

In the Bounty's administration, the secretary and treasurer were soon joined by a legal officer. As early as April 1707 the governors decided, in order to help in coping with the baffling problem of arrears of first-fruits and tenths, to appoint a 'solicitor of the revenue'. The secretary's clerk, William Taylor, was appointed, and seems to have been employed almost exclusively in the collection of debts and the initiation of legal

---

[1] Savidge, pp. 72–3.

[2] With the expansion of business their salaries later went up, under the authority of Letters Patent: the secretary's to £200 in 1718, £250 in 1725, £300 in 1780, £400 in 1805, and £650 in 1822; the treasurer's leapt to £250 in 1725, but stayed at that until 1827, when it was brought up to £500 a year.

[3] 1837 committee, Qs. 536–8, 936–941, 954–5.   [4] See below, p. 226.

proceedings. The heavier legal business—the preparation of conveyances, perusal of titles of land proposed to be purchased, and so on,
which was to become part of the Bounty's routine—was at first done by
the versatile treasurer. When he found the burden of it too great, it was
confided in 1719 to an eminent practising lawyer, Thomas Dalton.
Thus the Bounty's legal work was divided between two pairs of hands,
and this division became the rule.[1] The governors' 'counsel' attended to
the routine business of conveyancing land, purchasing tithes and rent-
charges, and administering wills and trusts; their solicitor looked after
their interests as a corporation, threatened (and warded off threats of)
legal actions, gave opinions on the construction of charters and statutes,
and so on.[2]

To the work of the Bounty Board was indissolubly linked that of the
First-Fruits and Tenths Offices of the Exchequer, situated in the Middle
Temple. Institutionally, the tie to the Tenths Office was the closer, for
the receiver of tenths owed his very existence to the governors' agitation;[3] he was paid by the governors (£300 a year) and drew most of his
office expenses from them also; and it is not very remarkable that
appointments to the post were always made on the governors' recommendation until 1827. What is more remarkable, is that the Bounty's
ties to the First-Fruits Office quickly became just as close. The Bounty's
treasurer was recommended by the Board for the receivership when it
fell vacant in 1718, and he got it. Throughout the eighteenth century the
Board's candidates for the office continued to be accepted by the Crown
without demur. By the seventeen-nineties a finance committee of the
Commons was reporting that appointment to this office was by the
Treasury 'upon the nomination of the Archbishops and Bishops'.[4] So
far as one can tell, none of the receivers thus appointed was inadequate
to the post, and at least one of them, John Bacon (receiver of first-fruits
from 1782 to 1816), filled it with some distinction. Everything that

[1] It seems, however, that one pair of hands sufficed immediately after Dalton gave
up the post on becoming Lord Chief Baron of the Exchequer (and thus a governor) in
1725. Taylor's successor since 1717, one Henry Bosvile, of whom nothing is known,
apparently took over Dalton's work.

[2] Most of this paragraph is based on Savidge, pp. 76–8.

[3] See above, pp. 84–85.

[4] *Reports from Committees of the House of Commons* (16 v., 1803) XII, 273 (Finance
Reports, 1797–8).

Bacon did was of concern to the Bounty, right up to the posthumous settling of his account with the Exchequer;[1] yet Bacon held no position in the Bounty Office. His *official* sphere of usefulness lay in the courts of the Middle Temple, not in Dean's Yard. It was through the other posts he held and interests he pursued outside the official administration, and because of this close connexion in practice between the Bounty Board and the First-Fruits Office, that Bacon made his particular contribution to the good of society.[2]

The fact that the governors were able to go on filling these two offices merits a little attention; as do also the sharp breaks made with this century-old practice, when a receiver of first-fruits was appointed in 1828, and a receiver of tenths in 1827, whom they had not nominated. The harmonious co-operation of these offices with their own mattered a lot to the Bounty, and it was therefore the more important that the receiverships were not turned into political jobs. For the governors' interest in the receivership of tenths there were obvious good grounds (though none of them strong enough to protect the office from a politician determined to get hold of it). But for the way the governors were allowed to establish a practice of nomination to the receivership of first-fruits as well, it is difficult to find a better explanation than that the administrations of the day were not so consumed with a lust for patronage and political jobbery as to be blind to the advantages of efficiency in the public offices, or to the natural justice of letting the Bounty Board share largely in the control of the department of state engaged in collecting the revenues so solemnly vested in them.[3] If they were brought into the system of patronage at all, it was for the governors' benefit, no one else's, and the Bounty seems not to have suffered from their use of it.

Some of their nominations, it is true, represented promotions for members of their official 'family circle'. Edward Barker, their first effective treasurer, became successively receiver of first-fruits, secretary, and receiver of tenths. There is no evidence that he was anything but a devoted and competent public servant. The receivership of tenths was

---

[1] Minutes, 19 February 1824, § 1.　　　　　　　　[2] See below, pp. 120-1.

[3] This latter position seems to be assumed in an undated document relating to a cognate matter, the appointment of the treasurer, in the Cholmondeley (Houghton) Papers, 78/20.

obviously the plum position, involving the least effort in proportion to its income. (In the eighteen-thirties the receiver was only in contact with his office two or three times a year.)[1] One after another the Board's favourite sons became the receivers of the tenths—first Barker (who was at the time receiver of first-fruits and secretary), then in succession Stephen Comyn (receiver of first-fruits), Thomas Parry (receiver of first-fruits), Robert Chester (solicitor and secretary), and Richard Richards (counsel). It was no doubt difficult for a man to 'go wrong' in such a post, particularly when it was built into the Exchequer; difficult also for a man to make any improvements in it. But Richards managed to accelerate the payment of his annual account by four months.[2] Of the origins of the men whose qualities became known to the governors as receivers of first-fruits little is ascertainable. Nothing, however, suggests that their appointments were 'jobs' in the common discreditable sense. One of them, Henderson, was their solicitor, and Edward Mulso, an official of the Excise Office, presumably got the post because of his family ties with Bishop John Thomas;[3] but John Bacon had risen from the lowest desk in the First-Fruits Office and his appointment was a recognition, not less sensible than honest, of his abilities.

It would be very interesting to know exactly why, in the early nineteenth century, the governors lost the right they had tacitly acquired to nominate to these posts, and why they were taken over by the government as ordinary pieces of political patronage. Such a seeming decline in administrative morality just at the time when the standards of probity and efficiency in the public offices were rising can perhaps be explained as a side-effect of that growing dearth of patronage which made life increasingly difficult for politicians throughout the age of Grey and Peel. This may explain how the receivership of tenths got into the hands of Thomas Venables when he was private secretary to Peel in 1827, and the receivership of first-fruits into those of another of Peel's secretaries, George Arbuthnot, a well-connected Treasury official whose influential uncle Charles Arbuthnot (husband of the beautiful Harriet, the Duke of

[1] 1837 Committee, Qs. 485–7.
[2] *Reports from Committees of the House of Commons*, XII, 53.
[3] See S. H. Cassan, *Lives of the Bishops of Winchester*, II, 273. He was son to the bishop's sister, and nephew to the bishop's wife; and his brother Thomas, a Commissioner of Bankrupts, acted as the bishop's secretary.

Wellington's confidante) got him the job in 1828.[1] There is no evidence that the Bounty Board was consulted about the appointments of either of them.

The receiver of tenths was subordinate to the receiver of first-fruits; and the latter was nominally subordinate in some way to two other officers, the remembrancer and the comptroller of first-fruits and tenths. It is difficult to find out exactly what they did in the eighteenth century; but it is certain that they did little or nothing. The office of remembrancer dated from Henry VIII's reign, and was still near enough to the front line for the villainous William Prettyman, remembrancer in the sixteen-sixties, to use the office for the diversion of its revenues into his own pocket. Prettyman's abuse of the office may have been responsible for its transformation, after he was out of the way, into a freehold patent office in 1680;[2] after which it sunk into as near a sinecure as makes no difference. All that the remembrancers in the eighteenth century had to do, after inheriting or purchasing their office, seems to have been to pay their deputies and sign particularly important documents, such as the annual accounts. In 1709 or thereabouts, when the Bounty Board was collecting opinions on the reasons for the inefficiency of the collection of their revenue, it was Butler the deputy remembrancer who put his office's point of view before them.[3] There is no evidence to suggest that the position recovered its earlier efficiency once it had become a freehold patent office. The last of the remembrancers was winkled out of his Somersetshire home by the 1837 Committee, and did his defensive best to make his job sound better than a sinecure, but convinced nobody.[4] Both the office of remembrancer and the first-fruits office were abolished together in 1838.[5] 'For though in life they were parted, In death they were side by side.'

[1] See the 1837 Select Committee, Qs. 82–7, 399–407: A. Aspinall, *Correspondence of Charles Arbuthnot* esp. p. xvii: and Mrs P. S. M. Arbuthnot, *Memories of the Arbuthnots*, p. 239. Venables, who was moribund at the time of the committee's inquisition, had been helped by his patron to a number of snug things. He was a clerk in the Home Office, deputy clerk of the Signet, and Receiver of the Police.

[2] Baxter, *Development of the Treasury*, pp. 119–20, and above, p. 23. When he died and was replaced, early in 1687–8, by Charles Porter, the place was said to be worth £800 a year. See the news-letter of 13 March 1687–8 in H.M.C., *Portland MSS*, iii, 406.

[3] Savidge, pp. 40–1.

[4] See especially Qs. 2, 28–32, 226–7.

[5] 1 Vict. c. 20 secs. 1 and 11–15.

The office of comptroller had by then already disappeared. This office (another freehold patent one, created about 1686) was allegedly designed to exercise a general oversight over the office and keep it from corruption, but it seems never to have done more than give its happy possessors an unearned income. There must still have been some slight function attached to it in the seventeen-nineties, for one F. N. Bacon (whom it would be imprudent not to suppose a relation of John Bacon's) was getting £25 a year as the comptroller's deputy. The small sum of the payment speaks for itself; and the Commons Finance Committee in 1797, looking for indefensible sinecures to abolish, could not miss it.[1] The last of the comptrollers died in 1818 and the office was then bought out and abolished.

John Chamberlayne, secretary to the Bounty from 1704 to 1723, had a finger in many pies. He had been educated at Oxford and Leyden, and was both a remarkable linguist and an amateur of science, who contributed to the transactions of the Royal Society, of which he became a fellow in 1702. Eminent among his many publications (most of which were translations) were the five further editions he published after 1703 of his father's indispensible *Angliae Notitiae, or The Present State of England*—a pioneering predecessor of *Whittaker's Almanack*. He was a minor court functionary under both Anne and George I, an active member of the S.P.G.,[2] first secretary of the S.P.C.K.,[3] and apparently a protégé of Archbishop Sharp's.[4]

Edward Barker, his successor, was an official of the opposite kind, a man whose life outside his offices seems to have had no public importance. His successive employments and promotions must have been largely, perhaps wholly, due to his business talents. He was a lawyer—'Edward Barker, Junior, of Mortlake and the Inner Temple', at his appointment as treasurer in 1708—and the tale of his official positions, remarkable though it be (for a glorious half-year he was treasurer, secretary and receiver of first-fruits all at once), does not of itself reveal the whole of his usefulness to the Bounty; for until 1719 he was also carrying out all the work that later fell to the governors' counsel, and the

[1] *Reports from Committees of the Commons* XII, 273; XIII, 318.
[2] Savidge, pp. 73–4.   [3] Cowie, *Henry Newman*, p. 25.
[4] Hatton-Finch MSS., in Brit. Mus. Add. MSS 29584 fos. 88 and 91, May and June 1702.

governors took him into consultation on legal matters for at least twelve years after his retirement from the secretaryship. One of these matters was the critical one of the Mortmain Act.[1]

Barker was not the only one of the Bounty's servants to make his mark as a man of business. Ecton, Bacon and Christopher Hodgson were at least his equals. But Barker's career seems not to have had that pleasant many-sidedness which characterized the most interesting of them. Not only were these men good at their jobs, they were doing several jobs simultaneously. Far from this pluralism's being discreditable, it seems in general to have provided a set of personal links between 'departments' of church and state, otherwise unable to share knowledge or labour, that was all the more valuable since some of these 'departments' were actually 'unofficial'.

The role of these 'unofficial' organizations in church and state is not easily appreciated by a modern collectivist, who has to take it for granted that the provision of services and facilities that are really important to the state will be subject to some kind of state supervision, if they are not actually state-run. In the eighteenth century (and, indeed, right into the mid-nineteenth) it was different. The main business of government was not to find out the needs of the body politic and satisfy them. If any such needs grew particularly pressing then they might, through the agency of parliament, be made the subject of legislation; but it was expected that the voluntary charity and social responsibility of the middling and upper orders (not unmixed, of course, with a good measure of political prudence) would act more or less spontaneously to meet most ordinary needs as they became apparent. As Pusey remarked, with institutions of higher education particularly in mind, 'It is a very remarkable peculiarity in this country, that the wants elsewhere provided for by the state, are here mostly supplied by private benevolence.'[2] Thus from the private enterprise of the eighteenth and early nineteenth centuries, not from 'the state' in any narrow definition of it, there sprang such apparatus of social welfare as those ages knew—the hospitals, dispensaries and lying-in charities, the orphanages, asylums and alms-houses, the seasonal distributions of coals, blankets and soup, many of

[1] Savidge, pp. 76–8. Barker retired from the secretaryship in 1730 but remained receiver of tenths until his death in 1759. (Minutes, 16, 26 June 1759.)
[2] *Remarks on the Prospective and Past Benefits of Cathedral Institutions*, p. 9.

the new churches, and most of the new schools. From 'the state' came only the church establishment, the parish poor-house, with its doles and doubtful hospitality, and the town and county gaols; and 'the state' meant, not central administration, but, under Crown and parliament, the higgledy-piggledy mosaic of local authorities, most of them parishes, boroughs and counties, self-governing within the large limits of statute law.

It is therefore not surprising to find that some of the most necessary business of the church was done by voluntary societies, nor that most men unquestioningly accepted them as part of the total provision for the safe maintenance of the constitution in church and state, nor that they were managed in part by men holding 'official' positions under government. Such men—and Chamberlayne, Bacon and Richards were among them—were able to do this because their official posts only took up a little of their time.

Queen Anne's Bounty nearly acquired the services of such a man as treasurer in 1724, after Chamberlayne's death and Barker's succession to his office. Henry Newman, secretary to the S.P.C.K., and a keen, busy churchman, was 'advis'd by some of [his] particular friends to make interest to succeed', first, Chamberlayne, and then, when Barker ('being an old servant, and desiring leave to exchange the place of Treasurer for that of Secretary') succeeded Chamberlayne, Barker himself.[1] Wake and Gibson both backed him, as a man 'well affected to his Majesty and the Government, and every way capable of Discharging that Trust',[2] and a month after his recommendation his hopes were still high;[3] but political considerations apparently intervened. Walpole wanted the office for one Mr Blackaby. To this man the governors strenuously objected, not unsuccessfully. Blackaby fell out of the running, but Newman fell out of it too. The treasurership went to Jeffrey Elwes, of a widely-ramified Hertfordshire family, who was knighted in 1744 and occupied the office for fifty-two years.[4]

[1] Letter of 4 November 1723, in the Brit. Mus. Add. MSS 47030 pp. 63–4.
[2] Cholmondeley (Houghton) Papers, 78/47.
[3] Letter of 2 December 1723, Brit. Mus. Add. MSS 47030 p. 84.
[4] Savidge, pp. 78–9, and L. W. Cowie, *op. cit.* On p. 155 Cowie, using Newman's S.P.C.K. letter-books, cites an interesting passage in which Newman, still expecting the treasurership of the Bounty, looks forward to the access it will give him 'to Privy

John Bacon was in some ways the most interesting of all the Bounty's servants in the eighteenth century.[1] He is remembered as the author of an improved edition of Ecton's *Liber Valorum*, alias *Thesaurus*, in 1786. In this work, Ecton's original authorship of which he was justly censured for concealing,[2] he incorporated particulars concerning the patronage of livings and, for several classes of them, the *actual* values; of which he seems to have got information from the political patronage secretaries (in the case of Crown livings) and from the Bounty Office (in the case of a few dioceses). His moderate celebrity as the producer of this work does not of itself reveal his true position in the eighteenth-century establishment, which was founded in the First-Fruits Office and the Corporation of the Sons of the Clergy. It was in the former that he made his career and fortune. He entered it as a junior clerk, assistant to his relative John Hetherington the deputy remembrancer and senior clerk. In 1778 he succeeded Hetherington in his offices, and in 1782 was appointed receiver in place of Edward Mulso, to whom (as to all receivers since his arrival in the office) he had been deputy.[3] Out of his official salaries and fees he managed to acquire (or to augment—the evidence is insufficient to say which) a modest fortune adequate to the support of a small estate at Friern Barnet and a seat on the county bench.

Bacon was also for a time treasurer of the S.P.G., for which he was paid £100 a year;[4] but it was probably as secretary and co-treasurer of the Corporation of the Sons of the Clergy that Bacon did the most good; and it was certainly in that honorary office that he expended the greater part of his zeal and energy.

By the reign of George III this society's regular anniversary proceedings, from the takings of which their charitable work among the widows of poor clergymen and (through the Clergy Orphans Corporation) their orphaned sons and daughters was mainly supported, were

Councillors, Bishops, and other great men in that Commission', and to the consequent opportunities for serving his friends.

[1] I have pieced together this account of Bacon from what is said of him by: the *D.N.B.; The Gentleman's Magazine*, LXXXVI (1816), pt. I, p. 276; John Nichols, *Literary Anecdotes of the 18th Century*, IX (1815), 5 ff.; and E. H. Pearce, *The Sons of the Clergy, passim.*

[2] See the several strictures upon him in *The Gentleman's Magazine*, LVI, 498, 939, 1027.

[3] Minutes, 11 February 1790, § 13.   [4] *Ibid.*

splendid and impressive. They comprised, first, a concert of sacred music in St Paul's, with a dinner for the stewards, musicians and others after it; then, later in the week, the anniversary sermon, also in St Paul's, as a preliminary to a gargantuan dinner—the heart of the festival—in Merchant Taylors' Hall; finally, a few days later, a return match on a smaller scale when the Archbishop entertained the Lord Mayor, sheriffs and stewards to dinner at Lambeth. Large collections were taken at both concert, sermon and dinner; a thousand pounds was not an uncommon total about this time. It was a very big show indeed. The preacher was always a distinguished clergyman, rising or risen, and the stewards of the festival, who left the actual work to deputies or, after 1800, a standing committee, were all 'top people' who were made to pay heavily for the privilege of appearing in this annual list of pre-eminent friends of the church.

The rise of the Corporation of the Sons of the Clergy to such social distinction in the reign of George III appears to have been due largely to the work of John Bacon, who was its secretary from 1769 to 1799, and a treasurer until his death in 1816.[1] The personal links between the Bounty and the Sons of the Clergy provided by Bacon and others like him (not to mention prelates and dignitaries of the church) were clearly important in articulating the otherwise unassociated bodies, official and unofficial, concerned in the same line of work. The church must have benefitted from all this. Its administration was slovenly and feeble enough and its poorer members' plight was wretched; but their plight would have been worse still had not the defects and gaps of the 'official' ecclesiastical system been partly filled by these semi-official voluntary societies and individual well-wishers. To ignore these latter in an account of the old constitution in church and state means failure to present it as it actually was. It is probably significant that John Nichols bracketed the First-Fruits Office and the Sons of the Clergy together as 'these prominent public departments'.[2]

Another link of the same kind was personified in the lawyer Stephen Comyn, who was register to the Sons of the Clergy from 1741 to 1759[3]

[1] See Pearce, *Sons of the Clergy* (2nd edn.), chh. 10–12, especially pp. 198–201, 231–2. He served as a steward at its festivals in 1779 and 1795.

[2] *Literary Anecdotes*, IX, 15 n.

[3] Pearce, *op. cit.* pp. 60, 287.

and steward at their festival in 1760;[1] receiver of first-fruits from 1754 to 1759, and receiver of tenths from 1759 until his death in 1773.[2] Robert Chester was another. He was a chancery lawyer, of sufficient standing and prosperity to marry into one of the leading families of his county.[3] In 1753 he was appointed the Bounty's solicitor; in 1773–4 he became receiver of tenths, and in 1779 secretary too;[4] and it looks as if his share in this nexus of associations went further still, for in 1760 the office of the Sons of the Clergy was moved to 'Mr. Chester's Chambers in the Temple', and he served as a steward in 1776.[5]

Probably the most remarkable of all was William Stevens, treasurer to the Bounty from 1782 until 1807.[6] Stevens was a city man, partner in a wholesale hosiery business in Broad Street.[7] He was a conspicuously pious and serious-minded man, systematic and unstinting in both religious devotions and charitable acts. He went daily (except on the fifth of November) to St Vedast's, Foster Lane,[8] and gave never less than half his income to the poor. At the same time he was attractive, lively and sociable—'a clubbable man' after Dr Johnson's heart, and founder of an exclusive and churchy dining club, Nobody's Friends. Being celibate as

[1] Lists of stewards since 1726 are appended to D. W. Garrow's *Sermon to the Sons of the Clergy* in 1818. There appear also James Comyn, 1737, Captain Philip Comyn, 1741; Thomas Comyn, 1742; and Valens Comyn, 1747.

[2] Minutes, 29 January 1754, § 2; 26 June 1759, § 1; 10 February 1773, § 1.

[3] In 1758, when he was 32, he married Harriet, second daughter of Charles Caesar. See R. Clutterbuck, *Hertfordshire*, II (1821), 287, whose ambiguity on this point is clarified by [R. Wilkinson] *Life of Sir Julius Caesar*, p. 63. I am obliged to Dr J. H. Plumb for guiding me to these sources.

[4] Minutes, 12 November 1753, § 12; 30 December 1773, § 3; 20 January 1774, § 3; 29 November 1779, § 4.

[5] Pearce, *op. cit.* p. 73.

[6] Minutes, 29 November 1782, § 22, record his appointment. It is tempting to read something into the fact that one of the sureties he produced was Anthony Bacon of Copthall Court in the City (*ibid.* 27 December 1782, § 18) who served as a steward at the festival in 1762.

[7] J. A. Park, *Memoirs of William Stevens* (from which most of my account is taken). The head of the business when he was apprenticed into it in 1746 was the father of that Jane Hookham who married John Frere; their son was the well-known diplomatist John Hookham Frere. Of the several books which have been written about J. H. Frere and his circle, unfortunately none seems to refer to Stevens or to Hookham's successor in the business, John Paterson.

[8] E. Churton, *Memoir of Joshua Watson* I, 30.

well as serious, he was free to give a great deal of time to the service of good causes. Among his intimates were Dr Morice, secretary to the S.P.G., Dr Gaskin, secretary to the S.P.C.K., Bishop Horne of Norwich, and most of the elders of the 'Hackney Phalanx', the high church pressure-group that offered the most principled opposition to the Evangelicals in the early nineteenth century, and more or less controlled whatever church societies and journals were not in the Evangelical camp. He twice served as steward of the festival of the Sons of the Clergy, was a governor of many socially valuable institutions (e.g. Christ's, Bridewell, and Bedlam Hospitals and the Magdalen Asylum), and played a leading part in the formation of the Scottish Episcopal Church Relief Fund in 1804 and of that Society (so nobly named!) for the Reformation of Principles, from which emerged the *British Critic*, the monthly hammer of the 'saints'. And he was treasurer of Queen Anne's Bounty. Of this part of his life his biographer wrote:

The indigent clergy and their families were the particular objects of Mr Steven's charities, and therefore, when in the time of Archbishop Cornwallis he was elected treasurer of Queen Anne's Bounty, it gave him peculiar satisfaction, as it was an office for which he was well qualified, in every respect suiting his temper and turn of mind; and it gave him the opportunity of mixing more with the Clergy in general, to many of whom he had been long attached, both from principle and the course of his studies; and of frequently meeting and conversing with the Bishops of the Church, of inquiring into the wants and distresses of that most useful body of men the Clergy; of relieving them from his own purse, when the funds of the Charity were not applicable to their case, and of treating them with tenderness and respect.[1]

The secretary and the treasurer were inevitably the men who 'stood for' the Bounty in the minds of the religious public. All the business was done through them. When hard-up clergymen, impatient benefactors, and too hopeful applicants had to be dealt with, it was the secretary or the treasurer, but usually the former, who had to do it. The secretary, moreover, lived in the Bounty's house in Dean's Yard. Naturally, therefore, he incurred much of the odium that the Bounty's operations, so slow and stodgy, were bound to excite. He could be attacked on either of two quite opposite grounds—as a 'strong man' who managed things his own way, or as a nincompoop whose incompetent stranglehold stood between the bishops and improvement. Suspicions like this are common

[1] Park's *Memoir* (1859 edn.), p. 31.

enough; they were to fasten in the eighteen-forties upon the first secretary to the Ecclesiastical Commissioners; but the suspicions of the Bounty's secretaries were apparently groundless. There were few opportunities anyway for those variations from established and complicated routine which give strong men their chance to impose on puzzled, part-time superiors; and control over the whole of the Bounty's operations rested unequivocally with the governors. What variations from and improvements upon existing practice were proposed, were proposed (so far as the evidence goes) by them, and the business was not so complicated, nor were their own attendances upon it so rare, that they could not keep up with it. The governors were the bosses; so the bosses were the bishops.

The Board need not by absolute necessity have become a predominantly clerical body. The original complement of governors was over two hundred. Less than a third of them were clerical, and when fifty-six additional governors were listed in the second charter every one of them was lay, so the proportion of clerical governors was reduced to a quarter. But already the trend towards clerical predominance was showing itself. Up to 1715 there had been, not indeed a predominance of laymen, but an average of over four lay governors at each meeting; for five years more the average remained at about four (usually Crown lawyers or judges), then it fell off never to recover. In 1720 'the first purely clerical meeting was recorded. In 1728 only one meeting had a layman present . . . in the years 1731-6 inclusive a single layman appeared, three or four times only'.[1] Lay governors never entirely ceased from turning up now and then. Sometimes one or two of the clerks of the privy council would come, or one of the civilians from doctors' commons, obviously there to advise on business. Sometimes a peer would attend, for reasons that one can only guess at; none ever came twice running, or more often still, except the earl of Harrowby in the early nineteenth century, whose reason for coming was the excellent one that he was the parliamentary leader of the church reform movement.

The falling-off in the attendance of deans was almost as remarkable. They continued to put in a fair showing until the early seventies. In 1772 there were fifteen dean attendances recorded, in 1774 ten.[2] An examina-

[1] This paragraph so far is drawn from Savidge, pp. 27-9, 66-7.
[2] As against 47 and 54 prelate attendances respectively.

tion of attendances in alternate years thereafter suggests that deans never again appeared in double figure numbers, and that it was extremely rare for there to be more than four separate dean attendances a year. Some years, there were no deans at all.

Thus were the bishops left in charge. For what the Bounty did or failed to do, the bishops were wholly responsible. They seem to have admitted this without hesitation. In 1829, when their wretched treasurer died and left them nearly twenty thousand pounds to the bad, they agreed between them to pay back what was owing by annual instalments out of their own incomes. The whigs and radicals on the 1837 committee ought not to have been surprised at the way the bishops had acquired complete control. The Bounty depended at several crucial stages of its operations upon their aid, or upon the aid of diocesan officials directly responsible to them. The actual value of livings, the material states of churches and residence-houses, the financial states of clergymen and benefactors—such necessary details could best, and sometimes could only, be found out through episcopal intervention, and right through the eighteenth century there was a running fire of inquiries and reports concerning them. The collection and assessment of this information being of necessity a diocesan task, and forming moreover so considerable a share of the Bounty's business, it was not surprising that deans and laymen should leave the work to the bishops, or be brought in only to make up a quorum.

There was another reason why the bishops should virtually monopolize the Bounty Board. They found it convenient as a meeting-place. Dean's Yard was only just round the corner from the House of Lords, at which they were on the whole assiduous in attendance, and its board room offered them a comfortable and appropriate council-chamber where the business of the church could be comfortably discussed, before or after General Courts or, in critical times, whenever they liked. Thus Archbishop Moore convened a meeting at the Bounty Office on 10 February 1787 (the day before a General Court) to sound his brethren's views on the attempt then being made to repeal the Test and Corporation Acts.[1] In March 1807, during the political storm that wrecked Grenville's administration, we have evidence of another such meeting. Bishop Moss, whose business it seems to have been to keep Bishop Tomline *au fait*

[1] Richard Watson, *Anecdotes of his own Life* (2nd edn., 1818) I, 261–2.

with Westminster affairs, wrote hurriedly from the House of Lords to say that 'the Archbishop has just told me that he thinks of sending notices to the Bishops tonight to desire they should meet him in Dean's Yard tomorrow'.[1] During the anxious first session of the reformed parliament, the bishops were meeting in Dean's Yard every Thursday.[2] While Convocation was in abeyance, and any conspicuous way of getting together was sure to invite anti-clerical suspicions of plotting and priest-craft, the Bounty's board room thus served the bench as their regular place of meeting; and when Convocation was, after a manner, re-suscitated in the eighteen-sixties, this tradition survived, for it was in the board room that the Upper House of Convocation met.

(ii) The Means

The Bounty's financial and administrative procedures in the eighteenth century hardly changed at all. Such changes as were of any importance came in the last two decades of the century, and are best considered part of the third church reform movement.[3] These procedures, numerous and complicated as they were, served the single purpose of collecting money from some of the clergy and handing it out, plus such freewill offerings as it had managed to attract *en route*, to others. Queen Anne's Bounty was really an instrument of income redistribution, so antici-pating, in a very faint fashion, the accepted practices of the modern state.

The first stage in this chain of procedures was the collection of the money by the First-Fruits and Tenths Offices. The First-Fruits Office was notified of the revenues it might expect by the lists of recent institutions which all the bishops were required to send in every half-year, and of which the remembrancer regularly reminded them. Clergy-men presented to livings that were liable to the payment of first-fruits were apparently expected to pay them and the Exchequer fees that went with them (£1 16s. 6d. if their value in the *Liber Regis* was under £40, £2 18s. 0d. if it was over) without being reminded. If they failed to do

---

[1] East Suffolk Record Office, Ipswich, Pretyman-Tomline papers, T.99/6, letter of 12 March.

[2] Bishop Van Mildert to Archdeacon Thorp, 14 March 1833, published by Edward Hughes, 'The Bishops and Reform, 1831–3', in *Eng. Hist. Rev.* LVI (1941), 481. He added, 'Three or four also come to me once a week for more confidential discussion. But do not *blab* this.'   [3] For which, see ch. 5.

so within three months then an Exchequer process would be issued against them, and they would be punished by having to pay the costs of the writ and an additional fee of a guinea to the remembrancer.[1]

The collection of tenths was in this manner. They were due annually at Christmas, but nothing was done about failure to pay them in to the Tenths Office ('over-against the Garden-Gate in the Middle Temple; where attendance is given only from the Hours of TEN in the Morning to TWO in the Afternoon, Holidays excepted')[2] until the end of April. If a clergyman had not paid by then he received a letter reminding him to do so and penalties for his tardiness began to accumulate. A fee of half-a-crown was payable to the Tenths Office until 1 June, for deleting the name from the 'non-solvent roll' which at that date went into the Exchequer; for some time thereafter, until the Exchequer had actually sealed and dispatched its writs demanding payment, an Exchequer fee of 5s. 8d. had to be paid as well.[3] The first reminder having been given, and the Exchequer writ having been issued, the matter passed into the hands of the First-Fruits Office, and fees naturally accumulated as time went by.[4]

The first-fruits and tenths revenues—the first of fluctuating, the second of fixed amount—having thus reached their respective receivers, had then to be transferred to the Bounty. This was never a quick process, although it was expedited about 1790, but it was a costly one, for the fees that the Bounty's treasurer had to pay to get them came to about £350. The receivers apparently kept the cash in private deposit accounts, and relied on the interest thereon for part of their income. In 1790 Bacon complained to the governors that the reforms then being demanded by the Commissioners of Public Accounts would prevent him from keeping about £4,000 constantly in hand, as had been the custom of the office,

[1] 1837 Committee, Qs. 67–81, 118–128, 503–525.

[2] From the instructions on the printed form of receipt. (P.R.O., Q.A.B./1/11.2.) It moved from the Temple to Portugal Street in 1823. (Minutes, 12 February 1824).

[3] 1837 Committee, Qs. 413–421, where the facts are not quite clear, and its Report, p. iv.

[4] *Ibid.* Qs. 421–461, and *passim*. Reminders were sent by the Tenths Office but the arrears had to be paid into the First-Fruits Office. Out of this division of duties a very cosy little racket was made in the early eighteen-thirties, much to the advantage of the First-Fruits clerks.

and making about £200 a year on it.[1] This was presumably the regular practice for both receivers, and it must have come to an end for the receiver of tenths as well at the same time; the said Commissioners directed him to pay in his balance before October each year, and under the efficient regime of Richard Richards it was paid in more quickly still, before the middle of June.[2] Once both these revenues were duly paid in, official notice was sent to the Bounty's treasurer (who could easily, of course, learn earlier and informally whether it was a fat or a lean year for first-fruits) who notified the Bounty Board that their income was ripe for collection. Then came the actual collection. The Board would instruct their treasurer to instruct the Treasury to instruct the Exchequer Officers to pay the money over to him; and, in a typical year, he would then at once put it to the purchase of gilt-edged stocks—Old South Sea Annuities usually, up to about 1780, and Three per cent Consols as soon as they became available. The secretary would be instructed to take firm security for the treasurer's doing all this. Every year up to their grand reform of 1831 the governors acted thus, taking special security from their treasurer each time he negotiated the collection and investment of their income. It was an extra, *ad hoc* security over and above the £6,000 security they took from their treasurer at his appointment and covered by sureties from a couple of prosperous friends. They were as careful about the reliability of the receivers, from whom they took security on as grand a scale. They had to be, with so much money coming and going through their officers' private accounts, and with the treasurer every now and then selling a few thousand pounds' worth of stock to keep himself in funds. So far as is known, nothing ever went wrong with this system until the wretched John Paterson defaulted in 1829.[3]

The Bounty put its money into gilt-edged stock bearing interest, and although some capital stock was sold each year to provide funds for the work of augmentation, the quantity of it grew and grew until in the early nineteenth century the amount of interest from capital overtook the annual income from first-fruits and tenths. All this, once the expenses

---

[1] Minutes, 11 February 1790, § 13. On 10 June (§ 4), they sought compensation for him by asking the Treasury to raise his salary by £150.
[2] *Reports from Committees of the House of Commons*, XII, 275.
[3] See below, pp. 224-5.

of the office and staff had been settled, was free for the work of augmenting the stipends of depressed clergymen.

Augmentations were of two kinds, by benefaction and by lot. The
governors always set more store on the former and dealt with them first.
The secretary would report the offers of benefactions he had received—
benefactions perhaps in lands, tithes or rent-charges, but usually in
money—and the eligibility of the living for benefaction would then be
checked. The promised grant of £200 to meet the benefaction would
then be made as soon as the proper character of the benefice (and of the
benefaction, if it was in kind) had been ascertained. The Board always
made as many augmentations as it could in this category before spending
the rest of what was available that year on its augmentations by lot. Lots
were drawn once a year among all the livings at that time eligible for
benefaction—those under £10 until they were all dealt with, then those
under £20, and so on. If a living thus augmented was still under value,
its ticket would go back into the lottery so that it could have another
chance; and new tickets were ever and anon being made out for livings
that, having been missed out of the original inquiries of 1705–8, were
later discovered by bishops and brought in under the provisions of
1 George I c. 10 s. 1.

Between the cup of benevolence and the lip of clerical need there
lay however a slippery and hazardous zone. Livings chosen for
augmentation by lot proved the more accident-prone. Persons who
proposed benefactions for particular livings usually knew well enough
what they were about. Often, indeed, they were only about their own
interest; nor were the lawyers who administered the several charitable
trusts founded to help the Bounty likely to make mistakes. There
could be delays in paying over the promised cash. A pious benefactor
having died, his heir might not feel as warm towards the church and
legal actions were occasionally threatened to make such a one pay up.
But the only trouble that much beset augmentations by benefaction was
sheer delay in executing the business; and that trouble was common to
the other class of augmentations as well, for the same kind of reasons.

Augmentations by lot, the principal business of the Bounty after 1736,
could sometimes prove very troublesome. In the first place, a living's
actual eligibility for augmentation had to be checked. It had a ticket in
the lottery because its certified value, in the original returns to the

Exchequer (or in a bishop's subsequent late return) gave it a prima facie claim on their charity; but a more serious check had to be made before the augmentation could be confirmed. An important and early item on the agenda of each meeting was the consideration of bishops' reports on the 'nature and value' of the livings provisionally allotted an augmentation. This practice of careful inquiry seems to have been a late development dating from the later seventeen-thirties, and probably attributable to the greater stress then perforce being put on aid to the poorest livings by the Bounty alone. The actual value of a living might, since the original returns were made, have gone up so much that it had lost its title to early relief. This had to be gone into. A more complicated question was the actual nature of the living. The governors had decided at the very outset of their career not to subsidize the avarice of patrons, nor to risk their money on recipients of uncertain legal status. Rectories and vicarages were, generally speaking, of certain enough status. Curacies and chapelries and donatives of all kinds gave trouble. The governors stipulated in their statute of 1715[1] that any cure they augmented, if it did not already give its holder a freehold for life (and thus freedom from the grossest tyranny of patrons), was to become a 'perpetual benefice' and so give its minister the security they thought proper; they stipulated also that the patron or impropriator of such a benefice should give a firm promise to continue to pay to its minister the stipend or 'pension' (often it was only an *ex gratia* payment, hardly yet an established custom) he had been paying thitherto. The governors further attempted to promote the reform of the church in a particular that had often been suggested as a proper matter for statutory enforcement but had not the slightest chance of passing an unregenerate parliament;[2] they took power to insist on an increased stipend or pension, and to withhold the allotted augmentation unless their condition was agreed to.

From all this two consequences followed. First, many impoverished livings never got an augmentation at all, because their patrons or impropriators refused to help. A slim account-book in the Bounty's records lists the livings over which patrons, impropriators, and ministers of 'mother-churches' were prepared thus to co-operate between 1737

[1] 1 George I c. 10, ss. 4 and 16.
[2] See e.g. the stillborn 'Act for the better providing for the serving of the Cures of impropriated Parishes', in the Tenison MSS at Lambeth, vol. 640, no. 8.

and 1809. They were not numerous. The diocese of Bath and Wells had the most to show, but it was only a paltry 21, and none of them later than 1784. Gloucester had only 10, Lincoln only 15, within similar periods. This part of the Bounty's work was not very successful. The second consequence was, that the discovery of the facts about such mean and, often, obscure cures might take the bishops or the secretary a long time, and the negotiations with their patrons longer still. The case of the curacy of Alvandley, or Alvanley, in the diocese of Chester, illustrates both consequences, and the administrative confusion that not surprisingly sometimes went with them. Worth not more than £5 10s. 0d. a year and perhaps nothing at all, its ticket was drawn in 1741, 1775, 1787, 1788, and 1792. The first time, apparently, the augmentation was considered a good one; something (which in the absence of the letter-books can only be guessed at) went wrong with the second; in 1790 the noble patron under pressure promised to give something himself, but in fact never did so; and in 1804 the Board learnt that the curacy lacked even a properly licensed curate, it 'being still considered by the Arden family as a private domestic chapel'. They agreed that to augment it in these circumstances would be improper, and set all the lots aside.[1]

The moment of augmentation came when these inquiries into the value and nature of livings had been satisfactorily completed.[2] The money was then transferred to the account, so to speak, of the cure agreed to be proper for augmentation, and a letter was sent to the incumbent apprising him of his good fortune and urging him to find, as quickly as he could, a piece of land or a tithe rent-charge to purchase with it. This was the Bounty's *idée fixe* throughout the eighteenth century, that their augmentations should go to strengthen the church's stake in the land. They may have believed that investments in land were safest; they must have subscribed to that belief in the moral and political superiority of endowments based on agriculture that was accepted by the majority of churchmen of their age. Several times they were urged to be more elastic in their principles, and to allow the investment of augmentation monies in gilt-edged securities;[3] but they held rigidly to

[1] Minutes, 19 January 1804, § 9.

[2] A printed form for inquiries about curacies etc. was produced in 1740—minutes, 2 March, § 5—and another for rectories and vicarages in 1775—minutes, 1 June § 8.

[3] See chapter v, below, p. 221.

their course, and moreover persisted until as late as 1830 in a policy of making it decidedly disadvantageous for clergy not to put their augmentation into real estate. They did this by paying a punitively small rate of interest on it while it remained in their hands. To begin with, they had paid a fair equivalent of 5%[1]. In 1720 it was reduced to 4%, and ten years later to $3\frac{3}{4}$%; by 1740 it had gone down by four small jumps to $2\frac{1}{2}$%; and in 1758 it went down further still to 2%, never to rise again till the eve of the death of George IV. Whatever other reasons there were for these drops, the main and public one was simply to encourage incumbents to find estates eligible for purchase. They never succeeded. The incentive to find an estate was at least as clear as the difference between £7 or £6 (the sums that the governors cautiously reckoned a £200 estate ought certainly to bring in in 1747 and 1758 respectively)[2] and £4; but the number of cures getting the benefit of their augmentations in half-yearly dividends at the Bounty Office increasingly outstripped the number of land-purchases made, and it is probably to be accounted one of the failures of Queen Anne's Bounty that its governors devised no fairer system.

The discovery and purchase of suitable lots of real estate could take a very long time. On 9 November 1715 an order was made 'that the Secretary do write to all the Incumbents of Augmented Livings and acquaint them that the Governors expect they should use their utmost Diligence to find out Lands or Tythes to be purchased with the Augmentation Money and to be annex'd perpetually to their respective Livings'.[3] Suitable lands and tithes were not easy to find and the delay in finding them was only the first of a series. The piece of land had next to be inspected. A printed form of inquiries[4] would be sent via the bishop to a small commission of two or three persons whom he had nominated.[5] Their return was received as the first item on the agenda at the next General Court, or was dealt with by a committee of two or three governors if it came in the late summer or autumn, during which off-

---

[1] Savidge, p. 61.
[2] Minutes, 6 April 1747, § 7, and 10 January 1758, § 6.
[3] Minutes, § 4.
[4] Printed in Ecton's *State of the Bounty* (1721 edn.), pp. 125–6 and Savidge, p. 149.
[5] This at least was the procedure established in 1738 (minutes, 8 May 1738, § 2). Earlier, it seems to have been more informal: see Savidge, pp. 87–8.

season the Bounty Board scarcely ever met. This would take perhaps eight or nine weeks. Then came the worst delays, while the title to the proposed purchase was examined, the deeds of conveyance prepared, and the purchase at last effected under the Bounty's seal at a General Court. Time and again they tried to speed up these legal formalities,[1] which discouraged incumbents and vendors alike and put a less efficient appearance on the Bounty than they liked. Savidge gives several instances of complaints about these delays in the Bounty's youth. That from the incumbent of Watenhall, alias Wetenhall, in the parish of Sandbach, Cheshire, well expresses many of the travails through which the poor clergy had to pass before they got their little piece of land. He warned the Board in 1720 that the vendor was impatient of the delays in completing the purchase, and anxious to sell to someone else, 'unless you send him such a threatening letter as will overawe him. . . . I am reflected on in my own house as a vile man as intending to cheat him of his estate and indeed it's a shame that the poor man cannot in twelve months have his money. . . . If this bargain miss, Cheshire won't afford such another.'[2]

While purchases pended—and often they pended perpetually— incumbents were entitled to interest on their augmentations. The rate of interest was low—only 2% from 1758 to 1830—but often a living would have been augmented two, three or four times, and the amount to be drawn from the treasurer's office each half-year would then be well worth drawing. The survival of the treasurer's 'Out' letter-book for 1807–11 enables us to put quite a lot of flesh on the bones of this part of the Bounty's work. Some of the facts it reveals are rather startling; and there is no reason for supposing that earlier things were not more startling still.

The treasurer at this time was John Paterson, William Stevens's partner in the business at 68 Old Broad Street, with whom the bachelor Stevens had continued to lodge after his retirement, and to whom he had entrusted the posthumous settlement of his affairs (which would of

---

[1] e.g. by Orders on 23 November 1716, 27 October 1719, 21 April 1721, 8 May 1738, 18 December 1783, 25 January 1787, 1 May 1794, 29 May 1800. In this latter period the delays were partly the fault of their own solicitor, Edward Chalmer, whom in the end they apparently sacked; see their minutes for 28 January 1802, § 23, and 22 June 1803, § 17.   [2] Cited by Savidge, p. 93.

course include his debts to the Bounty as treasurer). Early in 1807 Archbishop Manners-Sutton told the Board that on Stevens's death he had asked Paterson to act as treasurer temporarily; six items later in the minutes of the same meeting, Paterson was appointed as Stevens's official successor.[1] The suddenness of his appointment is a little astonishing. Paterson must have signified his readiness to do this before the meeting. Stevens obviously had been much attached to him. Perhaps Stevens had expressed a dying wish that his friend and partner should carry on his work. Whatever the reasons behind the appointment, anyway, it seems to have been a good one at the time.

One cannot imagine pleasanter letters coming out of a public office than the elder Paterson's. His manners were gentle, obliging and bland; to even the roughest questions he could return a soft answer. Queen Anne's Bounty, it must be remembered, was an easy target for suspicion and hostility. As a London office run by London men, it was at least suspect to every sound provincial and country-bred heart; for was not London perpetually engrossing profit and power, and did not Londoners assume a smart superiority over all others? All the public offices evoked these fears. Their demands for fees, their appetites for a rake-off, were insatiable. Few people enjoyed having business with them. Radicals and provincials alike were always ready to believe the worst of them. Indeed, one of the most interesting aspects of the report of the 1837 committee is its Radical members' reluctance—almost sheer inability—not to believe that the Bounty was corrupt. To their credit (for it showed large reserves of uprightness in men like Edward Baines and Tom Duncombe to set their names to a report affirming that an office of semi-ecclesiastical civil servants directly under the wing of the bishops was neither corrupt nor inefficient) they believed the evidence, singled out the Bounty's secretary-cum-treasurer for a compliment, and in general commended the whole concern.[2] The hostile suspicions with which they approached the Bounty were not at all new,[3] and were probably shared to some extent by most poor clergymen who approached it for the first time.

One example of Paterson's style in calming angry clergymen must

---

[1] Minutes, 26 February 1807, § 3.   [2] Report, pp. vii and ix.
[3] See e.g. the ultra-Whig *Collection of Letters and Essays in favour of Public Liberty*, (1774,) I, 8–9, or *The Gentleman's Magazine* LV (1785), 860.

suffice. The Reverend John Jones, curate (so he alleged) of Llangadwalader, near Oswestry, had apparently demanded to know why his interest
had not been paid for a long time. 'Reverend sir,' replied Paterson, 'I
this morning received your letter without any date and am rather surprised at the contents. What information you may have received
respecting the interest being kept is certainly extremely erroneous. I am
not the least aware that you ever applied for it, neither had I the least
information of your being the Curate of Llangadwalader.' He then
made several helpful suggestions and concluded thus admirably: 'I wish
your letter had not contained reproach for any Error on my part, as it
would have been much pleasanter had you written for information
which is what you seem to want and which at any time will with
pleasure be given by, Yours faithfully, John Paterson.'[1]

Jones's trouble was the inaccuracy of the information he had been
given, that his cure had been augmented some time ago. More often the
trouble was that clergymen succeeded to livings without realizing that
augmentation interest was payable to them. Nobody told them, there
were no records to enlighten them. Paterson seems not to have written
to remind any such but to have waited until, several or many years later,
they awoke to their situation and asked how much was owing. Three,
four or five year accumulations were not at all uncommon. The longest
in this particular book seems to be sixteen and a half years, owing to a
perpetual curacy in Wales.[2]

It was required of a clergyman at his first collection of interest to
present a certificate from the diocesan register, to the effect that he really
was the legal incumbent. Paterson had repeatedly to point out to clergy
that this was indispensable. Once he had received this certificate Paterson
was ready to release the money at the presentation of a signed and
stamped (4d) receipt for it. He would send these receipts to clergy who
did not know the procedure, and I think they were usually to be had also
at the diocesan offices, from the registrar or the bishop's secretary. Their
principal value was that they enabled clergy who could not call at the
treasurer's office themselves to get their dividend indirectly. Either they

[1] Letter of 4 November 1807, on fo. 6r. Another letter to Jones, of a very agreeable
and friendly character, followed soon after; copy on fo. 7v. These are in the one
surviving Letter-Book, mentioned above, p. 110.

[2] Letter of 12 December, 1808, fos. 28v-29v.

would sign their receipt and let a friend cash it for them, or 'pay it away as cash in the country'.[1] Whether they sold them at a regular discount or not, would be interesting to know. Paterson's letter-book is silent on the point.

[1] Letter of 3 November 1807 to the curate of Easington, Yorkshire, fo. 5v.

CHAPTER IV

CHURCH, STATE AND SOCIETY
1770-1840

By the end of the War of American Independence, the people who mattered in English church and state were becoming aware that the structure and quality of their society were undergoing drastic change: change mainly, they feared, for the worse. A new fashion of social and political anxiety spread among the upper classes as they faced this new domestic danger and got what comfort they could from theorizing about its sources and from preparing remedial measures. The changes that worried them were not merely those of the agrarian and industrial revolutions, although they, coming along with the explosive growth of population, were sufficiently disturbing to all who had eyes to see them, as preliminary warnings of fundamental social change.

During the seventies and eighties it needed no special sense of the implications of economic progress for men to feel that the tone and direction of society were not what they ought to be. Other, sharper, indications of this deplorable fact were easy to see. Hardly any sector of society was untouched by innovation. The ecclesiastical and constitutional sides of church and state were deeply disturbed, first by the anti-subscription movement with its culmination in the Feathers' Tavern petition, then by the progress of rational dissent hand-in-hand with political liberalism and their joint culmination in the attempts of 1787, 1788 and 1790 to repeal the Test and Corporation Acts. The hastening spread of Methodism and of the less aggressively political types of dissent was scarcely more comforting to men of the established church; and the progress through the same years of radical politics, with its menacing language about equality, representation, and the rights of men, was already a worry to some before it became a worry to all conservatives in the early nineties. It was no part of the accepted upper-class socio-political philosophy that the lower orders should engage in politics independently of their social superiors, and presume to think independent thoughts about them.

At the same time as these liberal and radical movements of men and ideas came to threaten the security of the old constitution in church and state, the pillars of the social structure were being shaken at the roots. Law and order were increasingly difficult to maintain. This was made clear by more commonplace and inescapable developments than great *émeutes* like the Spitalfields' weavers' forays and the Gordon Riots. The mere growth of population and the antique decrepitude of the ordinary machinery of police and administration were together bound to create dreadful difficulties; the seventeen-seventies seemed to mark an upward curve in the graph of crime and violence that was disturbing enough to provoke the first of several successive parliamentary inquiries and a vast quantity of literature. The gentry and clergy knew well (especially as magistrates) how difficult the maintenance of law and order was made as new suburbs of old towns, old villages turning into new towns, and worst of all, communities of miners springing up in moorland and forest, by-passed or stretched and broke the established system of local government; and this development, so dangerous to social order, became accentuated after the middle of the century.

Most important were the consequences and concomitants of the agrarian revolution. Enclosures brought much local resentment and national debate in their train; their social and economic consequences were ceaselessly argued. Above all, the poor laws demanded attention. Just as the family was the basic unit of society, so were the poor laws the foundation of the legal, administrative and police systems. An England without them was unthinkable. Every class of the poor, the destitute, and the down-and-out relied upon them. Whatever the cause of personal need—age, illness mental or physical, accident, widowhood, orphanage, unemployment—if private charity fell short, there was yet some relief to be had from the parish. J.P.s controlled it, churchwardens and the overseers of the poor supervised it, masters and mistresses of workhouses and constables managed it. A machinery entangled with all the other institutions of justice and administration, entrusted with functions so potent in respect of both the good of society and the happiness of men, could not but attract the attention of the legislator, the judge, the social reformer, and the economist, at any period of history. It was bound to attract their attention all the more magnetically in a period when the problems of society were multiplying, when the will to find new or improved solutions to them was growing, and when, moreover, the expense of this basic 'social machinery' was going up fast. In 1776 it was costing about one and a half million a year; by 1786 it was costing over two million; and by 1803 over four million. So sharp a rise was bound to be widely felt, and much resented. The poor laws had always shown a tendency to involve rate-payers in unwanted expenditure. Many and sometimes cruel were the expedients adopted to reduce their cost wherever the natural tendencies towards thrift triumphed over those towards extravagance. Whether they were costly or cheap, they were deplorable. It was the fate of the poor-laws of England, curious amalgam of charity and prudence, self-love and social, never to give satisfaction to all classes of the community at once, and always to be open to objections more or less serious.

The combined effect of all these factors, and of other lesser factors in the last two or three decades of the eighteenth century (the amazing development of newspapers, for instance, and the Sunday promenades and 'religious debating societies' that excited Bishop Porteus so extremely),[1] was to pose for the governing classes a major problem of social control. Its scale was unprecedented, and however immemorial the problem of containing extremes of riches and poverty, of cultivation and brutality, within one social structure, English history had no precedent (unless it was that of the civil war and commonwealth, which was often pressed into service as a dreadful warning) for the flood of unsettling ideas that was bred out of Locke by nonconformity and the *philosophes*. (For the insinuation that there was actually no God, freely made in France at this time and known about in England, there really was no precedent at all). Furthermore, one would gather from the dates and nature of the measures taken to answer this challenge that it was a fairly new and homogeneous one. The Sunday-school movement (late seventies) and the common primary school movement that soon followed

---

[1] 'The beginning of the winter of 1780 was distinguished by a new species of dissipation and profaneness ... a novel and a bold attempt, but not the less likely to succeed in this country and in these times.' Porteus's own words, cited in R. Hodgson, *Life of Porteus* (2nd edn., 1811), p. 71. Further testimony to their novelty and moral undesirability may be found in *Memoirs of Romilly*, 1, ff. 167–9.

it; the Acts promoted by the admirable Thomas Gilbert in aid of church reform (1777, 1781) and poor law reform (1776, 1782);[1] Bishop Lowth's successful assault upon the age-old abuse of resignation bonds (1780–3); the revival of sabbatarian legislation (1781, 1794); the campaign, renewed after a lapse of eighty years or so, for a 'reformation of manners' (c. 1787–8); the Society for the Suppression of Vice and Profaneness (founded in 1787), alias the Proclamation Society, particularly given to the prosecution of disturbers of the Lord's Day and of the publishers and vendors of racy and irreligious literature; and the beginnings of legislation in aid of the oppressed class of curates (1788, 1796): all these are examples of approaches by different routes towards the goal that other forces (the Evangelical and Methodist movements, for example, and the development of the professions) were approaching by other routes still—a more orderly, productive, and religious society, to be secured through the joint operation of better principles, better laws, extended education and a reformed church.

This goal of necessity involved the disciplining of the poor; but that was by no means the whole of it. It was possible for members of the upper orders to love those whom they chastened outside the family as well as inside it. The education prescribed for the children of the poor was very largely a course of indoctrination in safe principles. Even so, many people were worried lest it should make the poor less rather than more content with their subordinate station; but it would be stupid to make out that there was not often some benevolence or enlightenment mixed up with it too. Consider for example the 'Various Means of Doing Good Bodily and Spiritually' recommended by the moderately Evangelical Dr Stonehouse.[2] It is a remarkable blending of Tillotson and Venn, and the implication is clear: that the respectable believer (or, for that matter, the respectable elect believer) will not easily be saved if he neglects so many and so obvious social duties. The means of doing good spiritually were practical and imaginative. They included promoting

---

[1] The latter being 'the most carefully devised, the most elaborate and perhaps the most influential, for both good and evil, of all the scores of Poor Law Statutes between 1801 and 1834'. S. and B. Webb, *English Local Government* VII, 171n.

[2] Cited from his pamphlet *Considerations of some particular sins etc.* by Bishop Barrington in Appendix F. to his 1797 *Charge to the Clergy of the Diocese of Durham;* see his collected *Sermons, Charges and Tracts*, pp. 255–7.

schools and religious societies, helping the really talented to get on, the encouragement of private and family prayer and Bible-reading, and visiting the sick 'and comforting or admonishing them'; 'talking seriously and affably with children and servants, at any time or place, when a proper opportunity offers'; and 'dispersing printed or written slips of paper, against particular sins, as sabbath-breaking, swearing etc. in order to be given away occasionally, or enclosed in a letter, or put into a book, or dropt in any part of the house, where the reproved would be likely to meet with it . . .'. The means of doing good bodily were even more comprehensive and practical, and are worth citing in full because they illustrate very well the kind of activities which their sense of social responsibility was more and more to press upon the well-to-do. '1. By giving to the poor bread, coals, shoes, stockings, linen, coats, or gowns, which may be bought much cheaper than they can buy them. 2. By paying their house-rent or part of it. 3. By sending them wine, herb teas, or spoon meats, when sick, and sometimes proper dinners on their recovery, suitable to their weak state. 4. By paying their apothecary's bill, or part of it. 5. By giving rakes, prongs, or spades, to day labourers, or some implements of their trade to poor industrious workmen. 6. By seldom giving *money*, unless to those who live at a distance, and then we should be well assured that their case is truly stated, and that we cannot relieve them by any other method. 7. By subscribing to an Infirmary, where we may procure that relief for some real objects of compassion, which they cannot obtain elsewhere; and without which, perhaps, they must perish, or remain hopeless of any cure, and burdens to society. 8. By discouraging idleness in man, woman, or child; and by contriving work for those who are unemployed. 9. By defending the poor against oppression; especially such of them as are too often most grievously oppressed by hard-hearted parish officers, who have the power over them.'

Consider also the Society for Bettering the Conditions of the Poor, founded in 1796 by Bishop Barrington (than whom there was at that time no better prelate on the bench),[1] by his kinsman Sir Thomas Bernard, an eminent late Hanoverian philanthropist, and by William

---

[1] Barrington's definition of Christianity is of interest here; 'in truth, genuine Christianity is no other than THE UNION OF PURE DEVOTION WITH UNIVERSAL BENEVO-LENCE'. 1797 *Charge, op. cit.* p. 244.

Wilberforce. It was founded mainly to make good ideas for social improvement better known—a kind of philanthropic organization society, working by means of a standing committee, subscriptions, correspondence, and published reports. Its humane and benevolent sides were as clear to see as its obviously disciplinary ones, and were blended with them in a very homogeneous whole. Bernard believed passionately in social subordination and the duties the poor owed to the rich, but he believed also in the stewardship of money, and the duties the rich owed to the poor. Once he had improved, by a judicious marriage, the small fortune which his skill as a conveyancer had brought him, 'the endeavour to meliorate the domestic habits of the labouring class was', wrote his biographer-nephew, 'the first amusing occupation that occurred to him'.[1] The rest of his life was an unbroken series of endeavours to do good along these lines, and the eight volumes of Reports of the Society he helped to found show how many varieties of social improvement he and his friends were eager to make. He hoped his Society and others like it might be 'the means of creating more reciprocity of good-will and friendship between the different classes of society; of making the virtues and the distresses of the poor more known and respected; of impressing on their own minds a greater desire for character and reputation in life, and of teaching them the true value of those gradations of rank and condition which our Creator has thought fit to establish'.[2] At the same time as the general philanthropy of the age was entering the new phase typified by this Society—a phase of endeavour more dynamic, more imaginative, more scientific even, and certainly more humane—poor law reform was beginning to go in quite the opposite direction from that of the preceding century. From Gilbert's Act of 1782, write the poor law's greatest historians, poor law legislation 'increasingly dropped [its] disciplinary and repressive character; . . . the statute law as to the Relief of the Poor became, from decade to decade, more exclusively generous and humane in character and intention'.[3]

From all sides came evidence in the seventies and eighties of a quickening social awareness, concerned both for the sufferings of the poor and with the dangers that their sufferings and wrong-headed notions might,

[1] James Baker, *Life of Sir Thomas Bernard, Bt.*, p. 6.
[2] *Ibid.* pp. 30–31.
[3] S. and B. Webb, *op. cit.* VII, 422.

if not effectively checked, entail; and all this before the French revolution. Truly, that (and the run of bad harvests that came with it) made the situation more explosive, and gave added point to such further and deeper investigations of the condition of the lower orders as David Davies' *Case of the Labourer* and F. M. Eden's *State of the Poor*. Bishop Watson struck a powerful blow against lower-order discontent in 1793 by publishing a sermon on 'The Wisdom and Goodness of God in having made both Rich and Poor'—but it was one he had written and first delivered in 1785.[1] By the year the French Revolution broke out, the bishop of Salisbury could already call his clergy's attention to 'the progress of Sunday education; the exertions of private persons and societies for the promotion of piety, decency and good order; and, above all, the Royal Proclamation for the restraining of wickedness and vice; for the maintenance of religion and virtue; and, as the means of obtaining these invaluable ends, for the due observance of the Sabbath'.[2]

For some of this social responsibility and anxiety for the moral elevation of society the Evangelical movement was no doubt responsible, but not for all. Evangelicalism was not the only tributary sending down its flood of improving, moralizing ideas and energy towards the ocean of early Victorian respectability and public probity. It was not Evangelicalism that set the Quarter Sessions of Sussex and Gloucestershire, and Jeremy Bentham, to work on the reform of prisons; it was not conceivably Evangelicalism that was responsible for the administrative and economic reform movement begun by Lord North and carried on by each of his ministerial successors. The rise of the professions, the progress of sanitary ideas, had nothing to do with Evangelicalism. Plenty of the men (and there were many clergymen among them) who contributed to the great national debate on enclosures and on the causes, costs, and cures of pauperism, were scarcely if at all touched by the movement that gave William Wilberforce, Hannah More and Henry Thornton much of their similar concern with the same subjects. The Evangelicals have been held peculiarly responsible for impressing the observance of the Lord's Day upon the public conscience of the nineteenth century,

[1] R. Watson, *Anecdotes of his own Life* (1818 edn.), I, 438; *Miscellaneous Tracts*, I, 448 ff.

[2] Shute Barrington, 'Letter to the Clergy of the Diocese of Salisbury', 16 October 1789, in *Sermons, Charges and Tracts*, p. 103.

and yet the case made for it on grounds of social utility, as a civilizing and disciplinary measure, must have appealed to thousands of landlords and employers whom the Evangelicals' specifically religious arguments in its favour left cold. This vigorous statement of Arthur Young's, for example, was strictly non-partisan: 'Nothing tends more strongly (as Addison has well remarked) to civilize the lower classes, than the institution of a Sabbath; when their labours cease, and dressed in their best attire they assemble at the parish church to worship the common Father of all. The omission of this motive and opportunity of appearing clean, and mixed in a general assembly of the parish, entails dirt, slovenliness and rags; drunkenness, idleness, and consequent profligacy. . . . I know nothing better calculated to fill a country with barbarians than extensive commons [i.e. no enclosures] and divine service only once a month.'[1] Lord Brougham had not become an Evangelical when thirty-five years later he made exactly the same case for promoting 'the church-going habit' which helped at once to civilize the lower orders, to humanize the higher, and to bind them all closer in a conscious common society—'a matter which those who had best considered the subject had always deemed a public advantage'.[2]

The third church reform movement has its proper place in the story of how this social crisis of the end of the eighteenth and the beginning of the nineteenth century was handled. English society was felt to be in a bad way. The upsurges of production and commerce, the spread of comfortable ways of living among more and more people above the poverty-line, the growth in the quantity of lively religion (provided by the Evangelicals and Methodists), and other pieces of evidence that might have seemed heartening, did not seem to be matched by comparable increases in social stability and common acceptance of political and religious principle, nor by a diminution in the number of people below the poverty line. Methodism could indeed appear deplorable because its religious views and practices were so largely outside the structure of official establishments which should, ideally, contain the whole of the nation's religious activities (and 'religious', of course, comprised educational); it revived religion but sometimes so much in the wrong ways and wrong places that it looked more like a blight than a blessing;

[1] *General View of the Agriculture of Lincolnshire*, p. 438.
[2] *Hansard*, 3, xxv, 30–1, 17 July 1834.

and during the years of high excitability, the same came (albeit un-fairly) to be said of Evangelicalism. *These* were not the ways to make the red blood of real religion flow freely again through the arteries and cells of the body politic; they were dangerous expedients that flew in the face of political wisdom by neglecting to study where those arteries and cells lay. The great problem of social control, as men of the middling and upper classes were almost bound to see it, was at bottom a moral and religious one, that could only be met by making the religious institutions of the country efficient for their work of preaching salvation and (or, more usually, through) social subordination. 'Nothing is more certain', wrote the most influential conservative social theorist of the day, 'than that religion is the basis upon which civil government rests. . . . And it is necessary that this religion be established for the security of the state, and for the welfare of the people. . . . A state is secure in proportion as the people are attached to its institutions; it is therefore the first, and plainest rule of sound polity, that the people be trained up in the way they should go.'[1] How else could this be done but by restoring to the basic institution of the country's religious and political life, the parish, its proper vigour and vitality?

The church reforms of this period were nearly all designed to improve the parish, and they ought to be placed in the same picture along with the continual efforts to improve the poor laws, in their parishes or united groups of parishes, and with the 'select vestry' movement for the stream-lining of parochial government. Some saw more clearly than others, and some imagined more vividly, the possibilities that lay in the parish; all could see the desirability of making the parish an effective unit of government.[2] Even the church reforms that did not set the parish or its ministers in the centre of their propositions were aimed at the same end. More dioceses, for example, and fewer translations of bishops, were only

[1] Robert Southey, *Sir Thomas More: or, Colloquies on the Progress and Prospects of Society*, II, 47–8.
[2] I use the word 'government' in the broad sense in which it was, naturally enough, used by men who believed that a society was governed at least as much by ideas and conventions as by laws and orders. It was perfectly consistent, though short-sighted, to wish to strengthen the parish and at the same time to promote an *ad hoc* body that ran over parish boundaries.

thought desirable inasmuch as their achievement would enable bishops to keep a closer eye on their parochial clergy. The enthusiasm for primary education fitted into the same pattern. In the early years of both the Sunday-school and the common day-school movements there was a good deal of co-operation between churchmen and others, and the advantages of parochial organization were occasionally disregarded. But right principles soon re-asserted themselves. The Sunday-schools became either geared to the parish church or completely separated from it. The British and Foreign Schools Society, inclined towards inter-denominational fraternizing, was challenged and quickly overtaken by the National Society for Educating the Children of the Poor in the Principles of the Established Church. And indeed, how else in those years could a national system of anything have been more conveniently constructed than on the ready-made framework of the parishes? Even Whigs and radicals who had no particular love for the Church of England and no respect at all for the clerical order, were constrained to see that this was only common-sense. Both Whitbread in 1807 and Brougham in 1820, men who cared more passionately than most for the extension of education and who were certainly not simply out to enforce subordi-nation, proposed to establish their national school systems within the parochial structure.

Between the reformers and their ideal there lay, of course, innumer-able obstacles. The parish proved often a remarkably hard nut to crack. Some parishes were too large to function properly; they needed to be divided, sub-divided, sub-sub-divided. Some were too small; it was desirable that they should be united with small neighbours, or allowed to be held in plurality with them. Some parishes were peculiars, beyond the normal means of diocesan control, needing to be brought under it. No one parish was constituted in quite the same style as any other. They were fecund of vested interests. Often the chief opponent of reform was the incumbent himself. Vestries if 'select' (i.e. oligarchical) were often corrupt, if 'open' (i.e. democratic), disorderly. Churchwardens regularly perjured themselves in reporting on the condition of their church, church-yard, and congregation, to the archdeacon at his visitation. Some clergymen were abominably underpaid, some grossly overpaid; the underpaid one was just as likely to be detested by the tithe-payers as the other. Some parishes were, in the expressive words of so many vexed churchmen, 'riddled with dissent'; others already, or fast becoming, one-class parishes, unleavened by the presence of professional or 'gentle' people. Yet it was through the parish and through it alone that the established church could do the job it was established to do.

The best of all the writers on practical church reform between 1780 and 1830, was Richard Yates. He was obviously a remarkable character, son of the custodian of the ruins at Bury St Edmunds and a schoolmaster until he took orders at the age of twenty-seven in 1796 and became first curate, then chaplain of Chelsea hospital. He was a man of many committees, most of them charitable and philanthropic, and a preacher in many pulpits; and his frequent use of the phrase 'Gospel piety' suggests that his manner was mildly Evangelical. After reading his books it comes as a surprise to learn that he was quite a popular preacher in various of the fashionable chapels of the metropolis. Archbishop Manners-Sutton offered him the living of Blackburn, and Lord Liverpool that of Hilgay, 'in reward of his publick services'; but he refused both offers and stayed in the London area, with no doubt the greater ease for having married a modest heiress in 1810.[1]

Yates's only fault as a writer was pomposity. He could not touch lightly upon any subject, not even a light one. Allusion, irony, suggestion, were beyond his powers. But no one else seems to have held the whole of his subject so firmly in view, and certainly no one else cared as much for the facts. Facts and figures—the naked, rock-bottom facts, to be ascertained only by direct inquiry and to be tabulated whenever possible—did not apparently possess great natural attractions to churchmen of the early nineteenth century. They handled them sloppily and sometimes showed an astonishing inability to understand why anyone should want to know them. Perhaps this was because they talked so much about principle, perhaps it was because 'the best authors of antiquity'—upon whose style they were so proud to found their own—did not deal much in statistics; perhaps it was because facts were what your critics relied on; or simply because they were thought dull. Yates at any rate was so dull himself that he would hardly have felt the force of the last suggestion. By the time he was writing, indeed, the real facts

---

[1] This summary view of Yates's life and character is based on the 1843 Memoir (see p. 148 n. 3) and the *D.N.B.* entry, which most deplorably underestimates the ability of Yates's writings on church reform.

of the church's case were slowly being established, and to do his contemporaries justice it must be admitted that Yates was not the only church reformer to face the facts squarely and, instead of disputing them or shrugging them off, to see what could be done about them. Nor was his analysis of the church's state quite the most perceptive or imaginative; the anonymous *State of the Established Church, in a series of letters to Spencer Perceval* of 1809–10[1] and *Letter to the Archbishop of Canterbury on the subject of Church Property* of 1824[2] often go deeper, and get into the 'psychological' state of the church as the more sober Yates could never have done. Edward Berens's anonymous small book *Church-Reform: by a Churchman* (1828), was very good indeed, cool, comprehensive, and persuasive. But he was able to be so very largely through standing on Yates's shoulders. For sheer exhaustive honest investigation and methodical exposition, Yates had no rival. The reality of his concern and of his intelligence are unquestionable.

In 1815 Yates published *The Church in Danger: a Statement of the Cause, and of the Probable Means of Averting that Danger, Attempted; in a Letter to Lord Liverpool, etc.* Two years later he brought out *The Basis of National Welfare; considered in reference chiefly to the property of Britain, and Safety of the Church of England; in a second letter to Lord Liverpool;* and in 1823 Lord Liverpool was the nominal recipient of a third published letter, *The Patronage of the Church of England; concisely considered in reference to national reformation and improvement; to the permanence of our ecclesiastical establishments; and to its influence on the pastoral charge and clerical character.* He wrote also the *History and Antiquities of the Abbey of St. Edmund's Bury*, to the second (posthumous) edition of which was prefixed a short memoir.[3]

Yates's first two books made quite an impression on the public. Between about 1800 and the end of the wars the shortage of church accommodation was increasingly being recognized and deplored. Even the Primate noticed it. In the course of a debate on the dangers of dissent he admitted that 'the fact was, that our population had, particularly in

---

[1] First edition, pp. 88, 1809; second edition, pp. 151, 1810. The advertisement to the first says that the letters originally appeared in the *Weekly Political Review*, signed 'Senex'.   [2] 'By a Clergyman', signing himself 'W.W.' (pp. 102).

[3] A first part came out in 1805; the second part joined it in the second edition only in 1843.

some large towns, far exceeded the machinery by which the beneficial effects of our church establishment could be universally communicated'.[1] The next year, 1810, on the day after a long speech by Lord Harrowby on the church's deficiencies in general, Lord Sidmouth moved for returns by dioceses of the number and capacity of churches, the number of dissenting places of worship, and the population, in parishes of one thousand or over.[2] The *Quarterly*, reporting and praising Harrowby's Curates Act of 1813, said that these returns had provided incontestable evidence of the gravity of the church's danger.[3] The government appears to have intended to act as soon as Napoleon was safely out of the way, reckoning, presumably, that there would be no objection to a large grant of public money once the expenses of the war were over.[4] But the money was not so easily to be wrung out of a parliament intent on retrenchment and avid for economy. In the autumn after Waterloo, Sidmouth was discussing with Christopher Wordsworth how the urgency of the matter might be impressed upon the public. They agreed that an original essay would be best. Sidmouth proposed Coleridge or his correspondent's brother the poet, but the cautious Christopher thought they lacked the detailed knowledge that ought to go into it.[5] Presumably they wanted something lighter than Yates's *Church in Danger*, which did much to sway parliamentary opinion; for no public reference to the subject between its appearance in 1815 and the Church Building Act of 1818 did much more than restate, with varying degrees of loud or soft pedal, Yates's theme. When the Chancellor of the Exchequer introduced the bill into the House of Commons he lost little time in singling out for praise 'the very useful publications of Mr. Yates'.[6]

---

[1] 2 June 1809. *Hansard* XIV, 857.   [2] 19 June 1810. *Hansard* XVII, 770–1.

[3] *Quarterly Review* X (1813), 41 ff.

[4] In November 1814 Sidmouth told the Rev. Cecil D. Wray, who had recently published a *Statement of Facts* on the subject, that he trusted Parliament's attention would soon be drawn to it. A year later he wrote to Lord Kenyon that he had 'no doubt of Lord Liverpool's determination to submit a proposition to parliament, in the ensuing session, for an augmentation, to be progressively made, of the number of places of worship under the established church'. G. Pellew, *Life and Correspondence of Sidmouth*, III, 138–9.   [5] *Ibid.* p. 139.

[6] 16 March 1818. *Hansard* XXXVII, 1119. Other testimony to Yates's impact may be found between pp. 242–374 of his *Basis*, and in the advertisements at the end of his *Patronage*.

Yates's work shows well the value an intelligent, well-bred churchman set upon the church establishment: better, indeed, than in most writers of equal authority, because he was always ready to state the obvious. No better ground could be laid for a discussion of the role expected of the church in early nineteenth century society than by a catena of quotations from this admirable, intelligent, plain-speaking divine.

He recurred frequently to the paramount necessity of keeping the tone of society religious. 'Without the restraint of Religious Principle, Human Laws are unequal to the task of stemming the torrent of turbulent and selfish passions. Even the polished and philosophic Shaftesbury, as a Politician, has observed, that "a Devil and a Hell may prevail, where a Jail and a Gallows are thought insufficient".'[1] Looking at France, he wrote with shuddering distaste, 'We have lived to see a Government forming its measures upon the destruction and overthrow of all the Public Appurtenances of Religion, and proceeding in its functions upon the express and Public DISAVOWAL OF ALL EXPECTATION BEYOND THE PRESENT LIFE.'[2] This was wicked folly. It must be the ideal of the statesman to establish, 'upon the hope of Future Reward, and the fear of Future Punishment, that Moral and Religious Character, which leads to the highest improvement of the intellectual faculties, and is the only Basis of permanent Social Order, of Political Liberty, and of National Welfare and Prosperity'.[3] In England, something like this had been achieved; 'the institutions and regulations of social intercourse, and the political and legal establishments, are constructed with a regard to Future Existence, and with a view to the important influence which a due consideration of that Truth ought to have upon human conduct'.[4]

Obviously the diffusion and maintenance of religion in society ought to be the care of all Christian persons, and could be the work of many institutions; but it was peculiarly the work of the established church, and that meant the parochial clergy. In talking of them, Yates became quite eloquent: 'The Parochial Clergy—the Friends and Benefactors of the Community—the Promoters and Guardians of Piety, Decorum, and Good Order—the liberal, intelligent, and instructive associates of the Rich—the humble, candid, compassionate and charitable teachers of the Poor—the public and accredited Voice of the Church; to instruct the

[1] *Basis*, p. 100.   [2] *Basis*, p. 42.
[3] *Basis*, p. 21.   [4] *Patronage*, p. 7.

ignorant, reclaim the guilty, exhort the erring, confirm the wavering, and console the afflicted;—to diffuse and extend that knowledge of the Lord, which is the only true wisdom; and proclaim those Good Tidings, which are "Glory to God in the Highest, and on Earth, Peace, Good-will towards Men".[1] He summed up all his arguments thus:

If it be the part of profound and enlightened wisdom to appropriate a class of men to the Religious and Moral Instruction of the country: If the civil and public advantages of such an institution be evident to the slightest reflection, and apparent in the superior Civilisation, Order, and Decorum of Society: If Christianity be anything more than a cunningly devised Fable: If it be, in fact a system of truth most conducive to social and individual happiness: If the concerns of Eternity be superior to those of Time: If the influence of things present upon the mind of man be sufficient to weaken and obliterate the impression of future prospects, not frequently placed in view, and pressed upon the attention: If for this highly useful and most important purpose, it be advisable to call in the aid of Talent and Learning, Genius and Ability, as well as Zeal and Industry: Then these unanswerable and irrefragable truths will prove the wisdom and necessity of providing a just maintenance for such men, and the importance of the means of securing for them respect and attention.[2]

Therein lay the case for an established church and for its material reform, put into as much of a nutshell as Richard Yates could manage.

Here are two further aspects of the same case summarized by churchmen both different from Yates in status, party, and temperament— Bishop Watson, and William Wilberforce. 'The safety of *every* civil government is fundamentally dependent on the hopes and fears of another world which are entertained by its members; and the safety of every *Christian* civil government is brought into the most imminent danger, when infidelity is making a rapid progress in the minds of the people. . . . It may be difficult to find a full remedy for this evil; but the residence of a respectable clergyman in every parish and hamlet in which there is a place of established worship, appears to me to be more fitted than any other for that purpose.'[3] Finally, from an active reformer's jottings 'On the importance of legislative measures for promoting public morals'. He noted that morals and religion sank or swam together. 'Sanction of oaths, property, person, life, honour, depend on them; the very cement that compacts society together. . . . The necessity of religion among the bulk of the people, i.e. the lower orders, is the greater,

[1] *Church in Danger*, pp. 26–7.   [2] *Church in Danger*, pp. 215–6.
[3] Richard Watson, *Anecdotes of his own Life* (1818 edn.), II, 127.

because that great principle of honour, which it would scarcely be too strong to term the religion of the higher orders, does not exist among them. Consider then what the former would be without the restraint of honour, and estimate what the latter without religion.'[1]

The church's main function was social control. Sometimes this was admitted with great frankness. In the tense air of 1833 the *Quarterly* warned those landowners who were inclined towards clergy-baiting and resentful of tithes, that for all its imperfections the church had one great virtue—'it *maintains order*'.[2] To say this was not to imply that it had not also the function of saving souls. All Evangelicals, obviously, and presumably most high churchmen, would no doubt have agreed that saving souls was in some way a higher function. But even if they allowed a qualitative distinction of this kind, they would still have seen social control as a principal function of their established church, for these reasons: first, because a state without an established religion was almost— for some, absolutely—unimaginable, on common social and political grounds; second, because it was generally assumed that a nation of Christians was collectively lacking in religious seriousness if it did not have an established church, and would be punished by God accordingly; and third, because in the minds of virtually all the upper, and, one supposes, many of the middling and lower orders who were religious at all, the way to salvation lay through political good conduct. 'The best Christian', as William Otter remarked ,'was the most loyal subject.'[3]

Men of the governing class might argue among themselves about constitutional principle and might dare to oppose the will, and to question the wisdom, of the administration. To the orders of society that had no share in government except perchance in petty, local ways, these possibilities were not open. Theirs was to be content with their lot, and to do what they were told. Obedience to lawful authority was a common theme for the Hanoverian pulpit. All the standard texts were in constant use, especially at times of political disturbance.[4] The insistence upon the

[1] R. I. and S. Wilberforce, *Life of William Wilberforce*, II, 448–51.

[2] 'The Church and the Landlords', in *Quarterly Review*, XLIX (1833), 211.

[3] On p. 44 of the Sermon cited below, p. 159. Mathieson's use of this sermon, in *English Church Reform*, pp. 31–2, seems a little unfair.

[4] Much use was made of Proverbs xxiv, 21; Romans xiii, 1, 3–4; 1 Peter ii, 17; 1 Timothy ii, 2; Titus iii, 1.

religious duty of obedience was just as strong as it had been in the sixteenth or seventeenth centuries, and the arguments were much the same, except that Locke's 'civil magistrate' had usually taken the place of 'the Lord's anointed'. Just what figure was called into the peasant's mind by references to 'the civil magistrate', it would be interesting to know. Probably he thought it meant the local justice of the peace; and if he did, it would be very appropriate, for it was undoubtedly in the persons of the local magistracy (who would usually be doubling the roles of magistrate and landowner and would sometimes be titled) that most men in the humbler walks of life encountered the king's government. Obedience to *social* superiors as a religious duty does not seem to have been enjoined with the same explicit directness as obedience to political superiors;[1] but whether it was expressly enjoined or not made no difference in practice, because it was one of the signal advantages of English society then that political and social power were united in the same class and the same persons. A suffrage to God to 'bless the squire and his relations' was only equivalent to asking God to strengthen the hand of lawful authority. Where social and political power were *not* thus happily united, as so often in the larger towns and the mining districts, the clergyman was left to do his part of the job on his own, and this came to be seen in the early nineteenth century as one of the chief—if not absolutely the chief—danger of contemporary social change. The church had a political function to perform. All churches ought to preach political subordination; and established churches were especially bound to do so. Nor need their performance of this as a principal duty derogate in any degree from their spiritual character. Very few in the Church of England before the eighteen-thirties (and for that matter not many then) thought that the church, in its function as an established church, could have any higher aim than complementing the work of the civil power and—what it alone could do—toughening the fabric of society.

The education of the children of the lower orders became increasingly emphasized as an indipensable part of the establishment's work in these

---

[1] It was, however, by the vice-dean of Canterbury, George Berkeley, in his sermon on the 1785 anniversary of the death of Charles I, 'The Danger of Violent Innovations in the State, how Specious soever the Pretence'. He used the text Romans xiii, 7, and claimed the authority of Bishop Sherlock for his application of it. He presumably had in mind Sherlock's *Discourses* (6th ed. 1772), IV, 341 ff.

years. About 1780, a parish might or might not contain a primary school; if it did, it might or might not be attached to the parish church; and the questions of its existence and quality were not questions of great public interest. By 1830, it was almost universally accepted that a parish lacking a parochial school was gravely defective, and the kind of education given to children was generally recognized as a matter in which the statesman, no less than the parent, the clergyman, and the educationist, was legitimately interested. Some parishes seemed tragically incapable of supporting a school, and other parishes were still school-less with no good reason. Very few churchmen can still have doubted, by 1830, that a parish was incomplete without an educational apparatus.

In a way this educational function ascribed to the parish was only an extension, through the adoption of new devices, of the age-old establishment function of inculcating contentment and piety. But the old standard means of inculcating them, the sermon, the homily, the catechism, and the clergyman's pastoral energy, were increasingly felt to be inadequate without new institutional aids. For one thing, the clergyman was now often a cut or two above the bulk of his flock; the familiarity between superior and inferior, which he would sometimes most earnestly cultivate, could never be quite as close or affectionate as it had been a century or so earlier when their class distinction was usually less marked. For another thing, there was more going on—more movement from place to place, more news in the village of the rest of the world, more social aspiration and more likelihood of gratifying it. The country parish was no doubt sometimes as tranquil as it always had been; but there can be no doubt either that the heavy swell of social and economic change must often have tossed some intimations of an ever more restless and sophisticated society over the parochial boundaries. Yates clearly enough saw it happening.[1] Peacock's Dr Folliott, who abhorred 'the learned friend' and saw the March of Mind in the burglary of his house and the questionable proceedings of his cook and butler, was no mere fiction.[2] The mild and misanthropic incumbent of Camerton blamed Brougham for the troubles at his Somerset rectory. 'I understood at breakfast', he recorded in the summer of 1828 'that the servants

[1] e.g. *Church in Danger*, pp. 81–6, and *Basis of National Welfare*, pp. 60–1.
[2] See *Crotchet Castle* (1830), *passim*, but especially ch. 2.

154

made heavy complaints of their beds and accommodations, telling Anna that it was like a farmhouse more than a gentleman's. . . . This is the march of intellect with a vengeance. I wish Mr. Brougham had only a tythe of what I am obliged to submit to from the lower orders.'[1] How could the establishment keep control of these rising dangers but by a more resolute use of the old devices, and a bold introduction of the new— Sunday schools and ordinary schools, the Cheap Repository Tracts, distribution of Bibles and prayer-books, perhaps Bible-reading groups or cottage lectures, and non-stop parish visiting? This was the variety of old and new means by which the education of the lower orders, properly understood, was to be accomplished; and as the years went by, more and more such means were discovered—e.g. savings banks, benefit clubs, coal and clothing clubs and so on, allotments and district visiting societies; the value of which was not lessened by the power they gave to the clergy to discipline their parishioners by cutting off supplies.[2] By the end of the forties any good country parish might be expected to maintain the following: infant, day, evening, and Sunday schools; weekly lecture (M.W. or F., at 6), singing class, and Sunday lecture (2 p.m. in the Vestry); parochial library; school, coal, and rice funds; Provident Society (combining Savings Club, Clothes Club, and Sick Benefit Society); Baby Linen Society; allotments; and a branch of the S.P.G.[3]

The more disturbed the state of society became, the more urgent became the need for education. 'In times of public difficulty, such as the dearth of provisions,' said Bishop Barrington in 1797, 'we have too often and too recently discovered a tendency to discontent and disorder, not to be anxious for the application of some effectual remedy for so alarming an evil.'[4] Throughout his long and charitable life he set a good example to his clergy by taking up and using each new remedy that offered itself. Chief among those were the national schools systems that began to seem feasible soon after 1800. Barrington supported them with a nice mixture of zeal and caution; for their promise concealed the

---

[1] H. Coombs and H. N. Bax, *Journal of a Somerset Rector*, p. 172, entry of 5 July 1828.

[2] It was Dr Chalmers's eminence in this field of parochial organization, especially the principle of district visiting, that established his fame south of the border.

[3] Samuel Best, *Manual of Parochial Institutions* (2nd edn., 1849).

[4] *Sermons, Tracts and Charges*, p. 233.

danger that the wrong sort of education might 'indispose [the poor] to manual labour, and the more active duties of their humble, but most useful sphere'.[1] Even more eager, and even more resourceful, in the pursuit of social security was the celebrated Patrick Colquhoun, best known for his exact researches into London pauperism and crime, and much concerned with ridding society of both of them. The title of one of his works is an eloquent statement of the purposes of early nineteenth century education. In 1806 he promulgated *A New and Appropriate System of Education for the Labouring People as practised at the Free School at 19, Orchard Street, Westminster . . . with details explanatory of the particular economy of the institution, and the methods prescribed for the purpose of securing and preserving A Greater Degree of Moral Rectitude as a means of preventing criminal offences by habits of Temperance, Industry, Subordination and Loyalty among that useful class of the community comprising the Labouring People of England.* This was perfectly representative of the dominant attitude among the upper orders towards the education of the lower. It was both ideological and vocational. Some men would fasten more onto the one, some onto the other, branch of it. Colquhoun was more interested in its vocational aspect, the preparation of the children of the poor for the life of unremitting toil they must lead, and (which was an integral part of it in the minds of the humane) their training in the habits and attitudes that alone could make such a life bearable. The ideological side was obviously more to the front of the mind of that eminent lay churchman Lord Kenyon when, reproving Lord Liverpool for a certain laxness, he said he was sure Liverpool must share his own belief that 'if the mass of the Children of this Nation be not educated in the principles of the Established Church it is morally impossible that it, or the Government, can stand'.[2]

Both sides were held in a reasonable balance by Robert Southey, who time and again, in pamphlet, book, and *Quarterly* article, hammered home the necessity of education. In one of his crispest polemical pieces he said the children of the poor 'must be taught to "fear God and keep his commandments, for this is the whole duty of man". Mere reading

---

[1] *Ibid.* pp. 109–10, in the course of his recommendation of Sunday schools to the clergy of Salisbury diocese, 1789. The whole passage is a ripe example of the indoctrinating view of education.

[2] Letter of 31 October 1818. Brit. Mus. Add. MSS 38274, fo. 49.

and writing will not do this: they must be instructed according to the established religion; they must be fed with the milk of sound doctrine, for states are secure in proportion as the great body of the people are attached to the institutions of their country. . . . Give us the great boon of parochial education, so connected with the Church as to form part of the Establishment, and we shall find it a bulwark to the State as well as to the Church.'[1]

Southey combined this common view of education for political reasons—upon which he was emphatic indeed—with enlightened, even 'progressive', views about the value of education in helping its objects to happier and larger-minded lives, views more commonly found among the March of Mind men.

Here is the gist of the question [he wrote to a friend while working on his *Colloquies*]. The human mind is like the earth, which never lies idle. You have a piece of garden ground. Neglect it, and it will be covered with weeds, useless to yourself and noxious to your neighbours. To lay it out in flowers and shrubbery is what you do not want. Cultivate it then for common fruits and culinary plants. So with poor children. Why should they be made worse servants, worse labourers, worse mechanics, for being taught their Bible, their Christian duties, and the elements of useful knowledge? I am no friend of the London University, nor to Mechanics' Institutes. . . . But . . . my principle, is, that where a religious foundation is laid, the more education the better. Will you have the lower class *Christians* or *brutes*?[2]

The indifference of so many *soi-disant* friends of the church to real education saddened Southey; and, since he was so conspicuously a friend of the church himself, and so rootedly antipathetic to Brougham and his supporters, his statements about them carry the more weight.[3] Lamenting in 1812 the miserable quality of the bishops, he saw the church's only hope in the spread of education. If only the National Society (then very new) 'were formed into an outwork for the Church,

[1] *Letter to William Smith* (1817), pp. 35–6. Cf. the passage cited from his *Colloquies*, above, p. 13.

[2] Letter to the Rev. Neville White, 5 May 1827. *Life and Correspondence of Southey*, ed. C. C. Southey, v, 287–8.

[3] This, and the comment of Joshua Watson's next quoted, are two representative pieces of evidence that make it difficult to take, without a pinch of salt, H. J. Burgess's insistence that the National Society did not originate as a counter-stroke to the B. & F.B.S. and that it had a high educational ideal from the start. See his very useful book *Enterprise in Education*, ch. 2. A rather different approach to this question may be seen in the [*Cambridge*] *Historical Journal*, XII (1956), 155 ff.

you would breed up the great mass of people in attachment to its institutions. Perceval would have done this: but between indifference and bigotry the system at present has little chance. Something will be done while Lancaster[1] continues to frighten the higher clergy; take away that stimulus, and they will relapse into their former supineness.' The new bishop of London, John Randolph, and his party in the National Society 'would cram the children with the Catechism and be very glad, if they could, to teach them nothing else'.[2] Just a few years later, Joshua Watson, qualified above all others to speak the mind of the National Society, was corresponding with Bishop Ryder about it, and wrote that he was glad to find that they agreed 'that it matters comparatively little how much, or even how well, we teach our children in the week-day, if we do not carry them to church on the Sunday'.[3]

It is not surprising to find two Whigs, the one more, the other less, involved with the March of Mind, making criticisms very similar to Southey's. Francis Horner told Malthus, when the National Society was only just coming out of its shell, that he could not but 'feel strong suspicions against the sincerity of all recent converts, especially from a prejudice which seemed but very lately so inveterate, as that of church-men against the education of the lower classes'.[4] About the same time Sydney Smith told Lady Holland, 'We are about to have a meeting at York respecting the Education of the poor in the principles of Tithe paying, etc. etc. . . . it will never do. That the Church should make itself useful, and bestir itself to diffuse secular knowledge among the poor and continue to do so for any length of time is scarcely credible. I believe it is only a plan to prevent little boys from learning at Lancasters, and that a sort of Sham Multiplication Table will be introduced, teaching them all wrong. . . .'[5]

Sydney Smith thought it could not last, in which he was wrong. It not

---

[1] The founding genius of the British & Foreign.

[2] Letter to the Rev. Herbert Hill, 1 September 1812. *Selections from Southey's Letters*, ed. J. W. Warter, II, 291–2. He concluded, 'But this will never do; if the understanding and the hearts of the people are not with the Church, their hands will soon be against it.'

[3] E. Churton, *Memoir of Joshua Watson*, I, 217.

[4] Letter of 8 February 1812, in *Memoirs and Correspondence of Horner*, ed. L. Horner, II, 98.

[5] Letter of 7 January 1812, in *Letters of Sydney Smith*, ed. Nowell C. Smith, I, 219.

only lasted but it grew without stop. But Smith's estimate of the purpose of the movement for national education in its early years was substantially confirmed by what had later to be written in defence of education by two rather liberal Anglicans, more distinctly liberal than Southey, and more distinctly Anglican than Smith. William Otter, friend of Malthus, first principal of King's College, London, and bishop of Chichester for the four years preceding his death in 1840, published some excellent *Reasons for continuing the Education of the Poor at the present crisis*.[1] He was anxious to combat the notion that the bad spirit abroad in the nation was due to education. Rather, he maintained, was it due to insufficient education. The education given in the national schools surely could not be considered dangerous or too much. 'Of the propriety and, indeed, of the necessity of confining the Education of the Poor within such sober limits as their situation may require—of attending cautiously to the quality of the Instruction communicated to them—and of excluding everything which may give them a taste for the occupations, or a relish for the pleasures of the higher ranks—none can be more convinced than the Patrons of these Institutions. . . .' It was, in his view, scarcely consistent with that general liberty of which Englishmen were justly proud, to keep the poor poor and reduce them to total dependence on their superiors; and, in a noble phrase, it was hazardous 'to take refuge in ignorance from the terrors of sedition'.[2] And so he went on, to defend education on all grounds, including that of public economy: namely, that it would be cheaper in the long run for the community to spend money on education so as to reduce the cost of the prisons and poor-laws, which thrived on the fruits of ignorance and bestiality. This argument was to be more and more employed by educationists as the years passed.

Much the same point of view was pressed thirty years later in what amounted to a review of the National Society's progress to that date, and

---

[1] Shrewsbury, 1820. It was an assize sermon. Similar in sense and moderation, though far less elaborate, was the Vicar of Andover and Hursley, Gilbert Heathcote's *Address to the Principal Farmers, Churchwardens and Overseers of small towns and country villages on the subject of introducing Dr Bell's System of Instruction*, which gives one a vivid sense of the depth of prejudice there could be against even the most elementary education.

[2] *Op. cit.* pp. 5–8.

criticism of it, by Richard Dawes, the distinguished rector of King's Somborne, Hampshire, whose parish schools were a cynosure of the age and whose intelligence and educational enlightenment have never been seriously questioned.[1] Intemperately attacked by Archdeacon Denison's high-church backwoodsmen for not cramming his pupils with catechism, he took the side of the central education department against the obscurantists and doctrinaire high churchmen of the National Society and tore them limb from limb in 1850 in his *Remarks occasioned by the present Crusade against the Educational Plans of the Committee of Council on Education*. The bulk of the National Society's schools, judging from his description of them, were just the same as they had been in Otter's day—devoted to the ideals of subordination and indoctrination. The uneducated were kept by them so nearly uneducated as to be permanently sealed off from the higher classes—kept, in fact, as a permanent pool of peasantry for the convenience of the farmers and gentry. He described the National Society as, 'in some measure, a national deception', that had collected millions of money and wasted it through 'attempting to educate on a principle of forcing children into the church, not from a feeling that education is in itself a great good, and will add to the happiness of mankind and make them better in every social relation of life, even should they not be members of the church; nor have they succeeded in getting them to it. In this respect even they have failed.'[2] There is little doubt that Dawes was as right in his judgment, as he was certainly right in his facts. The agricultural labourer might have to go to church more often than his urban brother but his heart was not in it. The number of yokels present at church-parade in a well-disciplined country parish was no more reliable an index of real church feeling than the number of undergraduates attending compulsory college chapel; but it could deceptively seem so to churchmen like Denison and Manning who could imagine no good society but a strictly subordinated one. Dawes saw deeper and further, as did Charles Kingsley. It was just about this time that he put into the mouth of one of his characters the prophecy, 'Woe to Toryism and the Church of

---

[1] See the account given of his schools by C. K. F. Brown, *The Church's Part in Education*, pp. 32–4, Burgess, *op. cit.* pp. 135–6, and W. F. Connell, *Educational Thought and Influence of Matthew Arnold*, pp. 54, 66.

[2] *Op. cit.* pp. 7–12.

England and everything else, when it gets to boasting that its stronghold is still in the hearts of the agricultural poor!'[1]

Instruction in schools and by sermons was only the most systematic, formal means of social control practised in a good parish, and it was not necessarily as callous as it sometimes seems. Can Paley and all who practised the same persuasions really have been honest in their attempts to blarney the lower orders with *Reasons for Contentment?*[2] It is almost impossible to think so; but it is certain that they were often actuated by the most benevolent motives in preaching such stuff, and in preaching more powerful doctrine still.[3] If you unquestioningly accepted Christ's words, 'the poor will be always with you', as revealed truth, and understood 'poor' in a strictly economic sense; if you were well acquainted with the miseries of poverty, and depressed by the way the poor, with their ignorant, custom-bound, improvident ways, seemed so largely incapable of alleviating their miseries; if you could imagine (as the poor probably could not) the nature and consequences of a *jacquerie*, as well as sympathetically inderstand how natural it was for the lower orders to break out in one; if, after about 1800, you could not help believing that Malthus was rather right than wrong, and so on; if you were honestly of this way of thinking, it might seem the truest kindness to try to persuade the poor they were better off than they thought, and at all costs to keep them where they were, lest worse befall. Sensible and virtuous poor people, moreover, would co-operate with their betters in this endeavour to avert the dissolution of society, and not merely in a passive way. At the height of the 'labourers' revolt' of the winter of 1830–1, Hurrell Froude wrote, 'The labouring population, as well as the farmers, seem

[1] *Alton Locke*, ch. 32.

[2] The title of a much-valued sermon of Paley's, first preached in 1793, 'addressed to the Labouring Part of the British Public'. (*Sermons and Tracts*, p. 155 ff.). One of the most astonishing parts of Paley's argument is closely parallelled by Burke in his *Reflections, ed. cit.* IV, 112. One only doubts whether Paley did not have his tongue in his cheek, because he was capable of sly humour in the most unexpected places (see, e.g. the paragraph on the epiglottis in his *Natural Theology*, ch. 10, sec. v, for introducing me to which I am indebted to the Rev. G. F. Woods).

[3] Just as it is certain that the Tory gentleman who believed in strict subordination and was ready to go to any lengths to enforce it, might be devoting much of his income and energy to the pursuit of his idea of social improvement.

thoroughly indifferent to the welfare of the parsons and squires.'¹ This
inversion of the usual order of responsibility reads oddly, to a modern
ear. Given Froude's aristocratic outlook and gift for startling language,
it made sense enough.

Poverty, more or less (and in the England of Malthus and the decennial
censuses, rather more than less), was believed by most upper-class folk,
as it had been since the beginning of time, to be the natural state of the
majority of mankind. It was unpleasant, yes; but better poverty and
order, than anarchy and enslavement or extinction. Burke spoke of 'the
innumerable servile, degrading, unseemly, unmanly, and often most
unwholesome and pestiferous occupations, to which by the social
economy so many wretches are inevitably doomed'.² Sir William Scott
admitted in the Commons in 1812 'that the expense of the law, in many
cases, pressed with peculiar hardship on the poor; but still he feared, that
this circumstance was inseparable from the condition of human society'.³
Inseparable, inevitable, inescapable—these were the adjectives that most
conservatives and many liberals of the upper orders automatically
applied in descriptions of the hardships of the poor.⁴ 'It is a painful
reflection but not less true on that account that we can never get into a
good system, after so long persevering in a bad one, but by much
previous suffering of the poor. . . .'⁵ 'Circumstances are at work in every
part of this country, not more affecting its manufacturing than its
agricultural population, which leave little to expect for a large propor-

¹ Letter of 9 January 1831, in his *Remains*, I, 245. There is something of the same
tone in H. J. Rose's rejection of an American friend's notion that the English poor
were so depressed because the upper orders were so privileged. 'I am unable to trace
any necessary connexion between the two things', he naturally replied; 'in my mind,
the low state of our poor arises from the poor laws, which make the rich the slaves of
the poor, and the poor the slaves of the parish officers.' W. Berrian, in Memoir prefixed to *Bishop Hobart's Works*, I, 351, citing a letter of 16 March 1826.

² *Reflections, ed. cit.* IV, 177–8.

³ 23 January 1812. *Hansard*, XXI, 308.

⁴ Southey, as so often, held rather different views from the bulk of his party about
poverty. He believed cautiously but firmly in progress, and was inclined 'to think
there will come a time when public opinion will no more tolerate the extreme of
poverty in a large class of the community, than it now tolerates slavery in Europe'.
See, e.g., his letters of 30 November 1814 and 2 October 1816 in his *Life and
Correspondence*, ed. C. C. Southey, IV, 87 ff. and 213 ff.

⁵ Bonar and Hollander, *Ricardo's letters to Trower*, p. 25: letter of 27 January 1817.

tion of its inhabitants except hardships and difficulties. . . .'[1] 'Our civilisation has had the effect of dooming numberless millions of human beings to an existence of perpetual labour, to profound ignorance, and to sufferings as difficult to remedy as they are undeserved. . . .'[2]

The question here is not whether these men were right or wrong, sensible or silly, to believe these things, but how these beliefs were related to their ideas about the church establishment. Bishop Sumner continued thus, after recognizing the 'hardships and difficulties' of the poor, 'Religion is not more really necessary to these than it is to every man. But those are more really destitute without it, who in this world "have evil things". And further, it is the only remedy which we can offer.' But his definition of religion was very wide; for his 1829 Charge included much practical advice for helping the poor, by the staple means of efficient parochial oversight. J. B. Sumner was, after all, one of the greatest promoters of new churches and schools, a very practical and moderate Evangelical, unusually aware of what was going on in the great towns of his huge diocese; and in his early Charges he recommended to his clergy's attention almost every known device of establishment control. He was especially keen on District Visiting Societies, rather on the model of Chalmers's organization of his Glasgow parish, which was at that time much admired. They enabled an incumbent to manage a parish as he could in no other way; 'numerous parishes', he said, 'have been brought under such discipline with more or less success'. He went on to quote at length from the reports of the Brighton society, whose aims and conduct he especially admired: 'Experience has taught us that it is impossible to go among forty families [each Visitor's allocation] and exercise these acts of judicious kindness without insuring their respect and affection. The poor are found to be grateful beyond expectation; and get so attached to the Visitors as to resemble a large family. The Visitors are thus able to obtain a great moral influence over the district.' Thus, commented the bishop, would you keep a parish 'really *under pastoral superintendence*'.[3]

Exactly the same kind of attitude towards the lower orders was

---

[1] J. B. Sumner's *Charge to the Clergy of the Diocese of Chester*, 1829.

[2] Peel, according to the Comte de Jarnac's account of a conversation with him, in 1847. *Private Letters of Sir Robert Peel*, pp. 285–6.

[3] *Op. cit.* pp. 24–39.

displayed by William Lyall, Archdeacon of Colchester from 1824 to 1841, one of the most eminent and intelligent high churchmen of his day. In his 1833 Charge, in which he discussed (with a firmness of principle, depth of understanding, and moderation of language that were very rare in combination at that critical time) the nature of the establishment and the question of church reform, he turned in conclusion to the church's duty in respect of 'the labouring classes of the community'.

Take away the restraints of religion from their minds [he said] and immediately all the arrangements of society became changed in their eyes, as if seen through a distorting medium. . . . It makes all the difference in the view of a man who can with difficulty earn his daily bread, whether the subordination of ranks, and the inequalities of condition in society, be considered by him as founded upon God's will, or merely upon the will of his fellow men. Bid him understand that these things are of human contrivance—and rulers and superiors become in his eyes only so many taskmasters, whom he is compelled to serve—the laws under which he lives, merely the instruments of that oppression, by which his labour is exacted. The belief in God is, in the moral world, what the principle of gravitation is in the physical—that which binds all the discordant elements in one harmonious system.[1]

'One harmonious system' . . . the social ideal men have always longed for. Whether commercial or agricultural, sophisticated or simple, it was a harmony, a community of feeling between man and man, that the social reformers and the social stabilizers alike in the early nineteenth century sought to establish. Some of them had their model in a golden age gone by—Cobbett in his dream of a virtuous, prosperous, independent peasantry, Pugin and Lord John Manners and Peacock's Mr Chainmail in their dream (Cobbett's, seen from the postern gate) of an ideal feudalism; a few of them saw it coming through socialism and cooperation, more saw it in a general acceptance of the, as they thought, self-evident truths of political economy; and neither the socialists nor the political economists, confident of the excellence of their doctrine and the power of education, thought their ideal difficult of attainment. The more or less backward-looking men, the stabilizers, the men who assumed that 'every community, every individual, is interested in the *stability* of the times in which they live . . . times in which no fearful events occur to disquiet men's minds, or to interrupt them in the dis-

[1] *Charge to the Clergy of the Archdeaconry of Colchester*, p. 23.

charge of their duties',[1] from the medievalists to the conservatives of the landed interest, felt that a real community of beliefs between different classes of the community was not so easily to be had, and never expected to be able to do without some force to supply its natural weaknesses; but their ideal was the same as that of the progressives. They might see—as Lyall for instance saw—that the different classes of a community could come to dislike and fear one another; they were aghast at the idea of a state's having to live with such social dislike and fear embodied within it. Robert Owen preaching socialist co-operation, Harriet Martineau preaching individualist economics, and William Lyall preaching establishment Christianity, were all pointing, in their different ways, to the creation or restoration of 'the good society', one of whose main characteristics was its social solidarity, unmarred by envy, malice, and all uncharitableness.

In the churchman's idea of 'the good society', the parish and the parish clergyman had naturally an eminent place. Here was the little, manageable sphere within which social relations could be best regulated and improved, and here was the man—officer of both church and state—to supervise them. The more imaginative parochial idealists pictured the parson's relation to his parish as that of a father to his family. 'Every parish being in itself a little commonwealth, it is easy to conceive', wrote Southey in one of his big *Quarterly* articles, 'that before manufactures were introduced, or where they do not exist, a parish, where the minister and the parochial officers did their duty with activity and zeal, might be almost as well ordered as a private family'.[2] In Archbishop Howley's much more conventional mind the stereotype of the parson was of one who appeared 'in the midst of his Parishioners, like an Angel of God with a message of grace to each individual, administering commendation or censure, rebuke or encouragement, admonition or comfort, and adapting his language and manner, with parental consideration and tender-

[1] Bishop Van Mildert's *Durham Assize Sermon*, 1834, p. 9. He went on to remark that in times of commotion the poor suffered just as much as the rich 'in those private relationships which constitute the chief enjoyment of social life'.

[2] In a review of Yates's books etc., *Quarterly Review*, XXIII (1820), 564, where he also spoke, as a good establishment man naturally would, of 'the political as well as the religious purposes of our old parochial system, if we may be permitted to consider apart things which are, strictly speaking, inseparable'. A list of Southey's contributions to the *Quarterly* can be seen in his *Life & Correspondence*, ed. C. C. Southey, VI, 397 ff.

ness, to every man's particular condition'.[1] Bishop Sumner admired the way a parish might be turned into 'a large family'.[2] The rival *Reviews* could draw quite close together when imagining the ideal parish minister. The *Edinburgh*, lamenting the tendency of the poor laws to create unkindly feelings between farmers and labourers, found some comfort in the idea of the clergyman mediating between them;[3] the *Quarterly* spoke similarly of the clergyman's being ideally placed 'for bracing the upper and lower orders of society together. . . . His line is clear and precise . . . to plead for the landlord with the tenants, and for the tenants with the landlord—and so to encourage the one to be content, and the other to be considerate.'[4] It saw in this function an additional argument for endowments. It was the church's endowments that happily rendered the mediator independent of both parties, 'and thus above suspicion in his interference'.

But the clergyman was not, in what the church idealists considered a good parish, left on his own to run it properly. In his fancied mediatorial role, he was necessarily independent. As guide, guardian, and friend, however, he was to have the gentry of the parish by his side. The 'cultivated gentleman' idea of the parochial system—that it put mind, virtue, and refinement into the social structure by maintaining, in the person of the incumbent, eleven thousand or so pious and cultivated gentlemen up and down the land—made it possible for the church, at a pinch, to do its great work unaided; but the clergyman was better not left unaided, and it was taken for granted by virtually all expositors of the theory of the establishment, that squire and parson, pulpit and property, should sink or swim together. Their roles were complementary and equally indispensable in the churchman's ideal society. From the parson in his professional character came 'instruction in life and consolation in death'; from the squire (in 'the big house') came succour in time

---

[1] *Charge to the Clergy of the Diocese of Canterbury*, 1832, p. 29. Men like Van Mildert and Howley, who had been taught to refuse on principle to consider on their merits ideas or alleged facts that lay outside their rules, clearly had great difficulty in responding to new ideas and facts that beat their way through the barriers of set responses and defences, and imperatively demanded recognition on their own terms. They paid the penalty of seeming stupid for having done and said the correct thing for so long that it became nature to them. [2] Above, p. 163.

[3] *Edinburgh Review*, XLIV (1826), 501.

[4] *Quarterly Review*, XLIX (1833), 202.

of need, and hands and funds to run the parochial institutions; from parson and squire alike came valuable influences of personal cultivation and political good conduct, enforced partly by example, partly by what the statesmen of the time called 'the just influence of property'. They were, together, or *ought* to be, 'the influencing class'. 'Do I tremble at the Threats and wicked Professions of the Radicals in my native County and its Contiguities?' demanded one clergyman of Lord Liverpool when beginning to toady him for a deanery. 'I do not. But I lament their ignorance and delusion, which would never have existed had the influencing Class, consisting of the Clergy and Gentry etc. of those Districts caused a Portion of the immense Accumulation of Wealth created by their Labours to be appropriated to the erection of Schools and Churches. . . .'[1] 'As long as the country gentlemen continue what they are', wrote Lord Sidmouth in a time of troubles, 'the disaffected will never succeed in exciting rebellion, or in effecting a revolution.'[2]

Allusions to the role of the gentry in the ideal parochial system often displayed the same blend of fact and fancy and the same assured self-congratulation that gave to so many contempory descriptions of the constitution and its component parts a faint air of the ridiculous. Bishop Porteus found in his neighbourhood in Kent 'that judicious mixture of society and refinement, which constitute the true felicity of human life, and which so remarkably and so fortunately distinguish the gentry and nobility of England from almost all other countries in Europe'.[3] Vicesimus Knox in like manner lauded their respectability and usefulness, and scanned the continent in vain for anything like them; he also emphasized their affinities with the clergy, regarding the latter 'not merely as clerical and ecclesiastical persons; but as gentlemen, possessing the qualities of true gentlemen in mind, manners, and accomplishments'.[4] A *Quarterly* reviewer spoke of English country gentility as

[1] Letter from F. W. Holme of Fairford, Gloucestershire, to Lord Liverpool, 15 November 1819. Brit. Mus. Add. MSS 38281, fos. 30–1. The request for the deanery came on 10 December (*ibid.* fo. 255 ff.).

[2] Letter to Mr Loraine Smith, 3 December 1820, in Pellew, *Life of Sidmouth*, III, 336.

[3] R. Hodgson, *Life of Porteus* (2nd edn. 1811), pp. 30–1. He further remarked that most of them were 'not only polished in their manners, but of exemplary piety, probity, and benevolence'.

[4] *Remarks on a Bill to degrade Grammar Schools* (2nd edn. 1821), p. 14. Reprinted in *The Pamphleteer*, XIX (1822), 262.

'that pure retreat of simple pretensions, elegant sufficiency, and intellectual tastes, the proudest boast of our island. . . .'[1] This sounds a pretty fair description of the society of Netherfield and Mansfield Park, Ullathorne and the big house at Alington; but we know from the same reliable authors that have described these homes, that there was also the society of Rosings and Norland Park, Box Hill and Gatherum Castle. An author more satirical but much more pointed in his criticism, has assured us that besides Fitzwilliam Darcy, there was also Sir Simon Steeltrap and his like, who devoted themselves to 'game-bagging, poacher-shooting, trespasser-pounding, footpath-stopping, common-enclosing, rack-renting, and all the other liberal pursuits and pastimes which make a country gentleman an ornament to the world, and a blessing to the poor'.[2]

How large a proportion of the gentry at any one time were kindly and responsible, is a question that only the local historian will be able to answer. The biggest single factor in determining whether the big house was a blessing or not was the number of months for which it was occupied. Non-residence was as much a bane in the lay department of social control as in the clerical. Tories who cared, like Liverpool and Peel, Harrowby and Southey, attributed the greater part of Ireland's miseries to the lack of a regular resident gentry, and toyed with the idea of fiscal legislation to penalize non-residence. In the words of William Wilberforce, no one respected more than he the character of a 'nobleman or gentleman who lives on his own property in the country, improving his land, executing the duties of the magistracy, exercising hospitality and diffusing comfort, and order, and decorum, and moral improvement, and though last not least (where it has any place) religion too, throughout the circle, greater or smaller, which he fills'. Taxes ought to be differentiated to the advantage of such. 'For in fact your country gentlemen are the nerves and ligatures of your political body, and they enable you to enforce laws which could not be executed by the mere power of government, and often preserve the public peace better than a regiment

---

[1] Review of Mary Russell Mitford's *Our Village* in the *Quarterly Review*, xxxi (1824), 167.

[2] T. L. Peacock, *Crotchet Castle*, ch. 1. See also the more detailed account of Sir Simon in ch. 5.

of soldiers. London', he continued, by a very natural association of ideas, 'is the gangrene of our body politic . . .'[1]

London epitomized the general urban problem that became so acute, and so widely recognized as such, during Wilberforce's lifetime. The trouble with big towns was, that the ordinary machinery of social control, the quiet customary alliance of church and gentry, working more by attractive influence and unostentatious pressure than by bluster or bayonet, could not operate there. There the clergyman was destitute of the gentry's support. The middling classes might be dissenters. The occupations of the lower orders in towns and cities, and the relations they consequently stood in to their superiors, were not as conducive as those of the countryside to the maintenance of a more or less happy subordination of classes. Archbishop Howley despairingly said of 'the accumulated population of large towns' that, 'from its denseness and the peculiarity of its character', it could 'never enjoy the full benefits of religious instruction'.[2] Conservative churchmen, who very likely shared with Hurrell Froude 'that transcendental idea of the English gentleman which forms the basis of Toryism',[3] could not like or understand the growing towns and cities, or regard the wholly industrial way of life as anything other than a perversion of the proper course of nature. Their ideal parish was thus ill-suited to the new England. It was 'sweet Auburn, loveliest village of the plain', around whose supposed virtues of harmonious decent living and peaceful simplicity their imaginations passionately played, and to which their Victorian successors were wont to look back with pious nostalgia. G. M. Young, who has some excellent paragraphs on this theme, has neatly placed it in its proper and, it would not be too much to say, momentous setting. 'To this picture English sentiment clung, as Roman sentiment saw in the Sabine farm the home of virtue and national greatness. It inspired our poetry; it controlled our art; for long it obstructed, perhaps it still obstructs, the formation of a true philosophy of urban life.'[4]

---

[1] Letter to the Earl of Galloway, 3 December 1800, in his *Correspondence*, ed. R. I. and S. Wilberforce (1840), I, 219.

[2] Letter to Peel, 30 January 1835. Brit. Mus. Add. MSS 40412, fos. 207–8.

[3] Tom Mozley, *Reminiscences, chiefly of Oriel College and the Oxford Movement*, I, 226.

[4] *Victorian England: Portrait of an Age* (1936 edn.), pp. 21–2. It seems significant that

Certainly it obstructed the established church's attempts to fit itself into the slums and crowded dingy housing estates that were coming to shelter more and more of the lower orders. Dreams of a golden age were no preparation for an age of brass. In the new urban parish, nothing was the same, and not all the district visitors and paternal factory-owners in the world could make it so. Instead of 'the green and quiet churchyard', upon whose implicit poetry and patent charm Southey relied for much of the church's instinctive hold on men's affections,[1] you were likelier to have one of the nauseating, death-spreading burial-grounds that became distinguished among the menaces to public health. The very church-bell, in the town, was often more of a nuisance than an attraction. The incumbent was usually hard put to it in the new district churches of 1820 onwards to find a *locus standi* in his community; and what there was in the way of a community was increasingly likely to be made up of persons of one class only, and that the lowest. Whatever its class was, the one-class parish was from many points of view a distressing new phenomenon. None of its features was more regrettable, considering its mixed political and religious functions, than the absence from it of the gentry. Ideally, they and the clergy should co-operate closely to run a good parish and so create a good society. None saw this more clearly than Charles James Blomfield. Called to give evidence before the Commons' Committee on Sabbath Day Observance in 1832, he was asked whether it would not do much good if the higher classes 'concurred with the clergy and with the magistrates in acting by admonition and not by legal means?' 'I have no doubt,' he replied, 'except as to the towns. I do not think the higher classes have their legitimate influence there, as they have, or may have, in the country, where, if they could go hand in hand with the clergy, I have no doubt it would be so.'[2] And it was for calling his clergy's attention to this, that Sydney Smith thus caricatured Blomfield's first instructions to his clergy as bishop of Chester:

when Dickens wanted to portray the ideal Sunday, he set it in a moss and ivy-covered village church in the west-country, with a kind old minister who chatted to the healthy young parishioners as they left, and superintended their cricket in the evening. See Humphry House, *The Dickens World* (1942), p. 125.

[1] See his article in the *Quarterly Review*, XXIII (1820), 558.

[2] P.Ps. 1831–2, VII, 502; Q. 3875. See also Qs. 2827–8.

Hunt not, fish not, shoot not,
Dance not, fiddle not, flute not;
But it is my particular desire
That once a week you take
Your dinner with the Squire.[1]

It was generally admitted that the church, as it actually was, failed to carry out its vital role, most of all in the towns but also in the country districts to which alone the ideal pattern was suited. Those who knew or cared at all about the towns and cities were forced, as their size and condition became increasingly worrying, towards a sad recognition that their ideal could only with extreme difficulty be translated into terms that were at once appropriate and effective for them. It is possible for us now to see, what the furthest-sighted were already seeing by the eighteen-twenties, that the church's needs were desperate and the pace of its reforms, through this critical half-century, far too slow.

The first impediment to remedial action seems to have been that many did not see the problem in terms either clear or urgent—particularly country gentlemen with no direct experience of urban problems. Even Sir Robert Peel seems to have been surprised, in 1835, to learn that an impropriator could be getting two thousand a year from a huge parish while paying less than fifty as its vicar's stipend; and that the incumbent of the biggest parish in Nottingham (a disorderly, radical city) should be entirely dependent for his income on pew-rents and Easter Offerings.[2] These were typical examples of major church defects, which specialists in the subject had known about for over two centuries, and which could not have surprised Spencer Perceval, Richard Yates, or Robert Southey. But Peel was surprised when he came across them. He simply had not known. He could not believe his eyes when he read a pamphlet (sent to him by an anonymous well-wisher) about the work of the Society for Clothing Indigent Establishment Clergy. Were these things true, he

---

[1] There seem to be other versions of this. A longer one, related by the Rev. Arthur Hubbard to Lord Raglan in 1852, is given by Mark Boyd, *Reminiscences of Fifty Years* (1871), p. 341.

[2] Letter to Goulburn, 29 January 1835, in the Goulburn Papers, II/18, at Kingston. The version printed in Parkers' *Peel*, II, 283, is sadly mutilated. Mathieson, *op. cit.* p. 114, correctly points out that it was the principle involved in this Nottingham case that was distressing. The incumbent, a pluralist, was actually doing quite well.

asked the Archbishop? Howley reluctantly had to assure him that they were, and that the Society was genuine, though cliquey.[1] In like case was Bishop Kaye. He said in 1838 that until he saw the material for the second report of the Ecclesiastical Commissioners he 'had formed no adequate conception of the [spiritual] destitution of the manufacturing districts and of the large towns'.[2] It may seem to us that the material for forming that 'adequate conception' was available well before 1830, and that Kaye must have been stupid to miss it or disingenuous in saying that he had missed it. Nothing else in Kaye's life suggests stupidity, and dis-ingenuousness at that point of his argument would not in fact have assisted him in the polemical task he had in hand. Of Kaye the same must be believed as of Peel; he simply had not known.

There are other and more impressive reasons still to account for the slowness of the governing classes' response to the urgent demands of church reform: the aristocratic and authoritarian character of the old establishment; the adamantine fixedness of the antipathy towards change and reform in some sectors of the governing class; the high-principled denial by conservatives in general that the aristocratic institutions of church and state were politically accountable; and the intrinsic difficulties of church reform.

First, consider the authoritarian and aristocratic character of the idea of the old establishment. Its conservative exponents assumed that it possessed a natural, inalienable, and irrefutable title to deference. It was after all a teaching church, entrusted by the state with the responsibility of bringing up the people 'in the way they should go'; and by the common notions of the Christian world at that epoch, the teacher had to stand in an authoritative relation towards the taught. There could be (so ran the argument) no questioning the value of the establishment's func-tion, nor any discussion, except in the safe seclusion of common-rooms and learned journals, about the correctness of what it taught. Men might not like what it told them, either about their social and political duties or about themselves, but that was their fault, not the church's; and if they absented themselves from the services of the church, they put themselves clearly in the wrong. Charity might restrain the joint-managers of

[1] Brit. Mus. Add. MSS 40412 fos. 52–72 and 101–2, letters of 27 and 28 January 1835.
[2] Letter to the Archbishop of Canterbury, in *Nine Charges of Bishop Kaye*, ed. W. F. J. Kaye, p. 171.

church and state from imposing upon these absentees the sanctions demanded alike by political security and religious principle. Ever since 1689 the dissenters had enjoyed a rare and enviable degree of civil and religious liberty; but the freedoms that had been allowed them to worship in their own way, and even to hold public offices, were, on this theory, freedoms granted of grace, not of right. In theory these freedoms could be abrogated, and in principle they were contradictory to the idea of a national church. It pained good conservative churchmen to find that some dissenters could not appreciate the reasonableness of the establishment's necessary legal and political superiority. 'We concede toleration freely and fully,' said Bishop Van Mildert; 'we claim only to be equally unmolested in our own privileges, and thus to preserve the relations of peace and amity. What more does Christian charity require?'[1]

The dissenters were thus expected not only to recognize the value of the national church as diffusing morality and piety, but also to recognize the justice of its political ascendancy.[2] Along with this ascendancy went inevitably its claims on every class and member of the population for financial support. Dissenters might not like paying, but they could produce none but specious arguments against doing so. No one had a right to be let off. The national church existed for everybody's benefit, and stood under the same obligation to help and serve the people as they stood under to help and serve it. If they were unfaithful children, choosing to worship elsewhere or not to worship at all, it would not harry them; and they enjoyed common-law rights to the use of the church-yard, to a seat in the church (circumstances of course usually made this right nugatory), and to the clergyman's services in burial, marriage, and baptism. Citizens could insist upon the exercise of these rights.[3] The church, in return, insisted on its services being accepted in proper prayer-book form, and on the burden of its maintenance being shouldered by the whole community: which meant, in the main, church rates.

[1] *Charge to the Clergy of the Diocese of Llandaff*, 1821, p. 23.

[2] It was doubtless in this belief that Lord Sidmouth seriously expected the more respectable dissenters to approve of his Bill in 1811 to regulate religious toleration.

[3] Very high churchmen of course liked to deny them when they got a chance to do so. Their principles were reprobated, and their conduct pronounced illegal, by the Dean of the Arches, Sir John Nicholl, in the celebrated case of *Kemp* v. *Wickes*. See his *Judgment delivered on* 11 *December* 1809 and the account given of the ensuing controversy in the *Quarterly Review*, VII (1812), 201–23.

The maintenance of the national church, continued its conservative apologists, was not in truth a heavy burden, because most of its maintenance money came from its endowments of property, mostly in lands or in tithes. (The more absurd and wicked, therefore, to object to tithes as a burden or to say, as the Quakers always said, that they were an affront to conscience.) These endowments were viewed as particularly fortunate and proper, on account of the independence they gave the clergyman to tell his flock what they needed to be told. A 'stipendiary' minister, like the average nonconformist, would incline to tell his flock rather what they wanted to hear. He would thus do less than his duty by them; their faults would go unreproved; and the moral quality of the community would suffer. If he took too independent a line, he must risk losing his flock, and with it the fleece; fear of losing the latter was expected effectually to control the quality of his pastorate. But his established brother need fear no such penalty for free-speech, for the established ministry, securely based on its endowments, had an impregnable redoubt to which to retire in days of unpopularity.

Thus the theory. Its inherent difficulties and improbabilities need no comment. It only made sense on the twin bases of an exacting theory of human nature, and a close correspondence between the membership of the civil and religious commonwealths. Both bases were unsound in the later eighteenth and early nineteenth centuries, the first because it would hardly ever be sound anyway, the second because of the growth of nonconformity. The second, and more obvious, problem has attracted the more attention. But it was from the first that the greater difficulty came. What made the theory particularly difficult sensibly to apply was its requirement that the national church should at once be beloved of the people, and yet parentally critical of them. Just as the parish clergyman was imaginatively presented as a kind of father to the whole of his flock, without distinction of age or class, so was the church's relationship with society likened to that of a father's with his family. His duty was to educate, to guide, to reprove, and to chastise them (without distinction of age or sex) as became necessary; theirs was to submit and follow, and still to love.

There was thus embedded in conservative thinking about the national church a principle that kept its supporters (or most of them) from viewing without at least some tremors of concern its failure to be 'popular' or wholly acceptable to 'public opinion'. 'Popularity' was of course a pejorative concept in conservative circles; it was the concern of the demagogue, the dissenter, and the buffoon; a stern truth, a good government, could not possibly expect to be 'popular'. Peel spoke in 1833 of 'the necessary unpopularity of all government (particularly when Governments do their duty)'.[1] The claims made by Whigs and radicals for the control of Government by public opinion, *alias* 'the spirit of the age', were bound to seem to conservatives not just wrong-headed but immoral. Irish public opinion was obviously much in favour of 'catholic emancipation'; the established protestant church of Ireland was very unpopular with the great majority of the Irish nation; but plenty of Tories were ready in 1829 to risk a civil war rather than 'truckle to the mob'. The principle at stake was too precious, too imperative, to play politics with.[2]

Not all conservatives were as ready to deny that a government's or a church's acceptability was irrelevant when 'principle' was at stake. Peel took enough of his party into the lobby with him to make up good majorities for what was in fact concession. He above all conservatives felt the necessity of treading a politic middle path between what was, in abstract, 'right', and what would in the circumstances make for contentment and prosperity; that was why he was able to save his party's fortunes in the thirties and bring them back to office in 1841. Although he saw the advisability of coming to terms with respectable public opinion, it gave him little pleasure to do so. He presented his change of policy, not as a concession to existing pressure, but a prudent and timely avoidance of awful pressures in the future. As early as 1820 he had warned his more extreme friend John Wilson Croker that a gap was opening between 'the tone of England—of that great compound of folly, weakness, prejudice, wrong feeling, right feeling, obstinacy and newspaper paragraphs, which is called public opinion', and the policy of the government.[3] For Whigs like Lord John Russell and Lord Palmerston, if they

[1] Letter to Goulburn, in Parker's *Peel*, II, 222–4, where the date is incorrectly given as 24 June 1833. The Goulburn Papers at Kingston, Box II/18, show that it was actually 16 August.

[2] See my article 'The Protestant Constitution and its Supporters' in *Trans. Royal Hist. Soc.*, VIII (1958), 105 ff., especially p. 108 n.

[3] *Correspondence and Diaries of Croker*, I, 170. To describe it he called it 'liberal—an odious but intelligible phrase'.

were wholly sincere in their professions, this accommodation to public opinion was an honourable and statesmanly duty; to Peel it was a disagreeable necessity. The Whig would achieve the required accommodation by following, if he had to; the conservative would try to achieve it by leading if he could. The business of politics was inevitably a less agreeable one in such an age for the conservative than for the liberal. The conservative would be battling with the winds, lashed to the wheel, and worrying forever about the rocks ahead, while for the liberal it was more likely to be a fine fast run before a following trade-wind. Southey, whose remarkably original and far-seeing conservative mind found more to alarm it in the development of the newspaper press and the political influence of public opinion than in most other characteristics of his time, thought that their conjoint power was 'the worst evil with which, in the present state of the world, civilized society is threatened'.[1] It may be doubted whether Peel had a much higher view of it; but he knew that government had to pay its respects to it all the same.

Between the ultra-conservative's refusal on principle to accommodate his policy to the demands of public opinion, and the convinced liberal's perfect readiness to do so, lay a broad range of possible attitudes. They led men to see and to evaluate the problems that faced them in different ways; and the problems of church reform were no exception. You might admit that much was wrong with the state of the church. A liberal reformer and a conservative might agree on a list of agenda; and yet the conservative might not feel the same obligation to get on with the job, and would certainly not feel obliged to set about it the same way. He would be less apologetic. He would not hesitate to keep the mob— even a mob in the respectable dark clothes of the dissenting bourgeoisie— at bay with bayonet and truncheon while his reforms, prudently planned and cautiously undertaken, took effect. Most of the clergy, and most also of the more influential lay friends of the church, were very conservative. That was one big reason why church reform went so slowly, and, incidentally, why Peel was never wholly liked or trusted by so many of his party.

The extremer conservative's insensitivity to change was often coupled with an obstinate prejudice against it. Lord Liverpool pointed its existence out to Bishop Tomline when the bishop asked whether

[1] *Colloquies*, I, 233–4.

parliamentary sanction could be obtained for him to move the site of his official London residence. The prime minister feared there would be great opposition to such a proposal. 'In truth,' he replied, 'many of the staunchest Friends of the Establishment have a sort of Religious Respect for whatever is old, and connected with established Habits or preconceived Opinions, and they dread all Changes for this further Reason, that they are aware what Advantages may be taken of them by those whose only object is to destroy.'[1] In Ireland, where all the ordinary English conditions were exaggerated, this attitude was even more noticeable. Charles Grant met it soon after his appointment to Dublin Castle, when he wanted to effect some changes in the administration and objects of the Protestant Charter Schools, designed to make them at once more economical and more efficient. He was astonished at the opposition he aroused. 'To say the truth, it is not very easy to see how a measure can be deemed hostile to the Protestant interests or careless of them, the very object of which is to diffuse more widely a Protestant education. Nor ought the nature of the argument to which I refer be overlooked; for it goes to this, that a system allowed to be defective and expensive should be maintained, and the progress of improvement impeded, lest a change for the better should afford occasion for misconstruction.'[2] This kind of intransigence was not just the prerogative of the sillier members of the Eldonite party. It was a deeply ingrained, consciously high-principled part of the whole of their way of thinking. The archbishop of Armagh sent Liverpool a terrific denunciation of the Irish Tithes Bill which the prime minister and Goulburn had thought mild, reasonable, and necessary.[3] Among the many pejorative adjectives he used to describe it were: unjust, unconstitutional, irritating, vexatious, impracticable, theoretic, abstract, inapplicable, injurious. Croker, defending Eldon's court of chancery against those who wanted cases to get through it in less than the average five years or so, said it was 'the infirmity of human nature that falsehood, violence, and wrong are prompt and sudden; while the elucidation of truth, the proportioning of reparation, and the development of justice, are difficult, complicated, and

---

[1] Letter of 24 January 1821. Brit. Mus. Add. MSS 38289, fo. 45 ff.
[2] Letter to Liverpool, 13 January 1819. *Ibid.* 38275, fo. 51 ff.
[3] Letter of 14 February 1823. *Ibid.* 38292, fos. 196–7.

slow'.[1] There was no fruitful discussion between a liberal of any kind and a man who really could write of the unreformed court of chancery that way. He was in a different world. So was Richard Hurrell Froude, whose comments on foreign affairs in the revolutionary years 1830 and 1831 have the same flavour of political impossibility about them. On 1 August 1830: 'What a horrid affair this is in France. I admire the spirit of the King and Polignac . . .' Four weeks later: 'The fate of the poor King of France, whose only fault seems to have been his ignorance how far his people were demoralised, will give spirits to the rascals in all directions; though I sincerely hope the march of mind in France may yet prove a bloody one . . .' A year later: 'How atrociously the poor King of Holland has been used . . .'[2] The sprightliness of their expression apart, these views were perfectly representative of Froude's ultra-conservative world; they went very comfortably along with its 'transcendental idea of the English gentleman'.

The keystone of most conservative thinking, whether 'ultra' or liberal, was the conviction that the governing powers in church and state were not politically accountable to the public for their exercise of their rights and privileges, or performance of their duties. Accountability to the law, of course, they fully acknowledged. The law, by which their rights were defined and secured, could properly make sure they were not exceeded. The law, by which specific obligations were imposed on individuals or corporations, could legitimately be invoked to make sure they were fulfilled. A reforming radical might indeed insist that parliament could so alter the laws as considerably to limit those rights and could alter and increase those obligations. The conservative—and the 'ultra' much more than the liberal variety—objected to this; and the grounds of his objection, and of his adherence to a completely different idea of the relations of law and legislature, were mostly to be found in his abhorrence of the principle of direct political accountability.

The mere standing upon the ground of individual rights, which played so prominent and potent a part in the story of reform, was in fact subsidiary to this. Anyone, no matter how lowly his birth or condition, might oppose a change on *that* ground. An aggrieved cottager or vestry-

---

[1] *Quarterly Review*, xxx (1823), 272–3. Ascribed to Croker in Shine and Shine, *The Quarterly Review under Gifford*, p. 87.

[2] *Remains*, I, 243–4, 250.

man could make as much fuss in defence of an existing right (above all, of course, a property right) as could a prebendary or a peer. After all, by 1800 the English had had two centuries' drilling in the principles of inviolable individual rights and it was popularly held that they were the great glory of the world's best constitution. But still, the principle—for such it was, whether consciously recognized as such or, as was more usual, unquestioningly assumed—of political unaccountability lay deeper, for it armed resistance to the modification or abolition of old legal rights with better than merely legal arguments. It went behind the laws to jurisprudence, and defended them boldly within the precincts of the sovereign power, on what its supporters understood to be unanswerable ethical grounds, which were part and parcel of their aristocratic socio-political philosophy.

An aristocracy by definition could not be popularly accountable; still less could its authoritarian church establishment. Their direct responsibility was to God. They might admit an *ultimate* necessity of accommodating their government to respectable public opinion; but it was conceived of as a slow, barely perceptible process, cautious and controlled enough to keep principles intact while it was going on, and of course it was expected to be achieved more by the education, or direction, of public opinion, than by undignified gyrations of government. (Thus they were ill at ease in an age in which change was progressing as fast as in the later Hanoverian.) They did not necessarily mean there was to be no change at all, although many extremists would obviously have liked it that way. They did mean that changes in the established order, so far as they had to be made at all, were to be executed with enough deliberation to ensure that the precious fabric of the constitution was not jolted or jarred; no external pressure of public opinion was to be permitted to hustle the operation and so to involve the whole state in the risk of a holocaust.

These were orthodox and ordinary conservative ideas, easily recognizable as such. The principle of non-accountability gave them a couple of twists, not quite so well known. It was held, first, that such changes as were really desirable to be made, ought ideally to be proposed and carried out by those bodies themselves whose internal arrangements or external relations apparently needed to be changed. They alone knew the full difficulties of the case; they alone could understand the variety and character of the interests that depended on them. Moreover (and this was very important to the conservative mind) it had to be believed, as a necessary corollary of the principle of direct accountability to God, that they really wanted to behave conscientiously, which might well involve their adapting themselves to the changing needs of the community, and that they were only anxious to be shown how voluntarily to do so; parliament's part was not to compel them to reform, but to facilitate their self-reform. Sinecures did not matter, if sinecurists could be relied on to do the right, the decent thing.[1]

Great deeps of emotion lay beneath this principle that reform should not be forced, unnaturally, improperly, and unnecessarily forced, but brought on gently and safely by warm rays of public trust and encouragement. Unless you let it happen thus, you would destroy that atmosphere of confidence in public men and public institutions which was essential to the happiness and harmony of a society both aristocratic and free. Rudely to question their intelligence, disinterestedness, or sense of responsibility, was a kind of petty seditious libel. It was indecent to demand an account of them; it would indeed be better for everybody that no one should be in a position to do so.

Burke was no doubt responsible for much of this feeling about the indecency of calling the great officers and institutions of the land to account for themselves except on the gravest occasions and by the safest established means. Their lack of confidence in the good will and public responsibility of their traditional rulers was one of the faults for which he arraigned the French revolutionists. In one of his more pointed utterances on this theme he said (while defending the church establishment against the radical 'despoiler'), 'It is better to cherish virtue and humanity, by leaving much to free will, even with some loss to the object, than to attempt to make men mere machines and instruments of a political benevolence. The world on the whole will gain by a liberty, without which virtue cannot exist.'[2] It was cardinal to his political philosophy that the great natural powers in society, the landed proprietors and all the corporations, with the established church at their head, had it in them to wish to serve the best interests of their great community. They might not always quite see how best to do so, and the

[1] Pusey, *Remarks on the Prospective and Past Benefits of Cathedral Institutions*, p. 3.
[2] *Reflections, ed. cit.* IV, 113–4.

antiquated structure of laws that bound them together often prevented them from doing what they willed; in those cases parliament could help them, could show the way or clear it; but neither parliament nor, really, public opinion could call them like suspect servants to account, without sapping the confidence of the community, its most precious possession. To do away with that, was to hasten the demise of the age of chivalry.

One hears many echoes of Burke's thoughts on this theme in the literature both for and against reform in the early nineteenth century. At the Feast of the Sons of the Clergy in 1817, for example, the preacher, seeking to express in a few well-chosen words the most admirable qualities of English society, used very Burkean language about 'those deep-rooted, fundamental, principles of right ... those steady notions of honour, of integrity, of virtuous perseverance and of religion', etc.; and again, 'those sterling principles of right, those nice discriminations of honour, those attachments to the laws, and rights, and privileges of our country', etc.[1] A more particular application of the principle of trustworthy unaccountability was made in an anonymous *Letter to Sir William Scott*, 1818, defending both the newly appointed Charity Commissioners, and the nation's charitable foundations in general, against Brougham's insinuations that the former would simply play with whitewash, and that the latter needed a strict and exhaustive inquisition.[2] It defended both the Commissioners and the established charities with trenchant orthodox Burkean conservatism. Lord Sidmouth thought so highly of it, he called it an 'incomparable' production. Brougham had wanted the Commissioners appointed by parliament; the minister had however very correctly insisted that the Commissioners should be appointed by the Crown. 'The nomination of the Commissioners in the Bill would have been an implied suspicion of the justice and fair dealing of the Crown. ... The Ministers saw no analogy between an inquiry into the conduct of the officers of the Crown, and into that of stewards and trustees appointed by individuals amongst the people for the management of charitable trusts.' Brougham's bill had gone altogether too far and the Lords had done well to cut it down to size. The powers

[1] Lawrence Gardner, *Sermon at the Anniversary Meeting of the Stewards of the Sons of the Clergy*, 8 *May* 1817, pp. 15 and 21.
[2] Lord Sidmouth told Lord Colchester it was by a lawyer named Holt, in a letter of 27 October 1818 (P.R.O., 30/9.16, Bundle 1).

he had proposed to give the Commissioners 'trespassed too much upon the rights of property, the obligations of confidence, and the courtesies of life. . . . It is indeed a public and a proper principle that much should give way to the general good; but a suitable estimation of high character and office, and a just establishment of establishments and institutions, are no less a portion of the general good, than the particular objects of the charities themselves.'[1]

He went on to justify the Lords' excepting from the commission's purview all charities with special visitors, governors, and overseers, and recalled with grateful pride that the upper house was, 'as it were, the peculiar guardian of those fundamental principles which belong to the nature of all laws, no less than to the British constitution itself. Hence, in many cases in our history, their Lordships have interposed to correct the loose and large powers of popular Bills sent up to them from the Commons, and to recall them to principles more conformable with the nature of property and establishments, and more concurrent with the practice of common law.' Brougham's examples of alleged 'abuses in charities' did not in fact demand hasty interference; 'a wise and cautious legislature will rather continue to suffer the partial mischief of such temporary evils, until they submit to ordinary remedies, than violently root them out at the expense of principles which give certainty to law and security to liberty.' Finally, he castigated Brougham for hinting that the Commissioners would be partial to the conservative side. They should have been treated with greater courtesy. ' "Past services" are at least as good a qualification for ministerial preference as present insults. "Illustrious birth" might probably be some impediment in the way of new-fangled notions and practices. It might feel some disinclination to encourage and forward any breaking-up of the present system of property, and any redistribution of the funds of the church or charities, to the contempt of the established law or the will of the donor.'[2] It could, in short, be relied upon not to alter anything very much, and certainly not to cast aspersions on any trustees or officers of charitable foundations for having grossly neglected their duty and, as the inexorable investigations of the Charity Commissioners so clearly demonstrated once the 'ultra' ice-floes had begun to melt after 1830, for having converted public property to private advantage.

[1] *Ibid.* pp. 12–13, 15–16, 23.   [2] *Ibid.* pp. 24–5, 30–1, 95–6.

It may be doubted whether such a view of the case would have been within our expressive pamphleteer's range of imagination. To him and his powerful tribe, with their aristocratic and non-accountable principles, there was little distinction possible between the general public advantage and the private advantage of the right people. Their private advantages (but they would hardly have thought of them as exclusively private) were public benefits anyway; they only ceased to be so if the courts of law definitively condemned their use of their legal rights. Applied to the world of church and charities, and as a factor in the great debate on church reform, this meant that the richer the bishops and deans, prebendaries and parsons, were, the more good they would do to the commonwealth; and that insofar as their use of their emoluments and privileges, and the public relations of the religious and charitable foundations, seemed to be less than ideal, they needed only an encouraging hint from the legislature and such practical help as enabling legislation alone could give. The practical utility of an institution or office, more or less measurable and admitting public accountability, was not so much a bad test in their eyes as no test at all. What was right in principle was right in practice; and what was right in practice *must* be the most 'useful' thing going. There was no point in inquiring into its workings further.

Thus the reformer, whatever his political affiliations, might find himself at another dead end. His proposals for material reform of one kind or another might cannon off the walls that nearly enclosed him without making the slightest impression. But he was not completely hemmed in. The genuine deep-dyed 'ultra', the Eldonite proper, was as incapable of seeing the need for reform as he was unlikely to assist in it any way; but belief in the essentially authoritarian nature of the church establishment was not of itself incompatible with a zeal for reform, nor did the principle of non-accountability absolutely preclude some zeal for it, although it usually tended to do so. Many conservatives and other persons of aristocratic principles there undoubtedly were whose minds were kept open to the merits of the case for reform by their understanding or at any rate anxious awareness of the changes in which their society was inexorably involved, and by their assessment of the church's unfittedness to weather the storm they saw gathering. They were all for principle, yes; but, unlike the ultra-conservatives, and the waverers who finally came down through timidity or lack of imagination on the 'ultra' side, they took it into account that the result of too much standing upon principle might be a sad lack of soil for their principles to fertilize. They also found the principle of public accountability repugnant; but they saw too clearly how much was amiss and how much inexcusable in the unreformed institutions of church and state not to feel that the radicals and progressive liberals who demanded accountability had some excuse for holding views so erroneous and, ultimately, dangerous. It was from conservatives of this kind that church reform proposals and a certain amount of church reform (described in the next chapter) came, during the long years of the Whigs' not getting into place; and it was from them again, and most of all from Sir Robert Peel and his liberal conservative associates, that the greatest reform of all, the institution of the Ecclesiastical Commissioners, came when the Whigs were, for a few months, again out of place in 1835.

CHAPTER V

THE THIRD CHURCH REFORM MOVEMENT AND THE BOUNTY'S PART IN IT

Before examining the history of Queen Anne's Bounty during the years of the third church reform movement, it will be convenient briefly to sketch that movement's outlines, without pretending to replace the accounts of it given by W. L. Mathieson and, less pertinently, J. H. Overton.[1]

Overton's book is the less important. It now seems rather old-fashioned. A discursive narrative written from an admitted, though not immoderate, high church viewpoint, it is still valuable for its range of material (all of it however published), the quality of its judgment, and the charm and serenity of its style. Mathieson's *English Church Reform* is admirable. It has the bite and the irony that mark all his work, it is founded on a much larger body of knowledge than his minimal foot-notes admit, and it is accurate and judicious—except in its title. 1815 is a poor date to announce as the starting-point for a history of church reform, especially when the author himself does not believe in it. Mathieson freely refers back (as so good an historian had to) to events before 1815. It may be doubted whether he does so quite enough, and the arrangement of his material can be criticized. But his account of the church reform movement right through to the end of the eighteen-thirties seems unlikely to be much improved on, until those with the time and the inclination have patiently accumulated enough detail of particular branches of it, and local instances of it, to enable someone in the future to take a completely fresh view. M. H. Port has begun well by putting an interesting body of flesh on the bones of the story of church building in his book *Six Hundred New Churches; the Church*

[1] In their respective books, *English Church Reform 1815–1840*, especially ch. 1, and *The English Church in the 19th Century, 1800–1833*, especially chs. 5 and 9.

Building Commission, 1818–1856; and it is hoped that the account given within these covers of Queen Anne's Bounty and the Ecclesiastical Commissioners will prove an acceptable contribution.

Church reform up to 1831 may be summarily viewed under these heads: education, tithes, patronage, ecclesiastical courts, church rates, church building and division of parishes, episcopal revenues and diocesan boundaries, the collection of information, and poor livings (comprising the inseparable sub-heads non-residence and pluralism, residence houses, and relief for poor clergy).

Education

About 1780, it was through Sunday schools that the vital reforms were sought; after about 1800, through common day-schools as well. By about 1812 the movement for day-schools, expressed principally in the two great school societies, the British and Foreign and the National, had quite outstripped the Sunday-school movement in promise of social security. It cannot be too much emphasized that the Sunday-school movement was, like all the philanthropies of the eighteenth century, largely utilitarian. The Sunday School Union's 'Plan for the establishment and regulation of Sunday Schools' in 1805 was naturally given over mainly to questions of management, curriculum, and teaching technique; its tone was pronouncedly pious in the Evangelical style, its concern for souls unmistakeable; yet the note sounded at its opening was one of mixed benevolence and prudence, with prudence dominant. Crime and disorder were obviously the author's most immediate concerns. Human laws and penal sanctions were inadequate, he said, to 'secure our persons and property from those violent attacks or secret depredations to which they are now perpetually exposed'.[1] The same argument held for Sunday-schools and day-schools, often masked indeed by charity and delicacy, but always most fundamental. The idea of 'educating' the children of the poor in some sense seems to have gained fairly general acceptance by the eighteen-forties (except perhaps among the farmers and other close-fisted sections of the middling classes) but voices were always being raised to suggest that working-class children were being educated too high. It was not making them more industrious, nor, complained one commentator, did they seem to

[1] *Op. cit.* p. 4.

show a greater anxiety 'to provide for themselves without being an
expensive burden to their neighbours. Alas! the poors' rates speak
volumes, and if not speedily reformed, must involve the kingdom in
ruin and confusion. But . . . do we find more respect to their superiors
and gratitude to their benefactors? Do they order themselves more
lowly and reverently towards their betters? If these questions cannot
be answered according to our wishes, there must be something radically
wrong in our System of Education.'[1] Among the upper orders, the
question by the end of the French wars was not so much, Are the poor
to be educated? as, What kind of education ought they to be given?

Tithes

Tithes never ceased to embitter the relations of tithe-owners and tithe-
payers right up to the general Tithe Commutation Act of 1836.[2] The
arguments employed for and against commutation were no different
in kind from those that had been used for the past century and a half,
but they acquired additional force from the enclosure movement and
the growth of capitalised, scientific farming. Friends of the church had
much reason on their side when they reminded the farmers that tithes
would always in effect have to be paid to somebody, that they were a
species of real property, and that the clergy on the whole were easier
tithe-masters than the laity. But reasoned argument, unsparingly put
forth in sermon, pamphlet, speech and book, was powerless and inappro-
priate to allay resentment steeped in prejudice and meanness. One
grasping clergyman became multiplied by gossip, imagination and
anti-clerical censoriousness, to outweigh the examples of a score who
were more conciliatory. It was the more difficult for clergymen to be
conciliatory, since their successors might suffer from their softness.
Moreover they knew that even if they were conciliatory, they would
probably not make themselves the more popular, since it was the
principle of paying tithes to the clergy at all, in any shape or form,
that made them odious.

Lay tithes were felt to be different. The farmer who grumbled exceedingly in paying the parson, paid his tithes to the squire as a matter

[1] Montagu Burgoyne, *Address to the Governors and Directors of the Public Charity Schools* (2nd edn., 1830), pp. 4–5.
[2] For which very important measure, see ch. 10 below, pp. 465–8.

of course—'a fact,' drily commented Edward Burton, 'which may perhaps be explained by those who have studied human nature.'[1] The bishops were too much obsessed with the virtues of standing upon principle, and perhaps also, sometimes, too dull of mind and imagination, to accommodate their church's staple source of revenue to the facts of human nature, and to rid the pastor of 'the inauspicious appearance of a tax-gatherer.'[2]

In 1786 the younger Pitt told the Duke of Rutland that he was becoming increasingly convinced that tithes in any country were an obstacle to improvement, and that in Ireland they had become a severe and genuine grievance which it would be wisdom in the bishops to allay. Let them only look at it 'soberly and dispassionately, they will see how incumbent it is upon them, in every point of view, to propose some temperate accommodation'.[3] Towards the very end of his first ministry, he produced an ambitious plan for extinguishing tithes in England, which Watson and probably also Tomline supported, but which was frozen to death by the opposition of the rest of the bench.[4] Pitt's desire to settle the tithe-question on both sides of the Irish Channel rested mainly on political and commercial considerations.[5] Nor can there be much doubt that the agitation for the commutation of tithes into corn-rents, money-payments, or land, came largely from an interested party of landowners and farmers. Yet there were good, disinterested friends of the church who longed for an end to the bickerings and scufflings that went with the collection of tithes in kind and the jealousies and litigation that could not be avoided until the tithes were permanently and generally commuted. Southey, for instance, although he had nothing but abhorrence for Pitt's idea of selling the tithes, none the less earnestly sought some release from their endless

---

[1] *Thoughts upon the Demand for Church Reform*, pp. 31–2.

[2] Burke in the debate of 17 February 1772. *Speeches and Writings*, ed. cit., III, 391.

[3] Letter of 7 November 1786, in Earl Stanhope, *Life of Pitt*, I, 319.

[4] See Watson's *Anecdotes* (1818 edn.), II, 56–7 and the Pretyman-Tomline Papers 108/42 in the East Suffolk Record Office, Ipswich, which seem to be relevant. Pitt's idea was to convert the right to tithe into a title to an equivalent sum in the public funds.

[5] As was appreciated by the author of one of the better pamphlets of the period, *The Interests of the Church of England* (2nd edn., 1821), reprinted in *The Pamphleteer*, XIX (1822), 477 ff., at p. 485.

trouble-making.[1] This was so large a question, involving not only the interests of the church but also the economy and the balance of power in the countryside, and affording so many opportunities for assertion of principle and ostentatious legality, that the permanent general settlement was delayed until after the Reform Bill.

Patronage

This was increasingly recognised to be one of the root difficulties. By the time of the church reform crisis the more intelligent thinkers about church reform were putting it at the top of their lists of causes of inefficiency and occasions of scandal. 'There is not a single abuse, not a single defect in the Church of England, as at present constituted, but what might be fully remedied by a more pure and holy administration of its patronage, by the establishment of a more perfect code of ecclesiastical law, and a more vigorous and unfettered exercise of internal discipline.'[2] Of all matters it was the hardest to do anything about. Advowsons were property—often very valuable property—that not only carried a cash value in the market but meant even more in terms of social standing or family convenience. Patrons enjoyed an all but absolute control over their livings. If the living were a donative, it rested with the patron whether to accept an augmentation from Queen Anne's Bounty or not. In any change that altered the legal situation of the benefice (erection of chapels-of-ease, daughter churches, parish division, exchange of lands or buildings), he had a right to be consulted and a power to prevent any change he disliked. The best that the reformers could do was to press upon patrons the seriousness of their responsibilities and exhort them to guide their decisions by considerations of professional merit and the church's needs, instead of by family or political interest. It was the more difficult to sound convincing about this, because much patronage was in ecclesiastical hands, because of the church's political role (which everyone still frankly accepted), and also because so much had been made, in the late eighteenth century

---

[1] On the selling of tithes, see e.g. his letters of 12 and 30 May 1812, and 8 May 1822, in *Selections from Southey's Letters*, ed. Warter, II, 274–5 and 277, and III, 308, and on the amelioration of the system, his letters of 20 November 1816 and 7 March 1832, in *Life and Correspondence*, ed. C. C. Southey, IV, 220–1, and Warter's *Selections*, IV, 261 f.

[2] *Quarterly Review*, XLVIII (1832), 569.

and throughout the war years, of the affinity of interest and feeling between the lay and the clerical gentry. That great and reverent regard for the interests of the family, moreover, which was so characteristic of the Hanoverian age, was still full of vigour; and few churchmen (even of the highest principles) who had the chance of providing for a son or a son-in-law could resist the temptation to believe that their protégé was actually well suited for the clerical calling, and would have deserved a living quite apart from the family connexion which brought it so easily to him. In what was being said and written about patronage in the twenties and thirties one detects a certain unaccustomed awkwardness or conscious effort of boldness, the natural accompaniment of the clergy's growing sense of professional respectability and independence. To go against a set of tendencies and arguments so long unquestioned and so persuasive, indeed required an effort, for it meant unloosing some of the cords that tied the ancient connexion of church and state.

Patronage was not only a delicate, even an embarrassing question; it was also very complicated. The Crown was by far the largest patron of all. The clergy, whether as individuals or as members of colleges and chapters, were as much concerned as the laity. If you thought so ill of existing patronage arrangements as to rise to the brave heights of wishing to change them, you fell at once into the sticky difficulties of proposing improvements. Should the bishops' share in patronage increase? That idea frightened Evangelicals, who were weak in bishops; it appalled Whigs, who were against anything smacking of prelatical power; and it made indignant all constitutionalists who were of that cast of mind to fear the conferment upon individuals of discretionary (they would call it arbitrary) power. Yet it was for an increase in the bishops' powers that patronage reformers had to plead; there was no viable alternative. Various ideas for national or diocesan boards of patronage were quietly put forward but met with no response.[1]

---

[1] E.g. in *Blackwood's Magazine*, XXXI (1832), 187–9; *Church Patronage: a letter to Sir Robert Peel* (1828), pp. 59–64; Samuel Lee, cited in the Appendix to S. T. Bloomfield, *Analytical View of the Principal Plans of Church Reform* (1833), and *Letter to the Archbishop of Canterbury on Church Property* (1824), pp. 78–94. The two last-named are of more interest as containing suggestions anticipatory of the Ecclesiastical Commissioners: see below, p. 309.

Ecclesiastical Courts

The ecclesiastical courts mattered less at the end of the eighteenth century than they had done earlier, but were still not unimportant. They presented, it is needless to say, an involved problem to the would-be reformers. They could only be improved by cutting them loose from some of the functions and accretions they had gathered through the centuries, and standing them more on their own feet; by measures, that is, which looked, to conservative eyes, like sacrilege. Furthermore, the higher ecclesiastical courts were one with the courts of admiralty, and the very exclusive and monopolistic little knot of lawyers qualified to practise in them, the proctors of doctors' commons, did box and cox with one another, now pleading, now adjudicating, alternately in both ecclesiastical and admiralty cases; thus inviting the much misused Nathaniel Highmore, who had many reasons for detesting them, sarcastically to denominate them 'these Prize-Court Churchmen'.[1] Their fees were high, their pace deliberate, their independence in relation to both the executive and the other branches of the judiciary was extraordinary, and the amount of nepotism in them disgraceful. The lower levels of ecclesiastical jurisdiction displayed much confusion and pointlessness. Every archdeaconry had a court, and there were also nearly three hundred peculiars and manorial courts operating, or at any rate nominally operating, within the same 'system'. Some slight limits were set to their powers by statutes in 1787 and 1813.[2] The full enormities of the whole tangled network were made clear to the view by the series of investigations undertaken by order of the Commons from 1823 onwards.[3] Out of this public concern (which had much in common with the contemporary concern about the court of Chancery) came, first, an Act in 1829 regulating the duties, salaries, and emoluments of

[1] *Jus Ecclesiasticum Anglicanum; or, the Government of the Church of England exemplified and illustrated.* The title of this elaborate attack on the civilians of doctors' commons is misleading, but it is a racy piece of work, and some sense is mixed up with its fury. The section on the Revd. Lord Frederick Beauclerk (pp. 50 ff.) deserves to be better known.

[2] 27 George III c. 44 and 53 George III c. 127. The latter achieved one of Wake's and Gibson's frustrated ambitions, by abolishing excommunication for non-appearance or contempt of court.

[3] See the *Parliamentary Papers*, 1823, VII, 27–109: 1824, IX, 25–73, 75 ff.: 1826, XXI, 21–40: 1828, XX. 229–76, 741–5, 751–838: 1829, XVIII, 9–17, 19–137.

the officers in various of the courts;[1] and second, early in 1830, the appointment of the Ecclesiastical Courts Commission, which was renewed by William IV, and which made striking and reformatory recommendations.[2]

The best known of these was the abolition of the High Court of Delegates, the old court of appeal in ecclesiastical cases, and the transfer of their function to a judicial committee of the privy council, from which came so unexpectedly all the anguish of the Gorham case and its successors. This was the only recommendation of the Commissioners to be adopted, a special recommendation, made early on in response to an urgent leading question by the Lord Chancellor, and at the time was one of the least noticeable. But consider the rest: the abolition of every ecclesiastical court below the provincial level; the introduction of trial by jury and the admission of *viva voce* evidence in the few large courts that should be left; the abolition of peculiars; the clarification and settlement of the law regarding church-wardens, church rates, pews, dilapidations and sequestrations; and the introduction of an effective, cheap and speedy process of church discipline.[3] If only action had been taken upon these recommendations, how different might not the history of the Victorian church have been! No action was taken, and the ecclesiastical courts, their nuisance to the church increasing as their public utility shrank, remained a little longer substantially unaltered, to aggravate liberals, and obstruct bishops. They were perhaps never more notorious in the whole of English history than the dissenters made them seem in the great *fracas* of the later thirties about church rates.

Church Rates

As the Ecclesiastical Courts Commissioners remarked, the law on church rates was confused and uncertain; just how confused and uncertain, the public at large was made aware in the later thirties by the

---

[1] 10 George IV c. 53.

[2] P.Ps. 1831–2, XXIV.

[3] The minute book of this Commission is in the Church Commissioners' archives. It is clear that the lawyers did most of the work and it looks as if Stephen Lushington was the most influential of them. The thoroughness and boldness of their report ought not to make one forget Sir William Scott's attempts to make some changes along the same lines in 1812–13; for which, see the Commission's report, p. 22, and *Memoirs of Romilly*, II, 45, 113–15.

Braintree case. By then, it was too late for the church's friends to save the situation. The dissenters learnt from Dr Lushington all that they wanted to hear for the time being—that however legal it might be for churchwardens to make a rate, they had no power to enforce it against the will of a majority of the ratepayers. By this time church rates were the principal bone of contention between the establishment and dissent, an epitome for churchmen of all that establishment involved, a symbol for dissenters of all that it portended; and hardly a year passed between the breaking of the Braintree case and their eventual abolition in 1868, without some attempt to put church rates on a more rational footing.

There seems to have been no church rate legislation or judgment of any importance about church rates before the thirties. Quakers, presumably, had never paid them willingly. Some of the briskest engagements in the long campaign for a reform in the representative system were fought over church rates by political radicals in a number of midland and northern town vestries during the twelve or so years preceding the great Reform Bill; but they were not, before 1830, the outstanding cause of nonconformist grief they became soon after. Rather were they on the minds of church reformers because of the difficulties they caused in connexion with church extension and parish division, and the troubles they stirred up among churchmen.

The old establishment appeared at its worst in this respect. The rule was, that existing rights had to be respected by every innovator—a rule held sacred by the whole of the political community in the eighteenth century, and at any rate the early part of the nineteenth; and one not peculiar to the church. To the eye of the reasonable historian, it seems to have embodied much 'natural justice'. But this rule appears to have been often carried too far; its application amounted, sometimes, to a gross over-weighting of private individuals' claims as against those of the community, and helped to prevent the church's accommodating its parochial system to the needs of a changing society.

When a chapel-of-ease or a parochial chapel was built to take the pressure off a parish church—the mother church, as it would then be known—the directly remunerative church services, baptisms and burials and weddings, would probably have to be performed in the mother church; and provision would be made to ensure that the incumbent did not lose his fees or their equivalent. He would probably take the greater part, perhaps even the whole, of the Easter offerings. Those who went Sunday by Sunday to the chapel-of-ease could hardly feel comfortable in such conditions. Their regular place of worship was only half of a church. Their respect for their minister, and generosity to him, would be chilled by the knowledge that he was only an underling of the mother-church minister; and their interest in their little church and readiness to maintain or expand it, might be killed completely by their having to go on paying church rates (and of course tithes) to the mother-church although they rarely went near it. It is however possible that the undesirability of this would be somewhat cloaked by their always having to pay the poor-rate to the same centre.

Church Building and the Division of Parishes

Thus the questions of church building and of parish divisions were naturally bound up with church rates. Private chapels and proprietary chapels (as those chapels were known which were in law private but in fact open to the public and in some way money-making) were no more difficult to put up than nonconformist chapels. They seem not even to have needed consecration to have qualified for episcopal approval.[1] They made no interference with parochial law, they had no legal claim on anyone's loyalty or pocket. They might indeed be unwelcome to the parish minister as threatening to divert from his pocket some of his official flock's free-will offerings; but if the official flock was larger than the parish church could hold, the case for a provision of extra church accommodation, even at some cost, was not easy to refute. And *some* cost there was bound to be in the opening of proprietary chapels, as became increasingly recognised after about 1800. They hardly ever admitted the poor. How could they, when they had to make money? The minister wanted his income; perhaps a body of pious subscribers might reasonably wish to recover the capital they had put into it; perhaps some speculator or commercial partnership had bought it or built it simply as an investment. One need not ascribe the basest money-grubbing motives to all who had a hand in proprietary chapels (as hostile high churchmen often and unfairly did), to see that these chapels were at best an intrusion into, at worst a disruption of, the parochial system. The minister's flock was bound to be a select one;

[1] See James Baker, *Life of Sir Thomas Bernard*, p. 55.

he would rarely be preaching to the unconverted. His ministry was partial. He could only preach and pray; the administration of the sacraments, and the solemnization of matrimony, were normally beyond his powers. His chapel might run a Sunday-school and he might be an active organiser of Bible-classes; but there would be none of those organic connexions with the educational and governmental machinery of the parish that were essential to the improvement of society and the proper placing of the church in it. Proprietary chapels took virtue out of the parish; and if they did any good, the benefit was felt simply by those respectable persons who bought or rented the pews, and who went, perhaps because of the attractions of the minister, perhaps because it was fashionable or convenient, and perhaps because the lease of their house in a new square or terrace included a pew in the chapel provided to give the development a finished air.

Both proprietary and parochial chapels were thus inconvenient and irritating devices to supply the deficiency of church accommodation. It is characteristic of the state of the established church at this time, that the law allowed church extensions of deleterious tendency, and made almost impossible the only kind of church extension that was really adequate to the situation—namely, the proper division of parishes, and the building and endowment of complete parish churches. Before the Church Building Act of 1818, which was in effect a general church building act, it needed an Act of Parliament to do anything that altered parochial law and geography; and the necessity of respecting existing interests combined with the parish's 'secular' functions to make the proper division of parishes rather rare. In any case it could only be done at the cost of elaborately compensating existing interests and probably their posterity as well.

The Act of 1818, which established the Church Building Commissioners and laid down rules for the application of a million pounds of public money, made the provision of new churches and the division of parishes a good deal easier. It was followed by a series of statutes, of which the last that need be noticed here was Peel's District Churches Act of 1843, that progressively made these accomplishments easier still.[1]

---

[1] 58 George III c. 45: 59 George III c. 134: 3 George IV c. 72: 5 George IV c. 103: 7 and 8 George IV c. 72: 9 George IV c. 42: 1 and 2 William IV c. 38: and 6 and 7 Victoria c. 37.

Voluntary subscription came to the aid of the cause. The Church Building Society (which soon found it expedient to restrict its energies to church repair and enlargement) was started in 1817, and a number of diocesan church building societies were founded in its wake. There was soon no lack of churches, and the appropriate division of parishes was well advanced by the middle of the century.

Episcopal Revenues and Diocesan Boundaries

The inequalities of bishop's revenues and diocesan sizes were a field for church reform which remained untouched until the thirties. The inequalities of their revenues were the more obvious problem. Reformers worried about it, not because they thought equality desirable for its own sake, nor because they failed to see that for positions of admittedly varying difficulty and amenity, unequal rewards were quite reasonable. The real argument for some approach to equalization of most bishops' revenues rested on a different ground. While some were so much more lucrative than others, the poorer were regarded only as stepping-stones to the richer. Government could discipline the bench by leaving a Secker stranded for years in Bristol (£450 a year) and Oxford (£500) as 'the deliberate punishment for an early display of parliamentary independence',[1] and a Watson with nothing better than Llandaff (£550; but of course he held other, sub-episcopal, preferment). For bishops who discreetly remembered their makers, on the other hand, as well as for those who took the royal fancy or had influential friends at the critical moment, fine rewards were assured, and family fortunes most nobly founded. The pressures of politics thus joined the ordinary promptings of ambition to engage the bishops in a perpetual sedate game of musical chairs. Although other and impressive faults could be hinted at in this state of affairs, the main objection from the church reformer's point of view was that the poorer sees could rarely keep the same bishop for long, and the church's efficiency was crippled by this chopping and changing of its principal officers.

The other solid objection to these amazing contrasts between the

[1] Sykes, *Church and State in England in the 18th Century*, p. 61 ff. These were the estimated values of the sees in 1762. Their absolute values of course 'improved' thereafter but their relative values remained much the same until their radical readjustment by the Ecclesiastical Commissioners.

values of sees, was that it set a lamentable example of pluralism. To keep the poorer bishops solvent, and enable them to live up to their station—which meant a house in London during the session, hospitality there and in the country, contributions to charities both national and diocesan, the payment of secretaries, agents and so on—a custom had evolved of their holding certain preferments *in commendam*. To all the poorer sees, moreover, smaller preferments were permanently annexed. Some bishops no doubt held benefices *in commendam* simply to enrich themselves, or—to put it in the most sympathetic way possible—to enable them to live most comfortably up to the high station society allowed them.[1] But it was not always thus. The *commendams* were, in some circumstances, genuinely needed, and by Lord Liverpool's time were allowed only rarely. The bishopric of Llandaff (£924) was held *in commendam* with the deanery of St Paul's (about £5000 in all); Rochester (£1459) with the deanery of Worcester (about £1650) and the rectory of Bishopsbourne (£1240); and Bristol (£2351) with a prebend in Durham (about £1500); the vicarage of Almondsbury, permanently annexed to the see, appears to have been only an incumbrance.[2]

When the senior officers of the church had to pretend to be able to do several jobs at once, how could they convincingly answer inferiors who claimed to be able to do the same? A Blomfield, in full schoolmasterly flood, could attempt an answer; but he did not sound convincing. It was a messy, corrupting practice, which, despite the ingenuity of conservative apologists, could not be regarded by earnest churchmen in the reform era as better than badly *faute de mieux*. Richard Watson put the reduction of episcopal inequalities at the head of his very sensible proposals for church reform.[3] That it did not appear as one of the more exciting topics in the ensuing half-century only meant that the need

[1] See for instance the examples given by Sykes, *op. cit.* p. 162.

[2] These figures have been extracted, not without difficulty, from the 1835 report. I have no doubt they can be disputed. So hard is it to get the facts out of that report, and so far devoid of rhyme and reason was the whole ecclesiastical system, that nothing less than the personal co-operation of scholars side by side will ever bring their sums to the same answers.

[3] *Letter to the Archbishop of Canterbury* (1782–3), reprinted in *The Pamphleteer*, VIII (1816), 574 ff.; see also his *Anecdotes*, I, 116–17, 145–6, 175.

for reform was universally admitted. The Ecclesiastical Commissioners made it their care, and few presumed to criticise them.

The other aspect of the episcopate that needed reform was the inequality of the sees in size and weight. No one disputed the propriety of Canterbury's getting more than York; yet as a diocese it was nothing like as burdensome, having 343 benefices in it and a population of 403,000, as against York's 891 benefices and a population of 1,689,000.[1] Chester was not one of the wealthier sees, with only about £900 a year in 1760 and £3260 in 1830, which put it below the half-way mark; yet it was one of the largest, with 554 benefices, multitudes of chapels, and nearly two millions of people; and as the diocese which felt more than any other the impacts of popery and industrialisation, it was clearly one of strategic importance. Lincoln was huge, with 1234 benefices and 855,000 people; Ely was tiny, with only 149 benefices and 126,000 people; but the diligent Kaye with about £4500 a year (he was twelfth on the list) did not seem overpaid in comparison with the aged, disreputable and indolent Sparke, who was sixth richest bishop, with over £11,000. These disparities cried out for reform. It was equally an argument for reform, that in these larger dioceses, the volume of work was more than a good bishop could cope with—an argument the force of which grew *pari passu* with the rise of clerical standards and the progress of reform throughout the whole or the body politic. Several remedies offered themselves. The boundaries of the larger sees needed to be shrunk; there needed to be more bishops, either diocesans or suffragans. Like most other items in the programme of church reform, these needs were at least as old as the Reformation; but they were extremely difficult to supply. Clerical and regional prejudices and loyalties were quickly roused to withstand changes; the relations between the bench and the Lords presented difficulties and provoked arguments of a kind infinitely exciting to constitutionalists and lawyers; nor was it all that easy to see whence endowments for any new bishops might come.

The Collection of Information

The collection of information about the state of the church was not the least of the branches of church reform. It was singular in that the

[1] See Appendix 6.

need for it was only slowly recognized. So little was known for sure about the number, value, and conditions of benefices, that Queen Anne's Bounty had to inquire closely into each as it came up for augmentation; and the reason why there were still any livings under £50 a year in 1835, when the Bounty had had a hundred and twenty odd years to get rid of them, seems to have been that good bishops simply could not ascertain the facts about the obscurer livings in their dioceses, and that bad bishops would not bother to do so. Chapelries were often difficult to find out about; and more difficult still the donative livings, or livings in peculiars. The tendency of ecclesiastical legislation from the Bounty Act of 1715 onwards was to make it a condition of the extension of financial or legal advantages to donatives or peculiars that they should become more 'regular'; the ideal pursued was that donatives should be turned into perpetual cures, and that the bishop's writ should run throughout the diocese with no exceptions or exemptions. But whether these desirable changes took place or not rested entirely with the patrons of the livings concerned. If they preferred to keep them out of the ordinary course of church organisation, none could compel them; and in that case, their condition—perhaps even, in extreme cases, their existence—would remain hidden from the eyes of efficiency and reform.

Bacon's edition of Ecton's *Liber Valorum* in 1786 provided a good deal of up-to-date information about patronage and values, but it was patchy and of course not authoritative. Richard Watson, as one might have expected, seems to have been the first in this third period of church reform to have called for something better. The need for official inquisition was implicit in his plan of 1782–3 for soaking the richer, comfortable clergy in order to put a little fat on the poor 'working' clergy. In his evident dissatisfaction at having to rely so largely on guesswork,[1] he made it explicit in an interesting exchange of views with Pitt early in 1800, and published it all in his 1809 Charge.[2] The idea was so sensible, and the problems were in those years becoming so familiar to serious churchmen,[3] that it would be rash to ascribe to Watson the honour of

---

[1] *Letter to the Archbishop of Canterbury*, reprinted in *The Pamphleteer*, VIII (1816), 583–6.

[2] *Anecdotes*, II, 129, 135.

[3] Watson's demand for a full survey of present actual values is, for example, echoed in that excellent work already referred to (p. 148, above) *The State of the Established*

having originated the first of the official inquisitions. Nevertheless they started just a few years after he had been pressing an idea of this kind on Pitt. The collection of accurate information (or at any rate reasonably accurate information; the early returns were in many respects defective, and need to be used with great caution) at last began to make possible two things for lack of which the church reformers were half-paralysed— a comprehensive view of the actual state of the church that could not be dismissed as merely impressionistic, and an official machinery for correcting abuses.

Sir William Scott's Act of 1803, indifferently known as his Residence Act or his Non-Residence Act,[1] and excused by its author as merely a provisional or interim measure of church reform,[2] contained a clause requiring the bishops to return annually to the Privy Council a statement of the conditions prevailing in the benefices under their care.[3] The Council was given divers other tasks of ecclesiastical supervision, so onerous in the sum that a new office worth £500 a year was created to undertake them. The post was given to a clergyman, Thomas Brooke Clarke, who was to hold it for over twenty years. His main work was the analysis and tabulation of the bishops' non-residence returns, but the Council received also annual reports from the archbishops of the use they had made of their powers (conferred under clauses 19, 20 and 23 of Scott's Act) to hear appeals from their provincial bishops' decisions to refuse licences of non-residence. Clarke's branch of the Privy Council Office soon turned into a kind of miniature Ministry for Ecclesiastical Affairs. In 1807 the Council, or a committee of it, showed impatience at the dilatoriness of certain of the bishops (Ely, Hereford, Bangor, Norwich and St David's were the main

Church, in a series of Letters to Spencer Perceval.

[1] 43 George III c. 84, 'An Act to amend the Laws relating to Spiritual Persons holding of Farms; and for enforcing the Residence of Spiritual Persons on their Benefices, in England.'

[2] He sensibly reminded parliament that real reform would have to wait on the improvement of poor clergy's incomes, and the provision of residence-houses; see his *Substance of a Speech delivered in the House of Commons*, 7 April 1802, p. 50. Much subsequent criticism of his Act would have been avoided if it had been accompanied by the Curates' Stipends Act he had intended to put with it, according to Spencer Perceval (*Copy of a Letter to Dr. Mansel on the Curates Bill*, pp. 9–11).

[3] Clause 25. The first returns had to be in by 25 March 1805.

offenders), and some irritation at the failure of bishops and parochial clergy between them to send in accurately and fully the information the Council required. Obviously they wanted to check whether or not non-residence was diminishing, and to make sure that the bishops were correcting it with the rigour they desired. Some of the bishops thought this rigour ungentlemanly. The ancient Hurd of Worcester, for example, ingenuously stated that he had ceased enforcing the laws against non-residence because they caused his clergy such inconvenience. All of them were reluctant to issue the monitions the Council expected.[1] The Council, or its committee, wanted action, and was using these annual returns to make sure it got it; Clarke, who complained that the work was harder than he had anticipated, was continuously chivvied, and the improved form of return introduced in 1809 was the committee's work, not his.[2]

By this means a steadily more accurate picture of the state of the parochial clergy as regarded their residence was obtained; and it was natural—indeed it had presumably been intended all along—to extend the scope of inquiry to the clergy's financial state.[3] Lord Harrowby was no doubt a prime mover in all this. He was a Privy Councillor, and in these years quite often was present at the Bounty Board. Even more significant of co-ordinated planning were the occasional appearances at the Bounty of William Fawkener and Viscount Chetwynd, clerks to the Privy Council, and of Spencer Perceval. It is not rash to surmise that out of these meetings of the Bounty and the Privy Council from 1804 onwards, came the great inquiries that at last and irrefutably showed how rotten the material state of the church was.

First came an inquiry into the poverty of livings. Queen Anne's

---

[1] See especially the Privy Council's circular letter and the bishops' replies in P.Ps. 1808, IX, 247–50, and *State of the Established Church*, 2nd edn., pp. 120–1.

[2] This is mainly based on the Privy Council Registers in the Public Record Office, PC 2/166 pp. 1–2, PC 2/172 pp. 16, 144, 244–5, 407, 518–19, PC 2/173 pp. 162–3, 165, 506–7, 582, PC 2/176 pp. 280–1, 323, 336–7, PC 2/179, pp. 411, 559, 591, PC 2/180 pp. 124–5, 131, 177, PC 2/181 pp. 56, 434–5, 437–8, 471–2, 522.

[3] The non-residence returns for 1804–5, 1805–6, and 1806–7, with relevant official correspondence, were first published in P.Ps. 1808, IX, 237–60. They were reprinted along with those for 1807–8 in *ibid.* 1809, IX, 23–32. For the next years see P.Ps. 1812, X, 153, and 1812–13, XIII, 49.

Bounty elicited from the bishops[1] a new and detailed survey of benefices under £150 a year.[2] The accuracy of the returns on which this was based was impugned by the well-informed author of *The State of the Established Church*, who called them a 'gross and palpable imposition on the Bishops and on Parliament';[3] and even Morgan Cove, a heavy-handed but honest friend of the establishment whose judgment was un-balanced by his devotion to tithes, had to admit they were in many respects defective—'private pique, prejudice, interest and influence, prevented the return of a large number of livings; and many others were withheld, through an unwillingness to discover the inconsiderable and shameful compensations' made for serving vacant (often irregularly vacant) cures.[4] But they sufficed to indicate the scale of the problem, and they were used by Queen Anne's Bounty in its distribution of the parliamentary grants.[5] A year later, an abstract of these returns relating them to the non-residence returns was published.[6]

The year 1812 brought forth two very important bodies of in-formation, both collected and tabulated by the Privy Council's ecclesias-tical officer. First came an account of the church accommodation (and the dissenters' accommodation) in populous parishes—parishes, that was to say, of over a thousand souls—incorporating the population statistics of the recent census.[7] Soon afterwards came an account, very incomplete but poignant indeed, of the numbers and salaries of licensed curates, which gave Lord Harrowby his most persuasive arguments for the stipendiary Curates Bill he introduced that year, and succeeded in passing in 1813.[8]

[1] Or most of them; St. David's (whither Thomas Burgess had gone in 1803), Ely (where Yorke gave place to Dampier in 1808), and Norwich (a diocese whose diffi-culties Bathurst never managed to control), failed to make returns, as they had done to the Privy Council in the matter of non-residence. Rochester (where Dampier gave place to King in 1808–9) also remained silent.

[2] P.Ps. 1809, IX, 37.   [3] 2nd edn., pp. 93–6.

[4] *Essay on the Revenues of the Church of England*, 3rd edn. 1816, p. 119.

[5] See below, pp. 213–4.   [6] P.Ps. 1810, XIV, 95–7.

[7] P.Ps. 1812, X, 155.

[8] P.Ps. 1812, X, 157. The extent of its incompleteness as a description of how non-resident incumbents saw to the serving of their churches is partly indicated in the discrepancy between the number of incumbents returned that year as non-resident and not doing the duty of the living (about 4800) and the number of curates returned as serving non-residents' cures (3694).

The subsequent Parliamentary Papers of ecclesiastical import up to 1835 did little more than keep these tables up-to-date, improve them, and, by putting their contents into various combinations, throw into relief the deficiencies that were thought to be especially dangerous. Thus in 1817 the Council Office brought out an account of benefices returned as non-resident because of the lack of a residence-house.[1] A year later, it produced a refinement on its 1812 analysis of the shortage of church room in populous parishes,[2] and, as well, the most elaborate and nearly accurate paper yet, an account of the population, church room, and provision for residence in every parish, and its value if it came under £150 a year.[3] It is significant that the values and conditions of livings over £150 were never officially investigated, except as incidental to the later inquiries into curates' stipends, before 1832; nor were the capitular and collegiate clergy before then submitted to the indignity of an inquisition.

Clarke's prefatory explanation of his difficulties in compiling this last account illustrates the prevailing indiscipline and diocesan inefficiency. He said that the first returns on church accommodation had been found imperfect, and that the Council had asked the bishops late in 1814 to get better ones. Their attempts to do so were far from successful. Some of the clergy would no doubt, on principle, disobey their diocesan, and many see in these inquiries the forecast shadow of a threat to their comfort and independence. Whatever the cause of the bishops' failure, Clarke had to bring information together from a variety of sources—the census returns, the Bounty Office, the Land Tax Redemption Commissioners, besides the returns to his own office. He admitted that after all this, his findings were still far from accurate or comprehensive. They were however about the best that could be done before the Royal Commission of 1832-5.

The Poverty of Livings

This was in a way the greatest problem of all. The church's other defects would not have attracted such attention, and some of its characteristics might not have been denounced as defects at all, had not it been the fact that so many benefices were still incapable of supporting fully resident ministers. According to the 1809 returns, at least 3,300 benefices

[1] P.Ps. 1817, xv, 175-7.   [2] P.Ps. 1818, xviii, 93-134.   [3] *Ibid.* pp. 137-417.

were under £150 a year; at least 860 were under £50 a year; and those are certainly underestimates, though by how much it would be difficult to say. £150 a year hardly raised a married clergyman with a family above the poverty-line. £50 a year put him well below it. With so many cures so ill endowed, the arguments for pluralities, and the technical non-residence they entailed, looked watertight—until you realized how many livings held in plurality were not making poor clergy less poor, but comfortably-off clergy more comfortable.[1] For non-residence similarly, reasonable arguments could be produced. The proper meaning of non-residence was not always understood by radical critics. A clergyman's non-residence according to the statutes governing it and the diocesan returns that described it did not even mean that he was not serving the cure himself. It was a technical term, meaning that he did not for the greater part of the year occupy the official residence-house (or a house approved by the bishop) within the parish. The law thus invited misunderstanding, and the non-residence returns were soon taking pains to point how many clergy who were, for whatever reason, technically non-resident, were in fact doing the duty of the parish.[2] Apart from that, the non-resident's cure would almost certainly be served somehow or other; and it might be served by a fully resident curate. All kinds of persuasive arguments were advanced to excuse or justify pluralities and non-residence on these grounds and since there was often much sense in them they cut across the discussion on the poverty of livings and rather confused it. Nevertheless, there was little doubt by the turn of the nineteenth century that the principal causes of the church's material inefficiency were those that made it impossible or cruel, in practice and theory alike, to expect each benefice to support a resident clergyman without other assistance.

The lack of residence houses was one of the causes of non-residence, and was often the consequence of poverty. It was not inevitably so. The attempt made by some church defenders to believe, or to persuade

[1] See P.Ps. 1837–8, xxxviii, 183, where the values of livings held in plurality are abstracted from the Ecclesiastical Revenues Commission's report. They are of parochial pluralities only; the total picture, which would have to include prebends, is thus worse still.

[2] In those for 1809–10, published in P.Ps. 1812, x, 153, at least 600 out of 5435 were thus reported; by 1827 over 1500 were placed in this category. P.Ps. 1830, xix, 35–6.

the church's critics to believe, that the cupidity of pluralists and the negligence of archdeacons and bishops were not often to blame, was either ingenuous or dishonest. On the other hand, it is certain that many incumbents (whether pluralists or not is immaterial) during this period were enlarging or rebuilding old residence-houses, and making them adequate to the requirements of a gentry-clergy; and this must sometimes have involved disinterested generosity. The fact is, that the law on residence-houses, a leading branch of the law on dilapidations, was awkward and obstructive. It was an incumbent's responsibility to keep his residence-house in good repair. If he came into an adequate residence-house, and was reasonably paid, he could do it. But so often the residence-house was ruinous, through a long succession of failures to keep it up decently. Often there was no residence-house at all; it might have fallen out of use and then fallen to pieces ages ago; or it might have become a cow-byre or cottage, that brought the incumbent a small yearly rent. Once a residence-house had disappeared or become definitely too mean for contemporary ideas, there was absolutely no means of putting up a new one except for a benefactor (the patron, perhaps) to give one, or for the incumbent to pay for one out of the profits of the living.

It was the object therefore of a string of statutes to help incumbents find the cash, and to empower bishops to compel incumbents to build or rebuild residence-houses in certain cases. Gilbert's Acts were the first; then came two Acts in 1803, one putting Queen Anne's Bounty back in the position it had enjoyed before the 1736 Mortmain Act, and enabling it to offer its augmentations for the provision of residences;[1] the other generally encouraging gifts and bequests for 'the Promotion of Religion and Morality' by providing churches, chapels, glebes and residence-houses.[2] There were other, subsequent, statutes: but these seem to have been the main ones, and much progress was made after them.

The other reason why cures were often so ill-served was simply the insufficiency of the income of the clergyman who did the service. It is important here to distinguish between the states of poor incumbents and poor curates.

The poverty of incumbents was an old problem. Queen Anne's Bounty had been working on it ever since Anne's death, and the eleven

---

[1] 43 George III c. 107.   [2] 43 George III c. 108.

grants of £100,000 of public money made by Parliament annually from 1809 onwards went through the Bounty Board to the same end. Whether the Bounty, either in the administration of its own monies or in that of the parliamentary grants, did as well and wisely as it might have done, was questioned at the time and still allows dispute; but something, anyway, was done by these means. Another old expedient was taken up and improved in Archbishop Howley's Augmentations Act of 1831, which made it much easier for bishops, colleges and chapters to transfer properties to livings in their gift.[1] The clergy of the city of London, whose incomes had, since they were settled in Charles II's time, 'by the decreased value of money, the enhanced price of all the necessaries of life, and by various other circumstances peculiarly attached to the incumbents of the city of London, become greatly insufficient for the due support of their situation and character', were given what they regarded as a very insufficient rise in 1804.[2] Several other acts went by different and very unspectacular routes to the same end, and did a little to relieve the difficulties of incumbents. A series from 1798 onwards made it possible to redeem the land-tax on small livings and charitable institutions; Queen Anne's Bounty was enabled to lay out its augmentations, or part of them, in this way; and over the next two decades, nearly two thousand small livings were thus relieved, despite the formidable complication of the stipulated procedures.[3] An Act of 1801 partially exempted poor clergymen from the horse tax.[4] An Act of 1815 gave incumbents quite large powers to receive interest-free loans and gifts to help enlarge their residence houses and glebe lands, and to arrange beneficial exchanges of property already in their possession.[5] How much advantage was taken of an Act like this, it would need a very minute acquaintance with the history of livings to say. These Acts may be more interesting as evidence of the concern generally felt in these years for ecclesiastical improvement, than of improvement actually made.

---

[1] 1 and 2 William IV c. 45, passed on 15 October. The old expedient was that of the 29 Charles II c. 8.   [2] 44 George III c. 89, l. and p.

[3] See P.Ps. 1810, IX, 119–22; 1812, IX, 251–60; 1812–13, V, 527–37; and 1820, XI, 477–501.

[4] 41 George III c. 40. They had to be resident, and below the income-tax level.

[5] 55 George III c. 147, to which several amendments were subsequently made.

The Third Church Reform Movement and the Bounty's Part in it

Stipendiary Curates

This old problem had been hardly touched. The miseries of life as a poor curate were (incomes and other things being equal) harsher than as a poor incumbent, because the curate was likely to be completely in his parson's power. The laws that required the licensing of all curates, and gave bishops an opportunity (which of course they might not take) to insist on the payment of a reasonable stipend,[1] were generally evaded. Thomas Stackhouse's anonymous *Miseries and Great Hardships of the Inferior Clergy* is a description of the grimmer aspect of a curate's life about 1720, which would serve quite well, with only some softening of the brutalities, for the hundred years that followed it.[2] Quite apart from the difficulties of making those laws operative in a church as ungoverned and ungovernable as was the English establishment, there was such a glut of needy clergy ready to underbid each other that a non-resident could usually drive a pretty hard bargain. It was not so much a bold as a foolish curate who under such disadvantages, complained to his bishop and evoked the Act of 1713.

A similar Act was passed in 1796, and the same principle underlay Perceval's and Harrowby's attempts at Curates' Acts between 1803 and 1813.[3] Popular no doubt with the oppressed class of men they were designed to help, they excited much opposition among the oppressors, on two grounds in particular, one of them old and the other new. The old one—which had been valid in respect of the Act of 1713—was simply that the Acts were unworkable. Good men might obey them voluntarily; bad men could escape them if they wished. Sydney Smith's criticisms of Perceval's attempt of 1808 contain his usual mixture of wit, common sense, and unfairness. When curates were competing for employment,

Is it possible [he asked] to prevent this order of men from labouring under the regulation price? Is it possible to prevent a curate from pledging himself to his rector, that he will accept only half the legal salary, if he is so fortunate as to be preferred

---

[1] The Curates' Act of 1713, 12 Anne st. 2 c. 12, enabled bishops to order the payment of between £20 and £50 a year.

[2] Stackhouse's account of the oriental despotism of rectors receives some independent backing in A. Tindal Hart, *William Lloyd*, pp. 261–5.

[3] 36 George III c. 83. Perceval tried in 1805, 1806 and 1808. Lord Harrowby tried once without success in 1812 before passing the 53 George III c. 149.

among an host of rivals, who are willing to engage on the same terms? You may make these contracts illegal: What then? Men laugh at such prohibitions; and they always become a dead letter. In nine instances out of ten, the contract would be honourably adhered to; and what then is the use of Mr Perceval's law? Where the contract was not adhered to, whom would the law benefit?—A man utterly devoid of every particle of honour and good faith. . . . The law encourages breach of faith between gambler and gambler; it arms broker against broker—but it cannot arm clergyman against clergyman.'[1]

So long as the clerical was an overcrowded profession, so long as parsons could ignore the instructions of bishops with impunity, such objections could continue to be made.

The other, newer, ground of objection was the principle of the Curates' Acts. This foreshadowed, in miniature, the great objection which was to be made against the work of the Ecclesiastical Commissioners. Most of the arguments both for and against reform that agitated churchmen in the eighteen-thirties had their first airing before 1820. In each phase of the question, the same principles were in conflict. The advantages offered by the reformers were less harassment and more residence among the parochial clergy; the money to pay for this desirable end was to be taken from a better-off class of clergy to whose more or less enviable superiority of circumstances the poor curates' poverty could be attributed. Inevitably, there was argument over the fairness of this attribution, and whether you thought it fair or not depended on your premises. Of the curates, Smith for instance said that the fault was not in the parsons who paid the curates so little, but in the State that gave the parsons so little to pay the curates with. In the thirties, the parallel opposition of interests was that of the poorer parochial clergy versus the capitular clergy, whose 'responsibility' could be seen less directly in their relative idleness and undoubted affluence. The state could not be expected to provide further funds, and the capitular clergy as a class could afford it better, perhaps, than any other. Each time it was a measure of redistribution that was proposed, which was going to hurt the pockets of persons who could not possibly have expected it when they bought the advowson or accepted the presentation, or took holy orders. And, of course, such measures infringed the rights of property. Their supporters affirmed the superiority of the public interest over

[1] *Edinburgh Review*, XIII (1808), 33.

particular private interest; their opponents denied either that the two could be contrasted, or that the measure was in fact going to serve the public interest. Very often, in the church reform debates of the thirties, Harrowby's Stipendiary Curates' Act and its ineffective predecessors were adduced by the reformers as precedents for redistribution and interference with property. The battle for those principles was won, in a small way, before Waterloo.

Queen Anne's Bounty participated as fully in the third church reform movement as one would have expected of the outstanding creation of the second. It mirrored faithfully the reforming interests of the day, and shouldered particularly heavy burdens of reform. In the first three decades of the nineteenth century, indeed, its pre-eminence among the institutions on the ecclesiastical side of church-and-state was more conspicuous than it had been in the eighteenth century, simply because the volume and variety of its work were so much increased. So eminent did it become, that it seemed likely between 1820 and 1835 that the Bounty would be expanded still further and given the task of radically reforming the establishment; which, had it happened, would have forestalled the Ecclesiastical Commissioners and made them unnecessary. What the Commissioners were to church and state in the years of their greatest fame and peculiar achievement, from their foundation to the eighteen-eighties, Queen Anne's Bounty had been, more or less, in the half-century before—a focus of controversy about church reform, and the central instrument of church reform. It undertook important new tasks, at the same time as it showed an increasing readiness to correct various defects that had marred its earlier achievement.

The Bounty began to seek improvements in its operations about the year 1780. Its desire to do so should be viewed as one of the earliest manifestations of the church reform movement. An attempt was made to hasten the procedures for the purchase and conveyancing of land, and orders made to ensure that the Board was kept fully informed of what was going on in that department;[1] an order was made for the improved system of accounting introduced by Vincent Mathias (treasurer from 1776 to 1782) to be continued by his successor, and the secretary was at the same time instructed to collect and codify the

[1] Minutes, 18 December 1783, § 15 and 25 January 1787, § 33.

'rules, orders and resolutions' that the Board had made over the past seventy years.[1] These are sure indications of a livelier spirit in the Bounty Board. There had been nothing like them for fifty years. But there were to be seen still more impressive signs of an anxiety to exploit fully their potentialities for usefulness and to come out of the shell into which they had withdrawn after 1736. Early in 1787, when the new broom was at its most active, they embarked on a new financial policy that was quite adventurous in comparison with what they had been doing before; and, finally, they began to show some desire to remedy what had from the first been a defect of their system, the rigidity of their rules for augmentation compared with the fluidity of parochial finance.

Their regulations had from the start made provision for livings that escaped observation when their administrative bible, the original certifications into the Exchequer of 1707, was compiled. The first clause of the Act of 1715[2] gave the bishops power to make whatever inquiries into the values of benefices (including benefices in peculiars) they thought fit. But the second clause excepted from the wholesome operation of the first all benefices the values of which were given in the original certifications. (Was this well meant, to save the bishops trouble? It is difficult to see what other purpose can have lain behind it.) Benefices below £50 a year in 1707 might thus improve their value as time went by, while the bishops were precluded from obtaining any *official* knowledge of their improved value. The Bounty Board in fact always knew what these values were, because of their routine inquiries into the 'nature and value' of every living they started to augment. It seems that, whatever the Board's practice was in respect of improved 'certificated' livings (and the available records do not surely indicate), it occasioned no serious heart-searchings until the years 1775–82. Then, the problem was clearly recognized, and some desire to grapple with it shown.

The Board's practice with regard to the certificated livings had apparently, before 1775, been to inquire into their 'nature and value' only if they were described in Ecton's *Liber Valorum* as curacies or chapels, etc. Presumably the Board, concerned mainly to make sure that its augmentations were not intercepted and diverted from their proper object by grasping patrons, impropriators, and ministers of

---

[1] Minutes, 27 December 1782, § 15 and 27. [2] 1 Geo. I c. 10.

mother-churches, took it for granted that rectories and vicarages were safe from such dangers; but dealings in respect of them were now found to result in certain unspecified 'inconveniences,' and inquiries of the routine variety were ordered to be made about them.[1]

Whether those 'inconveniences' were found more in the natures or the values of certificated rectories and vicarages, it is impossible to say; but it is very probable that their improved values were the principal cause of the trouble, because three years later the governors found it necessary to minute a decision—rather a reluctant decision, to judge from its language—to augment 'certificated' livings drawn by lot even if their present actual value was ascertained to exceed the certificated value. They obviously felt bound to go by the letter of their founding laws.[2]

This problem continued to provoke discussion; as well it might, considering the practical absurdity in which it involved the governors. Despite their recognition of this absurdity, they found no way out of the legalistic corner into which prudence and, probably, counsel's opinion, had driven them. By 1782, 'Some doubts have arisen whether any new Certificates ought to be received from the Bishops of the several Dioceses of the Value of such Livings as were certified into the Exchequer'. The governors decided that augmentation by the Bounty or any kind of private donation to a certificated living gave them a good title to conduct an inquiry into it; but a few weeks later they withdrew again from the promising position thus adopted, by recording a decision to augment such livings so long as the sum of the value of the augmentation or donation added to the original certified value did not exceed the value of the class of livings they were then augmenting by lot (they were still trying to polish off the class of livings under £20 a year).[3] This marked a slight increase of breadth and boldness, but not much.

There the matter seems to have rested until the next spurt of reforming energy, which came not surprisingly between 1802 and 1805, and enabled the Bounty to overcome its worst diffidence and start on a course of activity from which it never afterwards fell away. In 1802 a committee of almost open membership was appointed to consider

[1] Minutes, 1 June 1775, § 8.
[2] Minutes, 30 November 1778.
[3] Minutes, 4 March 1782, § 11 and 27 March § 43.

drawing up a bill 'to give the Governors a discretionary power with respect to the Augmentation of Livings returned into the Exchequer . . . many of them being of considerable yearly value and as such improper for Augmentation with the Royal Bounty'.[1] A month later they had drawn up enough of a draft for it to be sent to their counsel 'for his further consideration'.[2] Then the project went dead for a couple of years. Their guiding principle of prudence, voiced perhaps by Sir William Scott, no doubt advised them to desist. In 1804, however, the committee was revived, and the bill taken off the shelf, refurbished, and printed for the governors' consideration during the recess.[3]

This draft bill in its second form surprisingly turned out to be a most ambitious and interesting measure. The release of the Bounty from the prison of the original certifications was the least of its contents. It included clauses enabling the Bounty's revenues of first-fruits and tenths to be paid directly to the treasurer, thus avoiding the costly delays of their detour through the Exchequer; encouraging benefactions of less than £200; seeking from the government a fund of £20,000 to help provide residence-houses on augmented cures; allowing the governors a discretion to augment particularly burdensome benefices over £100 a year, freeing them from the obligation to augment all livings under that sum without reference to the facts of area, population and so on; improving their still unsatisfactory procedures for land purchase; and, most remarkable of all, introducing revolutionary new rules for land purchase which would at once hasten the translation of their augmentations into real property—something they still set great store by—and their fullest exploitation. Two new arrangements were proposed: (1) that all the augmentation money not yet laid out in land purchases should be spent on large estates, diocese by diocese, vested in the Governors as trustees, the profits thereof to be distributed to benefices in due proportion; (2) that future augmentations be consolidated into respectable sums so as to purchase estates to be held and applied in the same manner.[4]

---

[1] Minutes, 28 January 1802, § 15. The committee was to consist of the prelates present at that general court (Moore, Porteus, Barrington, North, Cornwallis, Buckner and Majendie) or any 3 of them or any others who pleased to attend.

[2] Minutes 25 February 1802, § 10.   [3] Minutes, 26 April 1804, § 3 and 5 June, § 31.

[4] Minutes, 4 April 1805, § 5 and 6.

Here was enterprise! here was clarity of view and common sense! Had this plan been adopted, Queen Anne's Bounty would have stepped into the kind of position—business-like manager of large properties, trustee for the poor clergy who were relieved by the rents from them— that the Ecclesiastical Commissioners were to occupy forty years later. The benefits to church and clergy would have been incalculable. But next to nothing happened. Frightened by the scale of innovation their better selves demanded, and too well aware of the amount of opposition they might arouse, they drew back. They did pursue to final settlement the actual values of the certificated livings, so that within three months a statute had passed into law that gave the Bounty all the powers they needed to ascertain present actual values and free themselves from the bonds of 1707.[1] But everything else was 'postponed for further consideration', except the proposal to receive benefactions of less than £200, which disappeared at the next general court.[2] The great reform plan was, for the time being, dead.

Some less enterprising reforms along these lines there were indeed from 1809 onwards, when the Bounty's resources were extended by the eleven parliamentary grants. The Board was enabled to pick out, and favour first, certain classes of particularly needy benefices. In 1810 it took power to deal with 'strong cases of livings with laborious duty but inadequate income': when such a living was drawn in the lottery, its diocesan's recommendation would secure for it as many augmentations as the Board thought fit, at one go.[3] A year later the Board received discretionary power to give a preference in its distribution of the parliamentary grants to livings under £150 a year where the population exceeded 1000, bringing them without delay up to £80 if the population were between 1000 and 2000, and £100 if over 2000.[4] Thereafter they picked out necessitous benefices and augmented them on a sliding scale, bringing those with over 5000 up to £150, those with over 4000 up to £140, and so on down to those with over 1000, all of which (provided that their 'natures' allowed it) were brought up to £100. That done, they sought out livings of over 800—then 700—and so on

[1] 45 George III c. 84.
[2] Minutes, 16 May 1805, § 20.
[3] Minutes, 9 May 1810, § 2. Order dated 23 June 1810.
[4] Minutes, 29 March 1811, § 15. Order dated 30 May 1811.

down, by 1820, to 300, and made sure that all of them had at least £100 a year. They had discretion to do all this by simple augmentation, without tarrying for benefactors; but with regard to offers of benefactions their practice became in these years the same as in respect of livings drawn in the lottery—financial needs being equal, the more populous parishes were preferred.[1]

About the same time, the scandal of the persistence of livings under £50 a year came to weigh on them more and more heavily. A committee of at least four was appointed in 1822 to list them, and to make recommendations for at last getting rid of them. Its nucleus was Bishops Pelham, Van Mildert, Ryder and Law—the two last-named, at any rate, good men of business. They worked for a couple of years, discovering that nearly four hundred livings were still in this low class; and in 1824 the Board was enabled to bring them all summarily up to £50, and put them on the road to £60.[2] These heroic endeavours deserved more success than they met. Livings under £50 a year continued to appear in the official statistics for forty years to come, unfailing cues for the scoffer and the radical. In 1868, the best the Bounty's chief witness before the Commons' Committee could do was to point out that the number of livings under £50 was 'very much smaller than it was in the earlier years of their power'.[3] But this continuing scandal was really not the Bounty's fault. Sometimes an apparently poor living had been augmented with a residence-house, sometimes a brand new church had been put up regardless equally of expense in the building and of income for the incumbent. Most often, the fault was entirely that of a patron, who would not permit an augmentation on the very reasonable terms the Board required.

Thus the Bounty really came to life in the early nineteenth century,

[1] This account of the Board's augmentations in the eighteen-tens and -twenties is, I believe, substantially correct. The three sources on which it is based are all imperfect, and contain some slight inconsistencies. They are: the relevant Orders dated 25 May 1813, 14 May 1814, and 14 June 1820: Hodgson's evidence before the 1837 Committee, Qs. 625–30 and 1006–32: and the Bounty's reports on its administration of the first six parliamentary grants, in the P.Ps. 1810, XIV, 99–100; 1810–11, X, 471–2; 1812, X, 163–4; 1812–13, XIII, 53–5; 1813–14, XII, 149–50; and 1814–15, XII, 521–2.
[2] Minutes, 14 March 1822, § 11 and 21 March, § 1; 17 April 1823, § 1 and 16 May, § 1; 11 March 1824.
[3] 1868 Committee, Q. 260.

escaping from the antiquated cramps of its founding laws and the timorous quiescence that had followed the Mortmain Act. Up-to-date valuations of the poorer livings became available, a great new fund was placed at the Board's disposal, and the Board was enabled to deal with the most desperate and deserving cases without going through the hazardous delays of the lottery, or relying on the unpredictable vagaries of private benefaction. Nor were these the only directions in which the Bounty decidedly improved in this period. It began to attempt to deal also with 'undeserving' livings, and to use the prospect of augmentations as a means of influencing wayward incumbents to mend their ways.

The idea of attaching conditions to augmentations was not new. Tenison had suggested this very early in the history of the Bounty, and so had White Kennet, who found several instances of the practice under comparable circumstances in the late seventeenth century.[1] Their reasonableness was so obvious that several virtuous incumbents in the early days seem to have understood their existence, and to have accepted them voluntarily.[2] But they became no part of the Bounty's official policy until 1794. Then at last, 'the Governors, taking into consideration that many augmented livings are served by temporary Curates for small Stipends, and although the incomes have been much increased by augmentations ... they have but the ancient Duty performed which is generally once a Fortnight, and in many cases not so often; whereby the good intentions of her late Majesty Queen Anne are in great measure frustrated', agreed 'to make it known to the Clergy ... at their Visitations, or otherwise as may seem expedient', that they intended to require 'a more constant and regular performance of Duty'.[3] The principle, once adopted, was acted on and extended. It fitted neatly into the contemporary pattern of church reform activity, while so much piecemeal improvement was being made by the more progressive bishops in their own dioceses, urging the clergy to greater exertions and using such levers as the law of the church allowed (especially non-residence licences, licences for curates, and now the Bounty's augmentations) to put a little steel in their persuasions. The Board seems to have had no doubt that it had full discretion to attach conditions to its

[1] Savidge, pp. 54–5. Kennet, *Case of Impropriations*, pp. 411–12.
[2] Savidge, p. 96.
[3] Minutes, 1 May 1794, § 12.

grants, and extended their scope to include the provision by non-residents of properly licensed curates, as well as the performance of at least one service each Sunday.[1]

All this was done without recourse to higher authority. That came only with the parliamentary grants. On the great day when Lord Harrowby and Spencer Perceval came to Dean's Yard to frame the regulations for the distribution of the first grant, it was decided that the Board need not pay the interest of an augmentation but might reserve it and add it to the principal in cases where the incumbent was nonresident or possessed of another living of over £150, held in plurality.[2] This was indeed strong meat for a church so steeped in non-residence and plurality, and so apt to justify them. Within a year the governors had second thoughts. They decided that the rule was only an enabling one, not compulsory upon them, and that interest should be paid to all incumbents in the ordinary way unless the Board gave special directions to withhold it.[3] Soon after that they withdrew the restriction respecting pluralists whose other living was over £150,[4] and some years later, having found the remaining restrictions cramping to their style, they obtained large relaxations of them that enabled the payment of the interest unconditionally to non-resident or disabled clergy whose cases their bishop approved—to clergymen temporarily serving vacant cures—and to curates whose non-resident parsons were certified by the bishop as really unable to pay them decently.[5] Episcopal discretion was the mainspring of church reform in this period, and it was not surprising that the governors of Queen Anne's Bounty firmly believed in it.[6]

The Bounty came to have much to do with the provision of residence-houses in these years. Until the end of its independent existence they

[1] See, e.g., Minutes, 29 January 1806, § 29 and 31.
[2] Minutes, 23 June 1809, § 14/1. Order dated 12 September 1809.
[3] Minutes, 9 May 1810, § 2.
[4] Minutes, 21 February 1811, § 10.
[5] Order dated 11 May 1827.
[6] The position regarding augmentations in these cases of prosperous pluralists is not absolutely clear. The minutes that have just been cited are unequivocal, the soft practice they point to is exactly what one would have expected, and Hodgson's evidence to the 1837 committee seems wholly to confirm it. (Qs. 1036–47). Yet that committee in its report (p. vi) stated that the practice was quite tough. Perhaps the author of the report misunderstood the matter.

remained one of its principal cares. The Bounty's work in this department began very quietly with Gilbert's Act of 1777, 'to promote the residence of the parochial clergy, by making provision for the more speedy and effectual building, rebuilding, repairing or purchasing houses and other necessary buildings and tenements for the use of their benefices'.[1] Its preamble stated eloquently that 'many of the parochial clergy, for want of proper habitations, are induced to reside at a distance from their benefices, by which means the parishioners lose the advantage of their instruction and hospitality, which were the great objects in the original distribution of tithes and glebes for the endowment of churches'; and one of the several means it proposed for putting things right, was that incumbents might get loans from Queen Anne's Bounty at specially low interest-rates. The normal rate was 5% (but 10% in case of non-residents absent for more than twenty weeks of the year). The Bounty was empowered to lend up to £100 to livings under £50 a year without taking any interest at all, and up to two years' income to livings over £50 a year at only 4%.[2] Gilbert's second Act, of 1781, was an amending act only and did not alter these provisions.[3]

The Bounty Board appears to have done nothing under the Gilbert Acts for about thirty years. Why it should have taken so long is not clear. Certainly the Gilbert Acts were used in other ways.[4] But the Board was not eager to lend money as the Acts suggested. They decided late in 1781 that the calls upon their funds were so many and uncertain that they would have to postpone consideration of it for the time being.[5] Maybe their help was not much solicited: in the absence of letter-books, it is impossible to say. At any rate, nothing was done until 1811, when they suddenly embarked on an extensive programme of loans on mortgage under the Gilbert Acts and settled the procedure for handling them with great despatch.[6] This became at once a major branch of the Bounty's business. By 1826, £224,525 19s. 9d. was loaned on mortgage.[7] By 1836 the governors were reaping a harvest of about £10,000

[1] 17 George III c. 53.   [2] Sections 6 and 12.   [3] 21 George III c. 66.
[4] See e.g. Dr Whiteman's findings in the diocese of Salisbury, in *V.C.H., Wiltshire*, III, 52.   [5] Minutes, 29 November 1781, § 14.
[6] Minutes, 30 May 1811, § 6 and 20 June, § 27. Sydney Smith was one of their first clients (minutes, 29 April 1813).
[7] P.Ps. 1831, XV, 40.

a year on their mortgage loans.[1] All parties did well out of it. Incumbents got their loans more cheaply and with a good deal less accompanying anxiety than they could have done from private or commercial lenders; the church saw its residence-houses repaired or rebuilt; and the Bounty received about as much interest on its capital as it would have done from the gilt-edged securities in which exclusively it had thitherto invested.

This business was not indeed untroublesome. Many clergymen, finding it difficult to repay their loans in the specified period, expected the Bounty Board to deal with them leniently. In this hope they were disappointed. The Board had to be businesslike if it was to be benevolent. The money on loan was not from a fund that would otherwise lie idle, but was the property and source of income of individual clergymen, held and managed for them by the Board until they found property to buy with it. Defaulting mortgagers received from the Board's solicitor letters no less threatening than they would have got from any other solicitor. The amount of trouble the Board was put to by its loans under the Gilbert Acts may be illustrated from its proceedings in 1824, when the business had only been going on for a dozen years, and the rate of interest was reduced to 3%. 503 loans had been made, and on no less than 54 of them there were 2 or more years' payments in arrear. The Board decided that it was not usually worth badgering late payers until they were two years in arrear; instructed its solicitor to write firmly to those over two years in arrears, and to warn them that they must be punctual to qualify for the reduction in the interest; and resolved to bring actions against the incumbents of Newtown (St Asaph), Cannington (Bath and Wells), Newton Blossomville (Lincoln), and Childrey (Salisbury), who either owed excessive sums, or were known, on their own or their bishop's declaration, to be unable to pay unless forced by law to do so.[2]

Lending to incumbents under the Gilbert Acts was not the whole of the Bounty's concern with residence-houses. The Act of 1803[3] that freed Queen Anne's Bounty from the shackles of the Mortmain Act and extended the Act of 1715 so as further to encourage gifts and beneficial exchanges of lands and buildings, also authorized the Bounty's putting its

[1] 1837 committee, Q. 664.
[2] Minutes, 10 June 1824, § 29 and 17 June, § 1.
[3] 43 George III c. 107.

augmentations or parts of them to the purchase of residence-houses. Earlier in its career, the Board's practice in this respect seems to have been inconsistent. A minute of 20 March 1721 decided that augmentations could not be made for this purpose, and this decision was strictly adhered to throughout a protracted correspondence with the minister of St Edmund's, Salisbury.[1] In 1735 and 1739 the purchase of parsonages is known to have been sanctioned.[2] Yet when the 'inhabitants and neighbouring gentry' of Newton chapelry, near Manchester, asked if they could lay out half their proposed benefaction on a new parsonage ('the present being an old cottage not fit for a clergyman to live in') the governors told them that it could not be.[3] The causes of these seeming inconsistencies are not apparent. No augmentations were allowed to buy residence-houses during at any rate the second half of the eighteenth century. After the enabling act of 1803 they became quite common.[4]

The Bounty's interest in the provision of residence-houses thus became considerable; but its main business was still the augmentation of livings. It would be wrong to speak simply of poor livings. During the years of the third church reform movement, the distinction of value made from the very start between the livings augmented by lot and those to meet benefactions, was maintained and even accentuated.

The great events in this central department of the Bounty's work were the distribution of, first, the 'surpluses' in the closing years of the eighteenth century, and second, the parliamentary grants of 1809-16 and 1818-20.

The 'surpluses' were the consequence of the governors' insistence that augmentations should be put to the purchase of land, and that until suitable properties were found, they would pay only 2% interest on the capital while it stayed in their hands. But they were of course usually making more than 2% on it. The sum of interest they received on their capital thus exceeding, by amounts varying from year to year with the

[1] Savidge, p. 95.

[2] Savidge, pp. 95–6, and minutes, 5 June 1738, § 14, 2 October 1738, § 5 and 19 November 1739, § 13—the case of Barnsley, Yorkshire. The facts are not too clear, but it seems that the 'new-built stone house' coveted by the curate there was in the end bought.

[3] Minutes, 2 October 1738, § 15 and 6 November 1738, § 18.

[4] The governors settled their procedure in this new branch of business at the general court of 5 April 1804, minutes § 6.

ups and downs of the market, the sum they had to pay from it, there gradually accumulated a 'surplus' of interest. This 'surplus' they added every now and then to their year's clear revenue from ordinary sources, and so made mass augmentations of 238 in 1767, 119 in 1772, 135 in 1775, 185 in 1787, and 341 in 1792.

The parliamentary grants to Queen Anne's Bounty for the relief of the poor clergy attracted at the time, and have attracted since, much less attention than the church building grants of 1818 and 1825. Presumably this was because they were more humdrum, and men of taste could not find so much in them to argue about. But they were not less remarkable as pledges by the state of its confidence in the church and substantial proofs of their unbroken alliance; and they enabled the Bounty greatly to extend its sphere of usefulness. From 1809 on, it had two funds from which to draw, the Parliamentary Grants Fund, and the Royal Bounty Fund, kept strictly separate and administered under different rules. More enterprise was shown in the administration of the new fund. It was used as a hare to supplement the work of the steady old tortoise; which was moreover burdened after 1812 with the Gilbert Act mortgage loans. In 1810 its augmentations from the new fund were raised from £200 to £300 if met by benefactions of £200 in cash, lands or tithes, or rent-charge or annuity of £15 p.a.;[1] and in 1811 it was made the means of executing that plan for distinguishing the more needy, populous, poor parishes from the less needy and populous, that weighed so heavily on church reformers' minds about that time. They did not in fact establish satisfactory methods for picking out and helping the really needy, for the new church and parish divisions that followed the Act of 1818 introduced a set of new and changing problems that outmatched them. Yet the administration of the Parliamentary Grant fund was, undoubtedly, in these ways an improvement on that of the older fund.

In two other ways the Bounty's handling of its newer fund showed more sense and enterprise. The governors seem to have felt themselves free to do with it things that, for whatever reason, they could not bring themselves to do with the other. They were more liberal, for instance, in interest they paid to clergy whose augmentations were not yet laid out in land. Bounty Fund augmentations had been receiving their paltry

[1] Order dated 13 March 1810.

2% since 1758. Only in 1830 did this go up, to $3\frac{1}{4}$%. The governors then at last decided that 'the immediate investment of appropriated monies in the purchase of lands or tithes' was not 'a matter of paramount importance', and expressed a praiseworthy desire of 'improving the condition of poor incumbents'.[1] Some reformers had been suggesting these changes for ages; the idea was at least as old as Bishop Watson; and if the improvement of the condition of poor incumbents could be achieved in 1830 by raising the rate of interest, it could have been achieved a good deal earlier by the same means, despite their use of the capital for mortgages. The governors came out of this the less well, in view of their having raised the rate of interest on Parliamentary Grant fund augmentations (those at any rate that had been made to meet benefactions) from 2% to 4% in 1822, within a dozen years of its founding.[2]

Another overdue improvement made in respect of the new fund but not of the older was the making possible its investment in government stock instead of in land. This, again, had been suggested by Watson. The clergy of his diocese had joined in a petition to the Bounty, complaining of the difficulty of purchasing land and suggesting that they could get 5% on it, instead of 2%, if they were allowed to buy safe stocks with their augmentations instead of having to wait years and years for suitable land purchases. Watson presented their petition and approved of it.[3] The same change was advocated by the sagacious authors of *The State of the Established Church* in 1809, and *Letter to the Archbishop of Canterbury on the subject of Church Property*, in 1824.[4] Obsessed by the idea of rooting their church in the supposedly stable, 'natural', life of the countryside, and fearful perhaps lest they might be giving hostages to Erastianism and political exploitation, the bishops only decided to act along these lines in 1829 (by when of course the progress of their mortgage-loan business had progressed so far that it was out of the question to act similarly in respect of the Bounty Fund). They then adopted a plan drawn up by their efficient secretary, Christopher Hodgson, and promulgated two years later, by which their

[1] Minutes, 11 March 1830, § 1.
[2] Minutes, 9 May 1822, § 7. Hodgson's Memorandum of May 1824, given to the 1837 committee, Q. 764.   [3] *Miscellaneous Tracts*, I, 50–3.
[4] Of the former (2nd edn., 1810), pp. 102–3; of the latter, pp. 32–8.

augmentations and associated benefactions should be put to the purchase of blocks of 3% bank annuities, the dividend from each of which could be conveniently collected from the Bounty Office.[1]

Queen Anne's Bounty was thus booming in these years. It began to take on other tasks besides those named in its charters and the Gilbert Acts. In 1804, it was constituted a relief office for curates thrown out of employment by Sir William Scott's Non-Residence Act. Only a few applied, for the Act was so weak in itself and so weakly administered that hardly any non-resident clergy were brought back by it to residence on their cures; but neither the Bounty Board nor the framers of the Act could foresee this at the time, and the Board prepared for a flood of applications.[2] Hardly any of these curates lacked employment for long. The Board, granting them only about three-quarters of what they had been receiving, went out of its way to make unemployment less eligible than employment, and drove them back to stipendiary servitude.

One curate, Edward Gillespy, dismissed from a curacy at Blisworth, Northamptonshire, showed uncommon staying power. His bishop, Madan of Peterborough, continually backed his applications, and the Board at first treated him generously; in the winter of 1804-5 he got £52 10s., a year later £40. In 1807 he got £35 and in 1808, £30. By this time he was the only applicant, and the Board must have been uncomfortably aware that he was passing through the stage of an anomaly towards that of an abuse. When he applied again in 1809, they cut him down to £25; and that was all he got (his bishop, who was not present at the meeting, still 'duly recommending' him) in 1810. What subsequently happened to him, does not appear.

The Bounty was also put to work as a general ecclesiastical administrative department, in harness with the Privy Council's receiver of diocesan returns in 1809, when the Home Secretary directed it to find out how many livings there were under £150 a year. It could very easily have shouldered more work still, as plenty of church reformers thought

---

[1] Minutes, 2 May 1829, § 1; Order dated 13 July 1829; 1837 committee, Q. 766.

[2] 44 George III c. 2, setting aside £8000 for this charitable task—a pretty example of the legislature at its tenderest towards existing interests. The governors ordered their treasurer to draw £500 of it on 5 June 1804 (minutes, § 14), and relieved eight during the next six months. Thereafter they never had more than three on their hands at once.

it was fit to do. An anonymous barrister in 1829 published a short, brisk, and sensible pamphlet proposing the revaluation of first-fruits and tenths on a realistic basis and a large extension of the Bounty's powers to enable it properly to endow new churches.[1] His proposal, that funds should be provided for the church's urgent necessities by a realistic revaluation of first-fruits and tenths or a more justly proportioned, graduated tax on benefices, was common to many plans of church reform. Although controversial, and rejected as of bad principle by some reformers, it attracted a great deal of support, and was by far the commonest of all reformatory proposals *not* to be adopted sooner or later. Most of those who proposed it, by omitting to specify any new collecting or distributing agency, presumably intended it to be done by Queen Anne's Bounty.[2] Pusey remarked towards the end of his lengthy contribution to the debate on church reform, that he took it for granted that Queen Anne's Bounty was the natural instrument for the reapplication of sinecures to efficient purposes.[3] The rector of Beddington, Surrey, J. B. Ferrers, about the same time published a short pamphlet on *The Necessity and Advantages of an Immediate Increase of Queen Anne's Bounty;* he wanted all livings to be brought up at once to £300 a year, assistant curacies to be endowed on all parishes over 3000, and all district churches to be made full parish churches at the next vacancy; and Queen Anne's Bounty to provide the money for this radical and expensive reform, by immediately quadrupling tenths and first-fruits. An equally radical church reformer, Lord Suffield, said in debate on Howley's Pluralities Bill that he would have the Bounty Board assume the role of a wholesale redistributor of ecclesiastical revenues.[4]

Not only was the Bounty thus well to the forefront of the debate on church reform in its most critical years. It was in the same years going

[1] *Substance of a Letter to one of his Majesty's Ministers on the subject of First-Fruits and Tenths.*

[2] The respectability of this proposal may be judged by the quality of its advocates; they included Bishop Watson, the anonymous authors of *The State of the Established Church, The Interests of the Church of England* and *Letter to the Archbishop of Canterbury,* Archdeacon J. H. Browne, Charles Girdlestone, (who said Bishop Heber favoured it too), George Stoddart, and Edward Burton.

[3] *Remarks on Cathedral Institutions,* p. 117.

[4] *Mirror of Parliament* (1832), pp. 1394–6, debate of 23 March.

through a crisis of its own. One of its two principal servants involved it in great loss and scandal. The other did much to retrieve the situation, and made some radical improvements in the office organisation.

John Paterson, Treasurer to the Bounty, cannot have been a crook; not, at any rate, in his early years in the office. He began as partner and trusted friend of Stevens, of whom everything that we know suggests that he was businesslike and incorruptible. The one letter-book of his that survives, from the period 1807-11, gives a most attractive idea of him.[1] The governors left him completely on his own (except for the annual audit of his accounts), to get on with his job just as he pleased. He transacted his side of the Bounty's work from his business address at 68, Old Broad Street, and his son and partner William Paterson seems occasionally to have lent a hand with it.[2] His business in the days of his partnership with Stevens had been, or at least had included, wholesale hosiery. By the end of his life he had something to do, as had his son, with a coal and lime firm that traded under the style of The Penshurst Company.[3]

When John Paterson 'resigned' towards the end of 1830, he owed the Bounty £30,749 14s. 7d. Whether he merely retired, went abroad, or died, and at what date, cannot be exactly ascertained; the Board's minutes thereafter always refer to him as 'the late Treasurer'; but he was certainly dead by 20 March 1831.[4] This large sum he had in hand for the ordinary work of the Treasurer's department—the payment of interest to incumbents of augmented livings, loans on mortgage, purchases of estates; and as customary in offices like his, he held large sums in a deposit account and was able to make money on them for himself.[5] Hodgson, his successor, thought that he had probably been making more that way than he did on his official salary, which was £500 a year.[6] Undesirable though this practice might have been in principle, it would not have mattered if Paterson's estate had been substantial enough to have answered the heavy calls he had thus invited

[1] See above, pp. 133-4.

[2] E.g. letter of 9 August 1808, in letter book, fo. 18r.

[3] *London Gazette*, 1832, Part I, p. 665, advertisement of the bankruptcy of James Christie, 'partner in trade with Richard Wilson, John Paterson, William Paterson, and John Whyte'.   [4] See the Order of that date.

[5] In 1812 the Registrar of the Courts of Admiralty had sometimes about £200,000 in hand, to put to use. (*Memoirs of Romilly*, III, 43-4).   [6] 1837 committee, Q. 577.

to be made upon it. But no more was to be had from it than £5649 14. His unhappy sureties, Richard Debaufre and William Horton, lost their £3000 apiece, over £6000 more seemed to be on the way from one of his debtors, James Christie, and his son promised to repay all that he could. But first of all Christie, the coal and lime merchant, collapsed, and all they ever got from him was £319 16s. od.;[1] and then William Paterson collapsed as well. Early in 1835, 'the Governors agreed under the advice of the Secretary and Solicitor to abandon the security given by Mr William Paterson . . . in respect of a debt due from him to his late father and directed that his life policy effected in the Amicable Insurance Office should be sold and a Commission of two shillings in the pound accepted in full of all demands upon him.'[2]

The Governors were thus left some £15,000 to the bad. The manner in which they made it up to the Bounty was as much to the credit of their charity, as it had been little to the credit of their judgment that they allowed Paterson so criminally to mismanage their affairs. Feeling no doubt both uncomfortable and frightened at their situation—for there cannot have been many worse years in the whole century to un-leash an ecclesiastical scandal than 1831—they resolved to make it up out of their own pockets, at the rate of £1,100 a year. Canterbury, York, London, Durham, Winchester and Ely were to pay £100 a year each; the others, £25 a year; and new bishops, albeit wholly innocent of any responsibility for this débâcle, were to be expected to co-operate.[3] Thus was public scandal averted, and an answer made ready to turn away the wrath of unfriendly inquirers.[4]

It was a happy circumstance for Queen Anne's Bounty that during the very years that the worst officer in its history was letting it down, the best officer in its history was entering into the fullness of his powers. This was Christopher Hodgson, whom the Governors appointed to succeed Richard Burn in 1822.[5] In 1831, as part of the re-arrangements

[1] Minutes, 13 March 1834, § 1.

[2] Minutes, 14 May 1835, § 12.

[3] Minutes, 1 March 1832, § 17–18.

[4] The Paterson affair recurs frequently in the minutes between December 1830 and early 1835. See also P.Ps. 1831, xv, 43, and 1834, XLIII, 13.

[5] Minutes, 7 February 1822, § 1. The *D.N.B.* passes him over. Where no other source is specified or presumptive, my account of him relies on that given briefly in Boase, I, 1494; which is sketchy, and wrong in at least one of its dates.

consequent upon Paterson's collapse, the offices of treasurer and secretary were united; and Hodgson held the two of them until his retirement
at the age of 87 in 1871.[1] He thus held office for a very long time with
some distinction. He was already well versed in ecclesiastical business
when he was appointed secretary, at the age of thirty-eight. The evidence
seems conclusive that he was the son of John Hodgson of Bartlett's
Buildings, Holborn, an ecclesiastical lawyer, with an extensive practice
among the bishops and chapters; from whom he would easily enough
have got a good start in the same line of business.[2] In 1806 or 1807 he
became chapter clerk, registrar, and bailiff of the manors and bailiwicks
to the dean and chapter of St Paul's.[3] About 1809 he was appointed
secretary to the archbishop of Canterbury, and in the course of the next
ten years or so he became secretary also to the bishop of London and the
Archbishop of York, acting, as it would seem, as their solicitor, and
collecting their revenues for them. In 1817 he published a useful short
set of *Instructions for the Use of Candidates for Holy Orders, and of the
Parochial Clergy, . . . with Acts of Parliament relating to the same, and forms
to be used*, which went into its ninth edition in 1870; and in 1820 Archbishop Manners-Sutton conferred upon him a Lambeth M.A.[4]

He was thus a man of some standing and experience when he joined
the Bounty in 1822, and the office he held there was not his only place
of occupation and source of profit. When the 1837 committee, scenting
scandal, asked him whether he held 'any other appointment or situation,'

[1] His sureties as treasurer were the Reverend Dr Barrett and the second Lord
Harris. (Minutes, 14 April 1831, § 23). One is tempted to see some significance in the
fact that Lord Harris's sister Anne was wife to the eminent civilian Stephen
Lushington.

[2] Boase says our Christopher was elder son of John Hodgson of Bishop Auckland,
and was born at Bartlett's Buildings in 1784. The Archivist's Report of the Lincolnshire Archives Committee, 1950-1, p. 22, describes one John Hodgson of Bartlett's
Buildings as acting for the bishops, deans and chapters of Lincoln and Salisbury, the
bishops of St Davids and Chester, and other lesser clergy, in the matter of land tax
redemption, c. 1798–1808. A document in those archives shows that he was also joint
principal registrar of the diocese of Lincoln, and joint registrar under the commissiaries
of Lincoln and Stow. (Lincoln Reg. 39, p. 89.)

[3] G. L. Prestige, *St Paul's in its Glory*, p. 91. He held these offices until January 1869

[4] His *Instructions* were prescribed reading, along with Grey's *Ecclesiastical Law* and
Burn's, and the *Clergyman's Assistant*, for those who wished Bishop Burgess to ordain
them: see Appendix VII to his 1826 Charge.

he replied, 'only of a private nature. I am a Solicitor, a Professional man, and I have other professional business'. But he had given up all professional business save in respect of the three top prelates and the chapter of St Paul's, which he was perfectly well able to do outside the Bounty's office hours of 'ten to four, constantly'.[1] With this pluralism the 1837 committee found no fault, and went so far as to say, that they 'would not be doing justice to their own feelings if they omitted to express the favourable opinion which they entertain of the present secretary and treasurer, Mr Hodgson'.[2] The 1868 committee was less impressed. Hodgson by then was very old, and too ill to defend his Board in person. The assistant cashier and accountant, J. K. Aston, stood in for him. 'Speaking without any disparagement to Mr Hodgson, the Secretary is of great age, is he not?'—'He has reached the age of 84.' Too many others in the office were old as well: Hodgson's assistant secretary was 70; Mr Scott, about whom the interesting rumour, that he had been 60 when he was appointed, turned out to be a slight exaggeration, was about 75; and then, 'in the treasurer's office, there is the cashier, who has been there 56 years; he cannot be very young; what is his age?'[3] It is obvious that the Bounty Office had become Hodgson's private empire. The volume of business by the mid-century was not so great that one remorselessly industrious man could not keep the whole of it under his own control. Hodgson opened and minuted all the letters himself, settled the drafts, and signed the fair copies.[4] Hardly anyone ever retired; appointments were understood to be for life; the Bounty did not come under the Civil Service or the Superannuation Acts; Hodgson seemed indestructible and disliked change.[5] As he resided on the premises, as the secretary had been able to do since the Bounty first leased the Dean's Yard house in 1735, his home, his private office, and the Bounty Office were inextricably knotted together. Mr Bouverie tried to distinguish them. 'Has he a distinct residence, or does he live in the office?'—'The offices are in, under, and about the house, and annexed to it . . .: the board-room of the governors . . . at other times

---

[1] Qs. 531–8.   [2] Report, p. vii.
[3] 1868 Committee, Qs. 60–83. In answer to this last question, Q. 75, Aston said that the man had been there in Paterson's days, 'when the treasurership was a mere adjunct to the then occupant's other offices and duties'.
[4] Qs. 88–99.   [5] Qs. 68–73, 119–29.

... forms the secretary's private sitting-room.'[1] Somewhere in that hive were to be found also his nephew and partner, J. B. Lee, and the two clerks who helped them with their private business.[2] The committee found no fault with the Board's management of its business, but thought that Hodgson was overpaid at £1350 a year, and frowned severely at the use of a public office as a private residence and for the transaction of private business. It was the nineteenth century passing judgment on its predecessor, the new civil service replacing the old. Hodgson had to go. When, or how he went, is not certain. When he died in 1874, three years after he had left the Bounty's service, the place of his death was given in *The Times* newspaper as that smart new residential suburb, Spring Grove, Isleworth.[3]

To give the impression that Hodgson was in any way hidebound or incapable, however, would be very misleading. Although he may have become a reactionary by the eighteen-sixties, his character earlier had been very different. The new plan of augmentation out of the parliamentary grant fund in 1829 had been his. He, too, largely by his own efforts, had dragged the Bounty out of the mud and put its procedures on a better footing after the Paterson affair.[4] He published in 1826 a clear and serviceable (albeit starchy and legalistic) history of the Bounty and statement of its achievements to date, with instructions and advice to those who wished in any way to avail themselves of its services; and he brought out several later editions and supplements, to keep it accurate and useful.[5] These publications cost him nothing—the Board paid for

[1] Qs. 40–4. This seems to mean, that the Upper House of Convocation used to meet in Christopher Hodgson's drawing-room.

[2] Qs. 212–23, and Prestige, *loc. cit.*

[3] *Times*, 10 August 1874, p. 1a.

[4] Minutes, 2 May 1829, § 1; 17 February 1831, § 1 and 2; and 24 March 1831, § 13–16; Order dated 20 March 1831; 1837 committee, Qs. 576–7, 724–30. The main point of this reform of 1831 was that the Board opened an account of its own at Coutts's, got them to undertake much of the routine financial work, and introduced a foolproof set of regulations for checking the treasurer's efficiency and auditing his accounts.

[5] *An Account of the Augmentation of Small Livings by the Governors of Queen Anne's Bounty . . . and of benefactions by Corporate Bodies and Individuals; with Practical Instructions for the use of Incumbents and patrons of Augmented Livings:* 1st edition, 1826, 2nd edition, 1845; *Supplements* published (and usually bound in with the 2nd edition), 1856 and 1864.

them and the bulk of the work was no doubt done by his clerks—but other evidence suggests that the impression they give, of a man whose life and leading interests were absorbed in the Bounty's work, is not false. Hodgson, after all, to a large extent *was* the Bounty. In a late edition of his *Instructions* he asked the five thousand odd tenths-paying clergy, 'as a personal favour . . . kindly and considerately' to pay their tenths punctually without having to be reminded to do so!¹ And the Bounty's business *was* efficiently done. He defended it stoutly in a *Letter to the Archbishop of Canterbury* in 1865 and accused its attackers of ignorance and malice. Neither of the select committees was able to find any fault with it, and the first of these committees at any rate had every intention to find faults and expose them. They exposed the First-Fruits and Tenths Offices and recommended their instant abolition. But despite the needling of Baines, Duncombe and Philips, the Bounty Office showed no flaws. This was due partly to the good offices of Sir Robert Inglis, who several times took over from the unfriendly radicals and put questions that elicited facts to alkalise the acid of their innuendos; but even more was it due to Hodgson, who showed great firmness and resource in defence (one could as truly say, in self-defence). The other witnesses were uneasy and on their guard. Only Hodgson stood up for himself manfully and gave as good as he got. Edward Baines, prosecuting his interrogation from a hostile base of ignorance and prejudice, repeatedly tried to catch him out. It was to no avail. Hodgson was perfect master of his facts and the facts were not discreditable. Hodgson did particularly well towards the end of his examination (258 questions long) on the second day. Baines pointed out that the cost of running the Bounty had much increased since the beginning of the century. 'And it will continue to increase,' countered the secretary-treasurer, 'because it is like the accountant general's office in Chancery, the more suits there are, the more business he has to do, and the more business there is, the more clerks they must have.' (Point to Hodgson.) Baines: 'You have only three clerks now?' Hodgson: 'Yes, but they work harder than in any public office in London.' Baines dropped that line, and went back to the costs. After a short interlude of sparring, a quick jab by Baines was countered in a masterly fashion. 'Comparing these charges in 1805 with 1835, is there not an excess of £2469 17s. 4d.

¹ 8th edition. My italics.

a year?'—Hodgson: 'I make it £2416 18s. 8d.' The radical party temporarily collapsed, and the interrogation was taken over by another.[1]

The radicals could find nothing at fault in the way the Bounty Office did its business; but they put unerring fingers on some of the Bounty's weakest features, the fundamental principles that guided its work of augmentation. These were virtually as old as the Bounty itself, and for them, of course, the secretary-treasurer was in no wise responsible. With a consideration of these alleged failings, therefore, this section will conclude, leaving Christopher Hodgson the respected master of Dean's Yard, Westminster.

In spite of the important improvements that had been made in the Bounty's work since the time of the younger Pitt, several aspects of Bounty policy remained open to the general criticism that, in the process of augmenting the poor clergy's livings, a good many not so poor clergy profited as well, and three classes of persons who ought not to have profited at all in fact profited a great deal—impropriators, plura-lists, and patrons.

The not so poor clergy profited as well as the really poor, partly because of the Bounty's large tolerance of pluralities, more because the maximum value for livings augmentable in connexion with private benefactions was always so much higher than that for livings augmen-table by lot. The encouragement of benefactions was a principle very dear to the governors' hearts at all times, and one can see why it should have been so. Self-help by the responsible parts of the community was, after all, the common rule of the constitution at that time. By offering inducements to it, the governors were not only acting in perfect accord with a basic constitutional principle, but were stimulating sentiments of generosity and social responsibility whose value in any political community at any time can hardly be overrated. Thus, in 1809, when they were still augmenting by lot livings under £30 a year, they offered their grants of £200 to meet equivalent benefactions for livings under £80 a year, 'in order to preserve in some degree and continue a difference in point of value' between livings in the two classes. The year following, they put the maximum for the second class up to £120 a year, and offered grants of £300 from their new, parliamentary grants fund to

---

[1] Qs. 769–77. He was in great form again during his second examination and scored several more points off the radicals—see especially Qs. 1000–1013.

meet them. In 1820, while the problem of the under-£50 livings was still unsolved, this maximum was raised to £200. In 1836 the Board took power to cease augmenting livings, if it thought fit, otherwise than jointly with benefactors, and almost stopped augmenting them in any other way.[1] It is true that much more capital thus found its way into the church's endowments than would have done if the Board's grants were not meeting at least their equivalents and often more than their equivalents. It is true also that the Board, when considering offers of benefactions, would review the relative circumstances of the livings proposed and, in theory at any rate,[2] prefer the more necessitous; but the wisdom of persisting with this distinction was debateable, and caused some resentment among the unhappy holders of the poorest livings. There were still livings under £50 a year in 1868.[3]

More serious, though perhaps more unfair to the Bounty, since it was a matter over which the Board could have less control, was the criticism that patrons, impropriators and pluralists, classes of persons who had no claim whatever on the Bounty, were actually making a very good thing out of it. Let us deal with these in reverse order.

When considering the fitness of a poor living to receive an augmentation, the Board did not consider the fitness of the incumbent. The two things were, after all, separate. Benefices, so to speak, were there for ever; but incumbents came and went, their personal circumstances changed, their archdeacons and bishops had it in their power, a little, to moderate abuses and enforce higher standards. The task of enforcing the rule adopted by the Board in 1809 to prevent its augmentations swelling the profits of pluralists was formidable; and besides, pluralists were so much part and parcel of the church's system that they were practically sacrosanct. The Board quickly retreated from a position both invidious and untenable and virtually ceased to worry about pluralities, classing them among those circumstances of incumbents into which it was not *their* business to inquire.[4]

[1] Order dated 3 March 1836. Hodgson's *Letter to the Archbishop*, pp. 6–9, vigorously defends the Board's policy in this respect.

[2] See the Order dated 13 March 1810, Hodgson's evidence to the 1837 committee, Qs. 614 and 626, and the report of the 1868 Committee, p. iii.   [3] 1868 committee, Q. 260.

[4] On these points, see especially Hodgson's evidence to the 1837 committee, Qs. 1036–46.

Impropriators did very well out of the Bounty in an indirect fashion. Ever since Whitgift's day, they had been under moral pressure from the central body of church reformers to return to the benefice from which they drew their tithes at least enough to give its incumbent a decent subsistence.[1] No pressure other than moral was ever exerted. Parliament, in which the interest of the impropriators was of course well represented, never touched the subject except in two Acts, of 1677 and 1831, that facilitated the augmentation of poor vicarages and curacies by ecclesiastical corporations and colleges.[2] Lay impropriators, absolute masters of their property, needed no enabling legislation to do what the reformers expected of them. Bishops and deans, on the other hand, and chapters and colleges, all of whom were largely supported by impropriations, could not make any part of their impropriations over permanently to their original benefice, any more than they could give away any other part of their endowments, without statutory authority. This authority was at last fully conferred upon them by Howley's Act, and to some extent used; but it was left entirely to the bodies concerned to use it or not, at discretion.[3]

The secular lawyers' arguments in defence of lay impropriations, to which Gibson, Nelson, White Kennet and their allies had demurred in the eighteenth century, were if anything of even greater force a hundred years later, in the days of Howley and Peel. Sir William Scott reviewed the state of the poor clergy when he introduced his Non-Residence Bill in 1802, saying that whatever different course the law might have taken after the dissolution of the monasteries if only the friends of the church had been bold enough to take it, it had become 'settled law, in later times', that impropriations were lay fees. 'It is now too late, Sir, to undo what was done at the Reformation in this matter.'[4] In conse-

[1] See chapter I, above, p. 29.

[2] 29 Charles II c. 8 and 1 & 2 William IV c. 45.

[3] A very imperfect account of what was done under these Acts is given in P.Ps. 1866, LV, 129–44. The whole thing is a startling revelation of the state of diocesan records and efficiency. Returns were sought from diocesan registrars. Some failed to reply at all. Of those that did send in a reply, most are clearly deficient and only two went back before 1831. The impropriators of the eighteenth and the late seventeenth century were not as bad as that. White Kennet shows that the earlier statute was much used—see his *Case of Impropriations*, pp. 274 ff.

[4] *Substance of a Speech in the House of Commons*, 7 April 1802, pp. 29–32.

quence, impropriations could safely continue to appear in such contexts as this advertisement from *The Times* newspaper:—'GREAT TITHES and FARM. To be LET, on LEASE, a FARM of 110 acres, with the Great Tithes on Corn and Wood arising from 7000 acres of Land, comprising the parish of Cudham, in the county of Kent, of which 6000 acres are arable.... There is a farm house and extensive barns, stabling and other requisite outbuildings, affording every facility for collecting the tithes.'[1]

Despite this alleged unchangeableness of the law and the spirit of the law, however, the propriety of the impropriators' restoring their loot to the church still seemed so unanswerable and self-evident that several church reformers in the early nineteenth century went so far as to propose that government should compel them to do it. It is interesting that the idea should have seemed reasonable to some churchmen (including at least one 'ultra'), since it seemed so unreasonable to others. Lord Sidmouth, for example, a mild and conscientious church reformer although in his politics as ultra as could be, thought that whether or not incumbents ought to be forced to pay curates minimum stipends, impropriators should certainly be forced to do something of the same kind. He seems to have thought the cases fairly comparable.[2] Four respectable clerical writers on church reform, George Townsend, George Stoddart, J. Miller, and another, all had the same idea;[3] Lord Winchilsea spoke out impetuously in its favour in 1831 and 1832 in the House of Lords;[4] Southey thought it would be quite proper to get at them when they were descendants of the original despoilers;[5] and Bishop Phillpotts urgently pressed the idea on Peel. He went over all

[1] *Times*, 15 July 1830, p. 2e.

[2] See the debate on Perceval's Curates Bill, 1808 (*Hansard* n.s., XI, 1090, 1094). The civilian Dr Laurence was of the same way of thinking—*ibid.* p. 957.

[3] Townsend, *Plan to abolish Pluralities and Non-Residence*, p. 66 ff; Stoddart, *Evidence on the Necessity of Church Reform*, pp. 62–3; Miller, *Letter to Earl Grey on Church Property and Church Reform* (3rd edn.), pp. 112–13; *Letter to the Archbishop of Canterbury*, p. 52.

[4] 27 March 1832, *Mirror of Parliament* (1832), p. 1461. But no one took Winchilsea seriously. When he had said much the same thing a year before, Bishop Ryder, with some amusement, referred to him in a letter to his brother the Earl as 'poor dear Lord Winchilsea'. Letter of 11 February 1831 (Harrowby MSS, LXIII, 35–6).

[5] Brit. Mus. Add. MSS 40413, fo. 306.

the old ground and concluded that the law was not yet so indisputably against the church that it would not be worth the Crown law officers' investigation. 'Meanwhile', he said, 'Queen Anne's Bounty seems, in practice, to have withdrawn *general* attention from the claim on impropriators.'[1]

It is probable he was right; for ever since it began to work, the Bounty had been relieving the hardships of the poor incumbents of impropriated livings, without in general making any serious claims upon their impropriators. It was, indeed, the impropriation of their tithes more than anything else that had made so many livings so poor. The only case in which the Bounty would try to put pressure on an impropriator was that of a benefice (it would usually be a donative) of unsettled income. Under Section 16 of the Act of 1715 the Bounty, if such a benefice came up in the lottery, might refuse to make it an augmentation unless the impropriator settled a permanent income on the incumbent. But this did not often happen. The income of most impropriated benefices was 'settled', although contemptible; and in such cases the Bounty Board had no choice but to augment. Thus year by year, and reign by reign, the evils consequent upon impropriation were slowly and partially remedied; but at no cost whatever to the impropriators. It is easy to see why this was held against Queen Anne's Bounty by its critics. It appeared to go clean contrary to natural equity. There was really very little the Bounty Board could have done about it. The remedy could only come from parliament; and the average lawyer's and lay landowner's view of impropriations being what it was, there was no hope that, even if the governors had achieved the idea of seeking a statutory remedy (which, so far as one can tell, they never did), parliament would have been willing to do anything about it.

From parliament also, if from anywhere at all, had to come the remedy for the Bounty's defects in relation to the great and powerful order of patrons. They also profited from the Bounty, quite unreasonably. Here, as with the impropriators, it was unfair to criticise the Bounty Board for not taking a line that was politically impracticable, because remote from the prevailing climate of opinion in the upper orders of society. Advowsons were pieces of property. Lord Eldon's more distinguished brother may again be taken as an authority on the subject.

[1] Letter of January 1835, Brit. Mus. Add. MSS 40411, fos. 23-4.

Advowsons, he said, 'though originally perhaps mere trusts, are now become lay fees. . . . And they are not merely lay property *in law*, but a very large portion of them is so *in fact*.' Six thousand benefices, more or less, were presented to by private individuals. (Some of these individuals, of course, were clergymen). They were private property, untouchable upon any grounds except such as would open any other kind of private property to interference and spoliation.[1]

There is no doubt that Sir William Scott spoke for the great majority of patrons and proprietors. Again and again in the early years of the nineteenth century the impossibility of desirable reforms was urged on grounds of patrons' interests. The patron's voice was never silent. 'He could not consent to such an outrage upon those rights which every private man was supposed by law to have in his property. . . .';[2] 'it would diminish the value of livings, and was therefore a direct violation of property', it 'tended to vitiate the constitution, and subvert the establishment of the church . . .;[3] it 'would break in upon the right of advowson property'.[4] Yet there were those—and they appear to have been an increasing number through the years after about 1800—who thought that church property was not exactly the same as other property. Without wishing to damage that prop of manly independence, the parson's freehold, they would argue that it was not absolutely the parson's own, to do what he liked with, but a kind of trust property, and could be interfered with at least to the extent of making sure that the purposes of the trust were being fulfilled. This was the principal argument used by Perceval and Harrowby in pressing their Stipendiary Curates' bills; and by the twenties and early thirties it was the mainstay of the church reformers' case.

Some of the Bounty's friends made this their ground when they criticised the unearned profits that patrons made from its augmentations. Lord Redesdale, for example, gave the matter careful thought in a discussion with Lord Harrowby about the augmentation of poor livings. 'I have turned in my mind', he said, 'the possibility of taxing patrons for this purpose. They often now receive a benefit from aug-

[1] Sir William Scott, *op. cit.* pp. 41–2.
[2] Duke of Norfolk, 19 July 1804 (*Hansard*, II, 1069).
[3] Mr Barham, 21 and 30 May 1805 (*Ibid.* V, 44, 152).
[4] Lord Eldon, 18 June 1812 (*Ibid.* XXIII, 593).

mentation, without contributing anything.' He went on to consider several ways in which this might be done, and concluded, accurately enough, 'I fear this would be objected to.'[1] More interesting than his proposals in themselves, was the fact that he could conceive such a scheme of 'interference' at all, at so early a date.

Usually this subject merely excited helpless indignation in those to whom it seemed, for whatever reason, iniquitous; and it seemed so to men of more than one kind. Men who prized, and sought to recover, the church's independence of the laity were also likely to object to this enriching of the church's chief oppressors at the expense, very largely, of the clergy themselves. So H. J. Rose's *British Magazine*, a few months after loudly complaining on this score, printed a letter from a correspondent (subscribing himself 'R.W.B.') who had worked out from Hodgson's *Account* that between its foundation and 1834 the Bounty had added to the endowments of 2550 benefices in private individuals' hands, £2,059,300—an average capital accretion of about £877 each.[2]

Apart from the injustice of these subsidies for patrons from 'official' sources, the advantages that patrons inevitably drew from the improvement of the values of their livings tended also to deter private individuals from charitable deeds. The point of making, or organising, a benefaction to a poor living was considerably blunted when it involved benefiting also a patron who had made no move to augment it himself and who might, for all the benefactors knew, simply use the living's greater value as a reason for selling his advowson more profitably. All these points were in reformers' minds when they lamented the degree to which the Church of England was held in thrall by patronage. But what could be done about it, beyond urging patrons to be better men? The problem was so large and fundamental as to be in fact insoluble; and Queen Anne's Bounty, although its policy was indeed open to criticism for the extreme reverence it paid to the principle of patronage, was at any rate not more to blame in this respect than the most part of that church it existed to serve.

These criticisms of policy were, virtually, the only serious criticisms it had to face. Neither the officers nor the constitution of the Board were open to attacks other than the libels and slanders of ill-informed radicals.

[1] Letter of 5 June 1808 (Harrowby MSS, xII, fos. 114–7).
[2] *British Magazine*, December 1834 pp. 677–81 and May 1835 pp. 590–5.

Apart from John Paterson, all the Bounty's officers in this period seem to have given satisfaction. The 1837 select committee, which singled out Hodgson for special commendation, further stated, 'that the operations of the Board of the Bounty have been conducted with zeal and attention', and that the governors had made ample amends for that 'insufficient vigilance' that had led to Paterson's defalcation.[1] As for the constitution of the Board, although at least one member of the committee, Edward Baines, clearly thought it dangerous that the bishops had come to monopolise it, their report made no reference to the matter beyond recommending, mildly enough, that once a year there ought to be held a general board 'with a fortnight's notice of it given in the *London Gazette*'; which was presumably intended to give to the several hundred lay governors who never came, a chance to do so.[2]

The general approval given to Queen Anne's Bounty by the 1837 select committee was the more marked by contrast with the general censure then passed upon the First Fruits and Tenths Offices. These cost just as much to run as the Bounty Office but were productive of no public good whatsoever. All they did was to take the Bounty's revenues slowly through a circuitous by-way which cost both Bounty and clergy many hundreds of pounds they could ill afford. They were nests of sinecures and near-sinecures. The clerks did almost all the work, nor were their labours severe. 'Official hours are only from ten till two, and all red-letter days are holidays.' This was very unlike the Bounty Office, where they worked ten till four the whole year, except for Good Friday and Christmas Day, and where the treasurer's chief clerk had been occupied 'from ten till eight for three-fourths of every year since April 1831'.[3] The remembrancer of the First-Fruits Office resided in Somerset, the receiver 'holds two other situations, and transacts the business of the First-Fruits Office at Whitehall', and the receiver of tenths 'has been at his office only four times in eight years'. There were many absurdities and irregularities in their procedures, some of them smelling very bad, and furthermore, 'the complication of so many

[1] Report, pp. vii, ix.

[2] *Ibid.* p. x and Qs. 738–46, 984–90.

[3] 1837 committee, Qs. 536–8, 954–5. They had only worked this hard since the amalgamation of the treasurer's and secretary's offices, and the removal of the former from the city to Dean's Yard.

Boards is productive of much inconvenience. Their duties are confused, their transactions uselessly multiplied, and not easily traced; business is obstructed by references from one office to the other; and if a complaint is made it is easy for one Board to represent that the other is in fault.'[1]

There could be only one conclusion to a judgment so firm, so adverse and so just. These old offices had to be liquidated, and their functions absorbed in those of Queen Anne's Bounty, where they logically belonged. This was no new proposal, no late dawn of administrative light. The Commons' Committee on Public Accounts had commented on the same absurdities and extravagances, and had made very similar recommendations in 1797.[2] The consolidation of the three offices had been urged by the authors of *The State of the Established Church*[3] and the *Letter to the Archbishop of Canterbury on the subject of Church Property*,[4] both of whom picked unerringly on the church's most material defects. The Home Office seems to have had plans for their consolidation in 1824.[5] At last it was done, by Act of Parliament, in 1838.[6] This confirmation of the Bounty's place in the life of the established church, and stream-lining of its official machinery, was not least among the achievements of the third movement for church reform.

---

[1] *Ibid.* p. viii.
[2] *Reports from Committees of the House of Commons* (16 vols. 1803), XII, 273–5 and 452.
[3] 2nd edn., 1810, p. 101.   [4] Pp. 37–8.
[5] See the Bounty minutes, 12 February 1824, § 45.   [6] 1 Vict. c. 20.

CHAPTER VI

THE CRISIS OF CHURCH REFORM
1820-1835

From about 1820 onwards, the third church reform movement was in a critical phase. This was partly because it had already done so much, and partly because there was so much more to do; partly because a series of dilemmas or *impasses* then became clear, which could only be resolved or circumvented by heroic measures and the acceptance of heavy losses in the course of further advance; and partly also because of 'external' social and political developments that bore heavily upon it. Of these developments, the changes in the constitution between 1828 and 1832 had no doubt the most conspicuous and instant results; but their effect was simply to precipitate reforms that might otherwise have delayed for years longer, in the way that a sudden rise in temperature will bring a simmering liquid quickly to the boil. The first phase of this process had begun about 1780. The second and critical phase opened about 1820.

Much material church reform had been accomplished by the eighteentwenties. Dioceses varied, of course, but some of them could show by then a marked improvement on their late eighteenth-century condition. The diocese of Durham, for example, profited greatly from the reforming energy, no less than the charitable munificence, of Shute Barrington during his long episcopate from 1791 to 1826; and such was the momentum of church reform in those parts that the further progress made during the five years following his death included the building or rebuilding of 27 new schools, 8 residence-houses, and 27 churches or chapels, besides the division of 7 large parishes.[1] The diocese of Chester could not but be improved by the successive episcopates of three men as intelligent, conscientious, and active, in their very different ways, as G. H. Law (1812–24), C. J. Blomfield, and J. B. Sumner (1828–48). It may be doubted whether any diocese could escape being touched to some extent by

[1] Bishop Van Mildert, *Charge to the Clergy of the Diocese of Durham*, 1831, pp. 9–10.

the third church reform movement. Even where the diocesan administration was notoriously decrepit and the bishop inactive, as in Norwich under the long episcopate of Bathurst (1805-37), the atmosphere must have become somewhat less tolerant of the grosser scandals and abuses. The force of public opinion was on the reformers' side.

It was the force of public opinion that more than anything else precipitated the crisis in church reform. Conservatives naturally disliked the political claims made for public opinion. But if they were at all interested in reforms of any kind, as many of them (even some 'ultras') were, they could not help regarding it as in some ways a useful ally. Even if their interest in reforming the established church was restricted to bringing clergy, laity and all patrons to higher notions of responsibility, they were in fact promoting the very force they most declaimed against.

This was one of the several dilemmas that reforming churchmen were liable to encounter during this period. There was no doubt that public opinion could do at least as much good as legislation. Richard Yates, for example, recognized this when discussing the improvement of clerical standards so obvious in his own day. He referred to the 'Residence' Acts of 1803 and 1817, implying that the one had done little, and stating that the other had done much, good; but he noted also that 'The public and detailed discussion of the subject, like similar discussions of other important subjects, was productive of much benefit . . . and tended more powerfully perhaps than the enforcement of the laws themselves have done, to the promotion of their most useful object.'[1] Robert Southey, towards the end of a life devoted largely to combating the Whigs' and radicals' claims for the sovereignty of public opinion and the supreme value of the newspaper press, showed clear-headedness enough to recognize that their combined operations were far from wholly harmful. In 1829, surveying the losses and gains of the last half-century, he commended the higher standards that had come to prevail 'in every branch of the public service', and said, 'By whatever persons the government may be administered, they are now well aware that they must do nothing which will not bear daylight and strict investigation.'[2] A radical could not have said more. Half a dozen years later he was talking hopefully of the cathedral chapters reforming themselves 'under the wholesome fear

[1] *Patronage of the Church of England*, pp. 57-8.   [2] *Colloquies*, II, 421-2.

of public opinion.[1] That he could reach these conclusions was very much to the credit of his honesty and good sense; but it involved him, strictly speaking, in an inconsistency, because this public opinion could only be informed and articulated through freedom of speech and writing, and could still be safely ignored unless there could be brought to its aid the ultimate sanction of laws and orders.

Peel's famous half-distasteful recognition of the political force of public opinion[2] was made in 1820. That was just about when the tide turned.

> For while the tired waves, vainly breaking,
> Seem here no painful inch to gain,
> Far back, through creeks and inlets making,
> Comes silent, flooding in, the main.

Sometime between the end of the French wars and the formation of Canning's ministry, this new kind of public opinion became too strong, too vigorous, too determined, and too largely respectable, to be safely or even in good conscience ignored. Each man is entitled to date the pivot of change as he will: it can only be an impressionistic judgment: 1820 seems about right. Before that date a conservative might still think of suppressing or ignoring it without forfeiting his title to political rationality. Thereafter he had to work with it, somehow or other. And the established church felt this rough cold gale rising no less than did the government.

The principal evidence for this was the degree to which the church's relations with the more or less respectable parts of public opinion worsened. Till about 1820, the Tory side of the argument on the whole had the best of it, and for this good reason among others, that church reform had been seriously put in hand and defended against the ultra-Tory obstructives mainly by persons of impeccable conservatism. There was nothing Whiggish about Spencer Perceval or Lords Harrowby and Sidmouth. No important contribution had come from any of the big Whigs, whose hearts were not in such matters. They, with the radicals, would urge that the church's financial needs should be met from church funds, by redistribution and perhaps equalization.[3] They were much

---

[1] Letters to Charles Wynn, 8 February 1835, in Brit. Mus. Add. MSS 40413, fos. 305–7.　　　　[2] Cited above, p. 175.

[3] See, e.g., Lords Holland and Stanhope's contributions to the debate on the second

more interested in the church's constitutional status and in the question of religious liberty. The arduous and unspectacular practical business of church reform was not congenial to them, they had no contribution to make; and it was perfectly fitting that the *Quarterly* should, in the second decade of the century, have done much more to promote and educate a public interest in church reform than the *Edinburgh*.

Church reform went on after 1820 as before: its conservative backers were no less active, the *Quarterly* remained on the whole as friendly, and anxious churchmen could reasonably begin to cherish cautious hopes of a sufficient recovery of health and popularity. The outlook nevertheless became ever cloudier. This was partly because, inevitably, and as ultra-conservative churchmen had foreseen, the endeavours of their reforming colleagues were taken by the church's critics as indications of a guilty conscience, and served as much to sharpen as to deflect their darts. It was due also to the fact that, as the more easily removeable abuses became admitted as such and earmarked for reform, the more immoveable of them stood out in sharper, more offensive, contrast. And it was to be accounted for partly, no doubt, by the growth in numbers and assurance of classes of citizen more or less remote from the heart of the establishment—dissenters of all kinds and Unitarians most of all; uncommitted persons of liberal or radical turn of mind, whether Christian, deist, or secularist; readers of the *Edinburgh* and the *Eclectic*, the *Monthly Repository* and, after its foundation in 1824, the *Westminster Review;* men and women keen on things like education, economics, and parliamentary reform, not very well up in the court circular or 'ecclesiastical intelligence', but likely to sympathize with men like Sir Samuel Romilly, David Ricardo, and Henry Brougham, and to know, perhaps, a little more about Jeremy Bentham than that he was a fierce and exceedingly shallow critic of organized religion. Among these significant bodies of public opinion, the repute of the established church fell during the twenties; and the more churchmen of a controversial turn rallied to the counter-attack, the more such groups were confirmed in dislike and distrust of it.

Then there were the Evangelicals. They were of the established church, indeed, but, kept disdainfully at a distance by its ruling powers,

parliamentary grant, 18 June 1810, in *Hansard*, xvii, 751 f. and 768–9, or the *Annual Register* 1810, p. 146.

were increasingly resentful. That they should ever have come to add to the volume of respectable criticism of the establishment was a measure of the mixed stupidity and arrogance of the 'orthodox', for by the seventeen-nineties the Evangelicals had wholly shed that tendency towards ecclesiastical 'irregularity' that marked some of the founding fathers of their party, and throughout the two decades of war there had been no more devoted or effective sustainers of the establishment against the blows of radicalism and theological liberalism. But the orthodox had taken a dislike to them, and first in the *Anti-Jacobin*, then in the *British Critic*, had denounced them, and those they identified with them, with equal ignorance and rancour. Drubbing the saints became a fashionable diversion in orthodox conservative circles, to which their more ecclesiastical organs, the *British Critic* (established in 1793) and the *Christian Remembrancer* (founded in 1819), gleefully devoted a great deal of their space right up to the time of the reform bill.

The Evangelicals' chief organ, the *Christian Observer*, was naturally compelled to reply to the *Critic* and the *Remembrancer;* and it was not surprising, in the circumstances, that it should espouse causes that were gall and wormwood to them. In its early years (it was founded in 1801) it had betrayed little interest in the material aspects of church life. Church reform was not quite yet a major topic of public discussion; the Evangelicals always had a number of theological preoccupations; while the war continued, it was necessary at all costs to avoid giving the slightest colour of truth to the libels of the orthodox and Hackney churchmen; and besides, it was hoped in the drawing-rooms of Clapham that the expansive force of Evangelicalism would carry it into the higher orders of the church as rapidly as it was carrying it through the middling and lower orders. It was not unreasonable to have entertained such great expectations in 1800; but by 1820 it was clear that the campaign was not working out quite to plan. Far from conquering the upper orders of the clergy, the Evangelicals continued to encounter unrelaxed enmity or indifference from the bench, which reached its climax in Bishop Marsh's celebrated 'trap for Calvinists', the eighty-seven questions he put to candidates for ordination, institution, or licences, within his diocese of Peterborough. It was not to be wondered at that the *Christian Observer* thus came to blot the Evangelicals' copy-book still more by freely criticizing the bishops and the amount of irresponsible power they had over the inferior clergy. Nor was this the whole of its offence in hostile high-church eyes. From about 1818 onwards, the whole tone of the *Observer* was liberal and reformist. It judiciously applauded Brougham's investigations into the abuse of charitable endowments and denounced lawyer Holt's anonymous attack on him[1] as far more absurd on its side of the argument than ever Brougham had been on his.[2] It sought reform of the corn laws and wondered how long the victory of free trade over protection, which it regarded as ultimately inevitable and a very good thing, could possibly be delayed.[3] It dissociated itself from the fashionable idealization of the country parish with unusual objectivity: ...'Drunkenness and swearing, illegitimate connexions, sabbath-breaking, an almost general abandonment of the Holy Sacrament, a disregard for Scripture, and in many cases an open and undissembled denial of its truth, and all this coupled with, fostered, and perpetuated by, ignorance the grossest and most impenetrable—these are the fruits of our present system, these are the scenes which the lover of God and of his country is forced to contemplate in those villages celebrated by poets and orators as the abode of simplicity and purity and loveliness.'[4] It was a consistent friend to the oppressed and suffering. Despite its undeniable tendency to be over-pious the *Christian Observer* forms a most agreeable contrast to its hostile contemporaries the *British Critic* and *Christian Remembrancer*. Their controversial manners were much coarser, and their tone much more that of the coterie journal, with the insiders pausing from ladling butter from alternate tubs only to ladle slops over the outsiders they most disliked—Unitarians and secularists, anti-slave-trade sentimentalists, dissenters and Evangelicals. By this means, the orthodox controversialists succeeded through the twenties in undermining a good many of their own foundations. They kept party passions within the church at fever heat, and recruited for the army that was massing in readiness to besiege their ecclesiastical citadel not only the party growing most rapidly within the church but also such parts of the general public as might (if they had to choose between them) prefer the

---

[1] See above, pp. 181–2.

[2] *Christian Observer*, June 1818, pp. 413 f. and December 1818, pp. 798–817.

[3] See e.g. *Christian Observer*, XXII (1822), 326 ff., XXIII (1823), 400, XXVII (1827), 383 ff. and XXXI (1831), 126 f.

[4] *Ibid.* XV (1816), 479.

Christian Observer to the *Critic* or the *Remembrancer*, and might even have more respect for a solemn Simeonite than for a three-bottle orthodox man.

It was this rough aggressiveness in counter-attack against the church's enemies (or parties believed, albeit mistakenly, to be the church's enemies) that more than anything else provoked the greatest row of this period.[1] Born, obviously, of the orthodox churchmen's confidence in the reviving strength and *esprit de corps* of their order, it was as misplaced as a strike on a falling market and did the church nothing but harm. From the church's enemies' point of view, the battle-ground could not have been better chosen, for the principal contestants on the ecclesiastical side were the clergy of Durham, as notorious a group of prosperous absentee sinecurists as the canons of Windsor, and the more odious for their association with the last prince-bishop's palatinate. Their principal spokesman, Henry Phillpotts, was the hardest-hitting controversialist that ever fought the church's battles in the early nineteenth century, with an unbeatable set of claims upon liberals' detestation—husband to Lady Eldon's niece, an extensive and varied experience of pluralism, a vigorous and strict magistrate, a prominent enemy to 'Catholic emancipation', and (after the first phase of the battle) rector of what was certainly not less than the third richest living, and may have been the second richest living, in England, Stanhope.[2] The *casus belli*, moreover, was hardly religious at all but mainly political, identifying the upper clergy with ultra-Toryism, and thus the very last thing that church reformers who were trying to make the church again in some sense a truly national one ought to have desired. It needed the ultra-Tory cast of mind to fail to realize how easily the flanks of this position could be turned.

This great and significant row began with that affray in St Peter's Fields, Manchester, on 16 August 1819 which was within a week being called, and has been called ever since, the Peterloo Massacre. Lord Sidmouth the Home Secretary lost little time in communicating the government's approval to the responsible magistrates, two of whom were clergymen, one of them the most active of all magistrates in the

---

[1] Mathieson, with his eye for significant detail, devotes several pages to it—see *English Church Reform*, pp. 28–32.

[2] For his early history, see G. C. B. Davies, *Henry Phillpotts*, ch. 1.

Manchester district, and for long the government's mainstay there.[1] This injudicious display of reactionary solidarity excited respectable liberals all over the country to demonstrate, not their sympathy with the objects of the Manchester meeting, which though peaceful enough had been wholly radical and democratic, but their indignation at the government's white-washing the magistrates (who had been at best foolish and reckless, at worst vindictive and savage), and to demand a proper inquiry. There were demonstrations of this kind in Durham and Newcastle. The higher Tories in those parts countered them by signing and circulating a declaration of loyal confidence in government; and then Henry Phillpotts published his eloquent, abusive, and brilliantly partisan *Letter to the Freeholders of the County of Durham*, singling out for particular and personal abuse the member for the county John Lambton, alias 'Radical Jack'. Several replies were published, the weightiest being that in the *Edinburgh Review* for October 1819; after Phillpotts's rejoinder (*Remarks on an Article in the Edinburgh Review, No. 64, entitled 'Necessity of Parliamentary Enquiry'*) a brief lull ensued.

The second stage of the battle began in December 1820, when there issued from a liberal meeting in Durham a declaration, claiming to represent the views of the nobility, gentry, clergy, and freeholders of the county, and combining with a general censure of the government some particular references to its unfeeling treatment of Queen Caroline, whose rather seedy cause the radicals and extremer Whigs had enthusiastically taken up as a convenient means, presumably, of embarrassing that 'fat Adonis', their new monarch. This declaration was an ordinary political tactic, and its promoters could not fairly complain when the Durham clergy, with Phillpotts at their head, dissociated themselves from it and published a loyal declaration of their own. A storm of denunciation burst upon these Tory parsons, and Earl Grey said many hard things about them at a big liberal meeting in Morpeth, referring to them, *inter alia*, as 'animals'. This brought Phillpotts back into print with a long *Letter to Earl Grey* which, irrespective of the merits of its case, was an extremely effective piece of writing. More violent hands can never have been laid upon the reputation of a Whig

[1] This was W. R. Hay, who sent the official report on the day's doings to the Home Office. Soon afterwards he was rewarded with the rich living of Rochdale and a stall in York Minster.

grandee. The only trouble was, that some persons thought it a pity that it came from the pen of a clergyman. The Whigs even considered bringing a libel action against him.[1]

The third and last stage followed quickly. Queen Caroline died on 7 August 1821 and the bells of Durham cathedral, whether for good reasons or bad, deliberately or accidentally, were not tolled in mournful respect of her. No exasperated radical newspaper editor could ignore such an opportunity, and the very radical editor of the *Durham Chronicle*, John Williams, surpassed all his earlier efforts, and even Lord Grey's (where Grey had merely called the Durham clergy 'animals', Williams now specified their level in the brute creation as that of 'beetles'), in an article which the Durham clergy corporately prosecuted as libellous in respect of themselves, and calculated to bring the whole established church into contempt.[2] This was a grave mistake on their

[1] G. C. B. Davies, *op. cit.* p. 38. Davies cites many of the best passages from these writings of Phillpotts, between pp. 28 and 42.

[2] The article came at the end of a long leader on 18 August, 1821, about the death of Queen Caroline, whom it extolled as a pattern of all innocent virtues, a kind of radical saint and martyr. Then, after a vigorous attack on the *John Bull* newspaper, it turned to the cathedral clergy and the omission to toll the Durham bells. 'Thus the brutal enmity of those who embittered her mortal existence, pursues her in her shroud. We know not whether actual orders were issued to prevent this customary sign of mourning; but the omission plainly indicates the kind of spirit which predominates among our clergy. Yet these men profess to be followers of Jesus Christ, to walk in his footsteps, to inculcate his spirit, to promote harmony, charity, and Christian love! Out upon such hypocrisy! It is such conduct which renders the very name of our Established Church odious till it stinks in the nostrils; that makes our Churches look like deserted sepulchres, rather than temples of the living God; that raises up conventicles in every corner, and increases the brood of wild fanatics and enthusiasts; that causes our beneficed dignitaries to be regarded as usurpers of their possessions; that deprives them of all pastoral influence and respect; that, in short, has left them no support or prop in the attachment or veneration of the people. Sensible of the decline of their spiritual and moral influence, they cling to temporal power, and lose in their officiousness in political matters, even the semblance of the character of ministers of religion. It is impossible that such a system can last. It is at war with the spirit of the age, as well as with justice and reason, and the beetles who crawl about amidst its holes and crevices act as if they were striving to provoke and accelerate the blow which, sooner or later, will inevitably crush the whole fabric, and level it with the dust.'

This passage attracted much attention. It was quoted by *The Morning Chronicle* (and doubtless many other liberal-radical papers) and severely criticised by *The*

part. Williams's language was not stronger than much that was commonly used in the red-blooded politics of those days, and if the Durham clergy were going to participate so freely in politics, it could only be thought shabby in them, and sinister in implication, to skulk behind the laws when they were hit back. The Whigs made the most of their opportunity. Brougham turned his defence of the editor into a slashing attack on the abuses and naked Tory partisanship of the dignified clergy; the editor, although found guilty of libelling the Durham clergy, was for technical legal reasons unpunished, and lost no time in publishing a full report of the trial; and the *Edinburgh* backed up Brougham with a powerful article in its issue for November, 1822.[1] Phillpotts of course hit back, with a stinging *Letter to Francis Jeffrey, Esq.;* Jeffrey, evidently wincing under the lash, took the rather extraordinary step of defending himself in an editorial note at the end of his next issue, in February 1823, and Phillpotts hit him again in the April *Blackwood's*.[2] With that last shot, Phillpotts withdrew from the field, and the fracas was more or less over.

The importance of this controversy was very great, not for the Durham clergy or their terrible champion alone. Seen as a local trial of strength between the Whigs and Tories of the Durham and Newcastle district—which is all that it was—it left the honours about even. Editor Williams had not been wholly acquitted, and every sound Tory heart must have rejoiced at the severe punishment Phillpotts administered to his opponents. Editor Jeffrey had in fact been made to look slightly silly. Phillpotts himself no doubt was well pleased with his performance, especially when it brought him the offer of a lucrative Irish see.[3]

But for the established church as a whole, the consequences were unfortunate. What had begun as a local row, had been blown up into a matter of national interest. The trial of a Durham newspaper man for going too far in criticising the local clergy was turned into a trial of the established church for bigotry and corruption, conducted before a huge and fascinated audience through the fashionable media of immensely readable pamphlets and the much read *Times* and *Edinburgh Review*.

Guardian and other ministerial papers. *The Durham Chronicle* unrepentently repeated the most offensive parts of it on 8 September.

[1] 'Durham Case—Clerical Abuses', in *Edinburgh Review*, xxxvii, 350–79.
[2] *Ibid.* xxxviii, 265–9; *Blackwood's Magazine*, xiii, 476–8.
[3] Davies, *op. cit.* p. 43. He turned it down.

Nothing like this had ever happened before. Brougham's speech was really a speech for the prosecution. The *Edinburgh* cited several of his best passages at length, and very good they were—in turn droll, sarcastic, and denunciatory. Nor was this the *Edinburgh's* only attack on the establishment at this time. Phillpotts and his friends had asked for it, they should have it: and so the article on the Durham case appeared alongside Sydney Smith's on Bishop Marsh's Peterborough inquisition, and a shorter one ridiculing Bishop Howley's 1822 Charge. In the next issue came an odd article, headed 'Tithes' but devoted mainly to ecclesiastical abuses and to asserting that church property was public property, and another headed 'Church Establishments', similar in theme and particularly severe on Queen Anne's Bounty.[1] Some of the criticism in this unprecedented spate of articles was unfair, even vicious; but through it all there sounded notes which churchmen could in those years less and less afford to ignore—the failure so far to reform the greatest abuses and defects in the church, the contrast between the rich 'idle' clergy and the poor 'working' clergy, and the extreme difficulty of finding out the facts about the church's allegedly vast endowments. Nothing could have done the church more harm at this juncture than the position that the Durham clergy seemed to have adopted (as Brougham and the *Edinburgh* had no difficulty in showing), of shying away from public criticism and scrutiny.

Sydney Smith once remarked that the clergy were like a herd of cattle in that, when danger neared or one of them was attacked, all its brethren rallied round, heads down, and presented a menacing solid front of horns to the attackers. Something like this happened in 1823. Several pamphleteers hastened to the church's rescue. It cannot have been that they doubted Phillpotts's capacities; none was better able to look after himself. They must have sensed the true extent of the church's danger, and tried to save the situation. Two of them were very distinguished indeed. The younger Rennell, a shining light of Hackney churchmanship, published a long *Letter to Henry Brougham upon his Durham Speech and the three articles in the last Edinburgh Review;*[2] and

---

[1] *Op. cit.* XXXVII, 432–45, 457–61; XXXVIII, 1–26, 145–68. The latter has been cited above, chapter I, p. 33.

[2] The attribution to Rennell, who died the following year at the early age of thirty-seven, comes in his obituary in the *Christian Remembrancer*, August 1824, p. 490.

Archdeacon C. J. Blomfield published anonymously a *Remonstrance . . . by one of the 'Working Clergy'*.[1] Rennell, though severe, was much more reasonable than Phillpotts; Blomfield was in places almost apologetic. Their tone was significant. They had been put on the defensive, as the church had hardly been since 1736. There were also A. Campbell's *Reply to the Article on Church Establishments in the last number of the Edinburgh Review*,[2] and a *Vindication of the Church and Clergy of England from the misrepresentations of the Edinburgh Review: by a beneficed clergyman*. Mathieson says there were at least two more.[3] They cannot have done much good. The tide of public opinion was now going strongly against the church. It might not matter much to the upper clergy what low-bred radical publicists like Hone and Carlile said about the church, nor how much insidious fun Cobbett poked at 'the Botley parson', nor even how bad a press it got in papers like the *Durham Chronicle* or the London *Morning Chronicle;* but it mattered very much indeed in excitable years like the eighteen-twenties, when all but committed churchmen were ready to believe anything to the church's discredit, to have the *Times* and the *Edinburgh Review* persistently against you. That is why the Peterloo Massacre, the 'trial' of Queen Caroline, and the trial of John Ambrose Williams in 1822 for a libel upon the Durham clergy, did so much between them to precipitate the crisis in church reform.

Had the dilemma posed by the growing power of public opinion (so sinister in principle, so salutary in practice) been the only dilemma liable to confront loyal churchmen about this time, its importance as such might not have been very great. But in fact there were several others; and it was the coincidence of their impact upon the minds of churchmen that more than any other 'internal' ecclesiastical factor brought the crisis about. These dilemmas or *impasses*, as they became recognized, caused confusion in the clerical ranks. They brought forth a multitude of divided counsels; and, inevitably, under the 'external' conditions of the twenties and early thirties, a church divided against itself could not just stand still, even though every course of action presented dangers and disadvantages.

[1] Attributed to Blomfield in his son Alfred's *Memoir*, I, 85.
[2] In the same year, 1823, he also published, at Liverpool, an *Appeal to the Gentlemen of England, in behalf of the Church of England.*   [3] *Op. cit.* p. 31.

The most troublesome *impasse* to face conservative church reformers (radical church reformers, of course, encountered no such difficulty) was discovered in the gap between their ideal reformed church and the church as it actually was. On the one hand, they had a vision of an establishment little altered in its legal constitution but cleansed and effectively transformed by a spirit of self-sacrifice and devotion to duty, working through lay patrons and impropriators as much as through the clergy. On the other hand, there was the actual establishment they were trying to improve, so well integrated with constitution and society as to be changeable only with the utmost slowness and difficulty, and with the vast majority of its key positions in the hands of individuals whose preference for self-interest instead of self-sacrifice was the harder to detect and to censure because, under the old constitution, public and private interest in respect of men of property had been so much confused. The ordinary reformer was bound increasingly to recognize this gulf between ideal and actual as the years wore on. He found himself in the frustrating position of having all manner of good ideas to hand, yet no means of putting them into practice but through the voluntary co-operation of a multitude of almost uncoerceable, almost wholly independent local agents, who, even if they thought a particular idea a good one, would be likely, in any particular instance in which they were personally interested, to leave its adoption to everyone else and allow themselves the liberty of an exception to it.

This multitude of local agents upon whose intelligent and self-sacrificial co-operation the piecemeal plan of church reform so largely rested (all freeholders of benefices, and all other owners of ecclesiastical property in tithes and advowsons) were not wholly independent and autonomous. In practice they might be virtually so; but in theory their freedom of action was limited by the laws and, for the inferior clergy, to some extent by the discretion of their ecclesiastical superiors. The latter check was not perhaps of much importance. It could bear hardly on curates and it was one of the means by which non-residence and pluralities and skimped services could be, in certain cases, quietly discouraged; but an incumbent in his freehold could, if he chose, disregard his diocesan with near-impunity. Better checks upon individuals' misuse of the rights vested in them through their connexion with the establishment were imposed by the laws of the land, but neither were these very effective. Simony, for example, was illegal (which is not to say that it did not go on), and after 1783 the misuse of resignation bonds was considerably checked.[1] A clergyman who persistently and shamelessly failed to do his duty in his benefice could be suspended and deprived of it by a bishop willing to run the gauntlet of the courts and to pay the costs of at any rate his side of the action; so hazardous and expensive could such enforcement of ecclesiastical discipline be, that bishops seem rarely to have ventured upon this course unless they were unlikely to meet with opposition from the delinquent. The law forbade the clergy to engage in secular employments other than farming (teaching of course was not considered a secular employment) and imposed restrictions on that. It seems to have been somewhat disregarded,[2] but in theory the restrictions were good.

Ecclesiastical property was thus different from other property. It resembled trust property, given for a special end and (nominally) protected by the laws against waste or misuse. You could not do with it exactly as you wished. The principle behind these laws was, if you chose to deduce it from their as yet unrationalized labyrinths, that public policy had a concern with the manner of holding ecclesiastical property, and that certain public controls were accordingly placed upon it.

Such a principle was not readily recognized by conservative churchmen during the years of the third church reform movement. They were slow to recognize it, in part perhaps simply because of its strangeness and novelty, probably more because behind its strangeness and novelty they perceived some highly disturbing consequences which, in sum, threatened to lead them decisively from an age in which it had been possible to imagine stability into a turmoil of changes unceasing. All their prized familiar concepts—law, legislature, constitution, gentility—seemed sure to be caught up in this metamorphosis and given new meanings. Yet—and here they met their cruellest dilemma—from this principle they could hardly escape. It could be discerned in the laws by those who were not afraid to see it there—by Whigs and radicals, principally; it was the theoretical justification for each of the main lines

---

[1] See above, p. 57.

[2] Cobbett produced examples of clerical bankers and brokers in his *Legacy to Parsons* (6th edn., 1835), pp. 170–2.

of church reform being pursued in this period, whether it were the awarding of minimum stipends to curates, the further restriction of pluralities, non-residence, and clerical farming, or the division of parishes; and it was no less the theoretical justification for the more extensive, structural reforms that the furthest-sighted reformers like Richard Yates, Edward Burton and Lord Henley, were insisting on between 1815 and 1835. Conservatives could not forever blink so clear an issue, without absurdity or inconsistency; and the air of absurdity or inconsistency which attached to so many of their utterances and attitudes in this context (now maintaining, for example, that church property was the same as other property, now admitting that it was different) was mainly due to their persistence in doing so. What terrors did it hold for them? In what painful dilemmas did it place them?

In the first place, it offered a precedent full of danger to other kinds of property than ecclesiastical. If the sovereign legislature could interfere with the rights of the holders of church property, surely it could interfere with the rights of other categories of property-holder. To guard themselves against this, conservative churchmen would insist that church property did not essentially differ from other kinds of property. But in so doing, they cut the ground from under the feet of conservative, and thus moderately safe, reformers themselves. This most extreme point of view, although often and passionately employed in debate against unwelcome proposals, was in fact quite absurd, considering the interferences with private property regularly made by enclosure, canal, and public improvement acts; and Lord Liverpool himself had said, with Richard Yates's loud applause, that 'local interests, petty conflicts, and personal partialities' could not be allowed to stand in the way of essential reforms.[1] This dilemma thus became more painful year by year, as, defending the establishment against Lord John Russell, James Mill and their like, conservatives said that its property was not public but as private as any other body's. They might be sure of a cheer in the House, but an uncomfortably large number of their own actions could be adduced, to prove that they were talking through their hats.

It must be admitted that the more anti-clerical Whigs and 'philosophical radicals' were inclined to carry this argument to truly alarming extremes. It did not occur to a conservative church reformer to use the

[1] Yates's *Patronage*, p. 99n, and *Basis*, p. 199 ff.

legislature's power to make more adjustments to the terms of holding church property than were necessary to enable the church to function efficiently. He would attach conditions to its tenure and even take it from one side of the church in order to give it to another, but it would still be church property, directly serving church purposes. The really anti-clerical Whigs, and most radicals, whether of the philosophic or un-philosophic kind, were prepared to take it from the church and give it to some other body altogether. Their principle was the same; it was redistribution in both cases, justified by the same appeal to public policy and national need; the only difference was that whereas the more con-servative reformer believed it improper or unnecessary to put the pro-perty to other than strictly ecclesiastical use, the more radical believed it proper to transfer it to educational or charitable purposes. Carried to this point, redistribution appeared as 'appropriation' or 'spoliation', according to the way you looked at it. After many years of rumbling menace, it became a major topic of debate in 1833, when the appropria-tion of part of the Irish establishment's revenues to other purposes was advocated by some of the Whig ministers. It has remained a potential threat to the church ever since.

Out of such dilemmas and embarrassments came another batch of awkward and novel problems concerning policy. Once it came to seem inevitable or good that the church should undergo substantial alterations, the question might be raised, whether parliament was really fitted to decide what alterations. Now this question was a very novel and awkward one indeed. Parliament was legislative master, everyone knew that. The ideas of natural and fundamental laws were not quite dead, and voices were now and then raised to assert that parliament could not do this or that, where religion or property were concerned. Nevertheless, in the first two decades of the nineteenth century only a few high churchmen seem to have questioned parliament's legislative supremacy in church as well as state. Whigs and radicals, of course, accepted it whole-heartedly, and to most friends of the church on the other side of the house it seemed both natural and proper. Good Protestant Englishmen had at this time a great horror of independent ecclesiastical authorities. The Roman Catholic's split allegiance (divided between the temporal loyalty he owed his king and the supremacy in spirituals he acknowledged in the pope) was held against him as a disqualification from civil equality with Protestants, who were subject to no such scruples. The worst characteristics of the middle-ages and of 'backward' countries like Spain, Italy and Portugal since the sixteenth century were attributed to their hierarchies' independence of the civil power. Progress was believed to be dependent on Reformation. In this profound antipathy to popery lay much innocent Erastianism. Tories displayed it as much as Whigs. Nothing else, indeed, was to have been expected of a ruling class so keen on its property, so thoroughly Protestant, so proud of its success in identifying the interests of church and state and in assimilating the upper orders of clergy and laity. That the church's interests might ever much differ from the state's, or might better be elucidated by a convocation than by parliament, did not occur to them. Convocation was as good as forgotten. Some high churchmen kept the memory of its activity green and liked to remind their looser-principled contemporaries that the three estates of the realm were not, as was commonly held, king, Lords and Commons, but, properly, Lords, Commons, and Convocation; but they did this more to remind parliament not to do anything that might damage the church, than in serious hope of seeing Convocation ever revived.[1] For no other class of churchmen had the idea of an independent ecclesiastical estate or a separate ecclesiastical legislature of however limited powers much of an appeal.

Yet after 1815 or so, for one reason and another, parliament's suitability for the role of the church's legislature became more and more questionable. The character and consequences of its performance of this role were increasingly criticized. In many ecclesiastical quarters the beginnings of doubts seem to appear, slight and hesitant, as only to be expected in such a daring breach with established ideas and practices, and proceeding (without as yet any particular party colouring, which came only after 1833) from a variety of causes. Reflective clergymen were clearer at this stage as to what they disliked, than as to what they wanted instead. To suggest, as Richard Whately was to do in 1826,[2] that the

---

[1] See, e.g., C. Daubeny, *Guide to the Church* (3rd edn., 1830), II, 335–6; also H. H. Norris's letter of 18 April 1820, in W. Berrian, *Memoir of Bishop Hobart*, p. 235.

[2] In the anonymous *Letters on the Church: by an Episcopalian*. It is not wholly certain that it was Whately's, but it was commonly believed to be his; Newman, for one, had no doubt about it, and neither had V. F. Storr, half a century later. See Newman's

church could only recover its proper freedom of action by disconnecting itself from the state (which meant withdrawing the bishops from the House of Lords and relinquishing the status of most-favoured church) and establishing a proper governing body of its own, was to open a door to prospects almost terrifying in their novelty. We know that they produced effects quite galvanic upon two Oxford dons. Hurrell Froude, highly excited by them, told Newman that they would 'make his blood boil'; and one of their common friends told him 'that, after reading it, he could not keep still, but went on walking up and down his room'.[1] The book made quite a stir in Oxford. Not all of Whately's contentions would have been generally acceptable. He was too original and icono-clastic. His anti-erastianism was too trenchant and far-reaching, and his justification of the state's right to interfere, for the public welfare, with the property of ancient corporations ('for if we do not allow this right . . . we are in fact making the earth the property, not of the living, but of the dead'), was too suggestive of the Benthamite's frank assertion that 'no man ought to exercise rights of property six hundred years after his death'.[2]

Whately's analysis of the disadvantages the church experienced under the English form of church-state alliance must have approved itself by this time to many, for he was only saying 'what oft was thought, but ne'er so well express'd'. 'Can that be a *fair and reasonable* alliance', he asked, 'in which one of the contracting parties surrenders to the other part of his just rights, including his independence, as the price of receiving what was already his due?' He proceeded daringly to pull Warburton's much-vaunted theory of the alliance to bits, and then to examine how the connexion with the state had worked out in England. It had given rise, he said, to confusions, oppressions, and false impressions innumerable. The mass of the people, the unthinking in *all* ranks of society, got the impression that the Church of England was nothing but

letters to Hawkins in 1869 (Oriel College Library, Letters 376 and 377b), E. J. Whately, *Life and Correspondence of Whately*, I, 52 n., and Storr's *Development of English Theology in the 19th Century*, p. 98 n. The *Edinburgh Review*, warmly apprecia-tive, took it as a text for expounding its own idea of the established church—XLIV (1826) 490–513.

[1] Newman's *Apologia*, ch. I.

[2] *Op. cit.* p. 137, and the article on 'Corporation and Church Property' in *The Jurist: or, the Quarterly Journal of Jurisprudence and Legislation*, February 1833, p. 7.

that it would do so or not, churchmen had no doubt that the English and Irish church establishments were booked for trouble. The Irish church was obviously in hotter water than the English; but neither was going to be able to survive without great, perhaps revolutionary, structural changes. Many were its friends who, in the extremity of fear, proclaimed, in one form of words or another, 'the established church is finished'.[1] At Oxford it was even believed at the height of the excitement over the Reform Bill that the Birmingham Political Union, if it marched on London to enforce the Reform Bill at point of pike, would march via Oxford and sack the colleges *en route*.[2] Then, early in 1833, came the Irish Church Bill, confirming all the worst suspicions of anxious church-men,[3] and for all they knew—for they could not foresee the quick decline of the radical reforming impulse, and the revival of conservatism —marking the shape of things to come.

To these alarming developments of 1831–3, articulate churchmen seemed to react, generally speaking, in one of three ways. The first was the way of tough and contemptuous opposition to the march of events, conceding hardly an inch of ground, and responding to the hostility of liberal public opinion by lively counter-attacks upon it. This was the Tractarians' way. After the Tracts had started, and the 'apostolical' character of the movement began to be asserted, it acquired a special theological flavour and foundation; but for at least a year before that (and a very important year it was, too) it had been going strong, as a straight development of the *viae antiquae* of pious conservatism, under the principal direction of the same high churchmen who were associated

---

[1] Mathieson cites four expressions of it (by Arnold, Blomfield, Southey and Whately) on p. 58. A less familiar and very striking illustration of the degree of clerical apprehension is A. P. Perceval's retrospective description of how Church and nation seemed to stand in the middle of 1832, in his *Collection of Papers connected with the Theological Movement of* 1833, pp. 25–6.

[2] I have unfortunately lost the reference for this.

[3] 'The Government's real object', wrote William Palmer of Worcester College, 'was to gratify the priests by the abolition of the hierarchy of the Church of England, as a first step to the entire destruction of the Church's status and property, and the formation of a Roman Catholic establishment: but they did not venture to avow this motive, and pretended that the measure was for the purpose of reforming and strengthening the Church itself.' *Narrative of Events connected with the Publication of the Tracts for the Times* p. 45.

with the rallying of church opposition to Whiggism in 1833–4. So active were they, indeed, before the 'Hadleigh Conference' and Keble's Assize Sermon, that serious misunderstanding must follow from paying too much attention to Newman's remark that he 'ever considered and kept the day [of that sermon], as the start' of the Oxford movement.[1] Things were happening before the summer of 1833, as they happened after it, which quite rob it of its conventional aura of singularity. In 1830 Hugh James Rose had published his *Brief Remarks on the Dispositions towards Christianity generated by Prevailing Opinions and Pursuits*. In the following year he published in a South-East Anglian newspaper *Six Letters to the Farmers of England on Tithes and Church Property*, written in a vivacious, argumentative style, which attracted a great deal of attention and certainly did as much as *could* be done at that stage of the question to carry the war into the camp of the church's enemies.[2] A year after his massive *Origines Liturgicae*, William Palmer published some politely destructive *Remarks on Dr Arnold's Principles of Church Reform*. The Hon. Arthur Perceval followed up his high-principled *Reasons why I am Not a Member of the Bible Society* (1830) with a well-argued attack on Bishop G. H. Law's son-in-law (and, almost as directly, on Blomfield), *A Letter to the Rev. James Slade . . . containing remarks on his Letter to the Bishop of London on Church Reform* (1831). After March 1832 these hard-hitting high churchmen had a common platform in Rose's monthly *British Magazine*, wherein their contributions rubbed shoulders with Hurrell Froude's excellent articles on church-and-state and Keble's gloomy poetry. The *British Magazine* was attractively produced and certainly more 'popular' in style than the *British Critic* or the *Christian Remembrancer*. It combined keen contemporaneity with unblenching conservatism. On matters of church reform, it gave very little away.

The second of the three chief ways in which churchmen seem to have reacted to the liberal alarms and excursions of the very early thirties was that of a rather timid conservatism, bowing somewhat to the storm around them, and hoping that a show of reforming readiness might buy

---

[1] *Apologia*, ch. 1, last sentence.

[2] See the *Memoir of Rose* (1839), reprinted from the *British Magazine*, March 1839, pp. 327–47. These letters were singled out for commendation by the *Quarterly Review*, XLVII (1832), 386 n.; and a version of them was published in at least one other newspaper, the *Cambridge Chronicle*—1, 15, 22 and 29 July, 5, 12, 19 and 26 August, 1831.

off all but the most implacable of the establishment's foes. This was the 'safe' men's way, spiritless, unimaginative, falling leadenly between the cavalier young conservatism of the early Tractarians on one side, and the bold reformism of the Henleys and Blomfields on the other; this was the way of prudence. It is impossible to distinguish its merely prudential from its unadventurously reforming elements. The slightly mysterious 'Scheme' for a 'Royal Commission of Enquiry' early in 1831[1] was obviously compounded of both. It was designed by those who concocted it (Watson, Christopher Wordsworth, Howley, Van Mildert, and doubtless others of the Hackney Phalanx) to avert several dangers—Joseph Hume's yearning to conduct an inquiry himself, the growth of a lack of confidence between the lower clergy and the bishops, the further strengthening of the general public impression that the church was not interested in reforming itself; but not surprisingly it was, in political terms, grotesquely impractical, and Lord Grey must have been chuckling inwardly when, in the early stages of the negotiations, Van Mildert found him 'frank, disinterested, and gracious'. The Commission was to be made up entirely of clergymen, and its objects were to be strictly limited to suggesting 'the best practical remedies for the evils of translations, of unseemly commendams, and offensive pluralities'. This would not conceivably do. By March 1831, the good Joshua had to admit to a friend that 'it is all up with the Commission—certainly in the only shape I thought it worth having'. In conceding the idea of an inquiry at all, he had conceded enough.

The same compound of prudence and good-will showed itself in the more successful scheme for a Durham university. When the idea was still very new and secret, in the summer of 1831, one of the Durham prebendaries wrote thus to Gaisford, the dean of Christ Church, an influential dignitary whose support it was important to secure: 'It appears to be morally certain that as soon as the Reform Bill is disposed of, an attack will be made on Dean & Chapters and as certain that Durham will be the first object. It has occurred to us that it will be prudent, if possible, to ward off the blow and that no plan is so likely to take as making the public partakers of our income by annexing an establishment of enlarged education to our college. Most probably the general opinion would be favourable to the measure. No doubt sacrifices

---

[1] Of which we learn in Churton's *Memoir of Joshua Watson*, II, 3–7.

would be required of us. We regard them as a premium to be paid to insure the remainder.'[1] Another of the conspirators, Van Mildert's confidant, Archdeacon Thorp, in a politic letter to a local liberal leader, described his party as anxious 'to remove every ground of reasonable complaint', increase the church's efficiency, and present her as the faithful guide, 'instructress and comforter of the people'.[2] A pious high churchman of deeply conservative beliefs could go no further; this was already stretching Burke's principles to breaking point.

Archbishop Howley, who was closer to the line of fire than his brother of Durham, followed this same middle path and, with some half-contemptuous pats on the head from the prime minister, put on as good a show as he could as a church reformer. He may even have meant it. His position was unenviable and difficult, with pressure-groups trying to capture him on every side. It is certain that he was a 'real' reformer in the later thirties; it is not so certain that he was at this stage. On 24 June 1831 he announced in the House of Lords that he was going to begin. He would introduce three bills—one to facilitate and establish the firm legality of tithe compositions for short terms of years; another to facilitate the augmentation of small vicarages and curacies by ecclesiastical persons; and a third, to restrict pluralities. Only the augmentations bill passed.[3] Howley's language in moving its second reading reveals clearly enough his state of mind, well-meaning but unappreciative of the urgency of the occasion. The effects of his bill, he said, would be gradual, 'gradually brought about in the course of time . . . some of the small livings will be improved, without resorting to any objectionable measure to obtain that good end'.[4] He could not realize that there was not all the time in the world. Neither of his other bills became law. The one for tithe compositions seems to have petered out in the Commons, where Sir Robert Inglis moved its first reading on 14 October.[5] The pluralities bill, introduced into the Commons by Dr Lushington on 3 October, got no further that year, and was revived by Howley the

[1] Cited by Edward Hughes, 'The Bishops and Reform, 1831–3', in *Eng. Hist. Rev.*, LVI (1941), 461.
[2] Letter to James Losh, 12 September 1831, in *ibid.* p. 466.
[3] 1 and 2 William IV, c. 45.
[4] *Mirror of Parliament*, 1831, p. 929b.
[5] *Mirror of Parliament*, 1831, p. 3077b.

following spring when it was again lost in the lower house.[1] Even its friends could not find much more to say in its favour, than that it was at any rate a small start along the road to improvement.[2] Its opponents, who were either indignant at its interferences with property-rights, frustrated at its dealing so feebly with so immense a problem, or just professionally anti-clerical, were easily able to demonstrate that it was weak, muddled, and to some extent (as doing nothing to limit the holding of pluralities for profit) a fraud. But the archbishop was obviously anxious to make some improvements in this branch of the ecclesiastical system; and in the second of these debates, (which were rather confused and acrimonious, and ranged over the whole field of church defects and abuses), he ended with a plea for a full enquiry into church revenues. 'The Church', he said, 'has nothing to fear from inquiry; such an inquiry would, I think, be highly beneficial; and I have reason to hope that means will be taken to ascertain what its revenues actually are.'[3] Later in the debates Lord Grey did Howley the justice of admitting that the archbishop had told him, 'shortly after he entered office', of his desire that 'the general state of the property of the church' should be comprehensively reviewed, and assured the house that such an 'ecclesiastical inquiry' was on the way.[4] Two months later, on 23 June, the Ecclesiastical Revenues Commission and the names of its members were published. The finances of the whole ecclesiastical system were to be investigated, from the top to the bottom, without any exceptions whatsoever. The serious business of church reform had at last begun.

This momentous event introduces very conveniently the third main distinct class of churchmen whom the events of the early thirties stimulated to positive action of some kind. The ascertainment, at last, of the exact state of the church's finances could be viewed simply as a safety measure, a mere means of giving the lie to radical and anti-clerical libels: it was probably little more to the meek archbishop. But at the same time it was an indispensable first step towards the really extensive church

[1] Mathieson, p. 61, could find no reports of the 1831 debates. Some are given in the *Mirror of Parliament*, 1831, pp. 103–4, 589–90, 1768–71, 2079–84, 2249.

[2] See, e.g., Lord Harrowby and the Duke of Wellington on 27 March, in the *Mirror*, 1832, pp. 1460–1. [3] 23 March, in *Mirror*, 1832, p. 1393b.

[4] 2 April and 27 March, in *ibid.* pp. 1562a and 1461b. It is, however, possible that Grey was misleadingly referring to Joshua Watson's proposed Commission, which was not intended to go anything like as far.

reforms that a good many friends of the establishment had in mind. The reforms proposed by this class of churchmen were often far-reaching. Their ends were not at all new—how should they be, when the main material defects of the church were unchanged and unreformed after two centuries of intermittent effort? But in the means they proposed, and the anxious boldness they often showed in proposing them, there was much novelty. More reformers were prepared to go further, to take more drastic steps to secure larger measures of improvement, than ever before. They were either frightened or angry—frightened of the consequences of further delay in protecting the church from the assaults of its enemies, or angry after so long and, in some ways, shameful a failure to set the church to rights. Either way, they joined in seeking more substantial reforms than had yet been made. This was probably, indeed, as many of them sensibly appreciated, the establishment's last chance. It seemed also, by virtue of the Whigs at last getting into place and of their promise that they would make all things new, to be a long-awaited time of opportunity. Churchmen were not lacking to seize their opportunity with both hands.

Suddenly, the volume of publications on church reform swelled prodigiously. 1833 seems to have been the peak year. Their tone was often different from the general run of publications and views that had been publicly or privately expressed in the course of the preceding few decades. It was firmer, more positive, more detailed. General surveys of the church's material defects and needs were of course not new. Richard Yates, in his surveys between 1815 and 1823, had made appropriate, far-reaching suggestions. The anonymous authors of *The State of the Established Church, in a series of letters to Spencer Perceval* (1809–10) and the *Letter to the Archbishop of Canterbury on Church Property* (1824), although their investigations lacked the laborious depth of Yates's, had not less bold ideas for improvement.[1] The latter's proposals for the

[1] The latter, for example, who set the tone for his long pamphlet with an epigraph from Bishop Burnet about 'scandalous practices of non-residence and pluralities, which are sheltered by so many colours of law among us', proposed a wholesale re-organization and redistribution of church property that would, by reducing cathedral and collegiate church staffs to a mere three or four, and making first-fruits and tenths a realistic tax upon the richer clergy, raise curates' stipends to a minimum of £75 a year, and, by dint of large-scale unions of mean country benefices, raise the incomes of all poor incumbents to a moderate sufficiency.

reform of church leases went quite as far as any that were made in the thirties, and his suggestion of diocesan committees to administer episcopal and capitular property (pp. 86–9) anticipated one of the stock alternatives proposed by critics of the Ecclesiastical Commissioners ten years or so later. Yet there was about them all a somewhat unreal air. Politically, such thorough-going plans were still, in the early twenties, quite utopian.

By 1828, when Edward Berens published his small book *Church-Reform*, such plans had begun to seem rather more capable of execution.[1] The fountains of the political deeps were breaking up, and the old obstacles to radical reform were beginning to crack. 'The circumstances and the temper of the present times', wrote this admirable archdeacon, 'seem to be singularly favourable for it [i.e. reform]. . . . Public opinion has at all times had a claim . . . to be treated with respect; and in the present day public opinion is possessed of a weight and influence—a legislative weight and influence—which it never possessed at any former period . . . a spirit of general improvement has gone forth and pervaded the whole of our systems of legislation. Surely the Church ought not to be the only body not benefitted by the intellectual progress of the age.'[2] Such language did not endear him to the very conservative majority of his fellow-clergymen; and few of his detailed proposals for reform were calculated to reassure them that he was 'sound'. What principally rendered him suspect was his seventh chapter on the reform of the liturgy, wherein he mildly advocated, among other things, the excision of its damnatory clauses from the Athanasian Creed, the revision of the lectionary ('the Scriptures operate, not as a charm, but through the medium of the understanding'), and the removal from the prayer for parliament of its reference to 'our most religious' reigning sovereign; which was liable, he thought, in respect of—he was hardly able to put it delicately enough—George IV, to make people think the clergy were not wholly serious. But there was much else of a less deeply disturbing nature.

Berens dealt first with ecclesiastical law and discipline and proposed, as a means to correcting the gross defectiveness of the latter, an

[1] Although he published it anonymously, his identity as author was soon an open secret.

[2] *Op. cit.* pp. 10–11, 14–15.

ecclesiastical equivalent to the court martial. He suggested an exhaustive inquiry into church revenues, the redistribution of the revenues of most cathedrals prebends and sinecure rectories to poor and burdensome parishes, and a complete reform of the system of church leases. He sought the reduction of pluralities and an absolute end to their misuse for private profit and convenience. He would have improved ecclesiastical administration by making the office of archdeacon a full-time one, well-paid, and supported everywhere by active rural deans and churchwardens who really did their job. This was not the whole of his proposals, but it comprises their more prominent points. The comprehensiveness of his vision is not more remarkable than the firmness of his views. One need be surprised neither at his becoming unpopular at Oxford, nor at his being held in high respect by Blomfield and Peel.[1] All three of them spoke the same language.

Berens's was the last important work on church reform before the clouds burst about the clergy's heads after the general election late in the summer of 1830. He wrote with higher hopes of seeing something done than any of his precursors; those who followed close behind him and fired their ammunition during the great church reform debate of the early eighteen-thirties could be confident that action would at last be taken. Untold dozens of churchmen buckled down to the self-imposed task of communicating to the world their views, and their views on other writers' views, on this engrossing subject. They do not, on the whole, make bright reading. The same ideas necessarily turn up again and again, shuffled into an infinite variety of permutations and combinations; the style is often long-winded, the tone sometimes peevish; and the lesser men, lacking any original general views, in fact contributed nothing beyond particular proofs, based on their own local knowledge and experiences, of the merits or defects of the principles and plans that were most commonly canvassed. As the pamphlets poured out, and the periodicals began to comment upon them, two writers quickly came to the top. One was Edward Burton, the other Lord Henley.

---

[1] E.g. A. Blomfield, *Memoir of Blomfield* (1864 edn.) pp. 141–2, letter to W. R. Lyall, 21 November 1833; and Peel's letter to Herries, 21 January 1835, in Brit. Mus. Add. MSS 40410, fo. 303. There is also some Hackney gossip about Blomfield's approval of Berens, in a letter from Edward Churton to F. C. Massingberd, 19 October 1830, in the Massingberd Papers at Lincoln, 1/77.

Edward Burton was Bishop Lloyd's successor as regius professor of divinity at Oxford. Although very little is known of him, it seems likely that his early death in 1836, when he was only forty-two, was something of a tragedy for the Church of England; for not only was he a first-rate scholar and theologian with the advantage (rare indeed in those days) of continental study, but he was clearly also a man of unusually deep and cultivated understanding.[1] Certainly his three publications on church reform—*Thoughts upon the Demand for Church Reform* (1831), *Sequel to Remarks upon Church Reform* (1832), and *Thoughts on the Separation of Church and State* (1834)—are distinguished by their intelligence, courtesy, and elegance; and he had the rare gift of carrying a discussion easily and fruitfully to and fro between practical detail on the one hand and firm principle on the other, without relaxing his grasp of either. It was, indeed, the quality of his thought and writing that gave his contributions their celebrity, for he was not nearly so much of a blueprint-maker as Lord Henley and some others.[2] By no manner of means can he be called a 'liberal'; yet nor can he possibly be considered merely an exceptional specimen of the ordinary genus, 'Oxford divine'. He was a pupil and protégé of Peel's former tutor, Charles Lloyd, himself a theologian and teacher of original and enterprising mind; and it must mark him as at least a bit of a progressive, that Newman bracketed him with Hampden and a few others in 1830 as a man 'likely to make great innovations', whom he would not wish to see in control of Oxford's examinations.[3]

Three years later, when Burton's character as a church reformer was established, Newman told Pusey that he thought it a pity that the public mind had been excited and confused by so many publications on church reform and that people (he clearly meant, basically good people) like Burton had joined in; Burton's error, he said, 'surely was that of not understanding the age and the persons with whom he had to deal'.[4] He

[1] I have found no biographical information about him beyond what is given in the *D.N.B.* and its sources.

[2] In all this he seems to resemble William Rowe Lyall, of whom likewise one would wish to know much more.

[3] Letter of 9 January 1830, in Anne Mozley (ed.), *Newman's Letters and Correspondence*, I, 220. The other suspect dons were Cardwell, Mills, Short and Hampden.

[4] Letter from Rome, 19 March 1833, in H. P. Liddon, *Life of Pusey*, I, 249.

cannot have read Burton's pamphlets very carefully, if indeed he had read them at all. He ought to have liked the ironical compliment that Burton paid to the reforming zeal of the age at the outset of his first pamphlet: 'I have little doubt, that in a very few years it will be as difficult to meet with a dishonest man, as with a rotten borough.'[1] Burton was no fool. He knew that in many material respects the church was in urgent need of reform. He knew also, and plainly said, that many of those who clamoured for reform were ignorant and meddlesome. He affirmed, as did Archdeacon Lyall in his 1833 Charge, that the clergy were not, 'as a body, opposed to Reform', but merely given to distinguishing real reform from mere change. Most plans of church reform, he said, were either impracticable and injurious, 'or they have no tendency whatever to improve the morals and religion of the people. I repeat again and again, that this is the true, the only object of Church Reform. It is an object which is little appreciated by speakers at dinners and editors of newspapers. . . .'[2]

Burton's own proposals for reform went far enough to draw upon him a good deal of conservative criticism and abuse. His cardinal device was the reduction of the inequality of benefices ('that blot in our establishment')[3] by distributing among the poorer ones the proceeds of a fund raised by a graduated tax on benefices over £200 a year; it went up from a tax of £1 a year on £200, through £10 on £600 and £35 on £1000, to £167 10s. od. on £2000.[4] On no other points of reform was he as precise, although he brought most of the usual ones into his discussion. The graduated tax—an offensive, 'equalising', property-endangering device to the minds of many conservative churchmen—was his standby, as it was of some other reformers.

It would undoubtedly have done good; but it can be criticized for not going far enough. Unyielding in his principles, yet anxious to make salutary changes and unafraid to advocate a quite radical measure of reform, Burton was perhaps too shy of popularity. He was too subtle and refined for that rough-and-tumble debate. His position was like that of a polished swordsman who single-handed and with beautiful dexterity holds off a posse of ruffians, only to find after their withdrawal that while he kept them from the front door, their collaborators had broken in

[1] *Thoughts*, p. 5. [2] *Thoughts*, pp. 40–1.
[3] *Sequel*, p. 4. [4] *Sequel*, pp. 25–6.

through the servants' passage. All his hits against Lord Henley (to reduce whose popularity he particularly but courteously addressed himself in his *Sequel*) were good ones, his reflections and judgments on the many different aspects of church reform (whose inter-relations and constitutional implications he understood better than most) were serious and penetrating, but all too scrupulous.

Moreover, in two respects he misjudged the situation. Again and again he insisted that the church's fundamental problem was its patronage, and that higher standards of patronage (and particularly of lay patronage) would, almost unaided, solve the establishment's problems for it. This was too simple and optimistic, though characteristic of high-church attitudes at the time. It led him to neglect the importance of institutional reform. It must also be said, that his views, for all their quiet, firm reasonableness, seemed to be founded on too limited an experience. Burton was a scholar, a distinguished one, as it would appear; and as regius professor of divinity at Oxford, he was also rector of Ewelme. His church reform writings do not give the impression that he understood much of the world outside the studies and common-rooms of Oxford and the rectories of the old England that was still, one must remember, to all but the most perceptive or modern-minded of his contemporaries (as, for example, in their various ways, Richard Yates, Robert Southey, and Thomas Arnold) the only England thinkable for a cultivated gentleman. He must have known something of the social and economic revolution in progress, if only because he and his wife both came from Shropshire, where many of the things happened that marked the start of the industrial revolution; but there is no consequent note of urgency in his writings.

Lord Henley on the other hand was all urgency and sharp clarity. He saw the situation in black-and-white terms, knew what he wanted and said it. This was an approach well calculated to appeal to the mood of the nation in 1832; and it was doubtless largely on account of it that his name quickly became pre-eminent among the myriad church reform writers of the early thirties and that his *Plan of Church Reform* went speedily through eight editions after its appearance in the summer of 1832. Contributory causes of his vogue may have been the novelty of his appearing in this character (he was a lawyer, a Master in Chancery and well enough known as an authority on the bankruptcy laws, but never

heard of thitherto in any ecclesiastical connexion), his being a peer and
an Evangelical—'one who wears a coronet, and prays'—and perhaps
also his being Peel's brother-in-law. But there is no need to look far
beyond his *Plan* (which was his only publication of this kind excepting
*A Plan for a New Arrangement and Increase in Number of the Dioceses of
England and Wales*, in 1834) to understand why it became the focus of
attention. It was plain, direct, business-like, detailed, and very comprehensive; gave no hint that reform was, as Burton so painfully felt it to be,
a *delicate* matter; and admitted, as reformers who detested liberalism
were reluctant to admit, that there was indeed plenty to reform.

Lord Henley's aims and motives alike were simple. He believed that
the church was not functioning properly, and he had no doubt that its
function was, almost exclusively, the maintenance of a well-paid,
resident, full-time parochial ministry. He further believed that the
church was in great danger from the political tendencies of the times. He
wasted no time considering, what Oxford divines felt it professionally
incumbent on them to consider, whether those tendencies were good
ones or not; it was enough for him that they existed. As soon as the
question of parliamentary reform was settled, he said, there would be
a demand for church reform; it would be irresistible, and it would be
justified. The nation was 'thirsting for improvement and reformation';
better to give way gracefully to 'the just demands of the governed' while
there was still time to reform with prudence and moderation.[1] There
must be an end to pluralities and sinecures in church as well as state. He
had no time for the stock conservative clerical arguments that you had
to put up with them if you were to attract men of good family and
support a learned clergy; good men would come from good families
without such extravagant attractions, and as for the suggestion that
'sinecures' (for thus he brusquely denominated the bulk of cathedral and
collegiate preferments) supported learning—just look, he said, at the
clergy list, and see what kind of clergymen actually hold these positions!
Not more than a twentieth of them had any theological or literary
merit; they had got there through parliamentary interest, family connexions, or party gratitude.[2] The quantity of ecclesiastical revenue going
to waste in these places amounted to an 'immense misapplication'.[3] The
church, view her how you would, was a 'trustee invested with the

[1] *Plan*, 4th edn., pp. 4–5.   [2] *Ibid.* pp. 23–30.   [3] *Ibid.* Introduction, p. viii.

management and control of funds given for the discharge of a duty of the very highest and holiest nature. And, if by time, or accident, or neglect, or by the rise or improvement of property, or by the increase of population, any material impediment shall have arisen to prevent the due performance of this trust, it is the clear right and bounden duty of the Legislature to enforce its faithful execution.' He ended his muscular justification of the principle of redistribution with a flourish that placed him half-way between Macaulay and Bentham. 'No one now maintains the inviolability of corporate rights where a clear case of public necessity or expediency demands their sacrifice . . . it would be preposterous to contend that the embryo rights of any number of unappointed or unborn functionaries, can legitimately interpose to prevent a just or necessary measure of Reform.'[1]

His practical proposals, most of which he incorporated at the end of his pamphlet under thirty-four heads in a kind of skeleton parliamentary bill, were built around the reduction of cathedral and collegiate establishments and the redistribution of the greater part of their revenues to the poorer clergy. This was no new idea, although it seems never before then to have been proposed except on the one hand by the most extreme reformers (Bishop Watson, for instance, and Berens) and on the other by anticlerical bishop-baiters. What was more original was the proposal that capitular, collegiate and episcopal property (the last was to be pooled and redistributed more equally among the bishops) should be taken over by a body of Commissioners, who would manage it more efficiently than it could possibly be managed under the existing system of church leases by so many different hands, and superintend its application. These Commissioners would be partly 'official', partly 'salaried'; the latter were, of course, to do the day-to-day work. For the former he suggested the two archbishops, the Lord Chancellor, the First Lord of the Treasury, the bishops of London, Durham, and Winchester, the Home Secretary, the Speaker, the Master of the Rolls, the Prolocutor of the Lower House of Convocation, the three Lords Chief Justice, the archdeacon of London and the deans of Westminster and St Paul's. The Crown would appoint three salaried members to begin with, and might go up to eight subsequently. They were to make annual returns to parliament.

For this bold and rather original concept, only few and partial

[1] *Ibid.* pp. 16–17.

precedents can be found. The Church Building Commissioners were of course an obvious model to start from. The nearest approach in print before 1832 seems to have been the 1824 *Letter to the Archbishop on Church Property*. Whately, who had been concerned with the problem of church government for several years and had certainly travelled by an independent route, was pressing a similar idea for an Ecclesiastical Commission on Lord Grey in the late summer of the year.[1] Blomfield suggested 'a mixed commission of clergymen and laymen to consider what should be adopted in the way of Church reform' to Howley in December.[2] Clearly the idea of a body of Commissioners was becoming popular during 1832; equally clearly, it owed nothing whatever to the Benthamites. Compared with his suggestion of Commissioners, the rest of Henley's *Plan* seems commonplace. The bishops, their revenues more or less equalized, would not need to seek translation, and might moreover be expected to remain resident for nine months in their sees; to facilitate this, he said, it would be a good thing to take them out of the House of Lords, a removal which would at the same time shield the establishment from the reproach that it was political and worldly. Two new sees ought to be created, one at Southwell and one at Windsor. (His detailed plan for the redrawing of the ecclesiastical map came two years later.) He took up the old idea of a Commission (five prelates and five eminent and godly laymen) to administer the Crown's patronage; he made some conventionally sensible remarks about tithe-commutation; and he looked forward to some measure of comprehension of Trinitarian dissenters.

It made the blood of many churchmen boil, and not only because Henley referred to these dissenters as 'a large, an influential, and an excellent portion of the community'.[3] Bishop Van Mildert contented himself with telling Archdeacon Thorp that he was glad Henley was not

---

[1] See his letters of 25 August (in the Grey papers at Durham, Whately bundle, nos. 11–15) and 19 September (in E. J. Whately, *Life and Correspondence of Richard Whately*, I, 168–71.) The same papers contain quite a close anticipation of the Ecclesiastical Commissioners written out in the same hand as two draft bills on pluralities and non-residence. It seems likely that this scheme was drawn up for Grey's consideration, at Whately's urging. Unfortunately there is no indication as to date or authorship. See below, p. 310.

[2] A. Blomfield, *Memoir* (1864 edn.), p. 154. See below, p. 311.

[3] *Op. cit.* Introduction, pp. x–xi.

going to be in the first reformed parliament;[1] 'absurd and mischievous', 'impracticable and *most mischievous*', 'mischievous rashness and presumption', cried his friends.[2] The *Quarterly* found it very distasteful and alleged that its only certain result would be the destruction of the cathedrals and the extinction of the valuable race of curates.[3] And indeed Lord Henley's material proposals were as open to serious objection as his theological and political ones. It cannot be denied that he made a dead set at the cathedrals. They seemed to him (as they had also, though less sharply, to Richard Yates)[4] entirely to lack merit, therefore he was prepared to reform them altogether, and put their endowments to a more useful purpose. The present uselessness and waste of the cathedrals were not seriously contestable in 1832, but it was not as self-evident as Henley assumed it to be that they were incapable of better service in the future. Pusey's valuable *Remarks on the Prospective and Past Benefits of Cathedral Institutions* gave Henley the lie direct. Henley's downright opposition to pluralities and lack of concern for curates were understandable, in view of the amount of rubbish that had been written in their defence, but priggish and excessive. A sensible and thorough scheme of church reform could profitably have made room for both, in the right places and proportions; Henley, who was after all only a layman and professional lawyer, and moreover, as a rather angry 'outsider', was not inhibited by the modesty of conscious ignorance from saying very positive things, rather mistook their form for their substance. On another important point also his wisdom was contestable. He left the revenues of the richer parochial clergymen as he found them. Burton's graduated tax on *all* clergymen's revenues over £200 a year had a virtue and a boldness that was lacking in Henley's savage onslaught on the unpopular capitular and collegiate clergy alone.

But the strengths of his *Plan* were equally obvious. It is easy to see why it was the best known. It was radical, undertook to cut out corruptions,

[1] Letter of 15 December 1832, printed by Edward Hughes in *Eng. Hist. Rev.*, LVI, 477.

[2] Southey in letter of 10 April 1833, in C. C. Southey's *Life and Correspondence of Southey*, VI, 206. *British Magazine*, October 1832, p. 169. Edward Hawkins in letter of 4 February 1833, in Oriel College Letters, 412.

[3] *Quarterly Review*, XLVIII (1832), 564.

[4] *Church in Danger*, pp. 212–15.

and guaranteed results. It is easy to see also why Peel liked it—as one assumes he must have done, since his Ecclesiastical Commissioners followed so closely the lines of Henley's proposals. Henley's views on church reform were very like Peel's. The absurdity of questioning parliament's right to interfere—the wisdom of getting essential reforms done by friends of the church before it was too late for any but its enemies to do it—the express concern with the forlorn multitudes of the cities— the respect, unsoured by theological fault-finding, for dissenters' efforts in that field—the blunt political sense of recognizing that, in view of the way politics were shaping, the Church of England's security and influence for good would depend not on laws or privileges but on 'the habits and affections of the people, strengthened and confirmed by her own growing desire to work out her purity and efficiency and by her faithfulness in the discharge of the great trust which is committed to her hands'[1]—in all this one can see at work a mind very similar to Peel's. One might indeed suspect that Peel's brother-in-law was writing at Peel's instigation.

There is no need to spend much time on the rest of the mass of church reform literature. Lord Henley and Edward Burton were by far the best known of all the practical writers, and between them hit upon almost every practicable point. Two others, however, leaders of the second division, are worth a glance *en passant*. Charles Girdlestone, Vicar of Sedgeley, Staffordshire, came to Burton's aid in a very temperate and admirable *Letter on Church Reform . . . with one Remark* [a most discouraging one] *on the Plan of Lord Henley*. He agreed with Burton that the church's only hope lay in the redistribution of its revenues, and that this would be best accomplished by a graduated tax on benefices or a realistic revaluation of tenths; and he defended this position against the *British Magazine* in these forcible and realistic terms. Only consider, he said, '1. Whether we can reasonably expect any accession of wealth to the Church from without? Whether all hankering after the impropriate tithes is not worse than idle? 2. Whether we should not do well to distribute what we already possess, so as to secure the greatest possible number of resident incumbents? 3. Whether this would not be better for the spiritual influence of the Church, independently of any clamour which its enemies may have raised? 4. Whether this spiritual influence

[1] *Plan*, 4th edn., p. 53.

be not the sole end and object of our worldly possessions, and the best guide for their proper distribution?'[1]; for asking which pertinent questions, he was much abused.

The vicar of Pittington, Co. Durham, J. Miller, contributed a long *Letter to Earl Grey on Church Property and Church Reform*. Largely devoted to tithes, it advocated that taxation of the lay impropriators which seemed to Girdlestone—and, *a fortiori*, Henley—to be the idlest wishful thinking. In these respects Miller was off the main line; but there was much else in his pamphlet to recommend it and carry it through several editions. He got into the usual difficulties over church property. After asserting in conventional style that church property was not public property, and that it was to be treated by the legislature in the same manner as any other property, he laid it down that it was, in effect, public property, and could be interfered with by the legislature in order to secure the ends for which it was originally given. He spoke out nobly against non-residence and pluralities ('what *necessity* began, *interest* and other causes have continued')[2] and proposed a graduated tax on benefices above £300 a year, rising from 3% to 20%. Like Girdlestone, he was opposed to Henley's idea of a Commission.

Thomas Arnold's *Principles of Church Reform* chiefly concerned the fundamental principles of the establishment. The reforms he unblushingly advocated were constitutional in their essence, though theological in their implications. He would have made the established church at once less and more than many of its heartiest supporters imagined it to be or to be capable of being—less, by amending its articles and polity so as to take in the Protestant dissenters and admit the laity to a share in church government; and more, by affirming the ideal of a national church to the point of identifying church and state in their perfect forms. There was plenty here for high churchmen and orthodox liberals to get their teeth into, and several clerical controversialists took time off from their more accustomed intellectual pursuits to grapple with one or other of the startling propositions Arnold put before them.[3] In many ways, Thomas Arnold's *Principles* was by far the most important

---

[1] P. 10 n.   [2] *Op. cit.* 3rd edn., p. 108.

[3] E.g. William Palmer of Worcester College, on the one side, in his *Remarks on Dr Arnold's Principles*, and Archbishop Whately's domestic chaplain, Charles Dickinson, on the other, in his *Observations on Ecclesiastical Legislature and Church Reform*.

of all church reform writings in this period. It still attracts, and generously repays, study. But it was too radical (in the strict sense of the word) for the men and the circumstances to which it was addressed, and it seems to have had practically no influence at all on the material side of the question.

Such were the more conspicuous contributions to the great debate on church reform. How much effect they had, can only be guessed. It is difficult not to believe that Lord Henley's *Plan* and attitude corresponded closely to Peel's and Blomfield's; but whether Henley put much into their minds that was not there already, seems doubtful. His pamphlet and those of the others must have helped give form and direction to a good deal of diffused and vague feeling in favour of reform among the clergy at large. The majority of the poorer clergy, presumably, had no objection to proposals for raising their income; some of them might even have been wicked enough to resent their richer brethren's share of the good things of ecclesiastical life, and (secretly, no doubt) to look forward to their fall. It is noticeable that during just these years, between about 1828 and 1835, some who set themselves up as clerical spokesmen adopted that distinction between the 'working' and the 'dignified' or pluralistic clergy which Brougham popularized in his Durham speech.[1] It pleased well-placed conservative clergymen, who could use hard language about curates when they chose[2], to deny that this distinction had any currency among the clergy. That is difficult to credit. The case of the curates, the hardest-pressed of all classes of 'working clergy', had often been urged since the early eighteenth century, and always in the same terms. The extremity of their usual plight was common knowledge. That they cannot often have felt some resentment at their hardships and entertained profitable ideas of reform is hardly to be believed.

The poor clergy of France in 1789 surprised their superiors by the amplitude and promptness of their *cahiers*. In a weaker way (weaker,

---

[1] E.g. the anonymous author of *Church Patronage; a letter to Robert Peel, Esq., M.P.;* Stephen Cassan, in the appendix to his *Lives of the Bishops of Bath and Wells*, II, 267–8; Edward Duncombe's wordy but sometimes perceptive *Guide to Church Reform* and *Letter to the Hierarchy of the Church of England;* G. H. Stoddart, *Evidence on the Necessity of Church Reform;* and Scrutator's 'Letter to the Lord Chancellor on the Present State of the Established Church' in *Blackwood's*, XXXI (1832), 181 ff.

[2] See e.g. the contempt expressed for them in Rose's *British Magazine*, February 1835, pp. 207–8.

because something had already been done for them, and they had not absolutely lacked friends at court), the poor clergy of England got their chance about 1830. From Chipping Norton Sydney Smith sent news to Lady Holland that 'there is a strong impression that there will be a rising of Curates. Should anything of this kind occur, they will be committed to hard preaching on the tread-pulpit (a new machine) and rendered incapable of ever hereafter collecting great or small tithes.'[1] This was Smith's characteristic way of reporting that he had heard a lot of talk about church reform during his trip to the west country, and that the poorer clergy were hoping to get something out of it. On their ears, at any rate, many of Lord Henley's sentences must have fallen like music.

How much effect Henley and the other practical church reformers had on the more influential clergy can only be surmised. It may well be that Burton, Lyall and others who insisted that the majority of them would support sensible and genuine reforms, were right. Their ideas of what was sensible and genuine of course might not take them very far; they would undoubtedly feel readier to go further under a Tory government than under a Whig. But there is good evidence to support the Burton-Lyall argument. For example, when Peel became prime minister at the start of 1835, several obscure clergymen wrote to assure him of their support for whatever strong measures of church reform he might promote,[2] and the evening lecturer at Wakefield, John Lister, volunteered some constructive criticism of the working of the church building acts.[3] Sidney Herbert sent on to Peel a set of suggestions from a 'clergyman of the highest respectability', who alleged that almost the whole of his archdeaconry (Peel thought it was Salisbury) concurred with it. These suggestions, which were practical and thorough, look as if they were a selection of the best features of the many church reform plans that had been published, with perhaps rather more from Berens than anyone else.[4] Their main points were: 1. Absolutely no pluralities for holders of livings over £500. 2. No one to have more than two livings, and then

---

[1] Letter of 15 October 1830, in his *Letters*, II, 521.

[2] E.g. Matthew Vicars, incumbent of Allhallows, Exeter, and Thomas Powell of Tintern, in Brit. Mus. Add. MSS 40410, fos. 145–7 and 172–3.

[3] 27 January 1835. (*Ibid.* 40412, fos. 31–2.)

[4] Goulburn papers at Kingston, Box II/18. Peel sent them to Goulburn on 28 January 1835.

only when under five miles apart, joint population under 1200, joint income under £600, and second living provided with resident curate. 3. Abolish all peculiars. 4. Tighten up ecclesiastical discipline. 5. No preferment in more than one cathedral, unless over seventy and retired from all other work. 6. Annex cathedral dignities and prebends and sinecure rectories to their attached benefices or to needy benefices under ecclesiastical patronage. 7. No one to be bishop, dean or canon until he has done ten years' parish duty. 8. Reform the system of church leases. 9. All cathedral preferments and richer livings to pay graduated tax to Queen Anne's Bounty. 10. Build manses everywhere. 11. Divide and unite parishes as seems best. 12. Facilitate exchanges of patronage. 13. Amend simony laws so as to enable aged clergymen to resign livings on condition their successors paid them till they died a pension of not more than one-third of its value. 14. Enforce two services from all single-living men. 15. Tighten non-residence regulations. 16. Establish diocesan commissions to accomplish these reforms. Such suggestions were truly excellent. They could hardly have been better.

Further intimations of the same clerical readiness for action came from the influential high-church Archdeacon Bayley—'a most leading man among the Church party', as William Palmer described him to Newman.[1] He wrote to Goulburn (who forwarded his letter to Peel), 'Be assured that the best part of us are most willing to have a good and ample reform—and any of us would be glad to give information on any question proposed.' He referred him particularly to Archdeacon Goddard, 'the best informed and most talented of our body, though a queer fellow'.[2] Charles Goddard, archdeacon of Lincoln, was Bishop Kaye's right-hand man;[3] and Bayley, as archdeacon of Stow, was another of Kaye's willing assistants in the work of reform. He had, indeed, already been doing as much as could be done in that way before Kaye's translation to Lincoln;[4] in 1825 he was warm in praise of

---

[1] Letter of 27 October 1833, in *Newman's Letters and Correspondence*, I, 470. He further remarked that he was 'sorry to find the London clergy are generally quite of the Liberal school, and all under the Bishop of London'.

[2] Letter of 28 January 1835. Brit. Mus. Add. MSS 40333, fos. 293–4.

[3] As Kaye's correspondence, preserved at Lincoln, clearly shows.

[4] See his letters to Bishop Pretyman-Tomline, 1816–19, in the East Suffolk Record Office at Ipswich (Pretyman papers T99/109).

Blomfield's primary visitation;[1] he was obviously in the same class as a church reformer with Blomfield, Goddard and Kaye, and his central position in the Hackney phalanx strengthened still further his title to knowing what he was talking about. In view of all this it seems clear that during the early thirties, and especially during the winter of 1834–5 when the Whig frost seemed so unexpectedly to be thawing, there was much readiness for substantial church reform among the clergy, both the influential and the inconsiderable, and that they were looking hopefully to Peel to give them a lead.

Peel did not disappoint them. In a position to do much, he did it. He was able to do the more, for so little having been done during the past ten years or so. It must not be forgotten that although the reform of the English established church had been ceaselessly agitated during the early thirties, and was often brought up in parliament, hardly anything was done about it between 1831 and 1835. Howley's Augmentations Act of 1831 was the last important piece of legislation in this respect.[2] Much more would no doubt have been done had not all responsible politicians felt bound to wait for the report of the Inquiry Commissioners. Their labours took longer than they had expected, and their commission needed to be twice renewed. In mid-1834 they hurried out an interim summary report in an endeavour, no doubt, to put a stop to the wildly exaggerated estimates of clerical opulence that were, by then—and most unfortunately, from the church's point of view—articles of belief among the radicals; but their main report was not ready until a year later.

Loyal Church of England men did not rest in peace while the Inquiry Commissioners were at work, but were kept in a constant state of alarm and excitement. The Irish Church Temporalities Act of 1833 scared them stiff, with its wholesale reconstruction of the fabric of establishment, its executive Board of Commissioners, and its principle of 'appropriation' that disturbed even some members of the government that put it through.[3] From Oxford in the autumn of that year came the first of the

---

[1] Letter of 5 January 1825, in Churton, *Memoir of Joshua Watson*, I, 249–50.

[2] Apart from this, there were only a few acts altering the law of tithes, the weightiest being Tenterden's Prescriptive Rights Act of 1832 (2 and 3 William IV c. 100).

[3] Mrs Brose has a good discussion of this in her *Church and Parliament*, chapter 5, and Mathieson discusses it and its effects in *English Church Reform*, p. 75 ff. For the

Tracts for the Times. All through that winter and the spring of 1834 churchmen of the stricter sort bustled about in readiness to repel the hordes of radicals, dissenters and Whigs who were obviously about to come down upon them. Some 'Suggestions for the Formation of an Association of Friends of the Church', drafted by William Palmer, rewritten by Newman, and polished by Ogilvie, were widely canvassed.[1] A clerical Address to the Archbishop, which Joshua Watson approved as 'prevent[-ing] the reproach of unqualified opposition to all reform, without admitting the necessity of any',[2] received about 7000 signatures and, after a great deal of coming and going and clashing of temperament between Oxford, Hackney, and Cambridge, a loyal Laymen's Declaration was thrashed out and put into circulation, to receive in the end the signatures of over 230,000 'heads of families'.[3] Archdeacon Goddard, who was too busy running his archdeaconry, strengthening his bishop's hand, and advising both the archbishop and the government in their difficulties over church rates, was not impressed by it; he approved of the laity's coming forward, he said, 'only I wish them a better expression of their sentiments than is provided in the miserable printed Declaration left at shops in London for signature'.[4] But it certainly provided a ground-bass of support for the church during the ceaseless bickerings of 1834. During this year, attention turned ominously from the Irish church towards the English, and churchmen could derive little comfort from the fact that, by the end of the session, there had been no actual legislation about it. The dissenters were

background to Whig disagreements over 'appropriation', see my article in *History*, XLV (1960), 103 ff.

[1] *Newman's Letters and Correspondence*, I, 433. They may be seen in Palmer's *Narrative of Events*, p. 104 f. What they meant to Newman, and what impression Charles Girdlestone got of them, is vividly shown in the two very interesting letters printed in the appendices to W. Tuckwell, *Reminiscences of Oxford*, pp. 280–4.

[2] Letter of 1 November 1833, in Churton's *Memoir*, II, 30. H. J. Rose took violent exception to its last paragraph, as giving an impression that its signatories were ready to make reasonable changes: see his letter to Christopher Wordsworth snr., 30 November 1833, in the possession of Mr Jonathan Wordsworth, to whom I am indebted for permission to refer to it. The Address may be seen in Palmer's *Narrative* pp. 107–8.

[3] These figures, which may be exaggerated, are given in A. P. Perceval's *Collection of Papers*, p. 12.

[4] Letter to Kaye, 3 February 1834, in the Kaye papers at Lincoln, Cor. 4/148/3.

noticeably more vocal and vigorous than they had been in 1833, and were sounding new depths in their quarrel with the establishment. Church rates, admission to the universities, marriages and burials, were constantly debated, in parliament and out of it. Lord John Russell had a shot (which did not quite succeed) at settling the dissenters' grievances over marriages, and Lord Althorp made the first of what was to be a very long and tedious series of attempts to put the law regarding church rates onto a better footing. A private member's bill for the abolition of religious tests as qualifications for degrees got as far as the Lords. Each was accompanied by the usual paraphernalia of pamphlet, petition and counter-petition, and in the debates on the third of them, the universities admissions bill, the whole of the case for and against an established church was argued with a frankness and a freedom thitherto unprecedented, and highly shocking to establishment ears.[1]

Although churchmen in 1834 witnessed the abandonment or defeat of several bills intended to alter the church's structure or constitutional relationships, and although the main report of the Church Revenues Inquiry Commissioners was not quite yet published, they knew that action could hardly be long delayed. The proceedings of 1834 were alarming even to churchmen convinced of the need for major reforms. It was with great relief, therefore, that they heard of William IV's dismissal of the Whig ministry (by then having Lord Melbourne at its head) in November, and of his recall of Peel from Rome to form a Conservative government in its stead. The reservations which many of them had felt about Peel since his exploits of 1828 and 1829 were abandoned in hopeful joy at his party's return to office. The event was unexpected, not least by Peel himself, who was unconvinced of William's wisdom in acting as he had done. Churchmen were not on that account the less grateful for the respite thus offered to them. If only his ministry could have lasted four years instead of four months, Peel could have reformed the church very much as he pleased.

[1] A convenient account of these bills, and of Brougham's freakish introduction of his pluralities and non-residence bills, is given by Mathieson, pp. 102–10.

CHAPTER VII

THE FOUNDATION OF THE ECCLESIASTICAL COMMISSIONERS
1835-1840

Nobody knew what Peel would do in the way of church reform. His reticent character, no less than the new kind of conservatism he was trying to popularize, prevented him from making general pronouncements after the fashion of more officious politicians. Moreover, it is evident from his correspondence through the weeks of his ministry's formation that he himself had none too clear an idea what he would try to do. He approached the subject with an open and an inquiring mind, as one who considered he had been given a 'doctor's mandate'. He knew however that he would have to do something; and the nation knew it too.

All through the sessions of 1833 and 1834 Peel had been insisting that he was as ready to reform what really needed to be reformed as anyone else. He had taken pains to make this clear while censuring, as he felt bound to do, the more offensive features of Althorp's Irish Church Bill. He had actually supported Althorp's Church Rates Bill and Russell's Dissenters' Marriages Bill, and had made no secret of his anxiety to see the tithe question satisfactorily settled. Of all this he reminded his constituents (and through them, the nation at large) in his 'Address to the Electors of the Borough of Tamworth', familiarly known as the Tamworth Manifesto; wherein, turning to 'the great question of Church Reform', he said:

I cannot give my consent to the alienating of Church property . . . from strictly Ecclesiastical purposes. But I repeat now the opinions that I have already expressed in Parliament in regard to the Church Establishment in Ireland—that if, by an improved distribution of the revenues of the Church, its just influence can be extended, and the true interests of the Established religion promoted, all other considerations should be made subordinate to the advancement of objects of such paramount importance. . . . With regard to alterations in the laws which govern our Ecclesiastical Establishment, . . . It is a subject which must undergo the fullest deliberation, and into that deliberation the Government will enter, with the sincerest desire to remove every abuse that can impair the efficiency of the Establishment, to extend the sphere of its usefulness, and to strengthen and confirm its just claims upon the respect and affections of the people.

Here was an unmistakeable solemn undertaking to find out what needed to be done and to do it, but he gave the public no clue as to what was in his mind, beyond the reference—sufficiently ominous to some clerical ears—to 'an improved distribution' of church revenues. If Peel could approve of that in Ireland, why should he not do the same for England and Wales?

Blomfield, Howley, and Henry Goulburn (Peel's second-in-command in church matters) were the men he took into closest counsel while he was making his dispositions.[1] By the end of the first week of January 1835 he had decided to move forward on two fronts. On one side he would placate the dissenting and property-owning interests and save the church from the odium it quite unnecessarily incurred in respect of church rates, tithe commutation, dissenters' marriages and the inferiorities forced upon dissenters by the legal and medical professions. Here he would travel on much the same road as the Whigs. On the other side he would tackle the 'internal' reform of the church, church reform in the classical tradition. Here he was more original, in proposing (with Blomfield's and Howley's full approval) that the detailed plans of reform should come not from the government but from a semi-independent commission. About the middle of January, its members were being recruited, the clergymen by the archbishop and the laymen by the prime minister. Howley invited Archbishop Vernon Harcourt (as he had to, for the look of the thing) and Bishops Kaye and Monk, both respected for their piety and attainments, and each of them in his own way a church reformer. There was no need to write to Blomfield. Peel brought in Lord Lyndhurst, the Lord Chancellor,

---

[1] See, e.g. his correspondence with Goulburn, Brit. Mus. Add. MSS 40333, fos. 210–58 *passim*, Howley's speech in the Lords 10 March 1836 (*Hansard*, 3/XXXII, 134), and Peel's letter of 5 January to the King (in Parker's *Peel*, II, 276). There may be evidence of his taking others into consultation as close, but I have not seen it.

and Henry Goulburn, the Chancellor of the Exchequer; Charles Wynn, the Chancellor of the Duchy of Lancaster, who had been on the Commission of Inquiry into the state of the Public Records; and three non-ministerial men, Lord Harrowby, Sir Herbert Jenner, the Dean of the Arches, and Henry Hobhouse, Keeper of the State Papers since his retirement from active official life in 1827, whom Peel had come to know and trust as permanent under-secretary of state at the Home Office.

None refused, and the commission was thus ready to be published on 4 February. This was officially the Ecclesiastical Duties and Revenues Commission, the board that overlapped at each end of its brief span, first with the Ecclesiastical Revenues Commission, alias the Ecclesiastical Inquiry Commission (whose full report was only published in June), and then with the Ecclesiastical Commissioners proper, into whom it metamorphosed itself in 1836. Strictly speaking, the Ecclesiastical Duties and Revenues Commissioners and the Ecclesiastical Commissioners were different things. But since their membership was identical, and the latter form adopted simply to give effect to the recommendations made in the former, the Ecclesiastical Commissioners are most sensibly to be thought of as dating (in fact if not in form) from 1835 and Peel's first ministry rather than from 1836 and Melbourne's second. He had little time, but he left his mark. No one recognized this more forcefully than the simple, conservative clergyman who wrote, a few years later, that 'Sir Robert Peel in his short administration of 135 days did more mischief to the Church than 135 years will be able to repair.'[1]

The Commission was issued on 4 February. The Commissioners met for the first time on 9 February. After eight more general meetings and a number of committees, they had their first report ready for signature by 17 March 1835.[2] They went, indeed, rather too fast for prudence, and subsequently had to go back upon some of their first proposals. The reason for their haste was possibly Peel's anxiety to prove to the nation that his government, far from being averse to 'sensible' reform, could be relied on to make reforms, where they were really needed, with boldness and despatch. Blomfield and the others

[1] W. J. Aislabie, *Letter to Lord John Russell on the Church Bills.*
[2] Ordered to be printed by the House of Commons, 19 March.

might well have thought it wise to get as much done as they could before the defeat of Peel's government—which must have seemed inevitable from the start. But although it was Blomfield who became the Commission's dynamo later on, Peel himself seems to have been its initial driving-force; and, if one had not seen how seriously he took the matter of church reform, the leading share he took on the Commissioners' earliest deliberations would be surprising, in view of the immense amount of other work he had to do at the same time, as prime minister of a very new and shaky administration. The Commissioners' first meeting was in Peel's house. After that they met in the Church Building Commissioners' premises, the other side of the abbey in Great George Street. Peel certainly attended every general meeting until the signature of the first report, and it is not certain that he never attended the committee meetings (which, in order to make greater haste, became open after 21 February) in between. Moreover, they did not in these early, Peel-dominated days, confine their discussion to the matters dealt with in their reports. Peel meant them to go further still, and at the second general meeting asked them to take into consideration the whole state of the established church—which meant, to be precise, the pieces of legislation his government had been busily preparing. At the third general meeting, Goulburn submitted draft Marriages and Registration bills, and Peel outlined his Church Rates Bill. Later, they discussed pluralism, non-residence, church leases, and 'the Professional Knowledge of the younger Clergy'.[1] At the fourth general meeting, 'Some conversation took place, but nothing was definitely settled, with respect to the expediency of asking for this Commission powers to make such voluntary arrangements with Patrons of Livings, and so to deal from time to time with sinecure preferments as they may fall vacant, as best to secure the objects contemplated by his Majesty in issuing this Commission'.[2] Here was the germ of what they actually became fifteen months later. Had Peel's first administration only lasted, they might have become something even more powerful.

Peel's government however did not last. He resigned on 8 April, and, naturally enough, his resignation from the Commission came soon

[1] For the latter, see Howley's memoranda for Peel, 16 February 1835. Brit. Mus. Add. MSS 40414, fo. 272.
[2] Minutes, 14 February 1835.

afterwards. He was followed by its other ministerial members. The others—the five prelates, and the three laymen, Harrowby, Jenner and Hobhouse—decided to try to make terms with the new government and to stay on if they could. Howley acted as intermediary, and reached a satisfactory understanding with Melbourne towards the end of May.[1] The way was clear to the resumption of their labours.

Thus reconstituted, with Lords Lansdowne, Melbourne, and Cottenham, Lord John Russell and Thomas Spring-Rice in place of Lord Lyndhurst, Peel, Goulburn, and Charles Wynn, and none of them coming very often, the Commissioners lay low for nearly a year. They were busy collecting information, revolving plans, encountering their first whiffs of opposition from apprehensive chapters and stick-in-the-mud bishops, and discovering that, for all the inquiries of the Ecclesiastical Revenues Commissioners, the half was not yet told, nor yet understood, concerning the finances of the cathedral and collegiate churches.[2] Between the resumption of their meetings after Peel's resignation and the last meeting recorded in the minute book (27 January 1836), they met formally at least twenty-five times, and on several occasions two or three times a week.[3] It was during these months, obviously, that Blomfield came to take charge. His assiduity in attendance was matched only by the gentle and semi-invalid Lord Harrowby and the two archbishops, who both came with creditable regularity. None of these was the man to dominate a small group with Blomfield in it. The easygoing old Archbishop of York said later,' Till Blomfield comes, we all sit and mend our pens, and talk about the weather.'[4]

The bulk of the work of inquiry, tabulation and calculation, was done by the Commission's permanent staff; which meant, in chief, their secretary Charles Knight Murray[5]—one of the most remarkable men ever connected with the Commission. Charles Knight Murray was a capable, energetic, and pushing young lawyer, whose early prosperity

[1] See their correspondence, 18, 19, 23 and 30 May 1835, in the P.R.O., H.O. 73/11.
[2] See especially minutes, 18 November 1835.
[3] There was an intermission in their labours between 22 August and 14 November, and no meetings are recorded for December.
[4] A. Blomfield, *Memoir* (1864 edn.), p. 167.
[5] It has been difficult to discover much about him. The *D.N.B.* knows nothing of him, and the entry in Boase is flimsy.

was probably due to his or his father's political services. His father, another Charles, was a respectable Bedford Row solicitor. Either father or son seems to have been honorary secretary to the Constitutional Association, alias the 'Bridge Street Gang', which set itself in 1821–2 to promote the public welfare by putting down whatever liberal or radical publications might be actionable as seditious, blasphemous, or obscene literature. Murray was in his late twenties by then, and could perfectly well have done the work.[1]

The next steps in his progress were presumably made with the aid of Lord Lyndhurst, whom he served as 'principal secretary' during his Lord Chancellorship from 1828 to 1830, and very likely earlier as well. In 1829 he was made a commissioner in bankruptcy, and in 1830 one of the London stipendiary magistrates, sitting at the Union Hall police office. Sometime about this period he became also a 'Judicial Commissioner of Lunatics'.[2] These were all perquisites of the kind that a busy young barrister, intimate with the Lord Chancellor and acceptable to the party in power, might confidently look forward to. His next step was less predictable, and marked his entrée into the ecclesiastical world. He was named secretary to the Ecclesiastical Courts Commission which began to meet early in 1830. He continued however, as a magistrate until the eve of his appointment as secretary to the Ecclesiastical Duties and Revenues Commission. This conspicuous pluralism made Lord Melbourne hesitate slightly in 1831 before fixing his salary: how much work was Murray actually doing? he asked the commissioners. They replied that they could not say how long the work took him, but that it had been wholly satisfactory and, indeed, indispensable.[3] This compliment from his employers was only the first of many. It is one of the more astonishing things about Charles Knight Murray, that into whatever hot water he got outside the office, his employers always protected him and protested his excellence. Either he really was a first-rate administrator, or else (and some later evidence rather suggests this) he had a mesmeric power of making his employers believe he was so.

At any rate his work on the Ecclesiastical Courts Commission did

---

[1] He had entered Lincoln's Inn in 1812, aged 18. (*Admissions to Lincoln's Inn*, 1896, II, 48.)

[2] See Boase, the *Royal Kalendars* for these years, and P.Ps. 1847–8, xviii(1), 416–7.

[3] See their minutes, 17 and 31 January 1831.

not stand in the way of his being invited to act as secretary to the Ecclesiastical Duties and Revenues Commission; and his resignation from his police magistracy just five or six weeks previously (according to Boase) suggests that he expected it. Lyndhurst would of course have had a powerful voice in this appointment; and since Blomfield's voice would not have been a weak one, it must be significant that Blomfield thought highly of his clergyman brother, Thomas Boyles Murray, whom he had just recommended to Peel for an important metropolitan incumbency.[1] That the bishop already knew a good deal about Thomas's brother Charles is clear from his letter; and he would of course have met him on the Ecclesiastical Courts Commission. It was to be important both for Murray and the Commissioners, later on, that Blomfield had such a high opinion of him.

Thus Charles Knight Murray, the church's Edwin Chadwick, was part of the Ecclesiastical Commissioners from the start, as active and dominating in the management of their ordinary business as was Blomfield in their general meetings and committees. They worked quietly through the latter half of 1835, and then published the second, third and fourth reports quite close together, in the spring and early summer of 1836.[2] Their fifth and last report was delayed by the vigorous opposition of the deans and chapters to their proposals, and had still not come out when William IV's death brought them also to the term of their natural life. The draft was accordingly sent for by the Home Secretary and published late in 1837.[3]

The first report was almost wholly concerned with the reform of the episcopate. It proposed, in fairly general terms, the creation of two new sees, at Manchester and Ripon, and the union of two pairs of old ones— St Asaph with Bangor, and Llandaff with Bristol; a thorough reform of diocesan geography, to reduce the disparities between the various sees and rationalize the boundaries of each (e.g., by bringing the whole of the greater London area under the bishop of London, and transferring the county of Dorset from the diocese of Bristol, from which it was completely separated, to that of Salisbury) together with an ironing-out of such anomalies as parochial enclaves and overlapping jurisdictions;

[1] Letter of 2 January 1835. Brit. Mus. Add. MSS 40409, fos. 69–70.
[2] Signed 4 March, 20 May, and 24 June respectively.
[3] For the places taken by these reports in the Parliamentary Papers, see above, p. XIII.

the redistribution of the prelates' very unequal revenues among themselves, so as to pay each (including the two new bishops) not less than £4500 and not more than £5500 (except the Archbishops and the bishops of London, Durham and Winchester), and some redistribution of their patronage. These were its principal suggestions. It concluded with some important paragraphs designed to reassure both those who might think it was going too far, and those who were anxious for it to go much further. 'We respectfully beg it to be understood', they said, 'that . . . we assume that regard will be had to vested Interests, and that none of the proposed changes should take place, with respect to Bishops and Incumbents now in possession, without their consent.' Then followed the reassurance for eager reformers, in their narrative (surely intended to be exemplary) of what had just happened to the vacant stall at Westminster. Instead of filling it at once, Peel had made a test case of it, and proposed its annexation to the very populous and spiritually ill-provided parish of St Margaret's; which had been duly done, not without certain difficulties and doubts on the parts of Howley and the chapter, which were kept prudently hidden. Finally, they announced that the Crown, the Lord Chancellor, and the prelates Commissioners were going to suspend their cathedral and sinecure patronage rights until a plan had been produced for making better use of them.

The second report was the meatiest of the three, and from it most of the Commissioners' subsequent misfortunes sprang. They began with some further thoughts about the dioceses, and went more fully than before into episcopal revenues, making tentative suggestions concerning the exceedingly difficult and controversial question of church leases. The main section of the report, for which most church reformers and all Whigs and radicals had been eagerly waiting, concerned 'Cathedral and Collegiate Churches'. That they should have found the means for reducing clerical poverty and non-residence in the surplus of wealth in these establishments was almost inevitable. Their Commission had hinted heavily that these establishments were not as 'conducive to the Efficiency of the Established Church' as they might be, and that their revenues were ripe for redistribution. It was not the idea of redistribution itself, therefore, but the actual means proposed for its accomplishment, that were eagerly or anxiously awaited. In the event, the best hopes and worst fears of each side were fully realized. The Commissioners proposed, in brief, the abolition of all non-residentiary canonries, the reduction of the number of residentiary canons in general to four, where it exceeded that number, and the taking away from about half the deans and canons of the separate estates they held over and above their share of the corporate revenues.[1] Funds would thus be released from nearly four hundred assorted prebends, whether from their separate estates and impropriations or their shares in a corporate revenue or both; and the total sum to be expected from these sources under existing arrangements of leases and rents, supplemented by the revenues of sinecure rectories, was expected to exceed £130,000 a year. Beside these really radical reforms, which were worked out in detail, cathedral by cathedral, the rest of the second report seemed almost trivial. It included the suggestion that archdeaconries should be annexed to stalls and thus properly supported; urged the reduction in the numbers and improvements in the manner of remuneration of the lesser cathedral clergy—the vicars choral, minor canons and so on; advocated the transfer of most capitular patronage to the Crown or, more generally, the bishops; and came to an end with the summary of a bill Blomfield had prepared for the regulation of pluralities, residence, and the employment of stipendiary curates.

The third report resumed the main theme of the first, the reconstruction of the diocesan system, and urged speedy action to take advantage of 'the Number of Episcopal Sees at present vacant.' It made a few more revisions of its cartographical suggestions,[2] proposed a third union of sees—Carlisle with tiny Sodor and Man—and then produced its plans in the detailed form of a set of 'distinct Propositions' for an act of parliament. All but one concerned bishops, dioceses, and archdeacons, and that one was the first. It ran thus: '1. That Commissioners be appointed by Parliament, for the Purpose of preparing, and laying before Your Majesty in Council, such Schemes as shall appear to them to be best adapted for carrying into effect the following Recommendations; and that Your Majesty in Council be empowered to make

[1] To be precise, those of 'the old foundation'—York, London, Chichester, Exeter, Hereford, Lichfield, Lincoln, Salisbury, Wells and Windsor.

[2] Once again, its plans for the city and deanery of Bristol were changed. Now they were to be incorporated with the diocese of Gloucester.

Orders, ratifying such Schemes, and having the full Force of Law.' From this proceeded, a couple of months later, the statute establishing the Ecclesiastical Commissioners.

The fourth report followed close on the third and, like it, included a set of heads for a bill. It began with a polite acknowledgment of the criticisms that had been made of the second report and, while defending itself with the remark that some points of a scheme so vast would always be exceptionable to some people, made one substantial concession in respect of the means proposed for the reduction in size of the larger chapters. After a few paragraphs dealing with the peculiar problems of the Welsh sees and other matters, it presented its bill for the reform of cathedral and collegiate establishments; in which 'the Commissioners for carrying into effect [our] former Recommendations' were taken for granted.

The draft fifth report was simply a revised version of the bill suggested in the fourth, prefaced by a defence of their proposals in general, and sweetened by a few concessions on particular points.

Thus the Ecclesiastical Duties and Revenues Commissioners produced, between March and June 1836, the outlines for three statutes, together amounting to a broad reform of the establishment and dealing respectively with residence and pluralities, the episcopate, and the deans and chapters.[1] They hoped to pass all three at once. Had they succeeded, the year 1836 would have been a year of legislation unparalleled in the whole history of the Church of England, for it was the year also of the Registration and Dissenters' Marriages Acts[2] and the general Tithe Commutation Act,[3] which did away, at last, with difficulties so ancient and profound that they had become woven into the fabric of establishment, and which could only be removed by altering the character of the establishment itself.[4] But the Commissioners were disappointed. It was a busy session; their bills were not brought in till late, nor were they unopposed; and the result was, that only one of them became law that year. Their 'Act to abridge the holding of Benefices in Plurality and to make better Provision for the Residence of the Clergy' had to

---

[1] Respectively in the second report (pp. 15–17), third report (pp. 7–12), and fourth report (pp. 10–18, revised in the fifth report, pp. 6–13).

[2] 6 and 7 Wm. IV cc. 86 and 85 respectively.   [3] 6 and 7 Wm. IV c. 71.

[4] See ch. 10 below, pp. 465–8.

wait until 1838.[1] Although much watered down by parliament, it remained an effective and even a strict measure, going so far beyond its predecessor, the Act of 1817, as to mark something of a revolution in common clerical life. Its passage with, comparatively speaking, so little opposition, must have been due mainly to the diversion of attention from it by the contemporary furore over the other pieces of church legislation then being considered—the offensive attempt made by the government in 1837-8 to settle the church rates question on the lines of the 'appropriation clause' by finding an equivalent for rates in the 'surplus revenues' of better managed church lands[2]—and the 'Deans and Chapters bill', which had to wait, a standing object of fear and loathing in every close and college, until the government had dropped these plans of 'appropriation', the enactment of which would of course have foiled the Commissioners by putting the chapters' lands to another purpose. Only in 1839 was the way clear to proceeding with this bill; and in 1840, after four years of unremitting opposition from the great majority of the chapters, it was not permitted to pass until counsel had been heard pleading eloquently against it at the bar of the House of Lords.[3]

In pleasing contrast with the delays to which the Pluralities and Residence Act and the 'Deans and Chapters' Act were subjected, stood the ease with which was passed the Established Church Act, 6 and 7 Will. IV. c.77, embodying the propositions of the third report. Lord John Russell laid that report on the table of the House on 20 May 1836, and at the same time introduced a bill to carry it into effect.[4] Its parliamentary history thereafter is a little obscure;[5] but it got through both

---

[1] I and 2 Vict. c. 106. See Mathieson, pp. 132–3, and Bishop Monk's 1838 Charge, pp. 45–8.

[2] See Mathieson, pp. 136–7, and A. Blomfield, *Memoir* (1864 edn.) pp. 158–61.

[3] 3 and 4 Vict. c. 113.

[4] P.Ps. 1836, I, 589 ff.; *Hansard*, 3/xxxiii, 1133; and *Mirror*, 1836, p. 1571.

[5] Mathieson, p. 135 n., correctly notices 'several obvious inaccuracies in the Hansard reports'. But they are not the only difficulty. The bill introduced on 20 May appears to have petered out after its second reading on 17 June. (*Mirror*, 1836, p. 1949: not reported in *Hansard*). What happened on 8 July is difficult to make out; cf. Russell's speech as reported in the *Mirror*, p. 2278 ff., and *Hansard*, 3/xxxv, 13 ff., and the debate that followed it, with the bill apparently introduced on that occasion (P.Ps. 1836, I, 621 ff. and *Mirror*, p. 2295).

houses without much difficulty and received the royal assent on 13 August. It was opposed by three elements in parliament—by anti-clerical radicals, who thought it treated the bishops too well; by ultra-clerical conservatives, who scented spoliation and 'erastianism'; and by a Durham and Northumberland pressure group, who lodged thus early the first of a thirty-year series of protests against the reduction of Durham's revenues, and who were destined to give the Ecclesiastical Commissioners a great deal of trouble.

The Act began by citing the greater part of the third report's recommendations and then, right at the end of this immense first clause, named the existing commissioners and turned them 'for the Purposes of this Act' into 'One Body Politic and Corporate by the Name of "The Ecclesiastical Commissioners for England"', with all the ordinary attributes of such bodies—perpetual succession, legal personality, and the like. They were not tied up in a strait-jacket of statutory direction. The whole tendency of the Act was to recognize that this was only the beginning of a long, perhaps an endless, process of legal and administrative change; and it relieved parliament of much of the burden of directing these changes by delegating the direction of most of them to the Commissioners themselves. The better to prosecute the inquiries they would need to make, before proposing legislation, they were empowered to examine on oath and to compel the production of documents, and clause 10 expressly enlarged their legislative capacity to include 'such Modifications or Variations as to Matter of Detail and Regulation as shall not be substantially repugnant' to the recommendations of the report. The method of legislation prescribed for them was by Orders in Council embodying schemes they had prepared, of the same full legal force as if they had been included in the statute itself. These Orders were to be laid before parliament each January; apart from that annual opportunity to see what the Commissioners had been doing, with, of course, the power to ask questions in the House or demand the printing of papers, parliament came into it not at all. The Act, said its supporters, laid down principles for the Commissioners to apply. The working out of the details was left entirely to the Commissioners, and was, moreover, as some of its critics complained, not too closely defined.

Their number was small—thirteen, on the very rare occasions when all attended—and since they did most of their work in a general, open, committee, whereof the quorum was only three, it needed very few indeed to keep their machine ticking over.[1] Howley and Blomfield were almost always there. Out of 103 meetings, Howley missed only 8, Blomfield only 10. Hobhouse and Jenner, the 'legal members' whose experience was so often needed, were present 61 and 59 times respectively; Harrowby managed to be there nearly as often.[2] Their task was as yet quite simple and straightforward. They had only one big statute to put into effect and they were still blessedly free from the cares of landownership. They had powers to transfer pieces of property from one see to another or even to themselves, but never used them.[3] They were not even troubled with the revenues of the stalls and sinecure rectories that the ministers and bishops were obligingly leaving vacant. These were being collected and kept for them by Queen Anne's Bounty.[4] The work was neither so onerous nor so complicated that the Commissioners had difficulty in controlling it all themselves. Murray the secretary was kept in his proper subordinate place, managing the little office, drawing up draft schemes in consultation with the lawyers, submitting his actuarial and financial problems to Mr Finlaison of the National Debt Office or Mr Morgan of the Equitable Assurance Company, and taking his difficulties in the fields of church law and finance to Christopher Hodgson at the Bounty office nearby. Nothing in their office history or administrative functions during these years calls for comment.

Nevertheless they were years of the greatest importance for the future, because they witnessed the establishment of principles from which the Ecclesiastical Commissioners were never to depart. It was the same with them, as it had been with Queen Anne's Bounty. Their course was fixed, and the impression they would make upon the Church of England determined, from their infancy. Their troubles increased later, but no subsequent disputes about their constitution and principles of action matched these early ones in importance.

In the first place, objection was taken to their existence as a more or

[1] 1847-8 Committee, Qs. 322-3.
[2] *Ibid.* Appendix H.1.
[3] 6 and 7 Wm. IV c. 77 s. 1; 1847-8 Committee, Q. 36.
[4] 5 and 6 Wm. IV c. 30 and 3 and 4 Vic. c. 113 s. 60.

less permanent corporate body with delegated powers of legislation. The objectors were very often ill-informed, bad-tempered, emotional, and inconsiderate. Their besetting fault was a failure to take account of the political realities of the church's situation. We have already seen how much difficulty most churchmen of conscious principle had, during the years of the third church reform movement, in understanding that the test of 'Is this doing evil that good may come?' was not one they could expect continually to apply to legislation on ecclesiastical subjects. Many had learnt their lesson by the thirties; but many more had not, and it was largely by them that opposition was offered to the very existence of the Ecclesiastical Commissioners, in the form given them by the Act of 1836. They could indeed advance plausible objections to it, and some of them had some point; but they did not—often, doubtless, they simply could not—consider what was to be done if the Commissioners did not do it.

There was no hint in the original Ecclesiastical Duties and Revenues Commission of its being or becoming a permanent board. It seemed to be no more than another commission like the Ecclesiastical Courts Commission or the Ecclesiastical Revenues Commission, appointed to do a job and to expire when the job was done. And it could have been just that. Granted that a great deal of ecclesiastical legislation was needed—a proposition that would have received wide acceptance in 1834 and 1835—the government of the day could very well have decided to introduce the legislation itself and to have done it all by ordinary parliamentary means. The Privy Council Office and the Home Office were both experienced in various departments of church affairs; parliament was certainly in no mood at that time to decline interfering in the affairs of the church; temporary boards like the Church Building Commissioners or the Tithes Commissioners (who were only appointed for terms of years, and had to be periodically renewed) could have been created to handle specific matters of peculiar difficulty, local boards of the kind suggested in the 1824 *Letter to the Archbishop on Church Property* or by the 1832 Committees on Irish Tithes were a practicable alternative to the idea of a central board. There was nothing predeterminate about the Ecclesiastical Commissioners of 1836.

Their conception as a permanent board is probably to be found mainly in the circumstance of the church's lacking a 'government'.

It had recently become increasingly felt among the more reflective class of churchmen that this lack was a serious one. Parliament might for many reasons seem unsatisfactory as virtually the church's legislature, with ultimate authority over doctrine and liturgy as well as immediate authority over law and administration. It was inconvenient, and could be offensive. The ideas of convocation and of diocesan synods thus began to be canvassed towards the end of the twenties, by those who especially feared 'Erastianism' or felt that the clergy ought to band together and find in professional (or, to put it in the new Oxford way, apostolical) solidarity some strength to stand up to the laity. About the same time, others whose more immediate concern was with material church reform and church property, were thinking in terms of more or less permanent executive boards of commissioners. Something of this kind was proposed by the Commons' Select Committee on Irish Tithes of early 1832, who saw great practical advantage for the Irish establishment in the handing over to ecclesiastical corporations (each covering a diocese or a batch of dioceses) the general oversight of the church's property.[1] This did not go very far towards the Irish Church Commissioners as they were actually set up in 1833; and the Lord's committee that was considering the same subject at the same time went even less far.[2] Ideas of this kind were put before them by several witnesses, including Richard Whately, newly dispatched to the archbishopric of Dublin to manage the reform of the Church of Ireland. He told the committee that he would 'place all Church endowments, without exception, in the hands of boards of commissioners, to be administered by them as trustees'.[3] In correspondence with Earl Grey about this time he showed that he had yet bigger things in mind, to meet the church's perils. Of course it was the Irish side of the church that he was most concerned with; but his analysis of the disadvantages that the church suffered by its lack of a government, and the benefits to be gained by the institution of a mixed lay and clerical body with (delegated) legislative powers, was equally relevant to the English side. In the shadow forecast by this notion can be seen some of the lineaments

[1] P.Ps. 1831–2, XXI, 254. Mrs Brose's citation of a later passage in the Committee's report, in her *Church and Parliament*, p. 109, would seem to give the misleading impression that they were recommending a unitary corporation for the whole of Ireland.   [2] P.Ps. 1831–2, XXII, 185.   [3] *Ibid.* p. 114.

of both the Irish Church Commissioners and the English.[1] They can be seen even more clearly in what Blomfield wrote to Howley during the lull before the storm of the first reformed parliament, a time when the bishops were naturally worrying a great deal about the future of the church. 'I have long,' he said, 'been convinced of, and have for some time past been urging, the necessity of a mixed commission of clergymen and laymen to consider what measures should be adopted in the way of Church reform, whether as to the establishment of a consistent scheme of discipline, or the arrangement of ecclesiastical property.' He would not say whether it should be permanent or not, nor how far its powers ought to stretch; 'but I do not see how the final determination of the questions concerning pluralities, and cathedral establishments . . . can be made, with any prospect of a wise and equitable decision, except through the medium of a commission'.[2] He does not mention the Commissioners of Henley's *Plan*, which was by then in its seventh or eighth edition, but the similarity of their ideas is obvious. It was surely from these sources that the English Ecclesiastical Commissioners sprang, and the Irish Church Commissioners before them. The Irish National Board of Education of 1832 and the English Poor Law Commissioners of 1834 are of course also to be noticed, as evidence of the vogue enjoyed at that time by the idea of the executive commission, and as affording certain practical precedents for the Ecclesiastical Commissioners' constitution; but they bear no direct responsibility for it. They and it together were products of the *Zeitgeist*.

The particular origin of the Ecclesiastical Commissioners is thus mainly to be found in the proposals being made during the critical late twenties and early thirties to supply the church's grievous lack of any kind of self-governing power, and in the clear advisability (from the churchman's point of view) of removing the conduct of its major reforms to some distance from a House of Commons riddled (as it seemed to be between 1833 and 1837) with ribald radicalism. This obviously weighed with Whately and Blomfield, and probably weighed

---

[1] Not, however, as has incautiously been asserted, all: Whately went on to express his preference for a federal form of church government, with power shared between this central body and a set of diocesan or archidiaconal synods. See his letters to Grey, mentioned above, ch. VI, p. 286. n. I.

[2] Letter of 11 December 1832, in A. Blomfield, *Memoir* (1864 edn.), pp. 153–5.

with Peel too.[1] With Peel at the prow, and Blomfield at the helm, and with the Poor Law Commissioners making so promising a start at the other end of Whitehall, the Ecclesiastical Duties and Revenues Commissioners might very naturally let their minds turn towards acquiring a more permanent character; and this is in fact what happened. At their fourth general meeting, if not earlier, they discussed it.[2] It was clearly foreshadowed in their second report, where, contemplating the execution of their proposals for diocesan rearrangements, they said, 'It will be requisite ... that permanent Authority should be vested in some Persons, to be named in any Act of Parliament which may be passed for sanctioning those measures; who may be capable of inquiring into Details, more fully than would be convenient for Your Majesty in Council, with whom, we apprehend, the ultimate Sanction will rest.'[3] It was explicitly proposed in the sketch bill at the end of the third report, which moreover assumed, in its earlier parts, the existence of such a board, and entrusted to it not only the further inquiries that must precede legislation, but also a central place in their machinery of episcopal remuneration. Bishop Kaye tells that they had not themselves, in making these dispositions, expected to be turned into anything grander than a more durable form of Commission, but that the Crown law officers thought they would be better equipped for their work as a full-dress corporation[4]. This was the immediate background to the proposition that Russell and Peel between them shepherded safely through the Commons in 1836.

Of all this there were, from the start, serious criticisms. First, there were the strictly constitutional criticisms, proceeding no less from ultra-conservative Anglican quarters than from anti-clerical radicals. The radicals had long looked forward to exploiting parliament's power over the church, and were enraged to see the chance slipping away from them. The creation of the Ecclesiastical Commissioners was not the only factor in their frustration. The unexpected success of the Anglican

---

[1] See Mrs Brose's interesting suggestions, in her pp. 137–8. It must, however, be remembered that the actual conversion of the temporary into the permanent commission was done not by Peel but by Melbourne and Russell.

[2] Minutes, 14 February. See above, p. 299.

[3] Second report, p. 2.

[4] 'Letter to the Archbishop of Canterbury', 1838: in *Nine Charges, etc.* pp. 169–70.

revival, the unflagging vigour of 'No Popery', the Whigs' own refusal to go as far as the radicals wished, also helped to defeat them. The creation of the Ecclesiastical Commissioners was now yet another blow to their hopes. Those more adept at the manipulating of constitutional principles made the most of their opportunity. Charles Buller found fault with government's haste in pushing so important a bill through the House so quickly, a bill 'which, in fact, delegates the business of legislating upon this subject to another body'. They were being asked to sign a blank cheque, the encashment of which could benefit only the church. 'I wish to ask his Majesty's Ministers', he declaimed, 'under what species of insanity it is that they come forward to alienate from them their best supporters, in order to carry into effect the recommendations of a Committee appointed by the Right Honourable Baronet [i.e. Peel] opposite?'[1] Anticipating the replacement of a Whig by a Conservative government, another of them, Rigby Wason, remarked that the whole of the board would then be composed of men devoted to the principle of establishment, and that parliament would be given sad cause to rue its imprudence.[2]

Notwithstanding that Buller and Potter, and other radicals also, felt that the bill was 'very advantageous to the Established Church', and tended greatly 'to strengthen and consolidate it',[3] constitutional grounds of objection were found also by eminent churchmen. Sir Robert Inglis in the Commons said surprisingly little, and stuck mainly to what he perhaps felt would be his least unpopular ground, namely, that the principle behind the bill was one of interference with property. In the Lords, Phillpotts argued against the bill with great force and acuteness, and less tartness than usual. He maintained that an ordinary *ad hoc* Commission would have been sufficient to carry the report's recommendations into effect. This permanent Commission, however, was 'a machinery calculated to produce a perpetual change'. Its composition, moreover, was full of ill-omen. Only three of the Commissioners were independent, *ex officio;* the rest were either members of the government of the day, or were appointed by the Crown. 'I put it to you', he said,

[1] 19 July, *Mirror*, 1836, p. 2463b.
[2] 8 July. *Mirror*, 1836, p. 2292a. In this much longer report of his speech, no such startling remark occurs as is quoted from the *Hansard* report by Mrs Brose on her p. 139, lines 25–6.　　　　　　　　　　　　[3] 8 July. *Mirror*, 1836, p. 2292.

'whether you can find a single instance of the vast majority of a Commission being removable at the pleasure of the Crown.' Here he put his finger on one of the original Commission's weakest spots. He made his point in a characteristically exaggerated way, but it was true that neither Blomfield nor Kaye had approved the inclusion of the bill's second clause giving the Crown discretionary power to remove from, as to fill vacancies in, the two lower episcopal and the three non-ministerial lay places.[1] The Irish Church Commission was not open to the same objection. Phillpotts went on to indicate several evil consequences that might follow—for example, their taking control of church property themselves, and turning the clergy into 'stipendiaries'—and ended with a plea to alter the bill in committee.[2]

These themes, stated thus early by Phillpotts, were to be repeated, elaborated, and orchestrated endlessly over the next four years, and we need not dwell much upon them. They became the stock-in-trade of conservative ecclesiastical agitators, and were worked in with the many other objections that could be made to the Commissioners' practical proposals in order to whip up public sympathy for the deans and chapters, to humiliate Blomfield, and, variously, 'to free the church from state' (or 'parliamentary', or 'ministerial', or 'secular') 'dictation'. The degree of their wildness may be judged from the free use they almost invariably made of the bad old seventeenth-century ecclesiastical commissions, which were in truth no more like this one than Charles I was like William IV, and had nothing in common with it but the name. The most comprehensive and amazing of these indictments, incorporating the constitutional objections with all the others, was Pusey's, which presents the melancholy spectacle of a high-principled clerical mind almost unhinged by excitement and morbidity.[3] Manning's *Principle of the Ecclesiastical Commissioners Examined* also repays study, for similar reasons.

[1] See Blomfield's 1838 Charge, p. 25, and Kaye's 'Letter to the Archbishop', in *op. cit.* p. 170; though Kaye was mistaken in saying it was 'inserted' in the Commons. It was in the draft bill, and passed the Commons without comment.

[2] 29 July. *Mirror* 1836, pp. 2609–10.

[3] This was originally an immense article in the *British Critic*, April 1838, 455–562. It was at once published separately under the title *The Royal and Parliamentary Ecclesiastical Commissioners*. The attribution to Pusey is in Appendix A to vol. IV of Liddon's *Life of Pusey*.

One of the most ingenious and mischievous sallies against the Commissioners came in William Selwyn's *Substance of an Argument . . . against those clauses of the Benefices Plurality Bill which confer additional powers on the Ecclesiastical Commissioners* (1838). Most of the pamphlet was commonplace enough, but into the middle of it he inserted a correspondence between 'W. Dunelm,' and 'the Ecclesiastical Commissioners for England' so exceedingly lifelike and circumstantially presented that only the most careful reader will mark that it is, in fact, completely imaginary. It begins with a letter from 'W. Dunelm, Auckland, August 3, 1838' asking the Commissioners to use their powers under the 1 and 2 Vic. c.— to unite by Order in Council two contiguous livings whose eligibility for union he guaranteed. 'C. K. Murray' replies two days later, to say that the Commissioners will look into 'the circumstances of the case . . . as soon as the press of other business, with which the Board is at present overwhelmed, will permit'. Four months later the bishop, having heard nothing from them, asks for a decision. Murray delays ten days more before telling him abruptly that the board 'are not satisfied that the proposed union . . . may be usefully made'. The correspondence is closed by 'W. Dunelm.' thus:

Sir,

I beg you will inform the Ecclesiastical Commissioners for England that I cannot consider myself to have been treated by them with the respect and consideration due to the sacred office which I have the honour to hold in the Church.

At the same time I fully admit, that as the law at present stands I have no redress; and being the first victim of the Stat. 1 and 2 Victoria. c.–, under which the Commissioners act, I must set an example of bearing the indignity with patience.

I am, Sir,

Your obedient Servant,

W. DUNELM.[1]

So effective is this as propaganda, and so neatly extreme in its method, that one is reminded of Pugin's *Contrasts*, published only a year later.

One of the Commissioners' critics who was neither merely political nor too emotional, from whom such opposition was not entirely to be expected, was C. R. Sumner, Bishop of Winchester. In his 1838 Charge he, more coolly than the others, arraigned the Commissioners and their works. Besides saying everything Phillpotts had said in the parts

[1] *Op. cit.* pp. 20–2.

of his speech already quoted, Sumner pointed out, in strangely modern style, the despotic potentialities of delegated legislation. Such a constitutional arrangement as this, he said, 'facilitates the enforcement of measures vitally affecting particular and general interests, at the fiat of individuals, without opportunity being given for public and popular discussion, and without the concurrence—possibly without the concurrence—of the legally constituted and sworn guardians of the rights and properties with which it is proposed to interfere'. He also disliked it for including no ordained members of the church but bishops.

This last objection was frequently alleged to the composition of the board. Composed as it was of seven laymen and five bishops, the board was naturally likely to exacerbate the natural jealousy of the lower clergy, even had it not put forward proposals that seemed fully to justify some of their suspicions to the hilt. Peel perhaps expected this particular trouble. He wrote to Howley on 22 March 1835, asking whether it might not be a good idea to add to the commission three or four eminent dignitaries.[1] At first Howley agreed. He replied that a few archdeacons would be very useful, and that the reasons for their appointment would be so obvious that no one could possibly be jealous. Two days later he wrote again, to say that he had spoken to Blomfield and Kaye about it, and that they thought there would inevitably be such jealousies that the board would be better without them.[2] His hurried change of mind testifies eloquently to the respect—or fear—in which he held his brother of London, for it is as clear that it was a mistake not to include a few dignitaries, as that Blomfield was primarily responsible for their exclusion. One can hardly believe that the inclusion merely of a few archdeacons of the calibre of Goddard, Lyall and Bayley could have caused difficulties so acute as to outweigh the strength they would have brought to the board. But Blomfield was an autocrat, who, holding the episcopal office in high regard, expected every inferior clergyman to do the same. (This was something that Sydney Smith particularly would *not* do.) In his 1838 Charge, which he used to vindicate the Commissioners and his own part in their work, he went out of his way to justify the exclusion of all clergymen but bishops; but his arguments are not very convincing.[3]

[1] Brit. Mus. Add. MSS 40418, fo. 14.
[2] Letters of 23 and 25 March 1835. *Ibid.* fos. 24 and 83–4.　　　　[3] Pp. 24–5.

When the Commissioners were remodelled in 1840, the whole bench of bishops joined them, besides three deans. This did something to redeem the board with such of the lower clergy as had come to hold it in low esteem. At the same time the offensive second clause of the 1836 Act was repealed, so that the government had not the power (which it was however hardly likely ever to have used) to remove any members of the board at will[1]. As for the other respects in which the Commissioners' first constitution had been found objectionable, they remained unchanged, and did not subsequently give much trouble. The constitution of 1840 itself proved to be in certain new respects objectionable. Moreover, although in the forties the Commissioners were accused of just that tyrannical disregard of the subject's rights which Phillpotts and C. R. Sumner had prophesied, the cause of it was not found so much in the board's character as a semi-independent executive commission, as in its office procedures and the character of its secretary.

The Commissioners' policy with regard to the episcopate turned out to be controversial, more controversial by far than they had expected; yet in fact it was the least controversial branch of church reform. The actual state of the unreformed episcopate was admitted on all sides to be deplorable. Even diehard conservatives were prepared to admit the need for changes in it. The changes they sought were not often the same changes that the church reformers recommended. There was nevertheless something approaching general agreement that the episcopate needed refashioning. The irregularities and contrasts on the diocesan map had to be straightened out, new sees might be created, some bishops had probably too much money, some certainly had too little. The old system of translations to richer from poorer was scarcely defensible. These were reforms on which even prelates as earthbound in their conservatism as Van Mildert and Grey could agree.

The Commissioners' rearrangements of the diocesan map presented little difficulty and were, of all their reforms on this side of the establishment, the least criticised. The two maps facing page 154[2] show what the map was like before they began, and what it was like when, by about

[1] 3 and 4 Vic. c. 113 ss. 78 and 81.
[2] The first is taken from that appended to the first report, where it was accompanied by another map, showing the changes they wished to make.

1850, they had at last overcome, or given in to, their opponents. These territorial changes were the first reforms they agreed on. At their second meeting, the prelates formed themselves into a committee to draw up a plan and persuade the other bishops to agree to it. To speed them, Hobhouse and Jenner joined the committee on 21 February; and their draft report was ready to be laid before the board ten days later. Most of the other bishops fell into line. The minutes show that some of them came along in person between 25 February and 14 March, and that the rest sent letters or messages. Neither Bethell of Bangor nor Carey of St Asaph could see any objection to the union of their sees. The Archbishop of York obviously did not mind losing a good deal of his huge see to the proposed see of Ripon, and J. B. Sumner of Chester, who was to lose territory to both Ripon and Manchester, made only minor criticisms.[1]

The only real difficulties were raised by the bishop of Winchester, and in respect of Bristol. C. R. Sumner objected to losing 18 of his parishes. He remarked in his 1837 Charge that it was the quality of these parishes that bothered him, not their number, for they comprised two-fifths of the population of his diocese, one-tenth of his churches and chapels, and as many as one-seventh of his clergy. What he might well have added, was that it seemed odd that, when the talk was all of reducing overworked bishops' loads, the bishop of London was in one way actually increasing his load by taking in such parts of the dioceses of Winchester, Canterbury and Rochester as fell within the newly-defined metropolitan police district.[2] The Commissioners did not budge from the plan which Blomfield wanted, and Sumner was left to lament this breaking of old ties, of hallowed associations, and so on and so forth. Bristol's problems were less easily to be settled. As will be seen from the map, the diocese of Bristol was very absurd. It consisted of the city of Bristol, the county of Dorset, and a little enclave just over the border in Devon. Another factor, besides its geography, must have influenced the board's thinking. Bristol was one of the poorer sees and needed augmentation. It seemed sensible therefore to unite it with some neighbouring see of similar poverty. There happened, conveniently,

[1] Minutes, 26 February and 7 March 1835.
[2] The population of the diocese of London was to be put up by over half a million. But the number of benefices was to be much reduced. (See the first report, p. 12.)

to be two such, Gloucester and Llandaff. There was the greatest difficulty in coming to a decision. The Dorsetshire part of the diocese was
no problem; that obviously went in with Salisbury. It was the city of
Bristol that made the difficulty. Despite Copleston's clear warning that
he would not much like to take it in with Llandaff,[1] and although, as
the Commissioners pleasantly observed, 'it cannot be denied that the
interposition of the Bristol Channel between the two divisions of the
Diocese will produce some inconvenience',[2] that was the solution they
proposed in their first report. By the time of their second, they had
changed their minds, and had decided instead to incorporate it with
Bath and Wells. This might not have been efficient, but it would at
least have been cheap, for the bishop of Bath and Wells was well endowed and had a very adequate palace at Wells. There would thus be no
need to spend thousands replacing the old one that had been burnt in
the Bristol riots. The virtuous inhabitants of Bristol clamoured against
the indignity of losing their resident bishop, and so in the third report
the board reverted to the idea of a union with Gloucester.

These unions of old sees were proposed principally as means to the
creation of new ones. The only union that the Commissioners regarded
as good in itself was that of Sodor and Man with Carlisle, which they
proposed in their third report. More bishops were wanted in England
and Wales, not less. But it was not easy to see how to get them. The
Tractarians' notion of suffragan bishops was decisively rejected by
Blomfield.[3] To the increase of the number of diocesan bishops, which
the clerical commissioners at any rate seem all to have thought ideally
desirable, the insuperable objection was raised, that it would be quite
impossible to give them seats in the House of Lords. This need not have
been an insuperable obstacle to their creation. Lord Henley had felt
it desirable for bishops to abandon their parliamentary role, and had
positively proposed that any new bishops should be non-parliamentary.[4]
But among the bishops themselves it was still felt at this time that the

[1] Minutes, 3 and 12 March 1835.   [2] First report, p. 3.
[3] See his 1838 *Charge*, p. 27. 'The objections to appointing suffragans are so
obvious, that I need not urge them in detail.'
[4] Both in his *Plan of Church Reform*, and his 1834 *Plan for a New Arrangement and
Increase in Number of the Dioceses*. In the latter he suggested not two but six new sees,
at Ipswich, Bodmin, Huntingdon, Halifax, Lancaster, and Hexham.

dignity of their order and the nature of the establishment alike required their presence in the Lords, and that the introduction of non-parliamentary bishops would create difficulties and embarrassments. Room for new sees could thus be cleared only by unions of old. Ripon was created at once, as soon as the union of Gloucester and Bristol allowed it; Manchester was to wait for the union of Bangor with St Asaph.[1] There is no doubt that they would have proposed other new sees besides these, if only they could have made way for them.

No less important than the creation of new bishoprics and the redistribution of diocesan territories was the reform of episcopal finance. It was clear that the old system of subsidizing the poor bishops by giving them livings, prebends and deaneries elsewhere to hold in plurality had to go. On this, at least, few men of ordinary intelligence disagreed. There was less agreement on the means to be adopted for making up these prospective losses, and less still on the other changes in episcopal finance that might accompany them. It could be maintained, for example, that the incomes of the poorer prelates might be made up to some reasonable level by the annexation of sinecure rectories or supernumerary stalls within the diocese. No one any longer defended sinecure rectories, and there was wide agreement that the cathedrals' and collegiate churches' revenues could be put to improved uses. Why not begin reform in these branches of the church by bringing them to the bishops' aid? These arguments, cogent in themselves, had added attractions for those who were reluctant, for whatever reason, to see the revenues of the richer prelates diminished.

On the other side, there were those who wanted the revenues of the episcopate much reduced. All radicals of course were of this way of thinking. Whigs could easily simulate it, when declaiming against prelatical pride and reading lessons in humility and peacefulness to Blomfield and Phillpotts. Others, of less obvious partisan purpose, were apt to think the same. One was Fowell Buxton, the evangelical anti-slavery leader, who made two strong speeches against the Act of 1836. They were, indeed, the most telling of all that were made in the lower house, because he really cared for the Church of England and obviously had the interests of the parochial clergy sincerely at heart (which could not always be said of the radicals) and because he was not

[1] Which never happened. See below, pp. 436-7.

merely speaking for a particular threatened interest, as was the Durham lobby. The church, he maintained, was trying to be altogether too grand. It was reforming itself, yes, but the minds of its leaders were still too much impressed with considerations of prestige and social status, when they ought rather to be impressed by the quantities of spiritual destitution and clerical poverty that they admitted in their own reports. 'I will not say that the income of £15,000 a year proposed to be assigned to the Archbishop of Canterbury, is too much or too little', he said; 'but I wish the House to take into consideration, at the same time, that there are 300 of the working clergy whose united incomes do not amount to the sum of £15,000 a year . . .'[1] This line of criticism was a perfectly legitimate one for pious churchmen to take up, and men of all church parties, if they had sufficient imagination to conceive of a middle-class episcopate, continued to do so throughout the century.[2]

Between these two extremes, the Commissioners with a good conscience trod a middle path. Following the precedent of innumerable church reform writers over the past half-century, and of Lord Henley in particular, they worked out the total revenues of all the bishops from strictly episcopal sources—divided the total by the number of bishops—and then, by adding on a little extra here, and by taking off a little there, discovered that by means of such a redistribution of revenues within the episcopate, they could give Canterbury £15,000, York and London £10,000 each, and so on down a scale of desert to a minimum of £4000; than which, they thought, no bishop should get less.[3]

From the wealthier sees, therefore, the Commissioners creamed off their surplus revenues. Exactly how much, was left for them to work out. The Act merely empowered them to demand 'such fixed annual Sums . . . as shall, upon due Inquiry and Consideration, be determined on', so as to leave the payers their stipulated sums as an 'annual average

---

[1] 8 July; *Mirror*, 1836, p. 2287. See also his speech on 19 July, *ibid.* p. 2463.

[2] E.g. by Hubert McLaughlin, *A Tract on Church Extension*, 1851: Sidney Godolphin Osborne, in his letter to *The Times*, 3 November 1852: and H. S. Pinder, *A Plea for Country Bishops*, 1860.

[3] Third report, p. 10, and 6 and 7 Will. IV. c. 77, s. 1, just over half way through. Durham was to get £8000, Winchester £7000, Ely £5500, St Asaph and Bangor £5200, Bath and Wells, and Worcester, £5000. Thus those that were plums to start with retained a little of their flavour after the redistribution.

Income'. Variations in the fortunes of these milch-cow sees were prepared for by requiring a septennial review of their revenues, on the basis of which the Commissioners could make adjustments. From the fund thus built up, the Commissioners were to pay the rest of the bishops between £4000 and £5000 each.

Here was the origin of the Episcopal Fund, which became a fruitful source of annoyance and unpleasantness. That the board expected difficulties, was admitted in his 1837 Charge by Bishop Kaye. They had not, he said, been 'insensible to the inconvenience to which the possessors of the richer sees might occasionally be exposed, by having to pay a fixed annuity out of a variable income'; but in the interests of the poorer sees, they felt that a preferable course to requiring the payment of a variable surplus over a fixed basic income. This was reasonable enough, but hardly allowed for how very variable episcopal incomes could be. It mattered little that they came almost entirely from land and were subject to the common ups and downs of the agricultural market. The variations from that cause were not so marked or unpredictable as those involved in the system of church leases, which rewarded the lessor not so much by rent as by the fines taken for renewal; and of these leases, the most vexatious from the Commissioners' and the church's point of view were leases for lives. Leases for terms of years (usually multiples of seven) were after all more predictable and regular, although still undesirable in many respects. Leases for lives were altogether chancy, bringing huge profits to the lessor at irregular and quite unpredictable intervals; they well suited the Sparkes and Tomlines of the church, but their abolition was, as every one recognized, an indispensable preliminary to the rationalisation and improvement of church finance; it was necessary now to budget—dignitaries and rectors who wished to augment poor livings and sustain schools or charities had to budget no less than the Ecclesiastical Commissioners—and leases for lives made for so extremely variable an income that budgeting was quite impossible. Besides, leases for lives hindered the lessor from making the most out of his property. Some bishops and chapters had for a long time back been changing leases for lives into leases for years, but leases for lives still predominated,[1] and they gave the Ecclesiastical

---

[1] In the approximate proportion of 3 to 2: see Mr Finlaison's memorandum, early 1837, in P.Ps. 1837, XLI, 415–6.

Commissioners more trouble, by and large, than any other single aspect of ecclesiastical organization. Their conversion into more economical and profitable forms of lease was the greatest of all the problems the Commissioners had to face in the forties, and was not satisfactorily solved until the early fifties.

The Episcopal Fund, as it became known, fell for many years below its expected level. Such were the complexities of finance in many sees, that the estimates of their values, on which the Commissioners' calculations were based when they made their first assessments in 1836-7, proved later to have been erroneous. On balance, they seem to have been too optimistic, and furthermore the revenues at the bishops', and thus ultimately at the Commissioners', disposal were not enlarged by the more co-operative bishops' refusals to renew leases on the old terms. This had to be gone through as a first step towards the improvement of their property, but it brought a temporary shrinkage of income. Thus in the early years of the Episcopal Fund, some of the poorer sees needed to be subsidized more heavily than had been expected, while the holders of various of the richer sees at various times alleged difficulty in paying the fixed annual sums required of them .

Notable among these was Bishop Allen, who moved to Ely from Bristol late in 1836. He had not been very co-operative over the problem of Bristol,[1] and his translation had been a necessary preliminary to its solution. At Ely, he found considerable confusion and uncertainty, in which only one fact was clear, namely, that the leases from which the see drew five-sevenths of its ample revenues had been given on beneficial terms by the late bishop very largely to his relations and henchmen.[2] The board therefore in their dealings with Allen did not start off on the best of terms and since the Ely properties were clearly capable of much improvement, they may well have inclined not to take his protests too seriously. Yet, with the evil memory of Sparke fresh in mind, they were apparently too severe in exacting from his successor the penalty that the episcopate, sooner or later, had to pay for Sparke's misdeeds. Their first assessment of the value of the see was certainly too high. They began by requiring £4000 a year. Allen replied that this would ruin him, and said that if they stuck to this assessment, he would

[1] Minutes, 3 March 1835.
[2] This account is drawn from P.Ps. 1851, XLII, 176–219, 382–91.

have no choice but ask them to assume the management of the whole of his estates, and to reduce him to a stipendiary at his guaranteed £5500. The Commissioners, thus faced with responsibilities from which as yet they shrunk, thought again, and proposed a new plan. They would relieve the bishop of the estates the affairs of which were in the greatest confusion, and reduce their demand to £2500. By this time the unfortunate Allen was involved in litigation with his predecessor's receiver-general, who told the board that Allen had illegally sacked him, and forbidden his tenants to pay him their rents in the old way. It also appeared about this time that Allen was not paying Mr Serjeant Storks, the chief justice of Ely, his rightful salary. The board, thus given reason to believe that part at least of Allen's alleged difficulties were of his own making, stuck to their guns, and pointed out in answer to Allen's next agonized suggestion, that their founding statute gave them no power to let him keep a fixed annual sum instead of paying one. This was in April, 1837. Allen was now in real trouble, and his letters became almost distraught. During his first year at Ely, he told them, he had actually received less than they were asking him to hand over. But their hearts were hardened against him. By May 1838 they had put the case before the Crown lawyers, and were threatening him with a *mandamus*. This worked. Somehow or other he found the money and by the summer of 1840 he had put things straight. But Ely continued to give trouble, and by 1850 Allen's successor Turton was in even deeper difficulties.[1]

The merits of this case—the most extreme that the Commissioners had so far met with—are impossible to assess. It is improbable that Joseph Allen was dishonest, and fifty years of Yorke and Sparke had put Ely's affairs into a dreadful state; but he certainly seems to have made unnecessary difficulties, and to have managed his affairs injudiciously. After all, the money was in the end found, and the Commissioners had no choice but insist upon getting it, for, as they always pointed out to prelates who grumbled, upon their receipts depended the slenderer incomes of the sees on the other side of the Fund. Incidents like these helped to build up the impression, quite widely held during the forties, that the Ecclesiastical Commissioners were a group of ignorant, hard-hearted centralizing bureaucrats, comparable only with the 'three bashaws of Somerset House'. Needless to say, such incidents made bad

[1] *Ibid.* pp. 86–7.

blood between the bishops on the Commission and those off it. Allen cannot have found much to say to Blomfield or Howley, when he met them at the Bounty Board. Bishops Grey and Phillpotts had attacked them openly in the Lords. Bagot of Oxford viewed them suspiciously from the first, and after reluctantly agreeing to relieve the bishop of Salisbury of the care of Berkshire (which had to be done before the union of Gloucester and Bristol was achieved, so as to enable Sarum to take on Dorsetshire), tried to screw a new palace out of them and to get Cuddesdon severed from the see in return for taking on Buckinghamshire as well. When they replied that they had no powers to do anything of this kind, he closed the correspondence, and Buckinghamshire stayed with the bishop of Lincoln until Wilberforce succeeded Bagot in 1845.[1]

The Ecclesiastical Commissioners undertook to improve the condition of the episcopate in two other respects. The less important of them made a great deal of noise. The Act gave them power to find 'fit residences' for the bishops of Lincoln, Llandaff, Rochester, Manchester and Ripon, besides assisting the other bishops to 'more suitable and convenient' residences by purchase or exchange. Still larger use might have been made of these powers, had not the provision of palaces for the named bishops attracted so much uncomplimentary comment. Palaces they certainly turned out to be, costing between ten and fifteen thousand pounds each; and everyone who had any reason for disliking the Commissioners, and particularly everyone, lay or clerical, who thought that the bishops were making too good a thing out of it, found in these palaces a very convenient stick with which to beat the Commissioners. By the early forties it was as much an article of belief with the antiprelatical party that the bishops were making presents of palaces to one another, as it had been before 1835 that their wealth ranked them with the richest in the land. There was some justice in these allegations. The bishops Commissioners did believe that a bishop should live in state, and they allowed for incomes and residences accordingly. Those who felt with Buxton that the Commissioners aimed too high, had a legitimate and arguable case against them. Apart from this, the question attracted more attention than it merited. The wildest rumours circulated, and the Commissioners were alleged to have erred not

[1] See the correspondence printed in *ibid.* pp. 266–75.

merely by their pride and luxuriousness but also by unbusinesslike and wasteful management of the sales and contracts. The Commons' committee that investigated the doings of the Commissioners in 1847-8 went into all this with great diligence and no good will, but found little to the Commissioners' serious discredit.[1]

The other respect in which the Ecclesiastical Commissioners set out to reform the condition of the episcopate was in respect of its patronage. Some bishops had much patronage, others very little.[2] The effect of their Deans and Chapters Act whenever it should become law, would be to take away from some of them some of the most valuable patronage they had. The new sees of Ripon and Manchester would start off with none at all. It was undeniably awkward that some bishops' patronage lay in territories not their own. The Commissioners felt all this to need substantial modification. The principle which guided them was that a bishop needed to have patronage at his disposal if he was to function properly. The more he had, the better indeed could he do it; he would have the means to reward the deserving, to relieve the aged and ailing; and it would give him added consequence. They intended therefore so to shuffle the available patronage about that the more important sees should have appropriate portions of it—that Ripon and Manchester should have their fair share—and that the anomaly, as they viewed it, of bishops appointing to livings in other dioceses should be liquidated by exchanges or transfers.

These were reasonable propositions. It was not of course to be expected that they would meet with the unqualified approval either of the bishops due to resign part of their patronage to others, or of the clergy who saw their chances of advancement thus diminished. C. R. Sumner, who as dating from before the Act had a protected vested interest, withheld his consent to the last,[3] and the Durham lobby was to show itself particularly resourceful and energetic in opposition.[4] But these troubles

---

[1] Report, 1848, pp. v–vii. The only purchase which might, they thought, have been made on more advantageous terms, was that of the Riseholme estate for the bishop of Lincoln. The story of the estate they purchased for the Bishop of Gloucester and Bristol was, however, more discreditable. It had not reached its dismal conclusion by the time this Committee was sitting. See below, pp. 368-9.

[2] See Appendix 6.   [3] 1856 Committee, Qs. 646–51.

[4] See especially the correspondence printed in the Appendix to the 1856

were all to come later. No legislation was proposed for the redistribution of episcopal patronage until the fifties.

In some ways the Commissioners' handling of the patronage question was remarkably revealing of their state of mind. They proposed not merely to consolidate their own patronage but also to annex part of the deans' and chapters' patronage.[1] The deans and chapters naturally kicked against this, as they kicked against all the Commissioners proposals to benefit the church at their expense. The Commissioners drew back a little. By the time the Deans and Chapters Act at last got through, in 1840, they had withdrawn further still.[2] But to their main contention they adhered. The bishops, they said, needed every opportunity they could get of 'placing laborious and deserving Clergymen in Situations of Usefulness and Independence. It is to the Bishop that the Clergy of his Diocese naturally look, for Encouragement and Reward; and it is on every Account desirable, that the Connexion between them should be strengthened by all possible Means.'[3] Bishop Monk made a spirited defence of their policy in his 1838 Charge. 'A measure of church reform', he said, 'would have been incomplete, without some attempt to remove a defect in our system, which has always given pain and regret to the lovers of the Establishment. It frequently happens that unfriended and unconnected clergymen, however useful their ministry and however exemplary their character, pass the whole of their valuable lives without obtaining even the smallest benefice; particularly in those dioceses where the bishop has little preferment to bestow.' He explained to the chapters that their own usual means for the exercise of their patronage were unsuited to achieve the great end the Commissioners had in view, and added that the lay members of the board—'who in such a matter must be admitted to have been impartial judges'—were behind the bishops to a man.[4]

A bishop was at any rate likelier than a lay patron to bestow his patronage judiciously. He alone was in a position to know, as neither lay patron nor chapter could possibly know, the state of the diocese as a whole and the merits of its humbler clergy. But behind Monk's

Committee's first report, pp. 260–6 and 347–9, and their members' grilling of the board's witnesses before the 1856 Committee.   [1] Second report, p. 14.

[2] See its clauses 41 and 44, which marked the conclusion of the matter.

[3] Fourth report, p. 6.   [4] *Op. cit.* pp. 24–7.

words one sees a still deeper, and no doubt a less conscious, cause for his adherence to this policy of episcopal expansion. The bishops Commissioners had a good conceit of themselves. This showed itself in their every recommendation, whether for the scale of their salaries, the quality of their residences, the increase of their disciplinary and administrative powers, the magnification of their patronage, or whatever. Powers and salaries which they hesitated to allow to any other body, they thought both proper and safe in the hands of a bishop. And the lay Commissioners must have felt this too. Gentlemen all, and men of property, they believed in the propriety of equipping the heads of their church establishment to live on reasonably equal terms with the gentry. A seat in the Lords moreover meant a town house and perhaps a five months' sojourn in it; this alone added a thousand or so to a bishop's expenses. Bishops had to keep their residences in good shape, to subscribe to every diocesan charity, to hold hospitality at the episcopal table, to travel around their dioceses, besides educating their sons, portioning their daughters, and insuring their lives. There was every reason, in fact, to suppose a minimum of £4000 a year scarcely adequate for all that a bishop of the newly reformed Church of England had to do, let alone for what he ought to do. That minimum was all that the Commissioners proposed to give the bishop of Chichester, whose see was certainly not to be considered in the same class with Chester, Ripon, or Llandaff; but Bishop Otter, getting wind of this, called on the Commissioners and told them how difficult he would find it to manage with no more than four thousand. There were the three or four 'public dinners given to the noblemen, gentlemen and clergymen of the country in the autumn, which cannot without injury to the establishment be given up'. He had to come forward with a subscription for every new church, chapel, district or school; his house was old and the roof had just been blown off by a hurricane; the cost of living was higher south than north; immemorial custom compelled him to pay a £50 allowance annually to certain of the city's widows; and Maltby, who had just left Chichester for Durham, had told him 'that he could not have come to town at all, without the aid of the preachership at Lincoln's Inn'.[1] Otter was not avaricious, he was simply stating the facts of the case. A bishop *à la mode* could hardly make do on £4000

[1] Minutes, 12 June 1837: cited in P.Ps. 1851, XLII, 168–9.

a year. Most bishops, no doubt, married money or had money of their own.[1] A bishop of the reformed era, if he lacked private means, was bound to be a needy man.

It may therefore be argued that, far from the bishops doing themselves too well when their representatives on the board drew up their scale of remuneration, they were hardly doing themselves well enough. Of course they could not easily have gone further than they did. There would have been an outcry if they had brought money into the Episcopal Fund from any non-episcopal source. At least one of them showed a disposition to do so. Monk suggested that the new palaces might be paid for by the sale of the houses belonging to the prebends that they were going to suppress.[2] Nothing came of this. Their inclinations indeed ran in the other direction. Anxious for the creation of as many new sees as they could get, they were prepared to endow them out of their own fund. Had four or six been created, each member of the bench would have been proportionately the poorer.[3]

The lay Commissioners must have respected their clerical colleagues in this self-sacrificial mood, and for other reasons as well. A zealous, generous bishop, willing to take pains, risk opprobrium, and spend money, could do a lot in the way of reform before the eighteen-thirties. During and after them he was enabled to do even more; and if Howley, Blomfield, Kaye and Monk had some sense of conscious rectitude to encourage them in planning to increase their powers, they had it reasonably enough. They were not the only prelates who had distinguished themselves by good works, but none had distinguished themselves more. All were quick to make use of Howley's Augmentations Act.[4] Howley and Blomfield led the way in suspending the exercise of their cathedral patronage (which was worth a great deal to them) pending the settlement of the cathedrals question; each of the

[1] This assertion, which is *prima facie* safe enough, is substantiated by Bishop Short's public letter to the Marquis of Westminster cited at the head of *How to make Better Provisions for the Cure of Souls . . .* by 'Pauper Clergyman' (1857).

[2] Minutes, 22 January 1836.

[3] See Kaye's 1837 Charge and his *Letter to the Archbishop*, 1838; also Blomfield in *Hansard*, 3/cviii, 1326–7, 25 February 1850, and in his evidence to the 1847–8 Committee, 1847 Qs. 984, 1185, 1187.

[4] See Kaye's 1834 Charge in *Nine Charges, etc.*, pp. 111–12; Pusey's *Remarks* p. 120 n.; and Blomfield's evidence to the 1847–8 Committee, 1847 Qs. 993 ff.

Commission's reports recorded in its last paragraphs the preferments which had been left vacant by the Crown or one or other of the bishops; and their good example was followed by some—but not by all—of their brethren. It was necessary for the accomplishment of their financial reforms that bishops should not renew leases on their lands but let them run out, or renew them for only a very short period. Sometimes this involved large losses to them indeed, but they usually did it; Blomfield, for example, lost between six and seven thousand pounds by not renewing in the old way a lease on his large Rickmansworth property.[1] Voluntarily, these bishops on the Commission, and the better of their brethren outside it, gave up a great deal to get the reforms going. They knew what they were losing, and if they were seeking to enlarge their patronage, they set themselves high standards for its exercise.

Blomfield was exemplary in this respect. It was about the only aspect of his episcopate and character that Sydney Smith did not attack in his *Three Letters to Archdeacon Singleton*. Even his most fervent admirers must admit that Blomfield laid himself open to criticism. If these bishops were conscious of their rectitude and sure of themselves, Blomfield was the most conscious and sure. His character was large, strong, and confident. His diocese, already huge, was becoming huger; but he could manage it. His patronage was growing; but he would administer it fairly. His emoluments were princely; but they would be well used. Blomfield was not the man to doubt in these matters; and, of course, he was right. The Church in its despair, just waking up to the challenge of the new social order, cried out for leadership and direction. Its organization was still hopeless, full of gaps and hollows. Blomfield was so great a man as to be able to fill them and to bring his diocese under control. It was his nature to do this. Evidently such a man, at such a time, and in such a situation, laid himself open to the misrepresentations and misunderstandings of those who were out of sympathy with him. His colleagues got off much more lightly. Kaye withdrew in his old age to Riseholme, Monk became a recluse in the west-country. Howley faded away. But Blomfield stuck it out in London, and when at last he went, accepted a pension that invited yet more misrepresentations and insults. From no one had he to put up with so much as from Sydney Smith, the joker who failed to comprehend in the slightest

[1] 1847–8 Committee, 1848 Q. 2312.

330

degree the problems of the age he lived in, or what the Ecclesiastical Commissioners were trying to do about them. Having before him a target tailor-made for his darts, Smith did not miss his opportunity. But the joke misfired. As Blomfield himself remarked, Smith was not so amusing as might have been expected. The historian of the Ecclesiastical Commissioners may be pardoned if he adds, that Smith was not so charitable as might have been hoped. His attack was not indeed wholly unjust; but it cannot be cleared of the charge that it was, under the circumstances, somewhat indecent.

What brought Smith forward in opposition to Blomfield and the Ecclesiastical Commissioners was their proposals to reduce the establishments of the Cathedral and Collegiate churches and thus provide a fund for the relief of what became familiarly referred to as 'spiritual destitution'. Their second report had only approached the subject of the deans and chapters by way of some paragraphs describing the poverty of benefices (there were still, they found, 3528 under £150 a year) and the shortage of church room in populous parishes. They then reviewed the various agencies working to save the situation—Queen Anne's Bounty, the parliamentary grants, the Church Building Commissioners, and the many forms of private liberality—and concluded that even all this was not nearly enough. They proceeded to admit that they had entered upon their inquiry into the state of the cathedral and collegiate churches 'under a strong Impression, that if the Endowments of those Bodies should appear to be larger than is Requisite for the Purposes of their Institution, and for maintaining them in such a State of Efficiency and Respectability as may enable them fully to carry those Purposes into effect, the Surplus of those Endowments, whatever it may be, ought to be made available for the Augmentation of poor Benefices containing a large Population, and to the great Object of adding to the number of the Parochial Clergy.' Even so the church would still not have enough to do all that was needed, and the Commissioners hoped that the sacrifices required of the deans and chapters would stimulate the benevolence of other bodies and individuals.[1]

Here was a batch of assumptions made excusable only by the Commissioners' frank admission that they entered upon their inquiry with

[1] Second report, pp. 5–8.

their minds to some extent made up. Between 1836 and 1840 the noise of battle rolled continuously around the questions that the Commissioners begged in the report. What constituted 'efficiency' and 'respectability'? What *were* the purposes for which the cathedrals and colleges were instituted, and to what purposes might they not now be put? Was the parochial ministry so overwhelmingly important, after all? Many different answers were given. Even those who tried earnestly to be historical could not agree as to the original functions of cathedrals, and everyone had a different answer to the question, what was to be done with them now. On this question the Commissioners' position, while strong, was not so strong as to be perfectly unassailable, for some plans were put forward in opposition to their own which would have changed the character of the cathedrals perhaps as much. On most other points of church reform, the Commissioners could fairly argue that great changes were needed, and that no other body would or could go far enough. But in respect of the cathedrals, their superiority as reformers was not so self-evident. Pusey's notion of turning the cathedrals into centres of theological education found many followers. His respect for traditional ties and the principle of locality was widely shared. The dislike entertained by many churchmen for the Commissioners' drastic utilitarian proposals to introduce uniformity and efficiency into the cathedrals was exactly comparable to the country gentry's distaste for the radicals' vision of a uniform franchise and equal electoral districts; it did dishonour to feelings which they held in sacred regard. One can doubt neither that the Ecclesiastical Commissioners appeared at their most radical in this connexion, nor that the changes they enforced were of a truly radical kind.

It is worth ascertaining, therefore, how the Commissioners came to propose this particular plan, and why they stuck to it so gamely. So deeply were they convinced of its propriety that they showed some surprise and grief at the hostility they encountered. Not that they had been foolish enough to suppose that their reforms would make them universally popular. 'We knew from the first', said Blomfield, 'that we were undertaking an invidious and unpopular task.'[1] Made of stern stuff, he was not likely to shrink from unpopularity. It looks, indeed, as if he was one of those men who doubt whether they are doing their

[1] 30 July 1840, *Hansard*, 3/LV, 1154.

duty unless they make themselves unpopular with someone or other. Peel and Goulburn knew that Blomfield's participation was as likely to arouse suspicion of their Commission as was Howley's to allay it. Bishop Lloyd had warned Peel about Blomfield long ago.[1] More recently Goulburn had reported from Cambridge 'great jealousy lest the Bishop of London should lead the Government'.[2] But Peel was no more likely than Blomfield to be deterred from doing what was right by the fear of unpopularity, and, confident of Blomfield's judgment and ability, brought him into their counsels all the same. The other prelates, less daring pilots in extremity, were not so accustomed to meeting and returning blows. But they also anticipated opposition. Bishop Kaye, for example, in his 1838 *Letter to the Archbishop* remarked that 'The event has fully realized my expectations; the attacks upon us have not been confined to our measures; they have extended to our motives and intentions, and in some cases have even assumed a personal character.'[3] Monk, who made his defence in his 1838 Charge, referred with contempt to 'those who condemn indiscriminately everything proceeding from the Commission', and with pained indignation to the imputations levelled against him and his clerical colleagues of 'sordid and unworthy motives ... such as are inconsistent with the whole tenor of their lives. .... What may have been our adversaries' own motives, I presume not to judge. Some of them have thought it not unbecoming their station as Dignitaries, and their character as Christian Divines, to assail the heads of their Church with all the licence of personal invective and unbridled scurrility. .... Meanwhile, a sense of shame and humiliation affects every serious churchman, at beholding places which ought to be the seats of piety, learning, and dignity, occupied by the scoffer and the jester.'[4] Some of this obviously surprised him. Peel's letters do not show whether he was taken unawares by the elements of violence and malignity in the opposition; but his friend Goulburn was. 'I was quite surprised', he wrote

[1] Letters of 26 February and 19 November 1828. Brit. Mus. Add. MSS 40343, fos. 178–9 and 319–20.

[2] Letter of 2 January 1835. *Ibid.* 40333, fo. 212.

[3] *Nine Charges, etc.*, pp. 152–3.

[4] *Op. cit.* pp. 15, 23–4. No wonder, after this, that Smith turned on Monk towards the end of his *Third Letter to Archdeacon Singleton*.

to Peel in the early autumn of 1836, 'to find the strong feeling against it [the Deans and Chapters Act] among many reasonable men whom I had conceived the most ready to make provision for pastoral care by some sacrifices of less important ecclesiastical duties.'[1] The Commissioners' firm refusal to depart, in the face of all this, from the principle of their first plan (a refusal which Peel and Goulburn, after they had left the board, commended)[2] is striking evidence of the seriousness with which they took themselves and of their confidence in their convictions.

They came to these convictions between February 1835 and March 1836. Not all the Commissioners had gone into the business with their minds made up. They all, indeed, knew that something big would have to be done to the cathedrals and collegiate churches. Peel's mind was clear about this. He had little sympathy with them, and thought they were just nests of sinecures.[3] The wording of the Commission was such as to suggest the same.[4] Blomfield's episcopal colleagues must have known all this as clearly as Peel's political colleagues. None of the Commissioners can have set off without a pretty good idea of their destination. They were on the Commission to take revenues from the deans and chapters and redistribute them among the parochial clergy.

On the *mode* of redistribution, however, they were not at first decided; and it was in coming to a decision on this point that they took the course that made them particularly unpopular with the high church and the capitular conservatives. For some of the latter, in making their case against the Commissioners, claimed to be as ready as the Commissioners themselves for large modifications of the cathedral system. What they objected to above all was the Commissioners' almost total disregard of the principle of locality. The Commissioners' plan was for all the 'surplus revenues' of the cathedrals and collegiate churches to be pooled in a single central fund and redistributed by them according to need. This was, undeniably, a kind of centralization. It is possible

---

[1] Letter of 2 September 1836. Brit. Mus. Add. MSS 40333, fos. 361–2.

[2] See their speeches on the second reading of the bill, 6 April 1840. *Hansard*, 3/LIII, 602, 610.

[3] There is some evidence of what might otherwise have been well expected, that Blomfield thus early held similar views about chapters. See Phillpotts's report on his attitude in December 1832, cited by Mathieson, p. 171.   [4] See above, p. 303.

that, had the Commissioners not early concluded in favour of such a measure of centralization, they might have recommended some system of diocesan or regional synods or boards, for which there had recently been a good deal of support. It is certain that their pursuit of centralization damaged their reputation with two important bodies of public opinion—the capitular and collegiate clergy, who (if they were reconciled to changes at all) maintained that the redistribution of their revenues could be so contrived as to keep their establishments at their present level, and to bring the benefited benefices into connexion with themselves—and the strong sentiments aroused by the principle of locality, which were offended by the idea of giving Durham cash to Deptford curates.

Some of the accusations that issued against the Commissioners from these quarters strongly suggested that the Commissioners had plotted to do these wicked things all along. This was completely untrue. Several of Peel's letters during the weeks before the Commission first met show both that he was still uncertain what exactly to do, and that he had several ideas in mind which were subsequently abandoned.[1] Bishop Kaye admitted later that when he joined the Commission he had disliked the very idea he was driven, in the course of its meetings, to adopt.[2] Lord Harrowby held firm views as to what might or might not be done in many branches of church reform, but on this he confessed to Blomfield, sometime earlier that winter, that he was ignorant and undecided. 'When so many successive governments and parliaments have, right or wrong, carried into practice in every branch of the public service the principle of the abolition of *all* sinecures—it is impossible that the Church should be allowed to retain her present share of what will be called so, in spite of all the efforts of ingenious and, on many of the points, sound reasoners to prove, either that they are not so, or that they need not continue to be so. As to the best and safest mode of drawing upon this source, I feel even less competent to suggest anything than upon other parts of this subject. I hope that those

---

[1] See especially the letter in which he invited Harrowby to join the Commission, 12 January 1835, Brit. Mus. Add. MSS 40410, fos. 58–62 and Peel's *Memoirs*, II, 72–5, and his magnificent letter to Croker, 2 February 1835, in *Croker's Correspondence and Diaries*, II, 264–6 (of which a mutilated version appears in Parker's *Peel*, II, 284–5).

[2] See below, p. 339.

who are so [*sic*] will look to it seriously, and not flatter themselves that
it is possible to be avoided.'[1] A few days later, having received and
acquiesced in Peel's request that he should join the Commission, he
made himself one of those who had to 'look to it seriously'. Obviously
he had no idea what he would find when he looked.

The Commission's minutes tell the same tale. They are not very
revealing; but, so far as they go, they prove that the Commissioners
were not lying when, in self-defence, they later said that they had begun
by considering every possibility. At the end of March 1835, for example,
Murray was instructed to draw up statistics on which they might base
a decision whether each see could provide for its own poor vicarages;[2]
on 18 November, having moved on to the subjects of the second and
third reports, and with their minds still open, they were asking all the
bishops confidentially how best to apply sinecure prebends 'to the
objects of parochial instruction'. They did not draw only upon their
mitred brethren for ideas. Mr Finlaison the 'Government calculator'
and his son were requisitioned to work out the prospective values of
capitular estates, and Murray was kept busy abstracting facts and figures
from the Ecclesiastical Revenues Commissioners' Report to enable the
board to test provisional plans.[3] Only by the latter days of January 1836,
were they at last enabled to come to a decision, with Monk's draft for
the 'deans and chapters' section of the second report before them.[4]

Monk explained in his 1838 Charge that, although the Commissioners
had felt 'little difficulty' in deciding to appropriate the revenues of
'independent and non-residentiary' stalls, they had not lightly concluded that, in order to free further revenues, the larger residentiary
establishments should be reduced to four. He acknowledged the strength
of the many arguments advanced on their behalf—they were well suited
to support theologians, reward merit, attract gentlemen into the church,
and so on; would that they could be increased! 'But', he went on, 'when
I regarded the frightful deficiency of spiritual instruction under which
such numbers of my countrymen were suffering, when it was clear that
no earthly resource was available except what might be spared from

---

[1] Enclosed in a letter to Peel, 20 January, Brit. Mus. Add. MSS 40410, fos. 289–300.
[2] Minutes 31 March 1835.
[3] E.g. Minutes 18, 20, 23 November 1835, 20 January 1836.
[4] 20 January 1836.

cathedral appointments, it became a question, not of predilection or of taste, but of duty to the sacred cause of Christ's church. . . . The ornamental parts of our system, however beautiful they may be, and however comparable to the Courts of God's house, which our Lord himself delighted to frequent, are yet not to be put in competition with the souls of multitudes now abandoned to error, to ignorance, and to heathenism.'[1]

There were the reasons for the Commissioners' decision in a nutshell. They fell into three distinct parts. It was regarded as a matter of life or death that money should be found for the relief of spiritual destitution; it could be made available from no other source; and it seemed necessary to manage its redistribution from the centre, out of a common, central fund. These three elements in their decision are worth each a little comment.

Kaye spoke in terms even stronger than Monk's of the extent of the need the Commissioners discovered. 'It was in prosecution of our inquiries . . . that I became for the first time fully aware of the magnitude of the wants of the Established Church'. He had known the nature and needs of his own diocese, 'but I had formed no adequate conception of the destitution of the manufacturing districts and of the large towns until the Facts, detailed in our Second Report, were brought under my notice'.[2] They shocked and frightened him. Blomfield and Harrowby can have needed no such awakening, but if any of the other Commissioners had like Kaye not fully realized how perilous the church's position was in the populous districts, it may be presumed that Murray's abstracts from the Ecclesiastical Revenues Report, from the non-residence returns, the census and so on, converted them. We may think this right and proper, and marvel that any churchmen should not have been similarly impressed. But it is important to realize that the case made out for the cathedrals against the Commissioners rested partly on a denial of this, their major premiss; and that some clergy believed, or affected to believe, that the church did not need an extension of its

---

[1] Pp. 17–18. He added, 'It was indeed an obvious and easy road to popularity to have refused my concurrence with such recommendations, to have retired from the Commission, and declined all share in the obloquy consequent on such measures.' But conscience kept him on.

[2] 'Letter to the Archbishop', in his *Nine Charges etc.*, pp. 170–1.

parochial ministry to the degree the Commissioners alleged. J. W. Blakesley, for example, a Cambridge don, published in 1837 some *Thoughts on the Recommendations of the Ecclesiastical Commission . . .* in *a Letter to W. E. Gladstone* in which he roundly asserted, 'If there were no other order in the Church than parochial Clergy and Bishops, and we could give the former of these £150 a year each, and put one in every square mile of the country, I have no hesitation in saying that I believe the influence of the Church would be far less valuable than it was in the worst of times under the old constitution. Under that there have always existed channels, although at times perhaps partially choked up, by which every valuable talent has flowed into the Church, every rank of society been enabled to place its representatives in the ministry. We can as little dispense with the scholar, the metaphysician, and the antiquary, as with the preacher.'[1] However violently or persuasively this was argued, the Commissioners stayed staunch by their view of the case. Powerful though the inducements became to rat on the Commission, none of the Commissioners ever did so.

Whence might money have come to answer these necessities? Many of the Commissioners' enemies said it ought to have come from public funds. Perhaps it ought. Most of the Commissioners, probably indeed all of them to begin with, would have agreed. But it was politically quite impracticable. Sir Robert Inglis pressed this suggestion when the Established Church Bill was before Parliament, and it was Peel who gave him the straightest answer; 'If he or any one else', said Peel, 'believes that whilst Bishops have very large incomes, with livings *in commendam* at a distance, a Government can overlook that state of things, and imagine that it has nothing to do in order to silence the complaints of the public, that the working clergy with small livings are inadequately remunerated for their service, than to come and ask the House to vote large sums of money to make up the deficiency of their income, he will find himself grossly deceived.'[2] The wrath of the dissenters would have been terrific; the tithes question, just settling down, would have been stirred up again and the church rates question blown up to gigantic proportions; a government so high-principled or foolhardy as to propose it would have got into dreadful difficulties between the Irish papists on the one hand—who might reasonably

[1] *Op. cit.* pp. 35–6.   [2] 19 July. *Mirror*, 1836, p. 2465b.

have looked for a similar grant to themselves—and the British protestants on the other, who would by no means have tolerated such a
following of the precedent. The idea was one that retained its appeal
with certain high churchmen and devotees of the establishment for
years to come, and it was not indeed politically quite impossible;
but to have put it into effect would have meant some kind of a revolution.

Another possibility was the even more widely canvassed scheme of a
graduated tax on benefices above three or five hundred a year—the
scheme proposed by Burton, Miller, Girdlestone, and so many others.
The influential vicar of Halifax, Charles Musgrave, commended it to
Peel, just before the Commission first met, as a complement to the
tapping of cathedral wealth.[1] At least one of the Commissioners, Kaye,
embarked on his work with a strong predilection in its favour.[2] But
another of the Commissioners, Harrowby, had strong feelings against
it.[3] Peel was, one may guess, against it too. It was advocated by neither
Berens nor Henley, the two he seems to have respected above all other
writers on church reform,[4] and he would no doubt have agreed with
Blomfield, who said in his 1838 Charge that, although he had never
been strongly opposed to it and indeed thought it in some ways
advantageous, it was 'objectionable in this respect, that it goes to diminish the incomes of the parochial clergy and the values of livings in
private patronage'.[5] As powerful a party leader as Peel would not have
flinched from a row with the patron interest if it were unavoidable. But
in 1835–6 it was easily avoidable, by taking instead the money of the
chapters. The determining factor in Peel's and, more important, Blomfield's minds was probably not so much the respect in which they held
the rights of patrons, as the disrespect they shared for the deans and
chapters. Blomfield's great speech in defence of the Commissioners' bill

[1] Letter of 30 January 1835. Brit. Mus. Add. MSS 40412, fos. 235–8.

[2] *Nine Charges* etc., pp. 174–5.

[3] He had first declared his dislike of it in his 1810 *Letter to Spenser Perceval* and he told
Blomfield that he was still of the same opinion in the letter cited above, pp. 335–6.

[4] Mrs Brose errs on her p. 104 in linking Henley's name with Burton's as an
advocate of the graduated tax. It is true that in the Appendix to the eighth edition of
his *Plan*, wherein he attempted a union of his own proposals with Burton's, he
confessed himself 'in some measure reconciled ... to a taxation of livings'; but he
did not conceal his distaste for it.

[5] Pp. 42–3.

in 1840 made it clear that he had no patience with these bodies. Peel's letters of December 1834 and early 1835 show that he held them in contempt. Pluralities he would allow or ban on their merits, but sinecures he could no longer stomach. In 1836, in his place in the Commons, he used the phrase 'the working clergy'. When a churchman did that, in the eighteen-thirties, it meant that he had made up his mind to sink the cathedrals if necessary.

One other possible source of money there was: the revenues of the bishops. They were taken into consideration.[1] But the Commissioners' desire to increase the size of the episcopate, in the future if not at once, sufficed to ensure that no money was found available from this source.

Having decided to soak the deans and chapters, the Commissioners then faced the problem of redistributing their revenues. Could this be done without doing violence to the principle of locality? With all the available evidence on England's spiritual destitution before them, they concluded it could not. Their revenues from the cathedrals and collegiate churches must be brought into a common fund and then redistributed as need required. This proposition was violently attacked but it was not seriously open to criticism except on sentimental grounds— grounds which, however, were frankly raised by many conservatives to the level of principle. The cathedrals that had the most to give were not necessarily situated within the dioceses where help was most needed. Lancashire, Yorkshire, Staffordshire and South Wales would have come off very badly if the rule had been adopted that redistribution was to be intra-diocesan. Durham was one of the few cathedrals in respect of which this principle would have worked; significantly, it was from Durham that much of the hottest opposition came, both in the later thirties and subsequently. As for the proposal that some of the cathedrals' publicists were driven to put forward, that the redistribution should connect the cathedral clergy with laborious and important parishes in other dioceses where the home diocese had no need of their help—that entailed the extension of pluralism (no bad thing, of course, to minds like Pusey's and Inglis's) and administrative disorder. The cathedrals' advocates were ingenious to a degree, but never very convincing.

[1] See the Minute of 31 March, cited above, p. 336, and Kaye in *Nine Charges etc.*, p. 175.

The cathedrals did not, in truth, have much of a case.[1] Three took no part in the dispute (Gloucester, Chichester, and another) and of the rest, Winchester's arguments were several times complimented by the Commissioners, as sane and sensible. (Why three remained silent, and why the others ran the gamut from courtesy to calumny, would doubtless repay investigation.) For all the sound and fury of their opposition, it carried little weight. Parliament had tired of it, and the Ecclesiastical Duties and Revenues Bill, much changed in detail from what it had been four years ago but in principle and effect the same, ran easily through thin houses at the end of the session of 1840.[2] Excepting always dons, deans, canons and those elements in public opinion most responsive to the arguments of high churchmen and Tractarians, the public at large must have found it acceptable.

The character of the opposition was, after all, not at all free from the imputation of interested motives. The Duke of Wellington, never a bad index to what the plain man was thinking in the upper reaches of society, was full of contempt for it. He went so far as to dissociate himself with characteristic bluntness from an Oxford petition against the bill which, as Chancellor of the University, he presented to the House of Lords; he said the petition 'astonished' him, and that the Ecclesiastical Commissioners had only 'done their duty in recommending this bill'. When the duke so pointedly said that someone was 'doing his duty', he meant to imply that someone else was definitely not.[3] In a letter to Peel he had recently said:

I conclude that the object is to get a revenue for general church purposes out of the revenues of the deans and chapters, after the cessation of the interests of existing holders of dignities. But this will not be permitted. The subject will not be discussed on the ground of the necessity of providing from the funds in possession of the church more amply for that branch of the divine service in which we are most deficient, the cure of souls. We have archbishops, bishops, deans and canons, rectors, vicars, curates and others with benefices having cure of souls. But there is behind these another body

---

[1] He who wishes to understand the many-sided case they put forward may consult their exponents' original works, perhaps looking first at P. J. Welch's article 'Contemporary Views on the Proposals for the Alienation of Capitular Property in England, 1832–1840', in the *Journal of Ecclesiastical History*, v (1954), 184 ff. This does not unfortunately include any analysis of the different cathedrals' arguments.

[2] The main changes are conveniently summarized by Mathieson, pp. 152–3.

[3] 23 July 1840. *Hansard*, 3/LV, 903–4.

of churchmen in the universities and in the course of education to become churchmen, and throughout society; who consider that any reforms of this description . . . are neither more nor less than the robbery and plunder of themselves; and they make such an outcry as that the existing holders of dignities in the chapters, whose interests are not to be touched, think it necessary to oppose the measure. Then, as popularity is in these times the source of power, some of the bishops think proper to take the same course. But I hope [he concluded] the archbishop will proceed with firmness.[1]

Howley and Blomfield both flatly denied C. R. Sumner's and Phillpott's suggestions that the large number of petitions from the clergy against the bill, and the very small number for it, proved that the clergy as a whole disliked it. Knowing how easily petitions were got up, and knowing, moreover, exactly how several of these particular petitions had been got up, the archbishop wholly disregarded them.[2] The industry of the cathedrals men, and the fame of Sydney Smith (who privately despised them), combined to give the opposition's case, with all its misrepresentations and mis-statements, a degree of publicity that the Commissioners never enjoyed.[3] Yet pamphlets were written on the Commissioners' side. An admirer of Blomfield, A. Sayers, wrote quite an effective *Reply to the Third Letter to Archdeacon Singleton*[4]. There were others. The *British Critic* itself, which three years before had printed Pusey's frenzied onslaught, reviewed the passage of the bill and the whole controversy that had preceded it with a degree of philosophic calm and even of partial approval that spoke volumes.[5] Blomfield and the Archbishop must have been right.

T. S. Eliot has correctly characterized Blomfield as 'One who was

---

[1] 27 December 1839. Brit. Mus. Add. MSS 40310, fos. 318-9. I have rationalized the punctuation.

[2] 27 July 1840. *Hansard*, 3/LV, 1003-4 and Blomfield on 30 July, *ibid.* 1136-7. Howley is reported as saying, *inter alia*, that, 'He did not wish to undervalue the petitions of the clergy, but this he must say, that petitions were only valuable in proportion to intelligence!'

[3] Also, the mere fact that the bill was four years in passing gave the opposition a look of weight and success, whereas of course the delay through 1837 and 1838 was due not to the opposition but to the government's Church Rates Bill and the Committee on Church Leases.

[4] 1839. It includes a comic description of the average cathedral service and the 'intolerable strain' put upon the canon-in-residence.

[5] In an article titled 'The Cathedral Act', January 1841, 114-50.

usually right, And never intimidated . . .'[1] That Blomfield believed in the Deans and Chapters Act and fought for it so well—even taking on Phillpotts in single combat, and giving at least as good as he got—says much in favour of that measure. His last speech on it was truly great, and demands extensive quotation; not only does it put the case for the Deans and Chapters Act at its most unanswerable, but—as was only natural, considering the theme and the orator—in it can be seen better than in any other single speech or tract the whole case for the Ecclesiastical Commissioners, the emergencies that called them forth, the hopes that were held for their future.

It has been stated, by the learned counsel who were heard at the bar of the House, that a measure of this kind, which goes to suppress certain ancient offices, can be justified only upon one of three grounds, failure in the performance of duty on the part of those who hold those offices, misfeasance, or necessity. It is not necessary for me to dwell upon the first of these grounds. . . . I would rather take my stand upon the stronger ground of necessity. The state of things which constitutes that necessity is too notorious to be denied. It is admitted by all parties that there exists in this country at the present moment an appalling amount of spiritual destitution, and all parties are equally ready to admit the absolute necessity of making some provision for remedying that fearful evil. My Lords, there is no occasion for my troubling your Lordships with any details, in confirmation of that which none deny. But I may be permitted to say, that no person has more ample opportunities of witnessing that spiritual destitution, nor more frequent occasions to deplore it, than I have, as Bishop of the diocese in which this vast metropolis is situate. Weekly, almost daily, is brought under my notice some instance of the evil which results from the present state of things. I am continually brought into contact, in the discharge of my official duties, with vast masses of my fellow-creatures, living without God in the world. I traverse the streets of this crowded city with deep and solemn thoughts of the spiritual condition of its inhabitants. I pass the magnificent church which crowns the metropolis, and is consecrated to the noblest of objects, the glory of God, and I ask of myself, in what degree it answers that object. I see there a dean, and three residentiaries, with incomes, amounting in the aggregate to between £10,000 and £12,000 a year. I see, too, connected with the Cathedral twenty-nine clergymen whose offices are all but sinecures, with an annual income of about £12,000 at the present moment, and likely to be very much larger after the lapse of a few

[1] In 'The Rock'; cited by Mrs Brose at the head of her attractive chapter 4.

years. I proceed a mile or two to the E. and N.E. and find myself in the midst of an immense population in the most wretched state of destitution and neglect, artizans, mechanics, labourers, beggars, thieves, to the number of at least 300,000. I find there, upon the average, about one church, and one clergyman for every 8000 or 10,000 souls: in some districts a much smaller amount of spiritual provision; in one parish, for instance, only one church and one clergyman for 40,000 people. I naturally look back to the vast endowments of St Pauls, a part of them drawn from these very districts, and consider whether some portion of them may not be applied to remedy, or alleviate, these enormous evils. No, I am told, You may not touch St Paul's. It is an ancient corporation which must be maintained in its integrity. Not a stall can be spared. . . .

But to return to the question of necessity. It is stated by the Commissioners in their second Report, that the evils resulting from the want of sufficient provision for the religious teaching and pastoral superintendence of the people, far outweigh all the other inconveniences occasioned by anomalies in our ecclesiastical establishments. If I am asked what those evils are? I reply, Look at the examples of Newport, and Birmingham, and Sheffield. Inquire at the Gaol, the Hulk, the Penitentiary, what are the fruits of religious destitution and neglect. Read the Calendars at every Gaol delivery. Hear the charges of our venerable judges, and then determine whether, when we have the means of remedying those evils, in part at least, we shall suffer thousands and thousands of our fellow-creatures to live in ignorance and sin, debarred from those privileges which are their birthright as members of Christ's holy Catholic Church.

My Lords, it has been again and again alleged that the scheme of the Commissioners was adopted under the influence of fear. . . . I plead guilty to the charge. But of what fear? Was it the fear of popular clamour? . . . No, my Lords, the fear which swayed us was no such unworthy, unholy, fear as this. It was the fear of being found unfaithful to our trust, in leaving so many of our fellow-christians under the pressure of evils which it was in our power to alleviate, a prey to the emissaries of infidelity, and disloyalty, and vice; a fear, lest those classes of society which ought to be the basis and strength of the commonwealth, should become in the total absence of religious principle and moral restraint, its bane, and the instruments of its desolation. . . .

We have acted conscientiously in the performance of an ungracious duty, according to our own convictions of what was best for the real interests of the Church and the Country. We knew from the first that we were undertaking an invidious and unpopular task. We have submitted to much misrepresentation and obloquy, to which it was difficult to reply, without stating facts and employing arguments, which we would rather have forborne from using. I rejoice that I have now had an opportunity of stating to your Lordships the reasons which induced me (and I speak for myself alone) to give my hearty assent to the proposals of the Commissioners, as to all their leading features; susceptible as they may be of modification and improvement: and it is a great consolation to me to feel assured that, if Your Lordships should pass this Bill into law, many years will not elapse before the great body of the Christian people of this land will do justice to the motives and the prudence of the Commissioners, and acknowledge the benefits resulting from their labours. They will thank us for having done all in our power to lessen those evils which are now the bane of the Church, and if left unremedied will soon prove its destruction; they will be grateful to us for having set an example, on the part of the Church, of making a sacrifice—a sacrifice, be it remembered, only from one part of the Church to another—from the less useful to the more efficient. . . . If the measure now before your Lordships should fail of producing these anticipated benefits, it will fail from other causes than from a want of consideration, and caution, and careful deliberation, on the part of those, upon the strength of whose recommendations it has been now proposed.[1]

One fact seems to plead even more eloquently than Blomfield in justification of the Ecclesiastical Commissioners in general, and of their Deans and Chapters Act in particular; and that is the support which both received from Archbishop Howley. This support could not, in 1830 or thereabouts, have been predicted. Blomfield's could plausibly have been predicted, and his advocacy is therefore to that extent the less convincing; one is convinced by his arguments, that is all. But with Howley, it is not so much that the arguments carry conviction, as the fact that he ever came to use them. The Howley of the later thirties is quite a different figure from the Howley of earlier times. He was at best a moderate reformer then;[2] and his character seems to have been upright, unimaginative, amiable, unforceful. He gives the impression

---

[1] *Speech of the Lord Bishop of London . . . on the Ecclesiastical Duties and Revenues Bill, 30 July 1840.* Pp. 7–9, 14–15, 26–7. The *Hansard* version is in *Hansard*, 3/LV, 113–55.

[2] I do not think his church reform plans of 1829–30, so often subsequently referred to, can have amounted to much. No one knows just what they were; and Wellington's complete inability to remember anything whatsoever about them (30 July 1840; *Hansard*, 3/LV, 1131) suggests that they were not very exciting. As for his three bills of 1831, I have discussed them already—see above, p. 276.

of a good man too easily influenced by strong personalities to be called firm or strong himself.

After 1835 Howley veritably changes his spots. He may still have seemed 'the meek Archbishop' in private, but one would not gather that he was anything of the kind from *Hansard's* reports of his speeches in the House of Lords. Melbourne's speeches in the Commissioners' defence would be as long, and to Blomfield would inevitably fall the hatchet-work of debate; but whenever Howley was there, he had to lead for the prelates, and he always did it well. It is inconceivable that he did not believe in the Commissioners and their work, that he was only assuming a politic pose. Between 1832, when the majority of the bishops were huddling together at Lambeth and praying for a counter-revolution, and 1836, when he appeared as the inflexible supporter of quasi-revolutionary measures, Howley had apparently undergone a change of heart. Such things, we know, do happen. Gladstone underwent two such changes in his ideas about church and state between 1832 and 1868; they are intellectual analogies to religious conversion. What caused it, one cannot be sure. But Van Mildert's death in 1836 may well have had something to do with it. Van Mildert's prestige was higher with the clergy than any other bishop's, and his character was decisive and forceful. With Van Mildert urging firmness and rallying the bench on one side of him, and with a set of high church chaplains and satellites (Rose, Ogilvie, Norris, Harrison, D'Oyly) on the other, Howley was stuck. When Van Mildert withdrew in dudgeon to the north, Rose went into decline, and the progress of Tractarianism began to break up the old ecclesiastical parties, then Howley was freed. Perhaps, if there was to the last something in his character that required the support of strong-minded friends, he found that support in Peel and Blomfield. Himself twenty years older than the latter, and never so strong, he certainly came to lean on him heavily, and delegated responsibility to him.[1] The Howley who came so regularly to the Commissioners' meetings and spoke so well on their behalf was not ust a puppet pulled by Blomfield's strings. He believed in what he was

[1] See e.g. Graham's letter to Blomfield of 27 December 1842, about education, in which he said 'By the permission of the Archbishop ... I address your Lordship occasionally instead of his Grace on matters of business.' (Graham papers, bundle 56B.)

doing. The truth must be, that in the difficult circumstances of the eighteen-thirties, the Ecclesiastical Commissioners' measures, partial and painful though they were, could not be much improved on, by anyone who really tried to see church and nation as a whole, not abstractly nor in the terms of conventional rhetoric, but in the modern way, with the aid of maps, committees, circular inquiries, and tabulated statistics. This Howley did, however painfully, at the Ecclesiastical Commissioners' board. The result was infinitely creditable to him. More important, for our purpose, is the other conclusion to be drawn; which is, that to the institution of some body or other like the Ecclesiastical Commissioners, there was no serious alternative.

CHAPTER VIII

THE TIME OF TROUBLES

The Act of 1840 (usually referred to as the Cathedrals Act) could have initiated an era of better feelings for the Ecclesiastical Commissioners. The fiery animosities blown up against them seemed to be cooling down. The deans' and chapters' advocates had overplayed their hand. Its strength had lain in the prospective value of a remodelled cathedral system, and its weakness in the notorious abuses of the past and present cathedral system. In the excitement of communicating their visions of what the cathedrals might become, they too readily over-looked, or too prudently omitted to notice, what the cathedrals actually were like, and, by their irritable denunciations of those who, unable to overlook scandals so gross and inutilities so palpable, stood by the Commissioners, only stiffened the ranks of the latters' supporters. The Act, more popular than otherwise with the majority of the clergy, duly passed, but in a shape less offensive to the cathedral clergy than they had earlier feared. The clerical minority who had opposed it had therefore reason for satisfaction on their side as well, and could afford to view the Commissioners less implacably. The Commissioners helped them in this by reconstituting themselves in such a manner as to meet some of the constitutional objections that had been brought against them. The whole bench of bishops was put on the board, and the objection that the lower clergy were not represented was met—rather disingenuously, it may be felt, since two of them were also bishops—by adding the deans of Canterbury, St Paul's and Westminster, *ex officio*. The feature of their constitution that had brought Phillpotts and Blomfield together in criticism of it—the removability of part of the Commission at the Crown's will—disappeared, and all the Commissioners were given office *quam diu se bene gesserint*, which made them virtually irremovable.

These changes in their constitution helped to raise the Commissioners in the eyes of those who had not thitherto much appreciated them. At the same time the passage of the Cathedrals Act at last put them, apparently, in a position to do the work which all church reformers had so long awaited. A fund—the Common Fund, as the Commissioners called it—had been established for the financing of the church's activities where they were most needed. New churches, higher incomes, an abundance of better nourished curates, all the objects for which Perceval and Yates had argued and Harrowby and Howley so long endeavoured, were brought, in prospect, almost spectacularly nearer accomplishment. The Commissioners themselves saw many obstacles yet standing between the will and the deed. They could not know how many more obstacles were to interpose themselves before they were ten years older. But for the time being all was hope and harmony, which the Commissioners did nothing in 1840 or 1841 to disturb. Experiencing a kind of rebirth, they were able to make a fresh start.

How, after so fair a beginning, their reputation sunk ingloriously to its nadir in the next decade, is a depressing story. The Commissioners seemed to be dogged by misfortune. Things went wrong, they were blamed—as is the way of the world, especially with the clergy—for being in difficulties they could not conceivably have avoided, and for failing to deliver goods they had not yet got in stock. They found few friends and many enemies. It goes without saying that the dissenters believed them to be iniquitous and absurd. Radicals and economists thought them wasteful and unbusinesslike. The landed interest was suspicious. Within the church itself, opinion was divided. During their most unhappy decade, 1845–55, there seemed to be little to say in their favour, much to be said against them. Some bishops were permanently hostile. Cabinets were uneasy and embarrassed about them.

All in all, the Ecclesiastical Commissioners had an exceedingly bad time of it, so bad that one can only with difficulty believe that they were not themselves substantially to blame. Yet it really does appear that they were more sinned against than sinning. Their policies were not beyond question the best that could have been adopted, their ways of doing business were in some respects deplorable, and they certainly made mistakes. Nevertheless they were made to suffer far more than they deserved. To dissenters and radicals, the Commissioners were especially obnoxious as the guardians of that mass of property which ought, they believed, to be put to different and better uses. To many churchmen also the Commissioners were convenient as whipping boys. Churchmen who would not approve of change (and, once the pressures of the early

349

thirties were past, there were many such, as Peel, hustling to get things done when he had his brief opportunity, had clearly foreseen) naturally quarrelled with a body devoted to the process of perpetual change. But churchmen of more progressive mind also were annoyed by the Commissioners. The reforms they were engaged in did not go far enough, were not of the right kind. Poor clergymen like Amos Barton and Josiah Crawley, who were still denied the income that had been thought a tolerable minimum during the Protectorate, and men of every shade of churchmanship who saw with anguish the sands of national religion sinking fast, did not always pause to inquire how far the Commissioners were culpable before they laid the church's troubles at the Commissioners' door. The warmth of their feelings was understandable, and did them much credit; but they were none the less often unjust.

In 1850 the constitution of the Commission was again remodelled, the defects which had appeared in the operation of the 1840 constitution were remedied, and the board became, recognizably, what it remained till 1948. The years 1846–52 saw the virtual settlement, after much unpleasantness, of the vexed question of church leases, and attainment at last of a reasonable and not too inharmonious relationship with both bishops and chapters in respect of the management of their estates. In 1856, when the Commissioners' conduct was examined by the second of three Select Committees of the House of Commons within twenty years, they resumed the work of augmentation of poor livings which had been ten years suspended, never to suspend it again. Thus in every department of their work the Ecclesiastical Commissioners surmounted between 1850 and 1856 difficulties which might, had they run into even worse weather or managed their affairs less capably, have proved fatal. Boards like the Ecclesiastical Commissioners had, in the fifties, to make what headway they could against a very strong and constant gale of public opinion. There was every disposition in parliament to abolish them if possible. The fate of the General Board of Health was always before their eyes. 'Do you contemplate the Ecclesiastical Commission being a permanent body?', demanded the future Lord Salisbury of Spencer Walpole, a devoted Commissioner giving evidence to the 1856 Committee. 'It is so now', the latter replied, 'and I do not see how it can be otherwise.' The grand turning-point of the history of the Ecclesiastical Commissioners was epitomized in the question and answer that followed. 'You do not see any way of getting out of it?' 'I do not.'[1] Their survival was, like the victory at Waterloo, 'a damned fine-run thing'.

I. THE COMMON FUND AND ITS APPLICATION

The Common Fund of the Ecclesiastical Commissioners—which stood deliberately distinct from their Episcopal Fund until 1850—was established by section 68 of the Cathedrals Act, which directed them to apply it to making 'additional provision . . . for the cure of souls in parishes where such assistance is most required, in such manner as shall . . . be deemed most conducive to the efficiency of the Established Church'.

Revenues came into the Common Fund from two main sources. Where canonries were suspended, the shares of the corporate revenues they would have received if they had not been suspended were to be paid by the chapter to the Commissioners.[2] These were money payments arising out of property in the management of which the Commissioners were at first given no share.[3] But the rest of the revenue came from estates actually vested in the Commissioners—the *separate* estates of deans and canons, and the estates of non-residentiary prebends and suppressed sinecure rectories.[4] These were managed directly by the Commissioners, once the life-interest in them had expired or been commuted.

Existing interests were carefully respected by the Act of 1840, and its provisions for the suspension of residentiary canonries were calculated to soften the blow by slowing the process down. Instead of these canonries being suspended one after another as they fell vacant, until the number slid down to the uniform four which had been the Commissioners' proposal in the first place, it was conceded to the opposition that the reduction should proceed by the method of two steps forward, one step back.[5] It would thus be a long time before the Commissioners could come into the whole of their birthright and the Common Fund swell to its maximum proportions. They had great expectations, but

[1] 1845 Committee, Qs. 4901–2.   [2] Section 49.

[3] That came two years later, by the 5 and 6 Vic. c. 108, ss. 6, 18 and 20, 'An Act for enabling Ecclesiastical Corporations, aggregate and sole, to grant Leases for long Terms of Years.'   [4] Sections 50, 51, 54.

[5] Thus, at Winchester, where seven had to go altogether, the second and third to fall vacant were to be suspended, the fourth to be filled; the fifth and sixth to be suspended, the seventh to be filled; the eighth and ninth to be suspended, the tenth to be filled; and the eleventh to be suspended.

little ready cash. Christopher Hodgson had just over £30,000 in exchequer bills waiting for them, the accumulated receipts of suspended canonries etc. since 1835; but Murray told them at their fourth general meeting that they could not expect much more than £13,000 a year at first.[1]

The Commissioners got going without delay. Their first meeting under the new dispensation was on 15 August 1840. Not many were present—only Howley, Melbourne, Harrowby, Bishops Blomfield, Murray (Rochester), Bagot, Monk, Thirlwall of St David's and Sir Herbert Jenner. A few others were civil enough to apologize for their absence.[2] Almost at once they turned to the business of augmentation. There was no doubt where they should start. Their second report had drawn attention to the existence of 315 populous livings (2000 souls and more) under £150 a year. Not all of them were in public patronage (which they were to define, rather startlingly, so widely as to include patronage in the hands of the Crown, the prelates, chapters, and dignitaries and incumbents as such)[3] but those that were should claim their first attention. They directed Murray to check the correctness of those figures from the report of the Ecclesiastical Revenues Commissioners and to find out by diocesan inquiries how many new churches, consecrated since that report was drawn up, came into the same category.

The mode of augmentation was next to be considered. The Commissioners were faced with the same sort of problem as the Bounty Board had been. Should they proceed by allotting capital sums, by annexing lands and tithe rent-charges, or assigning fixed annual stipends? To review these alternatives and the other aspects of augmentation they appointed a committee to meet in between, and report to, their general meetings. All the pre-1840 Commissioners were to be on this committee, plus C. R. Sumner, Copleston, Bagot and Murray of Rochester; but as it turned out, and as might have been expected, few turned up. Howley and Blomfield were by far the most regular in attendance, with

---

[1] Minutes 2 February 1841, § 3a.

[2] *Viz.* Kaye, Phillpotts, Otter, Denison of Salisbury, and Stephen Lushington the judge of the Admiralty Court. Bethell, bishop of Bangor, wrote to say that the secretary might as well save himself the trouble of summoning him to meetings until further notice.

[3] Minutes, 24 November 1840, § 2/1a.a.

Harrowby, Murray, Hobhouse and the judges of the prerogative and admiralty courts, Lushington and Jenner(-Fust), in roughly that order, a good way behind.

From their meetings through the winter of 1840–1 emerged the outlines of the policy which guided the Commissioners for the next fifteen years. They would augment principally by means of fixed annual stipends, secured on their certain revenues; and would work according to a certain ratio of population to income. For livings in public patronage as they defined it,[1] their ratios ran thus, and were resolved to be made eligible on the following dates, as their funds became sufficient.

Population	Value to be made up to	Date of Resolution to start augmenting
2000 and over	£150	10 May, 1841
1—2000	£120	5 July, 1842
500—1000	£100	4 April, 1843
under 500	£80	25 July, 1843

Livings that came within this class were eligible for unconditional grants (i.e. grants irrespective of benefactions) provided that they were not sinecures, that they were at least district parishes under the Church Building Acts (i.e. distinct parishes for all ecclesiastical purposes), and that they were not held in plurality. The Commissioners carefully reserved the right to investigate the circumstances of each individual benefice as it came before them.[2]

This was the principal category of augmentations, but not the only one. Like Queen Anne's Bounty, they would make grants to meet benefactions for the augmentation of benefices in public or private patronage, provided they were of over 2000 souls and had less than £200 a year,[3] or over 1000 souls with less than £150 a year.[4]

[1] They soon stretched their definition still further, at J. B. Sumner's instance, to include churches in the patronage of perpetual curates, as such. (Minutes, 7 December 1841, § 19.)

[2] Thus, early in 1842, they declined to augment the vicarage of Newport Pagnell (over 2000 souls, income only £120) because the vicar was *ex officio* master of Queen Anne's Hospital in that place. (Minutes, 23 March 1842, § 3/5.)

[3] Minutes, 18 May 1841, § 5.   [4] Minutes, 2 August 1842, § 7.

A further class of augmentations were those in respect of local claims. Clause 67 of the 1840 Act had ended by obliging the Commissioners to give 'due consideration' to the 'wants and circumstances' of places, the tithes of which, or the lands given at some earlier date in lieu of the tithes of which, had become vested in the Commissioners. This express requirement, which the early Commissioners had not at all wanted, was the only restriction on their discretion to augment as they chose; and it constituted a kind of prior claim, parliamentarily recognized, upon their resources—of which interested parties were not slow to take advantage. The Commissioners set a limit to its potential nuisance value by resolving never to grant more than the actual value of the tithes (or whatever) on the basis of which a claim was made; but even so they were bound to make augmentations on this account to livings which would otherwise hardly have made the grade.

In one other way they set out to relieve clerical poverty. In 1842 they decided to make single grants of between a half and two-fifths of the cost to meet benefactions for the provision of residence houses, under the same conditions, as to value and population, as governed their ordinary augmentations to meet benefactions.[1] Since they undertook also to enter into all the contracts, supervise the whole of the construction, and pay all the legal fees, it was not unreasonable of them to insist upon the employment of their own architect, William Railton, and the adoption of one or other of his designs.

Thus ran the Commissioners' first augmentations policy. It was sensible, prudent, unimaginative, and inelastic. It was not often judged on its merits. Those have to be considered in relation to the whole state of church extension, which, by the forties, was booming. The Church Building Commissioners had little money left to distribute, but the demand for their aid and advice in the building of new churches and the assignment to them of proper parishes or districts was so great they could scarcely at times keep up with it.[2] Money was being poured into the construction and, to a much smaller extent, the endowment of churches by private individuals and diocesan societies. Church building, in fact, became fashionable. But church endowment did not. Too many

---

[1] Minutes, 29 November 1842, § 7.

[2] See e.g. their secretary's warning, recorded in the E.C. Minutes, 15 February 1842, § 3.

of these new churches were set on their way with negligible endowments, compelling their wretched ministers to exploit to an altogether deplorable degree the wretched system of pew rents. Some new churches went without ministers for months on end; few who had the chance to move on to something better failed to do so.[1]

Nor were these the only shortcomings of the church extension movement. The Church Building Commissioners were a deeply conservative body, and their assumptions were those of the *ancien régime* of before 1830. Their policy had been shaped between 1818 and 1825, when a degree of respect was paid to existing interests that crippled their potentialities for usefulness and had already by the forties come to seem unnecessary, even mistaken. But within their offices in Great George Street, this policy was as the law and the prophets. The world was changing rapidly around them but they either would or could not change. Most regular in attendance at their board was Joshua Watson, an old-fashioned conservative indeed, in whom there was no flexibility. Their secretary George Jelf told the 1847–8 committee that Watson had 'in every way laboured to maintain its character and the consistency of its proceedings'.[2] Almost as regular as Watson were the principal of King's College, Archdeacons Hale, Sinclair, and Harrison, Sir Robert Inglis, and Lord Bexley. The names speak for themselves. The Church Building Commission was a bastion of the old guard, where, just because they breathed the atmosphere of a vanishing civilization, their surviving members were able to keep active without compromising their principles. But even had they wished to modernize their policy, as other members of their board certainly did, they were virtually unable to do so. There were twenty-one Church Building Acts between 1818 and 1856, forming an almost impenetrable jungle of laws and orders; 'so complex and conflicting in their nature', wrote in 1857 one of the few men who understood them, 'as to have defied all endeavours to arrange or classify them, or render them at all intelligible to the general reader'.[3] Such an endeavour was made in 1842 when Jelf and Lushington prepared

[1] See W. Chamberlain, *Parochial Centralization* and John Livesey *Mechanics' Churches, passim*.

[2] 1848, Q. 2072. My views of Watson and, indeed, of the whole of the later years of the Church Building Commission, are rather different from Mr Port's.

[3] J. C. Traill, *The New Parishes Acts*, p. 22.

a consolidation bill of 211 clauses; but the government declined to wed itself to so bulky a bride, and no private member could be found with skill and zeal enough to make it his own.[1]

The conditions under which the insertion of new churches into the parochial structure was conducted were thus unsatisfactory—rigid, acephalous, hectic, uneconomic. The church extension movement exhibited all the characteristic failings of those partnerships between official, 'central' direction and voluntary, 'local' enterprise which were so often the nineteenth century's response to the demands of its new society; but it exhibited them to a peculiar degree, because the weight lay more than usually on the voluntary, 'local' side. Whether it had to be so by historical necessity is an open question not to be further discussed here. But it was so, and the Ecclesiastical Commissioners, when they hopefully first turned the flood of their Common Fund onto this confused field, were only accepting an existing situation, and working within it.

They were much freer and readier than the Church Building Commissioners to embark on new courses of action, and in 1843 did so. The initiative seems to have come principally from the prime minister and the home secretary, whom the state of the populous manufacturing districts—revealed at its darkest by the Chartist *émeutes* of 1841–2 and the reports of the inspectors of factories and schools—had exceedingly alarmed. By the autumn of 1842 the worst troubles seemed to be, for the time being, at an end, and Peel and Graham turned at once to the question of preventing their recurrence. While law and civil rights were in danger, they were prepared to uphold them by power; but they prepared at the same time, like the wise statesmen they were, to encourage the development of a happier and safer society. 'We must augment the means of education,' wrote Graham to Peel; 'we must keep down the price of articles of first necessity; we must endeavour to redress the wrongs of the labourer; we must mark an honest sympathy with his wants'. And, replied Peel, we must above all extend the church's parochial ministry.[2]

Through that autumn and winter they reviewed many means of

[1] P.Ps. 1856, XI, 473–4.
[2] Letters of 1 and 9 September 1842, in Parker's *Peel*, II, 546–7, corrected from the originals in the Graham papers, bundle 53 A.

church extension. Murray put figures and estimates before them; Goulburn and Gladstone were brought into consultation; so were Blomfield and Howley. They considered every possible way of finding money for church building and endowment—public grants or loans, improvement of church leases, a graduated tax on clerical incomes, private benevolence. The course by which they came to a decision cannot be exactly traced. Peel's lieutenants gave him bold counsels. Goulburn and Graham were both ready to impose a graduated tax, Graham was keen on public loans to the Commissioners, and Gladstone had advanced notions for the improved management of church property. These proposals failed to attract Peel, largely because they would have made his measure a controversial one, offensive to some interest or other. The prime minister, although second to none of his old-world, Erastian, more or less deist contemporaries in impatience with people like Inglis and Pusey on the one hand, with Sydney Smith and Edward Baines on the other, was at this juncture anxious at all costs to avoid trouble.[1] The measure he consequently introduced was tame compared with those he had recently been talking over with his colleagues. He simply proposed to increase the funds at the Ecclesiastical Commissioners' disposal by sanctioning their borrowing £600,000 worth of exchequer bills from Queen Anne's Bounty, with which to endow new churches; and he gave the Commissioners powers, similar to those of the Church Building Commissioners but more in keeping with the spirit of the age, to equip these new churches with new parishes.[2]

If it was indeed Peel's aim as much to avoid controversy as to help the church, then he certainly succeeded. His bill went through parliament with scarcely any comment. What was there to say about it? It touched no existing interest save that of ministers of parishes into which a new 'Peel district' might be intruded, and it provided for their compensation.[3] The radicals and dissenters found nothing to get their fangs into, and churchmen could only complain that it was not very enterprising.

[1] This paragraph is based on the correspondence between Peel and Graham in Parker's *Peel*, the Peel papers at the British Museum, the Graham papers, and Gladstone's memoranda, Brit. Mus. Add. MSS 44732, fos. 5–43.

[2] 6 and 7 Vic. c. 37, An Act to make better Provision for the Spiritual Care of Populous Parishes.

[3] Clause 19.

Lord John Russell had every justification for saying (perhaps sarcastically?) that 'it did not appear to be of vast extent or high principle, or to be likely to produce any extraordinary results'.[1]

The measure of its mildness was that, to a great extent, it gave to the Ecclesiastical Commissioners no larger powers than they had themselves already thought of getting. The loan from Queen Anne's Bounty was no new idea. An interest-free loan of public money such as Graham suggested would have been something new, but Peel apparently shied away from a proposal which, without satisfying Inglis, would certainly have enraged Hume and Bright. The Bounty Board had been willing to lend such a sum of money early in 1841, and the Commissioners had been anxious to borrow it; Christopher Hodgson drew up a bill to authorize it, which Hobhouse revised.[2] For reasons which are not clear, it was given up later that year.[3] But if it had gone through, they would have used it in just the same way as they used the loan of 1843, paying three per cent interest on it, selling blocks of it from time to time to finance their augmentations, and paying it back to the Bounty when their ships came home twenty or thirty years later. All that Peel's Act did beyond this was to set them up in a kind of rivalry with the Church Building Commissioners as dividers of parishes and makers of districts.

Such, however, were the demands upon the Commissioners for augmentations and endowments of new churches, that even with this extra £600,000 at their disposal, they very soon ran out of funds. The Bounty's loan, once gone, was gone for ever; the income of their Common Fund grew but slowly; and upon it was now charged, prospectively, the Bounty's loan's repayment. In August 1844 they were compelled to suspend all augmentations, except those in respect of local claims (which they felt obliged to continue, parliament having expressly favoured them and public feeling being strong in their favour) and for endowments of new churches already or at any rate very nearly completed. They sought a second loan from the Bounty but were refused. So unpopular were they by this time that to have gone to

[1] 5 May 1843, *Hansard*, 3/LXVIII, 1297.

[2] Minutes, 6 April 1841, § 4.

[3] No mention of it is made in the Minutes between April and 7 December 1841. Graham mentioned it without explanation in a letter to Peel, 7 January 1843, Brit. Mus. Add. MSS 40448, fos. 178–9.

parliament for help was out of the question. There was nothing for it, therefore, but to keep their good resolutions about augmentation in suspense (apart from an apologetic attempt to satisfy some of the myriad claims upon them, in 1849) until their income gave them a clear disposable surplus; which it did not until 1856. The story of their early promise and subsequent decline can be seen in Appendix 7a.

2. THE EPISCOPAL FUND AND ITS APPLICATION

The popular impression, that the Ecclesiastical Commissioners attended with particular care to the comfort and powers of the bench, gained strength and reached its zenith in the forties and fifties. It was not without foundation, although, inevitably, any cry that discredited the bishops was taken up and exploited by all sorts of men—both Christian and secularist, anglican and dissenting—who, disliking anything that smacked of ecclesiastical authority, were bound to dislike particularly those who personified that authority. Much of the criticism of the bishops has to be disregarded. Ultra-individualist liberals like Horsman and Buller recked little whether the facts they alleged against the bishops were true or not. Some of the Liberation Society's propaganda was of a kind that no respectable person should have touched. But mixed up with this dross were elements of truth; whether the bishops intended it or whether it just happened that way, the Commissioners' activities did nothing to limit the bishops' powers, much to strengthen them.

To a great extent, this was an inevitable consequence of the process of making the established church 'efficient.' The unreformed church had been inefficient for its mixed political and religious purposes mainly because it lacked government. Here and there, indeed, orders were given that had to be obeyed; but even if they aimed at public and not at private good, it could only be the local public good; and they were likelier, certainly, to originate with a layman—a big landowner, a prosperous merchant, a busy squire-magistrate-patron—than with a clergyman. There was no co-ordination of effort, nor any settled chain of command, in the anarchic congregationalism of the unreformed establishment. It was each for himself and, with luck, his neighbours, and the devil take the hindmost. Bishops intervened hardly at all in the lives of the parochial clergy, for the greater number of whom they were far too grand; able to do but little, bishops probably in fact did less to discipline delinquent clergymen than was done by local respectable public opinion. Their functions in the diocese were mostly formal, functions which their archdeacons, secretaries and registrars could execute for them. Bishops' seals and signatures mattered much more than bishops, whose natural habitats were the West End and the universities; in their dioceses, they were viewed as annual migrant visitors.

But from about 1780 onwards, the progress of church reform inexorably made the bishop matter more. Not that bishops began really to govern the church. Parliament governed the church and had no intention of ever ceasing to do so; the bishops merely did in their dioceses, with the executive assistance of their archdeacons and (in only a few cases at first) rural deans, what parliament told them to do. In this they closely resembled the lords lieutenant and their county magistracies, who carried out under much more advantageous circumstances the civil instructions of the sovereign legislature, and moreover formed, in their quarter sessions, a kind of local legislature for which the church had no counterpart. Yet even in their capacity as executives of parliament's will, bishops necessarily loomed ever larger in the clergy's life, whether the clergy liked it or not. They had to be more often consulted, the powers given them under the new statutes were definite and enforceable, public opinion compelled them to spend more time in the dioceses, to visit, ordain and confirm more often.

This was the start of the bishops' rise to new importance. It was accelerated by the independent part they took outside the parliamentary sector of the third church reform movement. As organizers or primary patrons of diocesan education and church building societies and such like they could show more initiative, and, in association with the leading clergy and laity of their district, actually initiate and direct the progress of reform; a reforming bishop with plenty of money to dispose of, like Shute Barrington or William Van Mildert, was personally able to subsidize some of the improvements he wanted to see made. The impact of such a prelate on a diocese could be great indeed. But it was not only independently, each in his own diocese, that the bishops began during the third church reform movement in some sense really to govern the church. They did it collectively as well, first at the Bounty

Board,[1] and then after the Cathedrals Act as Ecclesiastical Commissioners. They were still acting under parliament's authority and their actions were commonly criticized in parliament, but all the same their freedom of movement was great; it put them in a position to shape the strategy of reform and the pattern of church administration besides consolidating their powers as administrative lynchpins; by natural process they became, without sinister intention, both judges, jurymen, and executioners in the church's cause.

There were therefore elements of inevitability in the way the institution of the Ecclesiastical Commissioners bolstered the prestige and authority of the bench. Already (by 1840) important enough, the bishops made themselves even more so; and if there was some self-importance in them as well, that was only human nature. This had been evident enough in the higher estimates adopted for the standard of episcopal living, and for the settlement of bishops' incomes and palaces. The sums involved, as the following table shows, were sometimes very large.[2]

Palaces	Sum Expended	Dates of Authorisation	Sources of Funds	
Bath and Wells	4,000	1846	Q.A.B. loan	
Chester	4,800	1866	Q.A.B. loan, and sale of old residence.	
Exeter	3,526	1845–6	Exeter episcopal property	
Gloucester (Stapleton)	23,627	1840	Compensation for damage to Bristol palace, and sale of site	7,684
			Episcopal property	14,870
			Commissioners' funds	1,073
Gloucester (Gloucester)	14,411	1857–64	Sale of Stapleton ..	12,315
			Sundries	1,196
			Q.A.B. loan ..	900
Hereford	800	1848	Q.A.B. loan	
Lincoln (Riseholme)	52,185	1841	Sales of Estates ..	45,982
			Commissioners' funds	6,212

[1] See ch. 5 above, pp. 212 ff.

[2] It is adapted from P.Ps. 1867, LIV, 655–7. Sums of money are given to the nearest pound; the dates of authorization are the dates when the relevant Orders in Council were gazetted.

Palaces	Sum Expended	Dates of Authorisation	Sources of Funds	
Llandaff	9,054	1858	Commissioners' funds.	
Manchester	19,037	1854	Commissioners' funds.	
Norwich	7,745	1858	Q.A.B. loan ..	5,000
			Dilapidation monies	1,204
			Bishop's personal contribution ..	1,542
Oxford	6,819	1846-7, 1858	Commissioners' funds	4,800
			Q.A.B. loan ..	2,019
Peterborough	3,800	1865	Q.A.B. loan	
Ripon	15,492	1838-42, 1865	Commissioners' funds	14,622
			Q.A.B. loan	869
Rochester (Danbury)	30,530	1845-8	Sale of palaces at Bromley and Rochester	
Salisbury	2,000	1860	Q.A.B. loan	
Worcester (Hartlebury)	7,000	1846	Sale of palace in Worcester	2,085
			Commissioners' funds	4,915
York (Bishopthorpe)	2,000	1863	Q.A.B. loan	

TABLE 1. Spending of the Ecclesiastical Commissioners on Bishops' Palaces (before 1866)

Radicals and dissenters usually spoke as if the whole of these sums would otherwise have gone to relieve the wants of the poor clergy. This was not wholly true. Some of the money was borrowed; and the Bounty Board received as much interest from episcopal borrowers as from their regular gilt-edged investments. Other sums came from the sale of episcopal property. The Commissioners always denied that this was money snatched from the hands of the poor clergy; but that was not wholly true either, for they had an interest in the whole of the episcopate's estates, and at other times, in other arguments, were pleased enough to assert it. What they sanctioned to be realized from the sale of episcopal estates was only one degree less directly their own expenditure than what they contributed from their own funds.

Undeniably, the bishops treated each other generously in the execution of their policy, as in the making of it. Consider first the siting of the palaces, about which 'there were diversities of opinion in the Commission'.[1] Some maintained strongly that the most important thing about a bishop's residence was that it should be easily accessible to the clergy. This might mean that it ought to be in the cathedral town itself; it certainly meant that it ought not to be deep in the countryside, accessible only by carriage. 'Is your Lordship aware', asked a friendly member of the 1847-8 Committee of Bishop Blomfield, 'that the Commissioners, in deciding on sites for bishops' houses, do consult the convenience of the clergy of the diocese?' 'It is the first thing looked to', he replied.[2] Yet, on the evidence, it was neither always nor exclusively so. Blomfield, in fact, was shuffling. He had only just been remarking that it did not matter much where a bishop lived, so long as he kept regular days in the cathedral town and allowed the clergy to get at him there. Besides, the whole of the Commissioners' case for large episcopal incomes rested on the necessity of bishops' being able to consort on equal terms with the gentry, which meant, the landed gentry. It could therefore be maintained that the most important thing about a bishop's residence was that it should be a fine gentleman's residence in good grounds.

This consideration undoubtedly had much to do with Bishop Kaye's choice of the Riseholme estate—two miles or so out of Lincoln—for his new palace instead of utilizing the 'venerable remains of the ancient episcopal palace', with its 'site and grounds most salubriously and beautifully situate close to the cathedral'. These were the words not of a Horsman or even a Denison but of Phillpotts, in his old age more than ever like a thistle in the episcopal flower-bed. He himself had stuck close to his cathedral, moving the palace merely from an allegedly unhealthy and inconvenient site to a better one close by, and it really seems as if he earnestly believed that this was where a bishop ought to be. He therefore professed himself shocked at the way various of his brethren chose to live out in the country, and, when asked by the Cathedral Commissioners for his views on the proper relation between the bishop and his cathedral, he took the opportunity to list his brethren's delinquencies. Monk, he remarked, had settled on a palace half way between

[1] Murray's evidence, 1847-8 committee, 1848 Q. 553.
[2] 1847, Q. 1183.

Gloucester and Bristol, equally inconvenient for each[1]—'and this at a cost which it is painful to remember'; the old palace at Durham had been made over to the university, leaving the bishop out at Auckland Castle, ten miles distant; at Worcester, 'an old and excellent episcopal palace close to the cathedral has been assigned to the dean, and the residence of the bishop permanently fixed at his country mansion', Hartlebury Castle near Stourport; and the new palaces at Ripon and Manchester were both more distant from the diocesan centre than they need have been.[2] He might have added that Samuel Wilberforce stuck resolutely to the site of Cuddesdon, which his predecessor, when trying to move to Shotover, had declared 'inconvenient, in every respect', and perfectly inaccessible. 'There is but one road to the place,' he had said, 'and this at times during the winter nearly impassable, with the exception of the cart-road through the fields, which may be used in summer-time, but then with great difficulty.'[3]

Most bishops, clearly, preferred to live in the country or at least in the suburbs. Whether or not they ought to do so was something upon which men and even bishops disagreed. Phillpotts was not the only bishop to come out strongly in favour of a central site. Hartlebury, which was so far from Worcester, so remote from the geographical centre of the diocese, and so entirely deficient in accommodation for visiting clergy as to make it an extreme and scandalous case, seems to have been retained principally because Bishop Pepys (Lord Chancellor Cottenham's younger brother, jobbed into a bishopric just before Melbourne's government fell) and the influential Lyttelton family liked it. The Commissioners were never happy about it; and when Pepys at last disembarrassed the church of his presence, his higher-minded successor Philpott, supported by a great deal of local opinion, at once declared his wish to give Hartlebury up and move into his diocesan capital.[4]

Hartlebury ought never to have been kept, and most Commissioners must have known it. The plain truth was, that once all the bishops were

---

[1] This was a wild exaggeration; and anyway, Gloucester and Bristol were a special case.

[2] Cathedrals Commission, first report, pp. 568–9.

[3] Letter of 24 December 1836, in P.Ps. 1851, XLII, 272.

[4] 1862–3 committee, 1862 Qs. 424–38.

Commissioners, it was very difficult to stop any one of them getting what he had set his heart on. On principle, the bishops were claiming more and more discretionary authority over their dioceses. This was a central plank in their reformist platform; and it placed each of them in a good position for bargaining against the rest. One bishop, thwarted in his ambition for a new wing to his palace or a better set of stables, could easily turn awkward when another proposed a union of parishes or the redrawing of a diocesan boundary. The atmosphere at the board would have become most unpleasant if the bishops had not in general sunk their differences whenever they could. Inevitably they could most easily do this when the rights and advantages of their own order were under discussion, and, inevitably also, they found it difficult to avoid adopting a colleague's view of his case when he was there at the board to put it before them in person. For this is what in fact often happened. Even when their majority judgment (influenced perhaps by personal dislike, perhaps by the merits of the case, and probably—after 1845 anyway—by their anxiety not to give hostages to their enemies) ran contrary to that of a particular bishop, if he was prepared to turn up and argue it out with them he would, so long as his demand was within the limits of official policy and statutory sanction, be able to have his way.

This happened to Phillpotts. He was present when his formal application to move his palace to an allegedly healthier position was laid before the board. Graham, when commenting soon afterwards on some ignorant and inflammatory high churchman's bland assertion that 'the Commissioners' funds were exhausted', told Peel it was scandalous of Phillpotts to agitate 'to pull down his palace, to move it 100 yards, and to rebuild it out of Church Funds';[1] certainly in this echoing the Commissioners' view. With doubt and disapproval, they decided, when Phillpotts was *not* there, that they thought it more appropriate to do up the old palace; and Railton was sent down to investigate. His report, the report of a good and faithful servant, was in the sense they indicated; but when the board met to receive it, Phillpotts was back, to persuade

[1] 28 December 1842. Brit. Mus. Add. MSS 40488, fos. 148–9. He also censured Bishop Pepys for his insistence on spending thousands of pounds on Hartlebury, 'a country residence 12 miles off'.

them that it was full of fallacies. He stayed around long enough to see the board formally approve the scheme he favoured; thereafter, he did not need to do more than write occasional angry letters.[1]

It was the same with Cuddesdon. Bagot, once safe in the haven of Bath and Wells, and anxious to oblige his brisk young successor-elect, Samuel Wilberforce, who had set his heart on founding a theological college out there, changed his tune about Cuddesdon and enabled Wilberforce to quote to the board his opinion that it was in as good a situation as any and only needed quite modest improvements. The business thereafter went quickly. Wilberforce was in a hurry. No more than a week later he laid the report of his architect, Ferrey, before them. Struggling manfully against fate, they said they would accept it subject to their own architect's report, and moreover asked Wilberforce to consider whether Shotover House would not suit him better. This was almost their last gasp of independence in the matter. No more was heard of Shotover, and Railton had to be instructed to work overtime to keep up with Ferrey. On 28 January 1846, with Wilberforce present, they approved a grant of £3500 towards the new palace, and three weeks later, with him still present to see fair play, they granted a further £1300 for the improvement of the demesne.[2] No more was heard of Cuddesdon for a twelvemonth. Then, on 18 March 1847, came a letter from the bishop, saying that the improvements had cost £1836 more than the estimate, and could he borrow that sum on the security of the estates of the see? Greatly daring, they said No; but they might have saved their breath. A week later Wilberforce was back, to put the motion that the Crown lawyers be consulted as to the legality of granting the bishop of Oxford a mortgage loan. It was carried *nem. con.* Soon after that, Ferrey sent in his certificates of work done and asked to be paid. The board's normal practice was to have such certificates checked by Railton before accepting them; but Wilberforce assured them that all was in order, so the Commissioners took the extraordinary step

[1] Minutes, 22 November 1842, § 6 and 20 December, § 2/3; 7 February 1843, § 2/1 and 21 February, § 2/1.

[2] Minutes, 19 November 1845, § 18 and 26 November, § 13; 21 January 1846, § 14 and 28 January, § 15; 18 February 1846, § 19; partly printed by the 1847–8 committee, 1848 Qs. 564–645.

of dispensing with their usual regulations and accepting them on the spot.[1]

Not merely on account of the necessity or agreeableness of obliging each other did the Commissioners pursue a generous palace policy. By the later forties, indeed, when Cuddesdon, Hartlebury and Manchester were on their agenda, they were becoming anxious not to play into the Midianites' hands, and would rather have spent little than much; but in their early days they were quite magnificently open-handed. The new member of their exclusive club, Longley of Ripon, was made welcome to the tune of nearly £15,000. Originally, after paying £1111 for the site, they had decided not to spend more than £10,000 on his palace; but through a mixture of weakness and generosity the latter estimate was exceeded first by £2000, then by a further £1500.[2] The fact that Longley himself was putting several thousand pounds into it partly excused their lavishness, but the 1847-8 committee would seem to have been justified in complaining, mildly enough, that the original estimates ought to have been more strictly adhered to.

The most deplorable instance of waste and mismanagement was in connexion with the Stapleton estate, four miles from Bristol and more than thirty miles from Gloucester, where Bishop Monk designed to have his dwelling after the union of those two sees. Stapleton was not indeed the only cause of Monk's misfortunes. Before ever it had been mentioned, Monk had made a fool of himself and irritated both Blomfield, Hobhouse, and C. K. Murray by his inept interferences in the sale of the site of the old palace at Bristol; and after the bulk of the Stapleton business had been transacted, its sorry story merged into another episode not much to the credit of Monk's judgment, the affair of the Horfield estates. Glimpses of all this dirty linen were caught by the 1847-8 committee, but it had to wait for Horsman's hostile zeal before it was brought out and washed in public. It shows the Commissioners at their well-meaning worst, and yet, discreditable to them though it undoubtedly was on the whole, there were extenuating circumstances.[3] Most of the trouble came from the division of autho-

---

[1] Minutes, 18 March 1847, § 3 and 25 March, § 17; 6 May, § 22, 20 May, § 18, 3 June, § 22, 1 July, § 26.

[2] 1847-8 committee, 1848 Qs. 239-60.

[3] My brief account of it here is based on the Commissioners' Minutes; the 1847-8 committee, 1848 Qs. 2741-84; the 1862-3 committee, 1862, Qs. 346-54, 1863 Qs.

rity. Monk's architect, Pope, found himself competing with Railton; Monk's agents and solicitors in the west country did things that seemed injudicious or mistaken to the Commissioners and their solicitors; while Monk, who had a guiding hand in much of the business, showed himself to be rather an old woman. This division of authority was fatal. It was far more responsible for the waste and scandal that ensued than was the Commissioners' desire to treat Monk generously; and it was only an extreme instance of a difficulty from which the Commissioners at first could hardly escape. For full efficiency they needed to be sovereign masters in their own house. By the sixties they had become so. But in their early years they often had to share control and the making of policy with deans and chapters and bishops and their subordinates; and the Norwell case[1] showed how unpopular they could become by exercising such sovereignty as they at that period possessed. Usually they managed to come to satisfactory understandings with their enforced collaborators and to avoid frictions or mistakes. But fate ran against them in the Stapleton case, exploiting both their institutional and their human weaknesses to the full.

A history of the united dioceses of Gloucester and Bristol, no less than a biography of Bishop Monk, would have to devote many pages to the Stapleton affair, which was remarkable. The Commissioners had at first intended that the bishop should reside alternately in each of his cathedral cities. Monk, economically minded and determined at any rate not to live in a city that had shown itself so unhealthy for bishops as Bristol, decided in 1840 that if he could get Stapleton, it would suffice on its own. Tied by the terms of the Order in Council which had united the sees, the Commissioners could not oblige him. They approved it as his Bristol residence, and bought it, *without valuation or survey*, for nearly £12,000.[2] Then began the tragi-comedy of the alterations, with Monk's architect and the Commissioners' playing Box and Cox with each other (and Old Harry with the estimates). In the end no less than £12,000—enough to have built a fine new house— was spent in renovating the place. Monk cannot be held at all responsible for at any rate this part of the story. He never wanted so much

1178–1281; and the Returns ordered by Horsman, P.Ps. 1852, xxxviii, 121–329. For the Horfield part of the story, see also *Hansard*, 3/cxviii, 628–40, 656–61, 918–59.

   [1] See below, p. 377.   [2] Murray's evidence, 1847–8 committee, 1848 Qs. 2744–52.

done, and his architect's estimates were always by far the lowest. It was the Commissioners' determination to stick to Railton through thick and thin, and to do the job in style, that was primarily responsible for bumping up the costs.[1]

Thus Monk had Stapleton as his Bristol residence. His successor Charles Baring was as much against Stapleton as Monk had been for it. Very soon after his accession, the house and estate were sold for about £12,000, to be turned into a school. The citizens of Bristol professed themselves much hurt by the whole transaction, in pride and pocket; for £7000 had been raised by local taxation to indemnify the bishop for the damage to the old palace, and now, after all, they had no bishop resident. £12,000 of church money was as if it had never been. If the members of the 1847-8 committee, who were by no means too severe in their criticisms on this department of the Commissioners' work, had foreseen the conclusion of the story, they might well have spoken out more strongly than they did.

3. ESTATES AND LEASES

No part of their work in this period gave the Commissioners more trouble or a worse name than the management and improvement of the property in which they had an interest, direct or indirect. Their interest was direct in estates that became vested in them as existing beneficiaries died (that is, the lands and other properties of suspended stalls, the separate estates of all stalls, and of sinecure rectories); it was indirect and, to begin with, remote, in the cases of the estates of bishops, deans and chapters, whose revenues the Commissioners either shared in or had to augment. Whether they managed the property themselves or merely enjoyed an imprecisely defined power of interfering in some other body's management of it, they were soon embroiled in much difficulty and unpleasantness, because the changes they had to make were so big, and the interest they came into conflict with was so strong. This was the church-lessee interest, still persuading itself, as it had persuaded itself a hundred years before, that the church had no moral right to do what it would with its own, least of all to make as good a thing out of its lands as its lessees made. For well over a century bishops, dignitaries and chapters had been tending to improve their properties

[1] *Ibid.* Qs. 2756-83.

by raising the fines for renewals of leases and by converting leases for three lives into leases for terms of years; and even, though this would seem to have been very rare, by letting leases expire and exploiting their estates by ordinary tenancies at rack-rents.[1] The system of church leases was in most respects an absurd and deplorable one, but it was, before the Ecclesiastical Commissioners arrived on the scene, virtually unbreakable—partly because the breaking of it required of individual clergymen a degree of altruism greater than their age expected of them (greater, often, than they could afford). The system was that they plucked the fruits of their properties mostly in the form of fines; the 'reserved rents', payable annually, were negligible in comparison. This meant that harvests happened, at most, once every seven years, the intervals at which twenty-one year leases were usually renewed. But harvest-time came round less often, and less predictably, when leases of urban house property were granted for forty years,[2] or when leases of farm lands were made for three lives. As lives 'fell in', they might be renewed one by one; in which case the lessor would get his fine not, perhaps, too irregularly. Often the lives would happen to be unusually hearty, or else an individual lessor would 'run his life against theirs', backing himself to outlive all of them and hoping thus to get the maximum fine possible, the fine for a three-lives renewal— taking the risk, of course, of his dying first, and getting nothing at all. If that happened, his successor would walk into a fortuitous and un- deserved fortune.

The demerits of this system were gross and obvious. Nothing could be said in its favour, except that over many years and many clergymen it 'averaged out' fairly enough; one man's disaster was another man's goldmine, lean years had to give way in the end to fat, and so on. At a time when a career in the church was, by those who enjoyed its good things when they were addressing those who hungered for them, seriously likened to participation in a lottery, this argument did not sound too bad; at least it fitted in harmoniously with the rest of the case for leaving the ecclesiastical institutions of the nation alone. There

[1] This seems to be the implication of, e.g., the evidence to the 1837-9 committee on Church Leases, 1838 Qs. 499-503, P.Ps. 1837-8, IX, 42.
[2] Under the 14 Eliz. c. 11 all ecclesiastical corporations, aggregate or sole, except bishops, had power to do this.

was nothing else to be said for it, and everything to be said against it. For each bishop or dignitary who won by it, several lost. A bishop coming new to a see which had just yielded the best part of its fruits to his predecessor might be kept waiting years, and get heavily in debt, before the fines began to come in again. It was not difficult for a really grasping and unscrupulous bishop, or a bishop become imbecile and helpless in the hands of grasping and unscrupulous relations or officials, to milk a see almost dry by grants of 'concurrent leases' and so on. The incomes of all clergymen who relied partly at any rate on fines were bound to be erratic, besides being—as was admitted on all sides—lower than they might be if the land were exploited under the ordinary system of landlord and tenant. The case for change was unanswerable. But who was to make it? To refuse a large fine, a fine that was perhaps five or fifteen years' income in a lump, or to take the smaller fine that went with the conversion of a three-lives lease into a lease for twenty-one years, simply for the good of your successors (persons quite un-known to you) or of 'the church' (if you could conceive of it as an entity) required colossal self-sacrifice and might anyway be made impossible by debts and commitments acquired during the lean years of waiting. Corporations aggregate, who divided a common revenue between them, were in a better position to do what ecclesiastical economists unanimously considered the proper thing; and this no doubt accounts for the fact elicited by the 1837-9 Committee on Church Leases, that whereas bishops had nearly twice as many leases for lives as leases for years, chapters had about four times as many leases for years as leases for lives.[1] But that was as much of an improvement as they could make.

The lessees, on their side, were not so wholly enamoured of the system, which on the whole worked to their advantage, as to be wholly hostile to its reform. If their lease was for three lives, they had in common prudence to insure them. This was always expensive, often difficult, sometimes impossible; and whether their leases were for lives or years, lessees found it awkward and disagreeable to have to sink large lumps of capital in fines, when, for all they knew, they might die a month later. Even though they got the use of the land much more cheaply than if they had to pay rent for it (determining an equivalent to rent

[1] 1839 report, p. ix: P.Ps. 1839, VIII, 245.

by dividing the fine by the number of years it covered), they would often have preferred to rent it in the ordinary way, because the finances of that were simpler to manage. Lessees of church lands, moreover, might find themselves on a knife edge of uncertainty. The ordinary tenant knew just where he stood with regard to improvements, dilapidations and so on; his responsibilities and his landlord's were written into their covenant; and he never doubted that his tenancy could be terminated at any time. He was as clear about his position on the one side as was the freeholder on the other. But the church lessee's peace of mind was easily destroyed. Many lessees alleged, during their campaigns of the thirties and forties, that no shadow of doubt had ever crossed their minds that their tenure was not as secure as a freeholder's, and that their lessor might absolutely refuse to renew their lease; and some were doubtless speaking the truth. But others were certainly whistling to keep their spirits up, and exaggerating for bargaining purposes. The evidence given to the 1837-9 committee showed that on the whole church lands were not being improved in the scientific modern manner as much as freehold lands, that their timber was everywhere in a bad state, and that speculative builders fought shy of it. The reason could only be the uncertainties attaching to such property— uncertainties about the amount by which future fines would be reckoned or raised, uncertainty ultimately about this much-alleged security of tenure.[1] It was thus no wonder that lessees on their side looked hopefully, as did also the more progressive clergy from theirs, towards the idea of 'enfranchisement', the simplification of this unsatisfactory system either by the lessee's purchase of the fee simple of the land or by the lessor's purchase, on the termination of the lease, of the lessee's interest in it. How the terms of these purchases should be calculated, was a question on which lessor and lessee were likely violently to differ. Both really wanted to get rid of the doubts and difficulties attaching to church leases, and to improve the property more than the system permitted, but each saw his own and the other's rights in a different light. And whereas the system did not work wholly to the lessee's advantage, it did so sufficiently to make most clergymen feel that the lessees did well at the church's expense, and *per contra* to rally the lessees into a quite powerful subdivision of the great landed interest.

[1] *Ibid.* pp. xii–xiv/248–50.

Their time came to rally in defence of their rights, as they conceived them, when, from the eighteen-twenties onwards, church reformers began to approach the system of church leases with a new seriousness. Thitherto their wastefulness and irregularity had been deplored without any serious thought of reforming them. The younger Pitt's reform of the Crown's land system (which had been similar to the church's) brought the possibility of a change one step nearer; and indeed, when the talk in respectable circles was increasingly of the need to find funds for church extension and public education, it was inevitable that so obvious a source of additional revenue should attract attention. The 1833 Irish Church Act had contained elaborate provisions for the gradual abolition of the system,[1] aiming to promote as much the comfort of the lessees as the revenues of the church, and thus to benefit church and society at the same time. It was obvious thereafter that the time could not be long delayed when something similar would have to be done for the system in England, whether to raise money to compensate the church for the loss of church rates, to pay for church extension, or (as radicals and dissenters wished) to subsidize education. But the English system turned out to be a harder nut to crack than the Irish, partly because the Church of England was in a much stronger position to fight for its rights, partly because there was not, with regard to the English establishment, that tradition of large-scale legislative interference that there was in respect of the Irish, and partly because the English Ecclesiastical Commissioners (whose institution precipitated the conflict) got going before parliament intervened; whereas parliament's intervention and the foundation of the Irish Church Commissioners happened at the same time, as complementary measures.

The Ecclesiastical Commissioners precipitated the conflict because, as actual 'owners' of some estates and prospective owners of many more, they constituted a completely new kind of lessor, able to view the system in what was, from the lessees' point of view, a revolutionary and menacing way. Their difference from ecclesiastical lessors of the common traditional type lay in the facts, first, that as a corporation, they never died, and so were freed from the necessity to grab what they could whenever it offered; and second, that they were statutorily obliged to take the long-term interests of the whole church into

---

[1] Clauses 128–63.

consideration, which meant that they could be both tough and patient. Over the leasing policy of the ecclesiastical corporations who retained the management of their estates the Commissioners were given some control by an Act of 1842;[1] over their own estates, they were assured first by legal opinion and then by statute that they were absolute masters.[2] They conceived that their duty lay in terminating, so far as circumstances allowed, a system so uneconomic and wasteful, and catching up, so far as they could, on what the church had lost by it over the past three hundred years or so; they gladly admitted that their institution 'prevented the lessees from taking advantage from time to time of the weakness or poverty of the lessor, and . . . enabled [them], as trustees of that property, to do their duty to the Church, and to take care that renewals were not granted but upon fair terms'.[3] The lessees had enjoyed their beneficial leases for long enough. Now it was the church's turn to benefit from what was after all church property—although to listen to Henry Aglionby or John Abel Smith, lessees' spokesmen in the Commons, you would hardly have thought so.

Thus the Commissioners at first inclined to be tough. Some of them must have seen themselves as putting right a very old wrong; the restoration to the church's best advantage of its own lands was easily felt as analogous to the restoration of lay impropriations, which still exercised a fascination over a certain type of romantic pious high-churchman. All of them in any case wanted to increase their funds as quickly as they could. There was so much to be done, and so little money as yet to do it with. Even if a tougher leasing policy was sure to stir up opposition and even cause some hardship among the lessees, it was still their duty to adopt it. In all this they behaved very much in the manner of the Poor Law Commissioners, who were also entrusted by parliament with a task of the greatest public importance—a task very similar, in that it involved the breaking of some very deep-rooted and widely diffused bad habits—which committed them to making themselves unpopular if they were properly to perform it. And like the Poor Law Commissioners, too, they found they were not quite strong enough to do it.

[1] 5 and 6 Vic. c. 108. See above, p. 351. n. 3.
[2] See Murray's evidence to the 1847–8 committee, 1847 Qs. 378–9. The statute was 6 and 7 Vic. c. 37, § 6.
[3] Blomfield's evidence to the 1847–8 committee, 1847 Q. 1275.

But they tried; and it will surprise nobody to learn that Blomfield was apparently in this, as in so much else, their leader. He presented a front of iron to the lessees' representatives on the 1847-8 Committee and made his views almost tactlessly plain. Sir James Graham, who was on the Committee and who felt in exactly the same way, gave him a chance to state them.

Q.1201. Do you think, with reference to the sacred trust exercised by the Ecclesiastical Commissioners, that rules more favourable to lessees could have been granted, in fairness and equity, to the church property?—Most decidedly not; I would never, on any consideration, consent to rules more favourable to the lessees; I consider those rules as favourable to them as they can in equity expect.

Q.1202. Your Lordship, in assenting to those rules, went as far as your conscientious judgment would allow?—I did.

Blomfield was obviously as impatient with rule-of-thumb, traditional, provincial ways of doing business, as he was with the lessees' moans that they were being badly treated. He was sure that nothing lay beyond the powers of well-paid professional experts and a properly-managed bureaucracy. Much of the evidence taken by the 1847-8 committee concerned the wisdom of the Ecclesiastical Commissioners' administering their far-flung estates from a single, central, London office, and making decisions there about rents, leases and so on which—so all the lessees, and some, but by no means all, of the landed interest alleged—could only be properly decided on the spot, by someone familiar with local particularities. Blomfield, for one, thought this was bunkum, and more or less said so, even though his interrogators were mostly hostile and rather better versed in such matters than he was. Nicholl, Aglionby, and Denison brought the matter close home to him.

Q.1266. You are not prepared to recognize a difference between the real market price, whatever may be said of the marketable value, and the tabular price?—No, I am not prepared to give an opinion upon that subject without further enquiry.

Q.1267. If your Lordship were informed that in a large district of England the marketable value exceeded the tabular value by six or eight or ten years, would your Lordship think it right to adhere to the tabular value?—I should not think that we were bound by the practice in any particular part of England.

Q.*1268*. Then you do not give the market price?—I will not say that.

Q.*1270*. Would not that be much better ascertained by local inquiry than by taking down a book from the shelf, and ascertaining the tabular value?—I should say the value of the thing is to be ascertained by the valuation of the surveyor and the actuary, and not by the custom of this or that part of the country.

Q.*1271*. Does not that cease to be the market price, and become a tabular price?—It ceases to be the market price in your opinion, but not in mine, or in that of the Church Commissioners.

How the squires must have hated him!

Blomfield was not the only Commissioner to think in these terms. Some Commissioners, indeed, were softer, either through conviction or coercion. Bishop Kaye seems to have been put under pressure by Evelyn Denison to take a softer line, and this was advocated also by J. G. Shaw Lefevre, who though in some respects an opinionated busybody, was not likely tamely to swallow another man's doctrine.[1] Yet Graham and Goulburn were both for being tough,[2] and they did not lack outside support. Many churchmen presumably were of a mind with Roundell Palmer, the future Lord Selborne, who said at the close of the debate on the Episcopal and Capitular Estates Management Bill that the lessees' claim to beneficial terms of enfranchisement was 'a claim by private individuals, for their private interests, against the public; a claim founded on no legal or equitable right—founded on nothing but this, that a course of mismanagement by those intrusted with the administration of the public interests in respect of church property had existed for a considerable period, from which the lessees, as a body, had derived large benefits, and they, to a certain extent, had the expectation of continuing to derive those benefits.' To the argument that, whatever the merits of the case in abstract, the lessees in fact had a

[1] See their letters and statements, cited in the 1847–8 committee's report—P.Ps. 1847–8, VII, 530–3.

[2] See particularly Graham's contribution to the debate on the Episcopal and Capitular Estates Management Bill, 4 August 1851 (*Hansard*, 3/cxviii, 1869 ff.), and John Abel Smith's suspicions of Goulburn (*ibid*. 1907 f.) which Goulburn soon proved to have been perfectly correct when he tried, vainly, to convince Lord Chichester and Shaw Lefevre on the Estates Committee that they were not bound to enfranchise their own estates on the same terms as parliament had prescribed for those under episcopal and capitular management. (1856 committee, Q. 3067).

long-standing vested interest, he bluntly replied that a man could not 'acquire a vested interest in the mismanagement of public property'.[1]

It was not until about 1845 that the Ecclesiastical Commissioners' policy towards lessees began to be made a matter of notoriety. Most lessees in the early years accepted the terms the Commissioners offered.[2] Of course they must often have thought the terms hard—so much of the argument turned on what was 'fair', that inevitably there was much disagreement—but they received no public encouragement to stand up for themselves until the celebrated Norwell case came to a head in 1845. Norwell was a village in Nottinghamshire, roughly equidistant from Newark and Southwell. Nearly 2000 acres of the parish was leased from three Southwell prebends earmarked for suppression by the Cathedrals Act, and suppressed very soon afterwards. The land had passed to the Ecclesiastical Commissioners by the winter of 1841-2, and the more substantial lessees were beginning to ask the Commissioners how they intended to proceed. The property was occupied by half a hundred farmers, some very small, and it clearly needed rationalization; the Commissioners, therefore, beyond refusing for the time being to renew leases, and setting unacceptably stiff terms for enfranchisement, more or less stalled until they could get the estate properly surveyed and make a business-like decision on it; which was not finally accomplished until 1844.[3] What was happening at Norwell in 1841-2 stirred up only local waters, but in 1845 it began to excite a wider public, principally because Evelyn Denison, the strong-minded member for the West Riding, who was lessee of a small part of the property, acquired a strong impression that the Commissioners' policy was mistaken, that their ways of doing business were faulty, and that their secretary—whom he discovered to be the power behind their thrones—was not to be trusted. He argued his case with the Commissioners, their solicitor and their surveyor, more pertinaciously than anyone had yet done, and was the institutor of the 1847-8 select committee.[4] John Abel Smith, the member for Chichester, and then forty other members of parliament rallied to his standard, forming a

[1] 6 August 1851, *Hansard*, 3/CXVIII, 1909 ff.
[2] 1847-8 committee, 1847 Qs. 1203-5.
[3] See Murray's evidence to the 1847-8 committee, 1847 Qs. 358-80.
[4] 15 June 1847, *Hansard*, 3/XCIII, 596-7.

committee to foment opposition, by advertisements in papers, propaganda 'in Cathedral towns and in other neighbourhoods in which Church property was known to be situated', and so on. Six thousand lessees were soon banded together under the presidency of the Duke of Richmond, with the committee of members of parliament conveniently in London to conduct their lobbying.[1]

All this organized opposition grew up subsequent to the bursting of the Norwell case upon the public. The name of Norwell became, like that of Stapleton, a byword and a reproach. It was for the Ecclesiastical Commissioners what the Andover scandal was for the Poor Law Commissioners, and it had results exactly the same—parliamentary committees of inquiry, the stimulating of extra-parliamentary opposition, and the remodelling of their constitution. Denison's committee concerned itself as much with their constitution as with their management, and made important recommendations thereon.[2] The core of those recommendations lay in placing the management of the Commissioners' estates under a small permanent board of lay churchmen. As to the principles which should guide their relations with lessees, however, Denison's committee was vague; it merely remarked 'that either further consideration of their rules and practice by the Commission, or the interposition of Parliament, will be required in order that transactions between the Commission and the lessees may be carried generally to a satisfactory issue.'[3] The matter was left over for further and specialised consideration.

This it received at once from the Episcopal and Capitular Revenues Commission, which, appointed on 8 January 1849, made its two reports on 31 January and 30 July 1850; it consisted of the second Lord Harrowby, Dean Lyall, William Page Wood (solicitor-general, soon to be Lord Hatherley), Robert Armstrong, Richard Jones the tithes commissioner, and the ubiquitous J. G. Shaw Lefevre, who was probably its leading light.[4] Their commission instructed them to consider how

---

[1] E. J. Smith, *Two Letters to the Archbishop of Canterbury on the Origin and Progress of the Ecclesiastical Commission*, p. 21., and W. H. Grey, *Church Leases* (third edn., 1851), *passim*. Grey, an accountant of 48 Lincoln's Inn Fields, was the committee's secretary, enroller of recruits, distributor of propaganda and proforma petitions, etc.

[2] See below, p. 395.   [3] Report, 1848, p. xi.

[4] P.Ps. 1850, xx, 35–362.

church lands could be 'rendered most productive and beneficial to the Church, and most conducive to the spiritual welfare of the people, due regard being had to the just and reasonable claims of the present holders of such property'. This 'just and reasonable' clearly directed them to find in the lessees' favour. They did so, and a bill based on their reports was introduced into the Lords by the Earl of Carlisle in the spring of 1851. To the sterner kind of churchman this bill was unacceptable, because it gave the church only an inferior share of its lands' improved value; and although it gave the lessees nothing to complain about, a candid friend of theirs could maintain that they would be better off in the long run if the land were properly enfranchised and they were able to become either full owners or conventional tenants, instead of having to pay large perpetual rent-charges. With these arguments as well as their duty to the church to steel them, Blomfield and the arch-bishop had little difficulty in getting the bill extensively overhauled by a select committee of the upper house;[1] it was given a much more Blomfieldian look; and in that form, without significant alteration beyond the solicitor-general's insertion of the magic words 'just and reasonable claims' in the first clause, it became law for three years at the very end of the same session.[2] The lessees did not at first much like it, but at that stage of the session their strength was much reduced. Colonel Sibthorp sounded the dominant note of their opposition at the start of the debate on the second reading, by stating simply that it was too late for so important a bill, what with 'grouse shooting approaching, and Goodwood races on, and other amusements.'[3] Page Wood's insertion of their shibboleth, together with the limitation of the act to three years, went far to reassure them, and the dislike shown for Page Wood's amendment by the Ecclesiastical Commissioners' spokesmen, Cardwell and Graham, reassured them still more. The lessees' committee apparently gave it their blessing,[4] and by the end of the debate Aglionby and Abel Smith were under the impression that their side had won.[5]

---

[1] 22 May 1851 (debate on its second reading), *Hansard*, 3/cxvi, 1207 ff.; and E. J Smith's *Two Letters*, p. 25.

[2] 14 and 15 Vic. c. 104, passed on 8 August.

[3] 31 July 1851, *Hansard*, 3/cxviii, 1786–7.

[4] See Cardwell's comments, 4 August, on Aglionby's volte-face from hostility to approval: *ibid.* 1866–7.   [5] 6 August, *ibid.* 1907–9.

They may have been right; if they were, the bill—virtually Blomfield's last triumph—must be applauded as an example of that happiest species of legislation, which gives to every party the impression that its interest has been secured; for the Commissioners and their publicists seem subsequently all to have agreed that it settled the dispute fairly enough from the point of view of the church.

The Act did not directly affect the Commissioners' own estates. It was aimed rather at the estates still under the bishops' and chapters' management, as most of the church lands still were, and as they were then expected to remain. The Ecclesiastical Commissioners hardly came into it at all; bishops and chapters were to deal not with them but with the three new Church Estates Commissioners,[1] whose approval of the terms was indispensable to any enfranchisement. As members of the Estates Committee and managers of the Ecclesiastical Commissioners' estates, the Estates Commissioners were not bound to pay attention either to this act or to the resolutions of the Lords' Committee which had formed it. But Lord Chichester and Shaw Lefevre were sure they ought to do so, and Goulburn was not long in coming round to their opinion.[2] The whole of the church lands were thus brought under the operation of a single set of principles, and their enfranchisement proceeded quickly and quietly. The lessees' agitation dropped as suddenly as it had arisen; the terms of enfranchisement proved universally acceptable, and even Henry Aglionby, who, as Shaw Lefevre remarked, in a masterpiece of understatement, 'took a very strong interest in this subject, and maintained rather strong opinions in favour of the rights of lessees', was satisfied.[3] The progress of enfranchisement was rapid. By the eighteen-eighties it was almost complete, and a minor revolution in the English land system had been safely accomplished.

4. SECRETARIAL AND CONSTITUTIONAL DIFFICULTIES

The Commissioners' constitution caused far more trouble in this period than it had done earlier, but it did so for different and more interesting reasons. Earlier, the complaint had been that the board was too small and too exclusive. Exclusive after 1840 it might still be, but no one could complain that it was too small. From thirteen it swelled overnight

[1] See below, p. 396. [2] 1856 committee, Q. 3067. [3] 1856 committee, Q. 1833.

to forty-eight. Not all of them bothered to come. Some of the laymen were too busy: the ministerial members came but rarely, and the only one of the six judges to attend with any regularity was, understandably enough, the judge of the prerogative court. Some bishops kept right away. G. H. Law of Bath and Wells never came but once; he was very old. Bagot of Oxford and (after 1845) Bath and Wells hardly ever came. This is puzzling. He seems not to have been particularly decrepit,

	1840–1		1841–2		1842–3		1843–4		1844–5		1845–6		1846–7		Total
---	G	C	G	C	G	C	G	C	G	C	G	C	G	C	
Total	22	27	18	26	35	37	22	50	26	63	39	68	27	46	506
hbishop of Canterbury	22	18	16	16	32	32	21	16	21	16	31	1	19	4	265
ιop of London	19	21	14	20	22	23	18	30	20	31	31	26	25	26	326
ιop of Rochester	8	8	9	6	18	19	6	10	14	19	27	21	14	11	190
ιop of Bangor	5	6	8	13	15	16	11	11	8	24	18	24	10	18	187
ιop of Hereford	6	6	6	10	10	10	7	17	11	16	14	27	15	17	172
ιop of Ely	9	6	4	4	—	—	7	8	10	24	19	22	20	33	166
ιop of Salisbury	4	7	10	16	12	14	7	15	7	12	11	18	10	8	151
ιop of Winchester	5	7	4	8	14	13	4	9	8	17	13	15	8	8	133
ιop of Lichfield	9	7	—	—	—	—	16	30	13	25	9	19	4	6	138
ιop of Llandaff	4	3	4	2	13	12	10	9	11	15	10	2	10	13	118
ιop of Chester	4	1	5	8	13	12	4	6	9	15	11	4	8	5	105
ιop of Chichester	1	1	6	2	14	11	1	3	11	7	17	15	2	3	94
n of Westminster	—	—	—	—	19	19	19	40	17	34	6	2	2	4	162
of Besborough	7	—	11	9	28	28	15	30	14	36	21	32	—	—	231
ιry Hobhouse	7	12	7	11	8	9	7	17	7	25	12	32	13	23	190
ge of Prerog. Court	15	7	4	—	13	12	4	—	—	—	10	—	4	—	69
of Devon*	—	—	5	7	14	13	6	1	8	13	13	13	12	28	133
John Nicholl	7	3	7	3	16	13	3	6	9	29	6	14	4	8	128

pointed Feb. 1842.

TABLE 2. Attendances of commissioners who came to at least a quarter of the General and/or Committee Meetings, August 1840 to June 1847.

and since he was also dean of Canterbury he should have been doubly diligent in attendance; upon him, after all, as upon the dean of St Paul's (who was also bishop of Llandaff) and the dean of Westminster (who was soon to be bishop of Ely) the lower clergy relied for the safeguarding of their interests. But he was at only 20 general meetings out of 189, and 12 committee meetings out of 317. Davys of Peterborough and Carey of St Asaph were the other episcopal absentees.[1]

These defections were of little importance. There were plenty of other Commissioners, and on an average ten or eleven would be present, bishops always outnumbering the lay members by at least two to one. The charge was still brought against the Commissioners that, because of the continued preponderance of prelates, the interests of that class were given prior and undue attention—a charge in which there was, as we have seen, a little substance. Nevertheless this was not the main charge brought against them in respect of their constitution. What seemed more undesirable and ominous to the Commissioners' critics, and to some of the lay Commissioners themselves, was the lack of system and continuity in their management of their affairs, and the way in which that management consequently passed largely into the hands of their permanent staff; which meant, as the office was then constituted, into the hands of the Secretary, Murray.

This lack of continuity between meetings and in the conduct of business was one of the defects most conclusively brought home to the Commissioners by the Commons' Committee in 1847-8. It happened partly because the chairman was forever changing. The Commissioner 'first in rank and precedence' had to preside[2] This meant the archbishop of Canterbury, whenever he came; and since he came to the general meetings so often, they at least were usually conducted by a constant chairman. But he had many other calls on his time and intellect, and the Commissioners' business was expanding on every side. Even had he been a good man of business, he must have found it hard to keep abreast of all the work and understand it fully. As it was, his age and nature quite prevented him from doing what circumstances anyway made so difficult. When the Archbishop was away, the next in precedence took the chair, whoever he was; and if a senior came in late, the chair would be—*had* to be, according to the statute—yielded up to him. What a game of musical chairs could result from these observances was shown at the general meeting on 15 April 1845, when the chair was occupied in succession by the bishop of Winchester, the

---

[1] These figures are drawn from the tabular statement of attendances, 1840-7, printed as appendix H.2 to the 1847-8 committee's 1847 report.

[2] 6 and 7 Wm. IV c. 77, s. 6.

bishop of London, the earl of Devon, the Lord President of the Council, and, finally, the Archbishop of Canterbury.

This was ridiculous, and appallingly unbusinesslike, but not the only factor making for a discontinuity and flabbiness in the control of the Commissioners' business. The facts were, that the volume of their business was growing fast, and that they were constitutionally unsuited to control it. It increasingly required full-time attention, and none of the Commissioners was able to give it the whole of his attention, uninterruptedly. To begin with, the work had been light and simple. The small board of 1836-40 had no difficulty in understanding everything that was going on. As the work grew in scale and complexity after 1840, the Commissioners naturally had recourse to the expedient of committees. At first they rubbed along in a general committee. Particular members of the board would informally assume responsibility for particular pieces of business, and, as Murray explained to the 1847 committee in an incautious phrase, 'work them through the committee'.[1] Soon, however, this very informal way of running committees was found inadequate, and they began to meet in select committees, some standing (for estates, finance, new parishes, and episcopal incomes), some temporary *ad hoc*. But although many were committed, few made a quorum. It only needed three of its twenty-two members to make a meeting of the estates committee; and since Murray was secretary to all the committees, their existence did little to reduce his importance.[2] Indeed, they probably only made his omniscience and energy more obvious. A policy of *divide et impera* would have come very easily to him.

Murray the Secretary thus became a great man at the Ecclesiastical Commissioners. In the forties he became *the* great man, greater than Blomfield, as the 1847-8 committee correctly suspected. Blomfield's evidence to that committee showed that he had complete confidence in Murray, and that he was well content to leave him in absolute charge of the office and the finance, which, he several times remarked—as if to throw a smoke-screen around the secretary—were of only secondary importance in comparison with the great spiritual work on which the

[1] Incautious, because in early Victorian England the verb 'to work' could mean to exploit. ('I'll work him!' was how Soapey Sponge expressed to himself his intention to fleece one of his hosts.) The radicals made merry with this phrase later on.

[2] See his evidence to the 1847–8 committee, 1847 Qs. 120–54.

Commissioners were engaged. If Blomfield, who was not only an excellent man of business but had also peculiar claims to be regarded as the chief of the Commissioners, saw eye to eye with Murray, and was happy to leave so much to him, no other Commissioner was likely to object. Sir James Graham, than whom there can have been no harder head on the board, conspicuously stood up for Murray at the committee's hearings.[1] When Graham and Peel were discussing church extension in the autumn of 1842, it was to Murray they went for information, ideas, and the draft outline of an appropriate statute. In the course of preparing it, he went down to Dorset and spent several days at Henry Hobhouse's.[2] Whatever else he was, Murray was clearly a capable confidential servant, well on top of his work, wholly acceptable to his superiors.

Outside Whitehall Place, however, a different impression of Murray was entertained. His public image was that of a ruthless, heartless bureaucrat, engrossing power and using it for un-English ends—the aggrandisement of ecclesiastical power, disrespect towards the landed interest, the conversion of the good old landlord-tenant relationship (so easy to sentimentalize!) into hard business terms. This image was very similar to that entertained, not without some justice, of Edwin Chadwick, secretary to the Poor Law Commission; and Murray's reputation may well have suffered through its inevitable linking with his more famous contemporary. It was customary in most political circles, and virtually *de rigueur* outside them, to suspect the worst of the executive government and to call its zealous officers into contempt. The 1847-8 committee shared these tendencies and grilled Murray mercilessly. He seems to have stood up to it very well, and was never at a loss for an answer. They asked him 962 questions in all, spread out through the whole length of their sitting. Sometimes he was told to wait outside while they elicited, from other witnesses, facts or judgments that might, when they called Murray back, confound him. In front of other witnesses, his particular enemies (Denison, Smith,

[1] E.g., by intervening after a damaging barrage from Evelyn Denison or Smith to feed him helpful leading questions. Qs. 294-321.

[2] See Hobhouse's letter to Kaye, 19 November 1842, Kaye Correspondence 10/18; and, among various of the letters passing between Graham, Peel, Goulburn and Gladstone that autumn, especially Graham's of 1 December 1842, Brit. Mus. Add. MSS 40448, fos. 1-6.

Horsman) did not scruple to show that they not only disliked him and deplored his methods, but also doubted his honesty.

When the committee made their report, there was no division of opinion over their criticism of his actual official activities. Murray was obviously the target of their recommendation that steps should be taken to prevent 'a larger power' being thrown 'into the hands of the officers of the Commission than is fitting should fall to their share'.[1] Members of the committee could agree on this whether they disliked Murray or not. He had undoubtedly acquired virtual control of the Commission. This was not necessarily to his discredit. It pleased his personal enemies and the enemies of the kind of strong, centralizing executive power that he represented to believe that his power was the fruit of deliberate plotting and sinister ambition. It need not have been so. Someone had to hold all sides of the board's business together. None of the Commissioners had the brain *and* the time to do it. Murray, who was paid to give the time and who naturally had the brain, inevitably gravitated into his dominant position. 'Is not the only person who is cognizant of the train of business the secretary?' 'Yes,' answered Blomfield, 'in the proper sense of the term.'[2] They pressed Blomfield further but he steadfastly discouraged them from trying to push him into making statements damaging to the secretary's character. The committee's next witness, Bishop Short, was however of softer stuff and they became bolder, showing without reserve how far their suspicions went.

Q.1088, Mr. F. Baring. Does your Lordship believe there is sufficient control over the proceedings of the secretary of the Board?—I think there might be; but whether there is, I cannot pretend to say.

Q.1089. Who is it that really does the business, the secretary or the Board?—The secretary frequently asks the advice of the Board, but the detail business is of course done by the secretary.

Q.1090, Mr. Acland. Has he the power of selecting individuals whom he will consult?—Of course he has; but it is only in preparing business for the committee or for the Board.

Q.1091. Is it practically possible for the secretary to pack the committees who shall consider business, and get the decision of those committees subsequently confirmed by the Commission?—Certainly not.

[1] Report, 1848, p. iv.   [2] 1847, Q. 1060.

Q.1092, Mr Aglionby. Is it not practicable that the secretary might select the business to be brought before the Committee or the Board, and also to select the form and mode in which it shall be presented to them?—From the abundance of business it is almost impossible but that the secretary must have something of that power.

The bishop added, as a good Commissioner, 'I do not think it is possible that he could exercise any unfairness'; but several members of the committee were not so sure.

Many members of the public were not so sure either. One of them, inevitably, was Horsman, member for Cockermouth, self-appointed scourge of the establishment, and not a member of the 1847-8 committee until its second session. *The Times*, no friend to the establishment in the forties or fifties, thought Horsman went too far; but, accepting it as inevitable that so independent and inexhaustible a guardian of the public weal should embody elements of the buffoon and the liar, extended to him a patronizing, qualified approval. It likened him to the gadfly that chased Io (when Zeus had changed her into a heifer) all over the world. Horsman had become an 'ecclesiastical *aestrum*. Every now and then a whizz is heard, and the indefatigable tormentor digs his sting into the glossy coats of Bishops, Deans, Chapters and well-beneficed clergymen. Should they wish to enjoy any repose, and ruminate on the receipts of a plurality or a stall; should they show any disposition to enjoy themselves in a world of woe, or to consult their own convenience in a self-denying profession, the fatal buzz will be heard.'[1] The 1847-8 committee brought much grist to Horsman's mill. The lively picture he gave the Commons of Murray's ascendancy in Whitehall Place, while clearly extravagant and hostile, was not essentially too inaccurate; it was a caricature, but a good one. 'He was the sun of the whole system, round which the prelates revolved in turn; it was with him not *Ego et Rex Meus* but *Ego et Episcopi Mei*.' Murray was 'at once omniscient, omnipresent, and peripatetic'.

Did a prelate wish to sell an estate? He managed the Order in Council. Was another to build a palace? He found the cash. Had the Commission got into a scrape by what is vulgarly termed a job? The secretary 'made things pleasant'. Was it necessary to mystify and bamboozle Parliament? The secretary cooked the accounts. Was there an awkward question to be asked

[1] 18 May 1848, p. 4d, Second Leader.

in the House of Commons?—The secretary prompted the Prime Minister. In fact, concluded Horsman amidst laughter, 'I never yet gave notice of a motion respecting the Commissioners that I did not see in next morning's paper the unfailing paragraph—"The Secretary of the Ecclesiastical Commissioners had a long interview with the First Lord of the Treasury at his official residence in Downing Street".'[1]

Murray's position as both secretary and treasurer (for he combined both offices, under section 91 of the Cathedrals Act) did in fact put him in a position of this nature; and (the Commissioners' constitution and business being what they were) little blame need have accrued to them, and no shame at all to Murray, for its being so. It was explicable, it was undesirable, and it was remediable. All men of good will could have agreed on those propositions, and that would have been the end of the matter. But, unhappily for everybody concerned, it was not to be dismissed so easily. The committee, which hinted so much to Murray's discredit, signed its report on 14 August 1848. A twelvemonth later, Murray appropriated to his own use about £7000 of the Commissioners' money. There is no reason to suppose that he was lying when he told them that, being in great financial distress, he had only 'borrowed' it and that he meant to pay it back. In fact he proved unable to do so. The Commissioners got back about £1000 in all, and lost the rest. Every suspicion which had been voiced or hinted in the 1847-8 committee, and of which in the ordinary course nothing further might have been heard, suddenly acquired a new vitality. Was Charles Knight Murray a villain after all?

The evidence is uncertain, and insufficient to permit a clear verdict either way. 'Villain' *must* be too strong a word. But his record suggests that he was something of a buccaneer. He did his work too well and satisfied men who were far too sharp to be easily taken in (no one could have fooled Peel, Blomfield, Graham and Hobhouse over a course of fifteen years) for any straight indictment of villainy to stand. Yet he was not a simple character, and some parts of his history, which viewed in isolation would seem insignificant enough, when taken together make him either a bit of a rogue or else a most remarkably unlucky man.

[1] This is a conflation of the versions given in *The Times*, 6 February 1850, p. 3e, and *Hansard*, 3/CVIII, 348 ff., which are rather different.

In the first place he was virtually irremoveable. Clause 91 of the Act of 1840 united the offices of treasurer and secretary (thus reversing the Act of 1836) and named Charles Knight Murray as holder of the joint office 'so long as he shall well demean himself therein.' This very unusual provision secured him the job until he should resign or die. The 1847-8 committee took great exception to it.[1] They tried hard to discover how the clause—so extraordinary and improper—had got into the statute, but no one could tell them. Lord Seymour and Evelyn Denison one after another questioned Blomfield about it but he could, or would, remember nothing to the point.[2] They did not question Murray himself about it, presumably because they thought it indelicate and ungentlemanly, or because by his answer he might have incriminated himself; but they clearly concluded, as did the world at large, that Murray had slipped the clause in himself.

Then there were the other Murrays who appeared from time to time on the Commissioners' payroll. Principal among these was Charles's brother John Murray, solicitor, partner in the firm of Meadows White and Murray who did most of the Commissioners' routine legal work.[3] The circumstances in which he entered into that partnership are curious. A committee which met late in July 1842, only Blomfield, Goulburn and Lord Wharncliffe being present, complimented John Meadows White on the work he had just done for the board in respect of tithe commutation and advised that 'his services should be secured on behalf of the board'. Then they found 'that Mr John Murray, of the firm of Murrays & Rymer who have hitherto been employed by the treasurer in all other matters requiring such legal assistance as cannot be afforded by the solicitors to the Treasury, has entered into partnership with Mr White; and they accordingly recommend that Messrs. White and Murray be continued to be employed jointly as the attornies and solicitors to the Commissioners.'[4] This looks so much like a put-up

[1] They recommended that 'an arrangement should be made with Mr Murray by which he should hold office during pleasure, as he did when he was originally appointed'; and that the office should be held on those terms ever thereafter.

[2] 1847, Qs. 1044–6, 1061–5. I get a strong impression that these questions embarrassed him.

[3] The relationship was attested before the 1847 committee, Q. 1098.

[4] This was accepted by the board a few days later. (Minutes, 28 July and 2 August 1842, printed as appendix H.7 to the 1847-8 committee's 1847 report).

job, that one can hardly doubt it was one. But John was not the only brother to share the loaves and fishes. Another brother was briefed as Commissioners' counsel by Messrs. Meadows White and Murray when they opposed the Rye and Derwent Drainage Bill in 1846.[1] Horsman seems to have been strictly within his rights in speaking of 'a gathering of the whole clan Murray—Murray *primus* as promoter; another Murray as agent; and Murray *tertius*, in wig and gown, to conduct the case as counsel'.[2] An Adam Murray appears, very suspiciously, as conducting some of the Commissioners' estate management in Kent late in 1841.[3] There may well have been others.

Next, there were the 'misunderstandings' of May-June 1845, suggestive in themselves of unamiable traits in Murray's character, and introductory to the last and fatal phase in his official career. Murray and the assistant secretary J. J. Chalk had a row. It must have been going on for some time before Murray lodged a formal complaint against Chalk at the close of the general committee meeting of 20 May 1845, when the matter was referred to the committee on management. Chalk, in his turn, complained that Murray was spending too much time away from the office on other business. The committee, under the presidency of Lord Besborough, sorted it all out, and pronounced a general pacification on 5 June. They refused to comment on the justice of the charges that had been made but, by reorganising the office and awarding to Chalk a larger share of responsibility for his own department, and by stipulating that both of them 'should devote the whole of their time during official hours exclusively to the business of the office unless with the special permission of the Commissioners', indicated that Chalk's complaints were the more just.[4]

This was only the beginning of Murray's troubles; for it brought to the board's notice, what they seem thitherto to have been unaware of, that Murray was conducting an active business life outside the office, and particularly in that most fascinating but dangerous of all business

---

[1] 1847 committee, Q. 1139.

[2] 5 February 1850. *Hansard*, 3/cviii, 357, and *The Times* as cited in p. 387 n. 1, above.

[3] Minutes, 7 December 1841.

[4] Committee Minutes, 20, 23, 29, 31 May, 5, 18, 25 June 1845. 1847 committee, Q. 1128. The relevant papers are in C.C.F. 8034(1).

speculations in the mid-forties—railways. Late in 1844, Murray had become a director of the South-Eastern, or London and Dover, Company. The committee of management were quite right to be concerned about it. Before the middle of June, they had made him resign from the directorship; and that might have been the end of it, had there not almost at once been published, as a parliamentary paper, a 'List of Subscribers of £2000 or more to Railway Subscription Contracts deposited in the Private Bill Office, 1845'. Therein the Commissioners had the gratification of beholding that, although George Hudson was down for £319,835, G. C. Glynn for only half as much, and Mayer A. Rothschild for a beggarly £30,000, their secretary was down for £4500 as Murray of 5 Whitehall Place, and £574,800—all of it in the South-Eastern—as Murray of Notting-hill Square.[1] Hastily a special general meeting was called to consider this new aspect of their secretary, and the committee of management deputed to ascertain at once how Murray stood, and to consult the Treasury solicitors.[2] Murray's explanations seem to have been perfectly satisfactory. He had already resigned his directorship, and he had only allowed himself to be put down for so huge a sum in the first place because he had been assured by the lawyers who advised on the form of the contract that he would incur 'no liability beyond the actual amount of interest' he held in the company—i.e., that he had no liability for the several hundred thousand pounds' worth of stock he undertook to get taken up, but only for what he had in fact taken up himself. This account presumably was true enough.[3] But alas for Murray!—The Treasury solicitor opined that if the railway failed, he would be liable for the whole sum down against his name; and the committee can have had no difficulty in crediting Murray's 'anxiety to relieve himself, as far as possible, from the liability in which, as a trustee, he was placed'.[4]

Here was the beginning of the end, for Charles Knight Murray. His

---

[1] P.Ps. 1845, XL, 97. [2] 28 June 1845.

[3] It seems that the South-Eastern was peculiarly unhappy in its lawyers. No other railway undertaking listed in that Parliamentary Paper showed anything like so concentrated a degree of investment. See under Mills, Rich, Smale, Thomas and Winslow. They left the regular railway kings standing.

[4] The more important Minutes bearing on this episode are printed in appendices H.8 and 8b to the 1847–8 committee's 1847 report.

thirst for gold undid him. The anxiety under which he now lived must have been awful. The Commissioners too must have been anxious, however well he continued to do his work. He lived beneath the shadows of bankruptcy, gaol and failure. What his life was like outside the office, and into what other trouble he might have got, we cannot tell; but he sealed his fate as secretary and treasurer to the Ecclesiastical Commissioners when, sometime in February 1849, he diverted to his own account a draft for £2811 12s. od. from Canon Cust, a payment in respect of the suspended canonries at Windsor, and did away with the letter of advice that accompanied it. Thrice subsequently he repeated his exploit, covering his tracks by intercepting and taking from the office messenger, on his way to the post, the accountant's letters of reminder to these debtors-apparent. The truth came out when Murray either failed to intercept one of these letters, or the accountant, becoming suspicious, took care that they should not be intercepted. Whichever it was, the accountant had proof of Murray's defalcation by the latter days of September. He informed the prime minister, and a special meeting was called on the 25th. Murray, by now irrevocably broken, made a clean breast of it—'he could say nothing in extenuation; he knew the nature of his offence, and had not a word to say in extenuation; he threw himself entirely on the mercy of the Board, and only trusted that the Commissioners would not judge of his previous conduct as a servant of the Board by the sad event which had now occurred'. He resigned on the spot, and gave them £600 as a first instalment of his debt.[1]

The Commissioners did not prosecute him as they might have done. Inevitably, the Horsmans of this world did what Murray begged the Commissioners not to do—they read the whole of his history in the light of his fall, saw in clause 91 of the 1840 Act his first step towards fraud, and, by disregarding the chronological facts, managed to convince themselves that the financial rearrangements settled by the committee of management on 18 and 25 June 1845 were the consequence of the Commissioners' discovery of Murray's railway interests. The Commissioners were more humane towards their fallen servant, who, to do him justice, appears to have done everything he could to satisfy

[1] The Minutes and schedules relative to Murray's fall are printed in P.Ps. 1850, XLVII, 97–100.

them. His furniture and plate brought in £350 odd, the sale of his contingent interest in his wife's marriage settlement (she was 37, twenty years younger than he) brought in £128 more; a few more hundreds turned up; and when, like Mr Micawber, he sailed away with his wife and children to re-establish his fame in Australia, it was in the hope that he might thus the more quickly repay his creditors. The Commissioners made no objection to his going, and his last letter to them, in a hand rather less firm and dashing than it had wont to be, was not without dignity. 'I will not', he wrote from 14 Great Coram Street on 10 June 1852, 'look for any answer to this communication; but I will entertain the hope that your Board, so long as they find that my future career is consistent with that which preceded the painful disruption of my connexion with them, will continue to exercise the forbearance for which I have hitherto had reason to thank them.' In Australia he recouped both fortune and honour. His earlier experience quickly took him to the posts of parliamentary draftsman to the government of New South Wales and chief commissioner in lunacy. When he died, on 14 June 1865, at his residence four miles outside Sydney, he was senior member of the New South Wales bar.[1]

The character of Charles Knight Murray, seen through such scanty evidence as is available, still seems enigmatic. Was his fatal lapse in 1849 the only discreditable incident in an ambitious and bold man's otherwise honest career? Most likely, it was. The Commissioners' remarkable generosity towards him could hardly otherwise be explained. The other questionable aspects of his official career (except perhaps for that extraordinary clause 91 of 3 and 4 Vic. c. 113, if he really was responsible for it) are after all susceptible of a generous interpretation. He wanted money and position, he was forceful and ambitious to the point of recklessness, he could be an overbearing colleague or master, and, when in on a good thing, he made sure of letting his family in on it too. But in these things he was but a child of his age; Murray's jobbing of his brother into the solicitorship was neither better nor worse than Blomfield's, Kaye's, Phillpotts' and Sumner's gifts of good livings and archdeaconries to their sons. And whatever his faults, Murray was clearly a first-rate secretary. The Ecclesiastical Commissioners would

[1] This is taken from the *Sydney Herald's* obituary notice, which, with other material used for this account of Murray's fall and recovery, lies in C.C.F.8039.

hardly have been the same without him, and among the laymen whose names are listed in the Church of England's roll of honour, he is surely one of the more remarkable.

Murray had a conspicuous share in creating the three Church Estates Commissioners, and the Commissioners' Estates Committee. The Ecclesiastical Commissioners as set up by the Act of 1840 had been found too large, fluctuating and inexpert a body to do their job efficiently. Something smaller and more professional had to take their place, or (for men differed as to what precisely should be done) take up a place by their side. This was as necessary in the interests of efficiency as of political morality. Executive boards of commissioners were bad enough (to the common mind of the eighteen-forties) without being so ill-constituted as to throw power into the hands of a politically irresponsible man like Murray. The fresh memory of his secretaryship undoubtedly helped through parliament in 1850 the Act that prevented the recurrence of such a disaster, and he had to that extent some responsibility for it. Three others however were more directly and deliberately responsible—Lord John Russell, prime minister from 1846 to 1851, Sir George Grey his home secretary (and thus, virtually, minister for ecclesiastical affairs), and John G. Shaw Lefevre, one of the original Poor Law Commissioners and an Ecclesiastical Commissioner since 1846. It was their decisive advocacy that gave the idea of the Estates Commissioners and the Estates Committee such general currency and acceptability that it met virtually no opposition in the year of their adoption.

This quick acceptance was not indeed to be marvelled at. The composition of the Ecclesiastical Commissioners in the forties was patently defective, the cause of inconvenience, waste, embarrassment, and scandal. They were believed, especially by the lessee interest, to be unjust and irresponsible in their attitude towards the public, and, since they had no accredited parliamentary spokesman, they were not easily called to account. One possible course of action was to cut down the Commissioners' powers or, at any rate, decentralize them. Neither alternative was impracticable. The Commissioners were not yet, by the later forties, the owners of such an amount of property as to make their deprivation of it a major political or economic measure, nor was it yet apparent that the Commissioners were going to become property-owners on so great a scale. The decentralization of their power, by putting out to chapters or to new diocesan or regional boards a share of their work in management or redistribution, might have been more popular than otherwise with the friends of the church. But it would not have approved itself to those in every party who saw in the supreme power of a strong central authority, run mainly by unexcitable, long-headed laymen, their best guarantee that the established church would be serviceable and moderate. Even the most rabidly decentralizing of Mancunian administrative reformers would think twice before making a move that might play into the hands of the ecclesiastical pressure groups. Thus the Commissioners' critics to some extent cancelled each other out, and the road was cleared for those who, without wishing to reduce the Commissioners' powers or to decentralize them, felt increasingly sure that the Commissioners were not well-suited to exercise such powers under the Act of 1840.

It was with Lord John Russell and Sir George Grey that the idea of a nucleus of Estates Commissioners within the Ecclesiastical Commissioners proper originated. When the annual grant of £3340 for expenses came before the Commons in 1846, Grey agreed with a critic that the Commissioners' constitution was unsatisfactory and reiterated an opinion he had recently expressed, that there should be some paid person 'responsible for attendance on the Board; and to whom the House should look for the discharge of the duties of the Board'.[1] Russell, we know, was turning his mind to this question about the same time;[2] it is only reasonable to suppose they were working on it together. Early the following year Russell introduced a bill to place a salaried, full-time, Crown-appointed chairman over the Commissioners' Estates Committee, which was to be reduced to a business-like half-dozen.[3] He dropped it, however, partly because Howley told him that the Commissioners greatly objected to it (it was just like Russell to go ahead without consulting the bishops), and partly because Evelyn Denison's select committee was about to be appointed, with instructions

[1] 13 July 1846. *Hansard*, 3/LXXXVII, 1101–2.
[2] See what he said on 7 February 1850, *ibid.* CVIII, 463–4.
[3] 20 April 1847, *ibid.* XCI, 1048–9.

to take the composition of the Ecclesiastical Commissioners into consideration as well as their management.[1]

That Committee, as we have seen, bared the Commissioners to the bone, and elicited much evidence tending to the infusion of a professional element into their property management. The most important evidence on this point was Shaw Lefevre's. He had quite made up his mind in favour of a small body of paid commissioners—just two or three—to take the bulk of the routine work out of the Commissioners hands.[2] The inevitability of some such innovation was so obvious, and the idea itself by then so familiar, that no other witness was invited to comment on it, except Bishop Blomfield. He was generally disinclined to allow that there was anything seriously wrong with the composition of the Commissioners; but when asked, 'Do you think any permanent chairman or vice-chairman, or any permanent salaried Commissioner, would be an advantage for the practical working of the Commission?' he replied that he certainly thought so.[3] The committee accordingly recommended the division of the Commissioners' business into that part of it which was 'more purely ecclesiastical' (to be left to the whole body of Commissioners) and that part concerned with the management of property (to be conducted by three full-time, salaried commissioners) one to be nominated by the Archbishop of Canterbury, and the others by the Crown.[4]

A bill to give effect to these and other recommendations of the committee was introduced without success in 1849, successfully in 1850. It did not indeed follow the committee exactly, and for proposing to economize by having only two paid Commissioners instead of three, Russell, Grey and Goulburn got into great trouble with Horsman and 'Old Tear 'em'.[5] But no other dogs barked; other aspects of the bill distracted the fire of the high churchmen; and thus comfortably, with virtually no opposition at all, was made the greatest change in their constitution that the Ecclesiastical Commissioners ever experienced.

[1] *Hansard*, 3. CVIII, 463.
[2] 1847-8 committee, 1848, Qs. 932 ff., 975 ff.   [3] 1847, Q. 952.
[4] Their recommendation was not however made *nem. con.*; Gladstone and Stansfield wanted to recommend not three paid commissioners but 'one or more'.
[5] See especially the exchanges of 7 February and 29 April, *Hansard*, 3, CVIII, 460 ff. and CX, 938 ff.

The essence of the Act of 1850 was the partial replacement of a big part-time, amateur board by a small, full-time, professional one.[1] This was the Estates Committee, consisting of the three Church Estates Commissioners and two members (one of them a layman, not being a Commissioner *ex officio*) appointed by the Ecclesiastical Commissioners. Three constituted a quorum, so long as two Estates Commissioners were present. To this new board were entrusted two classes of powers. They were given, under the general rules and principles laid down by the Ecclesiastical Commissioners, absolute charge of the whole of the Commissioners' property, whether in respect of its 'sale, purchase, exchange, letting, or management'. This met all the objections of the lessee lobby, and reassured the landed and commercial interests that the church's property would be run by men of business. But their powers were much extended by clause 11 of the Act, which enabled the Commissioners to delegate to the Estates Committee any part of the rest of their business except only the affixing of their common seal. This opened the door to a much larger field of usefulness or, as it might be regarded, usurpation. The factors that gave the committee advantages over the whole body of Commissioners for the transaction of one class of their business were equally valid for all, and more and more was in fact to be done under this head, as Grey, Russell and Lefevre no doubt intended. Confidence and mutual understanding between the Commissioners at large and the Estates Commissioners were promoted by the requirement, in clause 10, that the Ecclesiastical Commissioners could do no business at all unless at least two of the Estates Commissioners were present.

The first three Estates Commissioners were the Earl of Chichester, Shaw Lefevre, and Henry Goulburn. Upon Lord Chichester may be said to have fallen the first earl of Harrowby's mantle. During over forty years' association with the Ecclesiastical Commissioners, he was the layman responsible above all others for the material reform and administration of the church. An Ecclesiastical Commissioner from 1841 onwards, he accepted without demur Lord John Russell's request to become the first First Estates Commissioner,[2] and remained at his post until 1878, shouldering a burden of work that was often very

[1] 13 and 14 Vic. c. 94, An Act to amend the Acts relating to the Ecclesiastical Commissioners for England.
[2] Letters of 16 August 1850. (P.R.O. 30/22/8 (pt. 2).)

heavy.[1] Chichester was the Crown's paid nominee. The Archbishop's was Goulburn, an old hand at ecclesiastical finance and administration, unimaginative, efficient, reliable, a useful man in a House of Commons rough-and-tumble, but beginning to look rather antiquated by the fifties. Shaw Lefevre accepted the Crown's invitation to the unpaid Second Estates Commissionership. He was not a man of independent fortune, nor was he without other employments. He was deputy clerk to the parliaments and in continuous demand on Royal Commissions and ministerial inquiries. Nevertheless he managed to attend two meetings out of three, and gave to the work of the Estates Committee a degree of attention that was quite remarkable.[2] The Ecclesiastical Commissioners appointed Bishop Blomfield and Sir James Graham (another survival, like Goulburn) to act with them.[3]

[1] E.g. P.R.O. 30/22/11; 13 and 16 September 1853.
[2] See Chalk's evidence to the 1856 committee, Qs. 607–17.
[3] For the membership of the Estate Committee, see Appendix 5d.

CHAPTER IX

THE HIGH VICTORIAN YEARS

While the Ecclesiastical Commissioners were going through these ordeals of frustration and unpopularity and experiencing radical constitutional changes, the Church of England was changing rapidly around them. The establishment on which they could act after their recovery of confidence and vigour about 1856 was very different from the establishment on which they had begun to act twenty years before. Some of this change was their own work. The pollarding of the chapters and the new division of the dioceses, for which they alone were responsible, together with the springing up of new churches in populous districts, for which they came to share responsibility with the Church Building Commissioners, altered the shape of the establishment almost beyond recognition. Other aspects of the transformation however were due to 'external' causes, affecting the Ecclesiastical Commissioners in common with the other parts of the establishment, and considerably altering its tone or ethos.

Through the eighteen-forties it was clear that the old church world was passing away. Into a church increasingly riven by ecclesiastical party strife, the worthless and worldly still gained an entry; but their academic qualifications had to be reasonably good, and their moral qualities, necessarily related to those of society at large, were bound to improve *pari passu* with it. Some landed clergymen still hunted or shot; whist and dancing were not anathema in every clerical household. But the riper scandals of the old establishment had gone—thoroughbred sporting parsons like 'the Dean of Tattersalls'[1] and the Hon. and Rev. William Capel; blackguard sporting parsons like the Rev. Sir Henry Bate Dudley, Bt., and Lord Frederick Beauclerk; underworld parsons engaged in the clandestine marriage business, money-grubbing parsons who were in the church simply for what they could get out of it;

[1] The Hon. and Rev. Fitzroy Stanhope; on whom see Bruce Dickins' article in the *Cambridge Review*, 8 March 1958.

bishops and dignitaries elevated simply for political and family reasons. Church and society had changed together, and the atmosphere of the mid-Victorian church was one in which vice, flaunting and brutish, could not breathe. Human nature had not perhaps changed all that much over the past sixty or seventy years. The selfish, lustful and worldly instincts were not forever banished. But there was a combination of forces at work to keep these dark sides of middle- and upper-class nature under control. Public opinion controlled them from without by its standards of propriety, respectability, manliness and purity; and from within, Evangelicalism and Tractarianism struck from opposite directions at the unregenerate heart, adding to the general voice their own affectionate insistence that the English clergy must be beyond reproach. Church discipline, moreover, was made stricter by the Act of 1840.[1] And so, while curiosities and eccentricities continued to luxuriate in the Church of England, conspicuous moral obliquity virtually vanished; and while worldliness and worthlessness still made their way in, they had to march under the colours of respectability or party zeal.

The mere elimination of disreputable elements from the established church was by no means the main part of the atmospheric change wrought between the beginning and the middle of the century. The whole tone of the establishment was changing, and not solely because of the Evangelicals and the Tractarians. Changes were taking place, the bases of which lay deeper than the church parties, and which should be seen as the manifestation, in the ecclesiastical sphere, of the general reforming spirit of the age, professional, pious, and (in no precise philosophical sense) utilitarian. Just as the medical profession in this period came to the front of so many movements in the direction of a more sanitary and humane society, often to its individual members' financial disadvantage, so did the clerical profession address itself with a new zeal of self-sacrifice to the gigantic task of social improvement and salvation. The old establishment was, indeed, committed to the same purposes. But, more and more as the nineteenth century wore on, the idea of the establishment as society's appropriately class-structured agency of moral control, and as an ancient corporation having interests and rights of its own, gave way to the idea of it as something more

[1] 3 and 4 Vic. c. 86.

399

mobile and malleable: unable in good conscience to insist upon its legal pounds of flesh, committed to self-sacrifice and to the service (rather than mainly to the moral supervision) of the community.

A few examples may serve to illustrate this moral revolution in establishment assumptions. Compare, for instance, the principles of the first batch of Church Building Acts (1818-1831) with those of the second (Peel's and Blandford's Acts, 1843 and 1856). The former were vitiated by the degree of respect they paid to existing interests—interests of patrons, interests of incumbents, interests of mother-churches, interests of pew-owners. Complete ecclesiastical divisions of parishes were rare under them; usually a new church began its life unpromisingly in a sickly kind of subordination to an old,[1] and private interests were allowed a quite unreasonable ascendancy over public. Peel's and Blandford's Acts asserted the superiority of the public interest and enabled new churches to get going in much greater independence of existing ones. Existing rights were not so much ignored as assumed to be morally unenforceable.

Other aspects of church extension illustrate the same transition. The earlier acts did only a little, and that grudgingly and ineffectively, to encourage prosperous individuals to build and endow churches by offering them the patronage or a share of it. The bench on the whole, and the whole high church party, feared this as likely to loose a flood of Evengelicals on the church. Rose and Pusey seem at times almost to have thought that to have no church would be better than to have an Evangelical one;[2] Blomfield got himself much disliked for presuming to think otherwise.[3] Blomfield, as usual, was on the side of the angels.

[1] The Church Building Commissioners assisted in the equipment of 1077 new church districts during their life-time, 1818–56; only 40 of these were wholly distinct and separate parishes. (P.Ps. 1861, XLVIII, 59).

[2] See J. W. Burgon, *Lives of Twelve Good Men* (new edn., 1891) p. 120, and Liddon's *Life of Pusey*, I, 329.

[3] See his advocacy of the Acts 7 and 8 Geo. IV c. 72 and 1 and 2 William IV c. 38, and Bishop Lloyd's opinion of the former as 'likely to do more real injury to the Church of England than any that has passed for a long time'. (Brit. Mus. Add. MSS 40343, fos. 178–9). The Evangelicals believed they were denied its benefits by the prejudices of the Church Building Commissioners who had the execution of it. See the *Christian Observer*, March 1831, pp. 181 f., and December 1831, pp. 771 f. But cf. Port, *op. cit.* p. 107.

The principle of rewarding munificence with patronage, already recognized by the Chester and Lichfield Diocesan Church Building Societies, was taken on also by his Metropolitan Churches Fund, and freely adopted by the later Church Building Acts; and the bishops and others who signed the remarkable 'Address on Church Extension' in the spring of 1851 went further yet, by interpreting 'the spirit of the Church Building Acts' to allow a voice in the nomination of ministers to subscribers above a certain amount, 'in such a manner as to avoid the evils of a popular election'. 'If the blessed truths of the Gospel', they continued, 'and its civilizing influences, can be brought within the reach of the great masses of our labouring population, no slight objections, arising from mere secular considerations, should arrest the steps of a Christian Government. . . .'[1]

'Mere secular considerations'—one wonders what Lords Eldon and Stowell would have thought of that way of referring to existing rights and aristocratic principles! Yet this was only what Richard Yates, Edward Berens and their like had been proposing while Eldon and Stowell still lived. All that had happened in the intervening twenty or thirty years was that what had been exceptional and radical in them had by now gained a wider acceptance. One of their contemporaries, for example, that excellent anonymous author of *The State of the Established Church* had, when old Bishop Hurd told the Privy Council that he had suspended the enforcement of the 1803 Residences Act because it caused such inconvenience, angrily exclaimed, 'Inconvenience, Sir! Is it for the convenience of the clergy that their revenues have been appointed? . . . It may be inconvenient to an officer to join his regiment or ship; but will the War Office or the Admiralty be amused with such a reason?'[2] The clergy, he maintained, ought to be giving value for money, and more than value. Thirty years or so later, his attitude had become quite general.

Furthermore, the need for adaptation and ingenuity in spreading the gospel came to be widely recognized. Before 1830, the high-and-dry men set the tone. 'Irregularity' was above all things feared and shunned. First, some of the early Evangelicals on their 'gospel rambles', then the Methodists, and then 1789 and all that, had burnt into the conservative

[1] P.Ps. 1851, XLII, 40.
[2] *Op. cit.* (1810), pp. 120–1. See above, p. 201

high-church mind an unreasoning rigid refusal to depart from the regular, the *correct* procedures, whether in preaching, in worship, in education, or in discipline. The establishment was strangled by a sort of moral red tape. Home missions and weekday evening services were viewed as dangerously radical; Bishop Law regarded two services on Sunday as an unpalatable concession to a deplorable popular thirst for excitement and innovation. By the fifties every kind of expedient was being canvassed, for bringing the lights of religion to those who were too dazzled by them to approach of their own accord. 'Ragged churches', to match the ragged schools;[1] 'Mechanics' Churches', to match the Mechanics' Institutes;[2] the use of schools, law courts, warehouses and theatres as churches on Sundays; the holding of liturgically startling special services; the acceptance of lay help in ministerial matters by instituting orders of lay readers and subdeacons;[3] such experiments were suggested, and some even acted on. The Act for securing the Liberty of Religious Worship, 1855[4] went some way towards legalizing these enterprising 'irregularities'. More still might have been done in 1858 but for Shaftesbury's impetuosity in pressing the Evangelicals' case, and the destructive reactions it provoked.[5] The full measure of the revolution in these respects is conveyed in the fact that, only thirty years after Howley left Fulham for Lambeth, his successor's successor was leading a metropolitan mission and preaching in the streets. All over the establishment the same new notes of self-sacrifice, service and adaptation were to be heard. It had been an article of belief with church

[1] See W. E. Richardson, *Letter to Lord Shaftesbury*.

[2] See J. T. Livesey's pamphlet of that title.

[3] See e.g. *Suggestions as to carrying out Lord Ashley's proposal for a Sub-division of Parishes*, by a Member of the Temple; *Church Organisation: a Letter to Lord Ashley*, by Amicus; G. S. Bull, *Sheep without Shepherds;* [Edward Monro] *The Church and the Million;* the *Quarterly Review*, CIII (1858), 139 ff., on 'Church Extension', and CIX (1861), 414 ff., on 'Spiritual Destitution in the Metropolis'. But this development is well enough known.

[4] 18 and 19 Vic. c. 86.

[5] It is not quite clear what happened; but the Evangelicals' enemies insisted on a more limited measure, allowing the bishops the final word; then the Evangelicals and ordinary anti-clericals seem to have joined to dish that plan as too flattering to the bench. See the reports in *Hansard*, vols. CXLVIII–CLI, on Shaftesbury's Religious Worship Act Amendment Bill and the Primate's rival Church of England Special Services Bill.

reformers and non-reformers alike before 1830 that gentlemen would not go into the clerical profession unless its rewards matched those of the other professions. Some still maintained this in the eighteen-fifties; it has not been unheard of in the nineteen-fifties; but there was certainly much less of it by the eighteen-fifties than there had been earlier, and the examples of good clergymen, of all parties and of none, testified to its error. Before 1830 it had been taken very much for granted that the incumbents of onerous urban parishes, the disagreeable importance of which was already well recognized, would need a country living in plurality, whereon to recruit their strength and rear their family. By 1850 this was no longer true. Villiers of Bloomsbury, Hook of Leeds, Bull of Birmingham—examples of the early Victorian urban clergyman at his best—had no country retreat, and neither themselves expected, nor were expected by others, to want one. They might indeed look forward to promotion or removal to less unhealthy surroundings as they got on, but that was quite different. Nor were they certain to want such a move. So radically was the tone of the establishment changing, that lifelong service of the most testing kind, even involving a deterioration rather than an improvement of worldly circumstances, was becoming an ideal for many of its members, to be voluntarily embraced, as it was by R. M. Benson when he founded the Society of St John the Evangelist in 1866 and by all the others who felt 'the call of the cloister'.

Marvellously although the establishment's tone changed between the twenties and the fifties, some notes of the old establishment still lingered. Bishops of the newly-reformed Church of England maintained the formidable reputation for longevity established by those of the unreformed, and there were still enough of them left in the fifties, like whales beach-stranded after a storm, to amaze the younger clerical generation. Not only in their persons did they bring echoes of the old world into the new. The Established Church Act of 1836 allowed to all office-holders at the time of its passing a vested right in their emoluments and preferments. Thus Blomfield remained in possession of London's old income until his retirement in 1856, and C. R. Sumner in possession of Winchester's until his retirement in 1869. Each of them was magnificently liberal and, by contemporary standards, judicious in his charities. No fair-minded observer could justly arraign them as old-style profiteers. Unfortunately, fair-mindedness was at a discount

403

in popular discussion of church affairs, and, with so much of a bishop's finances still his own private affair, not all the facts lay open to the public eye. The casual hostile critic in 1850 could therefore get the impression that Blomfield had been making an average £16,513 per annum out of the church and Sumner £12,216.[1] He would not bother to inquire, and could not indeed easily discover even if he tried, how many thousands each of them was putting yearly into church building, education, the relief of clerical poverty and so on; nor would he know, until some friend of the maligned prelates reluctantly stated it in his defence, how many thousands a year richer each of them would have been if he had renewed all his leases as he was legally entitled to do. Maltby of Durham was in similar case, even though he had gone to Durham after the Ecclesiastical Commissioners had started work and was bound to pay into the episcopal fund £11,200 a year. Even with that colossal charge upon his revenues, his average net income for the seven years ending with 1850 was £15,587. Like Blomfield and Sumner, he gave a great deal of it away, notably through the Maltby Fund which enabled the Commissioners over twenty odd years to apply more than £21,000 to the building of parsonages in his diocese.

The other conspicuous episcopal survivals from the prehistoric Hanoverian church were Murray, Bethell, Percy and Phillpotts. Murray, although he had spoken forcefully against the Cathedral Act, became quite an active Commissioner. He put in a lot of attendance in the forties (living so near London, he was well situated for usefulness) and made no difficulties about giving up the deanery of Worcester in 1845 and accepting an annual payment from the Commissioners in lieu. Phillpotts on the other hand hung on to his main supplementary source of income, the sixth stall at Durham, until his death in 1869. In 1850 it yielded him £2683.[2] His average yearly income from his see about that time was £1509, and as rector of Shobrooke and treasurer and residentiary of Exeter cathedral he received approximately £1300 more.[3] He would have lost very little had he given up these several preferments and let the Commissioners make his income up to their stipulated £5000, and he would have *looked* much less scandalous. Being Phillpotts, he was doubtless deterred from doing any such thing by the fear of popularity. Percy of Carlisle (who was also chancellor of

[1] P.Ps. 1851, XLII, 475–503.　　[2] *Ibid.* p. 52.　　[3] *Ibid.* pp. 489 and 73.

Salisbury and holder of the famous Finsbury prebend in St Paul's), and Bethell of Bangor, seem to have shared Phillpotts's prickly indifference to public opinion. Both became in due course public enemies of the Ecclesiastical Commissioners. Percy finally broke with them when, over-riding his protests, they cut his annual subsidy from £2000 to £1500 in 1846.[1] His chancellorship never brought in more than £100 and from his prebend he cannot have received much;[2] but he hung on to them to the end. Bethell of Bangor consented readily enough to the separation of the archdeaconries of Bangor and Anglesey from his see in 1844 and never made more out of it than was palpably decent;[3] but he never liked the Commissioner's early proposal to unite his see with St Asaph, and his fundamental dislike of the principles upon which they worked intensified until at last, in 1859, it burst forth in his *Remarks on the manner in which the business of the Ecclesiastical Commissioners for England has been carried on during the last three years.*

These few angry old men, charitable and conscientious enough after the fashion of a bygone age, were inevitably, in their own persons, conspicuous proof that the old establishment was an unconscionable time a-dying. Bishops whose long tenure of their offices enabled them to keep independent of the Ecclesiastical Commissioners, and to go on doing what they would with their own, were bound to attract both friendly criticism and commonplace libel to a peculiar degree. The conduct of all bishops, both old-style and new, was watched with hawk-like vigilance. Did they present a son or son-in-law to a living in their gift, the ensuing outcry was likely to be out of all proportion to the merits of the case, and it usually passed without notice that these relations were often employed in the executive offices (scarcely—if at all—remunerated, key posts) of chaplain, archdeacon and rural dean, upon whose efficiency the reformed diocesan system largely relied. Blomfield, Phillpotts, Wilberforce, the Sumners, were all, to a mild degree,

---

[1] *Ibid.* pp. 367–8.

[2] About 1830 it was worth £1489 (Ecclesiastical Revenues Reports p. 62) but in 1850 it seems to have brought him next to nothing. (P.Ps. 1851, XLII, 48). Anyway, the Commissioners would not have subsidized him so heavily had the revenues of his see not formed by far the greater part of his total income.

[3] His net income in the later forties was £4289 as bishop, and about £550 as rector of Llangristiolus and Llandyrnog. (*Ibid.* 482 and 46).

nepotists; but hardly harmfully, and the bitter-sounding complaints raised against them by the pauper clergy and their spokesmen, although natural enough considering their sad circumstances, had in them tragic elements of inevitability and failure. The *Guardian* newspaper, no great friend to the Sumners' theology, and well content to copy from the *Times* obituary its extraordinary and not too creditable account of C. R. Sumner's marriage (which no one wrote to deny), referred after his death to the way he had promoted his relations' interests, but made nothing much of it. Sumner had been a good man, and his relations were not at all bad.[1] *The Times*, reporting the death of Bishop Villiers in 1861, passed quickly over his celebrated nepotistic *faux-pas*—the presentation of his chaplain and son-in-law Edward Cheese to the rich living of Haughton-le-Skerne—as a mere misjudgment, an unhappy error that kicked the beam when weighed against the man's great virtues.[2]

On the whole the bishops were innocent of the charges (still made against them in the fifties, and with some circumstantial evidence) that they were old-style nepotists and profiteers. In fact the bench was probably the most reformed of all parts of the establishment. Elsewhere the survivals from the not-so-good old days, though less conspicuous, were rather less admirable.

Pluralism was not yet dead. Outcrops of ancient pluralism were common enough in 1850, as often as not recognizable under the names of former bishops. The *Clergy List* for that year shows that two Sparkes were still doing as well as their father could have wished. The Luxmoores and Beadons were flourishing, the Cleavers, Randolphs and Pretymans all going strong. Even on these hardy veterans, the new standards of clerical respectability were making some impression, and the holding of more than two parochial cures in plurality (not counting sinecures and stalls) seems to have gone almost completely out. The brothers Pretyman (who remained, respectively, the one chancellor of Lincoln, prebendary of Winchester, rector of Wheathampstead and Chalfont St Giles, perpetual curate of Nettleham; the other precentor of Lincoln, rector of Stony Middleton, Walgrave and Wroughton, master of

[1] *Guardian*, 19 August 1874, p. 1063.
[2] *The Times*, 10 August 1861, pp. 8 f. See the excellent cartoon in *Punch*, 9 March 1861.

Mere Hospital, Lincoln and St John's Hospital, Northampton) stood alone on their bad eminence.[1] Deans and canons still usually held a country parish as a necessary mark of gentility and a place to retire to when they were not in residence at the cathedral, and poor clergy still often needed a couple of adjacent livings as a means to a tolerable subsistence. But these forms of pluralism were harmless enough. Pluralism in its bad old forms, profit-inspired and destructive of efficiency, was fast disappearing.

What was not disappearing was the extreme disparity between the incomes and ways of life of the richer and the poorer parochial clergy. If this was a fault of the unreformed establishment (and there were of course those who had seen it rather as a virtue), it was a fault which the reforms of the early nineteenth century had scarcely touched, and had even, in some ways, intensified.[2]

It may seem startling that, with Queen Anne's Bounty carrying on steadily, with the increasing organization of voluntary benevolence, and with the Ecclesiastical Commissioners' own modest contributions in the forties, so many clergymen should still be so poor and, in relation to the rest of their profession, so wretched. Yet this fact is easily to be explained. The number of posts to be filled had simply gone up at a

---

[1] For the Pretymans, see my article 'The Road to Hiram's Hospital' in *Victorian Studies*, V (1961-2), 135-50.

[2] The facts are extraordinarily difficult to get at. Only two 'official' sets of figures were published during the whole of the nineteenth century: those so imperfectly compiled in 1809, and those published by the Ecclesiastical Revenues Commissioners in 1835. The Ecclesiastical Commissioners and Queen Anne's Bounty both had the means of finding out the revenue of any particular living whenever they needed to do so, and thus never needed to make another complete inquiry. The *Clergy List* (annual after 1841), which seems at first sight to contain all the figures one would wish to know, is in fact unsatisfactory since most of its figures, up to 1860 at any rate, were cribbed straight from the 1835 report, and unchanged in the interim; although it seems to have been fairly up-to-date on new benefices, created after 1835. The historian has to do the best with it that he can, as the Victorian church reformers had to.

	1809	c. 1830
Under £50	858	297
£50–100	1527	1629
£100–150	1006	1602
£150–200	not stated	1354

greater rate than the fund from which incomes were to be drawn. The standards of the reformed early Victorian Church required, in respect of populous parishes, either that the incumbent should get enough help by way of curates (and perhaps lay readers) to enable him to satisfy his parishioners' spiritual thirst, or that the parish should be divided and, if necessary, sub-divided. Either way, additional incomes had to be paid. Curates could still be miserably rewarded. There is no reason for supposing that the minimum stipend requirements of the 1 and 2 Vic. c. 106 were not often evaded. Many poor parsons, indeed, who needed a curate could get help from the Additional Curates Society or the Pastoral Aid Society; but these were never wealthy organizations and did no more than palliate, sometimes, the financial hardships always liable to hit both curates and those who had to hire them.

As for the incomes of incumbents of new parishes, they were often negligible.[1] Those 'Peel districts' which received the Commissioners' maximum endowment of £150 a year were among the more fortunate, and that income—equivalent to the income of a skilled tradesman or third-rate clerk—went nowhere in a district by definition spiritually under-nourished, at least partly pauperized, and usually deficient in the middle and upper-class residents to whom a parish clergyman had to look for support for his schools and parish charities, for district visitors and Sunday-school teachers, and for pew-rents to subsidize his own income and form a fund, perhaps, for church maintenance. The 'Peel district' churches had at least the advantage over the bulk of the Church Building Commissioners' churches, that they were not financially and legally subordinate to the old parish church. They started life under severe disadvantages all the same. As the great-hearted incumbent of one of them—William Rogers of St Thomas, Aldersgate Street, Charterhouse—remarked in his *Reminiscences*, 'The mother parish ate the oysters; the districts divided the shells.'[2] What had happened in the creation of his unappetising parish was that the tortuous boundary line between it and its neighbours had so been drawn as to leave them with

---

[1] The nineteenth century's new parishes and districts, and the clergy who served them—and who, it seems, were often of a new character—form a complicated subject which has as yet been scarcely touched by historians. My generalizations about it are based on no systematic research.

[2] *Op. cit.* p. 55.

the few better-class streets that ought, by the light of nature, to have been his; and to give him some particularly undesirable quarters that might well have been left with them.[1] His parish was destitute of almost every source of help, both financial and practical; and he was only able to put up schools, engage assistance, keep the church in repair and himself from despair, because of his Eton and Balliol connexions, who were themselves able to provide funds for his admirable schemes and were of a character to induce others to be generous as well.

A rather poor clergyman and former 'blue', who was 'Good old Rogers!' to many highly placed people and who could get the Duke of Argyll or Prince Albert to open his new schools, was *rara avis* indeed. His connexions enabled him to do what otherwise he could only have done with large private means,[2] or by attracting the interest of wealthy individuals or societies from outside (which was the more difficult to do in proportion as the parish's problems lacked a sensational or dramatic aspect). The pew-rents system, which bedevilled the whole business of church extension, inevitably did damage in one way or another. If there were enough parishioners of the pew-renting type to bring in a worthwhile sum, the church acquired an air of respectability that made doubly sure the poor would keep away. If there were not, and the church's endowments had been shaped in expectation that there would be, then the clergyman was pauperized; and quite apart from the difficulties of merely keeping alive and supporting a family (as Protestant predilections preferred clergymen to do) on something between £2 and £4 a week, sheer poverty kept a clergyman from making friends and influencing people in the way he should have done. Especially did it keep him from founding schools and hiring teachers. It is clear that, in lower class parishes without an upper class leaven, *education* was the primary means by which the clergy performed their function as they conceived it. Blomfield was quite positive about this. Where

[1] *Ibid.* ch. 3. C.C.F. 15450 contains the correspondence relative to this parish's formation. Its shape would have been plainer, and its character slightly more mixed, had the Commissioners stuck to their original plan and not given way before the complaints of the circumambient clergy and churchwardens. Presumably what happened in this case happened quite often.

[2] Rogers (*op. cit.* pp. 89–90) himself mentions that the first incumbent of St Mary's, Charterhouse, carved out of St Thomas's in 1862 and endowed with £200 a year, spent over £5000 of his own money within nine years.

funds did not allow church and school to be put up together in new working-class parishes, he said, the school should have precedence.[1] Schooling, naturally plus church-going, was their ideal; but it seems that, by the forties and fifties, the dull insistence on making church-going a condition of schooling, which marked the tens and twenties, had largely disappeared, at least on the active sectors of the establishment's front. William Rogers in Goswell Street and Golden Lane, Robert Gregory at St Mary's the Less, Lambeth,[2] the apparently heroic and all but anonymous clergy who fleetingly appear in the reports of commissioners and inspectors on factories, mines, education and public health, were all working and winning their contemporaries' praise primarily through their parochial schools; and schools cost money, which the Education Committee of the Privy Council was not always or sufficiently prepared to give.[3] Thus the continued poverty of the poorer clergy, whether they were in town or country, not only remained a scandal but gravely impaired the church's efficiency.

As a scandal it was not new; and the cause of its being a scandal was the same as it always had been. The contrast between the conditions of the more and the less prosperous parochial clergy remained stark, and continued to lack any relation to duties and burdens. The reforms of the thirties had enforced a strict relation between work and remuneration upon the bishops and the cathedral clergy. Upon curates, such a relation had been strictly enforced before that. But upon the parochial clergy these utilitarian reforms bore much more lightly. The Benefices and Pluralities Act of 1838, which alone of the church reform statutes affected them to any great degree, said what they might not do, but not (save with regard to curates) what they ought to do. To new churches, conditions of various kinds, both legal and informal, usually attached. Incumbents of 'old' churches were only likely to feel the effects of social change in so far as their parishes suffered mutilation; in consequence of which, sooner or later, fees and prestige were bound to sink. The conditions of life were thus liable to change quite con-

---

[1] A. Blomfield's *Memoir*, I, 247.

[2] See Gregory's *Autobiography*, pp. 55–9, 61–70.

[3] The Committee of Council had to insist on certain standards of building, equipment and teaching as conditions of its grants. But locally invaluable schools often came below these standards.

siderably for the incumbents of 'old' urban churches as the years went by, as daughter churches ran away, burial-grounds were closed, and lower orders moved into formerly respectable streets. In the country, such things very seldom happened. The conditions of clerical life there underwent hardly any forced change at all.

It was, indeed, among the better-off country clergy that the ways of the old establishment most lustily survived. Between them and the rest of the parochial clergy the gulf was as great in the middle of the nineteenth century as it ever had been, or greater. This was partly the mere result of economic disparity. None of the many proposals that had been made during the third church reform movement (and went on being made after it)[1] for taxing the more prosperous benefices ever came to anything. The chapters were fleeced and cut down to size, bishoprics were approximately equalized, but the incomes of the clergy of the 'old' country parishes were untouched (except in so far as they tended to lose a little in consequence of the commutation and the rating laws) and could remain perfectly adequate to a gentleman's support—which, of course, was exactly what the aristocracy and gentry, the unchallenged ruling class in the social sphere, wanted. Trollope's clergymen are not, perhaps, representative of the Church of England as a whole, nor do they, with the solitary and magnificent exception of Josiah Crawley, exemplify the best of which the English clergy were at that time capable; but they show to the life the clerical branch of county society, the established church at its most gentlemanly. Family livings, sales of advowsons and next presentations, resignation bonds,[2] stipendiary curates, all these features of the old establishment still flourished. It would be interesting though wearisome to find out whether the number of family livings actually increased in the course of the nineteenth century, as one suspects it did. A detailed study of episcopal and Crown patronage would likewise no doubt be rewarding. Professional merit seems still to have been more difficult to pick out,

---

[1] E.g. *The Augmentation of Small Livings to the minimal value of £200 p.a. by a Clerical Income Tax*, by 'Philadelphia', and *How to make Better Provision for the Cure of Souls ... by a Pauper Clergyman*, pp. 62–5. Robert Gregory had blocked his own path to preferment in Lincolnshire by proposing a voluntary self-taxation by the richer clergy in his *Plea on behalf of Small Parishes*; see his *Autobiography*, pp. 43–4.

[2] As controlled by the 9 and 10 George IV c. 94

and thus in fact was less frequently recognized, than rank and social connexion. Certainly, contemporaries said that even the best and most deserving young clergyman, if he had no 'family' or lacked influential friends, had a hard time getting out of the slough of perpetual curacy. 'What chance has a curate without interest, and without a family living to look to, of preferment?' asked W. G. Jervis in 1856; 'He can only expect it from his bishop, and the whole bench has but 1248 livings to divide among many thousand curates.'[1] Bishops were indeed likelier than private patrons to reward merit—this, it will be re-membered, had been the main argument in the thirties for increasing their patronage—but it may be questioned whether they always went to great trouble to do so: poor curates thought that a good many episcopal appointments smelled of Cheese.[2] The fact was, that the entrée to the delightful world of country rectories and county drawing-rooms, the world of Trollope's Grantleys, Robartses and Oriels, was jealously guarded both by bishops and private patrons; the potential supply of suitably respectable well-bred clergymen always exceeded the supply of eligible benefices; and very few who were not socially acceptable got hold of them. It may even be that, about the middle of the nineteenth century, the town and the country clergy were further apart than they ever had been, on account of the abolition of old-fashioned pluralism. That, at any rate, had often brought a clergyman from the country benefice where his heart was to spend some part of the year in an urban parish, and it meant that he would have some idea what life in the town was like. His mid-Victorian successor and counter-part had to read about it in the papers.

Influence, interest, and social distinction thus continued to set their stamp on the church, particularly by helping to perpetuate and perhaps even accentuate the eighteenth century's distinction between rich and poor parochial clergymen, between those whose lines fell in easy places

[1] *The Poor Condition of the Clergy*, p. 3 n. Jervis was a Surrey clergyman who con-cerned himself particularly with clerical poverty, and the ways in which it was being, and might better be, relieved. All his pamphlets are of great interest.

[2] See, e.g., that curious pamphlet *The Scrip; or, Smooth Stones out of the Brook, for the Forehead of Ism, the Modern Goliath and his Sons, Sch-ism, Roman-ism, Liberal-ism, Auto-ism, Despot-ism, Nepot-ism, and Euphem-ism:* by Sigmabetaphilus; H. J. Dixon, *Sad Experience of a Clergyman of the Established Church*, pp. 4 and 9; and *How to make Better Provision for the Cure of Souls*, pp. 36–41.

and those for whom life was, by any objective standards, hard and unpleasant. The poor clergyman in the nasty district would be just as aware as the easy country parson that only good schools and good teachers could really do the establishment's work well; and the need for doing it would be proportionately as much greater as the means at hand for doing it would be inferior. His ministry in such circumstances was bound to be ineffective—whether more or less ineffective, would depend on the nature of the district and on his own quality and strength. The lives of such clergymen must have been infinitely depressing, their work unromantic, and their connexions, almost by definition, undistinguished. Lacking leisure to write themselves up, they were as a class much less articulate than the country clergy who happily laboured to perpetuate the image of the village church as the characteristic, ideal Church of England church, and themselves its cream and glory. Now and then a Select Committee or a Royal Commission summoned some of these unknown crusaders as witnesses, sometimes a philanthropist or publicist brought their case forward. For a space the glare of publicity would reveal dreadful things in the darkest corners of the establishment—ancient cast-off curates starving in attics, clergy widows and children at the gate of the workhouse, hundreds of poor clerical families dressed in strange assortments of handed-down clothes, sons and daughters apprenticed to tradesmen or schooled on the cheap by one or other of the charitable institutions (Lowood and the like) existing for this end. The Crawleys of Hogglestock, in whom Trollope allows a glimpse (too uncomfortable to repeat) of real clerical poverty, at least had rich and influential friends; the Quiverfuls, who were nearly as badly off, were able to get their mess of pottage, at some sacrifice of self-respect. Poor country clergymen could be very badly off; but the state of poor town clergymen was likely to be even worse. William Rogers refers with tantalising brevity to those who tried to fight it out under such circumstances and 'fell in the fray, depressed, broken, ruined, patrons passing by on the other side and no good Samaritan taking care of them. . . .'[1] One can well believe it. This was the dark side of the establishment in the middle of the last century, which must be borne well in mind as we resume the history of the agencies existing above all for its enlightenment.

[1] *Reminiscences*, p. 55.

413

Temporal Pillars

The three Estates Commissioners, who had been intruded into the large body of the Ecclesiastical Commissioners by the Act of 1850, had been called into being primarily to improve the board's management of its property, which had, as we have seen, given the landed interest much dissatisfaction. This task of management was by the statute entrusted to the Estates Commissioners sitting as the 'Estates Committee', to which the Ecclesiastical Commissioners were permitted to add two members (section 7). It should be noted that they were not positively required to add them, and that *at least one* of them had to be a layman. These terms were hardly flattering to the bishops. The language of the statute seemed designed to give them as little voice in the committee's deliberations as was decently possible. The presence of two Estates Commissioners was needed to make a quorum for the dispatch of business; no business whatever could be discussed unless two of them were present (sections 8, 10). Even in the salaries stipulated for the two who were to be paid, the same anti-prelatical bias showed. The First Estates Commissioner, nominated by the Crown, was to get £1200 a year; the archbishop's nominee got only £1000; and the money was to come not out of public funds, as might quite reasonably have been expected, but out of the Commissioners' own funds (section 2).

In their management of the Commissioners' property, the Estates Committee could act quite on their own, within the limits of a general policy laid down for them by the Commissioners. The provision of the statutes that such rules and directions should be only general, and must be laid before Parliament, ensured that they could not be turned into a means of keeping the Estates Committee from the independence it was intended to enjoy (section 12). The management of its property was of course by itself a very substantial part of the whole of the Ecclesiastical Commissioners' work. To their control of all this, the Estates Committee was permitted to add whatever other parts of their work the Commissioners chose to delegate to them; and to do the whole of it save only the very last stage, the affixing of the Commissioners' common seal (section 11). Thus the Commissioners retained a power of veto; but it seemed clear from the start that this was a theoretical safeguard merely. All five members of the Estates Committee, after all, were

Ecclesiastical Commissioners as well, were likely to be among the most assiduous in attendance at their general meetings, and would know much more about what was going on than anyone else. They were bound to become the real controllers of the board. Their progenitors-in-chief—Lord John Russell, Sir George Grey, and John G. Shaw Lefevre —had obviously intended this; and this is what happened.

The Estates Committee quickly became a kind of inner cabinet. To begin with, at any rate, they met twice as often as the main board. The main board met fortnightly except during the 'recess' of September and October, when they met not at all; the Estates Committee met weekly through most of the year, and even broke into the sacred recess to meet once or twice.[1] Between 1851 and 1855 the board held 93 meetings. Only five Commissioners came to more than half the meetings, and the only one of them who was not on the Estates Committee was the Archbishop of Canterbury.[2] This pattern of attendance, which did no more than reflect the real balance of power, established itself as the rule, as may clearly be seen from this table of attendance (p. 416) at general meetings. Only since the First World War have the proportions changed at all, and that not significantly enough to matter. Until then, and particularly during the decades of the Ecclesiastical Commissioners' most important work, the Estates Committee was firmly in charge for most of the time.

It must have taken over almost at once. The take-over was complete by 1856, when both Lord Chichester, Shaw Lefevre and C. K. Murray's successor J. J. Chalk described its work to the Commons' Committee.[3] The hand was the hand of the Ecclesiastical Commissioners, but the voice was that of the Estates Committee. This mild and formal duplicity enraged Lord Robert Cecil, who put it to Chalk that he was abetting the practice of a fraud upon the honest common people of England by sending out papers in the name of the Ecclesiastical Commissioners when in fact the Ecclesiastical Commissioners—the men the public knew, the bishops they trusted—had often never set eyes on the business,

[1] 1856 Committee, Qs. 600–604.
[2] 1856 Committee, Qs. 162–3. Goulburn came top with 88, and Lord Chichester had 84. Blomfield, J. B. Sumner and Shaw Lefevre had 61, 60 and 56 respectively. Then came a big gap before Bishop Wilberforce's 34.
[3] Qs. 147–61, 2260–74, and 554–93 respectively.

	No. of Attendances each year				Average No. of other members at each meeting	
	1st C.E.C.	2nd C.E.C.	3rd C.E.C.	Abp. of C.	Clerical	Lay
1850—5 (av.)	17	11	18	12	5	1
1856—61 (av.)	20	11	23	18	5	1
1865	31	17	31	22	5	1
1870	34	16	31	22	5	1
1875	30	26	32	20	5	1
1880	32	20	32	13	4	1
1885	32	8	31	21	4	1
1890	19	4	20	11	4	1
1895	17	8	18	10	4	1
1900	21	19	19	16	5	1
1905	19	15	19	18	6	1
1910	20	14	16	14	5	1
1915	20	14	19	11	6	1
1920	17	10	17	4	5	1
1925	14	11	16	3	5	1
1930	13	7	14	8	7	1
1935	15	8	13	9	8	1

TABLE 3. Attendances at General Meetings, 1850–1935[1]

nor any understanding of it.[2] This was indeed a matter which excitable enemies of 'centralization' and 'bureaucracy' might take seriously. Other members of the Commons' Committee came to the Commissioners' rescue by pointing out that this sort of thing was constantly happening in the public offices; when the secretary, having laid papers before the Estates Committee and posted their decision, told the recipients that it was all the Commissioners' work, he used their name in a Pickwickian sense.

In the very nature of things, the Estates Commissioners through the

[1] Taken by permission from Dr Willson's thesis.
[2] Qs. 577–81. He came back to this point in his examination of Shaw Lefevre, Qs. 2263–8, 2270–1.

Estates Committee engrossed more and more of the Commissioners' work. They were there all the time (at least, two of them were; the Second, unpaid, Estates Commissionership presented special difficulties). They knew all the ropes as no one else, except the secretary, could. Bishops came and bishops went, but the First and Third Estates Commissioners went on more or less for ever. Largely independent of the general board though they were, it cannot be doubted that their formal semi-subordination was occasionally tiresome, and that the continuing division of the Ecclesiastical Commissioners' business into three parts— the part the Ecclesiastical Commissioners did by themselves, the part they delegated to the Estates Committee, and the part the Estates Committee did on their own—irked them as men of business. The stage was set for a recurrence of that ancient divergence of views between bishops and lay church leaders about what the clergy needed or deserved. It showed conspicuously in the case of the dean of York, 1858–1860, when the Estates Commissioners and such other lay Commissioners as came to support them were kept in a minority by the massed prelates, who were evidently making the most of so rare an opportunity to dish the politicians.[1] Lord Chichester, shocked and aggrieved, conceived it his duty to tell the prime minister and home secretary what they were about.[2]

No other such *cause célèbre* occurred to call public attention to the Commissioners' doings and to illuminate their domestic disagreements, but it may be taken for granted that the tensions which led to it were never wholly absent. It is not strange therefore to find Lord Chichester in 1864 caballing with the other Estates Commissioners and Sir George Grey to strengthen their hand at the general board's expense. In a letter covering a draft bill for this purpose he wrote to Grey, 'You will remember that the bill has *not* been submitted to this Board, but is suggested by Walpole, Bouverie and myself as requested by you.'[3] In other words, Grey—an anti-clerical of anti-clericals, and one who hardly ever mentioned the Ecclesiastical Commissioners in the Commons without remarking that their constitution left much to be desired —was to bring the bill forward, and the Estates Commissioners were

[1] See below, pp. 438–40.
[2] See his review of the affair, 9 August 1860, in *Hansard*, 3/CLX, 922–6.
[3] 20 June 1864, P.R.O. 45/7636.

going to pretend that it was a surprise to them. The main points of the bill were to give the Second Estates Commissioner a salary like the Third, and enable the Estates Committee to take over the sealing of schemes. Chichester calculated that this would raise the proportion of the Ecclesiastical Commissioners' business that the Estates Committee absolutely controlled from seven-seventeenths to eleven-seventeenths. The remaining six-seventeenths was virtually the committee's already, being detailed augmentation work done under delegation and quite unsuitable for the general board to do anyway. Thus did the Estates Commissioners plan to streamline the board's labours and eliminate the irritating duality of powers, with as little unpleasantness as possible. *Ils pleuraient, mais ils prenaient toujours.*

   This particular project did not quite come off; what went wrong with it cannot be ascertained. Something, however, had to be done about the status of the Second, unpaid, Estates Commissioner, and it was done in 1866. The Second Estates Commissioner, being unpaid, had not the same motive for attendance that the others had. He was a public man who accepted the post out of a sense of public obligation, who came when he could. Russell and Grey had originally proposed to pay all three Commissioners, and had been thwarted, principally on the ground of expense. But by the middle fifties, when Shaw Lefevre found himself increasingly unable to attend Estates Committee meetings,[1] the question revived, and the 1856 Committee heard evidence in favour of three, or even five, paid Commissioners, in order to secure a better attendance. The trouble was that not only did the Second Estates Commissioner find it difficult to attend, but that the two other members of the Estates Committee sometimes found it difficult too, and so the quorum of three was not all that easily reached. One answer to this, supposing that the cost of three paid Commissioners remained intolerable, was to increase the committee's membership; the other, the Estates Commissioners' answer, was to reduce the quorum to two, so that the two paid Commissioners could if necessary carry on by themselves; and it was this latter course which was followed in 1866 when the constitution of the Ecclesiastical Commissioners experienced its last, and least important, change.[2] This determined that the First

[1] 1856 Committee, Qs. 607–17, 1866.
[2] 29 and 30 Vic. c. 111.

and Third Estates Commissioners should become the businessmen of the board, more or less permanent, and the Second Estates Commissioner more the political member, who came and went with the government. He had not been so at first, nor did he become so all at once; Shaw Lefevre was appointed because of administrative talent, and Goulburn, the Third Estates Commissioner, was fully capable of representing the Commissioners in the Commons, when the prime minister or the home secretary needed support. But he was on the way to becoming so, presumably, when Palmerston appointed his loyal supporter, Edward Pleydell Bouverie, member for Kilmarnock, in August 1859, at the height of the excitement over the dean of York's case. His successor H. A. Bruce was replaced in August 1866 by the Tory Mowbray, and Mowbray early in 1869 by the Liberal Acland. The convention seemed by them secure. It had some utility, for although the Ecclesiastical Commissioners were by that time ceasing to be more than sporadically controversial, it was good that there should always be a well-informed representative of the board in the Commons, to answer questions if required. But until after the First World War he never had as much to do as might have been expected, because the archbishops' Commissioners were always members of parliament until Lord Daryngton succeeded C. B. Stuart-Wortley in 1926.

2. THE FIGHT FOR SURVIVAL, 1856–1863

The Ecclesiastical Commissioners came through their second trial by select committee very creditably. This committee of 1856 was indeed the least menacing of the three. The Commissioners were just then sailing with a good strong wind behind them, and the weather seemed to be improving. The lessees were on the whole well satisfied with the arrangements made under the Episcopal and Capitular Estates Management Act of 1851[1] and its progeny. The 1856 committee investigated the working of these Acts with minute care, and was able to make no suggestion for their substantial improvement. With the deans and chapters, the Commissioners' relations were certainly not good; but they were not more unpleasant than an armed truce has to be. The Durham and Northumberland interest, to whom it never ceased to seem iniquitous that so much money should be taken from their counties

[1] 14 and 15 Vic. c. 104.

for distribution elsewhere, remained implacably hostile; but by the mid-fifties, that hostility had become just one of the ordinary hazards of the Commissioners' life. No great criticism could be made of their augmentations policy, since, beyond carrying out their obligations in respect of local claims, they had made few augmentations worth speaking of since 1844. It was bound to tell in their favour that they had just got into a position to resume them. They did so in such a manner that, by the time of their next and final ordeal, in 1862-3, they lay open to attack. For the time being, however, they were safe on this score, and the committee prudently said no more about their augmentations policy than that it would require further consideration. It said the same of the modes of assuring the estates and incomes of the bishops and chapters. Two very contentious topics were thus kept hot for the attention of the legislature during the next few years; as we shall see, they caused great excitement. But where it was decisive at all, the 1856 committee was quiet and complimentary. It reflected no echoes of the suggestions, that issued now and then from aggrieved or suspicious bodies, that the Commissioners were extravagant and inefficient; and instead of limiting their expansive propensities the committee proposed to increase their load and, by giving a salary to the Second Estates Commissioner, to reinforce the Estates Committee's power to shoulder it. As for their constitution in general and ways of doing business, the Commons' Committee held a silence which signified approval.

But, although they had temporarily ceased to be acutely controversial, they were not yet popular, nor had they yet become positively indispensable. It was not certain that their work could not be done by other agencies. The Church Estates Commissioners indeed had the special business of enfranchisement to see to, and obviously had to carry on until they had finished it; but there was no reason why they should be continued after that. They were, in that respect, easily distinguishable from the main board; and the main board's more ferocious enemies, given ample ammunition by the board's policies, mistakes and misfortunes between 1857 and 1862, did not shrink from suggesting a complete dismantling. These, after all, were very dangerous years for central boards that got on the wrong side of the legislature. The Poor Law Board which had been brought to heel in 1847, was far too useful to the propertied classes to be a serious target for the dismantlers. The General

Board of Health, although handled in the same way in 1854, had still sufficient marks of the centralizing bureaucratic beast about it, to get itself abolished in 1858. The same fate could have happened to the Ecclesiastical Commissioners a few years later, and if some people had had their way, would have done so. The Commissioners were at this time not quite indispensable, only very nearly so. The ferocity of the last serious attack upon them suggests that their enemies saw this, and knew that it was their last chance.

It was not the Ecclesiastical Commissioners' constitution, but their alleged characteristics, that made trouble. Their constitution was now settled. The Estates Committee did much of the work by itself. The main board, mainly episcopal, met fortnightly through five-sixths of the year to go through the formalities of approving and sealing business prepared for it by the secretaries and the Estates Committee, and, exceptionally, for discussing and determining matters of general principle. These alternate Thursday meetings did not often matter much. At the Bounty Board, on the other hand, the bishops were in their element. They met in the Bounty offices also as the Upper House of Canterbury Convocation. Dean's Yard was their natural habitat. In Whitehall Place they became, to some extent, visitors on alien soil. The Estates Commissioners, the still influential secretary, the other important officers—actuary, solicitors, land agents, cashier, chief clerks— these were the real managers of the concern after 1850. It was really against them not the bishops, that the attacks were directed. The words most commonly used, in the attack, were 'centralization' and 'bureaucracy'. To the mid-Victorian these words had a deep, rich, and nasty meaning, many overtones of which are difficult to recapture a century after. They were often used in association with other pejorative epithets, like ruthless, wasteful, extravagant, sinister, heartless, inefficient, uncontrolled, arbitrary, narrow- and small-minded. These were the characteristics of which the men in Whitehall Place came to be accused.

At the heart of all this, lay the old freedom-loving, countryside-minded prejudice against the city[1] and Whitehall. Metropolitan civil servants, it was held, simply could not know how the church's business, spread out as it blessedly was through thousands of estates and glebes

---

[1] Not, of course, 'the City' in our financial sense.

and parishes up and down the land, ought to be handled. If they were good men, they would not know that they could not know, because it was only natural in executive men to pull as much power into their hands as they could and to imagine that this was desirable from the nation's point of view. If they were not good men, they would not care about not knowing, because they were promoting no one's interest but their own. They thought, or pretended to think, that their centralizing system was ideal. But no system was ideal. All systems were more or less faulty; and the system whose faults did the least damage was the one that left long-standing arrangements alone, that respected local and personal preferences and loyalties, that worked through gentlemen's agreements rather than lawyers' letters and that, above all, respected the principle of locality. The utilitarian tests of the accountant and the efficiency expert were, beyond a point, simply irrelevant. What mattered was that feelings should be respected, and that men should be dealt with face to face by men.

The anti-centralizers believed that the Ecclesiastical Commissioners were going against all their cherished principles. The Commissioners evidently panted for more and ever more responsibility. They sought to assume control of all the episcopal and capitular estates, and to 'reduce' bishops, deans and canons to 'mere stipendiaries'. They could not manage so vast a mass of property properly, nor could they, as distributors of the proceeds of this property, have the right qualities of tact, delicacy, and flexibility. From this empire-building came unpleasant, inevitable consequences—a high cost of management, a needlessly large staff, stiff, red-tape-ridden office procedures, and inhumanity in dealing with individuals. The Commissioners shunned publicity in order to get away with their sharp practice and acted, as far as they dared, in defiance of public opinion and parliament's will.

This picture had some truth in it. But the facts brought forward to support it were selected facts and, both in the way they were selected and in the way they were presented, they were 'looking-glass' facts, upside down and disproportionate. They appealed, moreover, to particular classes of churchmen, with particular axes to grind. The Durham-Northumberland group of members of parliament had always disliked the Commissioners' insistence on keeping their hands as free as they could in distributing the surpluses from their common fund.

What the men from Tees- and Tyne-side felt acutely, many others felt in lesser degree. A large group of metropolitan clergy were almost as keen as the north-easterners on the principle of local claims; the same feeling was common enough elsewhere; and to all such malcontents, the Commissioners' dogged refusal to admit more local claims than the legislature had forced upon them in 1840 branded them as bad-principled. Then there were those provincial churchmen who, either because they did not know, did not care, or had by some amazing scale of values honestly worked it out so, set no store on the fashionable concern about church extension in the towns and cities, and who preferred to trust the actual holders of church property, or at the most, local boards, to do good with it rather than to channel it all through a central board. Deans and canons, it seems, were much given to this way of thinking, and so were a few bishops. They eagerly grasped anti-centralization as a stick with which to beat the Commissioners. Decentralization was indeed the deans' and chapters' main hope in their long rearguard action.

No doubt the men of Whitehall Place did thirst for greater power. Lord Chichester and his colleagues on the Estates Committee were ready and willing to take over virtually the whole of the Commissioners' official duties.[1] Not all the bishops liked this. Some for local, others for personal, reasons would prefer to manage their own diocesan affairs more independently than the Commissioners' rules permitted. Bishops of Durham were bound to be decentralizers. Bishops of Carlisle seem to have been so too. Bishop Percy (1827-56) was permanently alienated from the Commissioners. Bishop Villiers' views are not known, but his successor Waldegrave (1860-69) gladly gave evidence against them to the 1862-3 committee.[2] Tait (London 1856-69), though fully aware of the importance and potential value of the Commissioners, recognized that their work was much misunderstood, expressed anxiety that their affairs and public relations should be put on a better footing, and seemed at first to wish that some limit should be set to their expansive propensities.[3] To Tait and Waldegrave and others who saw

[1] Above, pp. 414-7.
[2] 1863, Appendix 15, a memorandum of views he would have stated in person if the day he was to have appeared had not been changed without his knowledge.
[3] 9 August 1860, *Hansard*, 3/CLX, 926-31. Tait is obviously the dominant figure in

things the same way, the institution called the Ecclesiastical Commissioners, and theoretically run by the bishops to serve spiritual ends, had got out of control, and was pushing the spiritualty aside in an unseemly preoccupation with property.

It all depended which way you looked at it. If you valued above all things local self-government, administrative flexibility, the human touch, diffusion of resources and responsibility rather than concentration, then you would side with Tait, and regret that the church's finances were not being differently managed. If on the other hand you liked the ideas of uniformity and regularity, procedures founded firmly on known rules and regulations to the elimination, so far as possible, of the fallible human element, the certainty of impartiality, the management of the national church's resources by a single all-seeing, all-powerful body—then you would incline to take the professional administrators seriously. You might indeed feel that they took themselves too seriously, and object to details of their system, but you would not wish radically to alter it.

One of the commonest charges against them was their extravagance, extravagance with money and manpower alike, tending to promote their own private ends at the expense of the public's. Whitehall Place certainly gave an impression of family compactness. Tait had cause to characterize it as the 'centre of the establishment'. When the Commissioners set up business there, they modestly occupied half of No. 5, sharing it with the Office for French and Danish Claims. As their business grew and their connexions multiplied, they took more and more of Whitehall Place over. By 1845 Serjeant Mereweather of No. 7 had given place to T. E. Ripley, solicitor; J. Meadows White and John Murray, solicitors; J. S. Rymer and E. J. Murray, solicitors; John Murray and James A. Murray—an impressive houseful of Murrays and solicitors, to make sure the Commissioners did not lack for legal aid! Their solicitors took No. 7; their surveyors, Cluttons, took No. 8. And so it went on. In 1855 the Commissioners moved to No. 11 at the end of the street, where they could enjoy more elbow-room. Their friends and relations clustered ever closer, until by 1865 the whole

the mid-Victorian church, and I have only not examined his papers at Lambeth because Dr Peter Marsh (who has been all through them) assures me that, surprisingly, they contain virtually nothing relevant to my theme.

side from No. 6 to the end was involved in their business. At No. 6 were White, Borrett and White, solicitors; at No. 7 John, the last of the Murrays; more solicitors, Calthrop, White and Buckston, occupied No. 8; their architect, Christian, was at 8A; Cluttons were now in No. 9; and the Commissioners themselves at No. 10, which had swallowed up No. 11. Nor was that quite all. Just over the road at No. 14 were Smith and Watkins, their land agents, and Yool their actuary.[1] This concentration of partners was convenient, indeed to a great extent necessary, for the dispatch of the Commissioners' business; but it invited comment of an obvious kind.

The spirit of the age was not unfavourable to the employment of private firms to do public business. This division of the Commissioners' business between their own staff and private professional men had nothing intrinsically disturbing in it. Nor were these private firms anything but excellent. The Murrays (inevitably) only excepted, no breath of scandal, no convincing charge of ineptitude ever attached to them. The Cluttons, Pickering and Smith were at the top of their professions, and their conduct of the Commissioners' business could only improve as they grew ever deeper in the Commissioners' confidence until they spoke the same language and thought the same thoughts. They became, as indeed they and their direct descendants remain, like trusted old family lawyers or other professional men. E. J. Smith, the surveyor of their northern division, published the best pamphlet that ever defended the Commissioners against the assaults of their enemies; the extent of his influence and knowledge is self-evident.[2] Such confidential closeness of relations made for harmony and dispatch; but amateurs of public economy, and bureaucrat-baiters, inevitably suspected that it made equally easily for the multiplication of business and the great profit of the firms concerned.

> Jack Horner's christmas pie my learned nurse
> Interpreted to mean the public purse,
> From whence, a plum he drew; oh, happy Horner!
> Who would not be ensconced in thy snug corner?

[1] This natural history of Whitehall Place is based on the Royal Blue Books for 1840 and 1845, and the Post Office London Directory thereafter.

[2] *Two Letters to the Archbishop of Canterbury on the Origin and Progress of the Ecclesiastical Commissioners* (1863). He also appears in every relevant Blue Book.

Although in this case it was not the public purse but the church's that was alleged to be tapped, the principle was the same, and throughout the middle-years of the century this cry was continually heard.

Each of the three Commons' Committees paid some attention to the Commissioners' running costs and scales of remuneration. The general public of course was always ready to believe that they were excessive. The 1847-8 committee hinted that the Commissioners had been led into some extravagance through carelessness and generosity, and expressed satisfaction that this had stopped.[1] The 1856 Committee, which was by no means unfriendly, resolved 'That the present system of management by the agents of the Church Estates Commission should be reconsidered, with a view to its greater efficiency, and a possible diminution of expense'.[2] The 1862-3 committee, which the root-and-branch men managed to capture, went much further than that; they alleged that the system of management was still 'unnecessarily expensive', that the accounts were almost unintelligible, and they resolved that 'the legal business of the Board be conducted by the appointment of a Legal Adviser at a fixed salary, in the same way that the Treasury, the Admiralty, and other Government establishments, and some of the Railway Companies of the Kingdom, have their legal business conducted'.[3]

This last was the judgment of men determined to find fault. The fact that they were unconvinced by the official replies to their insinuations and questions does not mean that those replies were pointless. The official replies, whether made in parliament or before the Commons' Committees, always ran along the same lines. Admitting that their staff was large and their costs at any rate not cheap, they maintained that they were giving church and nation service of a quality it had never previously experienced. Law business could be done on the cheap, and often had been; preferring not to risk embarrassing their posterity, however, they preferred to make sure everything was in good order—and had to pay accordingly. Church estates, whether agricultural or urban, were notoriously in bad shape; money had to be spent on them not only to make them capable of rendering their full potential value, but often also to do justice to the folk who lived on them; agents had to be paid to superintend the improvements. Moreover, on coming

[1] 1848 report, p. vi.   [2] Third report, p. ix.   [3] 1863, pp. iii–iv.

into the Commissioners' hands, these estates had to be identified, mapped and surveyed, as they hardly ever had been, before the Commissioners could carry out any of their obligations in respect of them. Things that clerical individuals and corporations had done indifferently and spasmodically—often necessarily, because of their limited life-interests —the Ecclesiastical Commissioners were trying to do consistently and well. They wanted to do it in style; they believed in building to last; and although the cost of their management seemed excessive against the small yearly rents at first receivable, the solidity of their groundwork must in the end have saved the church a great deal of money.

Critics of official expenditures, given plenty of ammunition by the Commissioners' administrative thoroughness, made the most of it before an appreciative audience. The Commissioners were perhaps unusual at that time in declining to cut costs to a minimum. But it was not always wise or good to do so. Tragic mistakes were certainly made through trying to minimize public expenditure and central control; the Irish Famine, the cholera epidemics, the Revised Code, come quickly to mind. The Treasury's habitual meanness was something the Commissioners had often come across, and it is not certain that the Treasury was always right. To compel the Commissioners to pay all their expenses—including the salaries of the Estates Commissioners, and the expenses attendant on the Church Building Commission's work after they took it over[1]—was perhaps justifiable, on the grounds that one interference with the church's property justified any; but the Lords' 'Committee on Spiritual Destitution' took the Treasury severely to task for its refusals to sanction even a small grant of public money to aid the building of a church for the employees of Woolwich Arsenal.[2] The Ecclesiastical Commissioners, who were free from Treasury control in the expenditure of the church's money, may have been on the side of the angels after all.

One good contemporary guide there is to the merits of this argument over the Commissioners' expenses. In 1859 a Treasury Committee investigated the Commissioners' 'office establishment', interpreting its terms of reference broadly, and inquiring particularly closely into those matters which popular rumour held to be most at fault—the

[1] 29 and 30 Vic. c. III s. 19.
[2] Report, pp. xv–xvi: P.Ps. 1857–8, IX, 15–16.

auditing, for example, the secretary's alleged arbitrariness, and the employment of private firms of solicitors and surveyors. Their report was wholly favourable to the Commissioners. Considering the charges made against the Commissioners on these and similar heads, it was astonishingly favourable; and it may be considered a sad commentary on human frailty, that this verdict of 'not guilty' was actually printed by the 1862-3 committee as an appendix to their condemnatory report.[1] The only fault the Treasury men found was in the manner of the auditing, the only caution they uttered was against over-thoroughness and consequent extravagance in the registry. Far from criticizing the number of clerks employed, they thought the official establishment too small and proposed its increase. They found that the Commissioners' staff worked longer hours than civil servants in comparable departments, and for less pay. They thought Chalk did his job very well. They considered the pros and cons of employing outside firms, and concluded that the advantages outweighed the disadvantages. In sum, they dismissed the popular charges about extravagance and inefficiency out of hand. Unless this was a piece of official whitewashing, as the Commissioners' more rabid enemies did not hesitate to assert, the Treasury Committee's favourable report has to be taken at its face value.

The complaints about red-tape and the harshness of their official procedures may be quickly dealt with. No doubt some clergymen were hurt by the curt formal letters they sometimes got from Chalk or Aston. The Surbiton case,[2] and that of Mr Moss,[3] certainly involved some unpleasantness. But such things can hardly be avoided in the conduct of big concerns, and they are easily blown up into major grievances by the ignorant or offended. One of the chief witnesses for the prosecution in 1862 was a director of the Bank of England, William Cotton, a wealthy pious patron of good causes and a keen church builder. He had published his grievances against the Commissioners before the Cambridge Church Congress of 1861, and was brought before the Committee to repeat his charges. Those that were not based on misunderstandings turned out to be ridiculous.[4]

[1] 1862, pp. 293–307.   [2] See the 1862-3 committee, 1862 Qs. 4451–714.
[3] *Ibid.* Qs. 900–12, 1241–6.
[4] See the examination of Chalk on this matter, 1862 Qs. 616–64, Cotton's own evidence, and his cross-examination by Walpole and Deedes, Qs. 2204–425.

Those who thought the Commissioners in some way sinister came to that conclusion mainly, of course, because of the Commissioners doing things they disliked. The pleasure of imputing extravagance and arbitrariness to them was enriched by making the charges in a melodramatic key. There need not have been any material basis to the charge. But in fact there was some material basis, deriving from the peculiarity of their constitutional position. They were poised on the isthmus of a potentially uncomfortable, but actually rather convenient, middle state, between being on the one hand absolutely subordinate to parliament and without discretion of any kind, and on the other hand enjoying ordinary departmental discretion and being appropriately represented by a responsible minster. They were half represented, and they had some discretion; but their parliamentary representatives, whether the prime minister, the home secretary, one or other of the Estates Commissioners, or even a prelate, were none of them *wholly* responsible for the policies they had to defend; and as for the Commissioners' discretion, it was very largely circumscribed by the statutes that gave them their powers.

The anomalies of such a position, and the difficulties arising from it, seem only occasionally to have excited discussion. There were so many boards of different kinds in early Victorian England that the Commissioners—who, after all, although they sometimes made a stir, were nothing like as conspicuous as some other boards, and never cost the public more than a few thousand a year—attracted comparatively little notice. Their enemies on the 1862-3 committee, seeking to pare their claws, proposed to make over the whole property-managing side of the business to two paid Commissioners, ineligible for seats in parliament, and one unpaid Commissioner with a seat in Commons; that, they felt, would be quite enough for a board reduced satisfactorily to total dependence. On the other side, no one seems ever to have demanded that they should become a proper executive department under a responsible minister. Cardwell discussed the idea with Lord Chichester at the 1862-3 committee.[1] The conclusion of the discussion seemed to be that so radical a change in the Commissioners' constitution was not worth the trouble. So they went on in the old way, pursuing a middle course that could give offence on either side, and with their relationship to

[1] 1862, Qs. 447-50.

the legislature a trifle obscure. The Radicals, for example, cannot have been very pleased when, having successfully moved an Address to the Crown for returns of all the prelates' incomes during 1844 and 1845,[1] Murray palmed them off with the 1843 returns and the comment that 'the Commissioners are only authorized by Act of Parliament to call for returns of Episcopal Incomes at the expiration of every Seven years'.[2] But if it was convenient at times to stick tight to the will of parliament, it could be convenient at other times to ignore it. What principally divided the prelates from the lay Commissioners in the case of the dean of York (1858–60) was the laymen's feeling that the Commissioners should go back to parliament and ascertain its will before acting, and the bishops' refusal to do so.

There were thus some grounds for fearing that the Ecclesiastical Commissioners were more independent than they ought to be; and these fears were used by their particular foes to fortify a suspicion that as the Commissioners increased the quantity of church property under their control, and executed their policy of consolidating it, they would become able to influence voters after the normal way of landed pro-prietors. Excitable radicals and anti-clerical liberals were bound to take this seriously. In the debates on the 1860 Act, it was alleged that bishops and chapters would be able to meddle in politics better than ever before as they got their own estates consolidated and moved into convenient proximity for them by the Commissioners. Similar fears were ex-pressed with regard to the Commissioners themselves by some of the 1862–3 committee men.[3] Such fears have interest, as evidence of the way in which the minds of some of the Commissioners' enemies worked.

It remains in this section only to consider those enemies' constructive proposals. Their destructive criticisms rested to a great extent on grounds common to all who viewed the slow progress of executive power with misgivings. This talk about red-tape, waste, arbitrariness and so on was a *lingua franca* for individualist liberals. But the con-structive side of the case against the Commissioners was inevitably more specialized, for the cure prescribed for centralization in one depart-ment would obviously not do in all. The Ecclesiastical Commissioners

---

[1] 3 February 1846. *Hansard*, 3/LXXXIII, 449–50.
[2] P.Ps. 1846, XXXII, 1.   [3] E.g. 1862, Qs. 397–404, 1506–15.

were by this time a very big concern involved with property all over the country, engaged in financial transactions totalling millions each year, charged with the execution of important ecclesiastical policies. What was necessary and what was valuable in their work had to be taken care of, even if as the Ecclesiastical Commissioners they should cease to exist. It was not at all an easy problem to solve.

The majority on the 1862-3 committee[1] resolved that the Estates Commissioners in their present form were 'objectionable', not least because as a single central body they controlled so much property and decided upon the boundaries of new districts and divided parishes throughout the kingdom. The property side of the work they proposed to entrust to the three-man board that has already been mentioned;[2] the rest of it—parochial division, augmentation and so on—they proposed to divide between an enlarged Queen Anne's Bounty and 'local associations in each diocese, composed of clergy and laity' and naturally possessing 'an intimate knowledge of the spiritual wants and local circumstances of each diocese'.

The setting-up of such local boards had been pressed so prominently by the members of one family that they might almost be described as 'the Selwyn plan'. Charles Jasper Selwyn, a prudent and successful barrister, was one of the members for Cambridge University. He had led the opposition to the Ecclesiastical Commissioners' Act of 1860 and sounded a loud alarm against centralization. In 1862-3 on the Commons' Committee he assumed the role of counsel for the prosecution. One of his star witnesses was his brother William, Lady Margaret Professor of Divinity at Cambridge, vicar of Melbourne and canon of Ely, who had first broken a lance against the Commissioners as long ago as

---

[1] An odd combination, under odd circumstances. After an unusually long and rancorous closing session, five of the committee men wanted to report simply their 'inability to arrive at a satisfactory conclusion', and six insisted on passing the death-sentence. The five were Spencer Walpole, at that time Third Estates Commissioner; G. W. Hunt; J. H. Scourfield; Robert Lowe; and A. F. Kinnaird. The six implacables were P. J. Locke King; Alderman Copeland; H. Fenwick; C. J. Selwyn; C. N. Newdegate; and Lord Robert Cecil, who carried on the campaign for their destruction with a venomous article in the *Saturday Review*, 2 January 1864—'universal hatred', 'jobbing of a fossil, mammoth kind', etc. (Attribution by J. F. A. Mason, in *Bulletin of Institute of Historical Research*, XXXIV, 36 ff.)

[2] Above, p. 429.

1838,[1] and who between 1858 and 1860 published a series of very shrewd, amusing and admirably good-tempered attacks on them in his anonymous *Conversations on Legislation for the Church, between M.P. and Canon.*[2] Quite clearly the two brothers were working hand in glove. Close behind them stood their much respected brother-in-law George Peacock, dean of Ely, who with the chapter submitted petitions against the Commissioners, and made out the cathedrals' case in general for greater control over their own revenues and affairs than the Commissioners were inclined to give them. All the Selwyns were true-blue Tories, but, with the probable exception of Charles, they wore their Toryism with an agreeable air of enterprise and public spirit. The third brother, George Augustus, went as first bishop to New Zealand; Canon William made generous and judicious benefactions, and was a leading light on the Cathedrals Commission; their sister's husband was almost notoriously implicated with the reform of their university. They must all have disliked the Ecclesiastical Commissioners on many grounds, but it can hardly be doubted that the mainspring of their hostility about 1860 was their devotion to the idea of restoring the cathedrals to splendour and usefulness. The canon had had this on his mind ever since he first took a dislike to the Commissioners. One of his earliest pamphlets was *An Attempt to investigate the true Principles of Cathedral Reform* (1839); and he had written more on the same theme. The Commissioners' reduction of the cathedral establishments had from the start been the most controversial of their policies, opposed not only by the reactionary protagonists of chartered privilege but also by a much more respectable class of conservative reformers who, while usually holding different and distinctive views as to what could be done with the cathedrals, all agreed that nothing much could be done without men and money. The Ecclesiastical Commissioners deprived the cathedrals of both and were therefore more consistently disliked by the cathedral clergy than by any others. To the canons' aid came sympathy from that side of the public mind which responded to the appeal of the medieval and the picturesque, and, as the abuses of the unreformed cathedrals became increasingly forgotten, from a wider public still. The cathedrals'

[1] See above, ch. 7, p. 315.

[2] There were at least nine in the series. Only nos. 1, 2, 4, 5, 6, and 9 are in the Cambridge University Library.

revanche was signalized during the debates on the Act of 1850, when eloquent pleas were made on their behalf in both houses and an attempt by Sidney Herbert and Gladstone to secure a new deal for them was defeated only by 104 to 84.[1] Their claims were then forcefully and comprehensively stated by the Cathedrals Commission of 1852-4.

Of this Commission, William Selwyn was a member. According to his biographer in the *Dictionary of National Biography*, he was its guiding light.[2] The Commission heard no oral evidence but conducted all its inquiries through the post, taking opinions from none but bishops, deans, canons, minor canons and heads of houses. In these circumstances a keen man could more easily bring the evidence to back a particular case than if it were being taken orally. The rather antiquarian tone of the whole, and much of the supporting material, was identical with what Selwyn had been saying for years; and the idea of local or diocesan boards appeared in several places, although it was not made one of their formal recommendations. It was proposed by the deans and chapters of Durham (which was only to have been expected), Salisbury (where W. K. Hamilton's influence was ascendant), and Ely; the other capitular bodies, fearful of losing their autonomy, were more or less hostile to the idea. Old Bishop Monk let the cat out of the bag when he wrote, apropos of the Commission's delicate reference to this idea in their questionnaire, that they seemed to be referring 'to some scheme in agitation for extension or improvements, of which I have not been apprised'.[3]

The Cathedrals Commission, for all its antiquarianism and despite the self-interestedness which showed through the statements of some chapters, had much to report that was worthwhile, and its recommendations respecting the overhaul of Cathedral Statutes were sound. But nothing came of it. It was of too esoteric a character for the general public or the ordinary member of parliament to take note of. Church

---

[1] 15 July. *Hansard*, 3/CXII, 1410 ff.

[2] It is curious that the same suspicion of being dominated by one member attached to the next Cathedrals Commission. When Bishop Temple spoke roughly in the Lords of its report, he spoke with pleasing directness of 'the man who drew up this Paper': see his exchange with Viscount Cranbrook, 22 June 1882, *Hansard*, 3/CCLXXI, 9.

[3] First report, p. 578, referring to a document on pp. 560-1.

extension and religious education, subjects that would have attracted attention, hardly appeared in its pages. Of the many ecclesiastical blue books of the age, it was perhaps the most noticeably ecclesiastical; and there was moreover a strong presumption that it had been rigged.[1]

The Selwyns' seed thus fell on stony ground in 1854, and on ground not much more receptive in 1862 and 1863. Charles Selwyn confronted Lord Chichester with the idea of local boards during the committee's second meeting.[2] Chichester gave not an inch away. He thought such boards must either mean the duplication of work or the surrender to local influences. (This latter, of course, was what Selwyn wanted). If they were to be part of an efficient system, it would have to be an expensive one; if the system were not to be expensive—much more expensive, he maintained, than the Commissioners were at present—then it could not possibly be efficient. To Selwyn's arguments from his own experience, Chichester replied in like coin; he said that the diocesan association he belonged to, while active and capable as the best, would certainly not like to undertake the management of church estates, nor did it dislike dealing with the Ecclesiastical Commissioners. Selwyn tried to get him to damage his own case by aspersing the principle of local associations; Chichester said no one could value the work of local voluntary bodies more than he, but insisted there were some things that only a central board could do. The Committee came back to the same points later on, when Edward Cardwell helped Chichester make out his case for the greater efficiency and economy of a single central board.[3] It looked a sound case. Nothing that subsequently came up in evidence or discussion damaged it. But there were enough angry men beside Selwyn on the committee to get the local boards into their report. That however, was the full extent of their victory. No consequent action was taken, and local boards were never heard of again.[4]

With the practical neglect of this committee's report, the Ecclesiastical Commissioners were safely past the last ambush in which their enemies had tried to destroy them. Men had wanted to reduce their

[1] One wonders why Lords Harrowby and Blandford's signatures were not appended to the third report.

[2] 1862 Qs. 288–91, 308–20.

[3] Qs. 453–9.

[4] Until the diocesan boards of finance were created after the First World War.

importance, even to abolish them, before this, but had not so far sprung so large a mine—although the circumstances of the committee's report and the motives of its supporters were such as to place the explosion quite a long way off. The Commissioners were by now so active, so large a department (46 in all, from the secretary down to the super-numeraries), so ubiquitous in their interests and powers, that it was clearly for their enemies a question of now or never. The Commissioners moreover were bound gradually to become more popular with the parochial clergy; as with increasing affluence they escaped from the necessity of having to reject so many pleas for succour, they would cease to be accused of hard-heartedness or misjudgment. The bishops, on their side, had little choice but to accept them; and in any case the generation of bishops that had known the high old days of episcopal autonomy and land-ownership was almost gone. The last act of the Commissioners that seriously disturbed the harmony of the bench, the redistribution of episcopal patronage in the northern division, was accomplished in 1859.[1] Only some deans and chapters remained irreconcilable. They had cause to do so. Had their wishes been respected, both the Commissioners' funds for the augmentation of needy clergymen, and their powers to apply those funds where the need was greatest, would have been reduced. That was the principle upon which Chichester and Cardwell stood in their argument with Selwyn. It was a good principle. Whether their practice came up to it was another question.

3. AUGMENTATIONS: BISHOPS, DEANS, AND PARISH CLERGY

The Ecclesiastical Commissioners' policy in respect of bishops underwent no significant changes during the mid-Victorian years. The memory of the palaces of the Blomfield-Murray epoch lingered long, but the Commissioners went very gingerly indeed after all the trouble they had caused and never again gave grounds for believing that they were building fine residences for bishops at the poor clergy's expense. Bishops' incomes continued to draw unfavourable comment but with neither more nor less justification than earlier, for they remained substantially unchanged.

[1] Order in Council dated 29 July, gazetted 5 August 1859.

The only important events in the episcopal branch of the Commissioners' activities were the formation of a second new see, that of Manchester, in 1847, and the merging of the Episcopal and Common Funds three years later.

A bishopric of Manchester had been intended from the very beginning, and—since they could not see their way to the creation of a non-parliamentary bishop—room was to be made for it by the union of the sees of Bangor and St Asaph, in the same way that the see of Ripon had been created on condition of the union of Gloucester and Bristol. This union of Gloucester and Bristol was not accomplished without difficulty, but the difficulties were nothing compared with those that got in the way of uniting St Asaph with Bangor. The formation of the diocese of Ripon has been ably studied by A. M. G. Stephenson;[1] the formation of the diocese of Manchester would even better repay investigation, for not only was its building a longer process, but its launching was accompanied by a complicated and interesting controversy, in Manchester, over the proper mode for establishing it there (and over the whole question of church extension, of which under the peculiar local circumstances it could not help forming part).

Difficulties began with the longevity of the existing bishops of St Asaph and Bangor. William Carey was 61 when he moved from Exeter to St Asaph in 1830. Christopher Bethell was 57 when he went to Bangor in the same year. Neither of them was willing to take on the united dioceses, and so the Commissioners had to hope that when one died, the prime minister would appoint to succeed him a clergyman willing to do so as soon as the other died. Despite the legendary longevity of bishops, it was not unreasonable of the Commissioners to hope that death would clear the way. Their plan was completed and published early in 1839,[2] and although they later modified its financial provisions, from its principle they never budged. In the autumn of 1846, when Carey died and the co-operative Short was appointed in his place, they still meant to go on with it.[3]

But the plan had to be abandoned all the same. The clergy of both

[1] Oxford B. Litt. thesis, 1960. His main interest however is more the life of Ripon's first bishop, Longley.
[2] Order in Council dated 12 December 1838, gazetted 25 January 1839.
[3] See the minutes and correspondence printed in P.Ps. 1851, XLII, 343–5, 358–0.6

dioceses had always denounced its financial and administrative provisions as taking away from a dissent-ridden land the means of gradually
re-establishing the church there and of adequately rewarding the clergy.
Provincial and racial loyalties sprang readily to their aid. The earl of
Powis took the lead in pressing their claims on the legislature; and the
outcome of all this was, that in 1847 the separate lives of the two north
Welsh dioceses were reprieved and the creation of additional but still
parliamentary bishops made possible by introducing the principle of
seats by seniority.[1] This sensible compromise removed the worst
barrier from the creation of further sees; but no more were in fact
created until St Alban's and Truro in the seventies.[2]

The merging of the Episcopal and Common Funds, which was part
of the new constitution under the Act of 1850, was apparently designed
to reassure both lay and clerical publics that the bishops, by losing their
own fund, would be put under proper control. Most of the bishops,
including Blomfield, fought it, on the ground that only from such a
fund, specially kept distinct for the purpose, could come the means
for the extension of the episcopate—perhaps overseas as well as at
home, and perhaps also for complementary purposes such as the endowment of archdeaconries. When they saw that the government was
determined to have its way, they tried to insert a clause requiring the
surplus from the episcopal parts of the new combined fund to be set
aside for these purposes. That move failed also. Rightly or wrongly,
the bishops were popularly understood, by their conduct as Commissioners during the forties, to have rendered the episcopate ineligible
for special treatment. Thus the funds were merged, and any money
for the extension of the episcopate out of the Commissioners' Common
Fund was bound to come, in theory, at the expense of the Commissioners' other interests. It was this more than anything else that prevented the creation of new sees between 1847 and 1875. The matter
was too delicate. Blomfield, as usual, was right.

Not bishops but deans provided the *cause célèbre* for this chapter of the
Commissioners' history. The Acts of 1840 and 1850 rather put deans
into eclipse. This was nobody's deliberate policy, it just happened; as
the torrents of reform legislation washed away the silt of traditional

[1] 10 and 11 Vic. c. 108.
[2] 38 and 39 Vic. c. 34, 39 and 40 Vic. c. 54.

connexions and pluralities, the deans were left with little to do and, most often, little enough for doing it, by the standards of their social equals and professional inferiors. Just grounds for complaint were given when deans, who were required to reside for two-thirds of the year, were debarred from holding any benefice in plurality except one under £500 in the same town[1]: some of them were scarcely getting their statutorily minimal £1000 a year.[2] (Some deans were much better paid. The deans of Durham and Christ Church were guaranteed £3000, the deans of St Paul's, Westminster, Manchester and Windsor £2000, and most of the rest seem to have got well over £1000.)[3] It would appear that section 52 of the Cathedrals Act was intended to give the Commissioners discretion and means to make sure that the incomes of deans of cathedrals of the 'old foundation', some of which had been very lucrative, were not below £1500. Endeavouring to do this for the deans of Salisbury and Wells, the Commissioners ran into legal difficulties, which were not wholly settled by section 18 of the Act of 1850. The great dean of York's case arose when they tried to do the same for him and others a few years later.

Although the Hon. and Rev. Augustus Duncombe, whom Lord Derby made dean of York of 1858 in place of the disreputable William Cockburn, became the centre of the whirlwind, it was not at all his fault; and the whole affair was rather ridiculous. Dean Duncombe did not need money. He had been made dean precisely because he had plenty of money of his own, and could afford to live as high as his friends and relations among the Yorkshire aristocracy, who naturally liked to see someone of their own kind in the deanery. That the dean was only paid a paltry £1000 hardly mattered to such a man. He accepted the post as a sacrificial public service, and the radical Ewart's awkward question about it in the Commons was blandly and effectively put down by Disraeli.[4]

---

[1] 13 and 14 Vic. c. 94 s. 19.

[2] 3 and 4 Vic. c. 113 s. 66. Fees, taxes, and customary payments might reduce it below this.

[3] Their incomes were never officially returned. I go upon assertions in the correspondence on the dean of York's case (C.C.F. 19107, much of it printed in House of Lords Papers, 1860, no. 407) and the forecasts in P.Ps. 1840, XXXIX, I.

[4] 4 June 1858. *Hansard*, 3/CL, 1522–6.

That might have been the last of it, had not the possibility of using this long-awaited change to make some better financial arrangement occurred to certain Commissioners (bishops, apparently), and had not other deans of lesser means persuaded Duncombe to add his name, 'upon public grounds and as a matter of principle', to their memorial to the Commissioners protesting against the continuation of such disparities in decanal incomes, and asking for a rise.[1] This was reasonable enough. There might never be another Duncombe; and the whole position of deans was by this time, as Milman pointed out to Sir George Lewis in the most charming way possible, really very unsatisfactory.[2] The great majority of the bishops, and probably indeed the whole board of Commissioners, could see that, and wish to put it right. On the end, they could agree. But, unhappily, on the means for achieving that end they were deeply divided.

What divided them was the question how much respect should be shown, for reasons of political prudence or constitutional propriety, to parliament. The Estates Commissioners, the lay Commissioners with the House of Commons in mind and no doubt an instinctive preference for ecclesiastical subordination, and old bishop C. R. Sumner, subscribing to the Estates Committee's orthodoxy, were sure that it was wrong to press on with a scheme which had been, though not banned, at least deprecated by the Crown lawyers, and which ran flat contrary to an earlier decision of the legislature. The other Commissioners, the bishops, would not wait. They had the votes, they had the deans, they had the money too; and in the end they won. In 1858 Chichester easily persuaded Lord Derby[3] to get their Order in Council stopped by the Privy Council Office. In 1859, when the bishops had a second shot, Chichester brought Palmerston and Granville (who were ex officio Commissioners but had never been before) and Lewis (who as a secretary of state was eligible as a Commissioner and was, as Palmerston remarked, 'dubbed' specially for the occasion) along to the vital meeting to try and dissuade them.[4] They failed; and several deans' incomes were

[1] The others were G. H. S. Johnson of Wells, H. P. Hamilton of Salisbury, and Dawes of Hereford. (House of Lords Papers, 1860, no. 407, pp. 3–5).
[2] Letter of 26 June 1859. P.R.O., G.D./29/24.1.
[3] Chichester to Palmerston, 22 June 1859. P.R.O., G.D./29/24.1.
[4] Letter to Granville, 22 (?24) June, in *ibid.*

consequently raised to £1500, and that of the dean of York to £2000.

The sound of scuffling within the board-room could not but be heard outside, and this affair soon became matter for popular comment and surmise. What made it so rich, was that the dean who came out of it with the biggest increase was the very one who had been appointed in the first place because he did not need money. There were many things which lent themselves to misinterpretation. Duncombe was probably innocent of the plotting cupidity with which popular suspicion endowed him. Some deans really were ill-paid, by the standards the upper clergy set for themselves. But to press it in the way they did was imprudent of the bishops. Bernal Osborne called it 'the great job of the session'.[1] It was bound to look like that. G. H. Sumner, the bishop of Winchester's son, writing in defence of the Commissioners a few years later, did not attempt to deny that they had handled the affair very badly.[2] *The Times*, which was by this time more friendly towards the Commissioners and anxious to promote their work of augmentations, was saddened and disgusted. Why, it asked, should one dean have more than another?

This interesting and plaintive cry made its way into the House of Lords through the speech of the bishop of London, who added ill-used deans to the noble catalogue of sufferers from the world's injustice. It was a new aspect of them; but still none of us will know till the consummation of all things how many martyrs there have been in the world—though we may conjecture that the number will not be small, if the title comprehends all who wish particularly for £500 a year more than they have.

The truth, alleged *The Times*, was simply that Duncombe's appointment, and the improvement of decanal incomes in general, were meant primarily to maintain the connexion between the church and the aristocracy. There was enough truth in that to make it hurt. The conclusion that *The Times* drew from it had more uncomfortable truth in it still. Disraeli, defending Dean Duncombe's appointment in 1858, had rounded on the liberal opposition by blaming them for originally cutting down the incomes of deans to the point where only men of private means could afford to accept deaneries—'pleasant news', com-

---

[1] 21 August 1860. *Hansard*, 3/CLX, 1689.

[2] *The Ecclesiastical Commission* (reprinted from *The Churchman's Family Magazine*), pp. 52–4.

mented *The Times*, 'for the laborious clergy, who, having been shut out for a long time from these appointments because they were too good for them, were now shut out from them because they were too bad. It would seem as if the preferment of the Church never could be in that happy state of precise adaptation in which it would act as the reward of services. . . .'[1]

The dean of York's case was interesting and revealing; but it was only a storm in a tea-cup, in the context of the Commissioners' main work, the 'providing for the cure of souls, with special reference to the residence of the clergy in their respective dioceses'.[2] This work had been more or less at a stand since the middle forties. The bulk of their early augmentations rested on the loan from Queen Anne's Bounty, and the repayment of that and the interest upon it became the first charge on their funds. Only after 1856 did their income reach a level that enabled them to look again to doing something beyond that. With their resumption of ordinary augmentations, their popularity began to rise. 1844 to 1856 were their worst years, when, strait-jacketed by their obligations to the Bounty, committed to the mass of annual payments they had undertaken in 1843 and 1844 and embarrassed by the promises they were unable to honour, with their income rising but slowly on account of their difficulties over enfranchisement, they could do little to help the church in its great need. From 1858 to the nineties were in many ways their best years, when they really accomplished a great deal and did much to redeem their early and involuntary sloth. Now at last they were really working as William Selwyn's thick-skinned 'M.P.' described them, 'like one of those large clouds we sometimes see on a fine day, travelling from East to West, taking up into itself the rich moisture of the land in Durham, and dropping it unexpectedly in Lancashire or Staffordshire. Or take a humbler illustration, from our great sanitary works, it's like a steam-engine, pumping up money from all the chapters in England into the great central reservoir in London, thence to be distributed by pipes and conduits to every spot of the country'.[3] It is an interesting reflection of the re-

[1] *Times* second leader, 13 August 1860, p. 8 c–d. It had already dealt with the subject in a second leader on 28 July, p. 9b.
[2] The language of Peel's original commission, to which they commonly recurred.
[3] *Conversations on Legislation for the Church*, no. 1, pp. 12–13.

volution that has taken place in public opinion, that an illustration which Selwyn meant to be damaging to the Commissioners, should now seem apt and even complimentary.

The augmentations policy which the Estates Committee recommended and the Commissioners adopted in 1856 differed from their first policy, that of the early forties, in two important respects. It was different, just as—perhaps largely because—the times were different. The early forties had been anxious, angry years, revolutionary and rebellious; the condition of England had never looked, was indeed never again to look, worse. The Commissioners, face to face with crisis and egged on by a government that looked more to them than to any other agency to do something about it, acted somewhat precipitately. They repented at leisure over the next decade, and experienced the chagrin of having to refuse offers of benefactions to the total sum of £200,000, for lack of funds to meet them with.[1] When at last they sighted the prospect of resuming augmentations, they determined not to follow their spirited but exhausting early policy of making grants in the form of income, but to make capital grants, as Queen Anne's Bounty did. They may have felt the safer in doing this, for the greater social peace and prosperity into which they had moved. The fifties were golden years compared with the forties; the bite had gone out of politics, the fires of popular discontent were banked; neither the mood of the decade nor the attitude of the government pressed them to proceed in any but prudent ways. They were content therefore to go on the principle of slow but safe, husbanding their resources and distributing their largesse with discrimination. Capital grants would leave the Commissioners with an uncommitted revenue in hand against the expenses of their having, in consequence of the legislation of the fifties, to purchase church leasehold reversions.

This was not the only respect in which their new augmentations policy differed, to begin with, from their old. They determined to make grants only to meet benefactions. Thus would they make their funds go twice as far, or further still. Their early grants had mostly been 'unconditional'. Now they would rely on the great spirit of charitable giving that was swelling to its mid-Victorian climax. The Estates

[1] Estates' Committee Report, 4 December 1856, in Appendix to the 1862 report of the 1862–3 Committee.

Committee, from whom in the first place these plans came, cannot have been blind to the considerable drawbacks of this policy. They were not absolutely dogmatic in their framing of it. They spoke of pursuing this policy 'in the first instance'; they expected later on, when their funds were larger, to be able to make some grants to populous poor parishes where 'benefactions only of a limited nature can be procured'. But they were very nearly dogmatic and extreme in their reliance on churchmen's doing charitable duties, which, in truth, they did little enough to encourage. Their official manners towards benefactors in the ensuing years had a somewhat repellent quality; it seems that men must have wished to be benefactors very much indeed, to go through with it.[1] The Commissioners certainly viewed the affairs of the church *de haut en bas.*

Some people certainly thought they carried this loftiness too far. The prosecution brought witnesses before the 1862-3 committee to assert that the Commissioners' policy was mistaken and cruel, that they were generally distrusted, that men would not contribute towards church building and endowment because the Commissioners disgusted them. There must have been some truth in these allegations, but there may not have been nearly as much as those who made them liked to think. The Commissioners' policy was of a kind to displease almost all parties. That could have meant that it was, under the circumstances, pretty fair. Nor can it be held against the Commissioners that they made no attempt to play for popularity. Perhaps they were politically imprudent not to do so; particularly in their time of troubles, they could have avoided some odium by better public relations. But their failures in these respects were not moral ones.

The fact was, that some measure of aloofness was essential to their proper functioning. They had to be able to view the church from Durham to Penzance. They had to be free from those local pressures that sprang from such potent passions and principles, and went on obstructing the progress of collectivism right up to the end of the century. They meant to treat each case on its merits, to distribute from their single central fund to each case according to its needs and in relation to their annual budget. They were denounced, inevitably, for

[1] See, e.g. Chalk's defence of their charging the donors of land with the legal expenses; 1862, Qs. 1360-3. Queen Anne's Bounty's policy was exactly the opposite.

'centralization'; they courted unpopularity; but they clave to the course they thought right, in the belief that although some clergymen would wring their hands in the present, they would be better able to ring their bells later on. For the present, therefore, 'conditional' grants were the order of the day. In that course, they believed, lay the church's greatest advantage.

The disadvantages were obvious enough and were, indeed, identical with those that made the early Victorians' reliance on local initiative and generosity for local government and social improvement less than satisfactory. To those who could give, much might be given; those who had nothing to offer, might have to go without. God and the state helped those who helped themselves. This was always the chief defect of a system which had many virtues, and in which the men of the early and middle nineteenth century, devoted equally to the principles of social improvement, voluntary effort, and public economy, firmly believed. And it may be held to have worked well enough, except with regard to the very places that most lacked the services of the clergyman, the teacher, and the constable. The low-class division of a chopped-up parish, the squalid squatters' suburb, the forlorn, lordless rural settlement—such places could hardly raise the money to pay for private bills or, more commonly, offer enough to the Educational Committee of the Privy Council or the Ecclesiastical Commissioners to draw grants from them. Their residents would be too poor, too ignorant, too helpless. Their only hope lay in attracting the charity of outside bodies. This became increasingly possible, as diocesan church building and educational societies burgeoned and the movement for the organization of charity progressed; but the need was far greater than the supply, and all too often the needy clergyman found that charity not only began but also stayed at home, in some more desirable locality.

William Deedes, the Third Estates Commissioner and member for East Kent, who acted as counsel for the defence on the 1862-3 committee, answered a critic's objections on this score ingeniously and, it would seem, ingenuously, by supposing a system of unconditional grants to the neediest parishes and then calling all the hypothetical sums of money that would, under the Commissioners' actual system, have been attracted by them, 'money lost to the church'.[1] Although they

[1] 1862 Q. 4106.

444

were quite soon forced to make departures from it, this remained their orthodoxy for several years. The table in Appendix 7a shows what proportion of their funds the Commissioners granted to meet benefactions, and what unconditionally. In 1860, when they were first compelled to change direction, they seem also to have undergone a slight change of heart, for they set aside £16,000 to be distributed unconditionally, in capital lots of £300 each. The £10 a year that this brought to the clergyman could easily appear derisory. Does it not appear to be trifling, demanded a hostile inquisitor of Chalk, 'to give £10 to a man with nothing at all?'[1] Chalk agreed that it seemed very little, but pointed out that the Commissioners were only just getting going. Only the lightest shower of augmentation had so far freshened the fields of penury. The good, heavy, soaking rains were yet to come. This was the Commissioners' case in answer to their critics, and it was not a bad one, considering that the current needs of the church were far greater than they could hope to satisfy, and that they could not possibly please everybody.

To start with, then, they stuck to the policy of granting capital sums to meet benefactions and reserved the right to decide for themselves which benefactions to accept; each year they were offered more than they could accept, and many offers of course were in connexion with not particularly populous or laborious livings in private patronage that had no good claim. But it was not long before their policy was turned upside down. Parliament in 1860 at last sided decisively with the advocates of local claims, and required the Commissioners to attend to them in respect of any places whatsoever from which they drew revenue. The Cathedrals Act had only required them to attend to the local claims of places from whence they drew tithes or tithe rent-charges; now it was any place that provided any kind of revenue, and the operation of the clause was made retrospective, to include all the episcopal and capitular estates which had come into their hands over the past two decades.[2] Thus a heavy burden, the exact weight of which was only going to be discovered over the period of years in which such claims could be examined and dealt with, was placed upon the Commissioners' shoulders, and their freedom of action circumscribed. Three years later they made another drastic change of policy. This time it was of their own accord.

[1] 1862 Q. 1399.   [2] 23 and 24 Vic. c. 124 ss. 12–14.

Either the volume of complaints at the slowness of their proceedings had made them feel it was dangerous not to cut a more dashing figure, or else they had decided for themselves that their financial prospects were good enough to justify a bolder policy. It is unlikely that they were not influenced to some extent by public opinion. The 1862-3 committee evidently frightened them. About this time they were trying as they had hardly tried before to get themselves appreciated. Their report for 1863 was astonishingly forthcoming.[1] In effect it was an apologia, an admission of the public into their confidence, and an endeavour to gain the confidence of the public. It included an announcement of a 'five-year plan', and printed five documents calculated to raise their public standing—the report of their Estates Committee on the points of mis-management alleged against them by the 1862-3 Committee, a long 'Explanatory Statement as to the Accounts and the Financial Position of the Commission', the Estates Committee's answers to the 1856 com-mittee's questions about their principles of estate management, the 1859 Treasury Committee's report on them, and the report of their own recent select committee on their accounts. The public had never had such a chance to look into the heart of the Commissioners before; nor was it ever to get quite such a chance again, even though the Commissioner's reports retained this communicative quality for some years. At the same time as the Commissioners were sticking up for themselves in this fashion, friends were rallying to their support outside. In 1863 their loyal sur-veyor E. J. Smith published his *Two Letters to the Archbishop of Canter-bury;* in 1864 'A Clergyman in the Diocese of Winchester' published a pamphlet on *The Ecclesiastical Commission, its Origin and Progress; with some Examination of the Report of the Select Committee of the House of Commons,* in answer no doubt to the hostile and even more anonymous (but presumably Selwynian) Cambridge pamphlet, *Report of the Select Committee of the House of Commons on the Ecclesiastical Commissioners, with References to the Evidence.* It was a measure of the stature they had by now achieved that the Commissioners were able for the first time since 1840 to give as good as they got.

The tokens of their new zeal were twofold: the five-year plan, and the decision to augment by grants of income, on their original plan, instead of by grants of capital. Their revenue was going up fast, and they felt

[1] Signed 25 February 1864. P.Ps. 1864, XVIII, 19 ff.

confident they could carry the burden which the new policy would impose, besides reviewing and rewarding all the local claims which parliament had thrust upon them. Within five years (starting in 1864) they expected to raise to £300 a year all existing benefices with over 4000 inhabitants, by their own unaided efforts if they were in public patronage, by meeting benefactions with grants of half the required sum if they were in private patronage. They determined also to set aside enough to provide £200 a year (or £100 to meet the same amount from private sources) for the endowment of new churches.

Through the five years that followed, they held manfully to this course, despite the pressure that continued to be put on them to augment this or that exceptionally deserving class of clergyman; as they testily remarked in 1867 and again in 1868, they could not do everything at once. Yet in these five years they managed to do a very great deal. In half a decade they appropriated to the improvement of poor livings a sum of capital that made up nearly half the whole sum thus appropriated since 1840. They 'granted £650,000 to meet private benefactions of at least equal amount'; endowed 75 new districts of 4000 or more inhabitants with £200 a year; brought up to £300 a year all similar-sized livings in public patronage and met benefactions half-way if the patronage of the livings was private; and, finally, dealt with local claims in respect of the estates of six sees and seven chapters by relating incomes to population, so that benefices of 500 or more inhabitants were brought up to £300 a year, of 400 to £250, and of 300 to £200.[1]

Their five-year plan was accomplished but they went on in much the same way afterwards, reluctantly doling out preferential grants to answer local claims, revising their programme as successive censuses showed the shifts of population, and keeping 4000 in mind as the optimum population for a parish, and £300, more or less, as the minimum stipend for its incumbent.

4. QUEEN ANNE'S BOUNTY IN THE NINETEENTH CENTURY

The Ecclesiastical Commissioners' work had startling and controversial qualities of which the staid old Bounty was completely innocent;

[1] P.Ps. 1868-9, XIX, 6-7. The words of the report actually state that they brought livings up to £200 where the population was 'below 300 persons', but that is clearly a slip.

they dealt wholesale in staggering quantities and had a huge turnover, making the Bounty seem a very old-fashioned and small retail business beside them. The business of the two boards of course overlapped, and their amalgamation was frequently discussed; it seemed, indeed, sensible and obvious. The Estates Commissioners and their henchmen in Whitehall Place no doubt longed to annex the Bounty, and Christopher Hodgson's tone in the memoranda and pamphlet that he produced in the sixties in his board's defence shows him, indignantly, on the defensive. The majority of the 1862-3 committee knew of this spirit of rivalry, and, neglecting no means of spiking the Commissioners' guns, proposed to make over all their augmentations work to the Bounty board. But parliament acted on this suggestion no more than it acted on any of that committee's suggestions, and by 1867, the Commissioners having entered clear water, the suggestion of amalgamation came again from their side[1] A Commons' Committee was appointed next year to consider the question, and concluded that the Bounty had better be left alone.[2] Through the next thirty years, however, the case for uniting them gained strength, with the increasing overlapping of their work. In 1900-1 a joint committee considered it again, and came down in favour of amalgamation; but no more notice was taken of that, than was taken when the Archbishop's Commission under Lord Cave's chairmanship made similar recommendations in 1924. The Bounty remained independent to the end.

While the Commissioners' offices and outhouses in Whitehall Place swelled to contain ever more staff, the Bounty's establishment in Dean's Yard remained small and select. Nevertheless it too expanded, as much in the variety as in the volume of its business. From the first of Gilbert's Acts onwards, it was given by parliament, or obtained by its traditional means of Rules and Orders under the Royal Sign Manual, a growing body of powers and responsibilities regarding poor clergymen.[3] The

---

[1] See E. P. Bouverie in *Hansard*, 3/CLXXXVIII, 1623 (16 July 1867); the clarification of what he was getting at, in the Bounty's solicitors' letter to Spencer Walpole, 28 January 1867 (P.R.O., H.O. 45/7476); and the instructions given to the 1868 Committee on the Bounty, as stated in that committee's report. Bouverie was its chairman.

[2] It was appointed on 19 May 1868.

[3] Summary views of this growth of business are given in the Appendices to the 1900-1 Joint Committee and to W. R. Le Fanu's *Queen Anne's Bounty*.

provision and maintenance of residence-houses became a major pre-occupation. The Board made loans for their purchase, construction and improvement, and extended its powers to cover both lands and out-buildings contiguous to the residence and glebe, and farm-buildings and labourers' cottages on benefice property. The uses and abuses of such loans were equally obvious. The Bounty's rate of $3\frac{1}{2}\%$ or 4% was lower than any other lender would have asked, and the period of repayment could be stretched up to thirty-one years; houses might be built and alterations made, which would otherwise have been unmanageable. But the power thus given to an incumbent to burden his successor or successors (who might have less money of their own, or find themselves living in much harder times) with a share of the repayments could work to their disadvantage, and the Bounty certainly incurred much under-standable, though less than just, unpopularity, in its character of debt-collector. As its secretary wrote in 1921, 'The very name of Queen Anne's Bounty may well sound incongruous to incumbents whose sole connection with the Corporation is the demands from its officials for sums due on mortgage.'[1]

With the related and coeval question of dilapidations also the Bounty came to have more to do. The law on dilapidations had always been uncertain and unsatisfactory. At last it received some attention in 1871. The Ecclesiastical Dilapidations Acts of that year and the next provided for the compulsory survey of all benefice buildings at each vacancy, and the payment of the dilapidations money to the Bounty board, who were to superintend its application. This made sure that it was not frittered away by the new incumbent, but did little to cheer the de-parture of the outgoing incumbent, upon whom—or upon whose widow—the burden of dilapidations lay as heavy as ever. The Bounty's intervention made for efficiency rather than humanity; church reform could be promoted as much by screwing the poor clergy down tight, as by easing the pressures on them.

These were the main new lines of Queen Anne's Bounty's business in the later nineteenth century. There were others—superintendence of sales or exchanges of glebe lands and lands originally bought with Bounty money, the acceptance of gifts and managements of trusts for the augmentation of livings, the receipt and investment of funds

[1] Le Fanu, ed. Hughes, p. 64.

coming from the redemption of tithe rent-charges, and so on. With so many irons (some of them, admittedly, very small) in the ecclesiastical fire, the variety no less than the quantity of business passing through the offices in Dean's Yard required an expansion of staff. In 1837 Christopher Hodgson had been able to manage with seven clerks.[1] In 1868 he had twelve; in 1900 his successor had twenty-seven. The number of governors grew by the multiplication of *ex officio* members until by 1901 it exceeded six hundred. Of these, only fifty-two (which included all the prelates) received summonses or ever attended meetings, and none of the rest were ever even told, when *ex officio* they became governors, that they were entitled to attend board meetings. Notices of meetings were still announced in the *London Gazette*—a 'somewhat antiquated method'—in fact, 'an almost useless formality'—commented the 1900-1 committee. A small group of laymen had come to take an important share in the board's work since the 1868 committee recommended the breaking of the bishops' long monopoly, and most of the bishops now attended by rota; but the tone of the Bounty seems to have been very little different from what it had been fifty, an hundred, or a hundred and fifty years before. It remained a quiet, proud, independent, archaic little office, fiercely jealous of its bigger younger brother in Whitehall Place, and determined to surrender none of the functions which gave it a claim to usefulness.[2] Of these functions, the oldest remained the most cherished.

Queen Anne's Bounty continued to flow for the poor clergy's benefit in just the same kind of way and at exactly the same rate as it had flowed since Anne's death. The governors had a gross sum of £15,000, more or less, to dispose of each year. It came, as it always had done, from first-fruits and tenths, most of them assessed still at the rates given in the 1535 *Liber Regis;* the only changes before the twentieth century being in respect of the prelates, whose incomes were charged, in 1852, with a small annual tax of $1\frac{5}{8}\%$ in lieu of their ancient obligations.[3] No new

[1] For the purpose of this comparison I am counting the four clerks of the First-Fruits and Tenths Offices in with the three of the Bounty Office.

[2] For its resistance to the 1900-1 attempt at amalgamation, see below, ch. 10, pp. 463-4.

[3] Order in Council dated 27 November 1852; Ecclesiastical Commissioners' sixth report.

assessment of first-fruits and tenths was ever made, nor were any benefices created since 1535 ever brought under contribution. Its system, such as it was, was highly irrational and absurd; but it was all that it had, and there was no chance whatsoever of substantial improvement. The only alternative to continuing along its old paths was to give up altogether and sell out to the Ecclesiastical Commissioners, and that was the last thing it wanted to do. It therefore kept to the old paths.

The principal claim made on the Bounty's behalf to justify its continued independent course of augmentation was that it looked after a class of poor livings which the Commissioners ignored. These were in the main country livings of far too small a population to attract the Commissioners' attention, and they were always under £200 a year. In livings over that value, whatever their population or difficult circumstances, the Bounty had no interest until 1923; and until the last decade of the nineteenth century, at any rate, it proceeded for the most part simply by grants of capital sums of £200 to meet benefactions of equal or greater value.[1]

Its operations remained open to the same criticisms as had been made of them earlier. The use it made of its slender resources was in many ways uneconomical. Too many tiny country livings got augmentations which really served only to delay their death agonies. Not until the turn of the century did it begin to inquire into the possibilities of uniting parishes before augmenting them.[2] Patrons continued to do very well out of the Bounty. Only if they declined to meet the Bounty's modest conditions—principally, in donatives or sinecures, that they should cease to be such—would their benefactions for their own livings be rejected. The question whether there were not many more populous livings worth over £200 a year, which really needed augmentation sooner than less populous livings worth less, was never touched on. So far as the Bounty was concerned, that was not its concern but the Commissioners'.

[1] The only important changes in their practice were made in 1838 (which enabled them to make up to three grants to a particularly needy living in any one year); 1856 (providing for grants of between £100 and £200 to meet benefactions for residence-houses); and 1898 (extending that of 1856 to cover benefactions for endowment as well). See Le Fanu, ed. Hughes, p. 46. [2] Le Fanu, ed. Hughes, p. 39.

Within the narrow limits of its augmentations policy, the Bounty seems to have pursued a straight and conscientious course; and the defences it put forward in the sixties, when its policy and proceedings ran into a squall which ended as suddenly as it began, were, within their terms of reference, satisfactory. Hodgson's *Letter to the Archbishop of Canterbury, on the present Regulations for the Distribution and Management of the Funds of Queen Anne's Bounty* was dull to a degree, but unanswerable; and the charges made against the Bounty by the Lincoln Church Association, a country clergymen's pressure-group which alleged that the Bounty was not reaching the *really* poor clergy, lacked substance. Twelve livings under £30 a year had been cited in proof of the allegation that the Bounty was not doing its proper work. Hodgson dealt with them in the appendix to a lengthy set of 'Observations' which the governors prepared for the satisfaction of the home secretary in May 1866.[1] That two of these benefices had been created since 1836 does not, to be sure, *ipso facto* seem a justification for ignoring them; presumably the Bounty felt they came in the Ecclesiastical Commissioners' province. But so far as the other ten went, the Bounty was obviously justified. The church of one was ruinous; another, alleged to be a mere scandalous £7 10s., had neither church nor population, and its incumbent held in plurality a second benefice of £170. Five were donatives; two of them were held in plurality, the patron of a third had already refused two augmentations and the patron of a fourth had refused three. As for the first on the list, the income of which was nil, Hodgson commented that it 'is not a benefice, and the name of the Clergyman stated to be the incumbent is not in his handwriting: the Petitioner has signed lower down the petition in respect of a Benefice between £150 and £200 a year'. It looks as if this petition suffered from the characteristic defects of nineteenth century petitions—carelessness, excitability, and forgery. The Lincolnshire petition got nowhere. It was mentioned only twice during the meetings of the 1868 committee, and then only to be contemptuously dismissed.[2] It was not along *these* lines that Queen Anne's Bounty could be attacked in the later nineteenth century.

[1] P.R.O., H.O. 45/7476.
[2] By the Bounty's Solicitor, Qs. 879–81, and by Bishop Wilberforce, Qs. 1026–7.

5. ESTATES AND MANAGEMENT

With no body of men were the Ecclesiastical Commissioners less popular than with the clergy of the cathedrals. Of all who came in any way within the Commissioners' sphere of influence, they managed to carry on as they wished for the longest time. Their sense of corporate independence was strong and they had peculiar reasons for disliking the Commissioners. The Commissioners, from their side, had obvious good reasons for wishing to get at the chapters. Between this masterful central board, therefore, and this proud provincial interest, no love was lost, no quarter asked or given. From the thirties to the seventies the battle went on, with now the Commissioners, now the chapters, on top. In the fifties and early sixties this conflict was at its height. After the failure of the 1862-3 committee (with the success of whose majority recommendations the chapters sank or swam) it fell back into the Commissioners' files, and became, with the Commissioners themselves, uncontroversial and, from a public point of view, unexciting. The Act of 1868, establishing the rules under which the closing rounds of the battle were to be fought, and recognizing that the Commissioners had virtually won, went through parliament without comment.[1] The chapters had given up fighting, and the Commissioners had become respectable. Only five years earlier, the respectability of the Commissioners had been as questionable as the pugnacity of the chapters had not. 'Internal' factors alone cannot explain this sudden change. The course of English history at large must have shared responsibility with the Commissioners' growing tact and the chapters' mounting moderation; the concept of a community of interest against an increasingly hostile array of dissenters, Irishmen, agnostics and democrats may well have pushed out old familiar habits of internecine bickering, as the sixties wore on. Whatever its causes, the pacification of the chapters by the later sixties was a fact—which removed the last obstacle to the Ecclesiastical Commissioners' general acceptance and usefulness. They did not indeed become universally popular, the poor clergymen's fairy godfathers, the loyal toast of every visitation dinner, the beneficent patrons of college and cathedral. Each class of clergymen still found fault with the Commissioners, above all the fault of not giving

---

[1] 31 and 32 Vic. c. 114.

everybody what they wanted. But the difference from the seventies onwards was, that the criticisms now made of the Commissioners were of the same order and degree as have continued to be made ever since. About eighteen-seventy, after thirty odd years of growing pains and adolescent awkwardness, the Ecclesiastical Commissioners grew up, and settled down.

They could not do this until they had mastered, or amicably come to some understanding with, the deans and chapters. The poorer parochial clergy were safely under lock and key, the richer swam securely out of reach. Bishops, by the sixties, were no trouble. The early difficulties over their payment had been solved,[1] and the Act of 1860 at last gave the Estates Committee the powers over episcopal estates it had long yearned for. The effect of this Act was, in brief, to veil from the public the fact that the bishops had become, what earlier in the century they had determined never to be, 'stipendiaries', by re-endowing them with estates (which the Estates Committee might manage on their behalf) adequate to provide their statutory incomes, and providing for a revision of the system at every vacancy. The remainder of the bishops' estates passed into the Commissioners' hands, to manage as they would. Thus the huge potential of the episcopal estates was at last brought under firm control, and made ready to supply the church's nation-wide needs.

The potential of the capitular estates was almost as great. Bringing it under control proved much more difficult. The deans and chapters were not merely better fighters, they were also in a better position to fight. They could make out a case for themselves that was a good deal better, in some respects, than the bishops'. Yet as the years went by, it became increasingly intolerable that the Commissioners should be excluded from the management of the remaining capitular estates. These, it must be remembered, were the chapters' corporate properties, the revenues from which the deans and canons divided between them. Those separate properties, from which so many deans and canons had derived part—sometimes the greater part—of their income, all fell in to the Commissioners as existing holders died or resigned, and

---

[1] By the 13 and 14 Vic. c. 94, which substituted a fixed income and variable surplus for the original variable income and fixed surplus; and by the 23 and 24 Vic. c. 124, ss. I–II.

became merged in the common mass of their property, which they could move around and manage as they pleased. The absoluteness of their control over this part of cathedral property made all the more conspicuous and painful the limits of their control over the part that remained under the reformed chapters' management. The Commissioners were entitled to the suspended canons' shares of the corporate revenue. In early years, before many canons had expired, their income from this source was not large, and was very unlikely, in any particular cathedral, to come to more than half the chapter's annual income. But it was not long before some chapters were paying the Commissioners nearly as much as they kept for themselves. The Cathedral Act made no less than seventeen of them suspend at least half as many stalls as they were allowed to retain, at the same time as it pegged canons' incomes within the £500-£1000 bracket.[1] The Commissioners were drawing a large part of their income from this direction between about 1845 and the early sixties; and the share of it provided by the wealthier chapters—notably by Durham, Windsor, Westminster and Canterbury, which besides being wealthy had suffered more than most from suspensions—was very large indeed.

What, under these circumstances, came more and more to irk the Commissioners and their friends outside, was their exclusion from all but a nominal share in the management of properties so evidently important to them. They trusted the chapters no more than they were trusted by them. They suspected that the chapters tried to defraud them, and, in so far as some chapters had a romantic attachment to the old system of fines for renewals of leases,[2] a system which had by 1850 been condemned by everyone else, the Commissioners knew that their properties were not being made the most of. Right through the fifties, anxiety on this score grew; and much evidence was brought before the 1856 committee to show on how unsatisfactory a footing the Commissioners stood in relation towards the chapters.

Some chapters, for example, were prepared to keep their accounts in a form the Commissioners could understand, others not. The Commissioners' right to inspect capitular accounts was never denied, but

[1] s. 66, as interpreted by Chalk for the benefit of the 1856 committee, Qs. 392–3.
[2] About half of them were still renewing leases after 1860. See the 1862–3 committee, 1862 Qs. 14–16.

their rights to regulate expenditure was still not settled by 1856. Their relations with several chapters were deplorable. With that of Durham especially they were on the worst of terms. The correspondence between the Commissioners' secretary and the Durham chapter's clerk was a painful display of litigious brinkmanship.[1] Deans and chapters were jealous of interference in what they regarded, with some justice, as their own preserves. They invoked their ancient statutes, their customs, their social and ecclesiastical responsibilities, to justify items of expenditure to which the Commissioners objected. Already hamstrung and lowered by the Cathedrals Act, they considered it hard to be denied a few small extravagances. The Commissioners, from their side, as participators in the chapters' funds, believed they had a right to object to payments that seemed improper. They wished to know, and could not discover, what was done with the residences of the suspended canonries of Durham. Pieces of plate were presented to retired officers, donations made towards the building of public baths and wash-houses, pensions were granted to widows of deceased canons. One smart chapter, which Chalk giving evidence said he 'need not name', deliberately ran an overdraft and charged the Commissioners the 5% interest they had to pay on it.[2]

For all their indignation at the way the chapters used their small financial freedom, the Commissioners' anxiety to make them virtual stipendiaries, as most of the bishops were by the sixties, came rather from their confidence in their ability to make more of the capitular estates than the chapters could, and their evident resentment (justifiable on grounds of economy and convenience) that this great body of church estates should remain exceptional, beyond their own otherwise complete control. They viewed it as Blomfield viewed peculiars. They sought to take it all over, integrate it with the rest of their property, reorganize it on businesslike lines, and then re-endow each chapter with a convenient close-knit estate adequate to the provision of its statutory income, which they would manage on the chapter's behalf if the chapter wished. This was the policy they single-heartedly pursued, overtly or under cover, from the early fifties until their all-but-total victory in

[1] 1856 committee, first report, Appendix, pp. 250–60.
[2] Most of this paragraph is based on Chalk's evidence to the 1856 committee, Qs. 677–713. See also Lefevre's evidence, Qs. 1997–2033.

1868. It was a policy for which the chapters, in the fifties at any rate, when their pride was still high, showed much distaste.

Their motives for hanging on so persistently to their own estates were relatively disinterested. It was not the hope of financial gain that induced them to hold out for so long. They were not the gainers from the improvement of their properties and the increase of their incomes. Once the original deans and canons of 1840 had gone, their successors were on fixed incomes, and whatever their corporate estates brought in over and above the sum of their own incomes, and the not very generous amount the Commissioners allowed them for cathedral expenses, went to the Commissioners. The more they made above this minimum, therefore, the more the Commissioners would get.

The Commissioners' case against the chapters was that, having no personal interest in improving their estates above that minimum, they would not be brisk and businesslike in management, and would thus, inevitably, let the Church of England down. Part of the chapters' answer was that they could be at least as efficient managers of property as anyone else, and a lot more efficient than the spendthrift centralized Ecclesiastical Commission. They would indeed deal more sympathetically with hard cases than the Commissioners were wont to do, but that would not hurt the church in the things that mattered; better the good opinion of the people than a few shillings more in the bank. The Commissioners themselves had to admit that chapters were at any rate much better fitted for estate management than bishops who would not be so resident, and who might get away with things that could hardly happen when responsibility was split fivefold. The chapters' advocates said that no one had ever questioned the Cambridge and Oxford colleges' abilities to manage their estates, and that anything a college could do, a chapter could do better, since its members would generally be older men and men of greater experience. The Commissioners' replied that good bursars of colleges usually gave more time to the work than it would be proper for a canon to do.

But these arguments on the capitular side were only subordinate ones. The chapters most of all wanted to keep their estates because they liked running them—because it was an activity satisfying in itself, and eminently proper for an upper-class clerical institution. Through the ownership of property, they could do good. The reverend canon Lord

John Thynne, sub-dean of Westminster and its property expert, who gave much evidence to the 1856 committee and showed both spirit and intelligence in his defence of the chapters, told the committee outright that such a rearrangement of property as Lord Blandford and the Ecclesiastical Commissioners sought after 'would diminish the spiritual influence of the dean and chapter of Westminster very considerably'.[1] Lord Robert Grosvenor promptly asked, 'Considering the spiritual nature of a cathedral corporation, do you see any necessity, in order to the proper performance of its duties, that the cathedral body should manage landed property?' Lord John replied that he could not conceive it interfered with the discharge of their spiritual duties in the slightest. 'On the contrary,' he went on, 'my experience as a clergyman is, that no clergyman is more respected than one who in combination with his spiritual duties is able to give advice to his parishioners upon secular questions. . . .'[2] He further stated 'that there is not a single estate belonging to the Dean and Chapter of Westminster to the spiritual improvement of which they have not at one time or another contributed by assisting the incumbent of a church, or building a school, or finding a site for a school, and they have felt an interest therein'.[3] In subsequent cross-examination he withdrew from the position of holding that chapters and so on positively ought to own property and manage it themselves, but insisted that it was highly advantageous they should do so, more for the sake of their tenants than themselves.

Lord Blandford at any rate would not have believed him;[4] but it was a point on which zealous chapter men, by the fifties, prided themselves. No stronger or more remarkable vindication of their rights was put forward than by Dean Pellew of Norwich, on his own and the chapter's behalf, to the Cathedrals Commission in 1854.[5] Lord Sidmouth's biographer found himself opposed at every turn to the advocates of centralization and fixed annual incomes, and pulled out every stop to brand them as uneconomic, fallacious, unconstitutional and sinister. The spirit of the age pained him. 'Judging from the grievous injury to religion, through weakening the influence of the church and

---

[1] Q. 2643. [2] Qs. 2644–5. [3] Q. 2648.
[4] See, e.g., his attack on Westminster and other chapters for neglecting the spiritual wants of places dependent on them, 28 February 1855 (*Hansard*, 3/cxxxvi, 2035–6).
[5] P.Ps. 1854, xxv, 876–8.

her ministers, which is now resulting from the disrespectful manner in which the private affairs and pecuniary transactions of prelates and other dignitaries are discussed in public journals, we consider that it should be the anxious desire of every true churchman to bring the present agitation on ecclesastical subjects to an early close. . . .' The increase of the Ecclesiastical Commissioners' powers was no better a route to this haven than the Selwyns' diocesan or local boards.[1] The best course of action was simply to leave well alone. 'We consider the objection that the care of our estates . . . would withdraw our attention too much from higher duties, to be undeserving of serious answer; we would assert, on the contrary, that the communication with different tenants would bring us usefully in contact with the various classes of society, and by showing us their grievances, necessities and defects would enable us the better to relieve and remedy them, whilst our possession of lands in various parishes would give us an interest in the inhabitants, enlist our sympathies in their favour, and to a certain extent authorize our interference in promoting their welfare'.

This was strong stuff, but not perfectly representative, and of no avail. Some chapters obviously felt more strongly than others. To those that had been not fat but lean, the Ecclesiastical Commissioners and their great central fund must have appeared rather as benefactors than bullies. First York, then Carlisle, then Chester, Peterborough, Gloucester and St Asaph in quick succession came to amicable agreements with the Commissioners. Most of the others followed suit in the sixties, until in the end the Ecclesiastical Commissioners' Act of 1868[2] set the question to rest. Fines for the renewal of leases were at last abolished, and what had by then become the normal procedure was statutorily confirmed: chapters transferred the whole of their estates to the Commissioners and, pending the re-transfer of a convenient estate adequate to their statutory needs, received in lieu an annual cash

---

[1] 'As regards the constitution of the proposed board, we are of opinion that that delicacy of feeling by which real gentlemen are always distinguished, would prevent the leading laity of the diocese from belonging to a committee in which they must sit in judgment on the incomes, conduct, and affairs of the dignitaries of their own church, and that the only parties really desirous of acting on such commissions would be those opposed either to the church generally, to its cathedral establishments, or to individual members thereof.' [2] 31 and 32 Vic. c. 114.

payment. The re-transference of estates took no great time, and by the eighties the whole business was accomplished. Only the dean and chapter of Hereford, along with Manchester and Oxford (special cases), never participated, holding out until the Cathedrals Measure of 1931 brought all these properties back for good into the Commissioners' hands.

CHAPTER X

THE COMMISSIONERS AND THE BOUNTY IN THE MODERN CHURCH OF ENGLAND, 1880-1948

It was not to be expected of institutions as staid and respectable as Queen Anne's Bounty and the Ecclesiastical Commissioners that they should, even in a decade as full of novelty as the eighteen-eighties, indulge in sudden or dramatic change. They concealed their adaptations to changed circumstances behind a screen of polite conservatism. Queen Anne's Bounty, continuing to repel the Commissioners' advances, assumed no important new responsibilities until after the First World War. With the Ecclesiastical Commissioners it was much the same. Until at any rate 1907, they stayed on the tracks laid down in their heroic mid-Victorian years. Their policy inevitably underwent some changes and they took on additional responsibilities but these were all developments out of responsibilities already borne; they marked no major new departures. Men still questioned whether the Bounty Board was worth its keep, but no one after 1880 seriously suggested that the Commissioners could be dispensed with. The passage of each successive year saw the Commissioners bedded deeper in the church's system, and their claims on churchmen's recognition or even gratitude increased as they made livings more liveable on, parishes more manageable, and the church's properties more profitable. As their usefulness within the establishment increased, so did their position in general become securer. The Church of England was still involved in politics but more and more marginally, and more and more on one account alone, that of education. With this side of the church's life the Commissioners had nothing directly to do, and so none of the mud thrown at it by the nonconformists stuck to them. Their history from the eighties onwards is almost entirely clear of the violent quarrels and picturesque incidents which enliven the record of their early years. They became almost uncontroversial.

Almost—but not quite. Now and then old fires would burst up from some apparently extinct crater and show that although the Ecclesiastical Commissioners could not be done without, the old suspicions and resentments lingered on. The consolidation, improvement and protection of church property was one of their biggest responsibilities and by far their most troublesome. Their motives and powers were easily misunderstood by the ignorant or malevolent, and sometimes they suffered much from attacks made on them by the friends (often far from disinterested friends) of those whom they were thought to have treated badly. The case might be ostensibly a reasonable one, of a farmer perhaps who felt aggrieved at the termination of his tenancy, or of a group of working people made homeless by slum clearance;[1] it might be more hysterical and improbable, as for example when a farmer's friend alleged that the Commissioners' local agents were helping incumbents levy distress on Kentish farmers for non-payment of extraordinary tithe,[2] and when the ideas attained wide and eager acceptance, in the later eighteen-eighties and early nineteen-thirties, respectively, that the Commissioners were making money for the clergy out of public-houses and brothels.

Such attacks came from outside the church and had the effect, frequently a designed effect, of smearing the church as a whole; it was this unhappy consequence of calumnies otherwise contemptible that made the Commissioners so particularly anxious to answer them. Of the Commissioners' standing within the church, one can at least say that it was in general much higher than it had been in mid-century. No doubt many who loved the old cathedrals, and entertained golden ideas of what they might have become if history had run down different channels, never quite forgave the Commissioners either their share in the chapters' undoing or their continued inability to give the chapters

[1] E.g. *Hansard*, 3/CCXXXIX, 1081–3 and CCXLI, 744–52, and House of Lords Paper 1878 no. 74, for the case of the Godmanchester farmer Charles Armstrong; or the questions asked in the Commons in 1886–7 about the demolition of Bream's Buildings, Holborn: *Hansard*, 3/CCCVI, 502–4, CCCXIV, 1113–15 and CCCXVIII, 696–7.
[2] *Hansard*, 3/CCCII, 587.

all they thought they needed for structural repairs and improvements.[1]

The only internecine dispute of the old type in which the Commissioners were engaged after 1880 was in 1900-1, when the Commissioners had another shot at absorbing Queen Anne's Bounty. Since so many individuals were on the governing bodies of both institutions and a few of the most active habitually attended both, it is a little difficult to see how and why, after thirty years' peace, the spirits of departmental pride, jealousy and vested interest should have been allowed to make such a stir and to scotch the project after a joint select committee had reported in its favour. Frederick Temple, the prelate best situated for seeing both sides of the question, and Randall Davidson, who as the bishop on the Estates Committee and also one of the most assiduous attendants at the Bounty Board was also in a position to know what he was talking about, were both keen on amalgamation.[2] The evidence of the Bounty's secretary, Le Fanu, before the joint committee did not stand up well to cross-examination on this matter. The case for amalgamation was indeed unanswerable. Yet amalgamation did not happen. The main strength of the Bounty's resistance apparently came from the handful of lay governors who came regularly to its meetings and controlled at least its financial and administrative policies. These few laymen constituted much the most active and, doubtless, the dominant element on the Board; and they were almost all either peers, queen's counsels or members of parliament.[3] The Board's vote against Archbishop Temple's plea for amalgamation was carried by six lay and three episcopal governors (Williams of Bangor, Edwards of St Asaph, and Glyn of Peterborough) against the archbishop and two other bishops—Percival of Hereford and Kennion of Bath and Wells.[4]

[1] This aspect of the Commissioners' relations with the chapters can conveniently be studied in G. L. Prestige, *St Paul's in its Glory*. But it should be remembered that St Paul's was a special case.

[2] See especially Temple's evidence, to the 1900–1 committee, 1901 Qs. 1298–1377, and Davidson's work as one of the committee men.

[3] Lords Ashcombe and Glanusk, Sir Ralph Thompson, H. W. Cripps Q.C., Charles Gould, Q.C., Cyril Dodd, Q.C., Alderman Sir Joseph Savory Bt., M.P., J. S. Gilliat, M.P. and James Cropper were the ones who mattered. None of them had anything to do with the Ecclesiastical Commissioners.

[4] Minutes, 1 July 1901. Archbishop Maclagan of York and Bishop Davidson left before the vote was taken. Lord Ashcombe, who had been on the Joint Committee

The prelates had a foot in each camp; the lay governors' loyalties were undivided, and one gathers from some of the evidence that, without knowing a great deal about the Commissioners, they suspected them of being, among other things, unbusinesslike and untrustworthy.[1] What strings these men pulled, what prejudices and party interests they played on to frustrate the amalgamators, one can only guess. The pages of Hansard give one no clue. Lord Stanley of Alderley and Mr W. S. Caine attacked the Commissioners in language strongly suggestive of a Bounty brief; after much vacillation a bill to give effect to the Joint Committee's unanimous report was introduced on 18 June 1902, only to be withdrawn without further debate or explanation four months later.[2] Amalgamation was not again seriously talked of until after 1920, by when the old suspicions and jealousies had died away and rational planning was at last possible, although a curious fatality still seemed to dog its progress. The Archbishops' Commission of Enquiry into Church Property and Revenues recommended it in 1924 but no further steps were taken towards it. In neither office, busy as each was with post-war reconstruction and reform, did the recommendation inspire much enthusiasm; some people no doubt, with the example of the disestablishment of the Church in Wales so fresh in mind, felt it inadvisable to offer all the Church of England had as a pawn in the political game; and besides, the Commissioners' functions and the Bounty's no longer overlapped so grossly, with the latter's decision in 1920 to leave the business of augmentations entirely to the Commissioners. The peaceful and co-operative division of functions between the two boards, rather than their concentration in a single office, accordingly became for a while their official policy, and the legislation of the mid-twenties on dilapidations, pensions and tithes gave each of them more than enough to do.

Nothing further was heard of amalgamation until 1933, when a commission of the Church Assembly under the chairmanship of Lord Selborne reconsidered the question and made much the same recommendations as the Archbishops' Commission had made ten years

with Randall Davidson, and Sir C. L. Ryan abstained.

[1] See especially Dodd's and Savory's evidence, 1901 Qs. 1057–1106, 1111–1217, and 1244–97.

[2] *Hansard*, 4/CVIII, 1507–10; CIX, 238, 476–7, 981; CXI, 371–2; CXIII, 136.

before.[1] It suggested a revision of the Commissioners' constitution, cutting out most of the 'government' members, cutting down the prelates to ten and including ten each of clergy and laity; its tendency was to place the new single board under the Church Assembly's control. This was entirely to the liking of those of the clergy and laity who had long resented their exclusion from a board apparently dominated by bishops, administrators and politicians; not so much, presumably, to the liking of the existing managers of the church's business, who might well feel uneasy at the prospect of coming under a new set of sensitive and inexperienced masters. Such sweeping changes were sure to excite opposition, and this together with the unexpected death of Sir Stanford Downing (who alone might, as secretary, have won the confidence of all parties to a new united board) sufficed to render it for the time being nugatory. But the need for amalgamation was by now clearly admitted by both the Bounty and the Commissioners. Their joint committee met a committee of the Church Assembly and produced a generally acceptable modified scheme,[2] which might have been quickly enacted had not the hand of death again snatched away the man uniquely fitted to preside over the amalgamation of the offices. By the time the damage of his death had been repaired, the outbreak of war enforced another delay. Only in 1948 was amalgamation at last achieved.

I. THE LAST OF TITHE

The early and mid-Victorian Church of England was relatively untroubled by tithes. After centuries of wrangling and wrong, the Commutation Act of 1836 put them, as it was hoped, to rest. Whether any better staple means could have been found for supporting the established church, or whether the harm they did to the clergy's social relations was in fact outweighed, as many ecclesiastical apologists claimed, by the essential rightness and piety of preserving them, are questions which can be argued indefinitely. There seemed to be no end to arguing about them in the eighteenth and early nineteenth centuries. Many more books and pamphlets must have been written about tithes than about any other of the conventionally distinguished departments of church affairs; an impression was certainly given that

[1] Church Assembly paper no. 440.
[2] Church Assembly paper no. 479.

many clergy, especially the prosperous ones, worried more about their tithes than about anything else. As the scandal and inconvenience of tithes increasingly impressed themselves upon the public after about 1780, and the hour of settlement inexorably approached, friends of the establishment were not lacking to proclaim that it could not long survive the death of the principle of tithes-in-kind. Yet the Act of 1836 was followed, not by uproar and despair, but by calmness and relaxation, as if a great weight had been taken off the clergy's minds and a bone of contention removed from their society. For over forty years this calmness—not absolute, indeed, but pronouncedly in contrast with what had been the ordinary state of things before—continued, and the country clergy were therefore the better able to do their work and to cultivate harmonious relations with their flocks; their liberation from the old perennial irritations of tithe-collecting materially assisted their pastorates, which were so often efficient and attractive. The Church of England was better off with its tithes generally commuted, and with as little attention called to them as possible.

The clergy however had several reasons for discontent; slight in themselves, together they gave the clergy the impression that they were the victims of injustice before the events of the eighties made it clear they were also victims of a natural calamity. The Act intended the commutation of all tithes in England and Wales; it allowed tithe-owners and tithe-payers a reasonable time in which to agree to terms, and provided for compulsory commutation by the Tithe Commissioners wherever agreement was not reached voluntarily. The principle proposed for commutation was the old one of the 'corn-rent', a charge based on the value from year to year of a specified quantity of grain, and thus following more or less closely the real value of money. An average was struck, in each given case, of the value of tithes (whether taken in kind or by way of composition) over the preceding seven years, and the net sum then supposed to be laid out in three equal parts on the purchase of wheat, barley and oats according to *their* respective average values over the preceding seven years. In 1836, when the scale was fixed, this bought for the £100 tithe-owner 94.95 bushels of wheat, 168.42 of barley, and 242.42 of oats; for the richer or poorer tithe-owners it bought greater or lesser quantities proportionately. These proportions, as established in 1836, and converted into their money equivalent on the basis of the corn controller's official statement of the previous seven years' average in the *London Gazette* each January, were the means of reckoning of 'tithe rent-charge' for the rest of the century.

The Act's most obvious shortcoming from the clergy's point of view was its denial of the right, so profitably exercised by 'improving' clergy and lay tithe-owners of the past hundred years, to share in the increase of the land. This right had naturally been particularly resented by improving landlords and farmers, and agriculturalists at large were sure that it acted to discourage the enterprising farming of which the nation had such need. It had to go. Some compensation was offered to the tithe-owners in the fact that prices had in 1834 and 1835 been exceptionally low (so that they would tend to do well as and when prices went up) and in the provisions made in the Act for their recovering rent-charge from defaulting producers by the convenient and sure means of distress and occupation. It was also held out as in many ways an advantage to the tithe-owner to be sure of his fixed annual tithe rent-charges as he had never been able to be sure of his tithes. Nevertheless this fixity of his income was only obtained at the cost of his chance of improving it alongside whatever rise in productivity there might be, and by the later seventies clergymen were gloomily reading Sir James Caird's calculation that the effect of the Act in this respect had been to lose the church two million a year it ought otherwise to have received.

Not quite the whole of the nation's tithes were comprehended by these provisions of the Commutation Act. Exception was made of hops, fruit, and the produce of market-gardens, all of which required intensive cultivation and were of a fluctuating nature.[1] To have left them altogether out of account would have wronged the tithe-owners; to have lumped them in with the ordinary tithe rent-charge averages would have wronged the cultivators. Provision was therefore made for the imposition by the Tithe Commissioners of an 'extraordinary tithe rent-charge' on these products, from time to time and place to place as need arose and locally interested parties demanded. It was well meant; but it gave an extraordinary amount of trouble, mainly because

[1] An amending act of 1840, 2 and 3 Vic. c. 62 secs. 26–33 clarified and extended the relevant sections (40 and 42) of the 1836 Act.

it reintroduced into the relations of farmers and clergymen those elements of uncertainty and jealousy which the Act of 1836 was to have eliminated. The church's case was, as usual, good in law and reason; but hop-growers and market-gardeners newly assessed to pay a charge with so ominous a title were going to consider not what a lawyer or 'reasonable man', but what common-sense, humanity and prejudice, told them they ought to do. Clerical indiscretion appears to have made matters worse. The immediate cause of the 1873 Act[1] which exempted from extraordinary tithe rent-charge all market-gardens developed since 1836, was the vicar of Gulval's attempt to have it levied at the rate of 30s. an acre on some market-gardens newly reclaimed from waste for growing spring potatoes, broccoli and so on for railway delivery to the big city markets. He had at first talked of 45s. an acre; the Tithe Commissioners awarded him 1s. 6d.; and then Parliament annulled his claim altogether.[2] Thirteen years later this troublesome chapter in the modern history of tithes was laid to rest by the Extraordinary Tithe Redemption Act of 1886.[3] The brief history of extraordinary tithe rent-charge illustrates admirably the tragi-comic paradox that marks so much of the tithes controversy; the clergy were, substantially, in the right; but the way they had to assert their right, if they were to assert it at all, was certainly not worth the trouble and unpopularity it caused.

The denial of extraordinary tithe rent-charge was regarded as a grievance by the clergy; and so, with still greater justification, was the way that tithe rent-charge was rated. Clergymen naturally looked upon it as income. In the eyes of the law however it counted as land. Between the two points of view lay a fertile ground for misunderstandings, as clergy and laity approached the problem from opposite ends, and came to contrary conclusions as to what equity required. But apart from that, the mode in which tithe rent-charge was rated

[1] 36 and 37 Vic. c. 42.
[2] For the Gulval case see the Commons' Committee on the Tithes Commutation Acts Amendment Bill, P.Ps. 1873, XVII, 799 ff., evidence of Tremenheere and Bolitho. It is characteristic of H. W. Clarke's superficially scholarly *History of Tithes from Abraham to Queen Victoria* (1887 edn) that on p. 128 he omits to mention that the vicar asked for over twenty times as much as he got.
[3] 49 and 50 Vic. c. 54.

was unfair. Everyone knew how much the rent-charge was worth, and the clergyman was always rated at its full value; but the rental of land had not to be declared by the only people who knew (the payer and the receiver) but assessed by valuers, who conventionally assessed it at between 15 and 25 per cent below its actual value;[1] and besides, the rental was reckoned to be only about a third of land's gross value.[2] The country clergyman was thus placed in a position both unfavourable and invidious. He was rated at the highest rate possible, he could claim no special deductions on account of his profession, and he was likely to antagonize his land-occupying neighbours if he attempted to get out of anything, or to take advantage of such loopholes as the law offered him.[3]

With the steady increase of local taxation, the country clergy found themselves perhaps the most severely taxed class in the community. They were liable, with the rest of their profession, to pay income tax when there was any, and land tax on their glebes, and of course indirect taxes as everyone else did, but beyond those normal obligations they were liable in respect of their rent-charges to pay every conceivable local rate (poor rate, highway rate, general district rate, borough rate and so on) at a higher rate, effectively, than any other class of local property owner, because the deductions allowed in estimating their rateable values were so niggardly[4]—and because tithe rent-charge was not, as was every other species of property locally rated, the means of their making an income, but their income, *tout court*.

[1] Cornewall Lewis's evidence to the Lords' Committee on Parochial Assessments, P.Ps. 1850, XVI, 19, Q. 16, and Appendix H to the Lords' Committee on Spiritual Destitution, P.Ps. 1857–8, IX, 631.

[2] The other two-thirds being profits, and running costs. See R. Hobhouse, *On the Excessive Rating of Tithe Rent-charge* (a paper read at the Plymouth meeting of the Social Science Association) p. 9.

[3] See evidence offered to the Lords' Committee on Parochial Assessments P.Ps. 1850, XVI, 26, Q. 66, and to the Royal Commission on Local Taxation, P.Ps. 1898, XLI, 417 ff. and 1899, XXXVI, Qs. 10990 and 18810–11.

[4] Cripps, *Law relating to Church and Clergy* states in his sixth edition (1886) p. 342 that no deductions were allowed for landlord's property tax, land-tax, contributions (voluntary or otherwise) towards district churches or chapels within the parish, curates' stipends, or mortgage-loan repayments to Queen Anne's Bounty. Deductions for curates' stipends were allowed by the decision in *Regina v. Goodchild*, 1858, but that was reversed by *Regina v. the inhabitants of Sherford*, 1867.

The new tithe dispensation following the 1836 Act came thus increasingly to seem a mixed blessing. Upon the poorer country clergy, living always on the brink of destitution, the pressure of local taxation could (if they were reliant mainly on tithe rent-charge) come to bear very hardly indeed; the perpetual curate of Yarnscombe, Devon, for example, was in the mid-seventies paying £24 10s. 0d. poor rates on his tithe rent-charge of about £120 a year.[1] The question attracted much attention in the seventies. A committee of the lower house of Convocation issued a report on it in 1872, a year after the lower house itself, with some embarrassment, had conducted a debate upon it. It seemed to be the clergy's most pressing financial question. But it was as nothing compared to what was coming a few years later.

The one event which Lord John Russell, who framed, and everyone else who helped to pass, the 1836 Act had not envisaged was the total collapse of England's agricultural prosperity. The price of wheat was unprecedentedly low in 1834-5; it was confidently expected to go up and stay up thereafter; and in fact it did so. The repeal of the corn laws made no significant difference to the general run of cereal prices. They continued to fluctuate considerably; but only once in the following forty years (1851) did they ever go lower, and only once (1864) did they ever approach being so low again. The septennial average prices of the three cereals on which tithe rent-charge was assessed reflected this overall stability. The value of tithe rent-charge worth £100 in 1835 fluctuated over the next fifty years around an average of £102 11s. 9d., never falling lower than £89 15s. 9d., in 1855, and never rising above £112 1s. 7d., in 1875. The mid-seventies were a period of particular prosperity. But in 1878, because of a fall in world cereal prices due mainly to the lightning progress of American and Canadian prairie farming, railway and shipping developments, and a shortage of gold, the value of tithe rent-charge began a decline which was not to stop for twenty years. In 1886 it passed the low-water mark of 1855,

[1] [H. J. Dixon] *Sad Experience of a Clergyman of the Established Church*, p. 6. His other expenses are worth noting; they explain why small clerical incomes often went even less far than one might have expected. He found the living burdened with a Bounty mortgage for a new vicarage, and had to pay it off at the rate of £22 9s. 1d. a year. It being a Lord Chancellor's living, he had to pay £20 11s. 0d. in fees on taking it up.

and it went on dropping, dropping, dropping, until in 1901 it was worth only £66 10s. 9d.[1]

The whole agricultural community was shaken by this disastrous fall in staple prices. Rents fell into arrears, farms fell vacant, villagers left the land, the new rich moved in as the old rich moved out, the traders and craftsmen who were just as involved in the farming world as the farmers and labourers suffered with them. And, of course, the clergy, through their long-cherished connexion with the land, suffered as well. It was not uncommon for country clergymen's incomes to fall by a third or more. Not only was the value of their tithe rent-charge sadly sunk, they often had not the heart to enforce its full payment, and allowed it to fall into arrears. Those who farmed or let glebe lands were likely to be similarly hit. The Ecclesiastical Commissioners, who were by this time drawing over a quarter-million a year from tithe and corn rent-charges alone and who drew still more from agricultural rents, felt the depression too, and were driven by it to make a radical change in their augmentation policy; although their losses are scarcely revealed in their rental accounts, being for many years balanced by the acquisition of new properties.

All in all, this was the church's worst financial crisis since the middle of the sixteenth century; and the meeting of this crisis was the principal concern of the business heads of the church for over twenty years. For the established church as a whole it would have been much more disastrous if its revenues had still come mainly from agricultural land, or if the greater part of its properties had not been taken in charge, and the income from them redistributed, by the Ecclesiastical Commissioners. Fortunately for the church, the urban and industrial elements of the Commissioners' income were steadily improving right through their farmlands' worst years,[2] and the Commissioners were not only able to keep up their normal augmentation and endowment policies, but could also to some extent turn funds towards the relief of clerical distress, as and when necessary. The diocesan or local boards, which some church reformers had earlier wished to set in the Commissioners' place, would presumably have been much less well able to do all this; it was a happy thing for the poorer country clergy in the eighties and

[1] J. A. Venn, *Foundations of Agricultural Economics* (1933) pp. 173–4, 181, 387.
[2] See the tables in Appendices 7b and c.

nineties that the Selwyns and the 1862–3 committee had not won their point.

But even so, the poorer country clergy's situation was bad enough. Every Church Congress during these dark years at one or other of its sessions heard tales of clerical distress and discussed remedies. One of the most accomplished speakers on this theme was the rector of Wolsingham, County Durham, and chancellor of the diocese of Chester and Liverpool, Thomas Espinell Espin. He noted that of the 4173 benefices returned as under £200 a year in 1891, 1586 had fallen into that class within the last twelve years. He went on to particularise. 'Peterborough *had* 89 livings of less value than £200; it *has* 175 of them now; Bangor had 32, it has 62; Worcester had 115, it has 173. Coming down to individual cases, I have heard of £150 a year dropping down to £26; £800 a year to £200; incomes of £300 and £400 reduced to nothing; and, indeed, worse than nothing, for certain liabilities of an incumbent do not vanish with his income; he must keep his parsonage in repair, and pay rates and taxes still.'[1] From all quarters came the same story, worse in some places than in others, but everywhere gloomy and apparently tragic. What was most tragic about the situation, however, was something of which not quite enough was heard at these meetings or in Convocation—namely, that it was tragic for the farm-folk too. If some of the clergy and their lay protagonists now thought too much of their own troubles and too little of the troubles of those on whom they depended, it was in a way quite a fair reversal of what had in former times, when the tithe-paying lorded it over at any rate the clerical tithe-receiving interest, been the rule: one must, as Venn remarked, 'take long views in studying the economic history of agriculture'.[2] The problem was, moreover, insoluble without doing substantial injustice to one party or the other, and all the old rancour that had accompanied tithe disputes earlier began to flood back into these disputes over tithe rent-charge, and to embitter them more or less acutely until their tardy final settlement in 1935. Scenes occurred reminiscent of the Irish tithe affrays of 1831–3, the like of which had not been heard of since. Violence first showed itself in Wales, where farmers, whether or not themselves nonconformists (and most Welsh-

[1] *Report of the Church Congress at Birmingham, October, 1893*, p. 365.
[2] *Op. cit.* p. 172.

men were), were particularly responsive to the Liberationist arguments against the established church, and looked forward to its destruction; to which a certain Farmers' Tithe Defence League, formed in the autumn of 1886, positively contributed by organizing, first, refusals to pay tithe rent-charge, and second, when the non-payers' goods were distrained on, demonstrations of solidarity in their support. At first peaceful enough, despite the occasional appearances of gangs of quarrymen (who, having no direct concern in the dispute, were premonitory of the bands of Blackshirts who tended mysteriously to turn up on similar occasions after the First World War), these demonstrations soon became more menacing. Police and soldiers were called in to protect bailiffs, auctioneers and agents, and in the end the fervid local feeling led to a riot at Mochdre, in which fifty civilians and thirty-four policemen were hurt. The evidence taken by the special commissioner sent down to inquire into these goings-on shows that blame attached to all parties, the tithe-owners included. Some had made no reductions and others, absentees, had made smaller reductions than the local landlords. The commissioner commented on the 'serious evils' resulting. Calling in the police to protect the distrainers made bad blood between the police and the farmers and encouraged contempt for the law; tithe rent-charge payment only fell further in arrear; and local clergymen, who could neither economically nor humanly hold out for it as long as the canons of Christ Church, were obliged to take only a fraction of what was due to them, for fear of getting nothing at all and 'to keep on good terms with their parishioners'.[1] The same menace of violence, the same agents and auctioneers and parades of police, were all to recur in the twenties and early thirties. Tithe went on causing trouble to the last.

With this kind of thing in the background, the debate on the rights and wrongs of tithe rent-charge proceeded briskly through the eighties. The clergy sought relief from local rates, both because of their current hardships and peculiar national value and on the grounds which have already been listed; the representatives of the agricultural interest replied that the clergy, though often badly off, were not worse off than they were, and objected to the idea of their having to take any of

[1] Report of an Inquiry as to Disturbances connected with the levying of Tithe Rent-Charge in Wales. P.Ps. 1887, XXXVIII, 261 ff.

the clergy's burdens on their own groaning backs. They countered with a demand for the moderation of the clergy's claims on them and began to point out the unfairness of a situation in which what had originally been a tenth part of the produce of land became in effect a mulct on the capital of men who could not sell their produce at a profit; to which was objected, legitimately enough, that the clergy's claims in the later nineteenth century were a great deal lighter than they had usually been through the last thousand years, and that the clergy were only asking for the minimum that parliament had guaranteed them when it denied them the chance of more.

To summarize this argument thus simply is to fail lamentably to do justice to the cases put forward. If, however, it conveys the impression that there was a very good case on each side, it will have served its purpose. The argument was the more complicated for its being involved with other issues that agitated the public in the same years. The whole farming world was concerned in the great debates on the land question and local taxation. The clergy had a keen interest in the latter, and were moreover driven by the decline in so many of their incomes, and the inadequacy of the charitable apparatus they had to rely on, to turn with new energy towards the several long-debated, long-delayed expedients that might soften the blows of poverty or disaster—notably the union of small benefices, and pensions not for retiring clergymen alone, but for clergy widows and children as well. These interesting topics were often discussed in clerical assemblies and in parliament, and aroused much passion. Many speakers inclined to blame the destitute clergy for having married improvidently or imprudently; such heartless and romanizing strictures brought defenders of the principle of a married clergy quickly to their aid. Spokesmen for the ten thousand unbeneficed clergy complained that their interests were never cared for. Spokesmen for the poorer clergy at large showed that their class's ancient hostility towards wealthy incumbents and the family livings men was undiminished. Within and without the church the questions were raised: why are some incumbents so well off while others are so poor? and why is there no proportion observed between emoluments and labour? At these points, of course, the argument was brought up sharp against those ancient ambivalent obstructions to so much reform, the parson's freehold and the patron's interest. Complaint about their

474

practical consequences was foredoomed to frustration, and could only serve to exacerbate tempers; but that did not stop men from complaining.

Parliament intervened in 1891[1] to place responsibility for tithe rent-charge payment squarely and unmistakably on the landowner. Much of the unpleasantness, and most of the difficulty attending its collection, had arisen from the fact that land-owners were in the way of providing for it to be paid by their tenants, who were usually, in hard times, in a weaker economic position to do so. This sensible Act, poised gingerly between the three poles of land-owner, tenant and tithe-owner, apparently worked quite well. The farmers were freed from the irritation and hardship of paying tithe rent-charge directly to bodies against whom they often conceived themselves to have a legitimate grievance; tithe-owners got their rent-charges more regularly and from a class of men more generally friendly and amenable; only this class, the landlords, suffered at all, insamuch as the time-lags between movements of cereal prices and their seven-year averages, and between changes in prosperity and the adjustment of rent agreements to meet them, put the farmers, as things ceased to get worse and then, after 1901, began to get better, into a sunnier position. Both landlord and tenant however shared the advantage conferred, to the great disgust of the tithe-owners, by clause 8 which introduced the principle of relating tithe rent-charge to rental value, and protected rent-charge payers from demands happening to exceed two-thirds of the land's annual value.

Between 1891 and the First World War there was no other important legislation and the tithe question went back, comparatively speaking, into hibernation. The redemption of tithe rent-charge, first facilitated by statute in 1846 and feebly encouraged by subsequent legislation,[2] proceeded slowly under the auspices of Queen Anne's Bounty, by whom redemption monies were held in trust for the benefit of the livings in respect of which they were paid. This activity was one of the several new ones undertaken by the Bounty in the course of the nineteenth century and it was undoubtedly a useful one; but the chilling limits set to it by the enabling statutes, and the natural difficulties of bringing both parties to an agreement, prevented as much redemption

[1] 54 and 55 Vic. c. 8.
[2] 9 and 10 Vic. c. 73, 23 and 24 Vic. c. 93, 41 and 42 Vic. c. 42, 48 and 49 Vic. c. 32.

as could have been undertaken.[1] The sums involved were very small. The Bounty's annual report for 1890 recorded that it then held a capital fund of only £387,587 from the redemption of ordinary and extraordinary tithe rent-charge. Thereafter the pace quickened, but by 1914 the same fund was still worth no more than £1,216,239.[2]

The First World War marked an epoch in the modern history of tithe, and set in train the stirring events that led to its extinction. The arguments used were much the same as those that had been used during the agricultural depression of the late nineteenth century, and were marked by the same inevitable, destructive, and wholly tragic inability of each side to understand the other's case or to take a calm, long-term, philosophic view of the issues. Because so much of what was said after the war had already been said before it, there is no need to describe 'The Tithe War' (the title of Doreen Wallace's eloquent statement of the tithe-payers' case, published in 1934) in any detail; it will be sufficient simply to give the outline of its economic and legislative history. Few readers' imaginations can be so weak as to be unable to colour in the blanks.

Farmers did well—could hardly avoid doing well—out of the war. By 1918 the value of tithe rent-charge was well above parity, and it seemed certain that it would go higher still, above its mid-Victorian peaks, before coming down laggardly, if it *did* come down, in the wake of the actual yearly prices. Such circumstances alone would have compelled legislation; but they were made still more difficult by the fact that in 1918, '19 and '20, when farming was at its most profitable, a vast transfer of land was in progress between landowners (often only too willing to dispose of a form of property that had become very much of a liability) and their prospering tenants (who, rather too confident that prosperity had come to stay, were often eager to buy the farms they worked and ready to borrow heavily to do it). With their lands they took over also the attached tithe rent-charges, which they were only likely to be able to pay comfortably so long as they continued to prosper at the war-time rate. Whether or not that happened, it was clear that tithe rent-charge was soon going to cause trouble again; the clergy were as

[1] See the report of the Royal Commission on Tithe Rent-Charge Redemption, P.Ps. 1892, XLVII, 341 ff.

[2] P.Ps. 1914-16, XXXIV, 189.

anxious as anybody else that it should be prevented from doing so; and accordingly an Act was passed in the autumn of 1918[1] with the dual object of fixing tithe rent-charge at its present value for six years, and of hastening the healing process of redemption. It enabled land-owners to redeem their tithes without the tithe-owner's consent, if that was unobtainable, and offered among other attractive terms the possibility of paying the redemption money by a terminable annuity over not more than fifty years. The task of supervising these arrange-ments, and holding the redemption monies, was naturally undertaken by Queen Anne's Bounty, which had at once to handle a torrent of applications from tithe-payers anxious to take advantage of the specially favourable terms offered to those who acted within a couple of years. Between 1919 and the end of 1924, when the law was radically changed, the Bounty had managed nearly five times as much redemption as during the whole period 1847–1918.[2]

The 1918 Act had provided that when the six stable years came to an end, tithe rent-charge should be assessed on a new basis of a fifteen-year average. Already by the end of 1921 all men could see that this would never work. The high war prices came rocketing down and stayed down; rates soared, the landowners were grievously burdened by them, and the relief given, at last, to the clergy by the Ecclesiastical Tithe Rent-charge (Rates) Act of 1920 was due to come to an end at the same time as the 1918 Tithe Act. If parliament had not intervened, the open-ing of 1926 would have seen the value of tithe rent-charge spring up from its stabilised £109 3s. 11d. to £131 11s. 4d., and the clergy caught after their five-years respite for rates of a truly Egyptian oppressiveness. The clergy did not exactly look forward to such an event, the tithe-payers for their part were determined not to pay rent-charge at any-thing like the anticipated level. Tithe-payers' Associations were formed to organize opposition and put pressure on the legislature. It was there-fore inevitable that parliament should again intervene, and advisable that it should do so boldly.

The 1925 Tithe Act[3] fixed tithe rent-charge in perpetuity at five per cent above par value, and furthermore set up a machinery for the

[1] 8 and 9 George V c. 54.
[2] Report of the Royal Commission on Tithe Rent-Charge, 1936, para. 52. P.Ps. 1935–6, XIV, 884.　　　　　　　　　　　　　　　[3] 15 and 16 George V c. 87.

redemption of the ecclesiastical part of it, in the form of a sinking fund fed by an additional charge of four and a half per cent of par value and designed to extinguish it after eighty years or so. Tithe-payers were thus presented with a new stabilized rent-charge of £109 10s. od. a year, which was a great deal less than the proposed fifteen-year average would have taken from them, and the prospect that their great-grandsons might be freed from it altogether; ecclesiastical tithe-owners were freed from the necessity of paying rates by the arrangement that the Inland Revenue department should pay the rates, and Queen Anne's Bounty should pay five or sixteen pounds in every hundred (according to whether a benefice or an ecclesiastical corporation was concerned) to the Inland Revenue.

These provisions were far-reaching and, so far as the principle of tithe went, revolutionary. Of equal importance was the vesting in Queen Anne's Bounty of almost the whole ecclesiastical tithe rent-charge.[1] This was in a way the most revolutionary change of all. It turned the Bounty Office upside down, placing upon it a burden of administration and, as it turned out, litigation, far beyond anything it had experienced thitherto; and it put an end to those direct tithe dealings between incumbents and their tithe-paying parishioners of which tithe-mad churchmen had made so much during the third church reform movement. Administrative convenience, and the avoidance of parochial unpleasantness, were the principal reasons advanced for this provision, and indeed they were both cogent ones; but it could not but emphasize the deplorable absurdity of the situation to which the tithe question had attained, that the Minister of Agriculture in introducing the bill's second reading should express the 'hope that the Church will realize that some small sacrifice is worth making, in order to achieve the severance between the tithe-payer and the tithe owner', which his scheme proposed.[2]

So Queen Anne's Bounty, working through an apparatus of fifteen regional committees, came to stand between the farmers and the clergy. Whereas in the past the Bounty had had mud slung at it by the latter, it was now among the farmers that it was held in low repute and its

[1] Exception was made of existing incumbents who were actually collecting their rent-charges themselves and wished to go on doing so.
[2] 18 June 1925, *Hansard*, 5/CLXXXV, 838.

gracious name jeered at. The 'tithe war' soon broke out in real earnest, as the Bounty got to work and brought all the resources of an efficient centralized bureaucracy to bear upon matters which the individual clergy, when they had full charge of them, had often let slide. As the chairman of the Bounty's tithes committee reminded the too soft-hearted or soft-minded clergy at the Chelmsford diocesan conference in the autumn of 1933, when they introduced a resolution deploring the 'tithe war' and urging their chiefs to work out some quick and, if needful, self-sacrificial pacification, the church ought to keep out of it, and let the Bounty fight the battle on the church's behalf.[1]

Whether it was really any more satisfactory for the clergy to have Queen Anne's Bounty bringing in the bailiffs and distraining on farmers' property than to have to do it themselves, was doubtful. In fact the reputation of the church and clergy suffered as much under this new dispensation as under the old, and the hard-pressed farmers' resentments, whether reasonable or unreasonable, were as keen either way. In the end, the government set up a Royal Commission and then compelled a pacification by the 1936 Tithe Act[2] which extinguished tithe rent-charge altogether, compensating its expropriated owners with an issue of marketable 3% stock, and setting up the Tithe Redemption Commission to take charge of the business and relieve Queen Anne's Bounty (then, as it seemed, on the brink of marriage with the Ecclesiastical Commissioners) of the opprobrium attaching to it. Tithe-payers had to reimburse the government by paying annuities of value much below that of the extinguished rent-charge over a period of sixty years. Their gain was considerable, and so was the church's loss. 6900 benefices lost £475,000 a year between them, and the Commissioners' own income was reduced by £50,000. The stock issued in compensation and held on benefices' account by the Bounty represented a net loss of 18% compared with the tithe rent-charge, and since the Bounty board had to call on capital in order to pay sitting incumbents what the Act made their due, the loss to their successors was something more of the order of 26%. This loss was not made good until well after the Second World War.[3]

[1] *Times*, 12 October 1933, p. 7c.   [2] 26 George V and 1 Ed. VIII c. 43.
[3] I owe much to Sir Mortimer Warren and Mr Alan Savidge for assistance in writing this paragraph.

2. HOUSING AND ESTATES

At no point of their career were the Ecclesiastical Commissioners not being blamed for something or other related to housing. In the beginning, it was for doing the bishops too proud. Then fault was found with the size and splendour of the parsonages which the Commissioners allowed so many enterprising Victorian incumbents to build; first the burden of maintaining them, then the business of replacing them, took up a great deal of attention. But by the eighteen-eighties it was not ecclesiastical but secular housing that mattered more, and not that of the middle or higher but decidedly the lower orders of society. From the eighties onwards the Commissioners found themselves up against all the problems, including to an exceptional degree the exposure to vilification, that faced the urban and slum landlord; and the record of their response to this situation is particularly interesting because the Church of England's reputation was implicated. The charge that the clergy were living on the profits of pubs, slum tenements and prostitution was more insistently made, with more effect, than any popular hostile charge since that of the early nineteenth century against the church's alleged great wealth.

The injustice of the attacks made on the Commissioners on account of their connexions with pubs and slums was the more marked, in that the Commissioners, finding themselves saddled with these odious connexions, did their best to get free of them. Inasmuch as they succeeded, they were hooking out of the fire chestnuts placed there—often long ago—by parties upon whom blame had much better have been cast. In respect of both licensed premises and slum properties, it was equally true, that the grosser abuses often had their roots in leases made for long periods of years—forty, eighty, ninety-nine, even nine hundred and ninety-nine—by bishops, dignitaries and chapters who had made the estate over to builders for development in return for ground-rent. Even when conditions and covenants were written into the lease, they were almost impossible to follow down the eroded channels of letting and sub-letting that marked the degeneration of urban estates; usually, however, such conditions and the will to enforce them were lacking. The Ecclesiastical Commissioners' Act of 1868 brought at last to an effective point their policy of prohibiting such leases, and at the same time made sure that when existing leases ran out, the properties leased would come into their hands. Some bishops, as I mentioned earlier, were voluntarily refraining from renewing leases as early as the eighteen-thirties, but some (notably C. R. Sumner and Henry Phillpotts) went on to the end; and upon deans and chapters there was no restraint at all from issuing long leases until and unless they put their estates into the Commissioners' hands for reorganization, which some of them delayed until the seventies. Leases were thus falling in right through the later nineteenth and well into the early twentieth century. The estates that had been developed under them were often in a terrible state; and the public naturally but unjustly blamed the Commissioners instead of blaming the bishops, deans and canons who had issued the leases, and the laws of their country which had allowed such horrors to happen.

The eighteen-eighties saw an impressive intensification of interest in social problems and conditions. In some respects things had got worse, not better, as the century wore on. Overcrowding was certainly worse, intemperance and the sweated trades probably so; these three evils were well to the forefront of public discussion. Other evils that had attracted reformers' attention earlier on were no doubt being reduced. More children were going to school, juvenile delinquents were put in the way of reclamation, smallpox and cholera were disappearing, and so on. Since one could not draw up a balance sheet of social gain and loss and say that England was positively a happier or a less happy land for the lower classes to inhabit in the eighties than it had been before, the new mood of anxiety and urgency about their ways of life is not explicable by any more or less sudden deterioration in their position. Not that, so much as an increased, often conscience-stricken sensitiveness among the more fortunate classes of society, and a readiness to put up with more inconvenience in order to see these wrongs righted, seems to account for the new mood of the eighties. Preachers and popular writers on the one side, social workers and sociologists on the other, gave it breadth and depth; and although analyses of the problems were not always the same, and prescriptions for their solution often wildly divergent, they had to be faced as never before.

That the Ecclesiastical Commissioners should have to face these social problems and do something about them was inevitable. The

Paddington and Finsbury estates they inherited from the see and chapter of London, the Southwark properties that had linked the bishops of Winchester with vice and crime for half a thousand years, the dean and canons of Westminster's exceptionally seedy properties behind the abbey—these were only among the most troublesome elements of the *damnosa haereditas* they had to accept.

Public houses first attracted attention. As the battle against drunkenness and its all-too-common consequences (crime, imbecility, pauperization, cruelty) raged fiercer, the fact that the Commissioners drew revenues from licensed premises was bound to attract attention. The Church of England Temperance Society sent a memorial to them in 1878. Bishops Westcott in 1881, Frederick Temple in 1882, lodged complaints about certain aspects of their policy. These were private complaints, privately answered; but people were beginning to talk. In the summer of 1882 the Commissioners were driven to clarify their position by Archdeacon Basil Wilberforce's public letter to the Archbishop of Canterbury.[1] Archbishop Tait reported the incident to the Commissioners in November that year, when they appointed a committee to review their position and recommend a policy. Bishop Thorold (who was a member of it) asked for its report to be printed in the following summer,[2] and when he did so, took the opportunity to give a summary of it, the sooner to scotch the sensational charges being made by the press and in an American travel-book.[3] These charges contained the usual mixture of truth and falsehood. It was not true that the bishop of London, when going from Fulham to his town house in St James's, passed more than a hundred public-houses built on church property, but it was true that he passed at least two. The Commissioners were arraigned especially in respect of four notoriously profitable licensed premises, over which they had no control whatsoever; but it was true that two of them were on church property—two Knightsbridge gin-palaces, let years ago by the dean and chapter of Westminster on a beneficial lease which still had 16 years to run. Of the other

[1] C.C.F. 63362.

[2] House of Lords paper, 1883 no. 175. Its other members were the Archbishop, Earls Stanhope, Chichester and Brownlow, Viscount Emlyn, Bishops Jackson, Temple, Ellicott, Lightfoot and Goodwin, Sir John Mowbray, G. J. Goschen, Evelyn Ashley, and Wilbraham Egerton. [3] 2 August 1883, *Hansard*, 3/CCLXXXII, 1299–1301.

two pubs in the indictment, the Royal Oak at Notting Hill had never been connected with the church, and the Hero of Waterloo had been sold by the Archbishop of Canterbury to the South-Eastern Railway Company twenty-three years ago!

The Commissioners were in fact by this time suppressing beer-houses and the worse sort of public houses as occasion arose. It did not arise often enough for red-hot temperance crusaders' liking, because so many pubs were on long-lease property; nor were the Commissioners willing either to suppress every pub that came within their grasp, or to decline to allow the erection of pubs on the respectable estates they were developing. But, in common with the better sort of owners of large urban estates, they were aware of the evil of intemperance and were working in a steady, unexciting way towards reducing it. They continued to own a considerable number. The On-Licenses Return of 1890 revealed them as owners of at least 53 pubs in London,[1] bringing in a rental of about £10,000 a year. Finsbury was the district where their pubs lay thickest on the ground; they had suppressed 16 there within the past decade, but still owned 24.[2] The suppressions went on. When Lord Hugh Cecil asked ten years later for returns of the number of London pubs they had suppressed or determined to suppress since 1883, the Commissioners reported that they had suppressed 56 pubs and given notice to tenants of 44 more.[3]

The Ecclesiastical Commissioners became involved in slum problems in the same months as public attention turned to their interest in the profits of the sale of intoxicating liquors. Concern about the conditions under which the poor lived seems to have reached a higher pitch in the eighties than ever before. The year 1883 saw the publication of two small works which cast a particularly ghastly light on the housing of the London poor and had something to do with the Commissioners' making one of the most important and creditable decisions

[1] P.Ps. 1890–1, LXVIII, 107 ff. Returns were only made of owners of two or more licensed premises.
[2] W. H. Smith's reply to a question in the House, 10 March 1891, *Hansard*, 3/CCCLI, 601.
[3] P.Ps. 1901, LIV, 935–7. Cecil also asked for figures relating to beer-houses. The Commissioners said they had kept no account of their suppressions but that it was their practice to suppress them all.

of their whole history. G. R. Sims, whose best-known ballad 'Christmas Day in the Workhouse' embodies all his good-hearted, romantic, simple qualities, published in *The Pictorial World*, during the spring and summer, a series of illustrated articles on 'How the Poor Live', which was immediately brought out as a paper-back. It contained nothing that intelligent educated persons ought to have been surprised by, but, partly because Sims kept his sentimental proclivities well under control, partly because of the illustrations (Frederick Barnard, who did them, had something of Doré's gift for atmosphere, besides a greater talent for character than Doré ever showed), and partly because of the public's nervous receptivity, it quickly became famous. The other, smaller, work was to some extent a product of Sims's, and used some of the same material. It was well known to be by a congregationalist minister, Andrew Mearns, well acquainted with the problems of the slums, and it was dramatically entitled *The Bitter Cry of Outcast London*. Sims could be more easily shrugged off than what appeared to be a semi-official publication of the leading free church. What *How the Poor Live* and its increasingly fashionable *genre* of journalism had not already done, *The Bitter Cry* succeeded in doing. Both authors were called to give evidence before the great 1884 Royal Commission on the Housing of the Working Classes, whose more deliberate and exhaustive inquiries substantiated almost the whole of their story. Meanwhile, a self-appointed committee in Brompton, seeking earnestly to find out more about it, formed—and publicized—the impression that some of the most vicious, bestial and heart-breaking slums in the whole metropolis, in 'the Mint', Southwark, were the Commissioners' property.[1]

This was the first of the modern series of misunderstandings of the Ecclesiastical Commissioners made, not by the heedlessly hostile, but by those who, presumably considering themselves to be on the church's side, ran with swift feet to condemn the Commissioners unjustly. Archbishop Benson and the Earl Stanhope, the First Estates Commissioner, were conveniently able to deal with the Brompton committee's allegations, by the same manoeuvre that contributed to dispel misapprehensions about pubs. They moved in the House of Lords for the report of a committee which the Commissioners had recently

[1] Their report is reported in *The Times*, 3 January 1884 p. 4a–b, and 16 January, p. 7a–b.

appointed to consider their Southwark properties; and in so doing summarized its contents, making it clear not only that the Commissioners had nothing to do with 'the Mint' district, but also that even if they had they could have done nothing about it while they were only drawing ground-rent from it and waiting for the long leases which bishops of Winchester had granted to fall in.[1] Their brief speeches and the report of the Commissioners' committee disposed easily enough of the suggestions that the Commissioners were actively and knowingly implicated in the profits of Southwark prostitution and poor-grinding. But they had, or would have, other metropolitan properties not much better than Southwark, and although they did not own 'the Mint', what they did own was bad enough. Much more important than rebutting the current slanders was determining the policy they were to adopt towards such poor urban properties in general. Hitherto not many such properties had come into their hands. Those in the old 'Winchester Park' estate in Southwark, the shabbiest so far, only began to fall in after 1881. What were the Commissioners to do with them?

Their earlier handling of urban properties had not been bad. A large area in Shoreditch, part of the Finsbury prebend estate, and smaller areas in Lambeth and Westminster, almost all in 'a dilapidated and unsatisfactory state' and occupied mainly by poor people, had fallen in in the later sixties. These areas demanded instant redevelopment if the church was ever to get from them the improved revenues which it was the Commissioners' responsibility to secure. But there were ways and ways of redeveloping. The Commissioners could have bulldozered these properties flat and made a maximum profit by letting the land to the highest bidders. Thousands of poor people would have been made homeless and forced to compete with the masses already competing for relatively cheap lodgings in the central urban areas; but that was happening so constantly that it seemed to be almost a law of London's

---

[1] 24 March 1884. *Hansard*, 3/CCLXXXVI, 557–60. The report was printed as House of Lords paper, 1884 No. 41. It is interesting that its membership was predominantly lay. The clerical members were Archbishop Benson, Bishops Jackson, Temple, Thorold and Goodwin, and Dean Bradley of Westminster. The laymen were Earls Stanhope, Chichester and Brownlow, Viscount Emlyn, Lord Egerton of Tatton, and four M.Ps.—The Hon. Evelyn Ashley, Sir John Mowbray, Bart., G. J. Goschen, and T. Salt.

life, a particularly acute local manifestation of the natural economic law that the weakest must go to the wall, and the Commissioners could easily have let it happen in their case. They did not, however, do so. They acted in the manner then characteristic of the best class of urban landlord. In their redevelopment of the Shoreditch, Lambeth and Westminster properties they took care to demolish and rebuild bit by bit, so that the folk they had made homeless should have a chance of finding a new home without delay and nearby. At the same time they made that chance greater than it might have been by letting the land at reduced rates to philanthropic workers' dwellings trusts and companies, or to the better sort of builders who were willing to agree to the Commissioners' stipulations about giving a first refusal to local people, and prepared to accept the same level of rents as the four-per-cent philanthropists to whose buildings their own lay adjacent. But no one pretended that all, or even many, of the folk who necessarily lost their old homes were re-accommodated in the new ones, even where (as the Commissioners tried to ensure) there was nominally room for them all. The new rents might not generally be higher but only the 'respectable' would be allowed into the new flats and houses and, unhappily for the poor who tried to be respectable, they usually had to overcrowd their homes while they did it. Overcrowding and respectability could only be married by extremest virtue, and those who had the letting of what were called 'improved industrial or artisans' dwellings' were bound to set their faces against overcrowding. Housing being in such short supply, there were plenty of applicants for the new homes who could pay their rents without overcrowding; and consequently the benevolent intentions with which the Commissioners and other good landlords approached the problem of rehousing the sufferers from their redevelopments achieved much less than they might have done.[1]

The novelty of the policy that developed out of their committee and subsequent decisions on the Southwark estates question lay in their going several steps further than they had yet gone towards securing

[1] This summary of the Ecclesiastical Commissioners' redevelopment policy between 1867 and 1883 is based mainly on their agent Ralph Clutton's evidence before the Royal Commission on the Housing of the Working Classes, Qs. 6393–738 (P.Ps. 1884–5, xxx, 296–306) and on papers relating to Southwark in C.C.F. 65065 Pt. I.

the comfort and convenience both of the tenants sitting at the time of their take-over, and of the tenants on the redeveloped properties. Their committee itself did not go very far. It recognized that the Southwark case was a peculiarly hard one, inasmuch as the sitting tenants of the very congested and confused courts and streets there were both poor and unusually meritorious, and had moreover, in many cases, been there for surprisingly long periods. Influenced by their deserving character and impressed by a deputation from the Southwark Homes of the Poor Committee, led by Arthur Cohen, M.P.; moving no doubt with the contemporary climate of opinion towards greater refinements of good landlordship; and inspired no doubt also by a natural desire to avoid hostile publicity, the committee recommended that the land should be let by stages 'for the erection of labourers' dwellings'.

'Your Committee', they stated, 'are not forgetful of the fact that, the Commissioners being a body of Trustees, and the objects of their trust being specifically defined, they would not be justified in giving up their property for the promotion of other objects, however good those objects might be. The value of the land in question cannot be put entirely out of sight. At the same time your Committee think that considering the very special circumstances of this case and particularly the fact that the Commissioners have become, not through any action of their own, but under the system of tenure the abolition of which was a main object of the Acts they administer, the actual landlords of a number of poor people living in houses which must be replaced by other buildings, and depending for their subsistence on trades carried on in the particular locality, the Estates Committee will be justified in not requiring the full market price of the land, if they can thus facilitate the provision of substantial and healthy dwellings for the present tenants.

These (which when finished were named Stanhope and Mowbray Buildings) were to be erected by 'a builder of good repute . . . under the supervision of the agents of the Commissioners [i.e. Cluttons] . . . and will be so planned as to include a large number of rooms which may be let, either singly or in sets of two or more, according to the wants of individuals or families.' Their standing practice of demolishing piecemeal would be strictly observed, and every care taken to accommodate the sitting tenants in the new buildings with a minimum of transitional inconvenience.

Here was a nice mixture of benevolence and prudence, perfectly creditable in the committee that counselled it but devoid of daring. They considered, only to dismiss, the idea of building themselves; not only would such a course be 'inexpedient on financial grounds, but . . . as a matter of administration, it could not be carried out satisfactorily'. Yet within half a dozen years they were building workers' dwellings and managing them according to a very remarkable system. It is impossible to judge exactly what influences, in what proportions, led them to change their course thus radically; but it is obvious that the main influence was the lady who was the first, and the last, to matter at all in the Commissioners' history—Octavia Hill.

Octavia Hill was one of the great organizing women of the nineteenth century. The social history of Britain is thick with them, and many departments of social reform or improvement actually originated in the compassion, the persistence, and the devotion of a particular intelligent and capable female. Elizabeth Fry will always be honourably connected with prisons, Louisa Twining with workhouses; Florence Nightingale and Agnes Jones with hospitals, Mary Carpenter with juvenile delinquency, Josephine Butler with the outcast hordes of prostitution; these women were inventive, brave, indefatigable, pioneers in various branches of social reform so desirable that they have all, more or less directly, been gradually incorporated in the modern welfare state. Octavia Hill was one of the greatest of these women. Her name and fame are less than they deserve, partly because she was always a more controversial character than the others, principally because she stood for principles diametrically opposed to those of the modern welfare state. She was on one of history's losing sides, and, as is the way with losers who are in no way romantic, she has rather dropped below the horizon of modern knowledge. Yet in her day, which ran from the eighteen-sixties to the eve of the first world war, she was generally celebrated and either admired or detested as the inventor of a system of property management which tended to elevate at once the living standards and the characters of the less fortunate of the lower classes, and also to strengthen the social structure by knitting upper and lower classes together in mutual sympathy and respect. It is less important for our purposes that she was also virtually the founder of the National Trust.

Although a woman of grace and delicate sensibility, and although, pierced to the heart with pity for the poor, she devoted the greater part of her life to improving the circumstances of their lives, Octavia Hill was not soft. She was soft neither with herself, her friends, her helpers, nor the poor. Apart from the streak of original genius that led to what others would, against her wishes, call her 'system', her mind ran along fairly conventional and indeed increasingly old-fashioned lines—individualist, moralist, *laissez-faire*, anti-centralization, anti-State almost. She took it for granted that life was meant to be a rigorous business, that the poor would be always with us, that God had not intended the race to be to the slow. She rarely strayed far from the safe position of assuming that if you did not get on in life, there was something wrong with you, physically or morally; if the former, then you must be encouraged and helped to keep going at whatever economic level you could independently manage; if the latter, it was necessary you should be told your faults and shown how to be better. Character was far more important than comfort. Charity was the greatest of the Christian virtues and the most misunderstood and malpractised. Men were not being charitable, they were being idiotically blind and irresponsible, in understanding charity to mean doles, free hand-outs, instant heart-easing responses to the sight of misery. Real charity meant personal service, the giving of time, self and sense, not just money and emotion. The poor cried out for charity and it was the duty of the comparatively affluent to give it them. The poor must be charitably helped, if they would but submit to be helped. Most would. Some, however, were bound to be unhelpable, and for them—she contemplated the inevitable with sad but philosophic resignation—the poor law, the police, and the prison.

Her 'system' was simply an ingenious and fruitful application of the proper principles of charitable effort. It was directed to the improvement of poor people's homes, without ruining their characters by giving them something for nothing. Character, she believed, began to crack the moment it neglected the principle of desert. Getting what they had not earned was morally deleterious for the really poor because their low state of education and circumstances of life would normally combine to make them try to get more the same way, instead of appreciating it (as the educated classes were at least capable of doing) as a gift from God bearing responsible obligations with it. She therefore distrusted Peabody's philanthropic provision of homes for working people at uneconomic, charitably subsidized rents, and absolutely detested the idea of council houses, subsidized out of the rates at other people's expense, as it came into local politics in the eighties. Better by far that the poor should learn that amenities must be earned, economic rents paid, Christian capital given its unambitious return of four or five per cent. But—and herein lay her originality and distinction—the poor needed love, help, and education if they were ever to see these things and escape from both their loathsome environments and the loose ways of thinking and behaving that stood between them and the virtues expounded by Samuel Smiles. How better could this love and care be shown to them than in the regular, close, conscientious and kindly visits of a good landlord, collecting the rents in person and establishing a vital link between the denizens of the slum and civilization?

So in the middle sixties she began her great work by buying, with the help of a cheap loan from Ruskin, the long lease of three houses near the school she and sisters were running in Nottingham Place, Marylebone. Bit by bit she built up a good relationship with the tenants, weeded out the unhelpables, repaired and decorated the rooms, put in lights and water and so on in proportion as the rents came regularly in, and showed such of the poor as were willing to believe it that some at least of their social superiors took their well-being seriously to heart. News of her doings soon spread around the grapevine of the charitable world and other good women began to emulate her, either buying little slum properties themselves or managing such for well-intentioned owners. By the eighties she enjoyed a modest celebrity and was receiving regular financial support from admirers, to whom she scrupulously presented an account of receipts and expenditure each year, along with a survey of her activities during it; she found herself at the head of an informal association of female agents working more or less according to her own 'system', the object of increasing attention both at home and overseas.

In the early spring of 1884 she got her biggest chance yet, with the Ecclesiastical Commissioners. Just how she came into contact with them, whether Ralph Clutton and the archbishop were speaking the literal truth when they said she had 'volunteered her services as collector',[1] and who it was (there must have been someone) who ascer-

[1] Clutton's evidence to the Working Classes Housing Commission, 25 April, Q. 6453, and Archbishop Benson in the Lords, 24 March 1884, *Hansard*, 3/CCLXXXVI, 558.

tained for her that her offer would be well received, the evidence does not suffice to show. In May she took over several Southwark courts, officially figuring as one of Cluttons' sub-collectors. In November she took over some more, and in the following year an associate took a lease of forty-one houses nearby.[1]

Thus began the connexion which was to have such momentous consequences. Her standing with the Commissioners seems not to have been too secure for the first couple of years. They clearly started by regarding her as a useful and pleasant temporary helper, who would keep the Southwark courts warm pending the completion of their redevelopment plans, without interfering with those plans in any way. They wanted by degrees to get rid of all the old houses, and fill up the land either with decent Peabody-type tenements (their concession to benevolence) or profitable commercial premises.[2] Octavia Hill had other ideas. Her admiration for even the best tenement blocks was tempered by regrets at their bleakness. They never had grass or gardens nearby, and for all her respect for five per cent profits, she passionately wished to bring playgrounds and open spaces into the slums, to take the edge off their endless bricks and mortar. Little private court-yards or pocket-handkerchief gardens were rare blessings to be cherished and preserved; a rickety old cottage with one would facilitate happiness in poverty more than the most model 'model tenement'. Furthermore, she could see that some of the older people, and all the unfortunates to whom nature had given no power to help themselves, would not like and would certainly not be able to pay even the lowest rents in the new blocks going up. She found in these Southwark courts many feeble flickering lights of goodness and joy which the well-meaning but brisk and businesslike Commissioners threatened to extinguish. Perhaps to their surprise, considering her reputation for toughness, they found her urging them to go more slowly, to build and manage houses themselves, to give her and her friends a freer hand and security of tenure as a fixed element in the Commissioners' system of estate management.[3]

---

[1] Octavia Hill, *Letter to my Fellow-Workers*, 1884–5, pp. 4–5.

[2] See the last three paragraphs of their Southwark committee's report.

[3] See hints in her 1884–5 *Letter to my Fellow-Workers* and the letters printed in C. Edmund Maurice's *Life of Octavia Hill*, pp. 466 and 474–6. The latter may well have been written to the Commissioners' secretary, with whom she was later on the

She urged them to search their hearts and alter their policy; and, perhaps to *her* surprise, she succeeded. Frederick Temple, when her battle with them was over, jocularly described it thus: 'When she had talked to us for half an hour, we were quite refuted. I never had such a beating in my life! Consequently I feel great respect for her. So fully did she convince us, that we not only did what she asked us on that estate [Southwark], but proceeded to carry out similar plans on other estates!'[1]

The crisis of their conversion came at a meeting of the Estates Committee on 25 November 1886, when she persuaded them to give her a piece of ground to be turned into a public garden. The debris and rubbish was soon cleared away and replaced by lawns, flower-beds, pools and even a little fountain. Octavia's imagination, however, fired by this initial triumph, improved the site still further. Along one side of the garden she persuaded her friends to add a children's covered playground and balcony; along the next side she placed six picturesque model cottages; and in the angle between them, a sizeable hall to serve as a kind of community centre, complete with stage, piano, giant open fires, and murals by Walter Crane 'illustrative of heroic deeds' by railwaymen and nurses.[2] To this Red Cross Hall, Cottages and Garden, which must have been one of the earliest and most attractive of humanity's counter-attacks on slumdom, were soon added the White Cross Cottages, outcome of 'a *most* satisfactory interview' with the Commissioners' secretary, which led her to remark to her mother, 'Times are indeed changed!'[3] These six new cottages secured the garden's openness on the sunny side and—an excellent Octavia Hill touch—kept 'the passage to them clean and orderly by erecting a gate, over which we shall have control.'[4]

best of terms; if it was not to him, it was obviously written to a commissioner. But it cannot possibly have been written as late as March 1887. Since a friend of hers had succeeded in taking a lease of some houses by the end of 1885, her request that they should let her do so means it cannot have been written later than that; her reference to 'May 5th', *tout court*, makes it look more like some time in the second half of 1884.

[1] Speech at a C.O.S. meeting at Fulham Palace, early 1889, reported by C. E. Maurice, *op. cit.* p. 486.

[2] The Countess of Ducie gave £4000 for the development of the garden; the Hon. Henry F. Cowper gave £2000 towards the cost of the hall; and Lady Jane Dundas built the cottages.   [3] 12 November 1889, in C. E. Maurice, *op. cit.* p. 503.

[4] 1889 *Letter to my Fellow-Workers*, p. 6.

There is no need to detail Octavia Hill's subsequent dealings with the Ecclesiastical Commissioners. From the early nineties onwards, until her retirement in 1912, she had great influence with them. More and more work was made over to her and her helpers. She was taken into counsel when they drew up their plans;[1] and, most important of all, in 1893 they took the momentous step of deciding (nearly ten years after they had firmly decided against it) to become house-property owners themselves. This was Octavia's work. 'Encouraged by the satisfactory result of Red and White Cross Cottages and Gable Cottages', she wrote in her 1893 *Letter to my Fellow-Workers*, 'I suggested to the Ecclesiastical Commissioners that they should themselves build similar cottages on their own ground in Southwark. They met my suggestion most cordially, and, after careful thought, decided to build nine new cottages. . . . The sun comes brightly in at their back windows. We begged the Commissioners to leave small borders against the walls of the tiny yards, so that tenants may plant creepers, and, at least, a few crocuses and ferns.' From this miniature beginning sprang the most effective phase of Octavia Hill's connexion with the Commissioners. It became a real partnership and evidently gave the greatest satisfaction to both parties. The Commissioners had their new properties managed with exemplary care, and Octavia, who had never previously worked for such powerful and determined landlords, was able to operate on a really big scale. Within a decade, they had built 430 separate holdings (either cottages or suites in three-floor tenements) containing 1351 rooms. Cluttons were of course the official managers 'but', to use the Commissioners' own words, 'an arrangement has been made by which the actual supervision and collection of the rents has been delegated by Messrs Clutton to Miss Octavia Hill and assistants trained by her to deal with this particular class of property. To Miss Hill's part falls, besides the collection of the rents, the ordering of the necessary tenant's repairs and general watchfulness over the maintenance of good order and against abuse of privileges and joint rights among the tenants.'[2]

When they wrote this, the Commissioners were in the throes of extending their building schemes still further. Their operations in Southwark and Westminster had not been ambitious; 14 cottages and 44

[1] See especially her 1903 *Letter to my Fellow-Workers*, about the Walworth estate.
[2] 1903 report, p. 118.

three-room tenement suites in Southwark, 34 cottages and 81 tenement
suites of different sizes in Westminster. But now, in Lambeth, they were
spending £61,000 on the redevelopment of about $2\frac{1}{2}$ acres of dilapidated, overcrowded cottages and narrow streets. A wide new road was
driven through it, sites set aside for mission rooms and a parsonage
house, two pubs suppressed, and (how far had not their ideas advanced
since 1884!) half an acre was set aside for a recreation ground.[1] Hot on
the heels of the Lambeth estate came another and larger one in Walworth. This too was in such a state that it had to be redeveloped, at a
cost of over £200,000. Again Octavia Hill was taken into consultation, and employed to find managers both for the existing old properties
pending their demolition and for the 793 new cottages and tenement
suites the Commissioners put up there.[2] The same pattern of redevelopment was followed as in Lambeth. Three beer-houses and a pub were
suppressed, and one of them turned into a girls' club; a site was provided
for a new parish school; and over an acre of recreation ground placed
at the heart of it, which was publicly opened by the L.C.C.—for whose
collectivism Miss Hill had, by that date, acquired some dislike—in July
1905. The Commissioners' secretary Porter was present, and so was
Sir Lewis Dibdin, who, according to her, 'made a most satisfactory
speech, showing that he grasped the main points of the work'.[3]

Octavia Hill finally withdrew from active work in the spring of 1912,
and died in the summer. Her spirit, so strong, careful, and compassionate,
lived on. The Commissioners, in redeveloping their urban working-
class estates, continued to do so with an eye to their maximum possible
improvement as working-class homes, contenting themselves with a
profit of four per cent or less. Until the nineteen-thirties they undertook
nothing as large as the Walworth redevelopment, but then came big
schemes in Vauxhall, Lambeth, Southwark, Woolwich, Stoke Newing-
ton and Paddington. Their performance still classed them among the

[1] *Ibid.* p. 119. Cf. also Octavia Hill's 1901 and 1902 *Letters to my Fellow-Workers*.
[2] 1903 report, pp. 119–20, and Octavia's 1903 and 1904 *Letters to my Fellow-Workers*.
It appears from the latter that the Commissioners nearly shied off the responsibility of
rebuilding and retaining control of so large an area, and toyed with the idea—
iniquitous, in her eyes—of ground-rents. In the end, however, they decided to play
the man, and do as she desired.
[3] C. E. Maurice, *op. cit.* p. 562.

best urban landlords going.[1] Before Octavia Hill came into their lives, they had let land, at preferential rates, for redevelopment by the Peabody Trust, the Improved Industrial Dwellings Company and similar bodies who put up gaunt blocks of tenements wholly lacking in charm, light and amenity but at any rate healthier and safer than the decrepit hovels their tenants had often been living in before. Octavia Hill educated the Commissioners to a higher standard, taught them not to disregard the virtues of the cottage and to keep their own tenements down to three floors. Now, in the nineteen-thirties, the Commissioners advanced *pari passu* with the best contemporary municipal practice to more sophisticated standards still. Dibdin House in Maida Vale, a fine spacious four-storey block for 230 families opened by the Bishop of London in October 1938—the seven blocks for 89 families along Union Street, Southwark, opened by the Bishop of Southwark in May the same year—and the 214 flats and social service centre in the Ethelm Street area of Lambeth, opened by the Archbishop of Canterbury in June 1939—were each of them creditable to the church of whose reputation the Commissioners were sensitively jealous; and the Commissioners were careful to proclaim that the management of each would be 'on Octavia Hill principles'.[2] The Southwark blocks were actually placed under the care of Miss L. C. Mitchell, to whom Octavia Hill had made over her own responsibilities when she retired in 1912.

'When I am gone', Octavia Hill had said, 'I hope my friends will not try to carry out any special system, or to follow blindly in the track which I have trodden. . . . When the time comes that we slip from our places, and they are called to the front as leaders, what should they inherit from us? Not a system, not an association, not dead formulas . . . but the quick eye to see, the true soul to measure, the large hope to grasp the mighty issue of the new and better days to come. . . .'[3] She might not have liked their blunt reference to 'Octavia Hill principles'; she would presumably have very much disapproved of the government subsidies which the Commissioners could get for their redevelopment schemes if they worked with the socialistic L.C.C. and took their

---

[1] Independent testimony to its quality was paid by Mrs Cecil Chesterton in her plain-spoken book, *I lived in a Slum*, pp. 218–9, 224–6.

[2] See the Official Opening brochures, in C.C. Archives Box 'Octavia Hill'.

[3] 1898: in C. E. Maurice, *op. cit.* pp. 582–3.

tenants mostly from the slums which the L.C.C. were busily clearing; she would certainly have lamented the height at which the Commissioners had pitched the rents in those of their new blocks that were not subsidized, and which were often higher than the cleared-out tenants could afford. But better days had come for the working-classes than Octavia Hill could have imagined before the first world war, and the stiff individualist substructure of her thought had, for better or for worse, been made to seem old-fashioned and irrelevant. The world had moved on from her fixed points, and the Commissioners, lacking neither eyes to see nor souls to measure, had gone with it.

'The Commissioners' expenditure in connexion with their housing schemes for the working classes is not undertaken as a profitable investment but in conformity with a duty which they regard as laid upon them as landowners. The return which they expect to receive is approximately £3 per cent.' This statement occurs in most of their reports during the thirties, and they felt bound to make it, not in order to imply that they were not anxious to make profitable investments whenever they decently could for the church's advantage, but because the air had again become heady with wild accusations that they were grinding the poor.

The ghosts which the Commissioners found it so hard to lay—in part because they were related to the Southwark ghosts of the early eighties—were conjured up in the spring of 1930 by the publication of a fourpenny pamphlet on housing conditions on what was commonly known as the London Bishoprick Paddington Estate. A well-meaning voluntary body, the Westminster Study Group, had commissioned two ladies to conduct the inquiry. It was neither ill done nor uncomplimentary towards the Commissioners whose good quality as landlords proper was recognized.[1] But the report included some strictures on the Commissioners as ground-landlords, and its facts were at fault. The area they were most concerned about, the Clarendon Street area, was bipartite, and with one part the Commissioners had nothing whatever to do. Of the other part they were indeed 'owners', but only as ground-landlords and in conjunction with a body of private trustees. The property had been let by Bishop Randolph in 1812 for a fine and a ground-rent on a perpetually renewable lease. The Law of Property

[1] It was summarized, with excerpts, in *The Times*, 29 March 1930, p. 7 f.

Act, 1925, had indeed declared that perpetuity meant 2000 years; but that hardly helped the Paddington Estate Trustees to put things right. They were in fact powerless. Much of the property was in terrible state. Poor-grinding was endemic. But if anything was to be done, it had to be done by Parliament or by the local authorities using such powers as had been given them by the Public Health and Housing Acts.[1]

This was only the beginning of the Commissioners' embarrassments with regard to Paddington during the nineteen-thirties. On the principle that there was no smoke without a fire, some people assumed that the Commissioners had something to hide. The uninterrupted rise in the Commissioners' rental from the Paddington Estate, which actually derived from the improvement of its wealthy Bayswater Road side, was pointed to as evidence that the Commissioners were grinding the poor after all. And then there were the whores who were always getting under the guard of the Commissioners' lessees and carrying on business, undeniably, on the Commissioners' estates. This was happening all the time, of course, on all West End estates. It was, and is, beyond human power to stop. The Commissioners, as ground-landlords merely, could do nothing about it. But such considerations did not prevent the prurient and the anti-clerical from relishing the piquant idea of the Commissioners prospering on the notoriously high profits of prostitution.

Rumours, legends and tall stories continued to circulate so freely that in 1936 the Commissioners acquiesced in a suggestion made by J. G. Lockhart, chairman of Church Social Action, that the Church Union Housing Association should be invited to appoint an independent commissioner to examine their London properties as fully as might be thought necessary in order to settle the question for good and all. Marion Fitzgerald, a woman of some experience in sanitary and housing affairs, was agreed on, and her report, *The Church as Landlord*, was published in an abbreviated form by the S.P.C.K. in 1937. The Commissioners regarded it as, not indeed faultless, but on the whole 'very well done'. Unfortunately, however, this survey, which was meant to lay the dust, actually became the instrument of raising another cloud of it. At the autumn session of the Church Assembly that year, there appeared on the agenda paper a motion deploring the Commissioners'

[1] See the 1930 report, pp. vii–viii.

participation in the profits of Paddington prostitution and the exploitation of the Walworth poor, as allegedly shown in Miss Fitzgerald's report.[1] Only a very hasty reading of that report could have led to such conclusions being drawn from it, and the Commissioners had no difficulty in rebutting them, by letters to the newspapers and in a pamphlet, *The Ecclesiastical Commissioners' Ground Rents: a Statement with Reference to recent Allegations*. But all the good that had been designed to be done was undone, by the haste of an excited Church Assembly man. It was not the first, nor the last, time that the church has suffered from the unreflecting consciences of its friends as much as from the assaults of its enemies.

3. THE CHURCH'S BUSINESS

In their thirty-third report, for the year ending 1 November 1880, the Ecclesiastical Commissioners paused to review the purposes to which their Common Fund had been applied since its creation forty years earlier. About 4700 benefices had been augmented or endowed with about £620,500 a year in perpetuity, representing a capital sum of about £18,615,000. The sum of private benefactions handled by them through the same period was equivalent to about £145,000 a year. The Commissioners could thus reflect, that their office had so far been the means of adding about £765,000 income a year to the poorer and on the whole the more laborious benefices of the Church of England.

Augmentations of existing, and endowments of new, livings continued to be a main preoccupation through the rest of the Commissioners' independent lifetime. But it soon ceased to be, virtually, their only outgoing interest and *raison d'être*. Other responsibilities, relating at first to the poor clergy only and then, after the first world war, to the church at large, were pressed upon them. The need of a central and controlling financial and administrative institution became more than ever acute as churchmen sought to mobilize the resources of the church to meet the novel challenges of the early twentieth century. The conservative particularism that had for so long stood in the way of desirable changes increasingly gave ground before the rousing idea of the church as a whole, fighting the Lord's battles in an unaccustomedly alien land, and moving men and money freely from place to place as need arose.

[1] Church Assembly paper No. 578, item 26.

The Ecclesiastical Commissioners, to do them justice, had always sought to facilitate such a movement. Not they, but the hostility of diocesan interests and a strong parliamentary mixture of anti-centralization and anti-clericalism, had prevented their making more progress in this direction in the later nineteenth century. Now at last church opinion began to awaken to its desirability. For many years it seemed as if any schemes for increasing the church's control over its finances must involve the placing them under the direction of Convocation. This was to doom all such schemes, because Convocation's exclusively clerical composition made it odious in many churchmen's eyes; but once the Church Assembly was set up after the first world war, a much more acceptable 'directorate' was easily visualized and, by slow stages, brought into being. So, in the twentieth century, the Ecclesiastical Commissioners' funds began to be made available for other important purposes besides augmentation and endowment, and the church's property as a whole came at last to be mobilized and deployed to meet its overall needs.

Already by the eighteen-eighties, the Commissioners were doing an extraordinary amount of the church's business. No longer any talk of closing them down! Church building; sales, leases and exchanges of ecclesiastical properties; patronage; the adjustment of the boundaries of parishes, archdeaconries and bishoprics; and the housing of the clergy, had all to be looked after, besides the clergy's remuneration. It will perhaps be convenient at this point to describe, as simply as possible, the Commissioners' activities in a single year, to show how multifarious they were, and to indicate the basis from which their further expansion was to proceed. Let the year 1880 serve as an example. It was an ordinarily busy year, well representing the nature of the Commissioners' work during the vigorous period brought slowly to an end by the economic depression of the eighties and nineties.

In 1880 they had assisted in the endowment or permanent augmentation of 357 benefices. 164 of these had been in conjunction with benefactors, who had given lands, rent-charges, investments and cash worth in the sum nearly £200,000. To meet this the Commissioners had given capital sums, for the repair or construction of parsonages, totalling £51,423, and undertaken to pay annually to these livings the sum of £3529. The rest of their permanent grants had been made independent of benefactors. 173 of these were in respect of local claims; capital sums had been given for the repair of construction of parsonages, or in discharge or mortgages to Queen Anne's Bounty, totalling £62,373; and annual payments of £13,203 undertaken. 20 grants were to livings that qualified for unconditional grants under their regulations obtaining at that time—i.e. to new districts assigned since 1871 and containing a population of 4000 or more according to the census of that year.

These were only their main activities in this line. They had also (1) annexed to benefices, in respect of local claims, 34 tithe rent-charges, tenths and 'pensions' worth in sum £3431 and 20 pieces of land amounting to nearly 101 acres in all: (2) made temporary grants to benefices within the boundaries of the gigantic old parish of Manchester to the value of £1050 from out of the revenues of the collegiate church, and £317 from their common fund: (3) met benefactions of the same amount with 328 grants totalling £25,440 for the maintenance of assistant curates in districts with mining populations: (4) received capital sums, under the Lord Chancellor's Augmentation Act of 1863, for the augmentation by annuities of £33 and £76 respectively of two benefices formerly in the Lord Chancellor's patronage: and (5) contrived the augmentation of eleven benefices with tithe rent-charges (£505 16s. 10d.), 'pensions' (£900) or land (nearly 46 acres) from associated benefices.

They had managed the transfer, usually to benefactors, of the patronage of nine benefices, and the exchange of the patronage of 14 benefices.

Of new ecclesiastical districts, they had constituted 20 'district chapelries', 18 'consolidated chapelries', one 'particular district', one further subdivision of Manchester parish, and 12 'Peel districts' or 'Blandford parishes'.

The rest of their business in connexion with churches and parishes was extensive and peculiar. 18 parochial boundaries had been altered; two churches had been authorized for the performance of baptisms, marriages and burials; sixteen new churches had been substituted for old; scales of pew rents been fixed for four churches; and conveyances of 167 sites for churches, cemeteries, parsonage houses and glebes approved and completed.

Two new archdeaconries, Macclesfield and Warrington, had been constituted and endowed, and the internal geography of four arch-deaconries rearranged.

The prebends of Putson Major, in Hereford cathedral, and Leicester St Margaret, in Lincoln, marked down for suspension forty years earlier, had been taken possession of in consequence of the deaths of their long-lived occupants. (The preferment that lasted longest after the nominal axeing of 1840 was the prebend of Wiveliscombe in Wells cathedral, the owner of which held out until 1891. 1887 saw the falling-in of two Hereford preferments; Archbishop Howley's son-in-law only relinquished the precentorship of St Paul's in 1886.)

The rest of the year's work was all concerned with ecclesiastical property. In 1880 the Estates Commissioners were still busily engaged, under the Act of 1854[1], in the enfranchisement of estates either by selling reversions and copyholds or by purchasing leasehold interests and copyholds, with the general aim of simplifying their managerial problems and making possible an improvement of revenue at the same time as a concentration of resources. For their sales they had received a sum of £178,129 2s. 7d. and annual rents worth £2023 4s. 6d.; their purchases had cost them £115,107; two of their offers to purchase had been declined, while they themselves, seeing ways of making good use in the future of nine leased properties, had declined to sell their reversions. Of all these properties, the Ecclesiastical Commissioners had (or were on the way to acquiring) sole powers of binding and loosing. They had also the power of sanctioning, or refusing to sanction, the sale by ecclesiastical corporations of *their* land, the granting of long leases of it, or the leasing of minerals under it. Earlier on, this shared power had made a lot of bad blood between them on the one side and the bishops and chapters on the other. By the eighties, arrangements had been made with the bishops and chapters which took the greater part of their estate management away from the Commissioners' control, and most of the business that the Commissioners were still doing under this head was with individual incumbents, selling or leasing pieces of glebe land.

Let us now survey the development of their business from the eighties onwards.

[1] 17 and 18 Vic. c. 116.

The agricultural depression was not the only, nor even the most important, of the reasons why the Ecclesiastical Commissioners drew in their horns in the eighties. They noticed it, of course, and referred in their report for 1879 to 'the circumstances which have of late operated to the prejudice of agriculture and trade', trusting that their operation would be 'but temporary'; they saw no need to worry unduly. Thereafter they noticed it in every annual report, but it was not until it was joined after 1884 by other factors that they thought fit to alter course. In 1884 their income from mineral royalties and so on was down as well. Expecting it to stay down, they decided to reduce the scale of their augmentations. In 1883 they had gone bravely up to a perpetual charge of £25,000 a year; now they came back to £20,000. Their income from minerals, as it happened, quickly recovered; but by 1885 they had other things on their minds. The tithe rent-charge averages were still declining, the reductions they had made in many tenants' rents were hardening into permanencies, the farming community's difficulties were still getting worse. Moreover the geese that had laid their golden eggs were palpably ageing. For thirty years or so their prosperity, such as it was, and means of helping the parochial clergy, had floated on the tide of property that continued to rise as ancient bishops and canons died, as chapters saw reason, and, most important of all, as long leases fell in. Very soon now, their reservoir would be full and only an insignificant trickle would continue to feed it. They decided accordingly to reduce their scale of grants again, and accepted a charge of only £15,000. In 1886 the situation deteriorated still further; they came down to £12,500; and in 1887 they prudently adopted a new principle altogether.

Instead of charging the common fund with so many thousands extra a year, (between 1863 and 1888 the permanent annual charge upon it for benefices had gone up from £90,000 to £600,000) they would annually appropriate *capital* to the business of augmentations, and so make their augmentations absolutely secure. They began, in 1887, with a capital appropriation of £200,000, which meant a diminution in their scale of giving of about one-third. The shrinkage was widely noticed, and the prudence that had prompted it criticized by the hard-pressed clergy and their spokesmen. The Commissioners felt the winds of unpopularity blowing about them and explained the grounds for their changed policy in their report for 1888, when they lowered their capital appropriation to £150,000. The following table shows how it remained at about this figure for the next ten years; then it began to go up so hearteningly that there ceased to be so much point in criticizing the prudent principle on which the Commissioners were proceeding, and on which they continued to act for the rest of their days. Prudent measures only seem mistaken to those who immediately suffer by them.

1887	£200,000	1901	£225,000
1888	£150,000	1902	£250,000
1889	£150,000	1903	£150,000
1890	£160,000	1904	£250,000
1891	£185,000	1905	£300,000
1892	£150,000	1906	£325,000
1893	£150,000	1907	£315,000
1894	£150,000	1908	£400,000
1895	£150,000	1909	£400,000
1896	£150,000	1910	£480,000
1897	£150,000	1911	£400,000
1898	£185,000	1912	£400,000
1899	£200,000	1913	£400,000
1900	£200,000	1914	£400,000

TABLE 4. *Annual Capital Appropriations for Augmentation and Endowment, 1887–1914.*

Local claims continued until well after the First World War to absorb a great deal of the Commissioners' attention; in some years more than a third of their grants were in respect of them. If the Commissioners' had an Achilles' heel, it was this. They had stoutly resisted the principle of local claims in their early years and submitted in 1860 to the necessity of attending to them only under protest. Later on they seem to have ceased to resent them so much. They went indeed further towards meeting them than they were absolutely compelled to, and Dibdin the First Estates Commissioner and Downing the secretary put no element of the apologetic into their judicious paragraphs on the subject.[1] While endowing new parishes (which, by definition almost, were populous) with £150 or £200 a year, and helping make other

[1] *Op. cit.* pp. 86–7.

livings up to £300 if their populations were over 4000, the Commissioners would make an otherwise qualified local claim living up to £300, even though its population were only 500. As the years went by and the original objections to local claims became forgotten, they were accepted as just another of the illogicalities and anomalies taken for granted within the establishment. No Blomfield or Chichester appears to have tried to put an end to them, although the amount of money spent annually on their satisfaction could only be at the expense of poor parsons and good causes whose moral claims were often immeasurably superior. The Commissioners had imagination or sense enough to do something about the latter when they were prosperous enough to do it without reducing their local claims augmentations; they were not imaginative or brave enough to do it at the local claims' expense.

There were only two important developments in the Commissioners' augmentations policy before 1907. The first was their decision to help to provide assistant curates for the incumbents of large poor parishes. In 1888 they began setting aside a substantial proportion of their capital appropriation for the year (one-fiftieth, to begin with) for grants to meet benefactions towards the maintenance of assistant curates in poor parishes of a populous character. These were permanent augmentations. The Commissioners also made about two hundred renewable grants of £60 on similar conditions for the same purpose between 1899 and 1902.

The second development came in 1901, when they started making special unconditional grants (i.e. grants unconditional on benefactions being offered) to help incumbents in particularly hard cases. It might be more accurate to say, to rescue, for an incumbent with no more than £300 a year to support him while he managed a parish of over 15,000 souls can hardly have found it less than back-breaking. In 1902 they lowered the population qualification to 12,000, in 1903 to 8000, in 1905 to 7000, in 1907 to 6000 and in 1915 to 5000; at which level it met the augmentations made under their ordinary regulations, coming up fast after 1907.

The augmentations policy changes of 1907 were the most important since the early eighteen-sixties. They signalized the end of the cautious prudence that had marked the past two decades. Their comparative lavishness might indeed have been indulged in a few years earlier, for the Commissioners' revenues had been in a highly healthy state for some time; that they came no later was mainly because of Randall Davidson's succession to Frederick Temple at Lambeth, and his friend Sir Lewis Dibdin's assumption of the First Estates Commissionership in place of earl Stanhope.

The 1907 innovations were two. The Commissioners started a pension scheme. They had long been urged to do something in this line. The English clergy were notoriously ill-equipped to meet personal or family illness, and as for retiring on grounds of senescence alone, the mere idea of it seemed absurd to all incumbents and curates save those with rich preferment or private means. The statutory facilities for pensioned retirement offered by the Incumbents' Resignation Acts of 1871 and 1887[1] were wholly unsatisfactory. Only beneficed clergy were eligible, the amount of the pension was unpredictable, and it was paid out of benefice income to the successor's direct loss and annoyance. Church Congresses and the Convocations had given much time to the subject. The examples of the pensions schemes available to Indian civilians, to the commissioned ranks of the armed services and the clergy of various other churches (especially the free and the established Churches of Scotland) were continually cited; tales of hardships, sometimes of retired clergymen but more often of their widows and children, were never lacking. Spokesmen for the curates and poor incumbents usually urged a compulsory scheme open to unbeneficed clergy as well as beneficed, and providing also for widows and children. Speakers from the church's higher echelons in reply would usually laud the virtues of independence, prudence and voluntary participation, sail as near as they dared to saying that if curates married they had only themselves to blame for their family's hardships, and refuse to countenance any suggestion that the richer incumbents should be taxed for the benefit of the poorer. They would point out the existence of the Clergy Pensions Institution and the other organizations (most of them diocesan) existing to relieve actual hardship and to help thrifty clergymen provide against it. The work done by these agencies was valuable, and several of the diocesan schemes were always spoken of appreciatively. But all their efforts were insufficient to meet the whole of the clergy's needs,

[1] 34 and 35 Vic. c. 44, 50 and 51 Vic. c. 23.

systematically and 'officially'. The Commissioners took the first step towards making this provision in 1907 when they announced the details of their scheme and set aside a first instalment of £100,000 towards financing it. But their scheme was far from radical. It aimed 'to promote the efficient operation' of the existing Acts, and only improved on their principles. No clergyman could look forward to a pension as of right, nor could he know how much he would get if he got one at all. Dependents and unbeneficed clergy were still excluded, pensions were still to come partly from benefice income, grants towards them were not to exceed £50 a year, and they were conditional on incumbents' already possessing a firm title to at least an equivalent pension from the contributory Clergy Pensions Institution or something like it. None of this was calculated to put heart into poor clergymen. But in two respects the Commissioners' entry into the field of pensions substantially relieved their plight, before retirement as well as after it. Poor incumbents—i.e. by the Commissioners' current standards, those with under £250 a year—would not be made to suffer much because the Commissioners proposed in such cases to divide grants between the payer and the receiver of the pension, and even to make additional grants to 'very poor' incumbents (i.e. those with under £150) to make sure they did not suffer at all.[1]

More important than the pensions was the extension of their ordinary augmentation work which the Commissioners announced in their 1907 report. This was a great step forward, marking both the beginning of their modern policy for clerical incomes and the completion at long last of the mission they had originally been appointed to carry out.

Whether that mission could not have been accomplished earlier, is a question which may be endlessly debated. By a more levelling policy the average incumbent's income could obviously have been raised; but to imagine that the levelling principle was ever practical politics in the nineteenth century is to dream dreams. A little more practical, but probably not much, would have been the better organization and management of church members' giving. Nonconformists liked to allege that established churchmen voluntarily gave less than free churchmen. How much this may have been true proportionately of particular free churches, or of the free churches in particular places,

---

[1] Appendix 33 to the 1907 report.

or of one period but not of another, cannot here be investigated. But some at least of the figures brought to bear by establishment controversialists suggest that it was by no means to be taken for granted. Stanley Leighton, member for the Oswestry division of Shropshire, at the 1888 Church Congress extracted from the church's official year book figures so staggering as strongly to suggest that the case was, indeed, quite otherwise.[1] The discussion in course of which he did this was on church finance. Other contributors to the discussion bent their minds to practical proposals for harnessing the huge financial potential which went so largely to waste for lack of direction. Such a harnessing cannot have been wholly impracticable. But the rivalries of church parties, the independent spirit which led Victorian Englishmen instinctively to resent being told what to do with their own, the legal complications consequent upon establishment, would all have made it very difficult, and nothing of the kind came off. Churchmen's giving continued to be, from the would-be planner's point of view, perfectly random.

While voluntary national societies and quasi-official diocesan ones continued to assist private generosity and local joint efforts to build and restore churches and to improve their ministers' conditions of living, the Ecclesiastical Commissioners continued to attract casual abuse from men who imagined that the Commissioners could on their own have done more. It was certainly justifiable at any date after 1836 to complain that the mutual independence, and (for it was no secret) dislike, of the Commissioners and the Bounty brought in its wake waste and confusion. It could certainly be said at any date after 1860 that the degree of attention given by the Commissioners to local claims was extravagant, and that some of the money they paid out on this account could have been better spent. Those who, especially between 1844 and the eighteen-sixties and again after 1886, argued that the Commissioners were being too prudent, that present needs should be dealt with more adequately and the future left to fend for itself, were not all rash and feckless; a greater immediate investment in educational and pastoral work in the later nineteenth century might, for all one knows, have handed down to a necessarily less richly endowed church in the twentieth century a more numerous and devoted flock.

Despite the pressure put upon them to spend their income without

[1] *Report of the Church Congress at Manchester, October* 1888, pp. 544–5.

tarrying for the banker, the Commissioners decided to play safe. Besides substituting capital grants for grants of income in 1887, seven years later they began appropriating to capital a large fraction of their income from mineral royalties, etc. to secure the payment of income grants made before 31 October 1887; which was duly achieved by 1907, when, as has already been stated, the Commissioners' mood changed. The policy of prudence had paid off so well that they were able to embark on a vastly extended augmentations policy without relaxing precautions against the future. They decided to continue to augment for the most part by capital grants and to go on appropriating the reduced but still weighty sum of £80,000 to a minerals depreciation fund. But they decided also that they could afford to carry new income grants up to an aggregate charge of £50,000 a year. It was upon that no less than the £400,000 capital they felt able to distribute that their new augmentations policy was floated.

The basis of this policy, as of their policy ever since, was simple. They set their sights at a higher minimum income for incumbents and simply augmented almost everybody up to it. They would make up unconditionally to £200 a year all livings in public patronage with populations over 1000, and up to £150 a year all such with over 500 'provided, in each case, that it is not practicable to unite them with other benefices'. Within a year they were bringing *all* over 500 up to £200. To private patrons the Commissioners offered the same, provided they would either transfer their livings to public patronage or, alternatively, contribute half the needed sum. Meanwhile, the Commissioners continued, of course, to augment along established lines, endowing new parishes of over 4000, helping incumbents of large existing parishes with money, parsonage houses and assistant curates, and meeting local claims.

In 1909 they reported that all livings in public patronage and insusceptible of unions had been raised to £200, but that there remained 'a large number of otherwise qualified benefices in private patronage which so far have received no benefit from the scheme, its conditions not having been complied with'. The difficulty cannot always have been in finding a benefaction. Patronal self-interest and prejudice still held up the relief of clerical poverty as it had done since Queen Anne's Bounty had first begun augmenting poor livings two centuries before. But the circumstances were now very different. The call to the clerical profession was, by the reign of Edward VII, for most clergymen bound to be a call to the ill-rewarded performance of often unrewarding duties; the church no longer offered 'little to do, and plenty to get'. Even for patrons hardy enough to affront public opinion, the opportunities for mischief were slighter. Patronage was, simply, becoming increasingly difficult to abuse. The Commissioners in 1909 therefore were not guilty of selling out to the troublesome class of patrons when they announced their intention of raising all private patronage benefices of 500 or more souls to £200 a year, provided that they remained in the same hands. The moment patronage was transferred, the grant would cease; this provision was necessary, to prevent patrons profiting from Commissioners' grants by selling advowsons at a higher price on account of them. The same principles were extended in 1917 to bring all livings, whether in public patronage or private, up to £200 a year if their population was over 300.

The year 1919 saw the Commissioners take three important steps forward along the lines marked out in 1907. First, the Union of Benefices Act[1] soon strengthened their hand against demands for grants to 'peppercorn' parishes. Second, they announced their readiness to make retiring pension-grants to deserving unbeneficed clergy as soon as they should receive legislative authority to do so.[2] Third, they 'set before themselves for accomplishment, as and when funds should be available', a bigger and better augmentations policy working on this scale:—

Benefices with populations of	Patronage	Annual Income from all Sources to be raised to
10,000+	Public only	£400
4–10,000	Public only	£350
1–4,000	Public only	£300
300–1,000	Public only	£250
Under 300	Public and Private	£200

In 1923, having more or less accomplished this programme, the Commissioners moved on to bring all public patronage livings of 300 or

[1] 9 and 10 George V c. 98, soon amended and systematized by the Union of Benefices Measure, 1923.

[2] This authority was given by the Ecclesiastical Commissioners Measure of 1921.

more souls up to £300 a year; of 1000 or more souls, up to £350; and of 4000 or more souls, up to £400 a year. Private patronage benefices were very soon brought within the scope of this revised scale after the passage of the Benefices Act (1898) Amendment Measure of 1923, which ensured the ultimate, and encouraged the rapid, end of the sale of advowsons. Thereafter the Commissioners treated livings in both sorts of patronage alike, so long as the private patronage was un-saleable. If it could still legally be sold, they would make temporary grants only.

1927 and 1928 marked further progress in the same direction, under the direct leadership still of Sir Lewis Dibdin. The Commissioners announced in their report for 1927 a new scheme of augmentations which, as slightly modified in 1928, worked in co-operation with the diocesan authorities, first, to raise all un-united or un-uniteable bene-fices irrespective of population, to £200 a year by the Commissioners' efforts alone if need be, and to £300 a year by the Commissioners in conjunction with the Diocesan Board of Finance wherever the latter could contribute or convey half the sum required; and second, to bring all livings of 300 or more souls up to £350; of 1000 or more to £375; and of 4000 or more to £400. This scheme, with negligible modifica-tions, remained the spine of their augmentations policy until the Second World War, by when it was practically completed. But it must not be forgotten, that these figures were only minima, and that the Com-missioners' means of lightening the clergy's burdens and enhancing the church's efficiency went far beyond these simple income rises. In their report, for example, for 1934—a year when they made a special effort to help to endow new districts and extend the ministry in the suburbs—they allocated their total capital grant of £365,000 for 1935 thus:

(1) £150,000 to meet benefactions towards improved incomes, parsonage houses and the endowment of funds for maintaining curates in parishes of over 5,000 souls.
(2) £158,500 to endow new districts with not more than £250 a year in each case.
(3) £34,000 to meet local claims.
(4) £22,500 in grants of not more than £150 each to curates in new housing areas.

These capital grants were over and above whatever income grants they made to livings qualified solely by their population according to the scale of augmentations then in force.

Three other substantial departments of the Commissioners' work between the wars, in so far as it directly benefitted the clergy, must be mentioned. A comprehensive and compulsory pensions scheme was introduced by the Clergy Pensions Measure of 1926; it required all active clergymen to pay 3% of their incomes annually to a new body, the Clergy Pensions Board; and the Ecclesiastical Commissioners made it possible by providing at once a capital foundation of £350,000 and £100,000 a year in perpetuity. Under the authority of the Ecclesiastical Dilapidations Measure of 1923, they made over £500,000 to Queen Anne's Bounty to prime the pump of the new dilapidations machinery; and they came to the aid of the Bounty also by paying, under the Tithe (Administration of Trusts) Measure of 1928, the interest on the overdraft which the Bounty ran up in paying what was due to the owners of tithe rent-charge.

As the Commissioners thus enlarged their interests, extended their powers, and actively assisted in that fundamental change in the life of the church which accompanied the construction of competent diocesan authorities, they also came to a better understanding with the Bounty, achieving a more rational and economical division of the church's business between them. The Commissioners' bold and rapid inroads on clerical poverty after 1907 brought them well into the Bounty's territory and made the Bounty's *raison d'être* increasingly obscure. It was in the church's interest that first fruits and tenths should be abolished, as they finally were in 1926;[1] it was in the Bounty's interest no less than the church's that the Bounty should leave the business of augmentations entirely to the Commissioners and strike out into some new fields of usefulness. It made the change just after the first world war, ceasing to distribute its income by way of augmentations and putting it instead at the disposal of poor clergymen who were having difficulties meeting their dilapidations charges. They had already some acquaintance with the difficulties of this business, having been brought into it by the Ecclesiastical Dilapidations Act of 1871. Now the Church

[1] First Fruits and Tenths Measure, 1926. The amount of them had been made up to livings under £200 and £300 a year since 1903 (by the Bounty) and 1920 (by the Commissioners) respectively.

Assembly's Dilapidations Measure of 1923 constituted Queen Anne's Bounty the central authority to work a comprehensive new system through a network of Diocesan Dilapidations Boards. For a brief interval dilapidations preoccupied them. Then in 1925 they went through a still larger metamorphosis, by becoming, virtually, the church's Tithes Department; and for the next decade this was by far their heaviest responsibility. It would probably be no exaggeration to say that between the First and Second World Wars, the sheer volume and complexity of the work done by Queen Anne's Bounty was greater than all that they had done during the previous two centuries of their existence.

4. CONCLUSION

The conclusion of my book is inevitably the amalgamation of the Bounty and the Commissioners in 1948, and the merging of their traditions, staffs and interests in the unitary body called the Church Commissioners.

The reader may find himself wondering what the story of these two institutions, and their relations with church and society, adds up to. I would assure him that I have sometimes wondered too. The story is, after all, neither plain nor completely satisfying. Queen Anne's Bounty and the Ecclesiastical Commissioners had chequered careers. They began, on their very different levels, full of joy and hope, poor clergymen looking to them as secular saviours, progressive churchmen expecting the Commissioners at any rate to infuse reforming energy and economic principle into the system of a church not notably rich in either. As it turned out, neither body was able to do as much as such well-wishers, evidently over-optimistic, expected. But the pessimists were disappointed too. Both bodies survived sicknesses and assaults which could easily have proved fatal; at the worst they kept going, at the best they showed, so far as their respective constitutions and tasks permitted, resourcefulness and vigour. They were, in fact, remarkably like the church they existed to serve.

Their services to the church and through it to the nation are obvious enough. The modern Church of England could not possibly have become what it is without them. In that respect they have great historical importance. But just as the history of the Church of England, still so peculiarly 'national' and representative despite the teeming anomalies of its establishment, cannot except by the most narrow-minded be called merely ecclesiastical history, so also must the history of Queen Anne's Bounty and the Ecclesiastical Commissioners be seen in breadth and perspective, now showing brightly, now half-hidden, always however a part only of the receding landscape of history. Their principal historic interest accordingly seems to lie in the share they had in the socio-political revolution which has, during the last two centuries, accompanied the changes in the church's conditions of establishment and its endeavours to set its house in order. This process was indicated in the first, and elaborated in the middle chapters of this book; there is no need to recur to it. It will suffice to ask the reader, if he has kept patience to the end, to contrast the secular organization of the Church of England then and now—to compare the social, political and economic dimensions of the early eighteenth-century and mid-twentieth establishments—and to set side by side the lives, not of pre-lates or dignitaries, but of ordinary obscure parochial clergymen, with cares about families, money, homes and churches as well as about souls and services. The material circumstances of clerical life and established church function on either side of the revolution seem scarcely comparable.

And yet, after all, the ends pursued by church and clergy in 1948 are not so dissimilar from those pursued in 1700. Service to the national community, seeking necessarily the salvation of its individual members but much more besides, was then, as it is still, the grand end pursued by the Church of England. In 1700 the forms of service and means of salvation were understood quite differently, and were neither expected to alter nor thought to be much alterable. By 1948 the church had become used to the fact that in the modern world society changes all the time and rapidly, and that the forms by which its members are to be served and saved must, if they are to be appropriate, change too. (Significant, in its way, of this change, was the Commissioners' augmentation 'scheme K' of 1943, which offered grants on conditions which encouraged parochial church councils to rally the support of the laity to an unprecedented extent). In both 1700 and 1948 the Church of England was not ill-adapted to the task it understood itself bound to perform. Its difficult time came in between, after the old simplicity and relative stability had gone, before the nature and necessities of modern society became fully understood.

Whether the Church of England did well or badly during that testing time of transition, and whether it could conceivably have done better or worse than it actually did, are questions which each man will answer in his own fashion. All will agree, at any rate, that this period was a crucial one for the church; and it was in the heart of it that the Ecclesiastical Commissioners were founded, to help the church to survive it. Now, as in the middle of 1961 I finish writing a sketch of their history, I see them transmuted into the Church Commissioners and with the support of the church in a changing society still their great and onerous task. It is a heavy responsibility indeed to be the chief temporal pillar of a famous branch of the Christian Church.

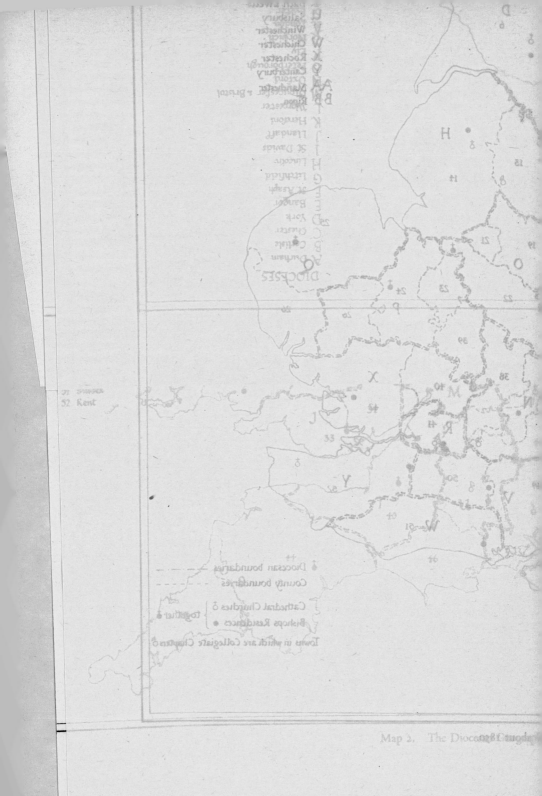

Map 2. The Dioceses

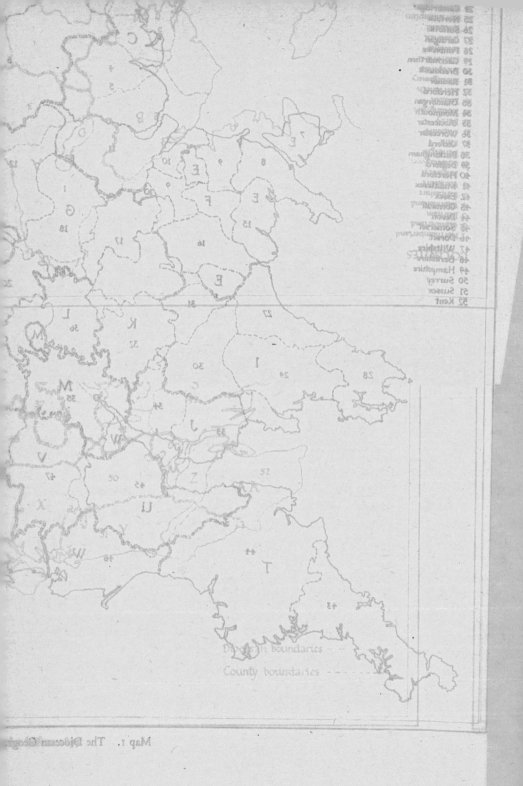

QUEEN ANNE'S BOUNTY'S
FIRST CHARTER

Sealed with the Great Seal of England,
3 *November,* 3 ANNE

ANNE, by the grace of God of England, Scotland, France, and Ireland, Queen, Defender of the Faith, &c., to all to whom these presents shall come, greeting. As the welfare and support of the Church of England, as by law established, have been always our greatest care, so we have, since our accession to the Crown, frequently reflected on the miserable condition of a very great number of the Clergy of this our kingdom, by reason of the mean and insufficient provision for their maintenance in several places, which tends very much to the ruin of this Church: and in regard that the arrears of Tenths due to our Exchequer upon small Rectories and Vicarages could not be answered without great difficulties and hardships to the poor Incumbents, and that several of those Churches, for fear of incurring the full payment of such arrears, were held in sequestration by temporary Curates, without being regularly filled with institution and induction, we were resolved to do as much as in us lay towards easing of the Clergy, and were graciously inclined to think that the Ministers who served those Cures might, in respect of their poverty, be true objects of our royal compassion, and that it would tend to the honour and good discipline of the Established Church, if those benefices were filled with able clerks, legally instituted and inducted; and to the charitable purpose aforesaid, we signed a warrant to authorize our Lord High Treasurer to discharge the arrears of Tenths due upon the small Rectories and Vicarages not exceeding thirty pounds per annum, by the most improved valuations of the same, on condition that the respective Churches were first filled with institution and induction; and our Lord High Treasurer signified our said bountiful intention by letters directed to our Archbishops and Bishops accordingly; and in order to settle a fund for increasing the maintenances of the poor Clergy, we commanded our right trusty and well-beloved counsellor, Sir Charles Hedges, knight, one of our principal Secretaries of State, to deliver a message in writing, signed by us, to our most dutiful and loyal Commons of England in Parliament assembled, declaring, that we having taken into our serious consideration the mean and insufficient maintenance belonging to the poor

Clergy in divers parts of this kingdom, to give them some ease had been pleased to remit the arrears of the Tenths to the poor Clergy; and that, for augmentation of their maintenance, we would make a grant of our whole revenue arising out of First Fruits and Tenths, as far as it then was or should become free from incumbrances, to be applied to this purpose; and if the House of Commons could find any proper method by which our good intentions to the poor Clergy might be made more effectual, it would be a great advantage to the public and very acceptable to us. And whereas by an Act of Parliament made in the second year of our reign, intituled, 'An Act for the making more effectual her Majesty's gracious intentions for the augmentation of the maintenance of the poor Clergy, by enabling her Majesty to grant in perpetuity the revenues of the First Fruits and Tenths, and also for enabling any other persons to make grants for the same purpose,' reciting, that whereas, at a Parliament holden in the twenty-sixth year of the reign of King Henry the Eighth, the First Fruits, Revenues, and Profits for one year, upon every nomination or appointment to any dignity, benefice, office, or promotion spiritual, within this realm or elsewhere within the said King's dominions and also a perpetual yearly rent or pension amounting to the value of the tenth part of all the revenues and profits belonging to any dignity, benefice or promotion spiritual whatsoever, within any diocese of this realm or in Wales, were granted to the said King Henry the Eighth, his heirs and successors; and divers other statutes have since been made touching the First Fruits and annual Tenths of the Clergy, and the ordering thereof; and whereas a sufficient settled provision for the Clergy in many parts of this realm hath never yet been made, by reason whereof divers mean and stipendiary Preachers are in many places entertained to serve the Cures, and officiate there, who, depending for their necessary maintenance upon the good-will and liking of their hearers, have been and are thereby under temptation of too much complying and suiting their doctrines and teachings to the humours rather than the good of their hearers, which hath been great occasion of faction and schism and contempt of the ministry: and further mentioning, that forasmuch as we, taking into our princely and serious consideration the mean and insufficient maintenance belonging to the Clergy in divers parts of this our kingdom, have been most graciously pleased, out of our most religious and tender concern for the Church of England (whereof ourself is the only supreme head on earth,) and for the poor Clergy thereof, not only to remit the arrears of our Tenths due from our poor Clergy, but also to declare unto our most dutiful and loyal Commons, our royal pleasure and pious desire that the whole revenue arising from the First Fruits and Tenths of the Clergy might be settled for a perpetual augmentation of the maintenance of the said poor Clergy in places where the same is not already sufficiently provided for: (to the end that our most gracious intentions may be made effectual, and that the Church may receive so great and lasting an advantage from our parting with so great a branch of our revenue towards the better provision for the Clergy not sufficiently provided for, and to the intent our singular zeal for the support of the Clergy, and the honour, interest, and future security of the Church as by law established, may be perpetuated to all ages,) it is enacted, that it shall and may be lawful for us, by our Letters Patent under the Great Seal of England, to incorporate such persons as we shall therein nominate or appoint to be one body politic and corporate, and to have a common seal and perpetual succession; and also at our will and pleasure, by the same or any other Letters Patent, to grant, limit, or settle to or upon the said Corporation and their successors for ever, all the revenue of First Fruits and yearly perpetual tenths of all dignities, offices, benefices, and promotions spiritual whatsoever, to be applied and disposed of to and for the augmentation of the maintenance of such Parsons, Vicars, Curates, and Ministers, officiating in any Church or Chapel within the kingdom of England, dominion of Wales, and town of Berwick upon Tweed, where the Liturgy and Rites of the Church of England as now by law established are or shall be used and observed, with such lawful powers, authorities, directions, limitations, and appointments, and under such rules and restrictions, and in such manner and form, as shall be therein expressed; the statute made in the first year of our reign, intituled, 'An Act for the better support of her Majesty's household, and of the honour and dignity of the Crown,' or any other law, to the contrary in anywise notwithstanding. Provided always, and it is hereby declared, that all and every the statutes and provisions touching or concerning the ordering, levying, and true answering and payment or qualification of the said First Fruits and Tenths, or touching the charge, discharge, or alteration, of them or any of them, or any matter or thing relating thereunto, which were in force at the time of making the said Act, shall be, remain, and continue in their full force and effect, and be observed and put in due execution, according to the tenors and purports of the same and every of them, for such intents and purposes nevertheless as shall be contained or directed in or by the said Letters Patents. Provided also, that the said Act, or any thing therein contained, should not extend to avoid or in any way impeach or affect any grant, exchange, alienation, or incumbrance at any time heretofore made of or upon the said revenues of First Fruits and Tenths, or any part thereof; but that the same shall, during the continuance of such grant, exchange, alienation, or incumbrance respectively, be and remain of and in such force and virtue, and no other, to all intents and purposes as if the said Act had not been made. And for the encouragement of such well-disposed persons as shall by our royal example be moved to contribute to so pious and charitable a purpose, and that such their charity may be rightly applied, it is enacted, that all and every person and persons having in his or their own right any estate or interest in possession, reversion, or contingency of or in any lands, tenements, or hereditaments, or any property of or in any goods or chattels, shall have full power, licence, and authority, at his, her, and their will and pleasure, by deed enrolled in such manner and within such time as is directed by the statute made in the twenty-seventh year of the reign of King Henry the Eighth, for enrolment of bargains and sales, or by his, her, or their last will or testament in writing, duly executed according to law, to give and grant to, and vest in, the said Corporation and their successors, all such his, her or their estate, interest, or property in such lands, tenements, and hereditaments, goods and chattels, or any part or parts thereof, for and towards the augmentation of the maintenance of such Ministers as aforesaid, officiating in such Church or Chapel where the liturgy and rites of the said Church are or shall be so used or observed as aforesaid, and having no settled competent provision belonging to the same, and to be for that purpose applied according to the will of the said benefactor in and by such deed enrolled, or by such will or testament executed as aforesaid, expressed, and, in default of such direction, limitation, or appointment, in such manner as by our Letters Patents shall be directed or appointed as aforesaid. And such Corporation and their successors shall have full capacity and ability to purchase, receive, take, hold, and enjoy for the purposes aforesaid, as well from such persons as shall be so charitably disposed to give the same, as from all other persons as shall be willing to sell or alien to the said Corporation any manors, lands, tenements, goods, or chattels, without any licence or writ of *ad quod damnum;* the statute of mortmain, or any other statute or law, to the contrary notwithstanding: Provided always, that the said Act, or any thing therein contained, should not extend to enable any person or persons being within age, or of *non sane* memory, or women covert without their husbands, to make any such gift, grant, or alienation, any thing in the said Act contained to the contrary notwithstanding, as in and by the said Act of Parliament may more at large appear.

Now know ye, that we, to the end our said gracious intentions may be made effectual, and that the Church may receive a great and lasting advantage from our parting with our said revenue of First Fruits and Tenths towards the better provision for the Clergy not sufficiently provided for, and pursuant to the said Act of Parliament, of our especial grace, certain knowledge, and mere motion have made, appointed, nominated, constituted, and established, and by these presents for us, our heirs and successors, do make, appoint, nominate, constitute, and establish, our most dear consort Prince George of Denmark, our

High Admiral and Generalissimo of all our Forces—the most reverend Father in God our right trusty and right entirely beloved counsellor, Thomas Lord Archbishop of Canterbury, and the Archbishop of Canterbury for the time being—our right trusty and well-beloved counsellor, Sir Nathan Wright, knight, Keeper of our Great Seal of England—the most reverend Father in God, our right trusty and well-beloved John, Archbishop of York, and the Archbishop of York for the time being—our right trusty and well-beloved counsellor, Sydney Lord Godolphin, our High Treasurer of England—our right trusty and right well-beloved cousin and counsellor, Thomas Earl of Pembroke and Montgomery, our President of our Council—our right trusty and right entirely beloved cousin and counsellor, John Duke of Normanby and Buckingham, our Keeper of our Privy Seal—our right trusty and right entirely beloved cousins and counsellors, William Duke of Devonshire, our Steward of our Household; Charles Duke of Somerset, our Master of our Horse; James Duke of Ormond, our Lieutenant-general and General-governor of our kingdom of Ireland; Charles Duke of Bolton; Mainhardt Duke of Schomberg; Thomas Duke of Leeds; John Duke of Marlborough, our Captain-general of all and singular our Forces, and Master-general of our Ordnance—our right trusty and right well-beloved cousins and counsellors, Robert Earl of Lindsey, our Great Chamberlain of England; Charles Earl of Carlisle, Earl Marshal of England during the minority of the Duke of Norfolk; Henry Earl of Kent, our Chamberlain of our Household; Charles Earl of Dorset and Middlesex; George Earl of Northampton; Charles Earl of Manchester; Thomas Earl of Stamford; Thomas Earl of Thanet; Charles Bodvile, Earl of Radnor; Charles Earl of Berkeley; Daniel Earl of Nottingham; Laurence Earl of Rochester; Montagu Earl of Abingdon, our Constable of the Tower of London: Ralph Earl of Montagu; Richard Earl of Scarborough; Francis Earl of Bradford, Treasurer of our Household; Edward Earl of Jersey; Richard Earl of Ranelagh in our kingdom of Ireland—our right trusty and well-beloved cousin and counsellor Thomas Lord Viscount Weymouth—the right reverend Father in God our right trusty and well-beloved counsellor Henry Bishop of London, and the Bishop of London for the time being—our right trusty and well-beloved counsellors Robert Lord Ferrers; Thomas Lord Wharton; John Lord Pawlet; Robert Lord Lexington; William Lord Dartmouth; John Lord Grenville; Heneage Lord Guernsey; John Lord Gower; Thomas Lord Coningsby of the kingdom of Ireland; Robert Harley, esquire, Speaker of the House of Commons, and one of our Principal Secretaries of State, and the Speaker of the House of Commons for the time being; Peregrine Bertie, esquire, our Vice-chamberlain of our Household; Henry Boyle, esquire, Chancellor and Under-treasurer of our

Exchequer; Thomas Mansell, esquire, Comptroller of our Household; Sir Charles Hedges, knight, one of our principal Secretaries of State; Sir John Holt, knight, Chief Justice of our Court of Queen's Bench; Sir John Trevor, knight, Master of the Rolls, and the Master of the Rolls for the time being; Sir Thomas Trevor, knight, Chief Justice of our Court of Common Pleas; Sir George Rooke, knight, Vice-admiral of England; Sir Edward Seymour, baronet; James Vernon, esquire; John Smith, esquire; and John How, esquire; and all and every the Privy Counsellors of us, our heirs and successors, for the time being—all and every Leiutenants of, in, and for the several counties within our kingdom of England and dominion of Wales, now and for the time being—all and every the *Custodes Rotulorum* for the several counties within our kingdom of England—the reverend Fathers in God Nathaniel Bishop of Durham; Peter Bishop of Winchester; William Bishop of Llandaff; William Bishop of Worcester; Thomas Bishop of Rochester; Jonathan Bishop of Exeter; Gilbert Bishop of Sarum; Humphrey Bishop of Hereford; Nicholas Bishop of Chester; Simon Bishop of Ely; John Bishop of Litchfield and Coventry; John Bishop of Norwich; Richard Bishop of Peterborough; Edward Bishop of Gloucester; John Bishop of Bristol; James Bishop of Lincoln; John Bishop of Chichester; William Bishop of Oxon; John Bishop of Bangor; William Bishop of Carlisle; George Bishop of Bath and Wells; William Bishop of St Asaph; and all and every the Bishops of the several Dioceses aforesaid for the time being, and the Bishop of Saint David's for the time being—the Deans of the several Cathedral Churches within our Kingdom of England and Dominion of Wales, now and for the time being—our trusty and well-beloved Sir Littleton Powis, Sir Henry Gold, and Sir John Powell, knights, Justices of our Court of Queen's Bench, and the Chief Justice and other the Justices of the Court of Queen's Bench for the time being—our trusty and well-beloved Sir Edward Nevill, Sir John Blencoe, knights, and Robert Tracy, esquire, Justices of our Court of Common Pleas, and the Chief Justice and other the Justices of the Court of Common Pleas for the time being—our trusty and well-beloved Sir Edward Ward, knight, Chief Baron of our Court of Exchequer—Sir Thomas Bury, knight, Robert Price, esquire, and John Smith, esquire, other the Barons of our Court of Exchequer; and the Chief Baron and other the Barons of the Court of Exchequer, for the time being—our trusty and well-beloved Sir Thomas Powis, knight, Sir Salathiel Lovel, knight, our Serjeants at Law; Sir Edward Northey, knight, our Attorney-general; Sir Simon Harcourt, knight, our Solicitor-general; and the Serjeants at Law, Attorney-general, and Solicitor-general of us, our heirs, and successors for the time being—Sir John Cooke, knight, Doctor of Laws, our Advocate-general, and the Advocate-general to us, our heirs, and successors for the time being—the Chancellors and Vice-chancellors of the two Universities of Oxon and Cambridge now and for the time being—our trusty and well-beloved Sir John Parsons, knight, Mayor of our city of London, and the Mayor of the city of London for the time being—all and every the Aldermen of the city of London, now and for the time being—the Mayor of the city of York for the time being; and all and every the Mayors of the respective Cities within our kingdom of England, now and for the time being—to be one body politic and corporate of themselves in deed and in name, by the name of 'The Governors of the Bounty of Queen Anne for the Augmentation of the Maintenance of the poor Clergy:' and them one body politic and corporate in deed and in name, by the name of 'The Governors of the Bounty of Queen Anne for the augmentation of the maintenance of the poor Clergy,' We do, for us, our heirs and successors, make, create, erect, establish, and confirm for ever by these presents; and by the same name they and their successors shall have perpetual succession, and shall and may have and use a common seal for the business and affairs of the said body politic and corporate and of their successors, with power to break, alter, and make new their seal from time to time at their pleasure, or as they shall see cause; and by the same name they and their successors shall be able and capable in law to purchase, receive, take, hold, and enjoy, for the purposes herein mentioned, as well from such person or persons who shall be so charitably disposed to give (as from all other persons who shall be willing to sell, alien, or assign) to the said Corporation hereby constituted, any manors, lands, tenements, hereditaments, goods, chattels, or possessions whatsoever, of what nature or quality soever: And further, by the same name of 'The Governors of the Bounty of Queen Anne for the Augmentation of the Maintenance of the poor Clergy,' they and their successors shall and may sue and implead and be sued and impleaded, answer and defend and be answered and defended, in Courts of Record or any other place whatsoever, and before whatsoever Judges, Justices, Officers, and Ministers of us, our heirs and successors, and in all and singular pleas, actions, suits, causes, and demands whatsoever, of what nature or kind soever, in as ample and beneficial manner and form as any other body politic and corporate, or any other the liege people of England, being persons able and capable in law, may or can have, take, receive, hold, keep, possess, enjoy, sue, implead, defend, or answer, or be sued, impleaded, defended, or answered in any manner of wise; and shall and may do and execute all and singular other matters and things by the name aforesaid that to them shall or may appertain to do by virtue of the said Act, or of these presents, or otherwise: And for the ends and purposes before expressed, and pursuant to and by virtue of the said Act of Parliament, we have given and granted, and by these presents, for us, our heirs and successors, do give and grant unto the said 'Governors of the Bounty of Queen Anne for the augmentation of the maintenance of the poor Clergy,' hereby constituted, and their successors, all the revenues of First Fruits and yearly perpetual Tenths of all dignities, offices, benefices and promotions spiritual whatsoever, payable to us, our heirs and successors, by virtue of the said Act of Parliament made in the six and twentieth year of the reign of King Henry the Eighth, or by virtue of an Act of Parliament made in the first year of the reign of the late Queen Elizabeth for restitution of First Fruits and Tenths to the Crown, or by virtue of any other Act or Acts of Parliament whatsoever, and all arrears of the said First Fruits and Tenths now due and undischarged (other than the arrears of the Tenths due upon the small Rectories and Vicarages under the yearly value of thirty pounds per annum by us as aforesaid directed to be discharged), to be applied and disposed of by the said Governors hereby constituted, to and for the augmentation of the maintenance of such Parsons, Vicars, Curates, and Ministers officiating in any Church or Chapel within the kingdom of England, dominion of Wales, and town of Berwick upon Tweed, where the liturgy and rites of the Church of England as now by law established, are or shall be used and observed, under such rules, restrictions, and directions, and in such manner and form, as shall be established pursuant to these presents. And for the better ordering, managing, and directing the affairs of the said Corporation, we do hereby, for us, our heirs and successors, grant unto the said 'Governors of the Bounty of Queen Anne, for the augmentation of the maintenance of the poor Clergy,' and their successors, and we do hereby ordain, will, and appoint, that as soon as conveniently may be after the date of these presents all and every the persons hereinbefore named and constituted Governors as aforesaid do assemble and meet together in the room commonly called the Prince's Chamber, adjoining to the House of Lords, or some other convenient place within our Cities of London or Westminster, or the suburbs thereof, as shall in that behalf be appointed by any seven or more of the Governors hereby constituted (whereof we will that any one of the Privy Council of us, our heirs or successors, and any one of the Bishops aforesaid, or any one of the Judges of any of the Courts at Westminster, or of the said Counsel learned in the Law of us, our heirs or successors, shall be three), to treat and consult concerning the business and affairs of the said Corporation, and the good rule and government thereof, and the faithful distribution of our royal Bounty aforesaid: And we do further, by these presents, for us, our heirs and successors, will, authorize, require, and command the said Governors and their successors from time to time to summon, appoint, hold, and keep four General Courts at least in every year, at any convenient place or places aforesaid (notice being in that behalf first given, by inserting the same in the Gazette, or otherwise, fourteen days before the holding of every such General Court); one of the said four General Courts to be held and kept in the month of December, another in the month of March, another in the month of June, and another in the month of September: And we do also and will by these presents, for us, our heirs and successors, do grant and ordain, that all the said Governors for the time being, or so many of them as shall at any time or times be assembled and met together as aforesaid, being not less than seven in number at one meeting or assembly in such General Court (of whom any one of the Privy Council of us, our heirs or successors, and any one of the Bishops aforesaid, and any one of the Judges aforesaid for the time being, or of the said Counsel learned in the law of us, our heirs or successors, we will shall be always three), shall be and called a General Court of the said Corporation: and that in such General Courts the said Governors and their successors shall and may do and despatch, by majority of votes, any busness relating to the government and affairs of the said Corporation, and also hear, debate, and determine any complaint or matter that shall be brought or exhibited in the said Court, touching the affairs of the said Corporation; and shall and may call to their aid and assistance such persons as the said General Court, or the major part of them assembled as aforesaid, shall think fit to aid, assist, and advise the said Governors hereby constituted, and their successors, in the due and effectual execution of the powers and authorities hereby granted. And for the better ordering and managing the affairs of the said Corporation, we do hereby, for us, our heirs and successors, grant, authorize, and appoint that the Governors of the said Corporation hereby constituted, and for the time being, or any seven or more of them (of whom three or more to be such as aforesaid) shall and may from time to time, as often as they shall think fit, erect, nominate, and appoint such and so many of the Governors of the said Corporation for the time being as they shall judge expedient, to be Committees of the said Corporation, for the better despatching and more easy managing and carrying on the purposes aforesaid, and the true intent and meaning of these presents; and to invest such Committees with such powers as the Governors of the said Corporation assembled in a General Court, or the major part of them so assembled, shall think fit to entrust them with, pursuant to the powers hereby given to the Governors hereinbefore named and constituted. And for the better effecting our will and pleasure in these presents declared, we do hereby, for us, our heirs and successors, authorize and command the 'Governors of the Bounty of Queen Anne for the Augmentation of the Maintenance of the poor Clergy,' at the first or some other subsequent meeting or meetings of the said Governors hereby constituted, or so many of them as shall then meet and be present (of whom any one of the Privy Council aforesaid for the time being, and any one of the

Bishops aforesaid for the time being, and any one of the Judges aforesaid for the time being, or of the said Counsel learned in the law of us, our heirs or successors, for the time being, we will shall be three at the least), to consider of, consult, advise, agree upon, draw up, prepare, and propose in writing, to us, our heirs or successors, such proper and necessary rules, methods, directions, orders, and constitutions as the said Governors, or any seven or more of them as aforesaid, for the time being, shall in their discretions judge most convenient to be observed for and towards the better rule and government of the said Corporation and the members thereof, and the receiving, accounting for, and managing all and every the revenues hereby granted or mentioned to be granted as aforesaid, and all arrears thereof, and also for and concerning the distributing, paying, and disposing of the same and all other gifts and benevolences that shall or may be given or bequeathed to the said Corporation for the charitable ends aforesaid, for the augmentation of the maintenance of the poor Clergy aforesaid; and such rules, methods, orders, directions, and constitutions as shall be so proposed, and shall be approved, altered, or amended by us, our heirs or successors, and such as shall be made by us, our heirs and successors, and so signified and declared by us, our heirs or successors, under our or their Great Seal, we will shall be the rules, methods, directions, orders, and constitutions by which the 'Governors of the Bounty of Queen Anne for the Augmentation of the Maintenance of the poor Clergy,' and their successors, shall receive, manage, govern, apply and dispose our said royal Bounty (and other gifts and benevolences which shall or may hereafter be given or bequeathed to the said Corporation, where the Donors thereof shall not particularly direct the application thereof), to and for the increase of the Maintenance of such Parsons, Vicars, Curates, and Ministers Officiating in any Church or Chapel within the kingdom of England, dominion of Wales, or town of Berwick upon Tweed, where the liturgy and rites of the Church of England as now by law established are and shall be used and observed, for whom a maintenance is not already sufficienty provided. And for the better enabling the Governors of our Bounty aforesaid to perform our will and pleasure hereinbefore expressed, we do hereby, for us, our heirs and successors, authorize and require our Keeper of our Great Seal of England now being, or the Lord High Chancellor of England or Keeper of the Great Seal of England for the time being, upon the request of the said Governors hereby constituted, or any seven or more of them (of whom any one of the Privy Council aforesaid for the time being, and any one of the Bishops aforesaid for the time being, and any one of the Judges or of the Counsel learned in the Law as aforesaid for the time being, we will shall be three), to issue out writs of inquiry, under the Great Seal of England, unto all and every or any of the counties and cities in England and Wales, to be directed to such and so many persons as the said Keeper of the Great Seal of England now and for the time being, or the Lord High Chancellor of England for the time being, shall nominate, assign, or appoint; thereby authorizing and requiring them, or any three or more of them, and giving them full power and authority, by the oaths of good and lawful men, and by all other lawful ways and means, to inquire and find out; and likewise the said Governors hereby named and constituted, and any seven or more of them, are hereby commanded and authorized to inquire, find out, and inform themselves, by all lawful ways and means, of the true yearly value of the maintenance of every Parson, Vicar, Curate, and Minister, officiating in any Church or Chapel within such counties and cities where the liturgy and the rites of the Church of England as now by law established are or shall be used and observed, for whom a maintenance of the yearly value of eighty pounds is not sufficiently provided; and the distances of such Churches and Chapels from our city of London, and which of them are in towns corporate or market towns, and which not, and how the several Churches and Chapels are supplied by preaching Ministers, and where the Incumbents have more than one living; that some course may be taken for providing for the augmentation of maintenance, where the same shall be found necessary: And we do further hereby, for us, our heirs and successors, authorize and require the said Governors now and for the time being, or any seven or more of them (of whom we will that any one of the Privy Council aforesaid for the time being, and any one of the Bishops aforesaid for the time being, and any one of the Judges aforesaid, or of the said Counsel learned in the Law of us, our heirs or successors, be three), from and after such inquiry had and made as aforesaid, to prepare and lay before us, our heirs or successors, a true state and account of the yearly values of the maintenance of all such Parsons, Vicars, Curates, and Ministers aforesaid; and also of the present yearly values of the said First Fruits and Tenths, and the arrears thereof, hereby granted for the augmentation of the maintenance of the poor Clergy aforesaid; and also of all such pensions, payments, or other charges as are now granted and payable out of the said First Fruits and Tenths by Letters Patents or otherwise therewith charged, to the end that the same being satisfied and discharged, our said Royal Bounty may be applied and disposed to and amongst such of the poor Clergy, the augmentation of whose maintenance will appear to be most necessary. And for the better managing, ordering, and governing the affairs of the said Corporation, We do, by these presents, for us, our heirs, and successors, grant to the said 'Governors of the Bounty of Queen Anne for the Augmentation of the Maintenance of the poor Clergy,' and their successors, and do hereby ordain and appoint, that there shall be, from time to time for ever, one able and sufficient person to be nominated and chosen as is hereinafter expressed, who shall be and be called 'Secretary to the Governors of the Bounty of Queen Anne for the Augmentation of the Maintenance of the poor Clergy,' and who shall act and perform all such matters and things, for and on the behalf of the said Corporation, as shall be found requisite and necessary to be executed and performed by him in such office: And for the better execution of our will and pleasure in that behalf, we have named, constituted, and appointed, and by these presents for us, our heirs and successors, do name, constitute, and appoint our trusty and well-beloved John Chamberlain, esquire, to be the first and present Secretary to the 'Governors of the Bounty of Queen Anne for the said Augmentation of the Maintenance of the poor Clergy,' who shall continue in the said office of Secretary during the pleasure of the 'Governors of the Bounty of Queen Anne for the Augmentation of the Maintenance of the poor clergy.' And we do further by these presents for us, our heirs and successors, grant unto the said 'Governors of the Bounty of Queen Anne for the Augmentation of the Maintenance of the poor Clergy,' and to their successors, that they and their successors shall and may have one able and sufficient person, to be nominated and chosen as is hereinafter mentioned, who shall be and be called 'Treasurer to the Governors of the Bounty of Queen Anne for the Augmentation of the Maintenance of the poor Clergy,' and also such inferior officers, substitutes, and servants, as the said Governors for the time being, assembled in a General Court, shall by a majority of votes think fit to choose and elect; which inferior officers and substitutes so elected, We will, and ordain, for us, our heirs and successors, shall continue in their several and respective offices during the pleasure of the said Governors for the time being: And we have also named, constituted, and appointed, and by these presents for us, our heirs and successors, do name, constitute, and appoint our trusty and well-beloved Edward Tennison, senior, gentleman, to be the first and present Treasurer to the 'Governors of the Bounty of Queen Anne for the Augmentation of the Maintenance of the poor Clergy,' to continue in the said office of Treasurer during the pleasure of the 'Governors of the Bounty of Queen Anne for the Augmentation of the Maintenance of the poor Clergy.' And further, We do by these presents, for us, our heirs and successors, grant unto the said 'Governors of the Bounty of Queen Anne for the Augmentation of the Maintenance of the poor Clergy,' and their successors, full power and authority from time to time, as often as it shall happen that any Secretary and Treasurer to the said Governors shall die or be removed from his or their respective offices aforesaid, or whose office or offices shall otherwise become void, to elect and choose, by a majority of votes of such Governors as shall be assembled in a General Court, some other fit person or persons into the office or offices of him or them who shall so die or be removed as aforesaid, or whose office shall otherwise become void; which person or persons so to be chosen shall continue in his or their office or offices whereunto he or they shall be so elected during the pleasure of the Governors. Provided always, and we do by these presents, for us, our heirs and successors, ordain and appoint that the said John Chamberlain and Edward Tennison herein before named and constituted to be the first and present Secretary and Treasurer to the Governors hereby incorporated and their successors, and also every other Secretary and Treasurer hereafter to be elected, shall, before they take upon them the execution of their said several offices, respectively take their corporal oaths for the due and faithful execution of their several offices before any seven or more of the Governors aforesaid, for the time being, in a General Court of the said Corporation, who are hereby authorized and required to give and administer the said oaths from time to time accordingly: and the present Treasurer, and every future Treasurer, shall give sufficient security to the said Corporation for his faithful accounting for the moneys he or they shall receive by virtue of the said office. And having no doubt that not only the Governors hereinbefore named and constituted, but also a great number of other our good subjects, will be disposed to follow our example, and will with great cheerfulness and readiness contribute to the further augmentation of the maintenance of the poor Clergy, we do by these presents, for us, our heirs and successors, authorize and empower the 'Governors of the Bounty of Queen Anne for the Augmentation of the Maintenance of the poor Clergy,' to take and receive from such of our good subjects as shall be piously inclined to contribute to the increase of this our Royal Bounty to the poor Clergy, all such voluntary gifts or subscriptions of any sum or sums of moneys, goods, or chattels, or of or for any estate or interest in any manors, lands, tenements, rents, hereditaments, or other matters or things whatsoever, which any person or persons, bodies politic or corporate, shall be willing to give, limit, appoint, or bestow for or towards the further augmentation of the maintenance of the poor Clergy; and further, to cause to be collected and received whatsoever shall be given, contributed, bequeathed, designed, or appointed for the purposes aforesaid, by the hands of the Treasurer to the said Corporation hereby constituted, who shall be appointed to receive the same: And to the end our royal intention in the premises may be better known to our loving subjects, we do hereby require the Governors hereinbefore named and constituted, or any seven or more of them, to cause public notice of this our Royal Charter, or the tenor or scope thereof, to be made in such places or by such ways and means as the said Governors, or any seven or more of them, shall think most conducible to the furtherance of the bounty and charity afore-said. And further, We do hereby, for us, our heirs and successors, give full power and authority unto the Governors aforesaid, and their successors, from time to time, and at all times hereafter, to admit into the said Corporation hereby erected and constituted, all and every such person and persons who shall be piously disposed to contribute towards the further augmentation of the maintenance of the said poor Clergy and the advancing so good a work, as the said Governors in a General Court of the said Corporation shall think fit to admit; which person or persons, when so admitted in the said Corporation, shall be and be deemed, called and reputed, members of the said Corporation, and from time to time shall and may vote and act in as ample manner and form, and have and enjoy such and the same powers, privileges, and authorities as other Governor or Governors of the said Corporation hereinbefore named may vote and act, have, enjoy, and perform by virtue of these presents. And we do hereby, for us, our heirs and successors, authorize and empower the Governors hereby constituted, and their successors, or any seven or more of them (of whom any one of the Privy Council aforesaid for the time being, and any one of the Bishops aforesaid for the time being, and any one of the Judges or of the Counsel learned in the Law of us, our heirs or successors, as aforesaid, to be three at least), in case they shall find the same necessary for carrying on and perfecting the pious intentions and designs of this our Royal Charter, by instruments or writings under the seal of the said Corporation, to depute and substitute such persons as they shall think fit to entrust to take such sub-scriptions as aforesaid, and to collect and bring in the moneys which shall be contributed, bequeathed, designed, or appointed for the ends and purposes aforesaid, to the hands of the Treasurer to the said Governors for the time being, and to displace or discharge such substitutes or deputies, or any of them, and to appoint others in the place of them or any of them, from time to time, as the said Governors, or any seven or more of them (of whom three or more to be such as aforesaid), shall see cause; and also to settle, establish, and appoint such cheques, comptrols, and orders as they shall think necessary or safe, for the full and due charging of the Treasurer, and also the said deputies, and all and every other person and persons whatsoever, who shall receive or be chargeable with any moneys or other profits for the said charitable use or purpose, to answer, pay, or account for the same. And we do hereby, for us, our heirs and successors, authorize, require, and command the said 'Governors of the Bounty of Queen Anne for the Augmentation of the Maintenance of the poor Clergy' from time to time to cause to be entered in a book to be kept for that purpose, the name of the persons who shall subscribe or contribute, give, advise, or appoint any moneys, or any real or personal estate, or other matters or things towards this charitable and good design, with the sums of money, goods, chattels, estates, or other things by them respectively contributed, given, limited, appointed, or devised, to the end a perpetual memorial may be made of such well-disposed persons who shall become Benefactors as aforesaid, and whereby the Treasurer to the said Corporation may be charged with more certainty in his accounts. And our farther will and pleasure is, and we do hereby, for us, our heirs and successors, give full power and authority unto the said Edward Tennison, and the Treasurer to the said Governors for the time being, from time to time, upon the receipt or receipts of any sum or sums of money or other profits for the purposes aforesaid or any of them, to give an acquittance or acquittances for the same, which shall be good and sufficient discharges to all intents and purposes whatsoever: And the said Treasurer for the time being, in his receipts, payments, and accounts, shall be subject to such inspection, examination, and comptrol as the said Governors for the time being, or any four or more of them (whereof such as are before appointed for a special quorum to be three at least) shall establish or appoint. And we do hereby for us, our heirs and successors, grant and declare that these our Letters Patent, or the enrolment thereof, shall be in and by all things good, valid, and effectual in the law, according to the true intent and meaning of the same, and shall be taken, construed, and adjudged in the most favourable and beneficial sense, and to the best advantage of and for the said Corporation, as well in all our courts of record as elsewhere, notwithstanding the not reciting, or not truly or fully reciting, of any Act or Acts of Parliament of or concerning the said First Fruits or Tenths hereby granted or mentioned to be granted, or any part or parcel thereof, and notwithstanding the not mentioning the true yearly value of the said First Fruits or Tenths, or any of them, and notwithstanding any non-recital, mis-recital, defect, incertainty, or imperfection in these our Letters Patent contained, or any other matter, cause, or thing whatsoever. In witness whereof, We have caused these our Letters to be made Patent. Witness Ourself at Westminster, the third day of November in the third Year of our reign.

By Writ of Privy Seal,
COCKS.

APPENDIX II

QUEEN ANNE'S BOUNTY'S
SECOND CHARTER

Sealed with the Great Seal of England, 5 March,
12 ANNE

ANNE, by the grace of God, of Great Britain, France, and Ireland, Queen, Defender of the Faith, &c., to all to whom these presents shall come, greeting. Whereas, in and by our Letters Patents under our Great Seal of England, bearing date the third day of November in the third year of our reign, We did incorporate the Governors of the 'Bounty of Queen Anne for the Augmentation of the Maintenance of the poor Clergy:' And for the better effecting our will and pleasure in the said Letters Patents declared, We did thereby, for us, our heirs and successors, authorize and command the Governors of the said Corporation thereby constituted, at their first or some other subsequent meeting or meetings, or so many of them as should then meet and be present (of whom any one of the Privy Council of us, our heirs or successors for the time being, and any one of the Bishops of England for the time being, and any one of the Judges of any of the Courts at Westminster for the time being, or one of the two eldest Serjeants at Law, or the Attorney or Solicitor General of us, our heirs or successors, for the time being, to be three at least), to consider of, consult, advise, agree upon, draw up, prepare, and propose in writing to us our heirs or successors, such proper and necessary rules, methods, directions, orders, and constitutions as the said Governors, or any seven or more of them as aforesaid, for the time being, should in their discretions judge most convenient to be observed, for and towards the better rule and government of the said Corporation and the members thereof, and the receiving, accounting for, and managing all and every the revenues thereby granted, and all arrears thereof, and also for and concerning the distributing, paying, and disposing of the same, and all other gifts and benevolences that should or might be given or bequeathed to the said Corporation for the charitable ends therein mentioned, for the augmentation of the maintenance of the poor Clergy in the said Letters Patents mentioned; and such rules, methods, orders, directions, and constitutions as should be so proposed, and should be approved, altered or amended by us, our heirs or successors, and such as should be made by us, our heirs and successors, and so signified and declared by us, our heirs or successors,

530

under our or their Great Seal, we would should be the rules, methods, directions, orders and constitutions by which the Governors of our said Corporation, and their successors, should receive, manage, govern, apply, and dispose our said Royal Bounty, and other gifts and benevolences which should or might then after be given or bequeathed to the said Corporation (where the donors thereof should not particularly direct the application thereof), to and for the increase of the maintenance of such Parsons, Vicars, Curates, and Ministers, officiating in any Church or Chapel within the kingdom of England, dominion of Wales, or town of Berwick upon Tweed, where the liturgy and rites of the Church of England as then by law established were and should be used and observed, for whom a maintenance was not sufficiently provided.

And whereas, in and by our said Letters Patents, a Secretary and a Treasurer to the said Corporation were constituted and appointed to continue in the said offices during the pleasure of the said Corporation; and upon a vacancy of either of the said offices, full powers were thereby granted to a General Court of the said Corporation to elect and choose others in their places, to continue during the pleasure of the said Corporation, as by the said Letters Patents, amongst other things therein contained relation being thereunto had, may more fully and at large appear.

And whereas, the Governors of the said Corporation have humbly represented unto us several inconveniences arising from the quorum by the said charter appointed, to the great delay and obstruction of the business thereof, by reason that by the charter of the said Corporation, no business could be done by the Governors unless seven were present, and of them one to be a Privy Councillor, and one a Bishop, and one a Judge, or one of our two eldest Serjeants at Law, or our Attorney or Solicitor General; and it having happened very often that at their meetings no business could be done, there not being three such as were by the said Letters Patent so directed to make a quorum.

And whereas, the Governors of the said Corporation have likewise humbly proposed to us, for our royal approbation, several rules and constitutions for the better rule and government of the said Corporation: Now know ye, that we have fully taken all and singular the premises into our royal consideration, of our especial grace, certain knowledge, and mere motion, have directed and appointed, and by these presents do direct and appoint, that the present Secretary and Treasurer of the said Corporation shall not continue in their said offices during the pleasure of the said Corporation, but shall from henceforth continue and remain therein during our pleasure. And further, that as often as it shall happen that either of the said offices shall become void, the nomination and appointment shall be in us, our heirs and successors, and not in the General Court of the said Corporation.

And for the better enabling the said Corporation to meet and do business, and to prevent the delay and obstruction of the business of the said Corporation, we have thought fit to increase the number of the Governors of the said Corporation; and we do hereby, for us, our heirs and successors, add to the Governors of the said Corporation the following persons—viz. the officers of our Board of Green Cloth, our Serjeants at Law, and Counsel learned in the Law, and our four Clerks in ordinary of our Privy Council for the time being: And we so hereby, for us, our heirs, and successors, declare and grant, that they shall be, to all intents and purposes, Governors of the said Corporation, together with the other Governors named in the Charter, as fully as if they had been expressly mentioned in the said Letters Patents of incorporation. And we do hereby also, for us, our heirs and successors, direct and appoint that any one of the persons in the said Letters Patents mentioned to be of the quorum, with six other Governors, shall make a quorum for the future, anything in the said former Letters Patents to the contrary notwithstanding; reserving nevertheless to us, our heirs and successors, the power of restoring at any time the old quorum, or making or directing any other quorum under our or their Sign Manual.

And for the better rule and government of the said Corporation, of our further especial grace, certain knowledge, and mere motion, we, having duly considered of the several rules, orders, and constitutions, humbly proposed to us by the Governors of the said Corporation, have made, ordained, approved of, ratified, confirmed, and established, and by these presents, we do for us, our heirs and successors, make, ordain, approve of, ratify, confirm, and establish the several rules, methods, directions, orders, and constitutions hereinafter mentioned, viz.

1. That the augmentations to be made by the said Corporation shall be by the way of purchase, and not by the way of pension.

2. That the stated sum to be allowed to each Cure which shall be augmented be two hundred pounds, to be invested in a purchase at the expense of the Corporation.

3. That the Governors shall begin with augmenting those Cures that do not exceed the value of ten pounds per annum, and shall augment no other till those have all received our bounty of two hundred pounds, except in the cases, and according to the limitations hereafter named.

4. That in order to encourage benefactions from others, and thereby the sooner to complete the good that was intended by our Bounty, the Governors may give the said sum of two hundred pounds to Cures not exceeding five-and-thirty pounds per annum, where any persons will give the same or greater sum or value in lands or tithes.

5. That the Governors shall every year, between Christmas and Easter, cause the account of what money they have to distribute that year, to be audited; and when they know the sum, public notice shall be given in the Gazette, or such other way as shall be judged proper, that they have such a sum to distribute in so many shares; and that they will be ready to apply those shares to such Cures as want the same, and are by the rules of the Corporation qualified to receive them, where any persons will add the like or greater sum to it, or the value in lands or tithes, for any such particular Cure.

6. That if several benefactors offer themselves, the Governors shall first comply with those that offer most.

7. Where the sums offered by other benefactors are equal, the Governors shall always prefer the poorer livings.

8. Where the Cures to be augmented are of equal value, and the benefactions offered by others are equal, there they shall be preferred that first offer.

9. Provided nevertheless, that the preference shall be so far given to Cures not exceeding ten pounds per annum, that the Governors shall not apply above one-third part of money they have to distribute that year to Cures exceeding that value.

10. Where the Governors have expected till Michaelmas what benefactors will offer themselves, then no more proposals shall be received for that year; but if any money remain after that to be disposed of, in the first place two or more of the Cures in the gift of the Crown, not exceeding ten pounds per annum, shall be chosen by lot, to be augmented preferably to all others, the precise number of these to be settled by a General Court, when an exact list of them shall be brought in to the Governors.

11. As for what shall remain of the money to be disposed of after that, a list shall be taken of all the Cures in the Church of England, not exceeding ten pounds per annum, and so many of them be chosen by lot as these shall remain sums of two hundred pounds for their augmentation.

12. When all the Cures not exceeding ten pounds per annum shall be so augmented, the Governors shall then proceed to augment those of greater value, according to such rules as shall at any time hereafter be proposed by them and approved by us, our heirs or successors, under our or their Great Seal.

13. That all charitable gifts in real or personal estates made to the Corporation shall be strictly applied according to the particular direction of the donor or donors thereof, where the donors shall give particular directions for the disposition thereof; and where the gifts shall be generally to the Corporation, without any such particular direction, the same shall be applied as the rest of the fund or stock of the Corporation is to be applied.

14. That a book shall be kept, wherein shall be entered all the subscriptions,

contributions, gifts, devises, or appointments made or given of any moneys, or of any real or personal estate whatsoever, to the charity mentioned in the charter, and the names of the donors thereof, with the particulars of the matters so given: the same book to be kept by the Secretary of the Corporation.

15. That a memorial of the benefactions and augmentations made to each Cure shall, at the charge of the Corporation, be set up in writing on a stone to be fixed in the Church of the Cure so to be increased, there to remain in perpetual memory thereof.

16. When the Treasurer shall have received any sum of money for the use of the Corporation, he shall, at the next General Court to be holden after such receipt, lay an account thereof before the Governors, who may order and direct the same to be placed out for the improvement thereof, upon some public fund or other security, till they have an opportunity of laying it out in proper purchases for the augmentation of Cures.

17. That the Treasurer do account annually before such a Committee of the Governors as shall be appointed by a General Court of the said Corporation, who shall audit and state the same; and the said account shall be entered in a book to be kept for that purpose and shall be laid before the next General Court, after such stating; the same to be there re-examined and determined.

18. The persons whose Cures shall be augmented, shall pay no manner of fee or gratification to any of the officers or servants of this Corporation.

19. That the salary of the Secretary of the said Corporation be one hundred and twenty pounds per annum, in full for his service, and for a clerk, and for stationery wares, to commence from Christmas, 1712, to be paid him half yearly by the Treasurer of the said Corporation.

20. That the salary of the Treasurer of the said Corporation, be one hundred and twenty pounds per annum, in full for his service, and for a clerk, and for all his expenses whatsoever (except the fees which he shall pay or allow in the Treasury or Exchequer), to be allowed half yearly, as aforesaid.

All and singular which said rules, methods, directions, orders and constitutions, We will and do by these presents, for us, our heirs and successors, signify and declare, shall be the rules, methods, directions, orders, and constitutions by which the Governors of the said Corporation and their successors shall receive, manage, govern, apply, and dispose our said Royal Bounty, and other gifts and benevolences in the said Letters Patents mentioned, according to the true intent and meaning of the said charter, and of these presents.

Reserving, nevertheless, to us, our heirs and successors, full and absolute power and authority from time to time, and at all times here-after, under our or their Great Seal, to make any alterations in the several and respective orders aforesaid, and to give and make in like manner such other orders, rules, and directions, for and concerning the better government of the said Corporation, and for the managing, governing, applying, and disposing, of our Royal Bounty to them granted, and for the augmentation of the maintenance of the poor Clergy, according to the true intention of the said Letters Patents of Incorporation, as to us, our heirs and successors shall seem meet.

Lastly, We do hereby, for us, our heirs and successors, grant that these our Letters Patents, or the enrolment thereof, shall be in and by all things good, firm, valid, sufficient, and effectual in the law, notwithstanding the not reciting or not truly or fully reciting the said Letters Patents of Incorporation, or the date thereof, or any other omission, imperfection, defect, matter, cause, or thing whatsoever, to the contrary thereof, in anywise notwithstanding.

In witness whereof, We have caused these our Letters to be made Patents. Witness Ourself, at Westminster, the fifth day of March in the twelfth year of our reign.

By Writ of Privy Seal,
COCKS.

THE ADVERTISEMENT TO THE 'NOTITIA PAROCHIALIS'*

To the Reverend the Minister of every Parochial Church or Chappel in England:

Reverend Brother, There being a Design form'd of publishing *The Present State of Parish-Churches,* giving an Account of all pious Persons who have been Benefactors to the Church since the Reformation; together with several other things that are worthy to be known: You are therefore humbly desired to contribute your kind Assistance to this so useful an Undertaking by returning a particular Answer (at the bottom, or on the back of the Advertisement) to such of the following Queries, as the Case of your Parish and any neighbouring vacant Parish (if such there be) shall require. 1. Are the Tithes, or any Part of them, impropriated, and to whom? 2. What part of the Tithes is your Church or Chappel endow'd with? 3. What Augmentation or other Benefaction has your Benefice had, when, and by whom? 4. If your Church or Chappel was founded since the Reformation, when, and by whom? 5. What Union or Dismembring (if any) has been made of your Church, and by whom? 6. What Library is settled or settling in your Parish, and by whom? 7. If the yearly Value of your Rectory, Vicarage or Chappelry be under 30*l.*, how much? 8. To whom does the Advowson, Collation, or Donation of your Benefice belong? 9. If it be co-nominal with any other Place, what is the note of Distinction? 10. If it be a Benefice that is not taken notice of in the *Valor Beneficiorum,* pray express in what Arch-Deaconry or Deaconry it is. The Account you'll be pleased to give of these or the like Particulars, shall be faithfully applied to the Service of the Publick. Pray take care that what you write be at the Foot, or on the Back, of this Advertisement, and not upon the Brief; and if that Paper be too little, you may affix more, and write upon't.

Any Notices relating to this Advertisement, upon the Return of the Briefs, will be taken care of and Lodg'd with *William Hawes,* Bookseller, at the *Golden Buck* over-against *S. Dunstan's* Church in *Fleet Street,* for the AUTHOR, a Divine of the Church of *England.*

* The notes are on printed slips of paper, approx. 15″ x 5″, detached from the bottom of a Brief soliciting contributions to the parish of All Saints, Oxford.

AUGMENTATIONS MADE BY QUEEN ANNE'S BOUNTY OUT OF THE ROYAL BOUNTY FUND

1713-1840[1]

	Annual Augmentations of £200 each[2]		Benefactions[3]			Annual Augmentations of £200 each[2]		Benefactions[3]	
	By Lot	To meet Benefactions	Capital	Annual Rent		By Lot	To meet Benefactions	Capital	Annual Rent
1713	—	—	2,127	—	1750	50	24	3,100	47
1714	19	9	6,860	5	1751	53	16	3,100	199
1715	20	10	4,773	—	1752	57	19	2,000	32
1716	—	20	5,148	112	1753	38	14	4,000	—
1717	2	25	4,260	10	1754	40	11	4,600	71
1718	21	49	7,660	65	1755	21	29	6,800	—
1719	6	57	11,707	10	1756	48	35	4,900	47
1720	4	61	10,350	15	1757	48	31	3,800	—
1721	6	47	9,105	28	1758	44	30	4,500	—
1722	5	57	9,498	85	1759	40	21	5,800	—
1723	13	77	18,097	12	1760	48	18	4,200	—
1724	1	54	12,502	104	1761	39	32	4,900	—
1725	8	61	10,420	20	1762	37	24	4,800	15
1726	16	53	6,330	26	1763	39	27	6,000	44
1727	4	35	7,933	25	1764	31	37	8,325	42
1728	6	51	9,940	30	1765	33	38	13,719	—
1729	10	46	8,520	24	1766	38	22	3,600	7
1730	10	34	5,150	28	1767	238	75	5,600	17
1731	18	32	6,950	12	1768	40	21	5,000	59
1732	12	38	6,720	6	1769	30	28	4,400	22
1733	16	29	5,460	20	1770	33	30	6,400	9
1734	8	37	6,600	20	1771	50	23	4,000	—
1735	29	21	5,000	30	1772	119	30	4,400	—
1736	—	—	5,400	13	1773	40	20	6,200	—
1737	72	36	2,310	—	1774	35	30	5,200	—
1738	37	15	6,400	—	1775	135	24	2,600	8
1739	38	24	3,700	20	1776	43	12	2,700	15
1740	40	20	2,500	18	1777	53	19	5,910	19
1741	45	15	3,800	39	1778	40	25	2,400	10
1742	41	19	2,600	7	1779	52	13	2,220	—

	Annual Augmentations of £200 each[2]		Benefactions[3]			Annual Augmentations of £200 each[2]		Benefactions[3]	
	By Lot	To meet Benefactions	Capital	Annual Rent		By Lot	To meet Benefactions	Capital	Annual Rent
1743	47	13	3,000	38	1780	52	13	1,400	—
1744	42	19	3,400	—	1781	48	6	1,000	10
1745	52	17	1,200	—	1782	52	6	2,400	—
1746	64	7	2,700	21	1783	52	11	2,600	53
1747	50	16	1,200	—	1784	48	10	4,300	—
1748	60	7	2,200	—	1785	50	18	1,410	40
1749	61	10	3,400	20	1786	61	17	3,000	—
1787	185	10	1,000	104	1814	43	6	7,900	35
1788	123	20	1,600	—	1815	43	1	10,391	83
1789	93	3	2,300	—	1816	52	1	11,500	60
1790	87	12	2,800	—	1817	36	7	11,000	55
1791	84	10	1,435	—	1818	25	4	12,390	30
1792	341	5	2,000	—	1819	26	4	15,290	60
1793	86	14	3,475	—	1820	23	4	4,400	116
1794	48	11	2,500	—	1821	—	—	3,600	8
1795	39	12	3,000	—	1822	—	3	9,200	—
1796	43	12	2,300	—	1823	—	1	15,500	—
1797	43	14	1,800	—	1824	200	—	15,400	—
1798	37	9	1,000	10	1825	98	—	20,000	30
1799	31	13	1,400	—	1826	82	2	24,190	35
1800	41	6	3,500	8	1827	131	25	18,805	53
1801	34	6	3,400	8	1828	89	76	19,450	30
1802	79	14	1,440	10	1829	43	38	5,970	45
1803	22	23	3,533	—	1830	62	84	19,498	—
1804	43	24	4,200	5	1831	10	66	17,236	—
1805	23	26	4,700	—	1832	83	47	15,472	300
1806	24	19	1,000	—	1833	5	25	23,707	1,212
1807	55	16	3,216	—	1834	34	42	13,414	544
1808	23	46	4,200	15	1835	22	29	11,684	312
1809	146	23	4,843	10	1836	4	46	23,208	205
1810	99	23	13,550	—	1837	4	65	21,856	285
1811	104	4	12,450	—	1838	15	56	20,191	233
1812	57	7	10,800	30	1839	4	58	20,437	400
1813	49	2	6,116	75	1840	3	57	22,407	169

[1] Excluding augmentations made after 1809 out of the Parliamentary Grants, and benefactions to meet them.

[2] Up to 1802, from P.Ps. 1803, VII, 419–21; 1803–1808, from P.Ps. 1814–15, XII, 388; 1809–1840, distilled from the table in Hodgson's *Account* (2nd edition).

[3] From table in appendices to Hodgson's *Account* (2nd edition).

LISTS OF THE PRINCIPAL OFFICERS OF QUEEN ANNE'S BOUNTY, THE ECCLESIASTICAL COMMISSIONERS, AND THE CHURCH COMMISSIONERS

A. SECRETARIES AND TREASURERS OF QUEEN ANNE'S BOUNTY

Secretary	Treasurer
John Chamberlayne, 1704–1723	Edward Tenison, 1704–1708
Edward Barker, 1724–1730	Edward Barker, 1708–1724
Thomas Moore, 1730–1737	Jeffrey Elwes, 1724–1776
Henry Montague, 1737–1766	Vincent Matthias, 1776–1782
Samuel Seddon, 1766–1779	William Stevens, 1782–1807
Robert Chester, 1779–1790	John Paterson, 1808–1830
Richard Burn, 1790–1822	
Christopher Hodgson, 1822–1831	

Christopher Hodgson, 1831–1871
J. K. Aston, 1871–1900
W. R. Le Fanu, 1905–1925[1]
F. G. Hughes, 1925–1935

W. G. Hannah, 1935–1942	Sir George Middleton and Lord
E. J. Hare, 1942–1945	Daryngton (jointly), 1935–1938
	Lord Daryngton, 1938–1939
	Hon. Richard Denman, 1939–1944

E. J. Hare, 1945 to the end.

[1] From 1900 to 1905, while the fate of Queen Anne's Bounty still hung in the balance, Le Fanu acted as secretary and treasurer.

B. RECEIVERS OF FIRST-FRUITS AND TENTHS, FROM THE LATE
SEVENTEENTH CENTURY UNTIL THE SUPPRESSION OF THEIR
OFFICES

Receiver of First Fruits
William Glanville,[1] to 1718
Edward Barker, 1718–1730
George Turner, 1730–1743
James Henderson, 1744–1753
Stephen Comyn, 1754–1759
Thomas Parry, 1759–1773
Edward Mulso, 1773–1782
John Bacon, 1782–1816
Charles Bicknell,[2] 1818/9–1828
George Arbuthnot, 1828–end

Receiver of Tenths
(William Glanville to 1718)
John Ecton, 1718–1730
Edward Barker, 1730–1759
Stephen Comyn, 1759–1773
Thomas Parry, 1773
Robert Chester, 1774–1790
Richard Richards, 1791–1827
Thomas Venables, 1827–end

C. SECRETARIES TO THE ECCLESIASTICAL COMMISSIONERS

Charles Knight Murray, 1836–1849
Sir James Jell Chalk, 1850–1871
Sir George Pringle, 1871–1888
Sir Alfred de Bock Porter,[3] 1888–1908
Sir Robert Carr Selfe, 1908–1909
Sir Stanford Edwin Downing, 1910–1933
Gilbert Henry Wheeler, 1933–1935

[1] Also a Treasury official: see e.g. *Calendar of Treasury Books*, vol. XXIV, part 2, p. 129; vol. XXVI, part 2, pp. 385, 423; vol. XXVII, Part 2, p. 161.

[2] Bicknell's name appears in the *Royal Kalendar* from 1819 to 1828, but I have been able to find out nothing definite about him. Bacon's death and replacement passed strangely unnoticed in the Bounty's Minutes, and Bicknell is never, so far as I can see, mentioned.

[3] 'Financial Secretary' from 1880.

Appendix V

Ernest James Davies, 1935
Sidney Somers Brister, 1936–1937
Sir James Raitt Brown, 1937–1947
John Stanley Collins, 1947–1948
Sir James Raitt Brown, 1948–1954
Sir Mortimer Warren, 1954–

D. THE CHURCH ESTATES COMMITTEE

Church Estates Commissioners[1]

	First	Second	Third	Appointed by the Ecclesiastical Commissioners[2]	
				Layman	*Bishop*
August 1850	Lord Chichester	J. G. Shaw Lefevre	Henry Goulburn, M.P.	Sir James Graham, M.P.	C. J. Blomfield
February 1856				Lord Harrowby	C. R. Sumner
January 1858			Spencer Walpole, M.P.		
February 1858		Lord Eversley		Sir J. G. Shaw Lefevre	
April 1858			William Deedes, M.P.		
August 1859		E. P. Bouverie, M.P.		Lord Eversley	
November 1859					
December 1862			Spencer Walpole, M.P.		
February 1864					
November 1865		H. A. Bruce, M.P.			A. C. Tait
July 1866			E. Howes, M.P.		
August 1866		J. R. Mowbray, M.P.			
November 1866					Francis Jeune
November 1868					A. C. Tait
January 1869		T. D. Acland, M.P.			
February 1869					John Jackson
April 1871			J. R. Mowbray, M.P.		
November 1872					
March 1874		G. Cubitt, M.P.			
December 1878	Lord Stanhope			Lord Brownlow	
March 1879		T. Salt, M.P.			
June 1880		Evelyn Ashley, M.P.			
February 1883				G. J. Goschen, M.P.	
February 1885					Frederick Temple

Date				
June 1885	Sir H. J. Selwyn-Ibbetson, Bart., M.P.			Duke of Richmond
July 1885	—			
March 1886	C. T. D. Acland, M.P.			
September 1886	Sir H. J. Selwyn-Ibbetson, Bart., M.P.			
June 1892	C. A. Whitmore, M.P.			
November 1892	G. G. Leveson-Gower, M.P.			
December 1892		Sir Michael Hicks-Beach, M.P.		
September 1895	L. Knowles, M.P.			
October 1895		C. B. Stuart-Wortley, M.P.		
January 1897				Mandell Creighton
January 1901				Randall Davidson
November 1901				A. F. Winnington-Ingram
March 1903	Sir Lewis Dibdin			Lord Burghclere
February 1905	F. S. Stevenson, M.P.			
February 1906	C. E. H. Hobhouse, M.P.			
April 1906	J. Tomkinson, M.P.			
March 1907				Lord St Aldwyn
February 1908	C. N. Nicholson, M.P.			
April 1910				Henry Hobhouse
May 1916	Sir W. A. Mount, M.P.			
March 1919	J. D. Birchall, M.P.			
February 1923				Sir W. A. Mount, Bart.
February 1924	George Middleton, M.P.			
December 1924	J. D. Birchall, M.P.			

D. THE CHURCH ESTATES COMMITTEE (continued)

	Church Estates Commissioners[1]			Appointed by the Ecclesiastical Commissioners[2]	
	First	*Second*	*Third*	*Layman*	*Bishop*
May 1926	—	—	—	—	—
July 1926	—	—	—	—	—
July 1927	—	—	Lord Daryngton	Henry Hobhouse	C. F. Garbett
July 1929	George Middleton	George Middleton, M.P.	—	—	A. F. Winnington-Ingram
January 1931	—	R. D. Denman, M.P.	—	—	—
March 1931	—	—	—	—	—
January 1939	Sir P. W. Baker-Wilbraham	—	—	Sir George Courthope, Bart.	—
November 1939	—	—	—	—	—
April 1943	—	J. D. Mills, M.P.	—	—	G. F. Fisher
July 1945	—	—	—	—	—
September 1945	—	T. W. Burden, M.P.	—	—	J. W. C. Wand
July 1948	—	—	Lord Tovey	—	—

[1] C.C.F. 11629/2/2   [2] C.C.F. 8089/1–4

544

THE STATE OF THE SEES, *c.* 1835

	Area, in Sq. Miles[1]	Population, to nearest 1000[2]	Benefices[2]	Net Income of See[3]	Patronage		
					Benefices, no. [4]	Benefices, value [4]	Dignities, no. and quality[5]
Canterbury	1,152	403,000	343	22,305	152	61,752	3P, 6C, 1A
York	5,300	1,464,000	891	11,725	54	14,889	52P, 5C, 4A
St Asaph	?	197,000	131	6,082	106	30,127	1D, 13P, 3C
Bangor	?	153,000	124	3,938	77	22,717	1D, 3C, 5P, 1A
Bath and Wells	1,642	404,000	441	6,011	27	7,969	49P, 4C, 3A
Bristol	1,005	263,000	254	2,161	10	2,171	1A
Carlisle	1,378	128,000	127	2,592	30	7,992	4P, 1A
Chester	4,138	1,902,000	554	3,022	35	6,507	6P, 2A
Chichester	1,463	237,000	267	3,560	28	9,859	30P, 3C, 2A
St Davids	?	373,000	407	2,915	98	14,328	42P, 5C, 4A
Durham	2,932	453,000	146	22,185	44	30,837	12P, 2A
Ely	858	126,000	149	9,597	78	30,270	8P, 1A
Exeter	3,906	793,000	632	1,571	42	12,446	19P, 3C, 4A
Gloucester	1,256	276,000	281	2,201	26	4,734	1A
Hereford	1,630	207,000	256	2,797	26	9,338	28P, 5C, 2A
Lichfield	3,344	984,000	606	3,660	22	5,512	23P, 3C, 4A
Lincoln	5,775	855,000	1,234	3,747	55	14,206	46P, 3C, 6A
Llandaff	?	184,000	192	1,043	6	1,459	11P, 2C, 1A
London	1,942	1,689,000	635	15,045	84	41,419	30P, 3C, 5A
Norwich	3,604	692,000	1,021	4,516	42	13,423	4A
Oxford	752	140,000	209	1,505	10	3,040	1A
Peterborough	1,166	186,000	290	3,363	6	3,698	6P, 1A
Rochester	384	197,000	94	2,180	20	8,198	1A
Salisbury	2,135	321,000	386	5,435	36	11,173	42P, 5C, 3A
Winchester	2,386	780,000	416	10,654	58	29,206	12P, 2A
Worcester	1,179	358,000	212	7,301	20	10,658	1A

[1] From Lord Henley's *Plan for a new Arrangement . . . of the Dioceses.*
[2] From first report of Ecclesiastical Duties and Revenues Commission.
[3] From P.Ps. 1851, XLII, 93 ff.
[4] From returns privately compiled for Ecclesiastical Commissioners, in the Church Commissioners' Library, 460.05.

[5] From *Patroni Ecclesiarum* (Rivingtons, 1831) and the lists appended to the main report of the Ecclesiastical Revenues Commission (1835: P.Ps. 1835, XXII, 1014 ff.). Their aggregate values could be worked out from this report but the result would be so approximate as not to be very useful. P=Prebend (including canonries); C=cathedral office, such as chancellor, precentor, preacher, sub-dean; A=archdeacon; D=dean. Chancellorships and Registrarships of the diocese were always in the bishop's gift, and are not here noticed; nor are vicars choral, minor canons etc. Prebends customarily held together with cathedral offices are counted as if they were separate preferments.

THE MAIN WORK OF THE ECCLESIASTICAL COMMISSIONERS, 1840–1938, WITH THEIR INCOME AND THEIR RENTAL RECEIPTS

A. MAIN LINES OF WORK IN AUGMENTING STIPENDS AND DIVIDING PARISHES[1]

AUGMENTATIONS[2]

Year	In Conjunction with Benefactions				Unconditional on Benefactions			In Respect of Local Claims (see note 7)			By Annexation of Tithes, Rent-Charges etc.			Annual Grants for Mining Districts[4]		PARISHES		
	Number	Gross Value of Benefactions[3]	Annual Payment Undertaken	Capital Sums Granted	Number	A.P.U.	Capital Grants	Number	A.P.U.	Capital Grants	Number	Value	Area	Number	Value	Annual Grants to Benefices under the Parish of Manchester Division Act, 1850	Districts and New Parishes under the New Parishes Act, 1843 and 1856[5]	District Chapelries etc.[6]
1841	—	—	—	—	91	3,771	—	1	300	—	—	—	—	—	—	—	—	—
1842	5	3,550	174	—	60	3,887	—	19	714	—	—	—	—	—	—	—	—	—
1843	22	17,415	878	—	158	10,042	—	5	214	—	—	—	—	—	—	—	71	—
1844	25	24,717	1,042	—	203	8,869	—	5	250	—	5	480	34	—	—	—	47	—
1845	5	8,215	239	—	5	347	—	2	115	—	—	—	—	—	—	—	76	—
1846	5	2,304	107	—	3	156	—	19	1,018	—	3	119	4	—	—	—	15	—
1847	1	3,195	30	—	3	305	—	6	470	—	3	—	20	—	—	—	10	—
1848	8	1,000	30	—	3	239	—	28	1,915	—	4	39	133	—	—	—	5	—
1849	8	2,000	237	—	108	4,099	—	25	2,935	—	—	—	—	—	—	—	4	—
1850[7]	4	2,650	184	—	11	483	—	6	430	—	5	54	51	—	—	—	5	—
1851	2	2,375	68	—	2	50	—	6	249	—	4	170	34	—	—	—	2	—
1852	2	2,733	66	—	1	45	—	1	6	—	1	—	9	—	—	—	—	—

THE MAIN WORK OF THE ECCLESIASTICAL COMMISSIONERS, 1840–1938, WITH THEIR INCOME AND THEIR RENTAL RECEIPTS

A. MAIN LINES OF WORK IN AUGMENTING STIPENDS AND DIVIDING PARISHES[1]

Year	AUGMENTATIONS[2] — In Conjunction with Benefactions				Unconditional on Benefactions			In Respect of Local Claims (see note 7)			By Annexation of Tithes, Rent-Charges etc.			Annual Grants for Mining Districts[4]		Annual Grants to Benefices under the Parish of Manchester Division Act, 1850	PARISHES — Districts and New Parishes under the New Parishes Act, 1843 and 1856[5]	District Chapelries etc.[6]
	Number	Gross Value of Benefactions[3]	Annual Payment Undertaken	Capital Sums Granted	Number	A.P.U.	Capital Grants	Number	A.P.U.	Capital Grants	Number	Value	Area	Number	Value			
1853	—	—	—	—	2	40	—	10	220	—	10	91	40	—	—	—	6	—
1854	1	1,875	30	—	2	130	—	3	19	—	1	—	3	—	—	—	1	—
1855	—	—	—	—	4	218	—	—	—	—	3	367	7	—	—	—	5	—
1856	—	—	—	—	18	386	—	—	—	—	11	550	29	—	—	—	2	—
1857	43	24,180	—	15,499	6	80	—	—	—	—	8	419	73	—	—	—	—	4
1858	—	—	—	—	20	290	—	—	—	—	10	192	24	—	—	—	5	52
1859	106	60,592	—	45,288	144	6,610	—	—	—	—	14	1,311	230	—	—	—	10	44
1860	129	81,938	—	72,187	17	281	—	—	—	—	25	2,774	180	—	—	—	5	72
1861	108	75,734	—	65,961	105	3,352	—	—	—	—	19	895	184	—	—	—	14	63
1862	139	93,974	—	85,113	11	221	—	33	3,291	—	27[8]	2,658	69	13	670	—	5	48
1863	168	111,813	—	97,598	59	6,744	—	75	9,440	—	16	830	316	31	1,755	2,293	24	74
1864	211	149,964	1,082	108,768	92	10,982	—	121	12,738	—	58	4,279	308	51	2,855	3,187	15	61
1865	146	129,465	3,115	19,131	89	10,794	—	125	14,869	—	26	2,520	42	59	3,750	3,429	19	75
1866	136	126,471	3,483	1,000	163	20,291	—	82	8,902	1,500	22	4,909	104	91	6,950	4,471	15	73
1867	182	158,231	4,520	12,885	115	16,727	4,500	156	11,336	135,453	44	5,130	70	91	7,125	3,444	10	72
1868	194	175,149	3,899	30,330	98	13,368	10,375	127	11,405	61,953	45	4,540	126	134	9,790	3,917	24	67
1869	150	152,887	3,382	21,550	57	10,697	5,814	156	14,452	72,279	83	6,110	172	161	11,440	3,095	19	74
1870	146	143,826	3,529	27,543	45	5,781	4,400	112	7,234	57,193	88	4,696	171	169	12,350	3,600	10	48
1871	144	118,244	2,792	26,366	47	6,307	8,325	141	8,482	71,451	57	5,181	64	183	13,500	3,602	17	62
1872	165	137,045	2,876	39,914	34	3,582	5,295	145	11,385	65,961	52	4,012	126	208	15,600	3,845	15	69

Year																	
1873	128	104,190	2,261	28,274	64	7,238	2,923	157	13,061	62,656	67	4,277	62	223	16,485	4,547	6	49
1874	141	139,693	3,194	31,626	85	9,693	1,585	133	12,017	53,701	72	4,087	317	238	17,775	4,622	26	45
1875	141	141,712	2,778	38,688	41	5,358	60	125	11,174	58,207	91	4,494	149	253	19,120	6,422	26	68
1876	140	151,955	3,129	28,441	116	14,059	51,081	4	46	3,000	49	4,439	22	259	19,620	4,408	10	49
1877	133	126,435	2,903	25,153	25	3,428	3,195	144	11,051	51,666	54	4,768	41	285	21,990	3,138	11	36
1878	155	147,265	2,942	35,571	27	3,732	2,225	119	9,636	50,312	45	2,223	131	296	22,990	2,147	19	57
1879	135	139,754	3,047	30,696	24	3,789	1,500	123	8,053	46,819	40	2,370	84	311	24,070	293	12	56
1880	164	190,348	3,529	51,423	20	3,055	600	173	13,203	62,374	54	3,531	100	328	25,510	1,374	13	39
1881	130	120,313	2,882	20,966	19	3,454	—	137	10,419	51,840	38	2,664	45	339	26,090	1,570	11	52
1882	185	190,391	3,827	44,390	23	3,780	—	173	12,458	48,901	40	2,378	55	357	5,712	1,438	9	29
1883	136	107,489	2,402	26,480	17	3,227	—	165	12,481	63,834	35	1,048	90	377	29,040	1,954	14	39
1884	157	129,926	2,835	28,479	72	8,576	—	147	11,931	56,333	31	1,592	35	378	28,950	3,530	10	46
1885	143	110,132	2,383	29,080	26	3,733	—	127	10,312	56,987	57	1,699	102	373	28,500	3,476	9	37
1886	127	94,115	1,705	30,004	21	3,504	275	98	7,600	33,325	390	1,274	95	363	28,180	16,299	4	39
1887	87	72,690	1,158	29,172	12	1,792	—	93	5,857	42,568	191	1,023	58	365	28,420	14,727	2	37
1888	83	72,949	512	39,884	11	2,230	—	37	1,876	17,103	20	540	24	370	27,960	18,320	5	39
1889	62	50,473	113	35,359	8	1,164	—	34	2,867	12,580	43	268	25	375	28,380	19,218	14	27
1890	60	54,855	240	34,580	7	1,000	—	24	1,783	9,437	11	299	5	369	27,900	19,069	3	27
1891	76	67,809	300	39,213	9	1,200	—	45	1,995	10,510	12	219	15	354	27,660	17,004	1	13
1892	84	56,914	320	36,476	10	1,382	—	33	1,692	13,000	9	17	11	372	27,660	17,053	5	31
1893	92	67,982	188	46,993	9	1,300	—	32	1,302	12,280	12	225	34	373	27,900	17,153	10	23
1894	92	53,090	240	40,376	9	1,075	—	57	4,061	7,615	8	—	23	353	29,580	17,641	4	25
1895	83	65,508	180	41,610	8	1,050	—	48	1,986	6,850	5	9	—	381	28,200	19,865	8	17
1896	104	67,984	180	47,022	7	1,000	—	47	2,899	8,112	6	9	1	379	28,200	19,695	6	15
1897	98	54,186	88	45,989	9	975	—	38	2,360	4,122	6	374	1	380	27,960	19,063	2	28
1898	98	63,327	290	41,810	10	1,395	—	43	2,019	6,900	4	—	4	383	27,960	19,149	14	26
1899	113	76,472	320	51,428	10	1,475	—	54	2,401	8,250	11	72	5	386	27,420	20,676	6	20
1900	118	70,100	189	54,577	14	1,482	—	64	3,119	6,526	5	30	5	383	28,020	21,679	7	28
1901	125	77,601	495	51,585	14	1,500	—	66	2,283	6,425	9	81	3	383	27,060	25,135	5	23
1902	135	83,552	—	65,733[9]	13	1,448	—	87	3,513	13,070	11	562	7	375	27,300	25,593	15	34
1903	152	96,823	—	77,205	17	2,050	—	90	3,351	15,532	8	61	8	379	27,240	26,507	6	27
1904	174	103,013	—	82,434	18	1,966	—	79	3,312	6,880	4	185	20	11	660	27,628	10	23
1905	179	102,807	—	75,687	19	2,178	—	73	2,939	13,737	9	19	21	353	9,816	28,208	9	27
1906	226	121,182	—	100,659	30	3,029	—	79	3,583	8,700	10	153	8	48	3,300	28,539	9	40

THE MAIN WORK OF THE ECCLESIASTICAL COMMISSIONERS, 1840–1938, WITH THEIR INCOME AND THEIR RENTAL RECEIPTS

A. MAIN LINES OF WORK IN AUGMENTING STIPENDS AND DIVIDING PARISHES[1]

Year	In Conjunction with Benefactions				Unconditional on Benefactions			In Respect of Local Claims (see note 7)			By Annexation of Tithes, Rent-Charges etc.			Annual Grants for Mining Districts[4]		Annual Grants to Benefices under the Parish of Manchester Division Act, 1850	Districts and New Parishes under the New Parishes Act, 1843 and 1856[5]	District Chapelries etc.[6]
	Number	Gross Value of Benefactions[3]	Annual Payment Undertaken	Capital Sums Granted	Number	A.P.U.	Capital Grants	Number	A.P.U.	Capital Grants	Number	Value	Area	Number	Value			
1907	235	120,683	—	103,297	29	3,131	—	90	3,985	14,071	8	98	8	23	1,380	23,646	7	21
1908	252	134,839	—	111,510	153	5,878	—	103	7,887	16,170	6	18	11	400	29,580	31,626	6	23
1909	234	119,826	—	92,560	428	24,635	—	83	3,844	11,700	9	224	6	10	600	32,606	5	27
1910	245	126,222	—	98,951	332	17,061	—	136	6,244	20,509	10	319	17	50	3,000	33,123	3	36
1911	247	137,274	—	111,392	72	6,352	—	78	4,862	7,604	7	59	12	17	1,020	33,884	3	38
1912	241	116,045	—	109,414	43	4,371	—	94	4,950	8,394	5	6	4	4	300	33,937	2	40
1913	224	118,515	—	101,400	70	6,174	—	96	2,733	10,738	11	26	4	400	31,620	34,708	6	32
1914	240	124,222	—	115,425	75	6,392	—	96	5,181	11,496	11	23	11	68	4,620	34,725	6	23
1915	247	118,417	—	118,417	50	4,630	—	94	4,950	8,394	7	95	—	1	60	34,475	2	20
1916	223	105,445	—	105,445	40	4,080	—	99	3,225	9,118	2	8	—	4	240	35,066	2	23
1917	184	89,039	—	89,039	59	4,820	—	69	2,897	7,366	4	25	49	2	120	37,426	2	17
1918	201	90,499	—	90,499	67	4,918	—	87	3,613	10,340	2	18	—	446	36,780	38,412	2	7
1919	305	148,218	—	148,218	439	21,818	—	119	4,834	18,162	4	—	2	52	4,500	42,240	2	7
1920	300	131,156	—	129,726	1,029	52,902	—	142	6,842	14,364	4	13	4	—	—	44,850	1	8
1921	320	129,102	—	128,202	903	48,683	—	126	4,407	16,944	5	165	3	391	28,880	42,576	2	12
1922	385	155,110	—	154,310	702	31,939	—	127	5,049	12,765	14	1,205	11	—	—	42,740	16	10
1923	480	187,913	—	188,413	196	11,223	2,600	133	5,285	18,663	5	655	—	—	—	42,825	11	14

PARISHES

Augmentation Grants

	Grants for Endowment of Livings in conjunction with Benefactions			In respect of Local Claims			Others[10]		Conditional on equivalent payment by or through Diocesan Board of Finance		Parsonage Houses (under whatever arrangements)			Curates' Grants					
Year	No.	Gross Value of Benefact'ns	Annual Payment Undertaken	No.	A.P.U.	Gross Value of Benefactions (approximate) under both heads	No.	A.P.U.	No.	A.P.U.	No.	Gross Value of Benefact'ns	Capital Sums granted	No.	Grants meeting Benefactions of approximately equal amount[4]	Other Grants	Gross sums[3]	No.	No.
1924	332	136,741	6,098	52	1,369	7,012	2,762	129,196	—	—	213	69,674	87,069	89	868	3,266	46,592	12	8
1925	327	135,753	6,110	30	751	8,755	530	30,275	—	—	238	81,348	105,317	76	951	2,719	48,073	15	7
1926	329	141,956	6,391	35	862	2,947	309	21,731	—	—	246	62,884	100,732	92	829	4,370	48,224	13	11
1927	324	135,063	6,083	48	1,479	9,314	206	13,433	—	—	284	64,603	112,527	84	960	3,090	49,172	11	9
1928	319	129,634	5,786	47	1,844	10,281	1,673	76,540	468	14,646	257	63,337	101,966	87	1,446	3,360	49,837	9	14
1929	324	132,483	5,989	44	1,223	4,470	1,127	38,337	143	4,116	265	64,189	102,059	102	1,429	3,790	51,650	10	19
1930	362	148,174	6,690	59	1,456	17,363	299	19,700	57	2,496	328	62,274	109,010	123	1,459	5,930	51,881	21	14
1931	300	128,429	4,846	59	1,313	15,777	267	21,123	27	741	257	78,219	90,989	96	1,265	4,496	51,462	18	15
1932	278	113,550	4,398	55	1,644	10,490	249	13,093	22	392	262	66,850	85,755	98	1,565	4,080	51,055	12	9
1933	273	106,528	3,904	44	780	8,235	271	13,703	20	458	244	61,353	70,693	116	1,432	5,210	52,506	11	5
1934	253	91,813	3,199	40	710	12,438	219	13,479	16	360	235	61,793	71,512	95	1,210	2,800	52,104	17	12
1935	222	84,123	2,717	37	479	9,003	171	10,459	21	499	309	60,379	67,224	102	908	4,560	52,442	6	19
1936	202	79,411	2,105	12	281	3,534	121	6,635	12	295	190	59,242	62,207	80	680	2,920	52,594	9	3
1937	180	74,172	2,199	21	858	2,998	171	13,555	13	221	199	56,560	59,888	63	562	2,520	52,202	19	19

[1] These figures, extracted from the Commissioners' annual reports, give less than a full picture of their activities. Their smaller or less sustained activities have had to be omitted. No full picture of their work in any given year (excepting only the year 1880, described on pp. 499–501 above) can be gained without going back to the annual reports. Pains have been taken to make these figures as accurate as possible, but some accuracy has no doubt been lost in the attempt to reduce a variety of forms to a single pattern, and to press the reports into a service for which they were never intended.

[2] All money sums are given to the nearest pound.

[3] Gross sums, including values of residence houses donated. Rent-charges have been counted as a 4% yield on gross property.

[4] Under 23 and 24 Vic. c. 124. Until just after the First World War (when temporary grants for curates ceased to be made separately under this head) they were grants of £60 to meet benefactions always of equal or greater amount.

[5] Including Districts under the Parish of Manchester Division Act, 13 and 14 Vic. c. 41.

[6] I.e. District Chapelries, Consolidated Chapelries, and Particular Districts.

[7] Year ending 31 October. Hereafter the Commissioners' year ran regularly

THE MAIN WORK OF THE ECCLESIASTICAL COMMISSIONERS, 1840–1938, WITH THEIR INCOME AND THEIR RENTAL RECEIPTS

A. MAIN LINES OF WORK IN AUGMENTING STIPENDS AND DIVIDING PARISHES

from 1 November to 31 October.

[8] From 1862, many and often most of these augmentations by annexation of tithes etc. were in respect of local claims, additional to those in the Local Claims column.

[9] From this year, they ceased to distinguish clearly between grants of capital for residence houses, and those for use as yielders of income.

[10] Including grants under both the Commissioners' ordinary regulations and their special scheme for populous districts.

B. COMMON FUND: ANNUAL NET DISPOSEABLE INCOME, 1861-1938[1]

	Rentals of Estates Vested in Cmrs.	Divs. and Interest on Govt. Securities	Interest from other sources	Surplus arising from Enfranchisements paid over by Church Estates Cmrs., plus interest	Sales of Land under 29 and 30 Vic. c. 111	Total for that Year
1861	146,927	13,214	7,805	10,000	—	251,075[2]
1862	174,646	9,435	15,947	330,000	—	619,662[2]
1863	201,335	13,408	30,716	100,000	—	403,049[2]
1864	246,763	20,442	27,128	100,000	—	436,336[2]
1865	277,973	38,200	20,851	50,000	—	432,574[2]
1866	286,013	51,472		50,000	100,000	536,441[2]
1867	325,613	50,593		30,000	100,000	515,992
1868	371,632	67,479		70,000	100,000	609,111
1869	398,440	47,726		50,000	100,000	601,746
1870	529,202	63,109		50,000	100,000	742,311
1871	574,571	87,770		30,000	100,000	792,341
1872	595,069	103,594		—	100,000	798,663
1873	740,242	84,894		90,000	100,000	1,015,136
1874	706,668	87,773		—	100,000	894,441
1875	733,426	97,424		—	100,000	930,850
1876	778,969	89,101		—	100,000	968,070
1877	827,553	81,621		—	100,000	1,009,174
1878	866,558	83,592		—	100,000	1,050,150
1879	864,562	83,175		—	100,000	1,047,737
1880	856,212	96,665		20,000	100,000	1,072,877
1881	879,887	94,543		—	100,000	1,074,430
1882	915,973	86,890		—	100,000	1,102,863
1883	936,705	102,830		5,000	—	1,044,535
1884	934,098	99,148				1,033,246
1885	906,994	90,173				997,167
1886	958,835	89,429				1,048,264
1887	971,738	87,204				1,058,942
1888	1,022,415	98,989				1,121,404
1889	1,031,712	97,172				1,128,884
1890	1,046,543	104,505				1,151,048
1891	1,107,318	112,097				1,219,415
1892	1,090,148	118,989				1,209,137
1893	1,054,202	131,861				1,186,063
1894	1,096,517	136,012				1,232,529
1895	1,119,988	139,008				1,258,996
1896	1,125,011	141,725				1,266,736

B. COMMON FUND: ANNUAL NET DISPOSEABLE INCOME, 1861–1938[1]

	Rentals of Estates Vested in Cmrs.	Divs. and Interest on Govt. Securities	Interest from other sources			Total for that Year
1897	1,125,495	161,307				1,286,802
1898	1,139,599	174,658				1,314,257
1899	1,178,955	192,626				1,371,581
1900	1,197,042	203,250				1,400,292
1901	1,247,792	219,148				1,466,940
1902	1,271,262	238,658				1,509,920
1903	1,256,088	261,715				1,517,803
1904	1,255,818	275,359				1,531,177
1905	1,288,246	297,701				1,585,947
1906	1,311,619	321,485				1,633,104
1907	1,328,847	357,324				1,686,171
1908	1,390,325	396,657				1,786,982
1909	1,449,396	407,957				1,857,353
1910	1,432,121	435,642				1,867,763
1911	1,406,288	457,239				1,864,527
1912	1,438,228	485,773				1,926,001
1913	1,436,568	517,839				1,954,407
1914	1,504,816	549,492				2,054,308
1915	1,481,441	567,384				2,048,825
1916	1,843,749	631,249				2,474,998
1917	1,558,447	662,052				2,220,499
1918	1,392,003	736,852				2,128,855
1919	1,529,116	767,399				2,296,515
1920	1,552,069	758,024				2,310,093
1921	1,523,839	838,913				2,362,752
1922	1,363,910	932,075				2,295,985
1923	1,559,164	964,068				2,523,232
1924	1,609,488	1,015,066				2,624,554
1925	1,624,954	1,086,929				2,711,883
1926	1,501,945	1,119,997				2,621,942
1927	1,459,830	1,201,765				2,661,595
1928	1,512,347	1,267,524				2,779,871
1929	1,549,983	1,346,734				2,896,717
1930	1,536,724	1,400,909				2,937,633
1931	1,484,894	1,450,056	250,000 ⎫	from Inland		3,184,950
1932	1,397,409	1,479,713	250,000 ⎬	Rev. towards		3,127,122
1933	1,341,082	1,526,449	100,000 ⎭	repayment I.T.		2,967,531

1934	1,424,720	1,553,809	100,000	from Inland	3,078,529
1935	1,475,068	1,598,333	103,000	Rev. towards	3,176,401
1936	1,494,189	1,671,566	95,000	repayment I.T.	3,260,755
1937	1,324,770	1,850,885	109,000		3,284,655
1938	1,231,295	1,924,188	126,000		3,281,483

¹ Until the early sixties, the form of the accounts, apart from being generally uncommunicative, varied almost yearly, and the extreme difficulty which contemporaries found in the way of understanding them seems now insuperable. Here, however, are some approximations to the Commissioners' annual income through the years 1840–60. It is regretted that they cannot satisfactorily be broken down to match those given for the period after 1860.

	£		£
1840	672	1851	102,132
1841	14,870	1852	126,513
1842	19,014	1853	135,873
1843	45,332	1854	156,391
1844	53,885	1855	176,676
1845	71,657	1856	192,957
1846	70,726	1857§	146,000
1847	67,201	1858	187,768
1848	102,304	1859	197,325
1849	111,622	1860	231,899
1850*	71,603		

* year ending 31 October.

§ in this year took place a particularly drastic recasting of the form of the accounts. There is no reason to suppose that income did not continue to rise as it had been rising all the time.

² Including shares of the corporate revenue of certain cathedrals: 1861, £72,129; 1862, £89,634; 1863, £44,381; 1864, £42,003; 1865, £45,550; and 1866, £48,956.

C. RENTAL RECEIPTS[1]

Year of Report	Rack rent Lands and Premises	Ditto in London[2]	Tithe and Corn Rent-charges	Royalties and Rents etc. deriving from Mining	Rents, Redeemed Land Tax etc. reserved in outgoing beneficial leases & copy hold grants for lives	Receipts from Manors of Inheritance	Ground Rents etc.	Paddington estate[3]	Total
1861	99,835	—	67,033	33,096	15,851	—	5,854	13,492	261,537
1862	125,681	—	74,460	44,779	16,646	—	6,743	14,113	304,478
1863	138,017	—	88,384	44,253	31,440	5,764	11,764	13,709	341,665
1864	158,269	—	104,141	51,007	34,764	6,035	22,374	13,774	399,760
1865	169,597	—	107,421	63,527	31,589	11,570	26,142	14,402	434,203
1866	168,298	—	113,274	61,270	29,928	6,473	29,942	16,872	438,109
1867	173,926	—	120,338	65,023	30,884	10,540	31,297	14,428	480,086
1868	186,717	—	119,459	71,670	38,397	15,197	36,009	17,815	523,182
1869	250,102	—	125,268	78,876	33,259	8,487	39,217	6,720	571,320
1870	266,195	—	139,080	79,798	41,497	11,405	64,642	6,847	643,493
1871	297,405	—	150,147	84,329	42,138	16,391	63,224	2,290	694,525
1872	217,392	88,899	160,699	97,425	39,735	17,091	54,414	15,407	723,024
1873	232,574	92,476	176,662	203,103	43,522	21,534	53,628	13,437	875,633
1874	244,232	95,392	191,043	144,123	42,721	22,910	56,103	13,545	846,018
1875	247,280	103,678	205,245	149,301	40,358	20,017	58,762	13,747	869,989
1876	258,099	108,617	218,028	164,148	37,503	23,954	61,628	14,679	920,777
1877	278,438	119,198	234,299	175,604	35,130	23,390	67,646	16,542	980,641
1878	295,321	126,910	240,917	198,387	32,614	18,279	70,926	16,733	1,028,938
1879	301,947	137,525	259,330	199,147	30,836	21,053	72,951	17,382	1,072,788
1880	280,832	141,327	260,433	180,707	29,244	25,648	75,133	15,822	1,065,213
1881	266,702	143,817	266,301	217,049	27,433	20,523	78,570	15,581	1,111,395
1882	250,766	163,960	270,994	220,009	24,603	19,257	81,576	14,399	1,143,695
1883	257,085	177,781	266,239	232,781	23,810	17,709	89,910	14,686	1,159,658
1884	264,491	187,828	272,228	217,972	21,401	21,541	94,129	13,457	1,167,505
1885	257,050	198,737	278,329	235,348	20,335	19,711	99,288	12,961	1,208,556
1886	241,762	206,639	275,595	306,002	18,332	17,885	102,887	13,189	1,270,987
1887	239,740	200,393	276,871	289,580	16,825	20,626	129,951	13,479	1,302,548
1888	233,063	203,032	277,629	300,677	15,552	15,105	137,595	13,450	1,331,554
1889	238,579	210,591	276,148	307,191	14,497	14,039	135,405	13,524	1,323,138
1890	239,833	224,215	269,384	321,325	13,808	16,838	141,751	13,509	1,343,481
1891	248,223	232,817	263,480	368,573	13,299	16,682	161,884	13,620	1,403,195
1892	251,679	230,049	256,829	332,977	13,403	17,789	164,651	13,512	1,370,261
1893	239,596	110,621[4]	257,821	270,811	10,818	21,073	284,129[4]	13,518	1,317,363
1894	232,800	110,084[5]	259,961	318,855	11,262	16,131	314,789[5]	13,800	1,363,976
1895	239,016	112,902	254,823	346,279	9,235	16,147	317,491	13,998	1,389,457
1896	236,670	115,764	250,590	320,891	8,739	17,122	328,482	13,911	1,386,855
1897	240,176	114,676	232,832	341,622	7,139	16,364	347,690	14,278	1,402,758
1898	244,194	114,335	227,393	342,047	7,795	17,794	355,844	14,732	1,410,385
1899	251,189	115,111	228,801	342,778	7,579	18,004	383,291	15,133	1,434,322
1900	254,525	118,241	218,966	388,137	7,006	18,177	390,565	15,398	1,467,439
1901	256,438	124,832	217,277	413,137	6,598	16,259	408,202	15,779	1,507,684
1902	256,240	147,219	219,171	409,707	5,700	15,374	431,550	16,352	1,535,012
1903	262,234	153,148	218,803	389,720	4,848	11,048	439,014	16,424	1,529,846
1904	258,890	156,974	226,211	394,863	4,553	11,477	454,164	16,766	1,558,264
1905	265,768	153,318	230,530	393,569	4,089	9,827	470,853	18,017	1,591,321

1906	268,338	157,371	229,860	405,213	3,806	12,918	483,055	17,558	1,619,197
1907	270,529	164,157	229,008	423,609	3,379	9,806	494,962	18,808	1,650,223
1908	273,284	165,984	232,309	463,439	3,000⁶	8,657	501,225	18,643	1,700,204
1909	273,351	170,833	234,684	468,673	—	11,402	512,987	19,986	1,729,016
1910	275,869	170,438	235,574	451,541	—	10,118	485,249	19,753	1,685,930
1911	278,415	169,521	241,377	446,552	—	9,008	521,499	19,926	1,722,331
1912	280,303	173,239	244,722	448,661	—	9,152	529,366	19,950	1,739,050
1913	279,292	172,725	250,345	432,872	—	10,433	535,139	19,955	1,729,102
1914	279,702	174,225	258,424	486,332	—	8,267	541,345	19,665	1,795,055
1915	281,941	176,952	262,781	443,221	—	7,378	544,138	19,749	1,765,544
1916	284,246	179,069	268,315	405,790	—	8,389	549,114	19,769	1,749,226
1917	288,373	184,230	289,170	427,836	—	8,038	549,479	19,902	1,804,187
1918	293,275	187,407	320,185	403,842	—	8,605	550,319	21,189	1,850,408
1919	297,186	195,554	379,330	374,693	—	7,753	550,762	21,267	1,881,382
1920	302,455	202,149	381,157	410,701	—	9,522	552,166	22,861	1,918,921
1921	279,814	225,074	354,602	451,854	—	11,965	554,549	24,141	1,946,810
1922	255,670	269,332	334,501	298,139	—	11,174	552,942	28,432	1,797,075
1923	249,597	308,625	319,032	425,751	—	10,558	557,244	31,983	1,944,061
1924	249,571	353,756	307,939	459,354	—	12,219	558,921	34,992	2,020,358
1925	247,667	367,674	305,695	464,823	—	8,758	567,125	38,526	2,040,390
1926	245,447	370,577	304,197	425,464	—	8,285	576,250	39,304	2,019,397
1927	242,938	356,588	413,841⁸	248,468	—	—	584,193	42,880	1,951,971
1928	238,115	363,793	292,112	375,469	—	—	604,948	44,240	1,993,827
1929	237,663	376,694	291,621	382,987	—	Timber	608,080	48,272	2,027,572
1930	234,050	378,417	290,870	417,357	—	etc. Sale⁷	618,080	53,395	2,071,893
1931	229,660	378,544	287,223	392,504	—	11,854	626,315	60,139	2,045,296
1932	221,836	378,180	289,122	315,135	—	11,635	634,849	60,654	2,002,190
1933	213,009	375,005	286,627	303,330	—	10,680	642,697	62,626	2,019,228
1934	207,353	371,954	281,844	282,507	—	10,664	650,540	67,020	2,042,491
1935	213,111	375,180	281,308	313,580	—	10,802	668,823	70,720	2,101,744
1936	216,773	367,558	282,554	309,754	—	11,638	674,575	74,687	2,110,826
1937	232,174	341,679	127,818	317,564	—	11,555	678,754	77,805	1,921,111
1938	237,481	344,596	—	337,620	12,763⁹	15,985	692,610	84,560	1,822,613

¹ Small miscellaneous rentals, although included in the Total, are not shown. The material does not exist for carrying these tables back towards 1840.

² Until 1883 this column was headed simply 'London'; in 1884 it changed to 'London and the Suburbs'.

³ Only from 1904 did the name of Paddington show in this column's heading. Earlier it was 'Net Receipts from Estates held jointly'.

⁴ A book-keeping transfer of certain rents in respect of leases granted on condition of rebuilding.

⁵ Another book-keeping transfer.

⁶ Hereafter this item becomes very insignificant.

⁷ This item was less significant before this date.

⁸ Sudden increase due to the synchronization of dates of payment, which brought in some rent-charges equivalent to a year and a quarter's, or a year and a half's, payments.

⁹ In this year 'Tithe Rates' are added to the other items in this column and the sum becomes again significant.

BIBLIOGRAPHY

This Bibliography lists no works that are not cited or referred to in the text. It is not a guide to the literature of the subject, which is vast; it is simply an aid to the identification of such printed books as have actually been mentioned, with certain exceptions: it does not include periodicals, novels, or newspapers, nor does it notice Parliamentary Papers and Debates, all of which are easy to recognize and locate. The place of publication is only given when it is other than London.

AISLABIE, W. J., *Letter to Lord John Russell on the Church Bills.* 1838.

ARBUTHNOT, CHARLES, *Correspondence:* see Aspinall, A.

ARBUTHNOT, P. S-M., *Memories of the Arbuthnots of Kincardineshire and Aberdeenshire.* 1920.

ARNOLD, THOMAS, *Principles of Church Reform.* 1833.

ASPINALL, ARTHUR, *The Correspondence of Charles Arbuthnot.* Camden Soc., 3rd. ser., xv. 1941.

Augmentation of Small Livings to the minimal value of £200 a year by a Clerical Income Tax . . . in a Letter to the Lord Chancellor, by Philadelphia. [1854].

BACON, JOHN, *Liber Regis vel Thesaurus Rerum Ecclesiasticarum.* 1786.

BAHLMAN, DUDLEY W. R., *The Moral Revolution of 1688.* New Haven, 1957.

BAKER, JAMES, *Life of Sir Thomas Bernard, Bart.* 1819.

BARRATT, D. M., *Ecclesiastical Terriers of Warwickshire Parishes:* i, Parishes A. to Li. Dugdale Soc. Pubns., xxii. Oxford, 1955.

BARRINGTON, SHUTE, *Sermons, Charges and Tracts.* 1811.

BAXTER, S. B., *The Development of the Treasury, 1660–1702.* 1957.

BENNETT, G. V., *White Kennet, 1660–1728.* 1957.

[BERENS, EDWARD], *Church Reform: by a Churchman.* 1828.

BERKELEY, GEORGE, *The Danger of Violent Innovations in the State, how specious soever the Pretence, exemplified from the Reigns of the two first Stuarts, in a sermon preached at Canterbury . . . 31 January,* 1785.

BERRIAN, W., *Memoir of Bishop Hobart.* New York, 1833 (in *Works of Hobart,* 3 vols.).

BEST, G. F. A., 'The Religious Difficulties of National Education in England, 1800–70', in *Cambridge Historical Journal,* XII (1956), 155–73.

—— 'The Protestant Constitution and its Supporters, 1800–1829', in *Transactions of the Royal Historical Society,* 5th series, VIII (1958), 105–27.

—— 'The Evangelicals and the Established Church in the early Nineteenth Century', in *Journal of Theological Studies,* X (1959), 63–78.

Bibliography

—— 'The Constitutional Revolution, 1828–32, and its Consequences for the Established Church', in *Theology*, LXII (1959), 226–34.

—— 'The Whigs and the Church Establishment in the Age of Grey and Holland', in *History*, XLV (1960), 103–18.

—— 'The Road to Hiram's Hospital', in *Victorian Studies*, V (1961-2), 135-50.

BEST, SAMUEL, *A Manual of Parochial Institutions.* 2nd. edn., 1849.

BETHELL, CHRISTOPHER, *Remarks on the Manner in which the Business of the Ecclesiastical Commissioners for England has been carried on during the last three years.* Bangor, 1859.

BIBER, G. E., *Bishop Blomfield and his Times.* 1857.

BLOMFIELD, ALFRED, *Memoir of C. J. Blomfield* (2 vols., 1863) 2nd. edn, one vol., 1864.

BLOMFIELD, CHARLES JAMES, *Sermon preached at the anniversary Meeting of the Stewards of the Sons of the Clergy . . . 23 May 1822.* 1823.

——*Remonstrance addressed to Henry Brougham, Esq., by one of the 'Working Clergy'.* 1823.

—— *Charge to the Clergy of the Diocese of London, 1838.* 1838.

—— *Speech in the House of Lords . . . 30 July 1840, on the Ecclesiastical Duties and Revenues Bill.* 1840

—— Life, see Biber, G. E., and Blomfield, A.

BLOOMFIELD, S. T., *Analytical View of the Principal Plans of Church Reform.* 1833.

BOASE, F., *Modern English Biography*, with Supplement. 6 vols., Truro, 1892–1921.

[BRETT, THOMAS], *An Account of Church Government, and Governors.* 1701.

BROSE, OLIVE J., *Church and Parliament: the Reshaping of the Church of England 1828–1860.* Stanford, Cal., and London, 1959.

BROWN, C. K. F., *The Church's Part in Education, 1833–1941.* 1942.

BROWN, SIR JAMES R., *Number One Millbank: the Story of the Ecclesiastical Commissioners.* 1944.

BUGG, THOMAS, *The Curate's Appeal to the Equity and Christian Principles of the British Legislature . . . .* 1819.

BULL, G. S., *Sheep without Shepherds: the Difficulties of Populous Parishes, and Suggestions as to Remedial Measures.* ?1852.

BURGESS, H. J., *Enterprise in Education: . . . the work of the Established Church . . . prior to 1870.* 1958.

BURGON, J. W., *The Lives of Twelve Good Men.* New edn, 1891.

BURGOYNE, M., *Address to the Governors and Directors of the Public Charity Schools.* 2nd ed., 1830.

BURKE, EDMUND, *Works* (World's Classics edition).

Bibliography

Burn, Richard, *Ecclesiastical Law.* 1760, with many subsequent editions.

—— *The Justice of the Peace and Parish Officer.* 1755, with many subsequent editions.

Burnet, Gilbert, *History of my own Time.* New edn, by O. Airy, 2 vols., 1897–1900.

—— *Life,* see Clarke and Foxcroft.

—— Supplement to *History,* see Foxcroft.

[Burroughs, Samuel], *Inquiry into the Customary Estates and Tenant Rights of those who hold Lands of the Church* . . . by Everard Fleetwood. 1731.

Burton, Edward, *Thoughts upon the Demand for Church Reform.* Oxford, 1831.

—— *Sequel to Remarks upon Church Reform, with Observations upon the Plan proposed by Lord Henley.* 1832.

—— *Thoughts on the Separation of Church and State.* 1834.

Campbell, Augustus, *Appeal to the Gentlemen of England, on behalf of the Church of England.* Liverpool, 1823.

—— *Reply to the Article on Church Establishments in the last number of the 'Edinburgh Review'.* 1823.

Cappe, Catharine, *Memoirs, written by herself.* 1822.

Cassan, Stephen, *Lives of the Bishops of Winchester.* 2 vols., circa 1827.

—— *Lives of the Bishops of Bath and Wells.* 2 vols., 1829.

[Cawdrey, Zachary], *A Discourse of Patronage.* 1675.

Chamberlain, Walter, *Parochial Centralization; or, Remarks on the present State of the Church of England in Provincial Towns . . . addressed . . . to Lord Ashley.* Bolton and London, 1850.

Chesterton, Cecil (Mrs), *I lived in a Slum.* 1936.

Church Organization: a Letter to Lord Ashley, by Amicus. 1850.

Church Patronage: a Letter to Sir Robert Peel, by a Son of the Church. 1828.

Churton, Edward, *Memoir of Joshua Watson.* 2 vols., 1861.

Clarke, T. E. S., and Foxcroft, H. C., *Life of Gilbert Burnet, Bishop of Salisbury.* Cambridge, 1907.

Clergyman's Vade-Mecum: or, an Account of the Ancient and Present Church of England. 1706 and subsequent editions.

Clutterbuck, R., *History and Antiquities of Hertfordshire.* 3 vols., 1810–27.

Cockburn, Harry A. (ed.), *Some Letters of Lord Cockburn, with pages omitted from the Memorials of his Time.* Edinburgh, 1932.

Colchester, 2nd. Lord, *Diary and Correspondence.* 3 vols., 1861.

Collection of Letters and Essays in favour of Public Liberty, first published in the Newspapers 1764–70 . . . by an amicable Band of Wellwishers to the Religious and Civil Rights of Mankind. 3 vols., 1774.

Bibliography

CONNELL, W. F., *The Educational Thought and Influence of Matthew Arnold.* 1950.

COOMBS, H., and BAX, H. N. (ed.), *The Journal of a Somerset Rector.* 1930.

COSTIN, W. C., *History of St John's College, Oxford, 1598–1860.* Ox. Hist. Soc., n.s., XII. Oxford, 1958.

COVE, MORGAN, *Essay on the Revenues of the Church of England: with an Inquiry into the ... Abolition or Commutation of Tithes.* 3rd. edn, 1816.

COWIE, L. W., *Henry Newman, an American in London, 1708–1743.* 1956.

CRIPPS, H. W., *Practical Treatise on the Law relating to Church and Clergy.* 1845 and subsequent editions.

CROKER, J. W., see Jennings, L. J.

DALE, A. W. W. (ed.), *Warren's Book.* Cambridge, 1911.

DAUBENY, CHARLES, *A Guide to the Church* (1798). 3rd edn, 2 vols., 1830.

DAVIES, D., *The Case of Labourers in Husbandry stated and considered.* 1795.

DAVIES, G. C. B., *Henry Phillpotts, Bishop of Exeter.* 1954.

DAWES, RICHARD, *Remarks occasioned by the present Crusade against the Educational Plans of the Committee of Council on Education.* 1850.

DEALTRY, WILLIAM, *Examination of Dr Marsh's 'Inquiry' ... in a series of letters to the Rev. Dr E. D. Clarke.* 1812.

DIBDIN, LEWIS T. and DOWNING, S. E., *The Ecclesiastical Commission: a Sketch of its History and Work.* 1919.

DICKINSON, CHARLES, *Observations on Ecclesiastical Legislature and Church Reform.* Dublin, 1833.

[DIXON, H. J.], *The Sad Experience of a Clergyman of the Established Church.* 1875.

DUNCOMBE, EDWARD, *Guide to Church Reform.* 1833.

—— *Letter to the Hierarchy of the Church of England.* 1834.

Ecclesiastical Commission, its Origin and Progress, with some Examination of the Report of the Select Committee of the House of Commons, 1862–3: by a Clergyman in the Diocese of Winchester. 1864.

ECTON, JOHN, *Liber Valorum et Decimarum, being an Account of such Ecclesiastical Benefices ... as now stand charged with, or lately were discharged from, the payment of First Fruits and Tenths* (1711). 3rd edn, 1728.

—— *State of the Proceedings of Queen Anne's Bounty* (1719). 2nd edn, 1721.

—— *Thesaurus Rerum Ecclesiasticarum* (1723). 2nd ed. by Browne Willis, 1764.

EDEN, F. M., *The State of the Poor.* 3 vols., 1797.

EVANS, FRANCIS, Diary, see Robertson, D.

FERRERS, J. B., *The Necessity and Advantages of an immediate Increase of Queen Anne's Bounty.* 1832.

FITZGERALD, MARION, *The Church as Landlords.* 1937.

BTP

Bibliography

FOXCROFT, H. C. (ed.), *A Supplement to Burnet's History of My Own Time.* Oxford, 1902.

FROUDE, R. HURRELL, *Remains.* 4 vols., London and Derby, 1838–9.

GARDNER, L., *Sermon at the Anniversary Meeting of the Stewards of the Sons of the Clergy, 8 May 1817.* 1818.

GARROW, D. W., *The Importance of the Sacerdotal Office. A Sermon preached . . . to the Sons of the Clergy . . . 21 May 1818.* 1819.

GIBBONS, A., *Ely Episcopal Records: a Calendar and Concise View.* (Privately printed) Lincoln, 1891.

GIBSON, EDMUND, *Codex Juris Ecclesiastici Anglicani: or, the Statutes, Constitutions, Canons, Rubricks and Articles of the Church of England methodically digested . . . with a Commentary, Historical and Juridical.* 1713.

—— *Of Visitations Parochial and General: being the Charges delivered to the Clergy of the Archdeaconry of Surrey.* 1717.

—— *Directions given . . . to the Clergy of his Diocese in the year 1724.* n.d.

—— Life, see Sykes, N.

GILL, HARRY and GUILFORD, E. L. (ed.), *The Rector's Book of Clayworth, Notts.* Nottingham, 1910.

GIRDLESTONE, CHARLES, *Letter on Church Reform, . . . with one Remark on the Plan of Lord Henley.* 1832.

GONNER, E. C. K., *Common Land and Inclosure.* 1912.

GOOCH, W., *General View of the Agriculture of the County of Cambridge.* 1813.

GORE, CHARLES (ed.), *Essays in Aid of the Reform of the Church.* 1902.

GREGORY, ROBERT, *Autobiography, 1819–1911,* ed. W. H. Hutton. 1912.

GREY, W. H., *Church Leases: or, the Subject of Church Leasehold Property considered, with a view to place it on a firmer Basis* (1848). 3rd edn, 1851.

HARROWBY, 1ST EARL OF, *Letter to Spencer Perceval . . . on the Augmentation of a particular Class of Small Livings without burdening the Public: first printed in 1810.* 1831.

HART, A. TINDAL, *William Lloyd, 1627–1717: Bishop, Politician, Author and Prophet.* 1952.

—— *The Country Priest in English History.* 1959.

HEATHCOTE, G., *An Address to the Principal Farmers, Churchwardens and Overseers of small Towns and Country Villages on . . . Dr Bell's System of Instruction.* Winchester, 1817.

HENLEY, 1ST LORD, *Plan of Church Reform.* Several editions, 1832.

—— *Plan for a new Arrangement and Increase in Number of the Dioceses of England and Wales.* 1834.

HERVEY, LORD, *Some Materials towards Memoirs of the Reign of George II,* ed. Romney Sedgwick. 3 vols., 1931.

Bibliography

[——] *An Answer to the Country Parson's Plea against the Quakers' Tythe Bill*, by a member of the House of Commons. 1736.

HIGHMORE, NATHANIEL, *Jus Ecclesiasticum Anglicanum: or, the Government of the Church of England exemplified and illustrated*. 1810.

[HILDROP, JOHN], *The Contempt of the Clergy Consider'd*. Dublin, 1739.

HILL, CHRISTOPHER, *Economic Problems of the Church, from Archbishop Whitgift to the Long Parliament*. Oxford, 1956.

HILL, OCTAVIA, *Letters to my Fellow-Workers*. Privately printed, almost annual.

—— Life, see Maurice, C. E.

History and Proceedings of the House of Commons from the Restoration to the Present Time. 13 vols., 1742–3.

HOBHOUSE, R., *On the Excessive Rating of Tithe Rent Rentcharge*. 1874.

HODGSON, CHRISTOPHER, *Instructions for the Use of Candidates for Holy Orders and of the Parochial Clergy* (1817). 9th edn, 1870.

—— *An Account of the Augmentation of Small Livings by the Governors of Queen Anne's Bounty* . . . (1826). 2nd edn., 1845.

—— *Letter to the Archbishop of Canterbury, on the present Regulations for the Distribution and Management of the Funds of Queen Anne's Bounty*. 1865.

HODGSON, ROBERT, *Life of Bishop Porteus*. 2nd edn, 1811.

HORNER, L. (ed.), *Memoirs and Correspondence of Francis Horner*. 2 vols., 1853.

HOSKINS, W. G., *The Midland Peasant: the economic and social history of a Leicestershire village*. 1957.

How to make better Provision for the Cure of Souls out of the present actual Finances of the Church, by a Pauper Clergyman. 1857.

HOWARD, H. F., *An Account of the Finances of St John's College Cambridge*. Cambridge, 1935.

HOWLEY, WILLIAM, *Charge to the Clergy of the Diocese of Canterbury*. 1832.

HUGHES, EDWARD, 'The Bishops and Reform, 1831–3', in *English Historical Review*, LVI (1941), 459–90.

HUGHES, EDWARD, *North Country Life in the 18th Century: the North-East, 1700–1750*. 1952.

—— *The Letters of Spencer Cowper, Dean of Durham*. Surtees Soc., CLXV. Durham, 1956.

Interests of the Church of England. 2nd edn, 1821, reprinted in *The Pamphleteer*, XIX (1822), 477 ff.

JENNINGS, L. J., *Correspondence and Diaries of J. W. Croker*. 3 vols., 1884.

JERVIS, W. G., *The Poor Condition of the Clergy and the Causes considered, with suggestions for remedying the same*. 1856.

KAYE, JOHN, *Nine Charges to the Clergy of the Diocese of Lincoln, etc.*, ed. by his son. 1854.

Bibliography

KENNETT, WHITE, *Parochial Antiquities attempted in the history of Ambrosden, Burcester, etc.* Oxford, 1695.

—— *The Case of Impropriations and of the Augmentation of Vicarages.* 1704.

—— Life, see Bennett, G. V.

KETTON-CREMER, R. W., *Country Neighbourhood.* 1951.

KNOX, VICESIMUS, *Remarks on the Tendency of certain Clauses in a Bill now pending in Parliament to Degrade Grammar Schools* . . . 2nd edn, 1821, in *The Pamphleteer*, XIX (1822), 249 ff.

LAMB, JOHN, *Masters's History of Corpus Christi College* . . . *with additional matter and a continuation.* 1831.

LAVROVSKY, V., 'Tithe Commutation as a Factor in the gradual Decrease of Land Ownership by the English Peasantry', in *Economic History Review*, IV (1932–4), 273–89.

LE FANU, W. R., *Queen Anne's Bounty: a Short Account of its History and Work.* 1921: 2nd edn, by Hughes, F. G. 1933.

Letter to Sir William Scott, in answer to Mr Brougham's Letter to Sir Samuel Romilly upon the Abuse of Charities. 1818.

Letter to the Archbishop of Canterbury on the subject of Church Property, by a Clergyman. 1824.

LIDDON, H. P., *Life of E. B. Pusey.* 4 vols., 1893.

LINNELL, C. D. (ed.), *The Diary of Benjamin Rogers, Rector of Carlton, 1720–1771.* Beds. Hist. Record Soc., XXX. Streatley, nr. Luton, 1950.

LIVESEY, JOHN, *Mechanics' Churches: a Letter to Sir Robert Peel on Church Extension in Populous Towns and Manufacturing Districts.* 1840.

LLOYD, WILLIAM, Life, see Hart, A. Tindal.

LOWTH, ROBERT, *Letter* . . . *to the Clergy of his Diocese.* Printed but never published; dated, 12 April 1784.

LYALL, W. R., *Charges to the Clergy of the Archdeaconry of Colchester, 1831 and 1833.* Published in the same years.

LYSONS, D. and S., *Magna Britannia.* 6 vols., 1806–22.

MCCLATCHEY, DIANA, *Oxfordshire Clergy 1777-1869.* Oxford, 1960.

MCCLURE, E., and ALLEN, W. O. B., *Two Hundred Years: the History of the S.P.C.K., 1698-1898.* 1898.

MCLAUGHLIN, HUBERT. *A Tract on Church Extension.* Ludlow, 1851.

MANNING, HENRY EDWARD, *The Principles of the Ecclesiastical Commission examined, in a Letter to the Bishop of Chichester.* 1838.

MARSH, HERBERT, *The National Religion the Foundation of National Education: a sermon preached at the annual Charity Schools Meeting* . . . 13 June 1811. Reprinted in *The Pamphleteer*, I (1813), 49 ff.

MARSHALL, DOROTHY, *English People in the 18th Century.* 1956.

Bibliography

[MASTERS, ROBERT], *Short Account of the Parish of Waterbeach*, by a late Vicar. 1795.

MATHIESON, W. L., *English Church Reform, 1815-1840.* 1923.

MAURICE, C. E., *Life of Octavia Hill.* 1913.

MILLER, J., *Letter to Lord Grey, on Church Property and Church Reform.* 1832.

MONK, JAMES H., *Charge to the Clergy of the Diocese of Gloucester and Bristol, August-September 1838.* 1838.

[MONRO, E.], *The Church and the Million.* 1854.

MOZLEY, THOMAS, *Reminiscences: chiefly of Oriel College and the Oxford Movement.* 2nd edn, 2 vols., 1882.

NELSON, ROBERT, *Works . . . all compendiously methodized for the Use of Families.* 1715.

NICHOLL, JOHN, *Judgment delivered, 11 Dec. 1809, in the case of Kemp v. Wickes.* 1810.

NICHOLS, JOHN, *Literary Anecdotes of the 18th Century; comprising Biographical memoirs of W. Bowyer.* 9 vols., 1812–15.

OTTER, WILLIAM, *Reasons for continuing the Education of the Poor at the Present Crisis: an Assize Sermon at Shrewsbury, 16 March 1820.* Shrewsbury, 1820.

OVERTON, J. H., *The English Church in the 19th Century: 1800-1833.* 1894.

PALEY, WILLIAM, *Sermon and Tracts,* 1808.

PALMER, WILLIAM, *Remarks on Dr Arnold's Principles of Church Reform.* 1833.

—— *Narrative of Events connected with . . . the Tracts for the Times.* (1843) 1883.

PARK, J. A., *Memoirs of William Stevens* (1812) 3rd edn, 1859.

PARKER, C. S., *Sir Robert Peel . . . from his Private Correspondence.* 3 vols., 1891–9.

Patroni Ecclesiarum: or, a List of the Patrons of the Dignities, Rectories etc. . . . . of the Church of England. 1831.

PEARCE, E. H., *The Sons of the Clergy* (1904) 2nd edn, 1928.

PEEL, A. GEORGE V. (ed.), *Private Letters of Sir Robert Peel.* 1920.

PEEL, ROBERT, *Life, and Letters;* see Parker, C. S., and Peel, A. G. V.

—— *Memoirs . . .* published by Lord Mahon and E. Cardwell. 2 vols., 1856.

PELLEW, G., *Life and Correspondence of Lord Sidmouth.* 3 vols., 1847.

PERCEVAL, ARTHUR P., *Reasons why I am not a Member of the Bible Society.* 1830.

—— *Letter to the Rev. James Slade, containing Remarks on his Letter to the Bishop of London on Church Reform.* 1831.

—— *Letter to Lord Henley, respecting his Publication on Church Reform.* 1832.

—— *Collection of Papers connected with the Theological Movement of 1833.* 1842.

PERCEVAL, SPENCER, *Copy of a Letter to Dr Mansel on the Stipendiary Curates Bill.* 1808

PHILLPOTTS, HENRY, *Letter to the Freeholders of the County of Durham.* Durham, 1819

—— *Letter to Earl Grey.* 1821.

—— *Letter to Francis Jeffrey Esq.* Durham, 1823.

—— *Correspondence between the Bishop of Exeter and Members of the Commission of Ecclesiastical Inquiry.* 1840.

—— Life, see Davies, G. C. B.

PINDER, H. S. *A Plea for Country Bishops, in a letter to a Friend,* 1860.

PITT, W., Life, see Stanhope, Lord.

POLLARD, A. F., *The Evolution of Parliament.* 2nd edn, 1926.

PORT, M. H., *Six Hundred New Churches: the Church Building Commissioners, 1818-1856.* 1961.

PORTUS, GARNET V., *Caritas Anglicana: an historical inquiry into those Religious and Philanthropical Societies that flourished in England 1678-1740.* 1912.

PRESTIGE, G. L., *St Paul's in its Glory.* 1955.

PRIDEAUX, HUMPHREY, Letters, see Thompson, E. M.

—— *An Award of King Charles I . . . settling a 2s. rate on the Rents of Norwich houses for the Maintenance of the Parochial Clergy . . . in lieu of Personal Tithes, etc.* 1707.

PUSEY, E. B., *Remarks on the Prospective and Past Benefits of Cathedral Institutions . . . occasioned by Lord Henley's Plan for their Abolition.* 1833.

—— Life, see Liddon, H. P.

—— *The Royal and Parliamentary Ecclesiastical Commissioners.* 1838.

PYLE, EDMUND, *Memoirs of a Royal Chaplain, 1729-1763.* Ed. Hartshorne, 1905.

[RENNELL, THOMAS], *Letter to Henry Brougham . . . upon his Durham Speech and the three Articles in the last Edinburgh Review upon the Subject of the Clergy.* 1823.

Report of the Select Committee of the House of Commons on the Ecclesiastical Commissioners, 17 July 1863, with References to the Evidence. Cambridge, 1864.

RICARDO, DAVID, *Letters to H. Trower and others, 1811–23:* ed. Bonar and Hollander. Oxford, 1899.

RICHARSON, W. E., *Letter to the Earl of Shaftesbury on the Establishment of Ragged School Churches.* 1852.

ROBERTSON, DAVID (ed.), *The Diary of Francis Evans, Secretary to Bishop Lloyd, 1699-1706.* Oxford, 1903.

ROBSON, ROBERT, *The Attorney in the 18th Century.* Cambridge, 1959.

ROGERS, BENJAMIN, Diary, see Linnell, C. D.

ROGERS, WILLIAM, *Reminiscences,* compiled by R. H. Hadden. 1888.

Bibliography

ROMILLY, SAMUEL, *Memoirs of the Life of*, ed. by his sons, 3 vols., 1840.

ROSE, HUGH JAMES, *Brief Remarks on the Dispositions towards Christianity generated by prevailing Opinions and Pursuits*. 1830.

SAUNDERS, ERASMUS, *View of the State of Religion in the Diocese of St David's about the beginning of the 18th Century* (1721). Cardiff, 1949.

SAVIDGE, ALAN, *The Foundation and Early Years of Queen Anne's Bounty*. 1955.

SAYERS, A., *Reply to Sydney Smith's 3rd Letter to Archdeacon Singleton, in a Letter to Archdeacon Wetherell*. 1839.

SCOTT, SIR WILLIAM, *Substance of a Speech delivered in the House of Commons, 7 April 1802*. 1802.

Scrip, The: or, Smooth Stones out of the Brook, for the Forehead of Ism, the Modern Goliath, and his Sons, Sch-ism, Roman-ism, Liberal-ism, Auto-ism, Despot-ism, Nepot-ism, and Euphem-ism. By Sigmabetaphilus. 1847.

SECKER, THOMAS, *Eight Charges delivered to the Clergy of the Dioceses of Oxford and Canterbury*. 1769.

SELWYN, WILLIAM, *Substance of an Argument . . . against those Clauses of the Benefices Plurality Bill which confer additional Powers on the Ecclesiastical Commissioners*. Cambridge, 1838.

—— *An Attempt to investigate the true Principles of Cathedral Reform*. Cambridge, 1839.

—— *Conversations on Legislation for the Church, between M.P. and Canon*. Cambridge, 1858–60.

SHERLOCK, THOMAS, *Discourses preached upon several Occasions* 5 vols., 1772.

—— *The Country Parson's Plea against the Quakers' Tythe Bill*. 1736.

SHINE, H. and SHINE, H. C., *The Quarterly Review under Gifford: identification of contributors, 1809-1824*. Chapel Hill, 1949.

Six Letters addressed to the Archbishop of Canterbury upon the Subject of Dilapidations, by A.M. 1801.

SMITH, ADAM, *The Wealth of Nations* (Everyman edition).

[SMITH, E. J.], *Two Letters to the Archbishop of Canterbury on the Origin and Progress of the Ecclesiastical Commissioners*. 1863.

SMITH, SYDNEY, *Letters*, ed. Nowell C. Smith. 2 vols., Oxford, 1953.

SOUTHEY, CUTHBERT C. (ed.), *Life and Correspondence of Robert Southey*. 6 vols., 1849–50.

SOUTHEY, ROBERT, *Letter to William Smith*. 1817.

—— *Sir Thomas More: or, Colloquies on the Progress and Prospects of Society*. 2 vols., 1829.

—— *Essays, Moral and Political*. 2 vols., 1832.

—— *Life, and Letters; see Southey, C. C., also Warter, J. W.*

SPEARMAN, J. and G., *An Inquiry into the ancient and present state of the County Palatine of Durham.* [Edinburgh], 1729.

[STACKHOUSE, T.], *The Miseries and Great Hardships of the Inferior Clergy in and about London,* by a Clergyman of the Church of England. 1722.

STANHOPE, EARL, *Life of William Pitt.* 4 vols., 1861–2.

The State of the Established Church: in a series of Letters to Spencer Perceval (1809). 2nd edn, 1810.

STORR, VERNON F., *The Development of English Theology in the 19th Century.* 1913.

STODDART, G. H., *Evidence on the Necessity of Church Reform* ... 1833.

STURGES, JOHN, *Considerations on the present State of the Church-Establishment, in Letters to the Bishop of London.* 1779.

Substance of a Letter to one of His Majesty's Ministers previous to the Session of 1828–9, *on the subject of First-Fruits and Tenths,* by a Barrister. 1829.

Suggestions as to carrying out Lord Ashley's Proposal for the Sub-division of Parishes, by a Member of the Temple, 1849.

SUMNER, G. H., *The Ecclesiastical Commission: reprinted from the Churchman's Family Magazine* [1864].

SYKES, NORMAN, *Edmund Gibson, Bishop of London, 1669–1748.* 1926.

—— *Church and State in England in the 18th Century.* Cambridge, 1934.

—— *William Wake, Archbishop of Canterbury, 1657–1737.* 2 vols., Cambridge, 1957.

—— *From Sheldon to Secker: aspects of English Church History, 1660–1768.* Cambridge, 1959.

TATE, W. E., *Parliamentary Land Enclosures in Nottinghamshire, 1743–1868.* Thoroton Soc. Record Series, v. Nottingham, 1935.

THOMPSON, E. M. (ed.), *Letters of Humphrey Prideaux to John Ellis.* Camden Soc., n.s., XV. 1875.

TOWNSEND, G., *Plan for abolishing Pluralities and Non-Residence in the Church of England ... in a Letter to Lord Henley.* 1833.

Tracts for the People: designed to vindicate Religious and Christian Liberty. 1840.

TRAILL, J. C., *The New Parishes Acts, 1843, 1844 and 1856.* 1857.

TRAPP, JOSEPH, *The Dignity, and Benefit, of the Priesthood ... set forth in a sermon preach'd before the Sons of the Clergy ... 8 December 1720.* 1721.

TUCKWELL, W., *Reminiscences of Oxford.* 1901.

VANCOUVER, CHARLES, *General View of the Agriculture in the County of Cambridge.* 1794.

VAN MILDERT, WILLIAM, *Charge to the Clergy of the Diocese of Llandaff, 1821.* Oxford, 1821.

Bibliography

—— Charges to the Clergy of the Diocese of Durham, *1828* and *1831*. Published at Oxford in the same years.

Venn, J. A., *Foundations of Agricultural Economics*. Cambridge, 1933.

Vindication of the Church and Clergy of England from the Misrepresentations of the Edinburgh Review. By a beneficed clergyman, 1823.

Warter, J. W. (ed.), *Selections from Robert Southey's Letters*. 4 vols., 1856.

Watson, Richard, *Letter to the Archbishop of Canterbury*, 1783. 3rd edn, 1816, in *The Pamphleteer*, VIII (1816), 574 ff.

—— *Miscellaneous Tracts on Religious, Political and Agricultural Subjects*. 2 vols., 1815.

—— *Anecdotes of his own Life* (1817). 2nd edn, 2 vols., 1818.

Watson, William, *Historical Account of Wisbech*. Wisbech, 1827.

Webb, Sidney and Beatrice, *English Local Government*. 9 vols., 1906–29.

Webster, William, *The Clergy's Right of Maintenance vindicated from Scripture and Reason*. 2nd edn, 1727.

Whately, E. J., *Life and Correspondence of Richard Whately*. 2 vols., 1866.

[Whately, Richard], *Letters on the Church, by an Episcopalian*. 1826.

—— Life, see Whately, E. J.

Whitaker, T. D., *History of the original parish of Whalley and honour of Clitheroe*. 4th edn, by Nichols and Lyons, 2 vols., 1872–6.

Whiteman, Anne, 'The Re-Establishment of the Church of England, 1660–3', in *Trans. Royal Hist. Soc.*, 5th series, V (1955), 111–37.

—— 'The Church of England, 1542–1837', in *Victoria County History, Wiltshire*, III (1956), 28–56.

Wilberforce, R. I. and S., *Life of William Wilberforce*. 5 vols., 1838.

[Wilkinson, R.], *Life of Sir Julius Caesar . . . with Memoirs of his Family and Descendants*. 1810.

Woodforde, James, *Diary, 1758–1802*, ed. Beresford, J. 5 vols., Oxford, 1924–31.

Yates, Richard, *The Church in Danger: a Statement of the Cause . . . in a Letter to Lord Liverpool*. 1815.

—— *The Basis of National Welfare . . . a second Letter to Lord Liverpool*. 1817.

—— *The Patronage of the Church of England, concisely considered in reference to National Reformation and Improvement, etc*. 1823.

Young, Arthur, *A General View of the Agriculture of Lincolnshire*. 1799.

Young, G. M., *Victorian England: Portrait of an Age*. Oxford, 1936.

INDEX

Index

Index

Index